Cognitive Processes in Spelling

Cognitive Processes in Spelling

Edited by

UTA FRITH

MRC Developmental Psychology Unit
Gordon Street, London, England

ACADEMIC PRESS   1980
A Subsidiary of Harcourt Brace Jovanovich, Publishers

London   New York   Toronto   Sydney   San Francisco

ACADEMIC PRESS INC. (LONDON) LTD
24/28 Oval Road
London NW1 7DX

United States Edition published by
ACADEMIC PRESS INC.
111 Fifth Avenue
New York, New York 10003

British Library Cataloguing in Publication Data
Cognitive processes in spelling.
    1. English language – Orthography and spelling
    I. Frith, Uta
    421′.52′019   PE1143   79–40788
    ISBN 0–12–268660–8

Typeset by Gloucester Typesetting Co. Ltd, Gloucester
Printed by Whitstable Litho Ltd, Whitstable, Kent

List of Contributors

BADDELEY, ALAN D. Medical Research Council, Applied Psychology Unit, 15 Chaucer Road, Cambridge CB2 2EF, England

BAKER, ROBERT G. Department of Electronics, University of Southampton, Southampton SO9 5NH, England

BARON, JONATHAN Department of Psychology, University of Pennsylvania, 3813–15 Walnut Street, Philadelphia, Pennsylvania 19104, U.S.A.

BARRON, RODERICK W. Department of Psychology, University of Guelph, Guelph, Ontario N1G 2W1, Canada

BRADLEY, LYNETTE Department of Experimental Psychology, University of Oxford, South Parks Road, Oxford OX1 3UD, England

BRYANT, PETER E. Department of Experimental Psychology, University of Oxford, South Parks Road, Oxford OX1 3UD, England

CHARD, JACKIE Department of Psychology, School of Natural Sciences, Hatfield Polytechnic, Hatfield, Hertfordshire AL10 9AB, England

COHEN, GILLIAN Department of Experimental Psychology, University of Oxford, South Parks Road, Oxford OX1 3UD, England

CROMER, RICHARD F. Medical Research Council, Developmental Psychology Unit, Drayton House, Gordon Street, London WC1H 0AN, England

DESBERG, PETER Department of Psychology, California State University, Dominguez Hills, Carson, California 90747, U.S.A.

DODD, BARBARA Medical Research Council, Developmental Psychology Unit, Drayton House, Gordon Street, London WC1H 0AN, England

EHRI, LINNEA C. Department of Education, College of Letters and Science, University of California, Davis, California 95616, U.S.A.

ELLIOTT, DALE E. Department of Linguistics, California State University, Dominguez Hills, Carson, California 90747, U.S.A.

FRIEDMAN, MORTON Department of Psychology, University of California, 405 Hilgard Avenue, Los Angeles, California 90024, U.S.A.

FRITH, UTA   Medical Research Council, Developmental Psychology Unit, Drayton House, Gordon Street, London WC1 0AN, England

HENDERSON, LESLIE   Department of Psychology, School of Natural Sciences, Hatfield Polytechnic, Hatfield, Hertfordshire AL10 9AB, England

HOTOPF, NORMAN   Department of Psychology, London School of Economics and Political Science, Houghton Street, London WC2A 2AE, England

KELLMAN, PHILIP   Department of Psychology, University of Pennsylvania, 3813–15 Walnut Street, Philadelphia, Pennsylvania 19104, U.S.A.

MARCEL, TONY   Medical Research Council, Applied Psychology Unit, 15 Chaucer Road, Cambridge CB2 2EF, England

MARSH, GEORGE   Department of Psychology, California State University, Dominguez Hills, Carson, California 90747, U.S.A.

MORTON, JOHN   Medical Research Council, Applied Psychology Unit, 15 Chaucer Road, Cambridge CB2 2EF, England

NELSON, HAZEL E.   Department of Psychology, The National Hospital for Nervous Diseases, Queen Square, London WC1 H 3BG, England

PORPODAS, CONSTANTINE D.   Department of Psychology, The University, Dundee DD1 4HN, Scotland

SEYMOUR, PHILIP H. K.   Department of Psychology, The University, Dundee DD1 4NH, Scotland

SLOBODA, JOHN A.   Department of Psychology, University of Keele, Staffordshire ST5 5BG, England

SMITH, PHILIP T.   Department of Psychology, University of Stirling, Stirling, FK9 4DA, Scotland

TENNEY, YVETTE J.   Department of Psychology and Social Relations, Harvard University, 1544 William James Hall, 33 Kirkland Street, Cambridge, Massachusetts 02138, U.S.A.

TREIMAN, REBECCA   Department of Psychology, University of Pennsylvania, 3813–15 Walnut Street, Philadelphia, Pennsylvania 19104, U.S.A.

VENEZKY, RICHARD L.   Department of Educational Foundations, College of Education, University of Delaware, Willard Hall Educational Building, Newark, Delaware 19711, U.S.A.

WELCH, VERONICA   Department of Psychology, University of California, 405 Hilgard Avenue, Los Angeles, California 90024, U.S.A.

WILF, JENNIFER F.   Department of Psychology, University of Pennsylvania, 3813–15 Walnut Street, Philadelphia, Pennsylvania 19104, U.S.A.

WING, ALAN M.   Medical Research Council, Applied Psychology Unit, 15 Chaucer Road, Cambridge CB2 2EF, England

Preface

Cognitive psychologists, for long fascinated by the study of reading, have largely ignored spelling and writing, which they have dismissed as having little connection with the intrinsic meaning of words. Furthermore English orthography is often derided as illogical and arbitrary. This book aims to encourage a more serious study of spelling by discussing it as both a skill and a problem, and by highlighting some of the hitherto ill-understood processes involved in learning to spell. Exactly how is spelling knowledge acquired? How is it used? Why do some people lose it, or never acquire it at all? This book attempts to answer these questions by examining the spelling of children at various stages of learning, in adults with nearly perfect spelling, in neurological patients, adult illiterates, and in children with special problems, such as deafness, dysphasia and dyslexia.

Active spelling production is a field of research that has been even more neglected than passive and often unconscious use of spelling knowledge in word recognition but in this book it receives particular attention. By comparing the perception and production of the letter-by-letter structure of words some new and surprising hypotheses are suggested which are relevant to the central issue in cognitive theory – namely the internal representation of words. Moreover, spelling, like reading, is a language skill and thus its study provides clues to the understanding of the phonology and etymology of words.

Many of the phenomena described in this book will be familiar to the reader, but from the studies here insight can be gained into such curiosities as why we all at times produce mis-spellings which we can immediately correct, why a competent speller can overlook mis-spellings, as for example when proofreading, and why it is sometimes necessary to write down a word before we can recognise and establish its correct spelling. The connection between normal spelling errors and language disorders is also examined.

This book concentrates entirely on English orthography – English having a long history of spelling and spelling reform and its basis in several other languages. English orthography is therefore very complex and presents an ideal testing ground for cognitive and psycholinguistic theories of spelling, which in turn will, undoubtedly, be applicable to other orthographies.

The study of spelling has only just started and many mysteries remain. With this book we hope to further the understanding of this everyday and ever-changing activity.

October 1979   UTA FRITH

Contents

and graphemic information to generate spelling patterns for real words?; Experiment 2: Can deaf children be forced to recode nonsense words presented in written form, in a phonological code for memory storage?; Experiment 3: Can deaf children graphemically represent nonsense words which they had to encode via lip reading, and if so, does their written output match their spoken output of the same words?; Summary and conclusion

BARBARA DODD

Introduction

UTA FRITH

This book does not try to present an authoritative survey of the psychological study of spelling. Instead it tries to open up a new field. A wide range of ideas and experiments is presented. From this a coherent picture has begun to emerge.

The context is set by considering historical, linguistic and cognitive approaches. Against the historical background the questions of spelling instruction and spelling reform are particularly relevant. For the status of spelling in schools, Venezky reveals a history of decline and fall. Spelling reform seems to be subject to fashion to an extraordinary degree and dependent on powerful personalities who occasionally take up its cause. The chapters by Smith and by Baker highlight both advantages and disadvantages of the present English orthographic system against a linguistic background. People who have learned to spell also have learned a great deal of linguistic information about words. This is richly demonstrated by Smith's and Baker's studies. People are sensitive to very subtle aspects of word spellings, in particular their etymology, without being at all aware of this. One delightful result was that people who were asked to act as spelling reformers judged words of Germanic origin (e.g. love) to be slightly more rationally spelled than words of Romance origin (e.g. move) – 'a surprising finding nine hundred years after the French invasion'.

On the whole, no strong argument for spelling reform can be made on the basis of this book. At first sight there might be a case for reforming the spelling of Black American English. Desberg, Elliott and Marsh consider and reject this possibility. They point out that everyone speaks a dialect and that speech is always imperfectly reflected in spelling.

A different perspective appears against the background of cognitive theories of spelling. Henderson reviews word recognition studies and relates these to studies on spelling. His anatomy of the word superiority effect allows deep insight into our ability to deal with orthographic structure. The experience of knowing immediately whether a spelling is incorrect, and conversely, the experience of missing errors when proofreading is analysed by Cohen in classic visual search experiments. Morton extends his logogen model in order to accommodate writing and spelling processes. This model has proved highly successful for investigations of the processing of visible language.

Since the study of spelling is set in this way in a historical, linguistic and cognitive context, the sources for methods and hypotheses of the more specific studies can be seen clearly. One common theme uniting all these investigations is the distinction between phonological and visual coding strategies. This distinction is clearly derived from the given theoretical framework. Phonological and visual aspects of spelling can be defined quite precisely. Spelling in alphabetical scripts essentially means representing speech sounds. Thus spelling is visible phonology. However, spelling also reflects other levels of language. Plainly, correct spelling especially in English depends on other factors besides sound. These may be called 'visual' to contrast them with sound factors However, they are not visual in the usual sense of the word. They are independent of the graphic shapes or forms of letters. The importance of these 'visual' factors can be illustrated by spellings of proper names. For instance, Marlene, made popular by Marlene Dietrich, gave rise to such new spellings as Arlene, Charlene and Darlene, which on other occasions have been spelled Arleen, Charleen and Darleen in analogy to other well-known forms such as in Kathleen or Eileen. Such is the power of 'visual' factors in spelling that an Arlene would consider her name to be utterly different from the name Arleen – even if they are pronounced identically. What shows that this is not simply visual appearance is that she would not be concerned to find her name written in different scripts. In order to become a skilled speller, this sort of letter-by-letter knowledge of words is essential. How it is acquired – by rote, by analogy, or by rule – is very puzzling. Mastery of sound-to-letter rules, though basic to the spelling process, is of little help here.

One interesting outcome of the investigations on spelling strategies is that there are marked individual differences. Baron, Treiman, Freyd and Kellman show that people can be classified into 'Phoenicians' who are good at spelling by letter-sound rules, and into 'Chinese' who are not. The historical Phoenicians were of course the inventors of the alphabet and with this the inventors of the highly artificial concept of phonemes as units of speech sounds. This concept is irrelevant and indeed difficult to grasp for readers of logographic scripts such as Chinese. Baron *et al.*'s 'Chinese' have a subtle deficit in analysing phoneme segments in speech. They apparently rely on whole-word recognition, just as if they were dealing with logographic symbols.

For schoolchildren, this distinction also turns out to be highly relevant. Barron demonstrates that good and poor spellers differ on these strategies in different ways for word recognition and production tasks.

Both visual and phonological factors play an important role in Ehri's theory of acquisition processes in reading and spelling. Barron and Ehri find intriguing effects on memory for so-called silent letters in words. The linguistic significance of silent letters is examined in detail by Smith.

Marsh, Friedman, Welch and Desberg conclude that 'visual' strategies take over from sound-to-letter decoding strategies from about age ten onwards. From then on new words are more and more spelled by analogy to old words. At the early stages of learning to read and write, Bryant and Bradley find convincing evidence for a specialisation of look-and-say strategies for reading and phonics strategies for spelling. Thus, a child may be able to spell a word, phoneme by phoneme, but not be able to read it back. However, the child can be made to read the word when tricked into using a phonics instead of a visual strategy. The same specialisation for reading by eye and writing by ear is considered by Frith. There it is suggested that the crucial difference between the two strategies may not so much lie in the contrast between eye and ear, but in the contrast between using partial and full cues. A partial analysis of visual orthographic structure is often sufficient for word recognition. For spelling, on the other hand, the full letter-by-letter sequence must be produced. Frith hypothesises that unexpectedly poor spellers (unexpectedly poor, because they do not suffer from reading problems) are so successful in reading by partial cues, that they never attend to the letter-by-letter structure of words.

All this is consistent with cognitive models of reading that assume that there are two distinct routes for getting meaning from print, via the eye and ear, and via the eye directly. This theory seems to apply just as much to writing and is relevant for the beginner as well as the highly literate. However, reading and spelling are not simply inverses of each other. Surprising asymmetry can exist, so that competence in one process can go together with incompetence in the other.

The popular belief that good spellers can see word spellings in their heads or that they 'just know' how to spell a word by some visual memory image has been tackled by Tenney and by Sloboda. The results of their experiments however do not support this belief. Instead they suggest that other factors are more important, for instance rote learning and linguistic sophistication. Thus, visual imagery and spelling ability do not necessarily go together. This is consistent with the notion that 'visual' factors in spelling have nothing to do with visual appearance, but concern letter-by-letter structure.

It is in everybody's writing experience that spelling errors can occur even though the writer knows perfectly well how to spell the words correctly. Wing and Baddeley provide a corpus of such errors from forty exam scripts. Interestingly enough, 'real' spelling errors are not very different from unintentional ones and this can be explained in terms of general attention and memory processes. The amazing similarities of slips of the pen and slips of the tongue are pointed out by Hotopf. His observations suggest that cognitive processes underlying the production of writing are surprisingly similar to those underlying the production of speech. This underlines the enormous importance of phonological factors in spelling.

The study of abnormal groups shows the relationship between speech and writing particularly clearly. Patients with language disorders almost always have spelling disorders. Morton vividly describes the case of a young woman with left hemisphere damage. She was apparently unable to use a phonemic code for spelling and therefore relied on a visual code which turns out to be extremely limiting. More patients with language problems as a result of left hemisphere lesions are described by Marcel who analyses characteristic spelling errors that involve consonant clusters. These same errors (e.g. GROUD for ground, HEPL for help) are also shown by some children retarded in reading, and by a large proportion of adult illiterates. Marcel demonstrates that these errors are not a result of order confusions as might appear at first sight, but that they are in fact due to phonological problems. He can explain these problems in terms of lack of phonological awareness and in terms of deviant acoustic feature selection.

Mis-spellings in the spontaneous writing of children with various language disorders are presented by Cromer. The mis-spellings of deaf and receptively aphasic children in particular show interesting similarities, but also differences, in line with specific hypotheses about the availability of visual and phonological codes in these groups. As Dodd shows, the deaf, without acoustic language experience, nevertheless possess a phonological code, and prove this in their ability to spell lip-read nonsense words.

A controversial topic of special interest to the study of spelling is developmental dyslexia. Seymour and Porpodas apply a sophisticated theoretical framework and analyse systematically the different points of possible breakdown in dyslexia within an extended logogen model. Thus they are able to throw new light on specific deficits in reading and spelling processes.

Nelson discusses the three most popular theories of dyslexia, none of which finds support from her analysis of spelling errors. She shows that if dyslexic children are compared with younger children of the same spelling achievement level, hardly any qualitative differences remain. Nelson provides an original spelling test that has the unique feature of quantifying the tendency of each word to elicit one type of error rather than another. This means that spelling errors can be compared even though they have been obtained from different words.

On the whole, normal and abnormal error patterns in spelling, with some exceptions, show many similarities. In both normal and clinical groups it proved fruitful to use models that contrast strategies and codes for reading and spelling. Strategies can only be inferred from normal skilled performance. However, they can often be demonstrated directly in abnormal performance.

What emerged as the most tantalising question still open is how spelling ability is learned and improved. Although there are suggestions in this book on the teaching of spelling, the research results are mostly not yet at a stage where they can be applied. The question of how to teach and how to learn is exceedingly important to the study of spelling, since spelling is above all an educational skill. It is possible that the problem of learning in general cannot be properly addressed in the present theoretical framework. This provides useful structural descriptions of skilled performance, but does not explain how a person passes from one stage of skill to the next. Perhaps a more appropriate framework can be developed through focusing on such a typically learned skill as spelling.

PART I

Spelling Instruction and Spelling Reforms

From: Noah Webster (1789).
The American Spelling Book.
Boston: Thomas and Andrews

I

From Webster to Rice to Roosevelt

The Formative Years for Spelling Instruction and Spelling Reform in the U.S.A.

RICHARD L. VENEZKY   *Department of Educational Foundations, University of Delaware, U.S.A.*

Neither spelling instruction nor spelling reform occupy central roles today in education or in public life. No major funding agency in the last 25 years has included among its highest priorities the improvement of spelling instruction or the development of a simplified spelling system. Few cognitive psychologists have confessed an interest in spelling processes and only a handful in the last decade have even suggested that this topic was worthy of serious investigation. Similarly, the public schools exhibit limited enthusiasm for spelling. Some have no systematic spelling instruction at all while the average class offers perhaps two or three 15-minute periods for it each week. And for spelling reform, the recent passing of Dr Godfrey Dewey, long time champion and sponsor of the cause in America, diminishes further an already sagging enterprise. With the abandonment by the *Chicago Tribune* recently of the remaining reformed spellings it had adopted in 1934 went the last token allegiance to a once grand and glorious movement.

But spelling was once a popular school subject and a matter of national concern. The most popular school book ever was the Webster 'Blue-backed Speller', for which at least 260 impressions are evidenced from the initial publication in 1783 until Webster's death in 1843, with perhaps as many as 100 million copies sold before the twentieth century (Skeel and Carpenter, 1958). In the school reform movement led by Horace Mann in the middle of the nineteenth century, the teaching of spelling was a central focus, and the earliest attempt on record to relate instruction time (time on task) to student achievement, done by Joseph Mayer Rice in 1895, was based upon the teaching of spelling. Spelling reform, which engaged the attention of both Noah Webster and Benjamin Franklin in the formative years of this country, was an active and organised movement at the beginning of this century, with national committees in America and England which listed on their governing boards the most prominent names from science, education, industry and public life.

But the fragility of the movement was exposed by its greatest triumph, an executive order in 1906 by President Theodore Roosevelt, directing the Government Printer to employ 300 simplified spellings in White House publications. Both the Congress and a vocal segment of the public voiced immediate and firm opposition and a well organised and highly financed drive sputtered off course, never since regaining its momentum. A little more than a decade later its principal financial support was severed and its highly visible offices on Madison Avenue in downtown Manhattan moved to the exclusive obscurity of the Lake Placid Club in upstate New York.

In the period from Webster's first speller in 1783 to Roosevelt's executive order in 1906, the unique character of American spelling was designed and firmly implanted, the role of spelling in school instruction established, and the public attitude toward spelling reform clarified. Yet much more can be learned from a careful analysis of this period. In the arguments and practices of Webster, and his main antagonist, Lyman Cobb, are portrayals of linguistic science of the late eighteenth and early nineteenth century, containing as they do phonologies of English and justifications for different renderings of sound into spelling. In the spelling reform proposals of both Webster and the early twentieth-century reformers are attitudes about orthography and its role in national life.

There are also excellent case studies for historiography, and particularly for the influence of great men on historical events. And for the study of educational change, events of this era are as valuable as those of the twentieth century for observing how educational practice is influenced by public pressures.

The plan of this chapter is to attend to these concerns through the activities of three of the men who were central to the events described above: Noah Webster, Joseph Mayer Rice, and Theodore Roosevelt, and through a review of the spelling reform movement which flourished about 75 years ago.

Since a single chapter, and perhaps even a complete book, is too short to analyse thoroughly all of the major issues involved, the emphasis here will be upon the influences which particular people had upon spelling and spelling reform and, where applicable, the psychological and linguistic principles upon which theories and proposals were based.

1 From Noah to Noah Webster

From the time of the earliest educational records until at least the end of the nineteenth century, spelling was intimately tied to reading. In the ABC method, which dominated reading instruction for over 2000 years, the names of the letters and their proper ordering were introduced and practised, followed by many if not all of the possible consonant-vowel and vowel-consonant combinations.[1] Then whole words were presented, to be both spelled and read. For the survivors of this regimen, sentences and stories, generally of a moralistic bent, followed. Hoole summarised the system thusly in 1660.

---

[1] On the history of reading instruction, and the role of spelling therein, see Mathews (1966) and N. B. Smith (1965). The former attempts to survey the entire history of reading instruction while the latter is concerned only with instruction in the United States. Hodges (1977) presents a brief, but highly readable sketch of spelling instruction in the United States.

The ordinary way to teach children to read is, after they have got some knowledge of their letters, and a smattering of some syllables and words in the hornbook, to turn them into ABC or Primar, and therein to make them name the letters, and spell the words, till by often use they can pronounce (at least) the shortest words at the first sight. (Hoole, 1660/1973, p. 20)

In this system spelling and reading were closely related, although for many teachers and educators spelling was considered primary. Noah Webster held, for example, that 'Spelling is the foundation of reading and the greatest ornament of writing' (Webster, 1783, p. 26). Textbooks for teaching reading and spelling, which began to appear in England at the beginning of the sixteenth century, generally included reading and spelling under the same cover. The first spelling book, Coote's *The English School Master*, was published in 1596 and in time the speller became the main classroom resource, from which not only spelling and reading, but also history, geography, civics and moral philosophy were taught.

The earliest American textbooks were either obtained from England or were local reprints of English texts, the most popular being Dilworth's *Guide to the English Tongue* and Fenning's *Universal Spelling Book*. These were the models which Noah Webster built upon (and borrowed liberally from) in preparing his own speller.

2 Noah Webster

Noah Webster, Junior, was born in Connecticut in 1758, the son of a farmer who later rose to be Deacon in the West Hartford parish and local Justice of the Peace.[1] Noah attended Yale University, graduating in 1778 after several brief stints in the Connecticut militia. Although he passed the Connecticut bar three years later, he found employment primarily as a school teacher. Sometime in the early 1780s he began work on a three-part series of texts for improving American education, the first of which was published in 1783 under the title *A Grammatical Institute of the English Language*, Part I.

The 'Blue-backed Speller', as this text was soon called, was motivated by equal measures of patriotism and educational reform. In the introduction Webster wrote, 'We find Englishmen practising upon very erroneous maxims in politics and religion; and possibly we shall find,

---

[1] Of the various biographies of Noah Webster, Warfel (1936), although sycophantic, is generally the most accessible. Less available generally are Scudder (1881) and Shoemaker (1936). Skeel and Carpenter (1958) is a complete catalogue of Webster's works.

upon careful examination, that their methods of education are equally erroneous and defective' (Webster 1783/1968, p. 4). The 'clamour of pedantry in favour of Greek and Latin' is attacked as is the lack of attention to standards for American pronunciation.

> Thus the pronunciation of our language . . . is *left* to parents and nurses – to ignorance and caprice – to custom, accident or nothing . . . and while this is the case, every person will claim a right to pronounce most agreably to his own fancy, and the language will be exposed to perpetual fluctuation. (*Ibid.*, p. 5)

Webster's pronunciation standard, rendered as an easy guide because 'The principal part of instructors are illiterate people' (*Ibid.*, p. 6), was intended to 'demolish those odious distinctions of provincial dialects' (*Ibid.*, p. 6). Although failing in this task, the book succeeded in every other purpose for which it was directed. Within nine months the first edition of 5000 copies was sold out. Within six years additional impressions were brought out in Philadelphia, New York, Providence and Boston. According to Warfel (1976), one and a half million copies were sold by 1801, twenty million by 1829, and seventy-five million by 1875.

In 1788 the title was changed to *The American Spelling Book* and the blue paper cover, upon which its common appelation 'Blue-backed Speller' was based, became a contractual component of the publication agreements. In the meantime, the remaining two parts of the Grammatical Institute were published; Part II, a grammar, was issued in 1784 and Part III, a reader, in 1785. Although both were revised several times, neither approached the popularity of the speller, and the reader in particular lost most of its market by 1800.

But even with the popularity of his spellers, Webster is best known for his contributions to lexicography. The *Compendious Dictionary*, published in 1806, established Webster as a competent lexicographer. The *American Dictionary*, published in 1828 with definitions for 70 000 words, established Webster as the father of American lexicography.

In these works, as well as in his seven other textbooks and in his voluminous philological, didactic, religious and political works, Webster reveals himself as a stern, humorless man, anxious for financial success and craving after acceptance by the political and intellectual leaders of the day. Much of his time was spent in hawking the virtues of his texts to schoolmasters, parents and any others who would gather to hear him. He campaigned vigorously (and quite successfully) for copyright laws to protect his royalties, and he solicited the approval and support of such men as Washington, Franklin and Jefferson, in addition to the presidents and leading professors at major universities.

3 Webster's spellings

Webster, though unreserved in his scorn for even the most minor inconsistencies in other authors, produced a continually changing set of
spellings in his major works. In the introduction to his first speller (*A
Grammatical Institute of the English Language*, Part I), he proudly announced his compliance with respectable British spelling norms. 'In
spelling and accenting, I have generally made Dr. Johnson's dictionary
my guide; as in point of orthography this seems to be the most approved
authority in the language' (Webster 1783/1968, p. 11). On the failings
of the English grammarians, and in particular Dr Dilworth, to articulate
a correct set of rules for syllabication and pronunciation, Webster is
unreserved in his criticism. But the remoteness of spelling reform from
his educational plan was unmistakably revealed in his criticism of those
who would delete the *u* from -*our* endings – a practice which Webster
himself was not only to adopt within a few years, but to defend as if
derived through divine revelation.

> There seems to be an inclination in some writers to alter the spellings
> of words, by expunging the superfluous letters. This appears to arise
> from the same pedantic fondness for singularity that prompts to new
> fashions of pronunciation. Thus they write the words *favour, honour,*
> &c. without *u*. But it happens unluckily that, in these words, they
> have dropped the wrong letter – they have omitted the letter that is
> sounded and retained one that is silent; for the words are pronounced
> *onur, favur* . . . (Webster 1783/1968, p. 11fn)

But while the first part of the *Grammatical Institute* with its conservative spellings was rapidly becoming an American standard, Webster
was changing into a radical spelling reformer, and in the style which
characterised most of his commercial ventures, was attempting through
personal appeal to America's elder statesmen to have his views imposed
upon the country. In 1786 Webster sent a plan for a phonetic alphabet
to Franklin, soliciting his aid in convincing Congress to adopt the
scheme as a national printing standard. Franklin, in part because he
favored his own phonetic alphabet, and in part from common sense,
gave little encouragement to the plan. Webster apparently dropped
completely the phonetic alphabet, but proceeded to advocate a less
radical reform, based on three principles which were first presented in
An Essay on a Reformed Mode of Spelling (1789/1908, p. 387f):

1. The omission of all superfluous or silent letters;
2. A substitution of a character that has a certain definite sound for
   one that is more vague and indeterminate.

3. A trifling alteration in a character or the addition of a point . .
[to] . . distinguish different sounds.

The first principle gave, for example, BRED, HED, GIV, and BILT for Modern English BREAD, HEAD, GIVE and BUILT. The second produced GREEF (GRIEF), KEE (KEY), LAF (LAUGH), DAWTER (DAUGHTER), KORUS (CHORUS) and MASHEEN (MACHINE). The third added a stroke across *th* to indicate (apparently) a voiced sound, points and macrons over vowels, and the joining of some digraphs.

These principles were used, although not consistently, in a Collection of Essays and Fugitive Writings (1790; cited in Warfel, 1936, p. 138); e.g. RITTEN (but WRITINGS), AZ, HIZ and HAZ (but PEECES, TIMES and EXCUSED), and GUVERNMENT (but OF). With this well-confined experiment, Webster withdrew from his extremist position and according to Warfel (1936, p. 158) concentrated on reform derived from 'uniformity on analogical principles'.

In 1804 Webster brought out the first major revision of the 'Blue-backed Speller' (since 1788 called the *American Spelling Book*). Included in the revision were various new poems and stories, 1800 census figures, and the beginnings of Webster's publicly advocated spelling reforms, here limited to deletion of *u* from terminal *-our* and *k* from terminal *-ick* (in polysyllabic words only). Two years later, however, he published his first dictionary, *A Compendious Dictionary of the English Language*, with the fullest range of spelling reforms that he would advocate for the remainder of his lifetime. The 'pedantic fondness for singularity' which he accused other writers of suffering from 23 years earlier now was in full corporal control of the father of American lexicography. *-or*, *-ic* and *-er* were clearly preferred over the British *-our*, *-ick* and *-re*, as were stress placements as a determiner of whether or not a final consonant is doubled before a suffix that begins with a vowel (REBELLING but TRAVELING). These and several other Webster reforms (see below) have become standard spellings, in contrast to such forms as AKE, CRUM, FETHER, ILE, and SPUNGE which also occurred in the 1806 dictionary.

The man who found earlier that Johnson was 'the most approved authority in the language' now could find little to praise in Johnson's orthography. And where spelling reform was once undesirable, now it was 'indispensable', at least under the proper constraints.

No great change should be made at once, nor should any change be made which violates established principles, creates great inconvenience, or obliterates the radicals of the language. But gradual change to accommodate the written to the spoken language, when they occasion none of these evils, and especially when they purify words from corruptions, improve the regular analogies of a language and illustrate etymology, are not only proper, but indispensable. (Webster, 1806, p. vii)

In time Webster rested his reforms upon two principles: etymology and the practices of great writers. '. . . I am guided by fixed principles of etymology, and endeavor only to call back the language to the purity of former times, supported by the authority of Newton . . . Pope . . . Gregory, Edwards and a host of other writers' (Webster, 1809, cited in Mathews, 1931, p. 48). It is a tribute to Webster's marketing capabilities that his major reforms were finally adopted, because the etymologies he invoked were often inconsistent or faulty and his citations of great writers obviously selective. For example, terminal *k* after *ic* is rejected because it was a Norman innovation, but *ch* for *c* when pronounced [č], *sh* for earlier *ss* (or *ssc*), and *th* for *eth* and *thorn*, which are also Norman innovations, are silently retained.[1] On the one hand Webster justified continual change to bring spelling in line with current pronunciation, but on the other hand justified specific re-spellings, such as FETHER and LETHER, by reference to Old English spellings for sounds which these words no longer contained.[2]

Webster's use of analogy was equally inconsistent, as pointed out by his most vocal critic of the time, Lyman Cobb. For example, Webster justified *-or* for *-our* on the basis of the *u*-deletion in such derived forms as LABORIOUS, RIGOROUS, INVIGORATE and INFERIORITY. But this same argument could be applied also to the *u* in *-ous* (CURIOUS–CURIOSITY, GENEROUS–GENEROSITY etc.), the *i* in *-aim* and *-ain* (DECLAIM–DECLAMATION, EXPLAIN–EXPLANATION etc.), and the *a* in *-eal* (CONGEAL–CONGELATION, REVEAL–REVELATION etc.) (Cobb, 1831). Similarly, *-re* should be justified over Webster's *-er*: CENTRE–CENTRAL, FIBRE–FIBROUS, LUSTRE–LUSTROUS etc.

Although occasionally careless and inconsistent, Webster nevertheless succeeded in giving America a unique and modern brand of

---

[1] Several examples of faulty etymologies can be found in the preface to the 1806 *Dictionary*. See, as an example, the historical sketch for the letter *c* (p. vii). Malone (1925) points out the faulty derivation of *provable*, *movable*, etc. (Webster incorrectly derives these from French verbs, rather than French adjectives.)

[2] Although Webster claims to have studied languages, and in particular the ancient languages, intensely in preparation for writing his major dictionary, he remained unaffected by the philological revolution that was occurring in Europe at the time. He either ignored or was unaware of the work of Sir William Jones, Grimm and Rask in comparative phonology. So far as his writings reveal, Webster never modified his Biblically-based view that all of the world's languages derived from the Semitic, with the three sons of Noah being the progenitors of the major language branches evidenced in Webster's time. The introduction to the 1828 dictionary is devoted almost entirely to establishing this view, complete with etymologies based on Hebrew roots for English words.

orthography. But in pedagogy Webster was Byzantine at best. As cited earlier, he held spelling to be the foundation for reading, which he justified by the claim that at the earliest instructional levels the child's mind was not ready to deal with word meanings. Therefore, spelling was the most appropriate topic for instruction. In general, Webster saw the five- and six-year-old child as nearly embryonic, with undeveloped mind and 'tender' vocal organs. Proper articulation of speech sounds was to be taught by instruction in the proper placement of the tongue and lips. Each lesson was to be learned to perfection before the next undertaken. Although Webster's word lists are graded by number of syllables and by spelling pattern, functional load was not a consideration in word selection. Rare geographic and Biblical terms received equal billing with the most common function words.

As unprogressive as were Webster's pedagogical urgings, he nevertheless made one major contribution to the teaching of reading and spelling, and this was to arrange his word lists not only by number of syllables but also by letter-sound pattern. The motivation for this derived from two American modifications in the traditional ABC approach to teaching reading. First, emphasis was placed on proper articulation and pronunciation and second, elocution was heavily stressed (N. B. Smith, 1965). The first change was probably motivated by an interest in reducing dialect differences in pronunciation and the second by the public advocacy role which citizens in the new democracy were assumed to play.

Webster's analysis of letter-sound correspondences, which is included in the introduction to his speller, shows little improvement over the analyses already published at the time that Webster worked, with minor exceptions. He noted, for example, that although *h* is written after *w* in words like WHALE, the *h* is pronounced first. He tabulated, as did others, the various pronunciations for letters like *c*, *g* and *x*, and showed an awareness of the problems of determining syllable divisions in words like MAGIC and ACID. Some of his patterns, however, like the syllable-dependent subpatterns for *c* and *g*, were faulty. Exceptions to letter-sound rules often included the bizarre, the arcane, or the obsolete, as, for example, the list of 'words in which *g* is hard before e, i, y', which included all of the common examples, plus a few oddities like ORGILLOUS (a variant of ORGULOUS, which itself was an obsolete borrowing from Old French, even in 1783) and PETTIFOGGER. To Webster, nevertheless, must go credit for the first pedagogically oriented tabulation of letter-sound correspondences.

4 The mid-nineteenth century reforms

Webster died in 1843 at the age of 85, having lived long enough to see many of his spelling reforms become American standards and to see his speller become an all-time best seller. But he also witnessed in his last years the beginnings of the new schooling methods that would make his texts obsolete. By the early 1800s the popularity of Webster's spellers had prompted a run of competitors, including such favorites as *The Young Ladies' and Gentlemen's Spelling Book* (1799), *The New England Spelling Book* (1803), and *The New Spelling Book* (1806). For the most part these were copies of Webster's speller, with variations in reading selections and supplementary materials, but with little originality in pedagogy.

Little change in the teaching of reading and spelling took place until the 1840s when under the influence of Horace Mann the whole-word method began to penetrate American education. Mann visited schools in Europe, particularly in Germany and Prussia where Pestalozzi's teachings had already had a major effect upon school instruction. Among other reforms, Pestalozzi advocated the teaching of reading through a word-centered approach that stressed the association between words and the objects they represented. Upon returning to the United States, Mann campaigned vigorously for the whole-word approach to reading and for the separation of spelling from other school subjects.

With the conversion of larger schools to an age-graded system in the middle of the nineteenth century, graded series of readers began to enter the classroom text trade. McGuffey's Readers, which were first published between the years 1836 and 1844, grew rapidly in popularity and remained dominant in American reading instruction until well into the last quarter of the nineteenth century. McGuffey presented a whole-word approach to reading, with words and sentences presented in the first lesson. (The letters of the alphabet and a three-page picture alphabet were displayed at the beginning of the book, but no lessons were built around them.)

The alphabetic-phonetic method remained popular, however, due in part to the availability of textbooks which were organised for this approach, and in part to educational conservatism. Nevertheless, the reforms of Horace Mann, Henry Barnard and others resulted in a reduction of importance for spelling in the curriculum and a change in the methods whereby spelling was instructed. Mann (1839) had advocated three principles for the selection of spelling words: 1. the ease of their use, 2. the pleasure they afforded the pupil, and 3. their potential for promoting progress in orthography, pronunciation and intelligence.

Mann advocated rote memory as the main approach to learning to spell, with words grouped by similarity of spelling pattern. At the same time the use of full sentences was being introduced for teaching (and testing) spelling and the emphasis on esoteric words was declining. This latter influence reduced the spelling-bee to an occasional diversion in many schools – a long drop from the position of importance it occupied at the beginning of the nineteenth century. But even with these changes, the teaching of spelling at the end of the nineteenth century was still far from scientific, as Joseph Mayer Rice discovered.

5 Joseph Mayer Rice

Joseph Mayer Rice was a surgeon turned educator who waged war through the public media on waste, inefficiency and ignorance in public schooling.[1] As part of this effort he carried out the first scientific studies in America on classroom learning, focusing first upon spelling. He also did the first major survey of teaching methods in American schools, founded the Society of Educational Research, and was quoted at length by Thorndike in his text *Educational Psychology* (Thorndike, 1903).

Joseph Mayer Rice was born in Philadelphia in 1857, the fourth child of Meier and Fanny Rice (Reiss). The Rices had arrived in America from Wachenheim, Bavaria, in the middle 1850s as part of the German–Jewish emigration wave that followed the failure of the German revolution in 1848. After attending public school in Philadelphia, Joseph Mayer followed an older brother (Isaac Leopold) to New York and enrolled in the Collegiate Course at the City College of New York.[2] After perhaps not more than a year's full-time study at City College, Joseph Mayer was admitted to Columbia College of Physicians and Surgeons, from where he graduated in 1881.

[1] A major source of information on Rice is the unpublished dissertation by Noble (1971), which is based in part on the Rice papers in the Teachers College, Columbia University, manuscript collection. Brief sketches of his life can be found in *Who's Who in America* (Chicago: Marquis, 1898–1932), *National Cyclopedia of American Biography* (New York: White, 1904), the *Encyclopedia Judaica* (Jerusalem: Keter Publishing House, 1971), and in a *New York Times* obituary (June 25, 1934, p. 15).

[2] Isaac Leopold Rice, who was six when his family immigrated to the United States, excelled in music, law, industry, publishing, and chess. He studied music in Philadelphia and Paris, and then taught for a short time in London where (apparently) he wrote the best known of his two books on the topic (*What is Music?*, New York: D. Appleton and Co., 1875). Returning to the United States from London, he entered Columbia Law School and received an L.L.B. in 1880. Until 1886 he was a lecturer in the law school and instructor in Political Science at Columbia. He resigned to practice corporation law and soon became a leading authority in the organisation of railroads. He was a successful inventor, founder of the storage battery industry in America, co-founder of the *Forum* magazine, and an expert chess player, after whom the Rice Gambit was named.

For seven years Rice alternated between private medical practice and positions in medical institutions. Then, without prior expression of concern, he turned his attention to the science of education and, following the example set by many other American students of the time, including James McKeen Cattell, Raymond Dodge, Frank and Charles McMurray and Lincoln Steffens, set out for Germany. Over the next three years Rice studied at both Leipzig and Jena. He worked with Wundt on the perception of small differences shortly after Cattell left the Leipzig laboratory, but his most enduring influences came from Jena, where in 1889, he enrolled in the Ph.D. program to study under the Herbartian, Wilhelm Rein. Although Rice dropped out of the program within a year, Rein's approach to modernising education through incorporation of current pedagogy and psychology provided a basis for Rice's own educational reforms.

Upon his return to the United States, Rice immersed himself completely in educational reform, primarily through the writing of articles and essays for popular journals. By July of 1891 he was referred to as an 'educational expert' in *Epoch*, a weekly family magazine and shortly thereafter was commissioned by *Forum*, the premier opinion journal of the late nineteenth century, to do a personal investigation of America's schools. For six months Rice visited schools in major cities of the central and northern states east of the Mississippi (or just across the river in the singular case of St. Louis, Missouri). The resulting reports, mostly unfavorable, were published over the next year in the *Forum*, and then issued together in 1893 under the title *The Public School System of the United States*.[1] However, Rice's most enduring contribution to American education derived from survey studies he did two years after the publication of his first book.

6 The futility of the spelling grind

Rice was not the first to use school survey data to promote educational reform, nor was he the first to engage in systematic classroom observations, or to use objective instruments to compare achievement across classrooms and schools. But when his total research program is examined, from hypothesis formation through research design, data collection, analysis, and reporting, his precociousness is strikingly evident.[2] More importantly, the issues he attended to, such as the rela-

[1] To the original articles Rice appended examples of written work gathered on a second field study of the four progressive school systems which he identified in the first study.

[2] E. L. Thorndike devoted about nine pages to Rice's studies of spelling and arithmetic in the first edition of *Educational Psychology*. In the revised, three volume edition of 1914, the Rice

tionship between time on task and achievement, and the approach he advocated for establishing a scientific basis for education, are among the ideas now being explored by educational psychologists. Competency based education, as an example, differs little from Rice's model for elementary education, but with one distinguishing difference: where competency levels today are often set by *ex cathedra* declaration or committee compromise, Rice devised an objective approach to determining expected achievement and collected data to demonstrate the practicality of his scheme.

Spelling was the first school subject to which Rice chose to apply his techniques, and his procedures, results, and conclusions tell us something about a wide range of subjects, ranging from research design to spelling itself. To understand what Rice found about the teaching of spelling at the end of the nineteenth century, however, we need to backtrack for a moment to Rice's philosophy of scientific education.

6.1 *Scientific education*

The educational practices which Rice observed in his various field studies were characterised primarily by rote (mechanical) drill, aimed towards what Rice called lower results, i.e. memory of facts and processes. Spelling, in particular, was simply drill, with little rationale for the selection of words. Fifth graders, for example, in one classroom which he visited, were being drilled on the spelling of EXOGEN, CYLINDRICAL, CONIFERAL, RESINOUS and WHORLS at a time when results from this same classroom on Rice's spelling test showed difficulties with such common words as RUNNING, SLIPPED, BELIEVE and CHANGEABLE. Rules or patterns were rarely taught and the allocation of instructional time bore no relationship to student outcomes (other than perhaps boredom).

Rice's remedy at first view appears simplistic and naïve. First, determine the results desired for each school subject at each level. Then, determine the results to be expected from a given period of instruction. Finally, allocate instructional time, beginning with the most basic subjects. But Rice was not totally ignorant of the reality of formal schooling and much of what he advocated seems to be concerned with orientation and goals as much as with specific mechanisms.

Results, for example, were carefully divided between lower results (rote memory), and higher results, which involved transfer of learning

---

discussion is retained. On the importance of Rice's work, Thorndike says the following: 'Dr. Rice's study is quoted at some length because it was the first of a series of studies of the actual results of school work, still few in number, but destined to increase rapidly with increasing scientific interest in school administration' (1913, p. 293).

and understanding of purpose of instruction. The latter was desirable for assessment while the former, though necessary for reaching true understanding, was not to be the limit of a teacher's interests. For determining the results to be expected from given amounts of instruction, Rice also had a simple answer, and one which might be beneficial to present-day educational planners; *viz.*, observe what the most successful teachers can accomplish. The average expectation will be set somewhat lower, but the process would still be the same. It was in support of these various steps towards scientific education that Rice initiated his spelling studies in February of 1895.

6.2 *Survey of spelling ability*

Rice's first survey consisted of a list of 50 nouns plus a questionnaire for the teacher on instructional methods and student backgrounds. These materials were mailed to an unspecified number of school superintendents in various sections of the United States. (In this as in almost all of Rice's school studies, emphasis was placed almost exclusively on school districts in major cities.) Twenty superintendents responded, returning data on about 16 000 children in grades 4 through 8. After the tests were scored and tabulated, Rice found that the subjective responses to his questions on instructional methods were not always interpretable, so he made personal visits to over 200 teachers who had used the test. Through one means or another he came to suspect that many of the highest class scores were not representative of the abilities of the classes involved. Although reserved in his criticisms of the school personnel involved, Rice's suspicions are evident; some teachers either overpronounced words to make clear their spellings or coached their students on the test items.

To overcome this problem, Rice prepared a second set of spelling tests. One, consisting of 50 words in sentences, was designed for fourth and fifth graders, and a second, consisting of 75 words in sentences, including most from the first sentence test, was designed for sixth, seventh and eighth graders. These tests were administered to about 13 000 students in eight cities, either by Rice himself or under his supervision. After the tests were administered, the students scored the papers. Then, Rice's assistants did final scoring and tabulating.

In addition to the sentence tests, 4000 children drawn from schools in seven of the cities were asked to write a composition based upon a story that was read by the classroom teacher with an accompanying picture. These were scored by Rice's assistants in terms of number of correctly spelled words per hundred text words. (Repeated mis-spellings of the same word were not counted as incorrect.)

Scores on both the word in isolation (column) test and the sentence test improved with increasing grade level. The composition test, however, had a pronounced ceiling effect at each grade level and therefore was not useful for comparisons across levels of independent variables. (The lowest class average was 95.9%.) One might interpret these high scores as evidence of superior spelling ability in functional contexts. A more conservative and probably more accurate explanation is that the students avoided words they couldn't spell with certainty.

In general, classes that scored high on the column test scored about average on the sentence test, validating Rice's judgment that many of the high scores were not true indicators of spelling abliity. But more interesting is Rice's analysis of independent variable effects, done primarily by a comparison of raw scores. What Rice found (i.e. concluded) was that neither instructional type (mechanical vs progressive), nor parentage (native vs foreign born), nor environment (an early form of SES) made a difference on spelling scores. Furthermore, time spent in teaching spelling (above a certain minimum) did not affect scores.

Rice's main conclusion, which is presented and elaborated on in Part II of 'The Futility of the Spelling Grind' (1897), is that the variance in spelling achievement is primarily under control of the teacher, that it cannot be attributed to age, nationality, heredity, environment or any other background factor. To uncover what teachers were doing to foster high spelling ability, Rice interviewed 200 teachers whose classes were assessed with the sentence test and the written compositions. In general, he found no direct relationship between the teachers' expressed methods and their results, but did derive from these interviews, plus his own analysis of spelling, a set of recommendations for spelling instruction which still retain a surprisingly modern ring. These were:

1 Use a variety of teaching methods.
2 Devote no more than 15 minutes per day to the topic.
3 Grade spelling words by orthographic differences and by use.
4 Give precedence to common words.
5 Omit instruction for words that are easily spelled from their sounds.
6 Separate regular and irregular words.
7 Stress rules for adding suffixes (final consonant doubling, retention or dropping of final *e*).
8 Begin drill as early as possible on difficult, small words.

Rice became so committed to the improvement of spelling instruction that he wrote and published a spelling program which incorporated the suggestions above (Rice, 1898). So far as can now be determined, however, the program enjoyed limited commercial success. Nevertheless, Rice articulated an approach to spelling instruction in 1895 that was thoroughly modern, rational and pedagogically sound. His influence on instruction was never large, unfortunately, and his role in the development of testing and curriculum evaluation mostly ignored. Long before his death in 1934 he withdrew from active involvement in educational study or practice, embittered by what he saw as a failure of the educational community to give proper credit to his contributions.

7 The organised assault on English spelling

While Rice labored to improve the teaching of spelling, a vigorous campaign to gain the same ends by simplifying English spelling was rolling into high gear on both sides of the Atlantic Ocean. With the exceptions of Noah Webster and Samuel Johnson, no single individual has succeeded in altering English or American spelling. However, the number who have proposed specific reforms, or who have advocated change in principle is not only large, but includes many of the most famous scientists and men of letters in the history of both England and the United States. Beginning with Sir John Cheke (1514–1557), the first Regius Professor of Greek at Cambridge, and continuing through Benjamin Franklin, Sir Isaac Pitman, Charles Darwin, Alfred Tennyson, Sir James Murray, Otto Jespersen and Leonard Bloomfield, the list forms an impressive register of the accomplished, and accounts for a significant percentage of the best known philologists and linguists of the past century.

The entire history of spelling reform, along with the logic of various reform proposals, and the political, economic and psychological factors which have blocked reform movements are too complex to present coherently here. What is of interest, however, is the organised spelling reform movements which were able to enlist the patronage and support of men (and women) such as those just named, and especially the reform movement in the United States which reached its zenith under President Theodore Roosevelt.

Sir Isaac Pitman, the inventor of the Pitman shorthand system, was the first to organise a reform movement. Through the Phonetic Society, which he organised in England in 1843, and through his *Phonographic Journal*, Pitman promoted a forty character phonetic alphabet which he had developed in association with the British philologist A. J. Ellis. Perhaps due to the radical departure which Pitman was making from traditional orthography, and perhaps due to the near religious fervor which Pitman displayed in his reform promotions, the Phonetic Society failed to gain broad support for its proposals.

In the United States, the lingering controversy over Webster's reforms and over the relationship of American to British spelling, created in the last quarter of the nineteenth century a receptive climate for a spelling reform movement. An American Philological Society committee, working in co-operation with a similar committee appointed by the Philological Society of England, reported an urgent need for simplification and made specific proposals for achieving this goal. In 1876 an International Convention for the Amendment of English Orthography was held in Philadelphia, and resulted in the formation of the Spelling Reform Association in the United States, and shortly thereafter, a companion organisation in England which counted among its vice-presidents Charles Darwin, Alfred Tennyson, Sir Isaac Pitman, James Murray (editor of the *Oxford English Dictionary*), and two of England's most renowned philologists, W. W. Skeat and Henry Sweet.

Through the 1880s both the Philological Society of England and the American Philological Association issued broad recommendations for simplifying thousands of spellings, but little progress in actual reform was made until 1898 when the board of directors of the National Education Association adopted, by an 18–17 vote, 12 simplified spellings for use in its proceedings (THO, ALTHO, THORO, THOROLY, THOROFARE, THRU, THRUOUT, CATALOG, PROLOG, DECALOG, DEMAGOG and PEDAGOG.) Both the moderation displayed by the NEA proposal and the presence on the proposing committee of W. T. Harris, U.S. Commissioner of Education, gave the reform movement an acceptability and rationality which the philologists with their endless lists of reforms had failed to achieve. The next major boost for spelling reform came in 1906 when, with a $10 000 a year subsidy from Andrew Carnegie, the Simplified Spelling Board was created.[1] Like the previous associations, boards and committees, this one also sported a star-studded list of officers and collaborators, including Andrew Carnegie, Samuel Clemens, Melvil Dewey, William James, the editors of most English language dictionaries, and many others. At once the committee issued a 15-page pamphlet (*Simplified*

---

[1] Andrew Carnegie, who was born in a weaver's cottage in 1835 in Scotland and died near Lennox, Massachusetts in 1919, was one of America's most generous and diverse philanthropists. The $311 594 230 which he is known to have given away, either personally, or through the Carnegie Corporation of New York, went to every imaginable human pursuit, from art to research on radium to the strengthening of educational institutions like the Tuskegee Institute and the Hampton Institute (see Lester, 1941 and Carnegie Endowment for International Peace, 1919, for a listing of benefactors). Carnegie established a $280 000 endowment for the Simplified Spelling Board and became himself an advocate of reformed spelling. He used simplified spellings, although not consistently, in personal correspondence and in the parts of his will which appear in his own hand (Hendrick, 1932, Vol. II, p. 263).

Spelling) in which it advocated the use of the simpler spellings of 300 particular words which were 'already spelt in two or more ways'.

Most of the reforms were based upon principles which rational people would have found acceptable. For example, 'If the choice lies between *e* and no *e* in words like ABRIDGMENT, LODGMENT, ACKNOWLEDGMENT, always omit the *e*', or 'Stick to *ense* in preference to *ence* when you have a choice'. Many of the reforms, such as the *-er* in CENTER, THEATER etc. and the *-or* in HONOR, LABOR etc. were already preferred American spellings. Others were acceptable alternatives (e.g. CATALOG, ACKNOW-LEDGMENT) if not the preferred spellings. Only a few, such as *pur* and *bur* and the *t* preterite after *s*, *sh* and *p* (e.g. DIPT, DRIPT, HUSHT) could be considered radical. The degree of departure which this list made from current practice was summarised by the Government Printer, Charles Stillings, in his introduction to the basic word list:

> The seeming difficulties of adopting copy to the new method will become greatly minimized when it is realized that of the 300 words recommended for immediate adoption 153 are at present in preferred use in the Government Printing Office; 49 of the others in this list are not preferred in Webster's Dictionary, but are used in the Government Printing Office wherever the author requests copy to be followed. (*Simplified Spelling*, 1906, p. 3)

As careful as the society was in selecting non-controversial spellings for reform, and in eschewing the radical and wide-sweeping proposals that had doomed previous simplification movements, it could not totally resist the hyperbole and exaggeration that has characterised most orthographic evangelists. 'Intricate and disordered spelling' was the only barrier to English becoming the 'dominant and international language of the world', announced Circular 1 of the Simplified Spelling Board. The consequences of this chaos were frightening to behold.

> It wastes a large part of the time and effort given to the instruction of our children, keeping them, for example, from one to two years behind the school children of Germany . . . Moreover, the printing, typewriting, and handwriting of the useless letters which our spelling prescribes, and upon which its difficulty chiefly rests, wastes every year millions of dollars, and time and effort worth millions more. (*Simplified Spelling*, 1906, p. 7)

The financial theme was to be picked up in a later circular, with exact figures on the savings which would accrue to education and industry through simplified spelling.

The Simplified Spelling Board deliberately chose a policy of gradual simplification, beginning with changes that had a high probability of popular acceptance. And success seemed to have been ensured when as soon as the 300 simplified spellings were published, President Roosevelt ordered the public printer to follow the Board's recommendations in all documents from the Executive department, and urged Congress to make them the standard for all government publications.

In Teddy Roosevelt the simplified spelling movement could not hope for a more sympathetic ally. A graduate of Harvard and the author of two American histories (*The Naval War of 1812* and *The Winning of the West*), Roosevelt became a progressive reformer in the early 1900s while governor of New York. As President, according to Goldman (1956, p. 127), he frequently entertained artists, writers and professors; 'wrote introductions to dissident books like Ross's *Sin and Society* [and] named that persistent nonconformist, Oliver Wendell Holmes, to the Supreme Court'. Spelling reform was a natural addition to the reforms which Roosevelt had already initiated by 1906 in anti-trust procedures, conservation, workmen's compensation, food and drug sales, and meat inspection.

According to Pringle (1931), Roosevelt's interest in spelling reform may have come from early difficulties in spelling. Whatever the validity of this claim, the link from the spelling reform movement to Roosevelt was certainly Brander Matthews, Professor of Literature at Columbia University, prolific writer of novels, reviews, essays and other forms of *belles lettres*, and Chairman of the Trustees of the Simplified Spelling Board. Matthews was a close friend of Roosevelt for many years before Roosevelt became President (Morison, 1951, Vol. II, p. 147, fn. 1). It was Matthews' invitation which led to Roosevelt's article on the history of New York City for the American Historic Towns Series (published in 1891) and it was Matthews who urged him to assist in promoting the Simplified Spelling Board's first list of offerings.

But the glory of the world has made no quicker transit than it did in 1906 for spelling reform. Roosevelt's order of August 27, 1906 to the Public Printer evoked an immediate and vociferous opposition from the public. In November of that year Congress received the President's special message on his visit to the Isthmus of Panama and on plans for the Panama Canal in the reformed spelling and quickly expressed its outrage. The Louisville *Courier-Journal* captured the flavor of the opposition in an editorial entitled 'Nuthing escapes Mr. Rucevelt', noting that 'No subject is tw hi fr him to takl, nor tw lo for him to notis . . . He now assales the English langgwidg . . .' (cited in Gardner, 1973, p. 71).

Roosevelt's political acumen had improved immensely from the time years before when he had stubbornly attempted to enforce the ɔunday liquor laws in New York City. On this occasion he decided that combat with Congress be reserved for more important issues and committed himself to rescind the order to the Printer if the House went on record against it. The House did just that on December 13 and Roosevelt, with Matthews protesting, fulfilled his promise immediately. 'I could not by fighting have kept the new spelling in', he replied to Brander Matthews on December 16, 'and it was infinitely worse to go into an undignified contest when I was beaten . . . But I am mighty glad I did the thing anyhow'. (Morison, 1951, Vol. V, p. 527.)

Roosevelt's backing, rather than accelerating the acceptance of spelling reform, produced the opposite effect by stirring to action the traditionalists who until then had considered spelling reform to be distant and abstract. Congress's refusal to go along with the President and the public outcry which resulted from the Executive order were as much reactions to the arrogation of linguistic authority on the part of the President as they were to the 300 innocent spellings which the Simplified Spelling Board had offered.

In the coming years Carnegie raised his subsidy to $25 000 a year, and various organisations, including the National Education Association and the Modern Language Association, officially adopted the Board's reforms, but the damage done by Congress and the public airing of the reform issue blocked the full acceptance which seemed so close at hand.

A few years prior to Carnegie's death in 1919 the Board's subsidy ended, and the staff was forced to move out of its Madison Avenue offices to a distant upstate New York resort.[1] In 1921 the National Education Association withdrew its support for reformed spelling, and in time most other organisations and publications did the same. The last holdout in the United States was the *Chicago Tribune*, which finally conceded in a front page announcement and editorial on September 29, 1975, that THRU, THO and THORO were through. 'From now on Webster's third will be our guide, first variants preferred. Sanity some day may come to spelling, but we do not want to make any more trouble between Johnny and his teacher.' Reform movements continued, and several exist today, but the potential for success which existed in 1906 has not

---

[1] By 1915 Carnegie had soured on the Simplified Spelling Board. To Henry Holt he wrote, 'A more useless body of men never came into association, judging from the effects they produced. Instead of taking twelve words and urging their adoption, they undertook radical changes from the start and these they can never make . . . I have much better use for twenty-five thousand dollars a year' (cited in Wall, 1970, p. 893). When the initial endowment ran out in 1917, Carnegie did not renew it. Wall (1970, p. 893) claims that 'of all of Carnegie's various ventures into reform, this proved to be his most complete failure'.

existed since, and neither the academic community nor the public seem at all interested in the issue of spelling reform.

8 Epilogue

In retrospect the spelling reform movement may deserve some credit for the current acceptance of spellings like PROGRAM, ACKNOWLEDGMENT and CATALOG. Yet it is undeniable that in terms of its own goals, the reform movement has failed. But why? Part of the answer lies in the naturally conservative attitude which most people have toward language. Just as we resist rapid changes in our phonology, syntax and vocabulary, so do we resist changes in spelling. Furthermore, schools, libraries, publishers and the public have large investments in printed materials which embody the current orthography; spelling reform is a potential threat to the utility of these holdings. Yet phonology, syntax and vocabulary do change, and spelling reform need not be so abrupt and extensive as to render existing materials obsolete.

Some of the fault for the failure of spelling reform must be placed on the reformers themselves, and in particular upon the evangelistic spirit and excesses of rhetoric which pervade the spelling reform tracts. The spelling reform movement has also suffered from an obsession with phonemic writing, an obsession which has occasionally led it to inconsistent and misleading defense of its proposals. English spelling now, as in 1906, is a phonemically based system that preserves morphemic identity wherever possible. It is not, nor was it ever (even in the beginning), a 'one letter, one sound' system as most reformers imply. Nor is there evidence for claiming that a phonemic writing system would significantly alter the rate at which children acquire literacy. After nearly a century of active reform agitation, no evidence has been produced to demonstrate that words with silent letters, as an example, are significantly more difficult to learn to read than words without silent letters.

Even more important, however, is the concern that by pushing English spelling more toward a phonemic system, the skilled reader will lose the advantage offered by the morphemic components of the present system. If CONE and CONIC, for example, were spelled KON and KANIC, their shared semantic base would not be so immediately obvious. Whether or not this feature has a significant influence on reading rate (or accuracy) has never been determined. If it does, then the gains from a more phonemic system would need to be weighted against the losses from removal of morphemic features. But since this argument does not apply to spellings like GNAT and PSYCHOLOGY, where no morphologically related forms are involved, we might ask 'Why not change these?' But given our tolerance of the current forms and the lack of convincing evidence for benefits from change, support for simplification is limited.

More enthusiasm for spelling reform might be generated if initial reading in a reformed English alphabet or in a language with a highly 'regular' orthography clearly progressed at a more satisfactory rate than is observed in this country. But 100 years of reading research have failed to even hint at such an outcome. If anything, we have learned that the perceptual-memory system can tolerate considerably more complexity and exception than English spelling presents to it and that the variation in reading abilities across any sizable population of learners is attributable to a host of factors, orthography being at most just one of many.

So now in the 1970s we are entrusted with an orthography that was last tampered with 200 years ago by Noah Webster, but that by the beginning of this century was so solidly woven into the national fabric that even Teddy Roosevelt, who led the charge up San Juan Hill, broke up the Northern Securities Company, and resolved the Russo–Japanese War, could not alter a thread of it. And the teaching of spelling, though susceptible to fluctuations in the importance it receives in the curriculum, remains today not very far advanced beyond where Joseph Mayer Rice brought it in the 1890s.

PART II

Spelling and Language

Further rules for true spelling, in which observe there are some letters that must be wrote in words, according to the right spelling, and yet are not pronounced in speaking.

There are several letters in words which are not pronounced, and yet must be wrote, because most of these words are of foreign derivation; as,

1) 'a' is written, but not pronounced, in *Pharaoh, marriage, parliament*

2) 'i' is written, but not pronounced, in *evil, devil, venison, Salisbury.*

3) 'o' is written, but not pronounced, in *Nicholas, carrion, chariot.*

4) 'u' is written, but not pronounced, in *intituled, guild, guile, guide, guest, disguise, guard.*

5) 'b' is written, but not pronounced, in *debtor, doubt, dumb, plumb, lamb, thumb, comb, womb, tomb, bomb.*

6) 'c' is written, but not pronounced, in *victuals, indictment, perfect, schism.*

7) 'd' is written, but not pronounced, in *Wednesday.*

8) 'g' is written, but not pronounced, in *deign, reign, feign, foreign, sign, design, sovereign, campaign,* &c.

9) 'h' is written, but not pronounced, in *honour, hour, herb, heir, honest, humour, Thomas, school, scheme, ghost, rhapsody, rheumatism, exhaust, exhort, Rhadamanthus, rhetoric, sepulchre, character, chemist, chimera, chaos, catarrh, catechism,* and others of Greek origin; as also at the end of all Hebrew words, as *Jeremiah, Hezekiah, Nehemiah,* &c.

10) 'l' is written, but not pronounced, in *Bristol, Lincoln, Holborne.*

Extracted from:
A plain and compendious English Grammar, Edinburgh, 1781

2

Linguistic Information in Spelling

PHILIP T. SMITH   *Department of Psychology, University of Stirling, Scotland*

1 What writing systems convey

Reading and writing consist of translating between three types of representation: the visual information on the printed page (graphemic information), a spoken version of this information (phonetic information) and the meaning of the text (semantic information). Modern cognitive psychology has tended to treat these types of representation as three distinct processing levels that are computed in the course of reading or writing, and psychologists have asked such questions as whether a phonetic level mediates the translation of graphemic information into semantic information, and to what extent semantic information is able to influence the extraction of graphemic information. This approach is limited: it gives us little idea about the detailed mechanisms involved in such translation processes, and it gives the misleading impression that each of these types of information constitutes a single homogeneous level. I shall argue in this paper that all of these types of information are much more complex and cognitively rich structures whose properties need much more attention before any psychological model of reading and writing can be constructed.

No writing system can represent all the corresponding phonetic and semantic information in a text: there is simply too much information, and much of it does not lend itself easily to linear transcription. Most languages, like English, use an alphabetic system whose symbols are in loose correspondence with the phonemes of the language; but in no language whose orthography is of any significant age is this graphemic-phonemic correspondence simple. It has been suggested that English is exceptional in the complexities of its orthography, but most languages use their orthography to indicate other than purely phonemic information: German uses initial capital letters to distinguish nouns from other parts of speech; many languages give syntactic information in their spelling (e.g. the present tense of DONNER in French contains the homophones DONNE, DONNES and DONNENT); even one of the most phonemically regular orthographies, Spanish, also transmits morphemic information (*b* and *v* alternate haphazardly in much Spanish spelling, but *b* is always retained for prefixes such as *ab-* and *sub-*); and several languages treat foreign loan words as special cases, both in pronunciation and spelling (e.g. Dutch puts stress on the final syllable of many words borrowed from French, and retains at the same time the un-Dutch-like spelling of the word: HORLOGE, BUREAU). The thesis of this paper is that such phenomena are not simply historical curiosities of little relevance to psychological phenomena in reading and writing: when we read a text we make decisions about parts of speech, about morphemic and syntactic structure and about the denotations and connotations of words, and it is natural that some of this information should be present in each language's orthography. Reading and writing are to be conceived of not as translations between the three isolated levels of representation (graphemic, phonetic and semantic), but rather operations relating to a single linguistic structure of many interacting levels.

TABLE 1   Some functions of 'silent' final *e* in English spelling

Graphemic	Presence of *e* is required after certain letters, e.g. GIVE, FREEZE. Absence after such letters indicates a foreign word (MOLOTOV, KIBBUTZ)
Graphemic/Phonemic	Presence of *e* is required after a syllabic liquid (*l* or *r*) that is preceded by a consonant, e.g. LITTLE, CENTRE. Absence only in rare foreign words (AXOLOTL)
Phonemic	*e* modifies preceding vowel (MATE, THEME, WINE, NOTE, CUTE, in contrast with MAT, THEM, WIN, NOT, CUT). *e* also softens *c* and *g* (ICE, RAGE, in contrast with MUSIC, RAG)
Phonological	The presence of final *e* in certain words, such as ECLIPSE, ARABESQUE, is claimed by some linguists to indicate a special underlying phonological form that is useful in predicting which syllable of the word will receive primary stress
Lexical	A final *e* can help to emphasise that the word is not a plural form, e.g. compare the homophones PLEASE, RAISE, ROSE and PLEAS, RAYS, ROWS. There are a few other homophones distinguished only by a final *e*: ORE, OR and CASTE, CAST; and there is also the fine distinction between such words as ARTIST and ARTISTE
Etymological	Silent final *e* often indicates Latin or French origin. This is not easy to predict with short words, though some homophonic pairs exist, e.g. LOOT (Hindi), LUTE (Old Provencal); MAIL (Germanic), MALE (Latin). In long words the existence of silent *e* in so many affixes all having Latin or French origins (*-able*, *-age*, *-ance*, *-ate*, *-ative*, etc.) means that silent *e* has a strong statistical association with words of Latin and French origins. In contrast, a pronounced final *e* suggests Greek (APOSTROPHE, PENELOPE) or some modern language (KARATE, CURARE). In general the 'rules' here are not very reliable, and indeed words with similar origins may have different spellings, depending on when they were first introduced into English: e.g. DEFINITE, EXQUISITE, DEFICIT, EXPLICIT are all Latin words, but the spelling without a final *e* indicates a more recent introduction into English

Evidence for this position comes from work I have done with Rob Baker and Anne Groat over the past six years, and which I will now try to summarise. A convenient focus is to consider the functions of final *e* in English orthography. Table 1 shows some of these functions. It can be seen that the same grapheme, *e*, can convey very varied information ranging from 'deep' to 'surface' level. The fact that it is silent certainly does not imply that it is unimportant.

Our research has been concerned with how functions such as these influence reading and spelling skills. One of our main techniques has been to construct nonsense words (NODUD, GEVESP) and embed them in sentences so that they appear as nouns or verbs:

The continent of NODUD spread out before them.

He decided to GEVESP the whole business.

Material is either presented in written form and the subject has to read it aloud, or the material is read aloud and the subject has to determine an appropriate spelling for the nonsense word. It is assumed that with nonsense words knowledge of rules is being tapped, rather than specific prior knowledge.

2 Stress assignment: results on reading aloud

Our chief interest here is where subjects decide to locate primary stress in 2-syllable nonsense words (e.g. NÓDUD or NODÚD). This is because stress is not directly signalled by spelling, and has been shown in linguistic analysis (Chomsky and Halle, 1968) to depend on a wide variety of linguistic factors. Some of these factors are shown in Table 2. The table is far from comprehensive, and is included simply to illustrate the range and complexity of the factors linguists consider relevant for a comprehensive set of stress assignment rules. Our concern was whether subjects were aware of these factors and were able to integrate them into a coherent response.

The subject read the sentence containing the nonsense word, the experimenter recorded the phonemic form that the subject chose to use (e.g. the subject might read NODUD with a tense final vowel, so that the final syllable rhymed with FOOD, or he might read NODUD with a lax final vowel, rhyming with BUD: lax (short) vowels, as in BAN, BEN, BIN, BONN, BUN, form a distinct set of vowels in English whose linguistic properties differ from those of tense (long) vowels (the vowels in BAIT, BEAT, BITE, BOAT, BUTE). The experimenter also recorded the location of primary stress in each nonsense word (each word in English contains a syllable that, under normal conditions of speaking, is more prominent than the other syllables in the word: this syllable is said to have primary

TABLE 2 Some distinctions important for stress placement in English

Level	Distinction	Examples	Comments
Phonemic	Vowel quality	TÉMPEST, ÉDIT vs DOMÁIN, SURPRÍSE	Tense final vowel attracts stress in 2-syllable words
Phonemic	No. of consonants	ÉDIT, CÁNCEL vs ADÁPT, ELÉCT	2-syllable verbs ending in 2 consonants have stress on 2nd syllable
		CÍNEMA, VÉNISON vs VERÁNDA, UTÉNSIL	In 3-syllable nouns the number of consonants following the second vowel can alter the stress pattern
Morphemic	Presence of affix	CÁNCEL, ÉDIT vs COMPÉL, ADMÍT	Prefixes such as com- and ad- can alter stress pattern
Underlying	Double consonant	CÍNEMA, CÓRSICA vs UMBRÉLLA, REGÁTTA	UMBRELLA behaves as if 2 consonants followed the second vowel, making it similar in structure to VERANDA; in fact only one consonant can be 'heard'
Underlying	'Silent' e	DÁMASK, ÁSTERISK vs BURLÉSQUE, ARABÉSQUE	Final 'silent' e can alter stress pattern
Syntactic	Noun vs Verb	SÚRVEY, CÓMBINE (nouns) vs SURVÉY, COMBÍNE (verbs)	Extra rules operate on nouns derived from verbs

stress; for example, with the noun THE PERMIT, primary stress is on the syllable *per-*, whereas with the verb TO PERMIT primary stress is on the syllable *-mit*). The concern in these experiments was the extent to which various linguistic factors influenced the location of primary stress, some factors being purely determined by the experimenter (whether the nonsense word appeared as a noun or a verb), some factors being partly determined by the subject (whether the final vowel was pronounced as lax or tense).

We were able to show that subjects indeed took account of several phonemic and syntactic factors in producing a response. Table 3 summarises some of the main effects obtained by Smith and Baker (1976) on adults (university students) and by Groat (1979) on seven-year-old children. Whether the final vowel is lax or tense, whether the word ends in one or two consonants, and whether the word appears as a noun or a verb, all have large and significant effects on the assignments of primary stress in the word. Roughly the same results are obtained for adults and children. These experiments show that graphemic-phonemic translation is not simply a question of turning small groups of letters into sounds, but the entire phonemic structure of the word, together with syntactic information, is used to obtain the full pronunciation that includes appropriate stress patterns.

TABLE 3   Frequency (%) of pronunciations with primary stress on the first syllable of two-syllable nonsense words, as a function of number of final consonants, quality of final vowel and grammatical category

No. of final consonants	Vowel quality	Example of phonemic form of nonsense word	Examples of similar English words	% first syllable stress			
				Adults		Children	
				Noun	Verb	Noun	Verb
1	Lax	nɔdʌd	CARROT, EDIT	85.0	50.5	89.3	78.2
1	Tense	nɔduwd	CHEROOT, INTRUDE	70.5	17.5	65.4	37.5
2	Lax	gɛvɛsp	TEMPEST, INVEST	50.0	27.1	87.1	55.9

3 The role of the final *e* in reading aloud tasks

Table 3 shows that the graphemic information that is rather directly connected with phonemic information (vowel quality, number of final consonants) is utilised even by seven-year-old children. This is not true for more sophisticated information, in particular for final *e* spellings. Figure 1 shows the main effects of a final *e* on the nonsense word (NODUDE, GEVESPE) in contrast with a 'normal' spelling where the *e* is omitted (NODUD, GEVESP). The data is based on words that were pronounced with the same sequence of phonemes in each condition: in this particular analysis both vowels of the 2-syllable nonsense word were lax (short). In other words, the phonemic structure is being held constant and the variations shown in the figure are entirely a function of the syntactic context (noun vs verb) and whether the spelling contained a final *e* or not. There are large and significant syntactic effects whereby nouns are more likely to receive first syllable stress than verbs, and clear differences in bias towards first syllable stress (children show a greater bias than adults). However, whereas children take no account of final *e* in deciding where to put primary stress in these words, the *e* has a marked effect on adult performance, reducing the probability of first syllable stress and abolishing the difference between nouns and verbs. The conclusion is that English speakers have acquired a sophisticated system of rules for determining the stress of the word, which involves the simultaneous integration of several linguistic levels; this skill is acquired quite early in linguistic development before reading is completely fluent, with the sole exception of readers' performance with final *e*, which appears to be handled in a special way by adults.

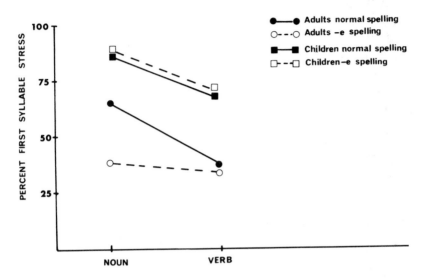

FIG. 1   Frequency of first syllable stress, as a function of spelling and grammatical category

Another aspect of this difference between adults and children emerges when we look at 3-syllable pronunciations. Words such as NODUDE and GEVESPE usually were pronounced as 2-syllable words, but occasionally the final *e* was pronounced to give a 3-syllable word. Table 4 shows that for adults this is a function of syntax (noun vs verb), but no such distinction is made by children. I shall try to explain these results after first considering complementary work on spelling.

TABLE   4   Frequency   (%)   of   three-syllable pronunciations of words like NODUDE and GEVESPE, as a function of grammatical category

	Noun	Verb
Adults	13.76	6.08
Children	5.00	6.43

4 Results on spelling

In this task subjects were asked to make judgments about the spelling of nonsense words, which were presented, as in our previous experiments, embedded in English sentences; however in the present experiment the sentences were read aloud by the experimenter. Factors such as the quality of the vowel, the stress pattern of the word and its syntactic function were systematically varied. There were two versions of this task: a selection task, where various alternative spellings were presented to the subject after each nonsense word had been spoken, and the subject had to choose what he thought was the most appropriate spelling; and a *production* task, where the subject was given no written alternatives and had to generate his own spelling. Surprisingly, the interactions between spelling, location of primary stress and grammatical category which we found in the pronunciation task appeared only in a much diluted form in the spelling task: sound-to-spelling rules seem less systematic (or perhaps simply less well practised) than spelling-to-sound rules. However one unexpected result involving final *e* appeared. In English there are two ways of signalling a tense (long) vowel in the final syllable of a word: either there can be a 'silent' final *e* (GATE, DISCRETE, RODE, LUTE) or a pair of vowels may be used (GAIT, DISCREET, ROAD, LOOT). This latter convention we call a *V spelling*, whereas a final *e* we call an *-e spelling*. Table 5 gives the relative frequency of *-e* spellings among *-e* and *V* spellings for nouns and verbs in the two experimental conditions.

TABLE 5 Proportion of *-e* spellings, as a percentage of *-e* and *V* spellings, for nonsense words ending in a tense vowel and a single consonant, as a function of grammatical category and experimental condition

	Noun	Verb
Selection task	50.7	55.0
Production task	67.1	72.5

There are gross differences between the experimental conditions (*-e* spellings are more popular in the production task than in the selection task), and also there is a small but significant tendency for *-e* spellings to be favoured more for verbs than for nouns. This latter result is at first surprising, since a quick check of the dictionary suggests no similar bias exists among real English words. One possibility however is that subjects regard low frequency verbs as more likely to be borrowings or inventions based on Latin and Greek (METAMORPHISE, SUPERANNUATE), whereas low frequency nouns are not so restricted. Again a check in the dictionary suggests that among words with silent final *e*'s a great preponderance come from Latin, Greek and French, whereas this is less true of *V* spellings; also, among words borrowed from more exotic languages, nouns greatly outnumber verbs. The intuition we are expressing here is that a subject is more likely to regard NODUDE (Latin spelling) as a technical verb meaning (say) to weld metals in a certain way, whereas NODOOD (non-Latin spelling) might refer to an article of clothing of a North American Indian. This interpretation now fits in with the strange result of Table 4: pronouncing a final *e* is rare in the Latin–Greek part of our vocabularies (just a few words ending in -*o*-*Consonant*-*e* (PENELOPE) which have Greek origins), and thus the 3-syllable pronunciations of words such as NODUDE may be taken to indicate that the word is perceived as deriving from a modern foreign language (like KARATE, VIVACE, CURARE, ENTEBBE). Table 4 indicates that adults are more prepared to ascribe a non-Latin foreign quality to nouns than to verbs, and this harmonises with the results of our spelling experiment. The fact that children do not show these effects suggests that we acquire late the ability to perceive our vocabulary as being constructed with the help of several different spelling systems of different historical origins.

Finally, the stress pattern data of Fig. 1 can also be handled by this concept of perceived foreign quality. In a separate experiment, when we asked subjects to guess what languages our nonsense words came from we were overwhelmed by the quantity of responses from our normally reticent subjects (56 languages, ranging from Albanian to Eskimo): this in itself suggests that the origin of a word is not something that subjects were unaccustomed to consider. Words with an -*e* spelling were often described as French, and French words have stress on the final syllable. The effect of -*e* spellings for adults in Fig. 1 therefore is to create a special class of 'French' words, which have low probability of first syllable stress and for which the normal English rule, that gives nouns a higher probability of first syllable stress than verbs, is blocked.

5 The perceived origins of words

We should explain more carefully here what we mean by a 'foreign' word. It seems to be the case that there is a continuum ranging from a clear perception that a word is totally foreign, to a complete acceptance of a word as standard English. In my vocabulary, for example, I use some (very rare) words with a careful non-English articulation (PAELLA, POUILLY FUISSÉ, SIMPATICO); other words remain 'foreign' but their articulation is less careful and more 'English' (ZEITGEIST, BEAUJOLAIS); other words receive a full English pronunciation although I am quite clearly aware of their foreign origin (MOSCOW, CHAMPAGNE); still other words I am faintly aware of their origins but lack detailed knowledge about them without the help of a dictionary: their pronunciation (for me) is fully English (MUGWUMP, JUNTA); finally there are words which seem totally English, even though an historical dictionary might assign different origins to them (WINE, WOMEN, SONG). When we talk of the foreign quality of words in this paper we are referring to the latter three classes of words above, that is, not to words which we given deliberate 'foreign' pronunciations, but to words which receive full English pronunciations even if these pronunciations occur in conjunction with partial awareness of the origins of the words. Subjects in our experiments very rarely pronounced our nonsense words in a foreign manner: the phonemes and intonation were entirely English and all that distinguished their performance from normal reading was an occasional hesitancy in uttering the word.

What we are claiming is that the studies we are reporting do not describe the performance of a very small group of language specialists who have an unusually detailed knowledge of English etymology; rather we are claiming that a large proportion of literate speakers of English are aware that the English spelling system is heterogeneous, and that different sets of rules apply to different parts of the system. Some linguists have explicitly proposed different sub-systems of English spelling (e.g. Albrow, 1972) and what we are claiming is that many literate English speakers are aware of these subsystems. It is not necessary in this case that such speakers are explicitly aware of the historical and comparative basis for such sub-systems: for example it is possible to grasp that a certain sub-set of English words spell the /k/ phoneme as *ch* (PSYCHOLOGY, CHLORINE, CHOLESTEROL, ICHTHYOGRAPHY) without being aware that all these words derive from Greek. When we talk of a subject using a 'Latin' spelling in this paper we do not mean the subject is making use of explicit knowledge of Latin, merely that the sub-system of English spelling that he is using can be conveniently described as of Latin origin.

In summary then, all of our results so far have shown that both in spelling and pronunciation tasks the presence of a final *e* influences subjects' performance, and a likely unifying explanation is the perceived foreign quality of the word. I would like to argue that although this is only one aspect of the functions of -*e* that are summarised in Table 1, it is not a particularly bizarre or isolated result: the Dutch examples with French loan words that I quoted at the beginning of the paper are instances in another natural lauguage where etymology is of significance to the reader and speller, and therefore will have psychological correlates.

6 Some differences between reading and spelling

A further result of our spelling task illustrates how there are different linguistic influences in operation in our reading tasks and in our spelling tasks. Frith (1979) has stressed the importance of a phonological component in spelling which is not present in reading. We have found support for this view. In our spelling tasks we compared normal spellings (NODUD) with -*e* spellings (NODUDE) when the final vowel was lax, and we also compared *V* spellings (NODOOD) with -*e* spellings when the final vowel was tense. The comparison we made was the ratio of -*e* to normal spellings and -*e* to *V* spellings, as a function of the final consonant of each nonsense word.

Now the graphemic rules of English in this case appear somewhat arbitrary. For final lax vowels, -*e* must follow *v* (GIVE, HAVE) and it may follow *t*, *m*, *n* (DEFINITE, TROUBLESOME, DETERMINE), otherwise it is very rare. For tense final vowels -*e* must follow *v*, *z*, *s* (HIVE, FREEZE, LOOSE), *V* spellings are possible for all final consonants though they are rare with *b* and *g* (BOOB, CRAIG); in addition -*ge* and -*ce* are not possible spellings of words ending in the phonemes /g/ or /k/, as these consonants are rendered soft by the following *e*. One might predict therefore that subjects' performance in this task would be erratic, with some trends towards favouring -*e* spellings following *v* and *z*, and avoiding -*e* following *g* (*c* was not used at the end of words in this experiment). This is indeed the case in the *selection* task (where subjects were given various spellings of the word to choose between): in comparing -*e* and normal spellings, no significant overall effect emerges, and when we compare -*e* and *V* spellings, there is a significant overall effect, but this is entirely due to the preference for *e* following *v* and the avoidance of *e* following *g*. This then is a case of knowledge and use of graphemic rules: *v* without *e* at the end looks wrong. Also subjects do know the rule of soft *g* before *e*.

The situation with the *production* task (where subjects were required to generate their own spellings) is quite different. Subjects appear to be overgeneralising graphemic rules on a phonological basis. Thus subjects show a preference for -*e* spellings with *all* fricatives, even though only *v* and *z* always require an -*e* spelling in the graphemic rules. In the case of tense final vowels, place of articulation of the final consonant is also important, and all front consonants are more commonly followed by -*e*, this tendency is reduced for middle consonants, and *V* spellings are favoured with back consonants (see Fig. 2). These results are highly significant, and nothing like this regularity is present in the English spelling system. However, with its regularity and emphasis on phonemic features (manner and place of articulation) this performance is entirely characteristic of a phonological system of rules. The conclusion is that while the *selection* task is largely a matter of reading, and does not involve a phonological component, the *production* task is basically a spelling task and involves a substantial amount of phonological over-generalisation.

7 *e* cancellation tasks

The final area in which a superficial view of graphemic processing can be seen to be inadequate is the letter cancellation task, first studied by Corcoran (1966), and more recently by Coltheart *et al.* (1975), Healy (1976), Frith (1979) and Smith and Groat (1979). The subject reads an English text, and is required at the same time to cancel every letter *e* that he notices in the text. A view of reading that puts emphasis on the importance of a direct graphemic-phonemic translation of single letters or small letter groups would predict that *e*'s not sounded out, and hence not directly associated with a phoneme (e.g. the *e*'s in GIVE, HOPEFUL) would more often fail to be cancelled by the subject than the *e*'s which were directly associated with a phoneme (e.g. the *e*'s in BE, RECIPE); this would be because subjects are likely to notice *e*'s that they have translated to a sound and fail to notice the others. What a theory predicts that emphasises direct graphemic-lexical translation is less clear, though presumably phonetic effects would be absent. In fact the data suggest a richer theory in which the boundaries between graphemic, phonemic and lexical information are not sharply drawn.

The *e* in *the* is very readily missed and is influenced by several task variables: e.g. Smith and Groat showed that subjects told to ignore meaning in reading the text cancelled more *e*'s in *the* than subjects without these instructions. Smith and Groat also showed that the *e* in the past tense morpheme -*ed* was much more frequently missed than other *e*'s in similar positions in words. These results show that syntactic and semantic factors are important in determining what features of a text a subject pays attention to. Phonetic factors also play a role in this task, but not in the direct way that Corcoran originally claimed. Our analysis goes beyond the simple distinction between sounded and silent *e* (BE *vs*

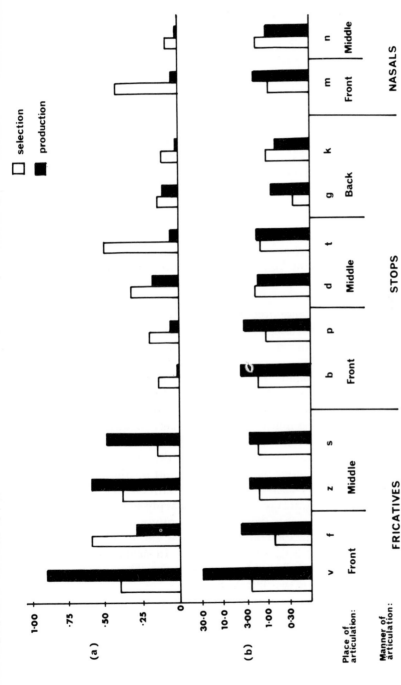

FIG. 2 Spelling preferences in the selection and production tasks: (a) shows the ratio -e to normal spellings for two-syllable nonsense words ending in a lax vowel and a single consonant, (b) (logarithmic scale) shows the ratio of -e spellings to V spellings for words ending in a tense vowel and a single consonant

GIVE), and looks in addition at other phonetic features (stressed vs unstressed *e*) and indirect phonetic effects (the *e* may alter the sound of a previous consonant or vowel. A careful control of all the relevant factors by Smith and Groat showed to be incorrect Corcoran's original claim that *e*'s directly associated with phonemes were more readily cancelled, but both Frith and Smith and Groat have shown that unstressed *e*'s (the *e*'s in OFTEN and EMIT) are more often missed than *e*'s receiving primary stress in a word (e.g. the *e*'s in OFFEND, EDIT).

Other phonetic effects of 'silent' *e* are best investigated in relation to the distinctions made in Table 1, and indeed Smith and Groat have used this table to compare *e* cancellation rates for graphemic, phonemic and lexical *e*'s. The particular classes of *e* investigated are shown in Table 6. These classes are (1a) *-ve no change*, where the *e* does not modify the preceding vowel (HAVE, GIVE); (1b) *-ve vowel change*, where the *e* modifies the preceding vowel (GAVE, HIVE); (2) -C*e*, where C is a consonant other than *r*, *s*, *v*, *z*: (2a) *consonant change* is where the *e* modifies the preceding consonant but not the preceding vowel (SINCE, EDGE), (2b) *vowel change* is where the *e* modifies the preceding vowel but not the preceding consonant (GATE, HOME) and (2c) *consonant and vowel change* is where the *e* modifies both preceding consonant and preceding vowel (ICE, RAGE); (3a) *-se no change*, where the *e* is not needed to modify the preceding vowel (RINSE, PLEASE); (3b) *-se vowel change*, where the *e* modifies the preceding vowel (RISE, CASE). Class (1a) we argue is graphemic, (1b) graphemic and phonemic, all of class (2) is phonemic, (3a) is lexical and (3b) is lexical and phonemic: the arguments for such classifications are presented in Table 1. *r* is omitted as a consonant from class (2) because of the many frequent function words ending *-ere* or *-ore* (THERE, WERE, MORE, BEFORE): *e* here could be said to have a lexical role in signalling this class of word but the case is not as straightforward as for *-se* words; for words ending in *-ze*, *e* would be classed as graphemic in our analyses, but no examples occurred in our samples.

Table 6 shows that lexical *e*'s are detected more readily than phonemic *e*'s, and phonemic *e*'s are detected more readily than graphemic *e*'s. The other significant factor is that *e*'s serving two linguistic functions [classes (1b), (2c) and (3b)] are more readily detected than *e*'s serving only one function. Thus the table shows that the deeper the linguistic level the more certain is the detection.

These data then support the view that while phonetic information does affect aspects of performance, not all phonetic information is equally effective. Since the analysis was based entirely on so-called silent *e*'s, it is clear that phonemic information in terms of a direct grapheme to phoneme translation is not involved. Phonetic information in terms of stress and of the consonant and vowel modifying functions of *e* is however very important in this task. Many lexical and semantic functions of *e* influence performance, but not all in the same way. For example, the *e* in THE is particularly influenced by changes in the instructions to subjects (to pay attention to or to ignore meaning), whereas the data in Table 6 are not influenced by such changes: this suggests that different levels of linguistic representation are being simultaneously computed (some levels associated with meaning, some with pronunciation etc.) and an ancillary task such as *e* cancellation can tap information at several different levels.

TABLE 6   Frequency of failure to cancel various classes of final *e*

Class		Role of *e*	Example	Omission frequency (%)
(1a)	-*ve* no change	Graphemic	GIVE	15.7
(1b)	-*ve* vowel change	Graphemic and phonemic	HIVE	12.0
(2a)	consonant change	Phonemic	EDGE	11.5
(2b)	vowel change	Phonemic	GATE	10.2
(2c)	consonant and vowel change	Phonemic	RAGE	5.0
(3a)	-*se* no change	Lexical	APSE	7.8
(3b)	-*se* vowel change	Lexical and phonemic	RISE	5.2

These different levels are independent to the extent that different task variables, such as instructions to subjects or the difficulty of the text, can influence differentially the amount of attention that is paid to each level. The reading process is not an inflexible system that always computes the same type of information to the same depth with the same order of processing.

8 Summary and conclusions

I have argued against a view of reading and spelling that conceptualizes graphemic, phonemic and semantic representations as simple single level structures, and which sees the processes of reading and spelling as simple direct translation from one representation to another. The evidence I have brought forward is as follows.

1   In determining the full pronunciation of an unfamiliar word, both adults and children go beyond simple grapheme-phoneme correspondences and use both syntactic information and information about the phonemic and graphemic structure of the entire word.

2 Etymological factors (whether the word looks or sounds foreign and from what language it might be borrowed) influence both the pronunciation and the spelling of unfamiliar words by adults. In particular, words ending in a final *e* are more likely to be judged French and more likely to receive final syllable stress; final *e*'s are more likely to be pronounced if they appear in nouns than in verbs; verbs are more likely to be spelt with a final *e* than nouns. This suggests that at least a tripartite division of our vocabulary into words of (*i*) Latin, Greek and French origin (*ii*) Germanic origin (*iii*) more exotic origins, makes psychological as well as historical and linguistic sense.

3 Reading and spelling skills tap different components of our linguistic abilities: in particular, spelling appears to have a phonological component that is absent from reading. Words ending in similar sounding consonants receive similar spellings in a spelling production task, but this effect is absent when subjects merely have to make visual comparisons of possible spellings.

4 Studies of *e* cancellation tasks suggest it is the linguistic functions of *e* that are primarily responsible for whether the letter is cancelled or not. While all levels of linguistic information exert an influence, each level behaves differently in response to such variables as the difficulty of the text and whether the subject expects to be questioned about the text. Direct phonemic factors are absent: it is irrelevant whether there is a direct link between the grapheme and the phoneme. However, indirect phonetic factors are important, namely whether the *e* occurs in a stressed syllable and whether the *e* is modifying a consonant or another vowel in the word. This shows clearly that a letter-by-letter or letter group-by-letter group translation into sound is a poor conceptualisation of the role of sound in reading. Surface level phonemic and graphemic factors are uninfluenced by difficulty of text or instructions. Higher level factors (missing the *e* in -*ed*, and missing the *e* in *the*) are affected by text difficulty, and such a result could be interpreted as suggesting that subjects with a difficult text are spending more time in computing a higher (syntactic, semantic) level of representation which treats -*ed* and *the* as unanalysed units.

These results suggest that a better conceptualisation of the processes involved in reading and spelling would be as follows. The reader or speller is to be conceived of as a multi-level information processor. The levels would be numerous (graphemic, phonetic, low-level phonemic, high-level phonemic, morphemic, lexical, syntactic, semantic, etymological, etc.) and any particular process (reading aloud, reading silently, proofreading, spelling, etc.) would utilise possibly different selections of levels, which would interact with one another in the course of the task. The problem for the student of reading and spelling is to determine which levels are used, how these levels interact and how the teaching of reading and spelling skills can be related to these insights. This is certainly a highly complex and daunting project in comparison with the neat and appealing compartmentalisation into graphemic, phonemic and semantic representations which has dominated much psychological work. However if we are ever to obtain some accurate idea of the intermediate stages following the visual presentation of linguistic material, this multi-level approach is surely necessary: we must seek psychological models that do justice to the sophistication of the readers and spellers we are studying.

Acknowledgements

This research was supported by a grant from the Social Science Research Council. Part of the paper was written while the author was visiting Max-Planck-Gesellschaft Projektgruppe für Psycholinguistik, Nijmegen: I am very grateful to Professor Levelt for providing facilities.

3

Orthographic Awareness

ROBERT G. BAKER   *Department of Psychology, University of Stirling, Scotland*

1 Principles of English spelling

Denouncements of English spelling as a graphic representation for spoken English are commonplace (see Follick, 1965; Pitman and St. John, 1969). English is said to be 'not a phonetic language'.[1] It must be conceded that English orthography frequently infringes the canonical principle of alphabetic orthographies – that of sequential matching of phonemic and graphemic units. However, the instances of anomalous and inconsistent spelling-to-sound correspondences can be dramatically offset by considering a set of hypothetical advantages recently suggested by a number of linguistic studies. Just as linguists are able to analyse language at a number of different levels of abstraction, so a writing system may be similarly selective in those levels of language it seeks to represent. The postulation of a principle of orthographic representation which is more abstract than one based purely on the phonemic level of description may render the would-be spelling reformers' criticisms invalid.

A few examples may illustrate how rigid adherence to a principle of one-to-one phoneme-grapheme representation can result in a positive loss of relevant linguistic information. Many people are surprised to learn that the spelling *-ed* in WALKED is not phonemically accurate. A more accurate representation would be WALKT.

Traditional orthography, however, prefers to maintain the parallelism with WAITED (more accurately WAITID), WARNED (more accurately WARND) etc. It may be argued that a spelling which disregards these phonemic differences (which are themselves phonologically determined) and signals the identity of the verbal past-tense morpheme *-ed* is logical and perhaps even helpful. We know immediately from their graphic form that we have in each case to deal with forms of the same syntactic class, i.e. past-tense verbs.

A similar example is provided by the plural morpheme *-s*. The *-s* in DOGS and CATS is spelled the same, but does not sound the same. Phonemically, the spellings should be DOGZ and KATS. It is unlikely, however, that many people would complain about this lack of strict letter-sound correspondence. It is surely useful to preserve graphically the identity of the plural morpheme, so that again this syntactic feature

---

[1] It is more accurate to say that English spelling is not a straightforward *phonemic* representation of spoken English. The term 'phonemic' is used to refer to the system of minimal linguistically significant sound segments of a language, its 'phonemes'. This is in contradistinction to the term 'phonetic' which has no such analytical consequences – the linguist's phonetic transcription is simply a maximally objective and detailed representation of language sounds without reference to their meaning or significance in the language. The term 'phonological' refers more generally to linguistically significant sound systems without necessarily assuming the unit 'phoneme'.

can readily be extracted from written material. Evidence that such syntactic morphemes are indeed treated as separate 'chunks' in tachistoscopic word-recognition experiments has been presented by Gibson and Guinet, 1971.

Another advantage of traditional spelling when it disregards the strict phonemic principle is in signalling lexical derivational relationships. If one were to omit the 'silent g' in the word SIGN, spelling it as SINE (or SIEN), the relationship to SIGNAL would be obscured. Jarvella and Snodgrass (1974) have demonstrated that subjects find it easier to make judgements of meaning-relatedness when pairs of words are minimally different from one another in written form, e.g. REVISE–REVISION than when they are not, e.g. DIVIDE–DIVISION.

Similarly, it may be very helpful that homophones can be differentiated visually. Thus in their written form, SIGN and SINE will not be confused, while they are indistinguishable in their spoken form, and would accordingly receive identical phonemic spellings. Lastly, traditional spelling allows differentiation of lexical and grammatical morphemes that sound identical. It enables us to distinguish a plural s from a singular s simply by requiring a final e to be placed when a singular form is indicated. This is the case with PLEASE vs PLEAS.

In all these examples, many people may agree that lack of one-to-one phoneme-grapheme relationships is to some extent justified. However, others may disagree and question why written words should 'improve' on the discriminability of spoken words and the information conveyed by speech sounds. One possible explanation is in terms of the total information content of language systems. Thus written language is necessarily lacking in its representation of some of the more subtle 'affective' distinctions conveyed by intonation – we have only '!' and '?' to represent a whole range of possibilities. Furthermore, written language is normally by its very nature isolated from the background of extra-linguistic cues which serve to enhance speech communication. It may be that the written language 'compensates' to a certain extent for this loss of information by rendering other linguistic distinctions and relationships less ambiguous. The question arises whether the type of compensatory information conveyed by written language is equal in value to that which is lost. At first glance, it appears not. Homophones rarely present problems of interpretation provided that there is sufficient linguistic context available. We know this because there are so many homophones in English which are *not* distinct in spelling, e.g. MINE and MINE. It seems unlikely that the knowledge that there is a derivational relationship between SIGN and SIGNAL would be of any use *except* as an aid to spelling the irrational SIGN (and as documentation for the historian of language). The value of each of the conventions exemplified above needs to be established empirically.

Linguists state that the representational principle of English spelling is morphophonemic (Venezky, 1970), systematic phonemic (Chomsky and Halle, 1968), or 'polysystematic' (Albrow, 1972). This latter notion of 'polysystem', or system of systems, in this case the co-existence of and interaction between phonological, grammatical and lexical systems of orthographic representation, derives from the work of J. R. Firth, who stated forty years ago that 'the main argument against phonetic spelling . . . [is that] it removes phonetic ambiguity and creates other functional ambiguities' (Firth, 1935, p. 61f). Similar statements can be found in Albrow (1972, p. 8f) and Venezky (1970, p. 122f). These writers see English orthography as a naturally evolved device for transcribing, albeit in a somewhat eclectic fashion, linguistic generalisations which may be of value to the reader.

However all but the most fortunate of English spellers have first-hand familiarity with the existence and persistence of spelling difficulties irrespective of our level of reading attainment; and one is inclined to ask whether the second-order, high-level regularities of English spelling, which may be patent (in both senses, perhaps) to linguists, represent anything other than an obstacle course for the average speller. One possible counterargument is in terms of the very obdurateness over time of the traditional orthography and its notorious resistance to all attempts at reform. Since it has survived, it must be superior. This explanation is inadequate in view of the many confounding political and socio-linguistic factors involved in spelling reform (see Haugen, 1966, for the Norwegian case). It is also inadequate since none of the proposed designs for a reformed orthography have been grounded in sufficient empirical research. This is true even for the 'initial teaching alphabet' (ita), one of the least radical and certainly most popularly successful reforms. In the first place, the designers failed to make explicit the differing demands made on an orthography by the reader and by the writer: ita was designed primarily with the reader in mind. Spelling-to-sound correspondences are with very few exceptions uniquely defined whereas sound-to-spelling correspondences are not. In the second place, the particular regularisations made appear somewhat arbitrary and without empirical justification (see Haas, 1970, p. 53f).

In the research to be reported below the point of view is put forward that such empirical work should take the form of an investigation into the psychological reality and intuitive plausibility of the conventions and rule-systems posited in the linguistic descriptions mentioned above. It was decided to examine the capacity of English spellers to reflect on their spelling and to provide their own solutions to the question of optimality in orthographic representation. With this in mind the initial approach was to ask competent spellers to play the part of spelling reformers.

2 The spelling reform task

Subjects are presented with sets of English words in traditional spelling, and after a short preamble on the 'rationality' or otherwise of English spelling, during which a note is made of the subject's own attitude to this general question, each word is given a rating on a 5 point scale according to the subject's own conception of 'rationality'. Then for each word rated less than 5 ('perfectly rational') the subject is asked to suggest an alternative 'more rational' spelling. Word sets have been selected from standard spelling tests (e.g. Schonell's Graded Word Spelling Tests) and from examples given in the abovementioned literature to illustrate the operation of spelling rules.

The assumptions underlying the task are that any spelling changes made will reflect a level of orthographic representation that has psychological reality for the subject in question. and that spelling conventions left unchanged are 'O.K.' i.e. they have psychological integrity. Thus particular conventions are evaluated by consensus. The rationale of the task bears some similarity to that of studies of syntactic acceptability (e.g. Hill, 1961) but there are still closer parallels with the work of Gleitman and Gleitman (1970) in which subjects were asked to paraphrase noun phrases such as 'black house bird' (with varying stress patterns), and the resulting paraphrases were taken to reflect the psychological reality of rules governing the formation of nominal compounds.

A selection of results from one such spelling reform study is presented in Tables 1–4. In this study, 11 subjects (university undergraduates) reformed the spelling of a total of 111 words taken mainly from the examples presented in Albrow (1972). The results were analysed according to the following spelling rules which are all motivated by non-phonological considerations.

1 Final -e after v and z.
2 Final -s and final -ed for specific grammatical morphemes.
3 Similar spelling for derivationally related words.
4 Different spelling for homophones.

2.1 *Final* -e *after* v *and* z

Table 1 illustrates subjects' attitudes to the graphemic rule that v and z do not regularly occur in word-final position in English.

TABLE 1 Spelling reform task. Treatment of graphemic final -*e* following *v* and *z*. (Number of subjects out of 11)

	-*e* preserved	-*e* dropped	Other solutions
(a) *v*			
SIEVE	1	10	—
LOVE	3	8	—
GIVE	1	8	-*f* (1), -*ff* (1)
NATIVE	2	7	-*f* (2)
DOVE	4	7	—
LIVE	3	7	-*vv* (1)
HAVE	—	10	-*vv* (1)
BELIEVE	1	10	—
RECEIVE	2	9	—
LEAVE	5	6	—
WEAVE	6	5	—
MOVE	2	8	-*f* (1)
Total	30	95	7
(b) *z*			
SEIZE	4	4	-*s* (3)
FREEZE	3	7	-*s* (1)
FRIEZE	3	7	-*s* (1)
Total	10	18	5

The results of spelling reform are that graphemic final -*e* following *v* is dropped more than three times as often as it is preserved, but that -*e* following *z* is dropped somewhat less often. In a few cases, instead of simply keeping or dropping final -*e*, an alternative response was observed (e.g. GIF for GIVE or SIES for SEIZE). These instances were treated as following the graphemic rule prohibiting final *v* and final *z*, since at least they avoided breaking this rule. Taking this into account, the proportion of rule-following and rule-breaking instances was computed for each subject and a sign test applied. The result was significant for final *v* ($p < 0.025$) but not for final -*z*. This result is surprising in view of the results of one frequency count (Dolby and Resnikoff, 1964) in which final *z* occurs 10 times (and -*ze* 55 times) in a total of 7000 words (*Oxford Universal Dictionary*) whereas -*v* occurs only twice (and -*ve* 113 times). Thus one must conclude that even though there are hardly any real-life exceptions to the graphemic rule in the case of final *v* (less than 2% exceptions), subjects nevertheless readily dropped the -*e* as a spelling reform (over 70% of cases). With final -*e* after *z*, on the other hand, real-life exceptions are far more common (15% exceptions) and yet subjects follow the rule about as often as they break it. These results imply that this particular graphemic rule is not highly valued by naïve reformers.

2.2 *Final* s *and* ed

In Table 2a morphemic -*s* (noun plural and/or third person singular verb) is seen to be well preserved in spelling reform. Treating both the use of -*z* instead of -*s* and the one instance of an alternative solution as rule-breaking, the sign test produces a significant result ($p < 0.025$). It should be noted that this result may be partially determined by reluctance to produce graphemically illegal final -*z*.

TABLE 2   Treatment of morphophonemic alternants of noun plural and/or 3rd person singular morpheme (-*s*) and past-tense morpheme (-*ed*). (Number of subjects out of 11)

(a) -*s*	Use of -*s*	Use of -*z*	Other solutions
HOUSES	11	—	—
DOGS	10	1	—
SEAS	9	2	—
WIVES	10	1	—
USERS	11	—	—
ALMS	9	2	—
STAIRS	10	1	—
USES	11	—	—
PLAYS	8	2	PLAZE (1)
SIGNS	6	5	—
COPIES	7	4	—
QUESTIONS	7	4	—
OCCURS	6	5	—
WAS	5	6	—
IS	5	6	—
Total	125	39	1

(b) -*ed*	Use of -*ed*	Use of -*d*	Use of -*t*
SHOPPED	4	5	2
HOPED	5	5	1
GUESSED	7	3	1
Total	16	13	4

NB In every case in (2a) a strict phonemic representation would *require* use of -*z*
In (2b) a phonemic representation would require use of -*t*.

In Table 2b, both - *ed* and -*d* may be taken as rule-following, since the phoneme /d/ is actually a more regular correspondence for the past-tense morpheme (e.g. AIMED = /eɪmd/) than is the sequence /ɪd/ (e.g FITTED = /fɪtɪd/).

The latter correspondence occurs only with verbs ending in alveolar stops. The use of final -*t* is clearly not preferred in spite of its phonemic accuracy in the cases tested (p < 0.01). These results suggest that the reformers felt inclined to continue the traditional practice of preserving the graphic identity of the morphemes -*s* and -*ed*. Alternative interpretations of these results are offered below.

2.3 *Derivationally related words*

In Table 3, pairs of derivationally related words are compared. Subjects may either maintain the relationships in spelling in spite of phonemic changes (e.g. SIGN–SIGNATURE) or they may destroy them (e.g. SINE–SIGNATURE). The critical graphemes and grapheme sequences that preserve the relationships are underlined in the examples in Table 3. The overall tendency is against preserving these particular visual relationships (p < 0.025), suggesting little support for this function of English spelling. However, there are obvious differences between individual pairs. Compare, for example, MUSCLE–MUSCULAR, where all subjects abandoned the graphic relationship and SOFT–SOFTEN, where many retained it. The grossly different biases for individual word pairs may

TABLE 3   Treatment of derivationally related word pairs. (Number of subjects out of 11)

	Relationship maintained	Relationship destroyed
SIGN–SIGNATURE	1	10
RESIGN–SIGNATURE	2	9
SIGN–RESIGN	6	5
EXHIBIT–EXHIBITION	3	8
RACE–RACIAL	3	8
MUSCLE–MUSCULAR	—	11
SOFT–SOFTEN	5	6
NATIVE–NATURE	5	6
NATIVE–NATION	2	9
NATURE–NATION	2	9
BOMB–BOMBARD	—	11
Total	29	92

be determined both by the perceived closeness of the derivational relationship and by the existence of differing possibilities for plausible change in different words. The former issue is not investigated directly in this study, although Derwing (1977) has produced some results which may bear on the matter. The problem of what constitutes plausible change (probably a complex function of such factors as word length and graphemic/phonemic structure) is of course precisely the object of this study. We have as yet no independent measure of this other than the subjects' responses to the reforming instruction. It is hoped that the idiographic methods outlined in Section 5 below will help to disentangle these factors.

2.4 Homophones

Table 4 shows a significant overall tendency to avoid identical spelling of homophones ($p < 0.025$). However, comparison of the results for

TABLE 4   Treatment of homophones. Total number of occasions on which subjects ($n = 11$) avoid and produce homographic forms when reforming relatively frequent homophones (AA words, acc. Thorndike and Lorge, 1944, $n = 19$) and relatively infrequent homophones (less than AA, $n = 19$)

	No change made	Homograph avoided	Homograph produced
Frequent	98	52	59
Infrequent	71	106	32
Total	169	158	91

frequent and infrequent homophones (e.g. RAIN vs REIGN) shows a relatively stronger tendency to avoid producing homographs when dealing with infrequent items ($p < 0.01$) than when dealing with frequent items (n.s.). Thus, given SEAM, subjects are unlikely to produce SEEM but will perhaps produce SEME (which is a real word only for some theoretical linguists). Given SEEM, on the other hand, the real infrequent homophone SEAM is a slightly more likely reform than SEME. Moreover, frequent homophones are slightly less likely to be changed in the first place, possibly as a result of an interaction between word frequency and perceived orthographic regularity. If this hypothesis is correct, then a possible interpretation of the frequent/infrequent homophone interaction is as follows: people are not happy about producing homographic spellings of homophone pairs, but if they do, they will tend to choose the less usual, less frequent, less 'regular' form. This may in turn reflect further uneasiness about the potential confusability of the resulting homographs.

In summary, this set of results for the four non-phonologically based rules shows little support for the psychological reality of purely graphemic rules regarding final -*e* or for the orthographic reflection of lexical derivational relationships. It shows strong support for rules intended to preserve the identity of the grammatical morphemes -*s* and -*ed* and to avoid homography. In other words, the reformers thought it rational for orthography to deviate from strict phonemic principles in two out of the four spelling conventions tested. Results of another spelling reform study in which the deletion of final -*e* was examined in greater detail in terms of a functional classification derived from Albrow (1972) are reported in Baker and Smith (1977). In the same study, the orthographic determinants of lexical stress placement, according to the analysis of Chomsky and Halle (1968), were also subjected to spelling reform. Results indicated significant tendencies both to preserve and to enhance spelling conventions on which the assignment of stress depends.

The rationality ratings provided by subjects prior to spelling reform are applied to whole words. Hence, it is somewhat dubious to draw direct inferences concerning particular spelling conventions independent of particular words. Nevertheless, the rating of whole words is a more meaningful task than the rating of rules and indeed this part of the procedure was intended to give the subject some help in conceptualising the instruction to reform. An earlier version of the task indicated that words were in fact being rated in a meaningful way, in that a significant positive correlation was obtained between subjects' rationality ratings and graded spelling simplicity accorded to Schonell's Graded Word Spelling Test A (Spearman's rho = 0.46, n = 100, $p < 0.01$).

A separate analysis of two particular *types* of conventions could be made by using the rationality ratings associated with a sub-set of the present words which could be readily classified into the separate orthographic systems defined by Albrow (1972). Albrow's contention is that the total orthographic 'polysystem' of English is most economically described by postulating three orthographic systems, each with its own set of conventions and spelling-sound correspondences. System 1 may be loosely described as consisting of 'native' or Germanic words, and System 2 of Romance words. System 3, consisting essentially of loan words (e.g. AXOLOTL, WELTANSCHAUUNG), is not considered here. One difference between Systems 1 and 2 is the letter-sound correspondence -*o*- as in LOVE (System 1) and MOVE (System 2). A set of 19 pairs of words of the LOVE–MOVE type were included in the spelling reform task, and since Albrow's polysystem is taken to apply to whole words, it is a simple matter to compare subjects' ratings of System 1 and System 2. The average rating for System 1 words was 3.52 and for System 2 words 3.42. This difference, though small, proved significant on a Wilcoxon test (n = 11, t = 10.5, p < 0.05). The apparently greater rationality of System 1 words cannot be accounted for by any simple frequency effect since the mean word frequency for System 1 words was actually lower than for System 2 words (60.83 versus 126.44 respectively, according to Kučera and Francis, 1967). Thus, there appears to be some difference in the degree to which the two systems are psychologically integrated into the total orthography, a surprising finding nine hundred years after the French invasion.

3 Phonetic transcription and the spelling reform task

There are a number of problems associated with the assumptions made about the subjects' mode of operation in the spelling reform task. Is phonemic realism the main reason for change? And is orthographic sophistication the main reason for refraining from change? It is unlikely that arbitrary changes would be made simply for the sake of making changes, since the option of 'okaying' a word is always open. On the other hand it is possible that the influence of the written norm is so strong that in particular instances subjects are unable to see beyond it. For example, the identity of the -s plural morpheme in DOGS /dogz/ and CATS /kæts/ may be preserved not for the orthographically sophisticated reason that this represents a useful morphographemic generalisation, but for the 'naïve' reason that the acoustic quality of the final phoneme is actually perceived as identical in both forms.

An attempt to test this possibility was made by asking the same group of subjects that had carried out the spelling reform task to listen to an auditory presentation of a set of words maximally similar in orthography to a sub-set (n = 36) of those used in the spelling reform task, and asking subjects to use the alphabetic symbols of English to represent all the 'sounds' they heard and only those sounds i.e. to produce a 'naïve phonetic transcription'. Thus if a subject phonetically transcribes LOGZ and yet produces DOGS in spelling reform, we would have a strong case for concluding that considerations other than phonemic realism are in operation in spelling reform. However, the within-subject comparison across phonetic transcription and spelling reform tasks resulted in only 69 instances (out of a possible 396, i.e. 17%) in which paired words in the two tasks differed on the spelling conventions of interest. As expected, in the majority of cases, the rule in question is preserved in spelling reform (e.g. DOGGS, LUVE, WASH, NATION, LEPPARD) and lost in phonetic transcription (e.g. LOGZ, DUV, WOND, POSISHUN, JEPERDY). Only a third of the cases showed the converse discrepancy. Thus the results suggest that there is a consistent tendency to be generally more conservative in spelling reform than in phonetic transcription.

Since, however, there was on the whole little difference in subjects' approach to the two different tasks, one cannot reject the hypothesis that phonemic realism is indeed the sole guiding principle of spelling reform. The issue of orthographic sophistication versus phonetic naïvity remains unresolved. Nevertheless, it may still be contended that we are obtaining, in both tasks perhaps, a *prima facie* assessment of the psychological reality of the orthographic system. Another similar task, designed to resolve this issue, in which subjects were asked to rank alternative reformed spellings of words, was abandoned as it could not be clearly ascertained what aspects of words were being ranked. A binary forced-choice version in which only the spelling convention of interest was varied produced the following bias: subjects almost invariably chose the form least changed from traditional spelling.

It may indeed be asked what kind of knowledge we are asking subjects to articulate in these tasks. Certainly the knowledge of spelling possessed by highly literate adults is likely to be a heterogeneous collection of generalisations picked up during the acquisition of reading and writing skills, when the spelling of words was learned through familiarity with alphabetic symbols and their associated 'soundings', memorisation of whole word shapes, word by word analogies, and perhaps a handful of mnemonic rules of the '*i* before *e* except after *c*' variety. (Similar reservations apply of course to syntactic acceptability studies.) Nevertheless the type of orthographic representation a subject chooses in spelling reform will necessarily reflect the *result* of this educational process, and we may further examine the generality and consistency of a subject's performance in order to judge the usefulness of his intuitive conventions (cf. Smith, Chapter 2, on the use of nonsense words in this context). The performance of individual subjects was consequently studied in greater detail.

4 Idiographic approaches

There are obvious gross individual differences in subjects' approaches to the spelling reform task. For example the total percentage of words changed by a given subject ranged from 16% to 90%. Similarly the number of orthographically illegal forms produced ranged from 1 to 45 out of a possible 111. Some subjects introduce quite idiosyncratic strategies such as using the phonetic values of alphabetic letter-names, e.g. RECV for RECEIVE, GRNT for GRANT (see Read, 1971, for an interesting parallel in the invented spellings of pre-school children), and using diacritic symbols to indicate, apparently, morpheme boundaries and/or vowel length e.g. YO-MAN for YEOMAN, WE-V for WEAVE.

An immediate difficulty in looking at intrasubject consistency in greater detail is the necessary selectivity of words, imposed by limitations of time and of maintaining the subject's interest. If, for example, we find a subject producing WICH for WITCH we would like to know how he would re-spell WHICH, since the dropping of -*t*- in WITCH constitutes a breach of one of a set of rules distinguishing lexical from grammatical forms. Or indeed if a subject leaves the testing-room with XP for EXPENSE on his answer sheet, we are immediately inclined to ask how he would reform EXPOUNDS (xlb, x£ or perhaps £x?). Short of inducing a subject to retranscribe the entire *Oxford English Dictionary* an alternative approach is an open-ended interview during which subjects can be asked such searching questions while they are carrying out the spelling reform task. However the insights obtained in this way are not easily amenable to quantification.

A highly structured approach to interview technique from which general principles of cognitive organisation may be deduced is that pioneered by George Kelly (1955). Although personal construct theory was originally developed in a clinical context, its fundamental postulates, which are concerned with how we see aspects of our world and how our perceptions, or 'constructs', are related to each other, are theoretically applicable to any aspect of rational behaviour. With this theoretical framework in mind we are presenting subjects with the spelling reform task and then asking them to explain and justify each of the changes they make. These explanations are then fed back to the subjects, after minimal editing and rephrasing, as scales on which all the reformed spellings are to be rated i.e. in terms of the relevance of the explanation, or 'construct,' to the reformed spelling, or 'element', in question. The ratings are then subjected to a principal components analysis by computer and the interrelationships between rating scales, between items rated, and between scales and items are described. The elements and constructs elicited from a single subject, a university research worker, who reformed 20 out of 40 words, are represented in graphic form in Figs 1 and 2, in which the proximity of points in two-dimensional space is considered to be a general reflection of this subject's approach to the spelling reform task. Rationality ratings obtained both before and after reform are included in the analysis and shown in Fig. 1. The constructs elicited from this subject, referred to by number

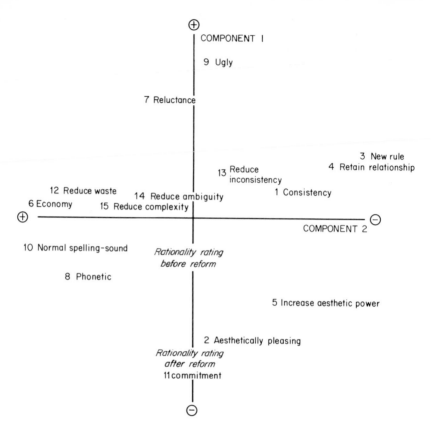

FIG. 1 Explanations of a single subject's behaviour in the spelling reform task expressed in terms of personal constructs. (The first two principal components with Varimax rotation)

in Fig. 1, are listed below in the order in which they were represented as rating scales:

1   I am aiming for consistency.
2   I am happy about the aesthetic effect of my reform.
3   I am instituting a new rule.
4   I am aiming to retain a relationship to related words.
5   I am aiming to increase the aesthetic power of the spelling.
6   I am aiming for economy.
7   I was reluctant to change the original.
8   I am aiming for 'phoneticness'.
9   I think the result of the reform is ugly.

10 I am using the most normal or common spelling representation of the sounds involved.
11 I feel committed to the reform made.
12 I am aiming to reduce unnecessary wastefulness of symbols.
13 I am aiming to reduce inconsistency.
14 I am aiming to reduce ambiguity of sound.
15 I am aiming to reduce unnecessary complexity (of sound-spelling relationship).

The words rated, i.e. the reformed spellings, are presented in Fig. 2. Ratings were on a 5 point scale throughout. The two principal components extracted by the computer analysis were subjected to an orthogonal rotation (Varimax method) and are represented by the x and y axes of Figs 1 and 2.

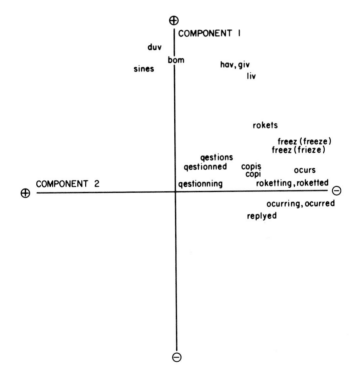

FIG. 2   Reformed spellings of a single subject rated in terms of the explanations in Fig. 1 (The first two principal components with Varimax rotation)

The interpretation of the first component, which accounts for 34.4% of the total variance, is straightforward. The highest negative loading

(NB No value judgement is implied by 'negative') is obtained on Construct 11 ('I feel committed to the reform made'). The highest positive loading is on Construct 9 ('I think the result of the reform is ugly'). We might accordingly label this as an 'aesthetic evaluative' factor. The alignment of the other constructs along this component shows a person for whom aesthetic considerations clearly have a major role to play.

The second orthogonal component accounts for 24.5% of total variance. The highest positive loading is on Construct 10 ('I am using the most normal or common spelling representation of the sounds involved'), and the highest negative loading is on Construct 3 ('I am instituting a new rule'). The alignment of the other constructs along this axis suggests a 'spelling reform dilemma' factor, according to which 'consistency' (Constructs 1 and 13) is quite strongly associated with higher-level orthographic principles (i.e. the subject's own rule system and the conservation of derivational relationships – Constructs 3 and 4) but not with the aim for a straightforward phonemic spelling-to-sound relationship.

Precisely what this subject means by 'new rule' is worth examining in more detail. Examination of the original rating scale reveals that 'new rule' is being construed in two very specific senses. The most highly rated items on this construct (ratings of 5) are QESTIONS, QESTIONNING, QESTIONNED, ROKETS, ROKETTED and ROKETTING, which all share the abolition of digraphs (*qu* and *ck* respectively). Overlapping with this new rule is one which doubles all single consonants directly preceding a suffix (QESTIONNING, QESTIONNED, ROKETTING, ROKETTED). OCURRED and OCURRING, which are not highly rated on this scale, are covered by an old rule, dependent on the presence of primary stress on the syllable preceding the suffix. We may conclude that the subject is generalising and extending an old rule which had previously made little intuitive sense to him, particularly in view of the real-life 'exceptional' case of morpheme–final letter *l* which, in British English although not in American English, doubles before a suffix irrespective of the position of primary stress (e.g. TRAVELLING, SIGNALLED, etc.).

The use of Construct 4 ('I am aiming to retain a relationship to related words) is also revealing. In fact, high ratings are given only to those words for which a semantically related item also occurs in the element list, i.e. OCURS, ROKETS, QESTIONS and their inflections. If we consider the item REPLYED, however, we observe that the subject has enhanced the graphic relationship to REPLY in contravention of the standard orthographic rule, $-y \rightarrow i/-ed$ (past). However, REPLY itself did not occur in the list and the subject has given REPLYED a rating of only 2 on the 'retaining relationships' construct. We are led to infer that the subject's conformity to this high-level rule in this case may not have been at the level of conscious awareness.

The position of 'rationality ratings before reform' is appropriately non-committal. It is not highly correlated with any other scale. Furthermore, the subject is gratifyingly satisfied with the rationality of the results of his own reform; the correlation between 'commitment' and 'rationality rating after' is +0.91.

In general, the reformed spellings themselves (Fig. 2) form two clear constellations. The first is an 'ugly' oversimplified group, where graphemic rules are broken to produce illegal final -*v* and where derivational relationships are ignored, i.e. BOM and SINES in spite of BOMBARD SIGNAL respectively (which did occur in the original list). The second group is an 'orthographically sophisticated' group where new rules are implemented, and graphic similarities between semantically related words are enhanced. It is significant that FREEZ (FREEZE) and FREEZ (FRIEZE) also occur here, indicating that this subject does not place a high premium on the orthographic differentiation of homophones.

Such results provide us with a clear picture of this subject's approach to the spelling reform task, and by extension from this a general summary of his conceptualisation of the ways in which an orthography ought to function. He would clearly not be happy with a phonemic system which disposed of all the higher-level regularities currently present in English spelling, and by introducing and elaborating his own 'intuitive' rule system, he is able to show us how he values a number of alternative solutions to orthographic problems.

The collation of results from larger and more representative samples of subjects should provide empirical grist for the real-life would-be spelling reformer's mill.

5 Conclusions

It is intended to carry out more extensive exploratory studies into the applicability of grid techniques to orthographic tasks. The spelling reform task (and its variants, such as asking people to suggest spelling errors they would consider characteristic for a particular word, or to discuss their own spelling difficulties or spelling errors) provides a conveniently flexible structure for interview, and the grid techniques derived from personal construct theory appear to offer an appropriate analytical tool. We are able to examine an individual subject's performance in depth, and we may further compare and contrast the conceptual systems of different individuals and groups of individuals. Moreover the task should be readily adaptable to spellers of any age or ability. Implicit in this writer's approach is the hypothesis that the nature of a speller's constructs about spelling will be closely related to his spelling ability. The nature of the relationship merits investigation. It has already been shown (Francis, 1973) that children who have a facility with the technical terminology of reading education (e.g. 'word', 'letter', 'sound') perform better on reading tests than those who are less 'metalinguistically sophisticated'. This chicken-and-egg issue has occasioned some controversy regarding the value of a 'metalinguistic' approach to teaching reading and spelling. Should children be formally introduced to the abstract concepts of 'letter', 'sound', 'spelling rule', etc., or are these best learned incidentally as a side-effect of a carefully structured curriculum? An investigation of how children put such knowledge to use should shed some light on this question.

Kelly's theory of personal constructs brings with it a complete theoretical orientation the espousement of which introduces many broader issues such as how spelling fits in with a person's total experience of learning to read and write. It has already been suggested (Reid, 1958) that a better understanding of early reading experiences could be gained by supplementing performance-orientated reading tests with structured interviews in which children are asked their opinions on the purpose and nature of reading (a valuable source of feedback for teachers, if nothing else). Similar research is currently being carried out within a personal construct theory framework (Beard, 1977). It is hoped that such work and the studies outlined in this paper will contribute to a drawing together of two extreme strands of thought in reading research – that of 'fragmentalists' (the majority of contributers to this volume) who examine in depth the various components and sub-components of the cognitive processes involved in writing and reading, and that of the 'anti-fragmentalists' (such as Goodman, 1970) who advocate a far more holistic model based on language-experience and heuristic meaning-seeking strategies.

Acknowledgements

This research was carried out while the author was employed on an SSRC supported research project at the University of Stirling. Thanks are due to Philip Smith and Stephanie Lee for comments and discussion. The computer analysis of the grid described in the text was provided by the MRC service for analysing repertory grids for which Dr Patrick Slater is responsible.

4

American Black English and Spelling

PETER DESBERG, DALE E. ELLIOTT and GEORGE
MARSH   *California State University, Dominguez Hills, U.S.A.*

1 Dialects

The term 'dialect' as part of the technical vocabulary of linguistics can be defined as 'a variety of a single language spoken by people in a particular region or in a particular social group'. This definition implies that if two people or groups of people cannot understand each other's speech, they speak two different *languages*. If they can understand each other, but the speech of one person or group is noticeably different from that of the other in pronunciation and grammar, then they speak two different *dialects*. Thus in theory two dialects must be sufficiently similar to be mutually intelligible, but there are degrees of similarity among dialects. The American English dialects of Georgia and Texas are so similar that someone from Minnesota might be unable to distinguish between them. On the other hand, the English of a Scottish lowlander and that of a Kentucky mountaineer can be sufficiently different from each other that to the untrained ear they may at first hearing seem to be two quite different languages.

It is important to notice that the definition of 'dialect' that we have given implies that *everyone speaks a dialect*. In popular usage, the term 'dialect' often seems to mean 'the speech of primitive or uneducated people'. According to the definition used here, however, an Oxford don and the president of General Motors, no less than poorer, humbler, and less educated people, are speakers of dialects. In all but the smallest and simplest societies, some dialect, as a result of its being used by people in high social, political and economic positions, takes on a special measure of prestige and becomes the *standard* dialect. In this way, Parisian French, southern British English, Peking Chinese, and the loosely de-fined 'General American English' in the United States have all become the standards for their respective societies. (In the United States, there is a much wider range of acceptable variation, especially in pronuncia-tion. The syntactic patterns that are accepted as standard are more rigidly fixed.)

Dialects inevitably arise within all languages because all languages inevitably change. No one is yet certain as to exactly why and how they change, and a discussion of the various theories would take us well beyond the scope of this chapter. The important point is that over long periods of time, all aspects of the structure of a language change: its pronunciation, its morphology, its syntax and its semantics. Perhaps a few examples from the history of English will help to clarify this:

1   six hundred or so years ago, the word MOUSE was pronounced in about the same way as the present-day word MOOSE, and WINE was pronounced like present-day WEAN;

2   at the same time, the word HUNTA (present-day HUNTER) could be used as the *subject* of a sentence, but the word changed its form to HUNTAN for use as the *direct object* of a sentence. Modern English has almost completely lost these *case* distinctions;

3   earlier English grammatical patterns of the form CAME HE? and WHAT SAW HE? have been replaced by DID HE COME? and WHAT DID HE SEE?;

4   the meaning of the word MEAT has been narrowed from FOOD IN GENERAL to EDIBLE ANIMAL FLESH. Conversely, the meaning of HOLIDAY has been broadened from A RELIGIOUS HOLY DAY to something like ANY DAY WHEN ONE DOESN'T HAVE TO WORK.

If groups of speakers of a language are separated by geographical or political barriers such as the Atlantic Ocean, the Blue Ridge mountains of Virginia, or the Rhine river, the form of the language spoken by each group will change in slightly different ways, especially if, as often happens, the geographical separation is reinforced by social separation. The result of these different variations of the same fundamental structure is two or more different dialects. If the geographical separation is sufficiently great and lasts a long enough time, the dialects may diverge from each other so much that they become distinct languages.

Over the centuries, the English language has developed a number of major dialects, each of which can be divided into sub-dialects. Dialectologists are fairly well agreed that historically there have been three major dialects in the United States: Northern, Midlands and Southern, each with its own regional variations. In the course of the great Westward migrations, the differences among these three were to a great extent levelled out, resulting in the 'General American English' spoken in most of the U.S. Our concern here is with a dialect which has in recent years come to be called 'Black English' (BE). There is much controversy among the experts over the origins of BE. Probably the most popular view at the present time is that BE began as a *pidgin*, i.e. a mixture, in this case of English and various West African languages, which then became a *creole*, i.e. it was adopted as a native language by later generations of southern Blacks. Some scholars do not accept this theory, however, and maintain that BE began as nothing more nor less than a variety of Southern American English, and that it has now become a social dialect because of the post-World War II migration of southern Blacks to other parts of the U.S. So far as our purposes here are concerned, this controversy is irrelevant.

1.1 *Phonological features of Black English*

We turn now to a discussion of some of the important differences between BE and Standard American English. Since we will be dealing
here only with possible implications of speaking BE for learning conventional spelling, we will concern ourselves primarily with phonological differences between the two dialects, and the interaction between phonological and morphological features.

1   Perhaps the most striking feature of BE pronunciation (from the
    point of view of a speaker of the standard dialect) is the strong
    tendency toward weakening of certain word-final consonants and
    simplification of word-final consonant clusters. Final voiced stops
    (/d/, /g/, and less often /b/, as in BAD, RAG and TUB) may be pro-
    nounced approximately like the corresponding voiceless stops (/t/,
    /k/ and /p/). Words which in the standard dialect end in a voiceless
    stop may be pronounced with a final glottal stop (/ʔ/) or nothing
    at all. In words ending in consonant clusters such as /-st/, /-sk/,
    /-nd/ and /-ld/, the second consonant is frequently omitted.
2   Pre-consonantal and word-final /r/, and less frequently pre-
    consonantal and word-final /l/, are also dropped.
3   Final and intervocalic /θ/ and /ð/ (as in WITH and MOTHER) are
    often pronounced as /f/ and /v/, respectively. Initial /θ/ and /ð/ may
    be pronounced as /t/ and /d/, respectively.
4   There are also differences in the vowel system. /ɪ/ and /ɛ/ (as in IN
    and PEN) almost invariably merge into /ɪ/ before nasal consonants.
    The diphthongs /ay/, /aw/ and /ɔy/ (as in BUY, BOUGH and BOY) are
    frequently simplified by omission of the /y/ or /w/, or weakened by
    replacement of these off-glides with the neutral vowel schwa (/ə/).

Often ignored in discussion of BE, but crucial to a correct understanding of this dialect, are the facts that (*i*) many of the features cited
as characteristic of BE can also be found in the casual speech of standard
dialect speakers; (*ii*) these features are the natural results of processes of
change that have been going on in the English language for centuries;
and (*iii*) these processes are by no means unique to BE or to English in
general, but examples of recurrent natural changes found over and over
again in the languages of the world.

Especially in informal circumstances, standard dialect speakers very
frequently simplify final consonant clusters, when the following word
begins with a consonant. Thus, the final /t/ in MISSED (phonetically
/mɪst/) is likely to be omitted in I MISSED MY BUS but not in WE MISSED
OUR BUS. In BE, however, simplification often occurs with a following
vowel, and even at the end of utterance. The tendency toward simpli-

fication is found in both the standard and the non-standard dialect; the only real difference is that it is found in the non-standard dialect more often and in a wider range of phonological environments.

The first and second of the standard vs non-standard pronunciation differences given above both exemplify a general tendency, found in both dialects, toward simplification, weakening, and eventual loss of word-final consonants and consonant clusters. This tendency has already led in standard English to the loss of the final /b/ in BOMB and LAMB, to the loss of the consonant sound represented by *gh* in NIGHT and BROUGHT, and to the loss of /l/ in CALM and PALM. Although we cannot go into the evidence here, it seems that the devoicing of final voiced stops is well under way in standard American English in many areas. Again we can see that the difference between the two dialects is less a matter of kind than of degree.

Finally, we may point out a few examples of the same processes of change in other languages. All final stop consonants (actually all final obstruents, a larger category) have been devoiced in German and Russian. Peking Chinese has no final consonants except /n/ and /ŋ/, and many languages lack final consonants altogether. However, no language is known which has only final consonants but no *initial* consonants.

1.2 *Sound-spelling correspondence*

We have concentrated here on some of the major phonological differences between BE and standard American English. Of course, other dialects differ from these two and from each other in various ways. Yet with a few insignificant exceptions, all the dialects of English share a common spelling. This common spelling is quite conservative, i.e. it often reflects earlier pronunciations. The retention of *gh* in NIGHT and BROUGHT is an example. As we have seen, BE has carried many phonological changes farther than the standard dialect. Thus the sound-spelling correspondence often appears to be more exact for the relatively conservative standard dialect than for the more innovative Black dialect. A question with fundamental implications for educational practice in elementary schools is: insofar as a close sound-spelling correspondence helps in learning to read and spell, does the child who speaks BE have a more difficult time acquiring these abilities than the child who speaks the standard dialect? If so, would it be a good idea to use a modified orthography in teaching BE-speaking children to read and spell, and then later shift gradually to the conventional orthography?

Fasold (1969) has argued that a special orthography for BE is unnecessary, and would in fact be educationally unwise. The BE simplification of final consonant clusters, mentioned above, results in pronunciations such as the following: /mis/ for MIST, /dɛs/ for DESK, /win/ for WIND, and /kol/ for COLD. Hence one can ask whether a special orthography should be used for reading instruction with BE-speaking children which would not indicate the final consonants, i.e. should spellings like MISS, DESS, WIN and COLE be used instead of the conventional spellings? Fasold argues against this, primarily on the basis of the fact that with rare exceptions BE speakers pronounce the final consonants when they are followed by certain suffixes, as in MISTY, WINDY and COLDER. There is no such suffix that can be attached to DESK, and hence it might be difficult to remember to write the final *k*. However, here the BE-speaking child is faced with the same spelling problem as that facing the speaker of any dialect in remembering to write the *b* in THUMB or the *s* in ISLAND.

As was also mentioned above, final /-θ/ is often pronounced /-f/ in BE. Would WIFF and BAFF therefore be better spellings than WITH and BATH? Fasold says no, pointing out that these words are sometimes also pronounced by BE speakers with final /-t/, but words with standard dialect final /-f/, such as OFF, are always pronounced with final /-f/ in BE, never with final /-t/. Thus if WITH were to be spelled WIFF, there would be no indication that WITH, but not OFF, can be pronounced with the final /-t/. If the two words are to be distinguished orthographically, then the conventional spelling is as good a way to do this as any.

No one, to our knowledge, has undertaken a thorough and systematic study of the question of the cross-dialectal adequacy of conventional English spelling. Our strong impression, however, is that for both practical and theoretical reasons, a special spelling for BE would not be a good idea.

2 Empirical evidence on the relation between dialect and spelling

2.1 *Naturalistic observations*

Naturalistic observations of dialect speakers' written compositions have suggested a possible relationship between dialect and spelling. An early study by Briggs (1969) studied the errors in essays written by 30 black high school students in Alabama, and Wolfram and Whiteman (1971) and Ross (1971) studied essays written by Black students in Maryland and California. While the major concern of these studies was the uses of syntactic forms found in BE, they also noted mis-spellings related to BE.

The most common type of error was the omission of grammatical morphemes, such as plurals -*s* and past tenses -*ed*.

The naturalistic studies, although suggestive, do not assess the degree of relationship between dialect and spelling. There was no attempt to assess the subjects' dialect directly, and no systematic observation of the kinds of mis-spellings which might be predicted on the basis of what is known about BE phonology.

2.2 *Correlational research*

Two of the present authors (Desberg *et al.*, 1977b) have previously run a correlational study to determine if dialect is a predictor of performance on a standardised test of spelling, reading and arithmetic. For this purpose we devised the Social Dialect Feature Inventory (SDFI), a performance measure based on the number of dialect features a child uses when answering structured questions. The SDFI correlates highly with previous measures such as the sentence repetition test used by Baratz (1969a), but does not have some of the difficulties associated with repetition measures (Desberg *et al.*, 1977a). The SDFI was administered to 120 black elementary school children at three grade levels: second (7 yr), fourth (9 yr) and sixth (11 yr). Intelligence tests and questionnaires measuring attitudes toward school were also administered in order to control statistically for the effects of these potentially relevant variables. The data were analysed by a stepwise multiple regression analysis using dialect, IQ and school attitude measures as predictors, and spelling, reading and arithmetic scores on the Wide Range Achievement Test (WRAT) as the criterion variables.

The results of this analysis for each grade level are shown in Table 1. The cell entries indicate the proportion of variance accounted for by one measure, e.g. dialect, with the contributions of the other 2 measures, e.g. IQ and school attitude, partialled out. To our surprise, the dialect measure accounted for a greater percentage of the variance in language-related achievement than either IQ or attitudes toward school. In contrast, IQ accounted for the largest amount of variance in arithmetic, except in the sixth grade.

At all grade levels, dialect accounted for more of the variance in spelling than in reading, and in all cases the relationship was higher the longer the child had been in school. Since non-standard dialect patterns generally decrease with years of schooling, a polarisation of the groups into children who still spoke BE and those who no longer did in the sixth grade probably increased the variance in the sixth grade sample. Hence correlations would be expected to be larger. One explanation for the relatively high relationship between dialect and arithmetic in sixth grade children may be the fact that arithmetic problems are more language-based at higher grade levels than the number problems at the lower grade levels. However in this case a higher relationship with the vocabulary score might also have been expected.

TABLE 1 Multiple regression analysis: proportion of variance accounted for (r^2)

Grade	2nd	4th	6th
	WRAT[1]-Reading		
SDFI[2]	0.1908	0.2214	0.4017
PPVT[3]	0.1294	0.0192	0.0732
SSI[4]	0.0016	0.0966	—
	WRAT-Spelling		
Grade	2nd	4th	6th
SDFI	0.2143	0.2422	0.5758
PPVT	0.0618	0.0027	0.0593
SSI	0.0187	0.0527	0.0104
	WRAT-Arithmetic		
Grade	2nd	4th	6th
SDFI	0.0587	0.004	0.3944
PPVT	0.1253	0.1795	0.1197
SSI	0.0057	0.1409	0.0042

[1] Wide Range Achievement Test (school achievement measure). [2] Social Dialect Feature Inventory (dialect measure). [3] Peabody Picture Vocabulary Test (IQ measure). [4] School Sentiment Index (attitude measure).

In general then, this study has established a sizeable correlation between dialect use and reading and spelling performance. The more dialect features a child uses the worse his score on the WRAT. The general congruence between reading and spelling may be because in this test both tasks depend greatly on phonological decoding. The reading sub-test of the WRAT is a measure of the recognition of words in isolation which presumably requires phonological decoding. Desberg et al. (in press) have argued previously that the effect of dialect should be greater in phonologically than non-phonologically based reading. Ehri (Chapter 14) has suggested that dialect speakers may acquire knowledge of standard English word pronunciations primarily by learning to read and to spell words. Hence, the relationship found here may be due to a direct and powerful effect of 'visual' language on speech. The reasons for the relationship between extent of dialect level and use of language-based academic achievement may seem straightforward, but correlational studies demonstrate only the existence of the relationship and not its causes. Some unknown basic factor that neither involves verbal intelligence, nor attitudes to school, which were both statistically controlled in the present study, may well account for this relationship.

2.3 *Other experimental research*

In order to determine the causes for the relationship, it is necessary to consider which features of BE might produce difficulties in spelling and then to examine dialect speakers' spelling errors to see if the predicted difficulties actually occur. This has been done in an important series of studies by Cronnell (1973).

As discussed previously, some phonological features of BE which might produce spelling interference are: (*a*) deletion or weakening of single final consonants; (*b*) deletion or reduction of final consonant clusters; (*c*) replacement of /θ/ and /ð/ with /t/, /d/, /f/ or /v/; and (*d*) vowel mergers (e.g. (ɪ) and /ɛ/ before nasals as in PIN and PEN).

These phonological features might result in the deletion in speech and spelling of morphological markers such as: (*a*) the past tense suffix; (*b*) the third person singular suffix (e.g. HE DRIVE A CAR); (*c*) the plural suffix; (*d*) the possessive suffix; and (*e*) contractions (e.g. SHE GOING).

In his first study, Cronnell (1973) used a multiple-choice spelling test in which the alternatives were the correct spelling, a mis-spelling based on BE features, and a mis-spelling which was not related to BE pronunciation. The subjects were 61 black and 61 white second grade children. Cronnell assumed that the black children spoke BE and that the white children spoke Standard English. The black children chose a small but statistically significantly larger proportion of BE-related mis-spellings than the white children. Both groups made more errors on the morphological features than on the purely phonological features, but again there was a small but significant difference between black and white children.

The initial study suffered from several flaws, the major one being that no measure of individual children's dialect was made. Dialect differences were assumed on the basis of race alone, which is questionable since many black children are not BE dialect speakers.

In Cronnell's second study, the children were classified as BE or SE speakers on the basis of a sentence repetition test. The subjects were 50 second grade black children from an urban school and 50 second grade white children from a suburban school. A dictated spelling test was used instead of a multiple choice test. The spelling test contained words which would be expected to produce dialect mis-spellings and control words which had spellings that were predicted not to be related to dialect. The outcome of the study is complex, with many interactions; however, several major results stand out. The BE speakers had more than twice as many errors as SE speakers on BE features as compared to control features. The BE speakers made more errors on morphological features than on purely phonetic features. However, when a correlation was run between individual children's use of a dialect feature in speech and their ability to spell that feature, the correlation was not significant.

In his third study, Cronnell restricted his investigation to the reductions in speech and spelling of word-final consonant clusters in various environments. The results indicated that there were considerable differences between the factors affecting consonant cluster reduction in speech and in writing. For example, whether the following word began with a consonant or a vowel affected reduction in speech, but not in spelling. There was a greater tendency to reduce monomorphemic forms than inflected forms in speech, but the opposite effect was found in spelling, where more suffixed words were reduced. There was a tendency not to reduce clusters which produced homonyms in speech, but no such tendency in spelling. Not surprisingly in the light of these results, again there was no significant correlation between a speaker's use of a particular BE form in speech and his use of that same form in spelling. A similar lack of relationship between spoken and written output was found by Dodd (Chapter 19) who concludes that speech and writing systems may be quite independent. Nevertheless a significant correlation between individual children's dialect use and amount of spelling errors was found in the Desberg *et al.*, (1977b) study. No one-to-one word analysis was carried out in terms of speech and spelling error overlap. The relationship can thus only be held to be a general and not a specific one. In other words, our dialect measure would predict achievement level on a spelling test quite well, but could probably not predict the individual spelling errors.

It appears evident that there are several other factors besides word specific direct dialect interference which might produce a general relationship between dialect and spelling. One of these factors is reading proficiency, since dialect is related to reading proficiency and reading and spelling are correlated. Reading is often thought to be one of the major ways in which children acquire knowledge about the spelling of words. Another possible factor is oral vocabulary. Spelling tests are often based on oral vocabulary counts of SE speakers. To that extent, the tests probably under-represent the oral vocabulary forms of BE speakers.

Finally there are considerably more homophonic forms in BE than in SE. Such tendencies in BE as vowel mergers (PIN – PEN) and final consonant reduction (PAS – PAST) will produce homophonic forms in BE. This might well make taking a spelling test more difficult where words are presented in isolation and hence give rise to apparent mis-hearing. Melmed (1970) found that BE speakers, although they could not discriminate pairs such as PIN and PEN in isolation, could easily do so in context.

O'Neal and Trabasso (1976) studied the effects of dialect on the spelling of words which are homophones in BE, but not in SE. Against their expectations, third and fifth grade urban and suburban white children tended to confuse the BE homonymous forms more than the urban black children. For all groups, a sentence context greatly reduced the number of homonym confusions, as might be expected.

O'Neal and Trabasso also compared the number of mis-spellings which would be predicted on the basis of other BE speech features in the three groups, with spelling ability partialled out by analysis of covariance. There were more dialect-related mis-spellings by black children than by white children at the third grade level. Five dialect-related mis-spellings were statistically significant in the Black urban sample, as opposed to only one each in the White urban and suburban samples. By the fifth grade, however, the difference had disappeared and the urban White sample actually made more BE dialect related errors than the Black sample. As the authors acknowledge, their dialect-related words were both longer and less frequent than the dialect-'neutral' control words. Both of these factors may have contributed to the unexpected pattern of results obtained. Furthermore there was no independent measure of the dialect their subjects spoke and to what extent the specific SE and BE dialect features overlapped. In general, therefore, we cannot take the results of this study as demonstrating direct phonological interference. When data concerning spoken dialect is available (e.g. Cronnell 1973), evidence for direct dialect interference in individual subjects is lacking.

3 Educational implications

The data indicating that BE interferes with spelling are at best only suggestive. Cronnell found an overall dialect effect, but did not find a one-to-one relationship between specific features of a child's dialect and his spelling. However, Wolfram and Whiteman (1971) and Briggs

(1969) found a substantial number of dialect-related spelling errors in the compositions of BE speakers. To the extent that BE does interfere with spelling, there are three possible strategies that can be used for improving spelling instruction:

1 Teach SE before reading and spelling instructions begin (Bereiter and Englemann, 1966). This idea is rejected here for a number of reasons, including the following: (a) the beginning of spelling instruction would be delayed, widening the existing gap between SE and BE speakers; (b) a number of social-psychological factors, such as a lowering of self-esteem resulting from forced dialect change; and (c) the lack of evidence that a child needs to speak SE in order to spell it.

2 Use BE materials for spelling instruction. Even the strongest advocates of using BE materials agree that BE reading materials should reflect the syntax but not the phonology of BE (Stewart 1969; Baratz 1969b). The argument for rejecting materials representing BE pronunciation is supported by the work of Desberg *et al.* (in press) demonstrating that BE speakers perform better on a phonics task with words represented in SE form than in BE form. Furthermore, there is no 'Standard Black English'. There is a great deal of variation from speaker to speaker, and no consistent way to represent BE forms for all BE speakers.

3 Changing the instructional procedures traditionally used. Whenever possible, present words to be spelled in a sentence context. This would reduce apparent auditory discrimination errors (Melmed, 1970). If a child makes spelling errors with consonants in word-final position, a problem word should be introduced followed by a word beginning with a vowel, rather than another consonant. When words are not presented in a sentence context, present words that are homonyms in BE but not SE simultaneously (e.g. PIN and PEN). In addition, it might be useful to highlight the differences visually by, for example, underlining or changing the color of the salient letters.

Wolfram and Fasold (1974) suggested a useful spelling strategy for words in isolation: attach suffixes to words where final consonants present a problem. For example, the word DUST is frequently spelled by BE speakers without the final *t*. This would occur less often if DUST were presented in the words DUSTY or DUSTING. This strategy will also help to distinguish potential homonyms for BE speakers. Consider the following examples: COAL/COLD/COLDER; FINE/FIND/FINDING; HOLE/HOLD/HOLDING; SIN/SEND/SENDER.

These three possibilities for teaching are based on the assumption that a student's performance on spelling and reading tasks is functionally related to the phonemic match between the dialect spoken and the dialect represented in print. Opposed to this assumption is the view that the regularities in spelling do not always relate directly to surface phonology, but often to an underlying form more closely related to meaning (Venezky, 1967; Chomsky and Halle, 1968; C. Chomsky, 1970). According to this view, English orthography is a 'near optimal' system (Chomsky and Halle, 1968) for representing all dialects of English. Consider the following pairs of words: SANE–SANITY, COURAGE–COURAGEOUS, DIVINE–DIVINITY, PRESIDENT–PRESIDENTIAL, RESIGN–RESIGNATION. As C. Chomsky (1970) points out, although the critical parts of each pair of words are spelled alike and have the same meaning, they are pronounced quite differently. Many such pairs can be found. From this point of view a close phonemic match would be undesirable.

Nevertheless most reading programs currently emphasise a phonemic-based word attack decoding strategy. In these programs, the students acquire a number of spelling-to-sound correspondences. The initial spelling strategy used may be a reversal of these to sound-to-spelling correspondences. The efficiency of this reversal strategy is in fact questionable. Berdiansky et al. (1969) identified 166 spelling-to-sound correspondences that efficiently predicted the pronunciation of 90% of the mono- and bisyllabic words in the speech-comprehension vocabularies of 6–9 year olds. Cronnell (personal communication) noted that less than 50% of these rules were reversible, i.e. were also sound-to-spelling rules. For a review of the relationship of reading and spelling rules see Cronnell (1970). In identifying rules that go from sound to spelling, Hanna et al. (1966) generated over 300 rules which predicted spellings of a 17 000-word lexicon with less than 50% accuracy. Simon and Simon (1973) found that fourth grade children could outspell a computer programmed with the Hanna et al. (1966) rules. What this points to is the general inefficiency of a phonemic-based system of spelling instruction. Thus there is a fourth suggestion for a spelling strategy to use in teaching BE speakers: This would be a de-emphasis of phonemic processing in spelling instruction. A recent article by Farnham-Diggory (1978) indicates that black children do prefer a visually based strategy in spelling while white children of the same age prefer a phonemically based strategy. However, in general it seems that good spellers seem to rely more on stored visual representations of words than on phonemic processing (Ehri, Sloboda and Tenney in this volume). BE spellers may be taught spelling 'visually' i.e. bypassing the in any case treacherous sound-spelling correspondence rules. Such a visual approach would demand a lot of rote learning but would certainly reduce any interference from the spoken dialect. Furthermore this approach might be equally beneficial to SE speakers as this dialect too is often misleading when a phonemic processing strategy is used.

PART III

Spelling and Word Recognition

5

The Reader's Implicit Knowledge of Orthographic Structure

LESLIE HENDERSON and JACKIE CHARD   *School of Natural Sciences, Hatfield Polytechnic, England*

They spell it Vinci and pronounce it Vinchy; foreigners always spell better than they pronounce. Mark Twain

It seems that the experienced reader has acquired a considerable body of knowledge about the graphemic structure of words in order to support his perceptual skill. Although this state of knowledge may be tacit, in common with much linguistic knowledge, we can infer it from experiments on the visual recognition of words.

There exist at least two sorts of reasons why the reader's orthographic knowledge may not equip him to spell. First, the knowledge may be merely tacit, able to be manifest in the relatively automatic process of word perception but inaccessible to the more deliberate processes that produce spelling. Second, the knowledge may be of a sort that is inadequate to allow the determination of particular spellings. It might, for example, be too general and abstract.

From their beginnings in the nineteenth century theories of word recognition have often centred on the finding that a letter array is most readily perceived when it forms a word. Two of the earliest distinguishable approaches to this word superiority effect assume that it is supported by rather selective knowledge of the visual structure of words. Different though the two theories are, they share damaging implications for the incidental learning of spelling in the way that they regard the use of stimulus structure in word perception.

One view asserts that word perception is holistic[1] (Cattell; Erdmann and Dodge). In such a view the identity of constituent letters in a word is obscured or ignored, since the features which determine the perceptual whole are gross or at least encompass a cluster of letters. The alternative view regards the letter as the unit of analysis but holds that perceptual skill involves economy in letter processing with attention restricted to critical letters or letter positions (Goldscheider and Müller; Zeitler; Messmer). Whatever the merits of these nineteenth-century views (reviewed in Henderson, 1977) it is not difficult to see in them implications for a divorce of reading and spelling competence. Such inferences were not drawn by early students of spelling, however, and it was not uncommon at the turn of the century for incidental learning during reading to be advocated as the primary vehicle for spelling instruction (see Peters, 1967).

Let us begin, therefore, with an examination of some of the evidence bearing upon the nature of the orthographic knowledge employed by the experienced reader.

---

[1] OED spelling from the Greek *holos* for whole. An interesting case for spelling reform since holistic refers to whole and not to hole. *Ed.*

1 Orthographic pattern and recognition thresholds

Recent studies of the reader's use of his knowledge of stimulus structure in order to facilitate word perception began with a small but important methodological improvement on the technique of nineteenth-century experimenters. They had shown that recognition performance appeared to be better on words than on random letters. However they had been unable to preclude the possibility that this superiority was attributable either to better memory for significant stimuli, once perceived, or to sophisticated guessing of incompletely perceived stimuli.

In the recognition task the perceptibility of a stimulus is diminished to a point where errors ensue by displaying it extremely briefly and, sometimes, by following it immediately with an irrelevant interfering stimulus ('masking'). Performance was traditionally assessed by asking for full report of the stimulus. More recent techniques have only required report of a designated portion of the display, chosen in an unpredictable manner. The new methods, by reducing greatly the amount to be reported and by controlling carefully the nature of the alternative responses confronting the subject, ensured at least that any residual 'guessing' which favoured word stimuli was of the sort inherent in skilled perception.

Controversy remains about the precise stage of information processing at which the subject brings to bear his knowledge of stimulus structure, though sometimes this debate presents itself in other guises, such as that between 'inference' and 'unitisation' theories (see the discussion on 'holistic perception' below).

Another general characteristic of this group of word recognition studies is the apparent sensitivity of the experimental outcome to the perceiver's particular choice of strategy (e.g. Johnston and McClelland, 1974). The uncertainties created by such susceptibility have tended to give the word recognition literature an appearance of irritably biting its own tail, an impression which is difficult to reconcile with that of forward progress. However, it is arguable that sensitivity to choice of strategy is a perfectly reasonable property to expect of any task calling upon complex cognitive skills.

What seems clear from the experimental comparison of stimuli possessing different amounts of structure is that recognition performance improves as the structure is increased from that possessed by a single letter or a string of random letters to that of a regular string comprising a pronounceable pseudoword, and improves again, though rather less substantially, for common real words. Controversy has centred on two issues: first, whether the perceptual advantage of pseudowords over random letters is due to pronounceability itself or to regularity of the spelling pattern and second, on whether the further advantage enjoyed by real words is a truly lexical effect.

The prevailing belief that the pseudoword advantage depends upon the purely visual structure created by spelling regularity rests largely upon a study by Baron and Thurston (1973). They found that the recognition advantage of pronounceable pseudowords was undiminished even when the subject chose between response alternatives that were pronounced alike. This suggests that the subject's perceptual decision is not based on an exclusively phonological recoding of the stimulus. Furthermore a similar advantage in perceptibility appeared to be enjoyed by regular over irregularly ordered chemical formulae, whose perception is unlikely to depend on articulation.

In another study Baron (1974) has shown that the perception of unpronounceable consonant strings can be facilitated by artificial spelling regularities created by exposing the subject to constraints on the sequential order of letters. Apparently subjects can pick up and use such structure in the course of a few experimental sessions. This finding for consonant strings has been extended to cover natural spelling regularities in a study by Spoehr and Smith (1975) who compared 'regular' sequences like BLST with irregular ones like LSTB.

Evidence for the use of a form of redundancy which goes beyond general regularities of the orthography comes from the demonstration of a *lexical* effect in recognition whereby common real words are more perceptible than regular pseudowords. This effect has been obtained by Manelis (1974), Juola *et al.* (1974), Spoehr and Smith (1975), McClelland (1976), and others who have used an analogous reaction time paradigm. What this seems to imply is that not only does the reader employ general knowledge of the statistical regularities of letter patterns but he can even bring to bear on the recognition problem knowledge of which particular letter sequences constitute real words.

One way in which both the general knowledge of letter combination statistics and the more constrained knowledge of the particular sequences which form common words might be used in recognition would be for the perceiver to search for elementary visual features which arise out of the conjunction of pairs of letters considered as a composite shape. This is an unusually explicit form of the sometimes mysterious notion of 'holism' in perception. It is therefore interesting to find that the available evidence is inconsistent with this simple solution. McClelland (1976) has shown that case alternation within a letter string does not generally reduce the superiority of real words over pseudowords. Since this manipulation should totally disrupt the conjunction of visual features across adjacent letters, survival of word superiority appears to be fatal for this particular holistic or 'perceptual units' theory. This result does not, of course, reduce the plausibility of the general view that the perceiver utilises his predictive knowledge of letter conjunctions. What it does suggest is that these predictions are applied to an *abstract graphemic code*, that is, one which is invariant over changes in particular visual form.

Further evidence for the existence of such an abstract graphemic code, as Allport (in press) has pointed out, comes from Saffran and Marin's (1977) study of a patient who was unable to translate print directly into sound. The authors showed that the patient was able to read successfully words mutilated by case-alternation, despite the fact that the stimuli did not permit holistic shape analysis and the patient's condition deprived her of phonologically mediated access to the internal lexicon. Access must therefore have been 'visual' but not at a level of code vulnerable to spatial perturbation.

2 Orthographic pattern and comparison times

By 'comparison times' we refer to a variety of tasks that involve measurement of the time taken to locate a target letter in a string of letters (visual search) or to compare two strings (same–different judgements).

Most of the major findings in these tasks are consistent with those of the recognition threshold task and so we shall not dwell on these details at length. Once again we find that performance is assisted by structure in the stimulus and in terms of its effect such structure can be ordered from real words down through pseudowords to random strings. This ordering of conditions is clearly established in the same–different task (Barron and Pittenger, 1974; Chambers and Forster, 1975). Furthermore, the facilitatory effect of lexicality survives even when the subjects are only required to match the initial letters of a pair of stimuli (Barron and Henderson, 1977). The same ordering of conditions also appears, though less reliably, in the letter search task (Krueger, 1970).

Much of the literature on these tasks has been devoted to a somewhat sterile and inconclusive debate as to whether the familiarity effects are attributable to perceptual encoding or to comparison processes. This concern has probably been motivated by several considerations. Foremost is the belief the familiarity effect is only of interest, if it can be shown to be truly 'perceptual'. If perceptual, it can be made to speak to the process of reading and, more generally, of pattern recognition, whereas if a comparison effect, then it might be an uninteresting by-product of the choice of task.

There are several ways in which this formulation of the alternatives is too simple. First, it is not clear why effects with the visual search task, say, should be any more susceptible to dismissal as comparison effects than those with the traditional threshold task using forced-choice recognition alternatives. A greater difficulty, however, inheres in the assumption that encoding and comparison are separable stages in these tasks. This assumption probably has least force in the single target search task. Even were the assumed separability of these stages to be granted it is not clear why we should reserve this (apparently honorific) term 'perceptual' for the encoding process alone. In a sense this dispute is irrelevant to our present purpose which is to examine the employment, by whatever means, or orthographic knowledge. But it has at least served the useful purpose of leading to the exclusion of one particularly uninteresting comparison-locus possibility, namely that orthographically structured stimuli simply owe their advantage to permitting a match at the name level (Besner and Jackson, 1975; Pollatsek *et al.*, 1975). More-over, another uninteresting locus appears to be excluded by Seymour and Jack (1978) who suggest that the familiarity effect is not attribut-able either to a response retrieval stage.

3 The active principles of orthographic regularity

A general characteristic of perceptual theorising which has sometimes been lamented has been the acceptance of many of the achievements of the perceptual system as *principles* whose details do not demand analysis. This has often been true of principles as diverse as those involved in the constancies, scene analysis and the utilisation of redundancy. But while reviewers of the word superiority effect have sometimes treated ortho-graphic regularity as an axiomatic elementary principle, there have also been attempts to analyse the underlying features of this regularity which are used by the perceiver.

At one extreme of these treatments lies the notion of 'orthographic rules'. This view has been persistently advanced by Eleanor Gibson (e.g. Gibson and Levin, 1975) who seems to assert that the actual forms of written English derive from a set of law-like structures which exist at another, more abstract level. 'The nature of these rules' Gibson and Levin argue (p. 172), 'behaves like a higher-order invariant in the language'. One implication of their view is that we can determine now with certainty what future forms are possible. Yet who would have sup-posed that we could have a word like LYNX which appears to arise as a direct adoption into English of a Latin transliteration of a nasal version of the Greek LUX (Partridge, 1966)?

At the other extreme from Gibson's strong claim for the existence of orthographic rules that support efficient recognition of words, is Coltheart's startling claim that there exists 'clear and reasonably abundant experimental evidence suggesting that inter-letter redundancy is *not* made use of during the process of word perception' (Coltheart, 1977, p. 161).

Only one of his arguments is pertinent here. In this he treats one particular measure of regularity, bigram and trigram frequency, citing three studies which fail to find a correlation between these measures and performance. As we shall later see, some authors (Mason, 1975) have argued that this is not the appropriate measure of regularity; nevertheless the absence of correlation of performance with the measure frequently used in generating regular stimuli is awkward and provocative.

We should first distinguish between pure transitional redundancy of the sort measured by the Underwood and Schultz (1960) norms, and transitional redundancy which is relative to a word position, such as that described in Mayzner and Tresselt's (1965) count of bigram frequency as a function of word length and letter position. The latter had some predictive value for performance in Gibson *et al.*'s (1970) study whereas the purely sequential measure did not. However, Gibson *et al.* confounded their positionally constrained bigram measure with the overall pronounceability of the item and a regression analysis showed that pronounceability was a slightly better predictor of performance than bigram frequency. Furthermore, the positionally constrained bigram measure failed to predict performance in the studies of recognition thresholds conducted by Manelis (1974) and by McClelland and Johnston (1977) and in the same–different task studied by Chambers and Forster (1975). Of these investigations, by far the most rigorous is that by McClelland and Johnston. Their work provides the only planned test of a bigram frequency effect, it uses an improved basis for estimating bigram frequency, and it involved comparisons of widely differing bigram frequencies. This last is no small matter since the earlier studies, cited by Coltheart (1977) as failing to obtain a relationship between summed bigram frequency and perceptual performance, had confined their search to post hoc correlations conducted *within a set of word or pseudoword stimuli* (Gibson *et al.*, 1970; Manelis, 1974; Chambers and Forster, 1975). This is unfortunate since the search for an identifiable regularity factor has its original motivation in the attempt to explain the superiority of word and pseudowords over single letters and random letter strings. It might be, therefore, that their examination of bigram frequency effects is obscured by truncation of the range of frequencies. Given the remedy, however, of these and other defects by McClelland and Johnston, it is difficult to avoid accepting their view that 'there simply is not a bigram frequency effect to be found' (1977, p. 259).

Before taking our leave of bigrams it is worth noting the comment of Chambers and Forster (1975) to the effect that it might not be continuous variation of bigram frequency that is effective but, instead the difference between zero and non-zero frequencies. There does in fact seem to be some evidence for such a dichotomous effect in the recognition of purely consonantal strings (Herrmann and McLaughlin, 1973; Spoehr and Smith, 1975). The question must be put, however, as to whether such an effect is best described as of bigram frequency. It might equally, for example, be regarded as evidence for a phonotactic factor.

On the other hand a quite different basis for regularity effects has been proposed by Mason (1975), who has suggested that the crucial agency is not sequential redundancy but positional redundancy as measured by single letter positional frequency within a string. She used visual search for single letter targets and found that performance was related to the summed single letter values for the string to be searched. Mason's method is interesting because it demonstrates how much apparent structure can be generated by such an elementary constraint. She cites the example of the letter set *a, b, d, e, i, r*, which, when arranged so as to maximise the summed single letter positional frequencies yields BARIED.

Unfortunately, it appears that positional frequency is not a *necessary* basis for facilitation since Krueger's many demonstrations of a regularity effect (cf. Krueger, 1975) were achieved with single letter positional frequency controlled. Worse yet, Mason provides no guarantee even that it forms a *sufficient* cause for facilitation since as we have seen with the example of BARIED, maximising positional frequency also affects transitional redundancy as well as syllabic and morphological structure. What is singularly absent from Mason's (1975) demonstration is a comparative or multi-variate approach in which different structural measures are pitted against each other.

McClelland and Johnston (1977) also reported an effect of single letter positional frequency in their threshold task, though this was based on a *post hoc* comparison of extreme frequency quartiles. Two points about their effect are of major interest. First, is the contrast with their failure to obtain a bigram effect. Normally when single letter and bigram frequencies are summed across the stimulus it is very difficult to vary stimuli on the two measures independently. However McClelland and Johnston get round this by performing their single letter analysis in terms not of the summed frequency for an entire stimulus but of the probability of reporting each component letter as a function of its frequency. (It is unclear from Mason's, 1975, discussion which of these procedures is most appropriate). Their rejection of a bigram effect is, however, based on both procedures.

The second point of interest is that once again positional frequency did not seem to be a necessary cause of the basic effects of stimulus type, since the positional frequency effect did not interact with a word vs pseudoword effect and since in a further experiment words were superior to random letter strings with positional frequency of target letters controlled.

At the time of writing, an interesting paper has been published by Massaro et al. (1979), highlighting several of these issues. They set out to compare the psychological reality of two descriptions of orthographic structure. Their 'probabilistic' description involves Mason's measure of single letter positional frequencies summed across the word. In contrast, their 'rule-governed' description uses criteria of pronounceability and graphemic context (e.g. initial TPR is unpronounceable, initial CC is orthographically illegal). In their study both measures of structure had some independent predictive power for letter search and recognition threshold tasks and the authors conclude that either both descriptions have psychological reality or that both should be brought together in some more general but as yet unformulated description.

Concerning the rule-based description there are two points to make. The first bears upon their inferred support for a rule-based measure. Inspection of Massaro et al.'s stimuli reveals that a virtually identical classification would be yielded by a purely probabilistic measure of trigram positional frequencies. There is, therefore, no basis in these data for supposing that a rule-based description is a necessity for the prediction of facilitatory effects of structure. A more secure basis for a rule-based system would have to come from either (i) a conclusive demonstration that probabilistic measures owed their predictive power to a discrete effect of zero vs non-zero frequencies or (ii) to the subtle prediction of anomalous facilitation occurring with zero frequency elements which nonetheless conformed to the rules.

Our second point relates to the nature of the rules treated by Massaro et al. Unlike the orthographic rules postulated by Gibson and Levin (1975) those of Massaro et al. do not pretend to be contained at a purely graphemic level of description. Thus they make reference to such morphological features as boundaries and form classes and to such phonological features as stress and phonotactic constraints (Venezky, 1970). Hence the perceiver's use of such rule-generated structure has in common with the lexicality component of the word superiority effect that it requires him to consult a higher order of entry in permanent memory than is involved in probabilistic organisations of graphemes. (Indeed, it might be that the facilitatory effect of lexical membership is due to use of the lexical information to gain access to orthographic rules).

In summary then, the superiority of pseudoword over irregular string stimuli in the recognition threshold task and in same–different and letter search reaction-time tasks offers strong evidence for an effect on perception of structural regularity. However, there is no positive evidence in favour of the notion that either positional or sequential redundancy is a sufficient cause for this effect. On the negative side there is some correlational evidence (with the reservations noted above) that sequential redundancy is not a sufficient cause and evidence that positional redundancy is not a necessary cause.

We have already touched upon the possibility that these variables do not act *causally* as continua but rather it is the presence or absence of of zero frequency bigrams, etc. which matters. This serves to reintroduce the candidature of an all-or-none factor of pronounceability.

4 Phonological factors in visual recognition

We have already reviewed evidence that seems to show that pronounceability is not effective simply by allowing performance to depend upon a phonologically recoded form of the visual stimulus (Baron and Thurston, 1973; Baron, 1975; Besner and Jackson, 1975; Pollatsek *et al.*, 1975). However, more recently the question of the role of pronounceability in visual recognition has been reopened in a subtle study by Hawkins *et al.* (1976). They re-examined the effect of presenting the subject with homophonic recognition alternatives. It will be recalled that Baron and Thurston had found no difference in performance between a homophonic condition in which the subject might be presented with BEAR and asked to decide whether it had been BEAR or BARE and a visually equivalent non-homophone condition in which DEAR might be presented, followed by the choice between DEAR and DARE.

Hawkins *et al.* (1976) made various methodological criticisms of the Baron and Thurston study but the main thrust of their argument was that by making half the response alternatives homophones, subjects were given little incentive to use phonetic recoding, if such an option were open to them. Accordingly, Hawkins *et al.* compared blocks of trials in which few homophones occurred (encouraging a phonetic strategy) with blocks containing a high proportion of homophones. They found that, in the condition that encouraged phonetic recoding, performance was worse with homophonic than with different sounding alternatives. In contrast, when a high proportion of homophones was used to discourage phonetic recoding no effect of homophony was found. This result implies that a phonetic recoding strategy *can* be used in visual recognition where the resultant code is appropriate for discriminating between the response alternatives. Nevertheless, Hawkins *et al.* go on to show that the word superiority effect does not depend upon the use of phonetic recoding for words. This follows from their finding that even when phonetic recoding was discouraged, words, whether homophonic or not, continued to be better recognised than single letters.

Hawkins *et al.*'s (1976) study goes some way toward clarifying the question of whether, and under what circumstances, phonetic recoding occurs; but it leaves unresolved several more fundamental questions, such as why words are better recognised than pseudowords, what the alternative form of code is that supports word superiority when phonetic coding is abandoned, and how it could be that phonetic recoding confers an advantage to word processing. We shall defer a comprehensive answer to the question of the basis of word superiority effects until Section 8. Meanwhile we shall restrict ourselves to a few comments on the significance of the manipulation of homophony.

First, it is worth making the point that the use of homophonic alternatives only prohibits the use of a low-level phonetic or articulatory code in which the orthographic information has been discarded. It seems to have been generally assumed without question that any phonological coding must take that form. In contrast it is quite plausible that a more abstract phonological representation could be used to decide between homophones. Such a phonological representation would have to conserve orthographic information. This would be achieved if what was represented consisted of translations between the graphemic and phonemic domains. Another possibility is that, at least for real words, this representation is like the abstract lexical level in Chomsky and Halle's (1968) generative theory of phonology. This lexical-phonological representation is quite lawfully reflected in the orthographic domain. If such a phonological code is possible then the homophony manipulation is not the conclusive test of phonological coding that it has been taken to be. By extension, the Hawkins *et al.* (1976) results would simply show that when homophones were few, subjects could be lulled into relying on a more superficial phonetic/articulatory code in which the orthographic information was discarded.

Our second comment on the homophony test is simpler and more direct. It is that the most appropriate conditions for searching for phonological coding occur not in the true word superiority effect (real words vs letters), for this superiority might be mediated by the use of some sort of non-phonological lexical code for words. After all, we already know that performance on words is superior to that on pronounceable non-words. Rather the place to look is the pseudoword superiority effect (pronounceable non-words vs letters). To be sure there are practical difficulties in defining pseudoword homophony (but how about FREWS/FRUISE?). Even so, if we want to isolate a condition in which the advantage in perceptibility might be exclusively dependent on phonological recoding then it is to the pseudoword that we should surely look.

Perhaps the most persevering attempt to develop a detailed phonological recoding theory of visual word recognition is that by Spoehr and Smith over the last six years (Spoehr and Smith, 1973; Smith and Spoehr, 1974; Spoehr and Smith, 1975; Santa et al., 1977). In a large measure this theoretical enterprise has been insulated from the various disputes about the word superiority effect. The theory is based on the correlation between pronounceability and visual perceptibility. Spoehr and Smith make the unquestioning assumption that pronounceability effects depend on phonological recoding. The theory attempts to relate pronounceability to perceptibility via a description of the steps required to derive a phonetic translation of the grapheme array and uses the syllable as a base unit.

One tacit and particularly vulnerable assumption of this theory is that phonetic translation takes place pre-lexically. This has two consequences. First, as Coltheart (1978) has cogently shown, such a translation process has to be implausibly clumsy. Indeed, it is questionable whether a translation that does not call upon lexical information can ever work consistently in English. A further consequence of this pre-lexical assumption is that the theory predicts no effects of lexicality on perception (Henderson, 1977).

One interesting implication of the syllabic model however, is the special role it assigns to vowel detection (Henderson, 1977), since segmentation requires that vowels first be 'marked'. In fact, James and Smith (1970) and James (1974) have found search for a specified letter target to be faster in a word when the target is a vowel. Furthermore Henderson and Chard (1978) found, using random strings, that presence of a vowel in a consonant string could be detected faster than the converse. Finally, Spoehr and Smith (1975) have shown that the perceptibility of a consonant string is quite well predicted by the number of vowels which have to be inserted to render it pronounceable.

5 Orthographic regularity and reading ability

Whatever the nature of the skills which support the superior processing or word-like stimuli, there is little consistent evidence that the individual's possession of these skills is a major determinant of reading ability. Leslie and Calfee (1971) required children of various ages to search through words for a pre-defined target letter. While search rate did increase with age, within each age group reading level did not appear to predict performance.

Krueger *et al.* (1974) investigated letter search as a function of levels of word-like structure in the search array. When fourth grade children were compared to adults both showed similar amounts of improvement in speed attributable to increased structure in the stimulus. Amongst the children, even though reading ability correlated with the overall search rate it was unrelated to the extent of improvement induced by stimulus structure. In a second experiment the authors found a tenuous correlation between undergraduates' reading comprehension (but not other reading tests) and the amount of improvement induced by orthographic structure. They conclude that 'there is no consistent relationship between reading ability and the ability to use the redundancy in words to speed letter search'.

Rather more positive results have been reported by Mason (1975) who found that whereas reading ability in sixth grade children did not predict the rate of letter search through random strings, good readers *were* faster when the search was through words. Also, only good readers were aided by letter positional redundancy in their search through nonwords. However, Mason's effects differ for target present and absent trials and some of them disappear with practice so that it is difficult to come to any simple conclusion about the relationship between reading ability and use of redundancy. On the whole her results are best summarised as showing that poor readers show no effect of positional redundancy whereas good readers often do show an effect, but not under circumstances that are well understood.

What are we to make of this developmental literature? Not only is it unclear at an empirical level what governs the ephemeral appearances of a relationship between reading ability and the capacity to use the various sorts of redundancy, at a theoretical level it is doubtful whether the existence of such a relationship is of major interest. There are few contemporary students of reading who suppose that purely visual processes play an important role in reading disability. On the other hand, while there is a fair amount of evidence that phonological recoding presents much of the difficulty in reading acquisition, there appears to be no reason to suppose that sensitivity to positional redundancy plays a significant role in deriving sound from text. Furthermore, even if we agree to entertain the hypothesis that a disability in the utilisation of visible redundancy plays a causal role in reading difficulties then even so the present studies would be logically incapable of lending positive support to that view, since any disability of redundancy utilisation might equally well be the product of rather than the cause of reading disability. Presumably good readers read more and are therefore exposed more to incidental learning of orthographic regularities.

One of the general findings of this developmental literature is that the normal reader has developed his full ability to exploit redundancy quite early in his reading career. This is true of Krueger et al.'s (1974) fourth grade children and Lefton and Spragins (1974) third graders. In our own work we have obtained further evidence to support this conclusion in a task which may more closely approximate the demands of reading.

We tested two groups of children (2nd and 4th grade) in a lexical decision task. Subjects were presented with a six letter display and we measured the time they took to decide whether or not it formed a real word. On half the trials the display consisted of a real word drawn from their reading vocabulary. These words were subdivided into a high and low frequency set. However, the main focus of our interest was on the rejection latencies for the remaining non-word stimuli. These stimuli were constructed by combining factorially high and low levels of mean single positional frequency with the presence or absence of vowels in the string. We were interested in whether the children could utilise either of these cues to speed rejection of non-word strings. Notice that in this task it is the *lack* of orthographic structure which can speed performance. The stimuli are shown in Table 1.

The results of the experiment are shown in Table 2 which presents the mean reaction times and percentage error for the grade 2 (n = 43; age 6–7) and the grade 4 (n = 30; age 8–10) children that we tested.

For the affirmative decision times to the words there is a highly significant frequency effect (p < 0.005) but no tendency for this effect to interact with grade level. For the rejection times to the non-words decisions are speeded both by the absence of vowels (p < 0.01) and by low redundancy, in terms of mean single letter positional frequency (p < 0.001). These data add general confirmation to the suggestion that even inexperienced readers can use lack of word-like structure to speed their decision that a string of letters cannot be a word. They are consistent with the finding obtained by Stanners and Forbach (1973), using adult subjects, that consonant bigram frequency within ccvcc and

CCCCC non-words was inversely related to rejection latency. Our findings also agree with Stanners and Forbach's ordering of conditions, with word-affirmative latencies intermediate between the fast rejection latencies for irregular non-words and the slow rejection latencies for regular non-words.

TABLE 1   The stimuli used in the lexical-decision experiment. Words are shown with their Thorndike–Lorge frequency in parenthesis. Non-words are classified according to presence or absence of vowel and single letter positional frequency (SLPF). Total SLPF values are shown for each stimulus. In addition, the mean bigram positional frequencies (BPF) are provided for each set of non-words

Words

High frequency		Low frequency	
KNIGHT (AA)	COURSE (AA)	COLUMN (49)	NORMAL (41)
SILVER (AA)	FAMOUS (AA)	GENTLY (46)	INSECT (40)
BRIDGE (AA)	SIMPLE (AA)	HUNTER (46)	FASTEN (40)
FAMILY (AA)	COMING (AA)	VOYAGE (45)	BISHOP (40)
DOUBLE (AA)	ANSWER (AA)	GLOVES (43)	NOVELS (39)
SINGLE (AA)	GROUND (AA)	THRONE (43)	GOVERN (39)
TRAVEL (AA)	KINDLY (AA)	CANDLE (43)	JOSEPH (38)
ITSELF (AA)	FIGURE (AA)	DRAINS (41)	UNABLE (37)
SHOULD (AA)	THROWN (A)	HASTEN (41)	DAMSEL (36)

Non-words

High SLPF			Low SLPF		
Vowels absent	*Vowels present*		*Vowels absent*	*Vowels present*	
SHRNLD 1530	TURILD 1542		DTSCFK 327	KUGAFP 308	
CHYTLD 1210	BELMOR 1155		NMDLBF 266	HGBAFL 284	
DRCKLS 1028	ARCOPT 888		FDJCBL 260	GSECFP 282	
BRTLDS 1010	FRINOD 1100		GBHJTM 248	NDEBKO 257	
THRDLF 956	GRILTS 865		TGBFHC 242	KCIBFM 256	
SPRNTH 878	FROMSE 1024		KGSBDP 232	JUWFAC 255	
FRGHLY 874	CHURKE 880		GDBCHL 225	DBECMI 252	
SCRNGH 864	CLASTY 868		JDWGCB 220	VBEJIC 212	
CLMPST 833	SCRUTE 1239		HGJCPL 213	UDBAFW 201	
$\bar{X}$ SLPF 1020	$\bar{X}$ SLPF 1062		$\bar{X}$ SLPF 248	$\bar{X}$ SLPF 256	
$\bar{X}$ BPF 91	$\bar{X}$ BPF 99		$\bar{X}$ BPF 1	$\bar{X}$ BPF 1	

One fairly clear conclusion that we can draw from these data is that both age groups can use their analysis of positional redundancy (either of single letters or of bigrams) to facilitate non-word-rejection decisions. This follows from the fact that even when the string is devoid of vowels and their structural implications, positional frequency affects decision times. Thus even six-to-seven-year olds are sensitive to quite subtle features of orthographic structure.

TABLE 2   Mean reaction-times and percentage errors in the lexical decision task as a function of word frequency and non-word orthographic structure

| | Words | | Non-words | | | |
| | High frequency | Low frequency | Vowel | | No vowel | |
			High SLPF	Low SLPF	High SLPF	Low SLPF
Grade 2 RT	1782	1929	2048	1846	1873	1668
(n = 43) E%	15	10	10	9	16	5
Grade 4 RT	938	1073	1178	956	1076	957
(n = 30) E%	11	15	21	6	9	7

Closer analysis of Table 2 suggests that in one respect the rejection latencies differ in pattern between younger and older children. For the older children the effect of vowel presence only occurs with high redundancy arrays. For the younger children the vowel effect is equal in both low and high SLPF arrays. The simplest explanation of this interaction (which was significant at $p < 0.05$) is that the combination of high levels on both orthographic factors yields items that are wholly plausible phonologically and orthographically (such as the 'pseudo-adjective' CLASTY or the 'pseudo-breakfastfood' GRILTS). Rejection of these must wait the outcome of a lexical search. The error rate is also relatively high for these pseudowords, implying a 'humility bias'. The child is disposed to accept the possibility that these *are* words, lying outside his vocabulary.

For these older children, the total absence of any effect of vowel presence when positional redundancy is low, suggests that low positional redundancy is a sufficient basis for a rejection decision. Either vowel detection does not contribute to the analysis of orthographic acceptability or its outcome is available too late to pre-empt the decision process. Since almost all the low positional redundancy stimuli have, for example, a zero frequency initial bigram this may trigger a rejection decision before the vowel detector has completed its analysis of the whole string. Because there is a vowel presence effect for high positional redundancy items we assume that some form of vowel-dependent analysis does exist in conjunction with the analysis that is sensitive to positional redundancy. This might be a system for 'marking vowels as a preliminary to parsing the string into syllables', as suggested by Smith and Spoehr's (1974) model of word perception. Or it might consist of a more global test of pronounceability.

What remains to be explained is why the younger subjects exhibit a vowel presence effect when positional redundancy is low. We assume this is a consequence of a less efficient decision process that requires more evidence of irregularity for a rejection response. This allows time for the detection of vowels, or the islands of local structure that they create, with a consequent slowing of the rejection decision. On this interpretation, what changes developmentally is not the nature of the underlying processes of stimulus analysis but the efficiency of the decision machinery. Expressed another way, the concept of word-likeness becomes more refined.

With adult subjects it is well established that when the non-words are all irregular then word-affirmative decisions can be made faster and appear to be based more on orthographic than on lexical considerations. It would be interesting to know whether children are also capable of adapting their decision criteria to the nature of the stimulus material in this way.

6 Does holistic word perception conceal spelling?

We began by considering the implications for the incidental learning of spelling of two nineteenth-century characteristics of word perception. One view concentrated on the recognition of individual letters but assumed economical, partial processing of the word. In a sense this approach is the parent of many of the redundancy utilisation notions. The other view, to which we now turn, held word perception to be holistic.

Early theorists were reticent in asserting what exactly holism entailed. For some, what mattered was the subjective quantity of the percept of a word, while for others holism was little more than the denial of a serial, letter-by-letter processing theory. More recent literature, however, has been distinguished by attempts to define holism more clearly both at an experimental and conceptual level.

One influential account has been provided by Smith and his colleagues. Smith and Haviland (1972) begin by attempting to distinguish two explanations of the word superiority effect in recognition. The 'inference hypothesis' holds that words are analysed in terms of individual letters but that the output of this analysis is interpreted by a system which applies knowledge of the redundancy of English. In contrast, the 'unitisation hypothesis' holds that words are more readily perceived than non-words because words can be analysed in terms of groups of letters and processing is aided by having to deal with fewer basic units. Smith and Haviland's attempt to adjudicate between these views rests on a claimed refutation of the inference hypothesis. Since that claim rests on the dubious assumption that a short period of training with redundancy introduced into consonant trigrams can be treated as equivalent to the reader's lifetime of experience with words, we shall consider it no further.

A more recent attempt to determine 'the functional units of word perception' has been reported by Santa et al. (1977). Their method is based on a task in which the subject is required to search a word or consonant string for a target which may be a single letter, a bigram, trigram, or so forth. (When the target is absent the string contains ingredients which differ only by one letter from the target.)

Santa et al. (1977) offer various arguments in support of the thesis that processing is based on units larger than the individual letter. First, they reject a serial letter-by-letter processing account on the grounds that there is no monotonic increase in reaction time as a function of number of letters in the target. However, this does no more than confirm the established view that multiple target searches can utilise parallel processing. (We must be careful to distinguish parallel processing models, in which the elementary units may be single letters, from models which are based on supra-letter features.) Nevertheless the authors appear to argue that a multi-letter target which is detected as fast as a single letter must thereby constitute a 'unit' of analysis.

A central difficulty with Santa et al.'s (1977) arguments, based as they are on the relative detection times for various sizes of target unit at various word positions, is that much of the variation of detection time seems attributable to the position of the target within the word. Thus, given that there is a bowed serial position effect with detection of single letter targets generally fastest at the beginning and end of words (and non-words), the finding that in BLAST the bl is recognised faster than the s can be accounted for without mention of target unit size.

Accordingly, the authors turn in their Experiment 2 to what they consider the crucial test for partitioning effects of serial-position from effects of the unit of analysis. To do this they compare consonant strings which begin and end with 'permissible' bigrams with those which do not (e.g. BLKST vs PFDGT). They report that whereas the medial bigrams were detected equally fast for both types of string the beginning and end bigrams were detected faster for the permissible string. Since this interaction was significant they argue that: 'Therefore, the RTs on the double letter-probes indicate that both serial-position and spelling-pattern effects contributed . . .' (Santa et al., 1977, p. 589).

However, since only the end bigrams were permissible in the so-called permissible strings, superiority of those items as compared to those of the non-permissible string does no more than confirm that bigram frequency affects detection times. This finding advances the target-unit argument not one whit. (Actually this argument is further complicated by the fact that the direction of this interaction between serial position and type of string is reversed when, within the same experiment non-permissible strings are compared with real words (Santa et al., Fig. 2).)

What this discussion shows is the futility of arguing directly from relative speed of detection to a theory of the underlying processes, in terms of the size of unit used by the comparison stage. It is difficult to escape the conclusion that the unit of analysis theory amounts to no more than a loose way of referring to (i) facilitatory effects of redundancy, and (ii) processes which are not serial in a letter-by-letter way. As with the nineteenth-century advocacy of holism (see Henderson, 1977) the unit of analysis view achieves little more than the denial of letter-by-letter processing.

A characteristic of Santa et al.'s (1977) view which makes it flexible, if difficult to test, is that they hold that analysis can use a range of perceptual units which may be of different size and overlapping. A much more radical position is that taken by Johnson (1975) who asserts that the entire word functions as a compelling unit of analysis so as to pre-empt analysis of constituent letters.

Johnson bases his holistic conclusions on two findings: (i) same–different RTs to pairs of words are unaffected by word length, and (ii) it takes longer to find a target letter within a word than to match a target letter to another letter or a target word to a word. From (ii) Johnson concludes that unitary word analysis must precede the analysis of constituent letters.

The first of these arguments has been criticised in some detail by Henderson (1975) who shows that the word length data are inconsistent with other findings but that in any case they can be reconciled with a class of parallel processing model operating on individual letter components of the word.

The second argument is also vulnerable both to empirical and logical assault. Thus it has been shown that the target size effect (whole words better than single letters) is an artifact of successive presentation of target and test stimulus (Marmurek, 1977; Henderson and Chard, 1976), and the effect is reversed by simultaneous presentation. Moreover, even were the effect to obtain consistently it could still be ascribed to processes other than stimulus analysis, since a general problem for arguments based on the time to match units of various size is that the situation potentially involves response conflict. One simple way to express this is to say that WORD/WORD is *more similar* than W/WORD. If matching performance is mediated by a device which responds to the overall amount of sameness then it is likely to be sensitive to such inherently different properties of the tasks.

Other whole word unit theories have rested their appeal on argument rather than experiment. Thus F. Smith (1971) in an influential general characterisation of reading, argues that the reader by-passes letter recognition; but instead of falling back on the rather discredited word-envelope (whole-shape) theory, Smith suggests that words are identified as a sequence of parsimoniously selected letter features. Thus READ might be analysed as, in sequence, left vertical and closed curve, rect-angular, pointed top, closed curve. (This is a crude example not intended to have predictive power.) Even ignoring the problem of how we recognise cursive script, this view encounters severe difficulties with out ability to cope with case ALTeRnAtIoN. More particularly, given McClelland's (1976) demonstration that the word superiority effect survives case alternation, the theorist is obliged to assert that word superiority and holistic perception co-exist but that the former is not caused by the latter.

Rozin and Gleitman (1977) provide a telling critique of the F. Smith model. The central difficulty which they bring out is the fact that the economy of feature detection in the model is offset by the extravagant feature-list memory required. They point out that while the alternative 'plodder' model requires an extra processing stage, that of letter identi-fication, redescription of the input data in terms of an abstract graphemic code with its restricted set of elements drastically reduces the storage and retrieval problem. 'Why all this torture' they ask 'to avoid noticing 26 inoffensive little squiggles?'

An extension of the case-alternation technique to same–different judgements has been made by Taylor et al. (1977). Two interesting general features of their data are the confirmation that word superiority is not reduced in magnitude by the disruption imposed by case variation and the demonstration that a case shift within a syllable is no more disruptive than a shift at a syllabic BOUNDary. However, the main thrust of their argument is that 'if spelling patterns are functional perceptual units, perceptual performance should exhibit a roughly linear decline with the number of case transitions'. This prediction is fairly well borne out in the data.

Must we then accept the perceptual units premise? Well in fact all we have to do to avoid acceptance is to show that the effect is predictable from a single letter unit model. As it turns out that is a simple matter. Consider a serial model, for simplicity of exposition. The processor scans the string translating letters one by one into an abstract graphemic code. As in many theories the translation process for each graphemic depends on a prior stage of 'normalisation'. It is reasonable to assume that normalisation is sensitive to case variation. Number of case shifts therefore has the predicted effect on perception.

In closing this examination of hypothetic perceptual units larger than the individual letter we turn to some search data reported by Healy and colleagues (Healy, 1976; Drewnowski and Healy, 1977). Their key finding is that when subjects search through prose for a target letter in a cancellation task they make a disproportionate number of omission errors in the common function words THE and AND. This effect is reduced when the words are placed in an inappropriate syntactic context and by various other manipulations designed to disrupt fluent reading. Drewnowski and Healy (1977) conclude that text can be processed at various levels (including phrase units), each of which involves units of a specific size: processing at these levels is conducted in parallel in a self-terminating manner so that completion at a higher level terminates all lower level processing.

In marked contrast to the foregoing accounts these authors are careful to deny that the units involved need be perceptual units. They echo the caution of several writers on speech monitoring tasks (e.g. Foss and Swinney, 1973) that *the order of processing different levels may not be the same as the order of accessing these levels in a detection task*. What these laboratory tasks require is access to a level of processing which is generally defined by the experimenter. As such they are constantly at risk of confusing limited access to the stages of processing (e.g. of word constituents) with the nature of the elementary units used in those stages; (see Henderson, 1977 and 1978 for a wider discussion of the problems of adjudicating between explanations in terms of levels of processing and levels to which the decision machinery has explicit access).

In summary, then, we can find no evidence whatever to suggest that the reader's use of redundancy involves holistic perception in a manner which obscures the identity of individual letters. The only way in which we have been able to invest holistic theories with a sensibly restricted meaning has been to construe them as asserting that the feature bundles which are extracted from the input and compared to the listings available in permanent memory are drawn from across the letter array. Furthermore, either these transgraphemic features must be assumed to be inadequate to specify the identity of an individual letter or if they are held to be adequate in principle then it must be assumed that they cannot in fact be applied to such an identification because of the size of the unit whose feature listing is retrieved from memory and entered into the perceptual comparator.

   This is the only formulation of the unit of analysis view which we can arrive at which makes sense of a contrast with the alternative theory that word recognition is mediated by a graphemic coding stage (and that this stage is affected by orthographic regularity). On the whole McClelland's (1976) and Taylor et al.'s (1977) case alternation experiments seems to refute the holistic view as formulated above. Furthermore we have been unable to discover any cogent evidence that is inconsistent with our alternative graphemic code theory. What we are left with is a variety of demonstrations from Cattell's nineteenth-century studies onwards that a serial letter-by-letter processing model is not viable. In addition, there are grounds for suspecting that many of the findings with the detection tasks employed may be idiosyncratic peculiarities of the tasks themselves, whether it be the effect of successive presentation or of response conflict on same–different judgements (Johnson, 1975), serial position effects in search (Santa et al., 1977) or the order in which response units become available to the decision process in detection tasks (Healy, 1976).

7 Reading and spelling

So far we have argued that the reader has acquired fairly powerful knowledge of the structure of English orthography to support the skilled perception of words. It appears that some of this knowledge is available early in the development of reading ability. Yet it turns out to be difficult to establish precisely what regularities are being used in the recognition tasks.

   Whatever the basis of these effects of orthographic regularity on recognition clearly there is no reason to be surprised at the co-existence of such orthographic sophistication in the reader with the usual difficulties encountered in the production of lexical spellings. There is a world of difference between the tacit employment in recognition of knowledge which may be largely statistical and the explicit use of full and determinate knowledge in spelling production. This gulf is hardly bridged by the demonstration that the reader's knowledge of orthographic structure includes a lexical component, as manifest in the superior perceptibility of real over pseudowords.

We began by considering two ways in which the reader's use of orthographic structures might obscure spelling information. Holism we found to be a poorly argued case and we could find no evidence to suggest that holistic perception might operate so as to prevent the identification of component letters. Partial or economical word processing was the other possibility. Despite the fact that partial processing in its most obvious sense does not appear to be responsible for the word superiority effect, (for that is one way of interpreting the guessing controls), there seems little doubt that some processing economies underlie fluent reading. This is attested by the ease with which confusional errors can be induced by context as well as the ease of reading mutilated text in which crucial SP–L—NG information is omitted. This difference between reading and spelling is sometimes characterised as being 'analogous to that between recognition and recall' (Gibson and Levin, 1975, p. 335). Unfortunately this analogy is not very helpful as the memory processes that distinguish recognition from recall are themselves the subject of major controversy (Brown, 1976). Furthermore, the nature of the recognition test in reading is highly uncontrolled. It is only rarely that closely matched alternatives exist (e.g. dependent, dependant) as real lexical items, and it may well be that their interchange would not be detected by many readers.

Where the dichotomies between recognition and recall and between reading and spelling converge is in the commonly held view that a generate – recognise loop is available to supplement spelling recall, that is, the supposition that we can efficiently utilise a test of visual familiarity applied to our own spelling output. We know of no experimental evidence in support of this intuition but the suggestion has been developed in several directions.

One of these directions has involved pursuit of a relationship between imagery and spelling ability. These studies range from the extraordinary claim of Radakar (1963) to have induced long-term improvements in children's spelling by two weeks of 'imagery training' to the failure to find a relationship between individual differences in imagery and spelling ability reported by Sloboda in Chapter 11.

We find several reasons to doubt that imagery plays a fundamental role in linking spelling and reading competence. Fisrt, even if the visual familiarity test-loop were to be viable there is no good reason to suppose that it is mediated by imagery in the usual sense of a *visible memory*. No more do we require to be able to generate from memory the seeing-experience of a face in order to go about recognising it. Second, we suspect that the relationship hypothesised between imagery and recognition testing is based on a primitive view of images as literally stored mental snapshots of words. In contrast, several current theories of imagery hold that the image is generated from stored abstract descriptions (see, for example, Pylyshyn, 1973). This might permit us to have images which do not serve as literal descriptions snch as the image of a building fronted by an *indeterminate* number of columns, or the image of the name of a Georgian chess master that we cannot spell or pronounce with certitude.

A rather more refined interpretation of the recognition test-loop has been advanced by Simon and Simon (1973). Farnham-Diggory and Simon (1975) have attempted a test of this model as follows. Words and non-words were presented to children for spelling after a brief interpolated task. Presentation was either by means of a visual display (of the word as a whole) or an auditory, letter-by-letter spelling. The main finding was that visual presentation was superior for the words but not the non-words. This the authors interpret as showing that visual presentation can be used more readily to access a visual representation of the word-spelling in lexical memory. [Actually they argue that with visual presentation alone, 'a chunk referencing the *visual* image in long-term memory can be retained over the interpolation' (p. 606); but the details of this claim need not detain us.]

Unfortunately the Farnham-Diggory and Simon experiment leaves open a number of other interpretations based on the possibility that visual presentation owes its superiority not to its allowing more efficient access to the visual spelling lexicon but instead to allowing more efficient on-line extraction of spelling information from the words. This might be due to its permitting examination of letter conjunctions, or to parallel presentation permitting the distribution of attention to the more difficult portions of the word. The lack of presentation modality effect for non-words could well have been due to their posing quite different problems since for some reason the non-words used included highly irregular items like EENGR, IXTYS and AMPST.

We have followed up these possibilities in a series of experiments on 8–9 year olds (the age range studied by Farnham-Diggory and Simon). First, in Experiment 2, we replicated the presentation modality effect. To do this we presented common 6 and 7 letter words to children. The presentation was followed by a six-second period in which the children read aloud three randomly chosen two-digit numbers. Then they wrote down the spelling of the word. The 87 children were divided into three groups which differed in the manner of presentation of the words. One group received parallel visual display for about six seconds. The second group received serial visual display a letter at a time, one second per letter. The third group received serial auditory presentation at one second per letter.

Performance with the parallel visual display was significantly better at 70% of words correct than with either serial visual (56%) or serial auditory (59%). These last two conditions did not differ significantly. This confirms the visual-parallel vs auditory effect previously reported. It also establishes that the effect is not one of sense modality but of full visual word display vs serial display. This is consistent with the idea that the conditions differ in the extent to which they permit extraction of spelling information from the display. But of course it is also possible that the serial displays cannot efficiently serve lexical access.

Accordingly we turned to manipulation of the duration of the parallel-visual display. This strategy was based on the assumption that access to the visual word lexicon could be accomplished within a second or so, so that any improvement with durations beyond that would indicate an involvement of information extraction from the display. Such improvement is actually precluded in the Farnham-Diggory and Simon theory, since they specifically deny that spelling information is held in STM during interpolation. All that their theory permits to be held in STM is the 'chunk' which is used as the lexical retrieval cue.

We ran two experiments (Experiments 3 and 4) with exposure duration manipulated. The second was essentially a replication of the first with some minor procedural improvements. Experiment 3 utilised 55 children and Experiment 4 utilised 57 children. All were 8–9 year olds drawn from two local schools. There were two variables. Exposure duration (1 second, 8 seconds) was a two-level blocked variable with the order of testing counterbalanced across two sub-groups. Lexicality (word, pronounceable non-word) was a two-level variable with alternating presentation within blocks.

TABLE 3   Performance in terms of percentage of correct items in two spelling experiments with lexicality and exposure duration manipulated

| Lexical status: | Word | | Regular non-word | |
Display duration:	1 sec	8 sec	1 sec	8 sec
Experiment 3 (n = 55)	34%	49%	21%	39%
Experiment 4 (n = 57)	50%	63%	41%	57%

On each trial the lexical status of the item was stated, a 'ready' signal was given, followed by projection of the item on a screen. Immediately after presentation the interpolated number-naming task began. Finally the item was named, as a signal to commence writing the spelling.

Performance is shown in Table 3. Clearly performance is superior on words. There is also an effect of exposure duration. However, there is no tendency for these factors to interact. In Experiment 3 words improve by 15% and non-words by 18% when duration is increased. In Experiment 4 words improve by 13% and non-words by 16%.

The finding of a substantial exposure duration effect confirms the suspicion that performance depends to a large extent on the on-line extraction of spelling information from the display. This seems to conflict with the specific claim made by Farnham-Diggory and Simon (1975) that the word spelling is not extracted and held in STM but 'the word is in long-term memory, and only a clue, or a pointer, is being held during the delay interval in short-term memory' (p. 606).

Furthermore when regular, pronounceable non-words are used a similar magnitude of improvement with exposure duration is found. Nevertheless there is a lexicality effect as well, since the real words were spelled more accurately at either duration. This lexicality effect was slightly smaller than the exposure duration effect but might have been underestimated due to the non-words containing slightly easier spelling patterns.

We conclude that given the impossibility of equating the opportunity for extracting spelling information between visual-parallel and auditory-serial presentation, the differences in the effects of these methods of presentation found by Farnham-Diggory and Simon (1975) cannot be used to support their particular theory of privileged visual access to the spelling lexicon.

The hypothetical visual recognition test-loop for spelling implies a psychological convergence of the processes underlying reading and spelling. However, in contrast to this inferred convergence there exists a demonstrable source of divergence to which much less attention has been paid but which is inherent in the nature of English orthography. This divergence has its base in the asymmetry of the correspondences between graphemes and phonemes.

Consider the analysis of mapping options for the spelling and sound constituents of the word FAKE (Table 4). There are a total of 19 options for the phonemic representation of the four graphemes. Conversely there are 27 options for the graphemic representation of the three phonemic constituents of the word. This exhibits the tendency for correspondences to be more ambiguous in the phoneme to grapheme direction.

Vowels are highly ambiguous in both directions, whereas, as the example shows, consonants are often very low in ambiguity in the grapheme to phoneme direction.

TABLE 4   Phoneme to grapheme and grapheme to phoneme mappings illustrated for the string FAKE. The table includes some minor simplifications. The examples draw upon the Hanna *et al.* (1966) corpus

(*i*) Grapheme-phoneme correspondences			(*ii*) Phoneme-grapheme correspondences		
Grapheme	*Phonemic options*	*Example*	*Phoneme*	*Graphemic options*	*Example*
f	/f/	FAKE	/f/	*f*	FAKE
				ph	PHONE
a	/ei/	FAKE		*ff*	BUFF
	/a:/	ARM		*gh*	ROUGH
	/i:/	EAT			
	/e/	MANY	/ei/	*a–e*	FAKE
	/ai/	AISLE		*a*	ANGEL
	/ɔə/	COAT		*ai*	AID
	/ɔ:/	ALL		*ai–e*	AIDE
	/ə/	CANAL		*aigh*	STRAIGHT
	/uə/	BEAUTY		*au–e*	GAUGE
				ay	WAY
k	/k/	FAKE		*e*	CAFE
	silent	KNEE		*ea*	BREAK
				ei	VEIN
e	silent	FAKE		*eigh*	WEIGH
	/ɛə/	THERE		*et*	BERET
	/i:/	FEEL		*ey*	THEY
	/e/	END			
	/ai/	EYE	/k/	*k*	FAKE
	/u:/	SLEUTH		*c*	ORC
	/ə/	ANGEL		*cc*	OCCUPY
				cch	SACCHARIN
				ch	ECHO
				ck	BACK
				cq	ACQUIRE
				kh	KHAKI
				qu	BOUQUET
				sc	VISCOUNT

Not only, then, are the total number of options unequal for the two directions of mapping but for an individual grapheme-phoneme pair the ambiguity of either item taken alone is unrelated to that of the other member of the pair. Moreover, there is asymmetry not only in the number of options but in the relative frequency of a given pathway. For example, on examination of the /k/ to *k* correspondence we find that the phoneme /k/ is the 'regular' sounding of *k*. That is, apart from a very few silent *k*'s all others are sounded as /k/. On the other hand, working in the opposite direction we find that the 'regular' spelling of the phoneme /k/ is *c*, which accounts for over 70% of instances: (these data are estimated from Hanna *et al.*, 1966, Tables 4, 5, 7 and 8). Again the path *ow*→/au/ has about 49% relative frequency whereas the path /au/→*ow* has only about 29% frequency and is pre-empted by /au/→*ou*, with 56% frequency. It follows that a simple translation device that operates in terms of an ordered stack of correspondence frequencies would encounter different difficulties according to the direction of its translation. Furthermore, in the case of whole words, some are irregular (in the relative frequency sense) in one direction but not in the other.

Now, to be sure, some of these asymmetries of choice can be reduced by applying other constraints, ranging from position within the syllable up to more complex linguistic considerations. But they cannot be eliminated. It should come less as a surprise than it frequently seems to, therefore, to find that there is little correlation between the ease of spelling and of reading (pronouncing) a given word.

8 Conclusions

Let us begin by summarising the various sorts of structure which are embodied in the printed word and which might be employed so as to facilitate performance in the range of tasks that one may loosely term 'perceptual'. As we review our conclusions on the efficacy of each form of structure, we shall lay particular emphasis on any role played by such structure in the word superiority effects. The primary motivation for this emphasis is that much of the recent literature on word recognition has centred on these effects and they have come to be regarded as paradigms for the investigation of the perceptual skills of the reader. Accordingly an incidental product of this summary will be the outline of a systematic account of the mechanisms underlying such effects. Moreover, the taxonomy of structures within which our summary rests may itself have some expository value. Finally, for each form of structure, we shall consider its relationship to spelling information.

8.1 *Redundancies at the graphemic level*

By these are meant constraints upon the set of possible letter arrays that can be defined without reference to higher-order (e.g. phonological, morphological) levels.

8.1.1 *Single-letter positional frequency.* Mason (1975), McClelland (1976), and McClelland and Johnston (1977) have shown that this form of structure assists perception in letter search and word recognition tasks. In addition, such structure enters into the young child's conception of wordlikeness. In the perceptual facilitation studies the structure is probably used to speed graphemic encoding. We argue below that this is not the way in which structure is being used in the word superiority effects. Furthermore, McClelland and Johnston (1977) have shown that even when this form of structure facilitates perception, such facilitation operates independently from the word superiority effect. By virtue of the fact that these SLPF effects truly depend upon *letter-positional constraints* (rather than simply involving the overall frequency of occurrence of letters) they imply a sort of spelling competence, but no more than a somewhat abstract sensitivity to statistical regularities that is unlikely to assist particular spelling decisions. Finally, it should be remembered that manipulations of SLPF frequently generate, as a by-product, other forms of structure, that may be operative in the situation.

8.1.2 *Sequential frequencies.* This refers to bigram up to n-gram frequencies, whether constrained by word position or not. This includes so-called orders of approximation to English. Reports of facilitation by such structure are most common in studies of consonant strings (e.g. Baron, 1974; Herrmann and McLaughlin, 1973; Spoehr and Smith, 1975; and, perhaps, Santa *et al.*, 1977). Generally these effects are absent in word perception (Manelis, 1974; Chambers and Forster, 1975; McClelland and Johnston, 1977). Where they might seem to occur with words as stimuli (Krueger, 1970), other variables such as pronounceability and lexicality are usually correlated with sequential redundancy. It follows that sequential redundancy plays no role in word superiority effects. As with SLPF, where sequence frequency is operative it probably acts by speeding graphemic encoding. Moreover, the implications of this sort of knowledge of structure for spelling competence are equally abstract and probabilistic.

8.2 *Lexical constraints on graphemic structure*

Such structure arises because of the existence of what are sometimes called 'orthographic neighbourhoods'. Consider the problem of identifying the first letters in -ELL and -NOB. In the first, the context places minimal constraints. There exist at least 10 lexically possible completions, whereas in the second example there are only two. The use of such constraints can therefore be advanced to account for the lexicality component of word superiority effects (see, for example, Wheeler, 1970, and Henderson, 1977). Recently, however, McClelland and Johnston (1977) and Johnston (1978) have subjected this idea to specific tests whose outcome has enabled them to reject lexical constraint as a factor in word superiority effects.

Whereas the lexical-constraint mechanism involves reference to a higher level of representation, it is like the preceding forms of structure in that any effect it might have would be upon the speed of graphemic encoding. As for the implications about the tacit knowledge of spelling possessed by a user of such constraints, these would be considerable: so rejection of lexical constraint as the structure responsible for word superiority is of special interest to us in the present context.

8.3 *Holistic encoding*

These preceding mechanisms for the facilitation of encoding speed, whether or not they involved consultation of levels above the graphemic, had their eventual effect at the graphemic level. In contrast, holistic encoding passes from elementary features to units which may be syllabic or lexical, without concern for the representation of individual graphemes. Holism is therefore a particularly discouraging theory of recognition in terms of its implications for the incidental learning of spelling during reading. We found that the evidence adduced for such theories did not bear scrutiny. Instead, we preferred the view that recognition was indeed mediated by an abstract graphemic representation. However, given the economies effected in arriving at a perceptual decision in rapid reading, such a graphemic code need not amount to the exhaustive specification of spelling which could serve production.

8.4 *Structures entering into phonological translation*

This refers to theories such as that of Spoehr and Smith that attribute variation in encoding speed to the difficulty of a phonetic translation stage. This theory is therefore a member of the class of encoding speed theories but is distinct in not being directly concerned with speed of *graphemic* encoding. We have discussed certain internal difficulties of this model and have rejected it as a means of predicting several aspects of word superiority effects. Some versions of the Spoehr and Smith formulation can also be regarded as *holistic encoding* models, based on a syllabic unit of analysis.

This theory might seem to have no very direct implication for spelling knowledge. However, insofar as it implies a discarding of graphemic information in the course of phonetic translation (see discussion of the homophony test, above) it suggests a discouraging basis in reading for the incidental learning of spelling. But it can be argued against the theory, in any case, that without spelling information, unequivocal lexical access is not possible. Furthermore, there is ample evidence (see Coltheart, 1978) that entry to the lexicon is *not* dependent on the use of a phonetic access code. We therefore reject the theory in this formulation. With this, we end our review of encoding-speed theories.

We turn therefore to a consideration of theories that appeal instead to the robustness of the eventual code for an explanation of word superiority effects. Perhaps the initial advantage of such theories is that the word superiority effect in the tachistoscopic threshold task appears to be based on the superior ability of words (and possibly pseudo-words) to survive pattern masking (Johnston and McClelland, 1973).

8.5 *Robust phonological code*

We assume that the pseudoword superiority effect depends on the use for pronounceable stimuli of a phonological code. If it is to be of use, such a code requires to preserve orthographic information, as we have already seen. We further assume that such a code survives masking which destroys isolated graphemic information. Finally we assume that the graphemic information that is unpacked from such a code can be more readily searched and matched in the various reaction time tasks that manifest pseudoword superiority. Even though such processing is conducted at the graphemic level, the availability of a phonological frame for the grapheme array facilitates access to the graphemic information.

8.6 *Robust lexical code*

We make similar claims for a lexical code, as the servant of the real-word superiority effects.

We are not able to divine any special implications for spelling in the use of these codes, either in terms of the tacit spelling knowledge that they imply or in terms of the implications for incidental learning of spelling. Clearly there are, in any case, other, and more direct grounds for accepting the existence of such codes, though not necessarily with the special properties that we have attributed to them.

Whatever the nature of the reader's command of orthography it has not been difficult to find reasons why this knowledge may not assist the production of spelling. Even if the form of the knowledge were in principle, pertinent to spelling it might not be accessible to the speller. We have seen that there is a vital distinction to be made between establishing that information is represented at some stage of processing (such as grapheme identities, in the course of word recognition) and establishing that the subject has conscious access to that information. Given the contrast between the automatic nature of many of the component processes in reading and the rather deliberate nature of spelling production this distinction is likely to be particularly important. In the present interpretation of the word superiority effects the moral might be drawn that the access to mental representations is at least as important as their speed of construction.

Acknowledgements

This research was supported by SSRC research grant HR 3301. Jackie Chard carried out the experiments reported and Avril Clark assisted in the conduct of Experiment 4.

We acknowledge the assistance of the Head Teachers and staff of Howe Dell School, Bishops Wood School and Broad Oaks School, Hatfield, Kingsmoor County School and Peterswood County School, Harlow, and Epping Junior School, Epping.

6

The Logogen Model and Orthographic Structure

JOHN MORTON   *MRC Applied Psychology Unit, Cambridge, England*

1 Introduction

This short chapter has been written by request of the editor who asked: 'How in principle could the logogen model be extended to take account of writing and spelling?' It is thus an exercise in the methodology of theory. I will start by describing the current state of the model together with the data prompting the most recent change. Then I will examine possible ways in which the model might in principle be extended to incorporate orthographical information. The model will not be totally described and the reader is advised to read the primary sources before drawing too many conclusions. There they will find many more details and justification.

2 The logogen model 1977

The model describes separable stages of processing of (mostly) linguistic material. In all except one publication (Morton, 1968) I have focused on single words; detailed accounts of the evolution of the model and data contributing to its form can be found in Morton (1969, 1970, 1977, 1979a, b).

An essential part of the model is the logogen system. This used to be a single system but the effect of the most recent changes has been to split it into three separate systems. The relations among these systems and between them and other processing systems are shown in Fig. 1.

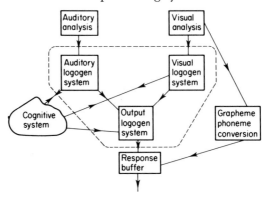

FIG. 1

The dotted line indicates the three systems which have taken over the functions of the single logogen system in the old model. They are called the visual input logogen system, the auditory input logogen system and the output logogen system.

2.1 Output logogen system

This system contains a defining feature of the old system – the units are terminally active when a particular word is available as a response. Thus, if you see the word TABLE, hear it spoken or see the object then if you say the name to yourself, the same output logogen is involved in all cases. The output logogen system produces phonological codes and sends them to the response buffer. It receives inputs from the cognitive system in a 'semantic' code (see Morton and Patterson, 1979) and from the input logogen systems by means of a one-to-one mapping at the morpheme level (cf. Murrell and Morton, 1974; van der Molen and Morton, 1979; Schwartz et al., 1979).

2.2 Input logogen system

The input logogen systems preserve the input functions of the old logogen system. They serve as passive categorisation systems which receive information from their respective sensory analysis systems. This information will include, in the case of visual inputs, which letters are present and in what positions but will also include more global information such as word shape, and more particular information such as individual visual features. In most cases there is redundancy in the input and so it is possible to get good performance when global cues are ABoLiShEd, as long as the stimulus information is clear. The important factor is that logogens are evidence collectors with thresholds – in fact two thresholds – and as such it is not *necessary* for all the letters to be recognisable in order for the word to be recognised. When a particular logogen has collected evidence in excess of its first threshold it sends a code to the cognitive system. Evidence beyond the second threshold results in a code being sent to the corresponding output logogen (see the debate on this route: Morton and Patterson, 1979; Shallice and Warrington, 1979; Schwartz et al., 1979). It is possible for the first threshold to be exceeded without the second being exceeded. Thus it is possible in principle to understand the word without 'knowing what it is' (cf. Marcel, in press). There is contextual feedback from the cognitive system to the input logogen systems in such a way that with continuous inputs contextual and sensory evidence add in a simple way (Morton, 1969).

Note that there is no semantic information in the logogen systems. As such they differ from lexicons in most uses of that term. Semantics is the province of the cognitive system.

2.3 *Response buffer*

The response buffer is the system which temporarily stores phonological codes. It has two outputs, one to the speech production system and another by which information is fed back to the other systems. This feedback would be used for silent rehearsal among other things. In this respect it shares some functions of working memory (Baddeley and Hitch, 1974; Morton, 1977).

Inputs to the response buffer come from the output logogen system in the normal production of speech and in reading aloud. There is also a route from the input analysis systems to the response buffer. These are the pathways which permit the reproduction of nonsense words. Since nonsense words have no representation in the logogen system, without this feature the model would not be able to account for our ability to read nonsense words out loud and repeat them, when they are spoken to us. The connection between the visual analysis system and the response buffer is via a system of grapheme-phoneme conversion where-in are represented the rules of conversion from letters and letter sequences to phonemes. The equivalent system on the auditory side converts acoustic codes to phonological codes which are fed into the response buffer.

2.4 *Cognitive system*

The cognitive system is the cognitive residue. It contains every-thing which is not explicitly included elsewhere. It has been expanded in Morton (1968) to indicate ways of handling continuous language, in Morton (1977) with respect to memory, in Morton and Patterson (1979) with respect to a number of features relevant for the discussion of deep dyslexia, and in Warren and Morton (in preparation) with respect to picture recognition. The only feature I will mention here is that in contrast with most lexicons I do not see all the information relevant to a particular word as located in the same 'place' and accessed simul-taneously. 'Meaning' is something to be computed as necessary, and not looked up as a unit. Other features of the cognitive system will be made apparent in the sections which follow.

3 Reasons for the change in the model

In the old version of the logogen model the same unit was active on input and output. Thus saying the word 'table' spontaneously and read-ing the word silently, involved the same logogen. The scope of the logogens was defined from the results of experiments in facilitation. In general these experiments involve a pre-training session, where subjects are exposed to particular forms, and then a testing session, where tachistoscopic thresholds are measured or the intelligibility of spoken words in noise is assessed. The intention is to look for transfer or lack of transfer from the pre-training to the test session. Thus Neisser (1954) found that reading FRAYS aloud had no effect on the subsequent recognition of PHRASE. This was taken as evidence for separate logogens with identical outputs to the response buffer. Murrell and Morton (1974) showed transfer from SEEN to SEES but not from SEED to SEES. We conclude that this result identified the critical recognition unit as morphemic and also established no transfer, over the time-scale involved (15–45 minutes), as a result of visual overlap. There are a number of reasons for rejecting the idea of *semantic* overlap as opposed to *morphemic* overlap in this experiment. Let us take just two. Firstly it isn't clear what the semantic relationship is between SEES and SEEN compared with the semantic relationship between PAINED and BORING to select two other of the stimuli in the Murrell and Morton experiment. And all the other cognitive activity in the half hour or so between pre-training and test could add semantic cueing on most common words in the logogen system. The second reason is more mundane, possibly more convincing but less valid. It is that with the auditory equivalent, Steven Kempley, working with me, has shown good transfer from BRINGING to BRINGS but none at all from BROUGHT to BRINGS. The semantic relationships between the pairs is not going to differ sufficiently to account for the data. (Doubt as to the application of this result for the visual logogen system lies in my suspicion that there are a number of profound differences in their operation – even if this is not one!)

Facilitation was seen as the result of the particular logogen having been active, the activity leading to a sensitisation of the logogen by lowering the threshold by some amount. But, by definition, there could be no distinction between a logogen firing as a result of sensory inputs and firing as a result of other activity. The same result would be required in all cases. The data turn out not to support this requirement. Winnick and Daniel (1970) found no effect on tachistoscopic thresholds for words as a result of having named a picture or spoken the word in response to a definition. Such a result is clearly impossible with the old model. Clark and Morton (in preparation) have replicated the Winnick and Daniel result and have shown that there is good transfer between handwritten and printed forms of words but poor transfer from auditory presentation to visual testing. They also showed no difference between conditions in which the response in the pre-training session was that of the word or its opposite. All these results tie the primary facilitation to the input portion of the divided logogen system. The auditory-visual symmetry was shown by Jackson and Morton (in preparation) who found only small effects of visual pre-training on auditory recognition. The result of these data has already been seen. There are three logogen systems and the primary facilitation effects are limited to the two input systems over the time scales of these experiments. In fact I believe there is facilitation in the output system over shorter time intervals and other facilitation effects at more than one time interval in the cognitive system, but they do not affect the structures already described.

Before proceeding we can note that Fig. 2 is completely equivalent to Fig. 1. In what follows I find it convenient to use expansions based on the second arrangement. I have included both versions to make clearer the derivation.

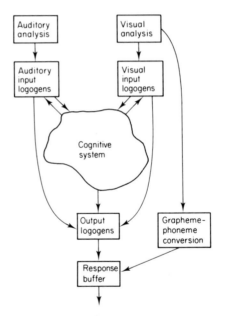

FIG. 2

4 Extensions to the logogen model

The clearest extension is due to Seymour (1973). He modifies the logogen model in order to incorporate separate access and exit channels for verbal and pictorial stimuli. In Fig. 3 I have redrawn the model as he gives it in his paper in a transformed and slightly reduced form to make it compatible in appearance with the earlier ones in this chapter.

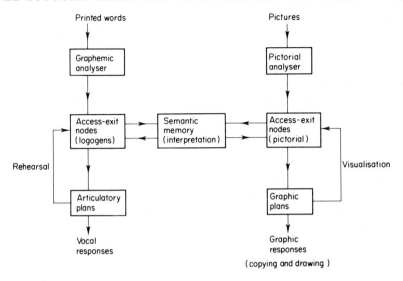

FIG. 3

The essential parts of his suggestions remain intact however. The model deals only with visual input as it stands but can be extended easily to incorporate auditory inputs. The power of the model in this extension is that it enabled Seymour to interpret a number of tasks in which we

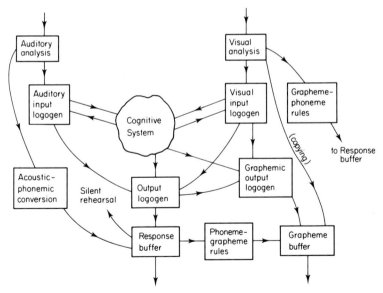

FIG. 4

measure how long it takes someone to read words, name objects or compare printed names and objects. The extension which Seymour has made is entirely within the spirit of the original model in that he separates out distinct coding stages and categorisation stages and attempts successfully to encompass a wide variety of data. You will see that in Chapter 20 in this volume Seymour and Porpodas have changed the format of his model somewhat. We have included the earlier version however so that the ancestral lines are more clearly visible.

An alternative way of representing the sub-systems is shown in Fig. 4 where I adopt Fig. 3 to allow for graphical output with connections from the visual analysis system, the visual input logogen and the response buffer. Let me justify these connections.

1   *Visual analysis system* – the direct connection to the grapheme buffer is labelled *copying*. This is the route which enables people to copy nonsense words, changing the format from print to script or vice versa. In principle this could be done by converting the letters into a phonological code going via the response buffer and thence via the phoneme-grapheme rules into the grapheme buffer. The argument in favour of the copying route is that there are patients with brain damage who can copy but cannot write to dictation, although they can repeat and understand spoken words (Weigl and Fradis, 1977). It is also a part of classical conduction aphasia, though in this case without the repetition ability (Hecaen and Albert, 1978, p. 43).

2   *Grapheme output logogen system* – the primary evidence for such a system would be from patients who could write words fluently but not copy nonsense syllables or write them to dictation. There are also patients who can only write fluently; as soon as they try to write with deliberation – even their own ideas – their writing goes to pieces. Connections to the grapheme output logogen have been made from the cognitive system, the output logogen system and from the visual input logogen system. The justification for the latter connection is purely the symmetry of the resulting system. It should be possible to find evidence to justify keeping or erasing that connection.

3   *Response buffer* – the main piece of evidence favouring a connection from the response buffer to the grapheme buffer via a system of phoneme-grapheme rules is our ability to write down nonsense words to dictation. Note here a patient reported by Beauvois and Derouesne (1978) who could write non-words to dictation but could not then read them. This justifies the separation of the grapheme-phoneme rules from the phoneme-grapheme rules.It is also going to be a possible route for talking about phonologically induced spelling errors in writing.

The reader who does not like the notation of information processing models will be at a grave disadvantage here. It would be possible to express all the relationships in Fig. 4 in verbal form; in doing this, however, one would simply lose the impression of simultaneity which the flow diagram expresses. The contents of the boxes are, in most cases, underspecified. And if the model has a grave fault it is that it underestimates the complexity of the mental processes it is trying to model. There are many degrees of freedom in the model at the moment with respect to writing, but as the model faces up to data these options should become reduced rapidly.

5 A little data with analysis

1   When I am writing I sometimes produce a word which is a homophone of the one I intend. The most common example in my own writing is a substitution of THEIR for THERE or the other way round. This happens when I am writing with a pen or when I am using a typewriter (see also Hotopf, Chapter 13).

2   Sometimes when I am asked how to spell a word I am not quite sure about I will write down the alternatives and will then be sure which one of them is correct by looking at them. It isn't that I know that one of them is right, it is that I know that one of them *looks* right (see also Tenney, Chapter 10).

These two observations about myself are common enough. What are we to make of them? While the first example will tell us a lot about spelling, I feel that the second piece of data tells us nothing about spelling but a little about reading. If we are not sure about the spelling of a word then we may proceed by analogy. The confirmation of the correct spelling, however, I would assume to be mediated by the action of the input logogen system. Only the correct word will correspond to the pattern accepted by a logogen. This will then arrive at a location in the semantic part of the cognitive system and thus be classified as word-like and give the feeling of being correct. The incorrect one will excite a logogen only inasmuch as its spelling resembles the correct spelling.

We can now take the first example. The fact that I produce a word which is a homonym seems to have a very simple explanation – namely that there is an intervening phonological code and this is simply translated into a graphical code by means of a set of phoneme-grapheme rules. In Fig. 4, this would pass via the response buffer. The rules would look like the grapheme-phoneme rules in reverse (see Smith, Chapter 2). These rules will admit of more than one way of converting a phonological code into letters and the wrong one gets selected.

This account has two flaws, one of them obvious – that I normally spell THERE and THEIR correctly. Thus we cannot conclude that we *always* go via a phonological code in a simple way, for in that case we would expect 50% errors of spelling. Thus the best we can say is that on occasion we go via a phonological code and convert it with some phoneme-grapheme rules. The second flaw in the premature conclusion is that the spelling errors of the type illustrated (i.e. caused by slips rather than ignorance) are not random. I never make spelling errors such as replacing HEIR by HAIR or BEAR by BEIR. If I ever used a simple set of phoneme-grapheme rules, taking a phonological string at one end and producing a string of letters at the other then I would expect to find errors of those kinds. This is because simple replacement rules could not know about a letter sequence actually being a word with a different pronounciation from the original and so could not detect that HAIR was not pronounced like HEIR.

Simple rules have no notion of wordness. This is why we can read nonsense syllables using the grapheme-phoneme rules. Deep dyslexics, who lack these rules can only read via a word representation and cannot read nonsense syllables at all (see Morton and Patterson, 1979). In the same way the rule system would not know whether the output string did indeed correspond to a real-word. So if we are going to use the idea of writing via the phoneme-grapheme rules at all then we have to introduce an extra stage in the sequence. This stage would take the letter string which the rules had generated and check this for its word-ness and for its pronunciation, to check whether it corresponded with the target in this respect. This could not, of course, be done using the grapheme-phoneme rules, for that system has no concept of word either (as already mentioned). Neither would it be sure of the pronunciation of HAIR and HEIR in any case. The checking would have to be done by passing through some word-based systems which took an orthographic input and produced a phonological output, such as the visual input logogen to output logogen route. The production of an output would guarantee that a word had been produced and the output itself could be used to check the pronunciation. Homophones are the only errors which would slip through this net.

If we elaborate the comparison system a little more we can return to the idea of using the phonological code all the time. All we need to do is run a second check of the 'semantics' of the word against the original intentions. The homophone errors would then be attributed simply to faults in that part of the check.

Another possibility is to avoid the idea of simple rules. Instead we could imagine that a phonological code is indeed produced first and that this code is used as a unit to access the letter code for the word. This would be like using a phonological code to access the grapheme output logogen system in Fig. 4. This could constitute an argument for a connection between the two output logogen systems.

In a perverse fashion I managed to produce a counter-example to my claim as I was in the act of writing about it. I was in the process of typing the word SURE and started typing *sh* before stopping in some alarm. There is no such word as SHURE (and I do not pronounce SURE to make it a homophone of SHORE). So in this case it looks as though I was simply going through a rule system. It isn't clear what checking procedures trapped the error.

Note that my case with simple and frequently used homophones is very different from performance with words which are either unfamiliar or rarely experienced in the written form. In such cases there is good reason for supposing that simple rules are being used – though it should be remembered that the same results would be obtained if one operated by analogy with words one knew. Thus, if the word CARE were heard, the novice might think that the word began with the same sound as the word KITTEN and ended with the same sound as BEAR. Then he might try the spelling **kear** as possible. Note that solving the problem by analogy in this way is equivalent to creating one's own phoneme-grapheme rules as one goes along. And note that Fig. 4 would need considerable elaboration to deal with problem solving.

6 Some evidence from a case study

The data in this section came from a young woman, Gail,[1] who suffered an embolism resulting in damage to her left temporo-parietal region. This patient was drawn to my attention by Margaret Hatfield and we have been studying her for the past four years. Complete descriptions of the patient are in preparation.

The earliest indication that Gail was going to provide clues regarding representation of orthographic information came when she was asked to generate instances from categories. In general we used one of two topics, asking her to produce as many names of countries or animals as she could. She was under no particular time pressure for this task but we did try to encourage her to continue to search for more names after it seemed to her that she had no more available. She had a pencil in her hand during this task and just after her accident would write down at least the initial letter before all her responses. Without this cue she did not seem able to produce any responses. So on one occasion she started

---

[1] Please note that 'Gail' is a pseudonym.

off a list of animals by writing a D and then saying 'dog', writing a C and saying 'cat' and so on.

The obvious interpretation of such behaviour is that she had access to the concepts but could not access the phonemic code directly from the concept. In terms of Fig. 4 we would say that the connection between the cognitive system and the output logogen system was damaged. The written code, however, was available, and the initial letter was in most cases sufficient to deblock the phonemic code via the grapheme-phoneme rules and the response buffer. Thus far one could imagine that the orthographic code was available as a string ready to be written, from which only the first letter need be produced. However her behaviour was not always so simple. On occasions, with rarer words in general, she had to write more than one letter before she could make any spoken response. The remarkable thing was that these letters were not always contiguous, and that she did not write them fluently but rather had to search for every one. Here are three examples from one session.

1   She writes an initial H; pause, then she writes a g some distance away from the H. Then she says 'hedgehog'.
2   Writes an initial P, then pauses and finally writes a k some distance away before saying 'peacock'. On another day she wrote P   c before getting 'peacock'.
3   Writes a series of things. The separate lines below indicate the result after each alteration.
    Pol
    Polar
    Polar (says: 'Is that right?')
    Polar R
    Polar B
    Polar Bear (and finally says 'polar bear').

Later in the same session she was trying to retrieve the names of countries. Among her responses were:
Pot l 'Portugal'
In   a
she then wrote down ABCD, and then inserted the d in the name of the country, added the i and said 'India'. (Note the case of the letters was correct.) Another string of countries included:
N   Z   New Zealand
Tur   y   Turkey
J p n   Japan
C   na   China

The last is a good indication that it is genuinely an orthographic code and not a translation from a partly suppressed phonemic code.

In the latter case we could not expect the initial C without the following *h*; and we have every reason to believe that Gail wrote down all the letters she could in sequence.

4   On one occasion she wrote down D T H before saying 'Holland' and on another occasion she wrote *Du* and then said 'Holland'. This complicates matters enormously since such a connection can only be made in the cognitive system. I am forced to assume that an internal code corresponding to DUTCH was fed back to the conceptual unit of HOLLAND. The block must in this case have been at the conceptual level *not* in the output system.

5   To allow the reader to get a better flavour of Gail I will quote a discussion we had about one country. Some of the dialogue is suppressed since it concerned my attempts to guess what she was aiming at.

Gail: writes SAR
Gail: Do you know it?
JM: I'm not sure what you are looking for
Gail: It's . . . it's 's' – its a very small place. It's a very small country
JM: An island?
Gail: Yes. I've been there

. . . .
JM: How did you get there?
Gail: By – er – by ship
JM: Where from?
Gail: Which countries? do you mean?
JM: Yes
Gail: . . . Gibraltar – er – Italy. . . . (. . .) on the map it's a long thing (draws it). Do you know what I mean?
JM: O.K. The next letter is D
Gail: Writes so she now has SARDINA, adding the INA without any prompting from me. She needed much prompting to read this out and couldn't say whether it was correctly spelled. When the additional *I* was indicated and written in she was still uncertain.

6   On occasions it was apparent that structural information was also available. Not only did she usually leave sufficient space for intervening letters when she wrote down parts of words but she also explicitly referred to word length. Thus we had this exchange in the course of a conversation:

JM: What kind of bird?
Gail: A swallow
JM: What kind of swallow?

Gail: Not a house swallow. It's a four-letter word. (wrote H) no, not H, it's B. Barn.

The examples above relate to Gail's output problems in the weeks after her accident. As time went on this problem virtually vanished and she only occasionally has recourse to a pencil when trying to find a word. Sometimes however, she will trace the beginning of a letter in the air before producing a word and claims that she visualises words she is trying to define.

More recently we have been looking at her receptive problems. In particular it seems as though, in terms of Fig. 4, she cannot get from the auditory input logogen to the cognitive system directly but has to go via a graphemic code.

The clearest evidence for the conversion of an auditory code to a visual one occurs when the conversion goes wrong. Two good examples of this occurred in one session when she was being asked to define words which were spoken to her. Note to start with that Gail has no problems whatsoever in repeating words or nonsense syllables. Any receptive loss must be central. Typically, she gives a definition straight away, or pauses, looks up in the air or starts to write the word down. Often she has no need to complete the words before saying something like 'Oh, I know it . . .' and then giving some kind of definition. Sometimes she goes through a different sequence, looking puzzled and asking 'Is it really a word?' and then trying to write it down. At this stage the reason for her puzzlement becomes apparent. In the particular session in question she was given the word ACUTE which she claimed not to know. She then wrote down **aquate** looked at it and then wrote down the word correctly. Later, with the word DESTINY she wrote down **dectiny** and again corrected herself spontaneously before giving a definition.

In the same session she wrote correctly PORTLY and CASUAL, and wrote parts of words on several occasions, including **compet** for COMPETITION; **trans** for TRANSPARENT; **opa** for OPAQUE. In cases like these she stops with the word incomplete, repeats it and then defines it.

In the cases of ACUTE and DESTINY, I assume that the phonological code is passed through a low grade conversion system to get an orthographical code, i.e. by way of the acoustic-phonemic conversion to the response buffer, through the phoneme-grapheme rules and to the graphemic buffer.

Similar findings were obtained in a dictation task. She was being asked to write down a mixed list of words and non-words. This might have biased the strategy she used but that does not invalidate our position. Among her responses were the following which were spontaneously corrected: **cride** (CRIED); **phome** (FOAM); **near** . . (NURSE). In addition DEEP was spelled **deap** without being corrected. In the same session she wrote correctly words such as AERIAL, SHIELD and POULTRY.

My interpretation of data such as these is that there is a method of conversion from an acoustic code to an orthographic one (via the response buffer in Fig. 4). From time to time this conversion operates at the level of the individual character. Only this way could the sound /s/ be converted to the letter *c*. It is equally clear that this cannot be the only way of operating as the following example shows. She was being asked to define the spoken word PLOUGH. She had no idea of its meaning but then wrote it down correctly – not as PLOW, which would have been the obvious result of a simple phoneme-grapheme conversion. She still seemed to have no idea of what it meant and then said, 'I've forgotten what it is – (pause) see it in a field – using some sort of machine – something to do with soil . . .'.

There are two choices here. Both of them require that the auditory input logogen is operating and, as always, produces a code relevant to the word as a whole. Then the spelling of the word could be obtained from the graphical output logogen system via the output logogen system. The other option is that there is a direct connection between the auditory input system and the graphical output system. This connection only exists in Fig. 4 via the cognitive system. By the conventions to date, passing through the cognitive system would involve accessing some, at least, of the semantics. It is not clear whether such information as she produced was available before she wrote down the word. The important thing about the example, though, is that it forces us to think in terms of the auditory input logogen system being used, rather than the acoustic-phonemic route.

7 Conclusions

I have explained how the logogen system might be expanded to take account of writing and have described and analysed some data to show how the model can be used. This analysis has not been sufficient to force us to take positions on the connections between the sub-systems. I hope that by the time this book has been completed that there will be enough information to force us to severely restrict the options. At the moment, however, there appear to be the following possibilities with respect to spelling and writing information. Not all of them have been covered in the discussion above but remain possible in principle.

7.1 *Visual input logogen system*

This system does not *contain* any accessible information with regard to spelling. It is responsible for recognising that certain letter strings correspond to words and for passing information concerning the identity of these strings to the cognitive system and the output buffers.

7.2 Grapheme output logogen system

This system contains spelling patterns for words (or possibly morphemes). It is addressed by the cognitive system by means of a semantic code (by analogy with the output logogen system) and by the visual input logogen system by means of some simple one-to-one mapping procedures. Its output goes to the grapheme buffer where output is coordinated and different plans are made for typing and handwriting. It is also likely that there is the facility to feedback information from this system to other systems, such as the cognitive system and the phonological output logogen system. In this way we can understand how Gail uses a visual code to access the meaning of a spoken word sometimes without actually writing anything.

7.3 Phoneme-grapheme rules

This system treats words and non-words alike and thus, if operated without any checking procedures, would fall foul of the one to many mapping aspects of the conversion rules. Clearly some spelling errors must arise from the operation of this system but the relative paucity of spelling errors resulting in non-words indicates that the outcome of the rules is checked for appropriate pronunciation and for wordfulness. This requires feedback which hasn't been indicated in Fig. 4 (or alternatively some device independent of the conventions of Fig. 4 which could perform monitoring and checking procedures anywhere in the system).

7.4 Cognitive system

The cognitive system is a kind of residual legatee. Anything not specified elsewhere is currently lumped in the cognitive system. We could imagine that it contains writing patterns of certain kinds such as one's signature or the motor pattern for certain words when typing.

7.5 A remaining problem

The model has most trouble in accounting for data from the patient Gail. It is easy enough to account, in general, for the way in which the graphemic code becomes available. The problem is that the grapheme output systems are supposed to produce a string of characters which are intended to be processed from one end to the other. What Gail did was to pick elements out of the string – always beginning with the initial letter, but missing out middle letters sufficiently often to constitute a problem for our explanation. Recall also that she always knew that letters were missing and left blanks accordingly. There appear to be two solutions. The first is to locate a pictorial record of the word in the cognitive system. This record would be a part of the 'lexical entry' for the word. Such a possibility is easier to include in other models (e.g. Forster, 1976) than it is in the logogen model, since at the moment there is no real concept of lexical entry. The other solution is to say that the output from the grapheme output logogen can be fed back (to the visual analysis system for example – but that would mean that the code would have to be compatible with a visual sensory code – not a likely thing, so some recoding would also be necessary) or scanned by some device which has not yet been devised. Neither of these solutions is a happy one because they rely on *ad hoc* devices whose utility for other purposes is unknown. The one saving grace is that the phenomenon resembles the tip-of-the-tongue phenomenon in which we seem to know something about the properties of words we cannot find. The difference between the two is that the tip-of-the-tongue information is very liable to error and uncertainty whereas Gail was almost never wrong and usually completely certain that the information she produced was correct. This does help to describe the phenomena in logogen terms, and for the moment we must end with this feeling of dissatisfaction.

Acknowledgements

I am grateful to Marie-Claire Goldblum, Karalyn Patterson and Cathy Skinner for discussions of the topic and comments on an early draft.

7

Reading and Searching for Spelling Errors

GILLIAN COHEN   *Department of Experimental Psychology, University of Oxford, England*

1 The search task

Visual search tasks have been widely used as a research tool to investigate visual information processing, but the read-and-search task described in this chapter has a different form, and a different purpose. In the conventional search task, the subject is required to search through a display and detect the presence or absence of one or more designated targets, such as a given letter or letters embedded in a background of non-target letters. He is not required to respond to the non-target items in the display, and these need only be processed to a sufficient depth to enable him to make the target-non-target discrimination. In the read-and-search paradigm employed in the experiments reported here, the search task differs in several important ways. The subject is asked to search for spelling errors which are embedded in meaningful passages of text. He has two tasks to perform concurrently. He must search for the targets, and at the same time read the text and process the meaning, so target search is combined with deep-level processing of the background. The aim is to find out how efficiently the search task can be combined with normal reading. By assessing the compatibility of search and reading it is possible to infer something about the nature of the processes ongoing during reading, so the search task here becomes a tool with which to probe the operations involved in normal silent reading. The requirement that the searcher should engage in deep-level semantic processing of the text turns out to produce a pattern of results in striking contrast to those obtained in tasks which only tap the lower levels of visual recognition.

These studies also differ from the typical form of search task in that the searcher is not given a specific target (such as the letter 'A') to look for. Instead he is asked to detect *any errors* in the text, and the experiments focus on the ease with which different kinds of error can be detected in conjunction with reading. The purpose is to explore the role of phonological coding in reading, and two different kinds of errors serve as targets. These are homophonic errors, which are phonologically correct but orthographically incorrect, so that they sound right but look wrong; and nonhomophonic errors which are both phonologically and orthographically incorrect, so that they both look and sound wrong. The predicted effects of detecting these two kinds of error depends on the extent to which the reader is employing a phonological code.

2 Phonological coding in reading

Whether or not the reader derives an internal phonological representation from the printed form of words when reading silently is a question which has been investigated extensively, but with inconclusive results. As a first step toward trying to resolve the inconsistencies of the findings (for a review, see Bradshaw, 1975) it is helpful to break down the problem, and to discuss the role of phonological coding at two different stages of the reading process – prior to lexical access, and after lexical identification. Nevertheless, the distinction between pre-lexical processing and post-lexical processing is not always clearcut. Some tasks involve a mixture of pre- and post-lexical processes; in other tasks optional strategies employing either pre- or post-lexical processing are available; and in some cases tasks are classified as pre- or post-lexical by the researcher on grounds that are somewhat arbitrary. As a general rule, pre-lexical processes include accessing a word in the internal lexicon and extracting the phonological and semantic information stored with the lexical entry: post-lexical processes consist of semantic and syntactic analyses applied to words in structured combinations. Tasks which require recognition of single words, or same–different judgements over pairs of words usually interrogate levels of processing up to and including lexical access, and may provide evidence of pre-lexical phonological coding. Tasks which require semantic judgements to be made over whole sentences which are held in memory include post-lexical stages as well. In my read-and-search tasks whole passages of text have to be read and understood, so the reader must integrate successive words in memory and process semantically. Post-lexical processes are therefore involved as well as pre-lexical ones, and any phonological coding which is revealed could be occurring at either the pre- or post-lexical stage.

2.1 *Pre-lexical phonological coding*

It is usually assumed that a written word is recognised and understood by accessing the lexical entry corresponding to that word in the reader's internal lexicon. The evidence suggests that there are two alternative routes into the lexicon, a visual one and a phonological one. Either the visual representation of the word may be directly matched with the lexical entry, or the written word may be converted to a phonological representation which is matched with the phonological properties of the lexical entry. Evidence for this pre-lexical phonological coding comes from the pseudohomophone effect. Using a lexical decision task, in which the subject has to indicate whether a letter string is a word or a non-word, several studies (e.g. Rubinstein *et al.*, 1971) have demonstrated that it takes longer to reject a letter string as a non-word when it sounds like a real word (e.g. a pseudohomophone like BLUD) than when it does not sound like a word (e.g. a nonhomophone like BLID). This result suggests that the non-word is being phonologically coded, and the negative decision for pseudohomophones is delayed because a real word match (BLOOD) exists in the lexicon. Patients suffering from brain injuries resulting in the syndrome known as phonemic dyslexia are thought to have incurred damage to the phonological route into the lexicon (Saffran and Marin, 1977). Hence they cannot formulate a pronunciation for a novel but pronounceable non-word; they have difficulty in judging whether two differently spelled words constitute a rhyming pair; and in the lexical decision task they are not affected by pseudohomophones. Nevertheless the intact visual route allows an extensive reading vocabulary to be retained.

In another task (Meyer and Ruddy, 1973; Meyer and Gutschera, 1975) subjects were asked to decide if a word was a member of a designated category. The category decision task is generally classed as pre-lexical on the assumption that category membership information is stored with lexical entries. Following a question like 'Is a kind of fruit?', a test word which was either a category member (PEAR), a homophonic non-member (PAIR), or a nonhomophonic non-member (TAIL) was presented. Since it took longer to reject PAIR as a non-member than to reject TAIL, this result suggests that phonological lexical access was taking place and that the judgement was being influenced by phonological characteristics. Meyer *et al.* have put forward a horse-race model of lexical access with visual and phonological routes operating simultaneously and in parallel. Their results support the conclusion that phonological access to the lexicon is generally slower than visual access. But if phonological access 'races' visual access on some proportion of the trials the average time to reject homophonic non-members would be inflated above the time to reject nonhomophonic non-members. The horse-race model is supported by the fact that the evidence for phonological coding in other experiments emerges most strongly from responses to non-words, where visual access is impossible because there would be no corresponding visual representation already stored in the lexicon. With real-word stimuli, the faster visual route would normally achieve access before the slower phonological route so that the phonological properties of real words have less demonstrable effect.

Another task which yields some evidence of phonological encoding seems intuitively to straddle the border-line between pre-lexical and post-lexical processing. Baron (1973) and Baron and McKillop (1975) asked subjects to evaluate phrases as sense or nonsense. Three kinds of phrase were presented; phrases which did make sense (TIE THE KNOT), homophonic nonsense phrases (TIE THE NOT) which are orthographically nonsense, but sound like sense, and true nonsense phrases (I AM KILL) which are orthographically and phonologically nonsense. Responses to the homophonic nonsense phrases were only slightly slower but produced more errors than responses to true nonsense. Again the difficulty in evaluating homophonic items is indicative of phonological encoding. In spite of the fact that the task involves a semantic judgement, both Kleiman (1975) and Coltheart (1979) class it as a pre-lexical task because the phrases used are short cliches which impose little load on memory and require little semantic processing. In a further version of the task, Baron and McKillop investigated individual differences in the use of phonological coding. In one condition the phrases had to be judged visually (Did the phrase look right? – Respond 'No' to homophonic phrases). In another condition the phrases had to be judged phonologically (Did the phrase sound right? – Respond 'Yes' to homophonic phrases). And in a third condition only true sense and true nonsense phrases were presented (the neutral condition). Comparing the relative speed of the condition requiring a visual judgement with the condition requiring a phonological judgement they found that, while the majority of subjects had faster visual access, there was a group of individuals who appeared to use phonological access more often and more rapidly. These subjects were less efficient at the neutral task than those with faster visual access, and the authors concluded that reliance on phonological coding is an inefficient strategy which is more typical of the slow reader.

Green and Shallice (1976) also concluded that access to the lexicon is primarily by the visual route. They asked subjects to judge whether pairs of words (a) rhymed, or (b) both belonged to the same semantic class. The words were either correctly spelled (DOTE-STOAT), or misspelled so as to preserve the correct phonological form (DOAT-STOTE). Semantic decisions, but not rhyming decisions, were delayed by the misspelling, suggesting that when the words were correctly spelled the semantic information was accessed via the rapid visual route.

The important point to note about pre-lexical phonological coding is that it appears to be the exception rather than the rule. It functions in processing non-words since the faster visual route is unavailable, but in accessing real words it is stigmatised as slow, inefficient and indirect. This stigma may arise, at least partly, because of the nature of the tasks studied since the use of pseudohomophones in lexical decision tasks, and homophone nonsense phrases in the evaluation tasks ensure that phonological judgements yield wrong answers. It is worth noting that the psychology of reading and spelling often lacks a historical perspective.

Standardised spelling was only adopted late in the eighteenth century. Before then, words were freely spelled as they sounded, with several different spellings of the same word sometimes appearing on the same page. Also, printers commonly used quite arbitrary abbreviations of words so as to produce justified margins. Both of these practices have implications for a theory of lexical access. The use of varied homophonic spellings suggests that the phonological route must have been commonly used in reading, since for the visual route to be employed the internal lexicon would have had to contain all possible orthographic representations, which seems unlikely. The use of abbreviations would also militate against visual access. Were the readers of that period less efficient as a result? Was the adoption of standardised spelling designed to make reading easier? Studies of reading mis-spelled texts like those reported in this chapter can help to shed some light on these questoins.

2.2 Post-lexical phonological coding

The role of phonological coding emerges as a much more positive one when post-lexical stages of processing are experimentally interrogated. That is to say, the evidence of its occurrence is stronger, and it appears in a more favourable light as serving a useful function.

The use of EMG measures provides a direct index of phonological coding by recording activity in the speech muscles during silent reading. Hardyck and Petrinovich (1970) showed that activity increased when the material was difficult either because it was unfamiliar or syntactically complex. Moreover, the amount of activity was positively correlated with scores on comprehension tests administered after reading. Conversely, efforts to reduce sub-vocalisation resulted in reduced comprehension. Since it is well established that in short-term memory a phonological code is more easily maintained than a visual code it is likely that the improved comprehension results from the use of the more stable memory code. When complex sentences are being read component parts of the sentence have to be held in temporary storage before combinatorial processes can be applied to yield a complete semantic representation, so that a temporary holding store with the greater stability conferred by phonological coding constitutes an advantage.

Other experiments have demonstrated the occurrence of phonological coding during post-lexical processing by combining a primary reading task with a secondary task of auditory shadowing. Kleiman (1975) compared reaction times for various kinds of pre-lexical and post-lexical decision in conditions with and without concurrent shadowing. Shadowing produced only small increases in time for graphemic decisions (Are two words spelled alike? e.g. HEARD–BEARD), for synonymy decisions (Are two words alike in meaning? e.g. MOURN–GRIEVE), and for category decisions (Is the word a member of a given category? e.g. PEAR–PAIR for the fruit category). But when a phonemic decision was required (Do two words sound alike? e.g. LEMON–DEMON) the ongoing shadowing and the phonological coding required by this task interfered with each other and reaction times increased very markedly. Kleiman found a similarly large interference effect was produced by shadowing when the primary task consisted of judging whether a 5 word string formed an acceptable sentence. He concluded that the tasks which showed little or no interference were pre-lexical, and involved little or no phonological coding, while the sentence acceptability task made heavier demands on memory, and so invoked the post-lexical processes which depend on phonological coding. His failure to find any substantial evidence for phonological coding in category decisions conflicts with Meyer's results, and his sentence acceptability task seems to reflect a much greater reliance on phonological coding than Baron found in his rather similar phrase evaluation task. Possibly this is because Kleiman's sentences were longer, more complex and less familiar than Baron's phrases. However, these discrepancies reinforce the conclusion that the use of phonological coding is liable to vary as a function of individual differences and task specific strategies.

The shadowing paradigm has also been used by Betty-Anne Levy (1975) who found that comprehension of material which was read silently was severely impaired by concurrent auditory shadowing. Since interference with phonological coding appears to be damaging, again the conclusion to emerge is that comprehension of sentences or text leans heavily on the phonological code.

The read-and-search experiments reported below produce results which run counter to the pre-lexical studies, but fit well with the findings derived from post-lexical tasks. That is, they give evidence that a phonological code is being employed and that it serves a useful function.

3 Experiment 1: A comparison of the detectability of semantic, phonemic and orthographic errors in text

The first of the read-and-search tasks was originally designed to compare the relative detectability of different kinds of error embedded in continuous text. Previous studies suggested that orthographic, phonological and semantic analyses all contribute to the judgements involved in detecting spelling errors, although in most of these studies items were presented out of context and the role of semantic processing was negligible. The pseudohomophone effect in the lexical decision tasks described in Section 2.1 leads to the prediction that mis-spellings which sound right will be harder to detect than mis-spellings which sound wrong as well as being orthographically incorrect. A similar result was also obtained by Mackay (1972) who asked subjects to reproduce letter strings after a brief tachistoscopic exposure. He found that mis-spellings were harder to detect when the mis-spelled word was a pseudohomophone (e.g. WERK) than when it was a nonhomophone (e.g. WARK), but this difference was only present when the subjects were 'set' to expect a specific word (in this case, WORK), Mackay proposed that tests for orthographic legality, phonological legality and identity with the expected word were all performed, and that it was harder to detect the misspelling when the letter string matched the phonological representation of the expected word. These tasks tested recognition of de-contextualised errors, but in another set of studies (Corcoran and Weening, 1968) subjects were asked to search through a text detecting either target letters or mis-spellings. They found that target letters such as k or l were more often detected when sounded than when silent. Unsounded final e's were often not detected, and missing initial k's were unnoticed, again suggesting that the search is conducted on the phonological representation. However, this was a proofreading task in which the subjects scanned the text, rather than reading with comprehension, so it is difficult to estimate whether context exerted any influence, and whether any post-lexical semantic processing was being carried out. The finding which emerges from most of these experiments is that mis-spellings which preserve the correct sound pattern are harder to detect than those which change the sound pattern. (See the chapters by Sloboda and Tenney, Chapters 11 and 10.)

The present experiment aimed to examine a wider range of types of error, and to discover whether the same pattern of results appears when error search is combined with reading for meaning, so that post-lexical processes are operating, and contextual information is potentially available.

Three passages of prose were prepared on separate typewritten sheets. The first two passages consisted of 500-word uncorrupted extracts from Rider Haggard's *King Solomon's Mines*. A third test passage was constructed which was the same length and similar in style and content. There were four different versions of this test passage, one for each condition. In each version 30 words spaced throughout the text were replaced with error substitutions. The same 30 words were replaced in each version, but a different type of error was substituted.

In Version A – the error substitutions were real word homophones

(REIN for RAIN, BEECH for BEACH), i.e. they were phonologically identical with the correct word.

In Version B – the error substitutions were real word nonhomophones (ROAN for RAIN, BIRCH for BEACH), i.e. they were phonologically different from the correct word.

In Version C – the error substitutions were compatible pseudohomophones (RANE for RAIN, BLOO for BLUE), i.e. non-words which sounded like the correct word.

In Version D – the error substitutions were incompatible pseudohomophones (RONE for RAIN, BLOE for BLUE), i.e. non-words which sound like a real word but not the correct one.

For further examples of error substitutions see the Appendix, Experiment 1.

The number of letters changed by the substitutions was equated as nearly as possible overall for the four versions, so that differences in detectability could not be attributed to differences in the visual similarity of the error to the correct word. Since the same words were always changed in each version of the text, the contextual information was also constant across the conditions.

Forty students served as subjects, 10 being allocated to each of 4 groups, A, B, C and D, corresponding to the 4 versions of the test passage. Each subject was tested individually. First the 2 passages of uncorrupted text were read silently. For each passage, comprehension was tested and reading time measured and a mean reading time was derived for the uncorrupted texts. Subjects were allocated to groups so that the mean reading speed for the groups did not differ. Then one version of the corrupt text (A, B, C or D) was presented and the subject was instructed to read it silently, maintaining the same speed and level of comprehension as before as far as possible, and striking out any words that appeared to be wrong. No information was given as to the type of errors that would be present, but the importance of not missing any errors was stressed. Comprehension was also tested after the passage had been read. The comprehension test was designed to induce the subjects to try to read with understanding rather than simply proofreading the text. It was not used in the analysis of the results.

For each subject the mean reading time in seconds for the uncorrupted texts was subtracted from the time taken to process the corrupt version so as to give a measure of the extra time taken in processing the errors. The results are shown in Table 1.

By analysis of variance the time scores differed from each other ($F_{(3,36)}$ 2.9, $p < 0.05$). A *post hoc* pairwise comparison by the Newman–Keuls test showed that all the time scores differed significantly ($p < 0.05$)

from each of the others. There is no sign of a speed-error trade-off, since the error scores are in the same direction as the time scores.

TABLE 1

Version of text	A	B	C	D
Mean extra time	46.1	52.0	30.1	39.6
Mean number of omissions (errors not detected)	2.5	7.1	1.5	1.9

The first point to note about these results is that both the non-word types of error (C and D) are detected faster than real-word errors (A and B). That is, errors which are orthographically incorrect, so that there is no corresponding orthographic representation in the lexicon, can be rapidly rejected. This means that a visual matching strategy is being employed, but a phonological strategy is also in operation, as shown by the effect of phonological compatibility, which is evident in both the non-word errors and the real-word errors. The real word homophones (A-type errors) which are phonologically compatible with the context are detected *faster* than the B-type errors which are phonologically incompatible. Similarly, the compatible pseudohomophones (C-type errors) are detected faster than the D-type incompatible pseudohomophones. The phonological identity of the error and the correct word appears to assist, instead of retarding, the detection of the mistake. Clearly, this result is at odds with the findings reported by Sloboda and Tenney (Chapters 11 and 10) since their subjects had more difficulty in detecting phonologically compatible mis-spellings. However, I shall be arguing that mis-spellings encountered in reading text are treated differently from mis-spellings which are, like those of Sloboda and Tenney, de-contextualised. In trying to formulate an explanation for the findings in this present study it is helpful to consider the following examples.

1   The sky was a brilliant BLUE   (correct)
2   The sky was a brilliant BLEW   (A type error)
3   The sky was a brilliant BLOW   (B type error)
4   The sky was a brilliant BLOO   (C type error)
5   The sky was a brilliant BLOE   (D type error)

Several possibilities suggest themselves.

(a) *A priming explanation.* The contextual information building up as the sentence is processed primes the lexical entries for the correct word, and for all phonologically identical representations. So BLEW would be primed, and BLOW would not, giving faster lexical access for BLEW. The semantic information signalling that BLEW does not fit the sentence frame would therefore be available earlier. This explanation might account for the A/B difference, but cannot apply to the C/D difference since no lexical entries exist for non-words, so they cannot be primed.

(b) *A frequency explanation.* Another possibility is that homophones and pseudohomophones are simply the kind of errors that are more frequently made, and so are more familiar. If, as seems to be the case, the kind of spelling errors made by writers are more frequently errors that sound right than errors that sound wrong, then perhaps people are accustomed to correcting such errors and watching out for them.

(c) *A semantic compatibility explanation.* A third possibility is suggested if we remember that the subject is engaged in reading for meaning as well as for error detection, and he is trying to attach a satisfactory semantic interpretation to the sentences of the text. Each successive word is being checked for semantic and syntactic compatibility with the currently held semantic interpretation. If we make the further assumption, following Kleiman and Levy, that this process of semantic building and checking is carried out *within the phonological code* it is possible to explain the results as follows. When the reader encounters an item which is phonologically identical with the correct word (BLEW or BLOO), he retains his current semantic interpretation of the sentence and rejects the error as orthographically incorrect (BLOO), or semantically incompatible with his sentence interpretation (BLEW). When he encounters an item which is phonologically different from the correct word (BLOW or BLOE) he suspends his current semantic interpretation, and backtracks to re-check or re-compute it in an effort to accommodate the phonological representation /BLO/. So BLOW cannot be rejected until the re-check confirms the original semantic interpretation, and even though BLOE could be rejected on orthographic grounds this judgement may be delayed, especially if the re-computation involves regressive eye movements. Note that this explanation does not necessarily claim that B and D type errors take longer to recognise as errors, but that they interfere with reading and so inflate the combined read-and-search times. In putting forward this explanation I have shifted my ground and am suggesting that the different types of error have their effect on reading times, rather than error detection times. Subjects in this experiment frequently reported that the demands of the read-and-search task were such that it was not enough simply to detect an error. To ensure comprehension they also needed to decide what the correct word should have been. With A and C type errors the correct word was immediately apparent by simple substitution of the phonological equivalent. With B and D type errors the correct word was less obvious, and a search for contextual clues was necessary.

This explanation may seem somewhat laborious, but is quite consistent with the nature of silent reading where speed is often achieved by minimising perceptual processing and relying on contextually guided constructive processes. When a mis-match between perception and construction occurs the construction needs to be re-checked, and the reader experiences a sort of mental 'Whoops!' and is aware of going back to re-read earlier parts of the text. An interactive model of reading can readily accommodate the semantic compatibility hypothesis. According to the interactive model, information at every level of processing (orthographic, phonological, semantic and syntactic) is combined, with each level constraining the interpretation of information at every other level. Neither a strictly top-down nor a strictly bottom-up model of reading is consistent with the kind of to-and-fro interplay between semantic context, orthography and phonology that is suggested by the semantic compatibility hypothesis.

Experiments 2 and 3 are designed to supply some tests of these explanations.

4 Experiment 2: Detecting spelling errors in normal and scrambled texts

This experiment aimed to compare the effects of two different kinds of errors. These were the C-type pseudohomophones which sound right but look wrong (e.g. RANE for RAIN), and E-type nonhomophones which sound wrong and look wrong (e.g. ROIN for RAIN). The two kinds of errors were embedded in normal text and in scrambled text. The use of scrambled text was designed to weaken semantic constraints. If the semantic compatibility explanation is correct then the advantage for pseudohomophones should be reduced or absent in the scrambled text, since no acceptable semantic interpretations can be formed. The priming explanation cannot apply since pseudohomophones are not represented in the lexicon and cannot be primed. However, if the frequency explanation is correct then the difference between the two kinds of error should be unaffected by the degree of semantic constraint in the text in which they are embedded.

Texts of 500 words were constructed for use in 4 conditions, (i) A story text containing 30 pseudohomophone C-type errors, (ii) A story text containing 30 nonhomophone E-type errors, (iii) A scrambled text with 30 C-type errors, and (iv) A scrambled text with 30 E-type errors.

(More examples of errors are shown in the Appendix, Experiment 2.)

To control for any differences in difficulty between the texts these were interchanged across conditions. Half the subjects read the first story text in condition (*i*) with pseudohomophone errors and half the subjects read the first story text condition in (*ii*) with the same words mis-spelled as nonhomophone errors. The other texts were similarly interchanged. The two different kinds of error were matched overall for number of letters changed. The order of conditions was balanced across 16 subjects, and each subject read one text in each condition. With the story texts in conditions (*i*) and (*ii*) they were instructed to read silently and understand the text while cancelling any errors they detected, and were tested for comprehension. With the scrambled texts in conditions (*iii*) and (*iv*) they were told that the text would be unintelligible, and they should not bother to try to make sense of it. They were just to read it through silently and cancel any errors.

The mean read-and-search times for the 4 conditions are shown in seconds in Table 2. The mean numbers of omissions (failures to detect an error) are also shown for each condition.

TABLE 2

| | Story texts | | Scrambled texts | |
| | *Pseudohomophones* | *Nonhomophones* | *Pseudohomophones* | *Nonhomophones* |
	Condition (*i*)	Condition (*ii*)	Condition (*iii*)	Condition (*iv*)
Times	126.9	140.5	162.3	150.6
Errors	1.7	1.8	2.0	1.9

By the Wilcoxon Matched Pairs Test the error rates were compared for conditions (*i*) and (*ii*), and for conditions (*iii*) and (*iv*). Neither comparison yielded a significant difference. The read-and-search times were also compared by the Wilcoxon Matched Pairs Test. Condition (*i*) was significantly faster than condition (*ii*) (n = 16, t = 26, $p < 0.05$, two-tailed), condition (*iv*) was significantly faster than condition (*iii*) (n = 16, t = 28, $p < 0.05$). Clearly it is easier to detect errors which sound right but are spelled wrong when reading for meaning. With the scrambled texts, where the task is more like proofreading, it is easier to detect the errors which both sound wrong and are spelled wrong. This result confirms that the detectability of different kinds of error depends on the contextual background and on whether the concurrent task involves semantic processing. Following the semantic compatibility explanation offered above, the occurrence of phonologically compatible errors can be handled more rapidly in the read-and-search paradigm of conditions (*i*) and (*ii*) because they do not interfere with the process of semantic interpretation. Phonologically incompatible errors delay comprehension, so in the examples below (6) is processed faster than (7).

6   We rested during the heet of the day   (C-type error)
7   We rested during the hent of the day   (E-type error)

However, in the scan-and-search paradigm of the scrambled texts in conditions (*iii*) and (*iv*), (9) is processed faster than (8),

8   I thing ferst the came I when heard   (C-type error)
9   I thing finst the came I when heard   (E-type error)

The results in the scrambled text conditions parallel the results of the lexical decision tasks, and of Sloboda and Tenney in that the E-type errors which are phonologically as well as orthographically incorrect and so have no corresponding phonological entry in the lexicon, can be rejected faster than the phonologically legal items. In the scrambled conditions, as in the lexical decisions, no post-lexical semantic processing is required. The fact that the two different kinds of errors have different effects when embedded in normal and in scrambled text indicates that it is not just the nature of the error itself which is critical, but the way in which the particular type of error interacts with the concurrent task. So the frequency explanation can be discarded. However, the results of Experiment 2 are quite consistent with the semantic compatibility explanation.

5 Experiment 3: The effect of errors on sentence acceptability decisions

This experiment investigates the effects of A-type errors (real-word homophones) and B-type errors (real-word nonhomophones) in a sentence acceptability decision task. Subjects viewed short incomplete sentences which were exposed one at a time in a tachistoscope. Each sentence was lacking its final word. The subject was allowed to study the incomplete sentence for as long as he liked until he was satisfied he had thoroughly understood it. He then initiated the exposure of a final word, and was asked to make a Yes-No key press response to indicate whether the word completed the sentence so as to make acceptable sense. Reaction times were measured. An example of one of the sentences with three different completion words is given below.

10   She looked in the mirror and combed her HAIR   (Yes)
11   She looked in the mirror and combed her HARE   (No – an A-type error)
12   She looked in the mirror and combed her HIRE   (No – a B-type error)

(More examples are shown in the Appendix, Experiment 3.)

The two different kinds of error completion were carefully matched over the whole set of sentences for visual similarity to the correct word, and for frequency, although slightly more of the homophone endings differed from the correct word in syntactic class. A list of 24 sentences was compiled and 18 subjects were divided into 3 groups. Each group received 8 sentences with correct endings; 8 with A-type error completions; and 8 with B-type error completions. The 3 kinds of completion were mixed in a random sequence. For each individual sentence, each group received a different completion word so that when the scores of the three groups were amalgamated, the differences between the three kinds of completion could not be due to variations in the difficulty of individual sentences. A practice session with a different set of sentences was given before the test session.

If the priming explanation is correct then the incomplete sentences should prime the correct word, and also the phonologically identical A-type error, giving rapid lexical access for both (10) and (11). The semantic features associated with HARE would be accessed faster than those associated with HIRE because there would be no contextual priming of lexical access for HIRE. So the priming explanation predicts that sentence endings like (11) should be recognised as nonsense faster than sentence endings like (12).

The semantic compatibility hypothesis, which was advanced to account for the delay caused by B-type errors in Experiment 1, is unlikely to apply in this task. The subject has unlimited time to form and confirm his semantic interpretation of the incomplete sentence before the final word appears, so he is unlikely to need to re-check it when he encounters the B-type error completion. If there is no difference in lexical access time for HARE and HIRE there is no reason why the time required to judge their semantic compatibility with the sentence should differ. In Experiments 1 and 2 the time taken to read and comprehend the text, and the time taken to detect the errors were confounded in a single time score. It was suggested that the delay caused by nonhomophonic errors might be affecting comprehension time rather than detection time. In Experiment 3 the sentence comprehension and error detection are separated out so that error detection time can be isolated. Consequently, if the homophone–nonhomophone difference is acting mainly on comprehension, it should disappear in Experiment 3. This is exactly what was found. Reaction times in msec are given in Table 3 overleaf. The mean numbers of errors are also shown.

No statistical analysis was carried out since there is quite obviously no difference between homophone endings and nonhomophone endings. Clearly the correct endings are being primed, but there is no sign of priming for homophones. The results therefore suggest that the advantage for homophonic errors evident in Experiment 1 and with the story texts in Experiment 2 are unlikely to be due to phonological priming, leaving the semantic compatibility explanation as the most plausible account of homophonic facilitation. While it is, of course, unsatisfactory to adopt this explanation in default of any viable alternative, the results of the three experiments reported here are all consistent with it.

TABLE 3

	Correct endings	Homophone endings	Nonhomophone endings
RTs	773	879	879
Errors	0.8	0.5	0.4

However, a number of difficulties arising out of Experiment 3 ought to be acknowledged. The task is quite similar to the categorisation task of Meyer and Gutschera, and to the phrase evaluation task of Baron and McKillop described in Section 2.1, yet in their studies homophones were more difficult than nonhomophones. If it is harder to decide that PAIR is not a fruit than that TAIL is not a fruit, why is it no harder to reject HARE in sentence (11) than to reject HIRE? If the phonological route sometimes races the visual route into the lexicon, we might expect that reaction times to homophones like HARE would, on average, be slower because of the misleading phonological identity of the homophone with the correct word. Why does this not happen in my sentence completion task? A possible explanation for this discrepancy can be found if the sentence completion task is analysed in more detail. The subject has two alternative strategies. Either he can access the completion word, extract its semantic features from the lexical entry, and match these with the semantic interpretation of the first part of the sentence; or he can match the completion word visually against the expected target word generated by the contextual constraints of the sentence. The second of these strategies would not produce any difference between homophones and nonhomophones. The match-to-target can be carried out by orthographic comparison, so it would not be any harder to decide that HIRE and HAIR are a mis-match, than to decide that HIRE and HAIR are a mismatch. The large priming effect for correct sentence endings like HAIR does suggest that specific expectations are formed. Reaction times to correct endings are 106 msec faster than for incorrect endings even though the ratio of 'correct' to 'incorrect' trials is only 1:2. Although this hypothesis does appear to be consistent with the results it can only be advanced as a tentative suggestion since there are other difficulties in interpreting experiments of this kind. The reaction times for the negative responses showed a large variance and much of this is probably due to massive variations in the semantic distance between the incorrect ending and the sentence frame. Failure to equate semantic distance effects could easily obscure differences between homophonic and non-homophonic items in the present experiment, and may account for the lack of agreement with Meyer and Gutschera, and with Baron and McKillop.

6 Conclusions

Taken as a whole, the three experiments reported here yield some insight into the relationship between reading and orthographic characteristics of the words. Homophonic spellings do not disturb comprehension of the text. Non-homophonic spellings interfere with comprehension. However, it is always possible to argue, when distorted texts are used to investigate reading processes, that the particular nature of the distortions forces the reader to adopt a strategy which may not be representative of his normal reading. So in Experiments 1 and 2 it is possible that the texts containing homophonic mis-spellings artificially induce the reader to employ a phonological code so as to preserve comprehension. The results suggest that he is able to 'switch off' the visual code and still read for meaning fairly comfortably. Such a conclusion agrees with the findings reported in Uta Frith's (1976) study of child readers 'How to read without knowing how to spell', in which she noted that good readers made fewer mistakes in reading aloud when the text contained homophonic errors like NITE and CLIME than when it contained non-homophonic errors like NGHT and CLMB. It also confirms the views of Kleiman and Levy concerning the role of the phonological code in reading, and suggests that readers in the pre-eighteenth-century era of non-standard spelling would not have been much handicapped by homophonic spellings.

If the semantic compatibility hypothesis is accepted, then acceptance of the interactive model of reading, as opposed to the top-down or bottom-up models, is also entailed. The importance of the distinction between pre-lexical and post-lexical stages of processing is underlined

by the fact that the relative difficulty of homophones and nonhomophones can be reversed when post-lexical processes play a larger part in
the task. It is only when heavy demands are made on memory and
comprehension that homophones and pseudohomophones are easier to
handle. Pre-lexical stages of processing reflected in the experiments
reported in Section 2.1, and in the scrambled conditions of Experiment 2
favour nonhomophones, but this advantage is cancelled in the post-
lexical task of reading because nonhomophones produce anomalies in
the phonological code which resist semantic interpretation. Homophonic errors yield acceptable phonological encodings and allow
semantic interpretation to proceed unhindered.

The experiments reported here serve to emphasise the enormous
flexibility of the reading process. Strategies are selected according to the
demands of the task, and the contribution of orthographic, phonological
and semantic analyses shift and change as the reader exercises his
cognitive agility to fulfil these demands.

7 Appendix

Error substitutions used in Experiment 1

Correct	A-type error	B-type error	C-type error	D-type error
week	weak	wake	weke	waik
blue	blew	blow	bloo	bloe
scene	seen	soon	sean	scune
shoot	chute	sheet	shute	sheat
some	sum	same	sumb	saim
shore	sure	share	shaw	shair
night	knight	nought	nite	nawt
slow	sloe	slew	slo	sloo
rain	rein	roan	rane	rone
bear	bare	beer	bair	beir
stare	stair	store	ster	staw
right	write	wrote	ryte	roat
beach	beech	birch	beche	berch
taught	taut	tight	tawt	tite
pale	pail	pile	payl	pyle
call	caul	cull	cawl	kull
whole	hole	whale	whoal	wayl
pair	pear	peer	payre	peir
grown	groan	green	grone	grean
great	grate	greet	grait	greit
plain	plane	place	playn	playce
straight	strait	street	strate	strete
feet	feat	fate	feit	fayt
been	bean	bone	bene	boan
ball	bawl	bowl	borl	boll
peace	piece	pace	peece	paice
paw	pore	pew	por	pugh
lane	lain	lone	layn	lown
sail	sale	soil	sayl	soyl
board	bored	beard	bord	beird

Examples of errors inserted in the texts in Experiment 2

Correct words	Pseudohomophone errors	Nonhomophone errors
quietly	kwietly	quintly
thousand	thowsand	thoisand
spears	speers	spoars
regiments	rejiments	repiments
ready	reddy	roady
guard	gard	gurd
shirts	sherts	shists
ordinary	awdinary	owdinary
surprise	serprise	sorprise
frame	fraim	frome
people	peeple	penple
waisst	waysts	walsts
turn	tern	tarn
path	parth	porth
imposing	impozing	imporing
conceive	conseeve	conselve
perfectly	purfectly	porfectly
poured	poored	puored
majestic	magestic	mapestic
plumes	plooms	plames
shields	sheelds	shrelds
earth	erth	enth
circle	cercle	cincle
wailing	waling	wanling
company	cumpany	campany
warriors	worriors	werriors
awful	orful	anful
white	wite	whote
snake	snaik	snape
bones	boans	bomes
crawled	crorled	crewled
heavy	hevvy	henvy
cool	kool	sool
lonely	loanly	lonnly
whistle	wissel	whintle
girl	gerl	gorl
afterwards	afterwoods	afterweeds
compass	cumpass	camposs
sailor	saylor	soilor
leading	leeding	lerding

Sentences used in Experiment 3 with alternative endings

The children played on the sandy – beach–beech–birch
The wounded man gave a loud – groan–grown–green
He hated flying and never travelled by – plane–plain–plant
In the orchard he picked a juicy – pear–pair–pure
The car drove down a narrow country – lane–lain–lean
We poured the water into an empty – pail–pale–peal
The animal held a nut in its furry – paw–pore–pew
The game stopped because we lost the tennis – ball–bawl–bale
She heated the iron and got out the ironing – board–bored–beard
The crowd was soaked by the drenching – rain–rein–roan
The generals wanted a just and lasting – peace–piece–place
Inside the tower we climbed a steep – stair–stare–store
The waves crashed on the rocky – shore–sure–share
He went to the Antarctic to study the polar – bear–bare–bore
The treasure was buried in a deep – hole–whole–while
The trapeze artist performed a daring – feat–feet–foot
Their holiday abroad lasted for one – week–weak–wake
Her new dress was of pale – blue–blew–blow
They prepared the fruit discarding pips and – peel–peal–pile
In the jungle we could hear the lions – roar–raw–rare
When it was painted the car looked like – new–knew–knee
After his illness he was careful what he – ate–eight–ought
The deer roamed the mountain in a small – herd–heard–hoard
She looked in the mirror and combed her – hair–hare–hire

PART IV
Spelling Strategies

CHINESE CHARACTERS
FOR THE SOUND: chiao

叫	to call, cause, let, ask, tell
教	doctrine, religion, to teach
校	to revise, collate
窖	cellar
覺	sleep in
較	to compare
轎	sedan-chair
酵	yeast
醮	Buddhistic offering

EARLY PHOENICIAN ALPHABET

𐤀	aleph	𐤋	lamed
𐤁	beth	𐤌	mem
𐤂	gimel	𐤍	nun
𐤃	daleth	𐤎	samek
𐤄	he	𐤏	ayin
𐤅	waw	𐤐	pe
𐤆	zayin	𐤑	tsade
𐤇	heth	𐤒	qoph
𐤈	teth	𐤓	resh
𐤉	yod	𐤔	shin
𐤊	kaph	𐤕	tau

8

Spelling and Reading by Rules

JONATHAN BARRON, REBECCA TREIMAN, JENNIFER
F. WILF and PHILIP KELLMAN *Department of Psychology,
University of Pennsylvania, U.S.A.*

1 Rules in reading and in spelling

In the study to be reported here, we examine individual differences among adults in the ability to use spelling-sound correspondences or rules. We ask where these differences arise and what tasks they affect. Although the study is correlational and therefore does not permit us to draw firm conclusions about cause and effect, our results tell us where to look further for causal antecedents of these individual differences.

The existence of spelling-sound rules in English is best viewed in terms of the history of alphabetic writing (see Gleitman and Rozin, 1977). The earliest writing systems relied heavily on relations between symbols and their meanings. If there were a symbol for 'think' and another symbol for 'study', the combination of the two might be used to indicate 'psychology', even if the phonological form of 'psychology' were unrelated to the phonological forms of the two other words. Such techniques are used in modern Chinese writing. Later writing systems used symbols to stand for syllables, regardless of whether the meaning of a syllable was preserved in different words. Like logographic writing systems, used in Chinese, syllabaries have been invented independently several times. Syllabic systems are used in modern Japanese (along with a logographic system for frequent words) and in indigenous African languages such as Vai (Scribner and Cole, 1978). The use of symbols that stand for units smaller than a syllable apparently began with the transmission of the alphabet from the Phoenicians to the Greeks. All known alphabets based on correspondences between symbols and phonemes (or minimal sound segments) were derived historically from the Greek alphabet, with the possible exception of Semitic writing systems, which indicate vowels with diacritic marks added to what is essentially a syllabary.

Originally, in Greek and Latin, spellings were closely related to pronunciations. This was often true when the Roman or Greek alphabet was adapted for a new language. But English spelling was quite chaotic from the start. 'Caxton, for example, spells the town where he spent the major part of his life before returning to England in at least six different ways: *brugges, bruges, brudgys, Brugis, bruggis, brudgis*' (Venezky, 1976). In the early sixteenth century, the scribes of the English chancery at Westminster were able to promulgate a standardised spelling system (Venezky, 1976), but no effort was made to make the alphabet phonetic. Rather, the spellings of many words were based on spellings of Latin words or other English words to which they were related. In some cases, spellings were modified for the sole purpose of distinguishing homophones. And many idiosyncratic spellings were standardised and made part of what the English schoolchild was expected to learn.

The lack of correspondence between English spellings and pronunciations has been so severe that some have advocated teaching English as if it were Chinese – as if each whole word stood for its meaning, and as if spelling-sound correspondences did not exist at all. It is certainly true that someone who learns the rules must learn several different possible pronunciations of most letters or letter clusters (often depending on context) and several different possible spellings for each sound. Some rules account for so few examples that they are probably not learned at all by most readers, and there are some words – true exceptions – that follow rules of their own, shared with no other words in the language (e.g. ONE, TWO, FOUR). English thus provides an interesting set of stimuli for a psychologist who wants to study the learning of spelling-sound rules in general. (Chomsky, 1970, has argued that many spellings actually map into psychologically real lexical forms that are abstractly related to phonetic forms. However, the psychological reality of these forms is in doubt, especially for children, and Chomsky must admit the existence of exceptions and unproductive rules, especially in frequent words.)

Despite the complexity and irregularity of spelling-sound rules, there is considerable evidence that rules are used from the start in both reading and spelling. Many studies have found high correlations between ability to read nonsense words (which must involve use of rules) and other measures of reading ability, especially in the early grades. Firth (1972), for example, found a correlation of about 0.90 between reading nonsense words and reading words in sentences (aloud) in first- and second-graders. In Firth's study, ability to read nonsense words was hardly correlated with IQ once reading ability was held constant; thus it seems that the correlation between use of rules and reading is not the result of similar general abilities being used in both tasks.

Not only is use of rules important in the early stages of reading, but it might be more important than use of rote associations between printed words and their respective spoken words. Baron (1979) found that children's ability to read regularly spelled words is correlated more highly with ability to read nonsense words than with ability to read exception words such as SWORD, ONE and HONOR, which violate spelling-sound rules.

The importance of rules extends even into the higher grades. Perfetti and Hogaboam (1975) found that good and poor readers (selected by tests of comprehension) differ more in speed of reading nonsense words than in speed of reading familiar words aloud. Calfee et al. (1973) found correlations between knowledge of rules and reading ability even in high school students. Frederiksen (1976) found that good readers in high school are more affected than poor readers by the complexity of spelling-sound correspondences when reading isolated words aloud. And Baron and Strawson (1976) showed that rules are used by adults in reading words aloud; specifically, words violating the rules took longer to read than regular words. While some evidence (Calfee *et al.*, 1969) suggests that other determinants of reading ability become more important once a reasonable level of knowledge of the rules is achieved, the evidence is clear that normal reading requires the learning of spelling-sound rules.

Rules seem to be used in spelling as well as reading. Read (1975) found children who invent their own phonetic spellings according to consistent rules, before receiving formal instruction in spelling. Literate adults seem able to produce credible spellings of new words, such as names. Whether differential knowledge of rules is related to differences in spelling ability is less clear. Boder (1973; see also Camp and Dolcourt, 1977) examined spelling in children diagnosed as dyslexic and found that dyslexics could be distinguished according to their knowledge of spelling-sound rules as indicated by both reading and spelling performance. Dyslexics who did not know the rules made spelling errors that seemed senseless in terms of the rules, while the few dyslexics who did know the rules made errors that were good approximations to phonetic spellings.

Boder's work suggests that there are individual differences in ability to use spelling-sound rules. Baron and Strawson (1976) have demonstrated such differences, in the course of attempting to show that rules are used in reading isolated words aloud. In that study – a precursor of the present study – the terms *Phoenician* and *Chinese* were used to characterise the two ends of the individual-difference continuum of interest. Phoenicians were those who rely heavily on the rules. Chinese were those who rely heavily on word-specific associations between each word and its associated pronunciation. (It is an open question as to whether the Chinese use the meaning of a word to extract the sound; in any case, besides a limited set of rules, they rely on thousands of specific associations between entire strings of letters and entire meanings or sounds.) The idea of the experiment was to look for a correlation between the Phoenician–Chinese dimension as measured by these tests of *use* of rules and specific associations in reading words and the dimension as measured by *knowledge* of rules and specific associations. The tests of use required subjects to read exception words and regular words aloud; use of rules was indicated by slower reading of exception words than of

regular words. Baron and Strawson attempted to measure both knowledge of rules and knowledge of word-specific associations. In the test of
knowledge of rules, subjects were given a list of nonsense words such as
SAIF, CENNEL, MAGOR, WHURM and were asked to say which of these
sounded exactly like words when pronounced by the rules (here only
SAIF and WHURM). The test of knowledge of word-specific associations
was more complex. It was reasoned that a person who knew word-
specific associations in reading would use them to check his spelling.
Such a person would do better at spelling when he could look at alternative spellings than when he had to make decisions without looking at the
word he was writing. Thus, the measure of knowledge of specific associations was the difference in scores between a test in which a subject
chose which of two spellings was correct and a test in which he had to
spell without looking at what he was writing. The results of the study
were as predicted. That is, subjects who knew many rules, as indicated
by the nonsense-word test, but few specific associations, as indicated by
a small difference score between the two spelling tests, were slow at
reading exception words aloud relative to regular words. This was not
true, however, of subjects who showed the reverse pattern of results on
the nonsense-word and spelling tests. Thus, it was possible to predict the
magnitude of the exception vs regular effect from tests that were very
different and that concerned the knowledge hypothesised to be involved.

However, subsequent reflection (and comments of others) revealed
that the spelling tests were not very useful, in principle. They measured
only a particular kind of word-specific association, which is not necessarily the same kind used in reading. In particular, it was possible to do
well in the spelling-recognition test not because of specific associations
between printed words and sounds or meanings but rather because of
recognition of the spelling as familiar or not. Thus, the measure of
specific associations between printed and spoken words might have had
little to do with the kinds of specific associations presumably used in
reading aloud.

It is in fact hard to find a good measure of knowledge of word-
specific associations for adults. In the present study we abandon the
effort to find such a measure. Instead, we measure only ability to use
rules. We also assume that the ability to use rules is largely uncorrelated
with the ability to use word-specific associations. Thus, our Phoenicians
and Chinese ought to differ more in rule-using ability than in specific-
association ability. In other words, by selecting people who are good at
using rules we are also selecting people who are better at using rules
than word-specific associations, and by selecting people who are poor at
rules we are selecting people who are better at specific associations than

at rules. By selecting on only one of the two abilities of interest, we can still argue that we are looking at the same individual-difference dimension as the Baron and Strawson study, *relative* ability at rules vs specific associations.

The Phoenician–Chinese dimension has also been examined in children. Baron (1979) asked children to read lists of exception words (such as PUT, GONE, SWORD), regular words (CUT, BONE, SWEET) and nonsense words (LUT, MONE, SWORP). Chinese, in essence, were those who correctly read more exception words than nonsense words; Phoenicians were better at nonsense words. There was in fact a higher correlation between ability to read nonsense words and ability to read regular words than between ability to read nonsense words and ability to read exception words. Also, ability to read regular words was more highly correlated with ability to read nonsense words than with ability to read exception words. Phoenicians tended to make sound-preserving errors when reading words (e.g. pronouncing the *h* in HONOR or the *w* in SWORD), while the Chinese tended to make meaning-preserving errors (e.g. pronouncing TWELVE as TWENTY or DONE as DID). This study generally supported the conclusions of Boder (1973) about individual differences in use of rules, although this study was restricted to reading, ignoring spelling.

Treiman and Baron (1978) discovered a correlate of the Phoenician–Chinese dimension in children. They asked children (in first grade and kindergarten) and adults to decide which two of three syllables (e.g. /bɪ/, /vɛ/, /bo/ – as in BIT, VET, BOAT) 'went together'. Two of the syllables had been rated as being similar overall but identical in no sound segments (e.g. /bɪ/, /vɛ/). Members of a different pair of syllables were identical in a segment but were rated as being dissimilar overall (e.g. /bɪ/, /bo/). Subjects could thus classify the stimuli by overall similarity or by 'dimensional' identity. (The common segment is analogous to a common value on a dimension, and the choice of this term ties this research to other studies of perceptual development such as that of Smith and Kemler, 1977.) A subject who put together the syllables with a common segment is thus said to make a dimensional classification, based on identity of a part of each syllable, and a subject who put together the similar syllables with no common segment is said to make a similarity classification, based on similarity of whole syllables. The other possible classification (e.g. /vɛ/, /bo/) would be made only if the subject misunderstood the task or if the stimuli were poorly selected by the experimenter; this 'anomalous' classification was chosen on only a small proportion of trials. Treiman and Baron found that adults were more likely than children to make dimensional classifications, and children were more likely to make similarity classifications. This was true even when the children were instructed that the dimensional classification was correct and given feedback on their responses. Thus, adults seem to be more influenced by the presence of identical segments. Further, of the children who could read at all, those children who made a higher percentage of dimensional classifications were able to read more isolated words correctly. And the errors made by these children tended to be those that characterised Phoenicians in the study of Baron (1979), i.e. sound-preserving errors. Those children who made few dimensional classifications tended to make meaning-preserving errors, which had characterised the Chinese in the Baron (1979) study. In sum, it appears that the tendency to classify syllables dimensionally, by common segments, correlates with the Phoenician-Chinese dimension, i.e. with the use of rules, and that this use of rules correlates with reading ability in children. The hypothesis that Phoenicians and Chinese *adults* differ in segmental analysis ability will be tested again in the present study.

We should comment on the possible relations between use of rules in reading and use of rules in spelling. There are two reasons why use of rules in one of these tasks ought to be strongly related to use in the other. One possible relation between reading and spelling is based on the 'Principle of Associative Symmetry' (Asch and Ebenholtz, 1962). By this principle, associations formed in one direction should be usable in the opposite direction. Thus, if a person learns to respond with a certain sound segment or group of segments to a letter or groups of letters, this learning should be equally accessible whether the letters or the segments are given as the stimuli when the learning is tested. Learning to respond with sound segments to letters as stimuli is a possible description of learning to use rules in reading, while learning to respond with letters to segments as stimuli is a possible description of learning to use rules in spelling. The Principle of Associative Symmetry thus implies that there ought to be complete transfer of learning from one use of rules to the other. One problem with this account is that the Principle of Associative Symmetry sometimes fails. Asch and Ebenholtz in fact found that when subjects are taught response B to stimulus A in a list of paired associates, recall of B given A is usually more likely than recall of A given B. However, they argued that such asymmetry could be attributed to differential learning of the responses themselves, as opposed to the stimulus-response associations. When they equated stimuli and responses by making sure that subjects had learned the lists of possible responses equally well before any associative learning, associative symmetry was found. By this argument, associative symmetry should apply in the case of sound segments and letters, since children have presumably learned both the letters used and the segments used before any associative learning occurs.

A second reason why reading and spelling should be related is that it is possible to use one skill to check the other. When we spell, we frequently read what we have spelled to make sure it is correct. We might also check possible readings of a word by using our knowledge of spelling. In principle, we might be able to learn to spell by trial and error, based on our knowledge of reading, even without any backward associations from segments to letters.

There are also reasons not to expect relations between reading and spelling in the knowledge of rules. For one thing, the Principle of Associative Symmetry might not apply. Waugh (1970), for example, has shown that the *speed* of recalling a practised association is faster than the corresponding backward association, even when response availability is controlled. This result suggests that after practice, associations are stronger in the direction in which they are learned. The Principle of Associative Symmetry might apply only to unpractised associations. If so, the Principle would probably not apply to reading and spelling. Further, the asymmetry found by Waugh may manifest itself in other ways than speed. Stronger associations (those originally learned) might be less readily forgotten, for example. It is also possible that associative symmetry is not the result of a basic mechanism of learning, but rather is due to subjects' use of special strategies for retrieving responses from memory when they are faced with the task of producing backward associations (as suggested by the results of Spyropoulos and Ceraso, 1977). For example, subjects might search (serially or in parallel) through the list of stimuli to find the one associated with the response (see Baron, 1978). When faced with a difficult task such as spelling, in which use of such a strategy might require more mental resources than are left over from other components of the task, this strategy might break down.

Another argument against strong relations between reading and spelling is the possibility that children, at least, do not check as often as they should. Holt (1964), for example, reports an incident in which a child spelled MICROSCOPIC as MINCONPERT, and later laughed at her own mistake – thinking it was someone else's – when asked if what she had written spelled MICROSCOPIC. The student evidently failed to check.

It is to be noted that the arguments against a strong relation between reading and spelling apply largely to children. Adults presumably will use strategies such as checking and searching their memories for stimuli corresponding to a given response. Therefore, we would expect use of rules in reading and use of rules in spelling to be largely indistinguishable in adults.

Although we may be unable to separate use of rules in reading and use of rules in spelling in adult subjects, we chose to use adults rather than children for several reasons. First, it is easier to use adults. This allows more tests to be given and greater risks to be taken in testing unlikely hypotheses. Second, there is no reason to think that the determinants of individual differences in rule using ability will change with age. Third, there is a sense in which adults' learning of rules is more 'natural' than that of children. The rules we test in our selection test are for the most part not taught in school. These rules concern complex vowel clusters and relations between subsequent consonants and the pronunciation of vowels, for example. Thus, our experiments are likely to tell us about the determinants of spontaneous acquisition of spelling-sound rules rather than about the ability to profit from explicit instruction.

In the experiments to be reported, we selected subjects who were good (Phoenicians) or poor (Chinese) at spelling and reading by rules. We tried to test hypotheses about the origin of these individual differences by giving other tests to these subjects. In general we consider two classes of hypotheses. One type assumes that the difference between the two groups arises from different kinds of reading experience. In particular, if Phoenicians have more experience extracting speech codes from printed words, they might have more opportunity to learn spelling sound rules through simple repetition of the associations. By this account, we might expect Phoenicians to use speech mediation in reading silently for meaning. Such mediation would give the Phoenicians extra experience at associating sounds and letters. Conversely, Chinese might use associations between printed words and meaning even when reading aloud; they may mediate extraction of sound with meanings rather than extraction of meaning with sounds. For these reasons, our battery of tests included tests of the use of speech codes in reading for meaning and of the use of semantic codes in reading aloud. We hypothesise that Phoenicians should rely more on speech codes in extracting meaning and less on semantic codes in extracting sound. (However, we shall see that the hypothesised results have other interpretations.)

The second type of hypothesis concerns general abilities or tendencies. One tendency of interest is simply the tendency to learn rules. There are many learning situations in which people are faced with the choice of learning rules or memorising examples (e.g. English inflections, see Berko, 1958). Perhaps Phoenicians are more likely to learn spelling-sound rules simply because they are more likely to learn rules of any sort.

For this reason, our battery includes a test of propensity to learn rules. We use a paired-associate learning task in which there are rules that can be used to derive elements of the responses from elements of the stimuli. This task is as close as we could come to actually asking the subject to learn spelling-sound rules, except that the responses are letters rather than sounds.

A second general ability we consider is the ability to perceive speech segments as identical attributes of different words; we call this ability *segmental analysis.* In order to learn that the letter *b* is associated with the sound /b/, however this is learned, it is necessary to recognise that the same segment /b/ can occur in different words. For example, this segment occurs in the beginning of both BOY and BANANA. If the learner is not prone to perceive the initial sounds of these words as identical, he may have difficulty learning that this common sound segment is associated with a letter. The same goes for groups of segments and groups of letters. Of all the hypotheses we test, this is the only one with prior empirical support, as described earlier (Treiman and Baron, in press).

2 Rationale for the tests and description of methods

We gave our subjects quite a number of tests. (Most tests are shown in the Appendix.) Some tests were developed after some subjects had become unavailable. Other subjects, especially Chinese, repeatedly failed to show up for experimental sessions. And some tests were abandoned because they seemed unpromising or because nobody wanted to run them. Thus, there are different numbers of subjects run in different tests. Also, with one exception to be explained, tests were given in different orders to different subjects. Nonetheless, we shall argue that the results present a consistent picture of the difference between Phoenicians and Chinese. Most subjects were run in most tests.

3 Tests used for selection of subjects and validation of the selection

3.1 *Selection test*

In this test, subjects were asked to re-spell a number of words so that someone else would give the correct pronunciation of the word they had written as the only legal pronunciation. Subjects then did a multiple-

choice version of the same test; they had to indicate which of several
re-spellings of each word were correct. The total score consisted of the
mean percent correct on the two parts. This test was supposed to measure
knowledge of spelling-sound rules and ability to use them. Note that in
the first part of the test, the production part, the number of responses
given was not necessarily correlated with the percent of correct responses.
Intuitively, it would seem that the number of responses given is an
interesting measure in itself, perhaps comparable to the number of
responses given in response to Rorschach cards (see Baron, 1978, for
discussion). However, the number was not our concern here.

In the test, it was possible to give correct answers on the basis of
analogies. For example, the response HAMN as a re-spelling of HAM was
counted as correct, even though it is supported by only a single analogy,
DAMN. The rationale for accepting this response comes from our
instructions to the subjects. Another person, presented with HAMN,
would pronounce it correctly if he did what most people do when they
follow spelling-sound rules in pronunciation. Much evidence (Baron,
1977a, 1979) indicates that analogies are commonly used when reading
nonsense words. Further, the only alternative pronunciation in this case
would involve pronouncing both the *m* and the *n*, which would yield
a sequence of sounds that is illegal in English. Otherwise, scoring was
done as follows: Analogies to each response were sought by breaking the
response between the initial consonant cluster and the first vowel
cluster and trying to think of words containing these parts in these
positions. If there were only a few exceptions to the intended pronunciation, the response was counted as correct. Also, the pronunciation of
some letters depends on the succeeding vowels. Thus, SCULE was a not a
correct re-spelling of SCHOOL because of MOLECULE (MOLEKYULE), and
SKULE was not counted. Responses that were familiar proper nouns were
pronounced as in the name. JAYNE was not counted as a correct or
incorrect re-spelling of JANE. Nor were otherwise correct responses that
were impossible as spellings (e.g. ROOOLL, SSOLE) counted as correct or
incorrect.

The selection test was given to 94 subjects under a variety of conditions. In some cases, the test was handed out in classes; in other cases,
it was given to subjects in other experiments after the experiments were
completed. Subjects were given as much time as they wanted to complete
both parts. It was hoped that the increased variability resulting from
this opportunistic method of selecting subjects would be compensated by
the use of subjects with extreme scores on the selection test in the other
tests; this hope was fulfilled, it seems. The convenience of the test is also
in its favor; it usually took less than ten minutes (although one

graduate student apparently spent quite a while on it, producing over a hundred responses in the first part). Subjects did not see the second part (the multiple-choice part) until they had completed the first part. The subjects were regular undergraduate students at the University of Pennsylvania, graduate students and summer school students.

Phoenicians were originally defined as those who scored 85% or higher correct on the average of the two test scores. Chinese were those with less than 70%. Midway through the experiment, these cutoffs were changed to 90% and 65%, respectively (when it appeared that the reliability of the selection test was low – a matter we shall discuss later). However, in all the analyses reported, the Phoenician-Chinese dimension will be treated as a dichotomous variable. Data from 18 Phoenicians and 16 Chinese were actually used, although the numbers of subjects who met the criteria were somewhat larger. (Data from one subject were dropped because that subject knew English as a second language. Another subject met the criterion for being Chinese in part as a result of giving only three responses on the first part of the selection test, one of which was an error; this subject was dropped. A third subject was a research assistant who had run the free classification test using other stimuli; her data on this test were dropped.) The number of subjects run in each of the different tests ranged from 16 in the speech interference test to 29 in the segment comparison test.

3.2 *Word spelling*

Subjects were given a spelling test consisting of a number of commonly mis-spelled words. The words were both exception words and regular words. Errors were scored according to whether or not these errors followed the rules. If our selection of subjects has been successful, a simple prediction would be that Phoenicians would make more phonetic errors than Chinese.

The spelling test consisted of commonly mis-spelled English words. There were 42 words – 29 regular words and 13 exception words. The experimenter pronounced each word, giving a short phrase, if necessary, to specify the meaning of the word (e.g. a military colonel). The subject was asked to use the word in a sentence to indicate that he knew its meaning, and then to spell it. All subjects could use all the words correctly.

Errors were scored as phonetic or nonphonetic. Phonetic mis-spellings are those that when pronounced according to rules and/or analogies give the correct pronunciation. Nonphonetic mis-spellings are those that lead to an incorrect pronunciation.

3.3 *Illegal spelling*

If Chinese really have difficulty associating a sound segment with its corresponding letter, we might expect them to have trouble spelling spoken 'words' that contain segment sequences that are illegal in English, such as /tlee/ or /zdree/. Two measures are of interest here: the number of correct repetitions of the stimuli and the number of times the subject's spelling agrees with his own pronunciation of the stimulus. The former measure relates to the segmental analysis hypothesis; if Chinese have trouble analysing sequences of segments, perhaps this deficit will make it difficult to learn new sequences of sounds. The latter measure bears on the generality of the selection test. If Chinese make errors in spelling single phonemes, this indicates that their deficit is not due only to difficulties with complex spelling patterns.

Twenty-one syllables beginning with consonant clusters that are illegal in English and ending with the vowel *e* were constructed. The syllables were recorded on tape by a female experimenter (R. T.), each syllable being repeated twice. Subjects were asked to listen to each syllable, repeat it, and then spell it. The experimenter recorded the subjects' pronunciations phonetically. The first three syllables were designated as practice items and were not scored. For each subject three measures were calculated: number of correct repetitions, number of correct spellings and number of times the subject's spelling agreed with his own pronunciation.

4 Tests of the hypothesis that Phoenicians have had more practice using rules

4.1 *Speech interference*

By one of our hypotheses, Phoenicians might use speech mediation more than Chinese when reading silently for meaning. One way to measure reliance on speech mediation in reading for meaning is to ask subjects to read for meaning while simultaneously hearing nonsense syllables. The nonsense syllables might be expected to make reading difficult, as indicated by slower speeds. Reading speed was measured in a task in which the subject had to check which of two alternatives fit best in each sentence in a list. The sentences were constructed so that some sentences did not contain the phonemes corresponding to *s*, *f*, *ch* and other sentences did not contain the phonemes corresponding to *p*, *t*, *k*. The nonsense syllables used as interferences contained either the first set of phonemes or the second. The measure of speech mediation is the difference between the times with different-phoneme interference and the times with same-phoneme interference. This technique assures that the interference effects found are not due to general properties of the nonsense syllables. The effects must be due to the fact that the nonsense syllables are related to the phonemes in the sentences. We consider this technique an improvement over previous uses of interference to measure phonemic mediation (Levy, 1975; Kleiman, 1975; Baron, 1977b). In many cases, the results of other interference manipulations could be due to other factors than interference with the phonemic properties of codes used in reading.

The reason that this specific interference interferes is not entirely clear. The mechanism may be related to the effect of phonemic confusability on short-term memory (Baddeley, 1966). However, this is not an explanation, since that effect is not understood either.

In the speech interference test, subjects were given sentences of the sort shown in the Appendix. (Only some of the sentences are shown; a complete list is available on request.) Each sentence contained a blank and two word choices; subjects were told to circle the word that made more sense in the blank. Times and errors were recorded for each page of 10 sentences. Two sorts of sentence lists were alternated in presentation. One type of list had many words containing the phonemes corresponding to *t*, *p* and *k*, and no words with the phonemes *s*, *f* and *ch*. The reverse was true of the other type of list. Throughout the experiment, all subjects heard taped nonsense words through headphones at a rate of about 6 syllables per second. Volume was set so that the stimuli sounded quite loud, but induced no discomfort. Subjects run in one condition heard nonsense words formed from the consonants *t*, *p* and *k*, combined with various vowel sounds (e.g. *ta*, *po*, *kee* . . .). In the other condition the phonemes *s*, *f* and *ch* were combined with the various vowels. On both tapes, syllables were read together in triplets, giving the impression of discrete 3-syllable nonsense words.

4.2 *Homophone sentences*

A second measure of speech mediation required subjects to decide whether each sentence in a list of sentences was true or false. In one type of list, the false sentences would be true if they were read aloud and listened to by another person. For example, the sentence, A BEECH HAS SAND, is true when listened to, but not when read. If a person uses speech mediation in reading silently, we would expect him to have trouble deciding that this *homophone sentence* does not make sense. This would be reflected either in errors or times. Similar techniques have been used by Baron (1973), Baron and McKillop (1975), and Meyer and Ruddy (1973). The present version of the procedure contains an improvement over previous versions. The control condition, in which the sentences do not make sense even when read aloud, contains words equally similar, visually, to the word that would make the sentence true. For example, a *control sentence* for the one above would be, A BENCH HAS SAND.

The control condition for this test and the speech interference test also provide us with measures of reading speed. If any measure of reading speed would be related to the Phoenician-Chinese dimension, it would probably be the speed of reading isolated sentences, since the reading and comprehension of whole paragraphs would be influenced by factors having even less to do with knowledge of spelling-sound rules. Thus, this test is a good one for our purposes.

Twenty-eight pairs of homophone and control sentences were constructed. The pairs of sentences differed in just one word, the word being a homophone of a word that would make the sentence true in one case, and a nonhomophone in the other case. The homophone and control words were always nouns. They were equated for visual similarity to the correct word, and they differed from the correct word in approximately the same number of letters in approximately the same positions. The homophone and control words were also equated for frequency according to Kučera and Francis (1967). Twenty-four unambiguously true sentences were also constructed. All sentences were short, simple declaratives (mean length, 5.5 words).

Lists of ten sentences were constructed by randomly interspersing seven false sentences with three true sentences. In homophone lists the false sentences were all homophone sentences; the control lists were identical except that the homophone sentences were replaced by their controls. One set of eight lists contained four homophone lists and their control lists; another set of eight lists contained the same homophone and control sentences, but in a different order and interspersed with different true sentences. Four practice lists, two containing homophone sentences and two containing nonhomophone sentences (different sentences from those used in the test lists), were also constructed.

Each subject received four practice lists followed by sixteen test lists. Half the pairs of lists occurred with the homophone list first, and half with the control list first. Each subject received one complete set of homophone and control lists, followed by the other set; order of sets was balanced across subjects. Within these constraints, order of test lists was randomly chosen for each subject.

Subjects were instructed to read each sentence silently and to say

'Yes' if it was true and 'No' if it was incorrect in any way. Their time for each list of ten sentences was measured with a stopwatch.

4.3 *Categorised words*

Another way in which Chinese might get less practice with spelling-sound rules is their using meaning to extract pronunciation, thus circumventing the rules. Our measure of whether semantic codes were used in extracting sound from printed words consisted of asking subjects to read lists of words aloud. The categorised word list contained eight groups of five words in each group, all five from the same category (e.g. furniture, utensils, etc.). The control list contained the same words rearranged so that each group no longer contained words from the same category. If a person uses meaning in reading aloud, he ought to read aloud more quickly when the words are in categories, either because meanings are activated more quickly when related meanings have been activated (Meyer *et al.*, 1975) or because the subject can use knowledge of the category of a word to speed reading it aloud. There are other ways of interpreting such an effect. For example, it might be that phonemic codes of semantically related words are associated in memory, so that activation of one code permits activation of other related code more quickly. However, it is hard to see why Phoenicians and Chinese should differ in the magnitude of such an association effect. If the groups differ in the effect of categorising the words, the most likely interpretation would seem to be that they differ in use of semantic information in reading aloud. Whether this difference is a cause of or a result of their differential knowledge of spelling-sound rules is a much more open question.

In the categorised word test, subjects were asked to read four typed lists aloud as fast as possible without error. Two of the lists contained the words grouped into categories, in a vertical column, with spaces separating the groups. The control lists had the same format, but the words within a group were never from the same category. Two versions of each type of list were used. Each version contained the same words, but the order was changed, within the constraints described. The four lists were presented in a balanced order (either categorised-control-control-categorised or control-categorised-categorised-control) twice. Subjects were told in advance how the lists were constructed.

4.4 *Ambiguous patterns*

To test whether Chinese use rules to a lesser extent than do Phoenicians when reading aloud, we used the paradigm of Meyer *et al.* (1975). In their experiment, subjects were asked to read pairs of words aloud, such as FREAK-BREAK or COUCH-TOUCH. These words contain ambiguous spelling patterns (in some cases because one of the words is an exception word, such as TOUCH). Subjects were slower in reading the second member of each pair than when the pairs were rearranged to avoid the confusion, e.g. FREAK-TOUCH, COUCH-BREAK. We would expect such an effect to be larger in subjects who rely more heavily on spelling-sound rules in reading words aloud. (This test and the categorised word test thus measure together the use of rules and meanings in reading aloud.) Such a difference between Phoenicians and Chinese was in fact found by Baron (1979) for fourth grade children. The lists used were slightly different from those of Meyer *et al.* Instead of rearranging the pairs of words, the first word in each pair was always a homophone that could be spelled with or without the ambiguous spelling-pattern. Thus, one list would contain pairs such as MAID-SAID, and the control list would contain pairs such as MADE-SAID, in the same positions. Thus the actual sequence of sounds produced by a subject was identical for the two kinds of lists. These lists were used in the present experiment. This test can show that the groups differ in their use of rules in oral reading.

In the ambiguous pattern test, the four lists shown in the Appendix were given in the order indicated, four times, with the procedure otherwise identical to the categorised word test.

5 Tests of the segmental analysis hypothesis

5.1 *Free classification*

To measure segmental analysis, subjects were given triads of the sort used by Treiman and Baron (in press) (e.g. /bɪ/, /vɛ/, /bo/) in studying age differences in segmental analysis. Treiman and Baron had also found that this test could predict whether children would be Phoenicians or Chinese. Children who made more dimensional classifications (/bɪ/, /bo/) were more likely to make sound preserving errors in reading isolated words aloud.

In the free classification test, the subject heard triads of syllables and were asked to decide which two 'went together on the basis of sound'. Two types of triads were included. In the first type, classification on the basis of shared segments and classification on the basis of overall similarity of syllables gave different results. For example, in the triad /fI/, /se/, /fo/ (as in BEET, BAIT, BOAT) classification by shared segments would group together /fI/ and /fo/. These syllables have the same initial consonant, but have very dissimilar vowels. Use of overall similarity would lead to the classification /fI/ and /se/. These syllables are similar in both the consonant and the vowel, but identical in neither. Twenty-four such triads were constructed, as described in Treiman and Baron (in press). In sixteen, the shared segment was in the same position in the two syllables (e.g. /fI/, /se/, /fo/). In eight, the shared segment was in a different position in the two syllables (e.g. /fI/, /se/, /of/).

In triads of the second type, none of the three syllables had any segments in common, but one pair was more similar overall than any other pair. For example, in the triad /Is/, /ez/, /bo/ (as in BEAT, BAIT, BOAT) the first and second syllables are most similar. Twenty-four such triads were constructed.

The triads were recorded on tape by a female experimenter (R. T.). One tape contained two occurrences of each Type One triad, the second tape contained one occurrence of each Type One triad and one occurrence of each Type Two triad. (The purpose of the second tape was to reduce the number of dimensional responses to Type One triads; however, this purpose was not achieved.) The syllables were spoken slowly and distinctly, and each triad was repeated twice.

Before beginning the test, subjects were given practice triads of the types they would hear on the test tape. All subjects heard the two tapes in the same order, and results from the two tapes were pooled.

For Type One triads, each subject's number of 'dimensional' classifications, or classifications based on shared segments; 'similarity' classifications, or those based on overall similarity; and 'anomalous' classifications, or those apparently based neither on shared segments nor on overall similarity, was calculated. For Type Two triads, number of correct classifications, which are by necessity based on overall similarity, was calculated.

5.2 *Segment comparison, word comparison and word reading*

A second measure of segmental analysis was designed to be as close as possible to the hypothesised ability in question, the ability to recognise that two different words have the same segment in the same position. It is this recognition that would seem to underlie the recognition of the significance of the fact that these two words are spelled with the same letter in the same position. Thus, our idea was to ask subjects to judge whether or not two words had the same segment in a prespecified position (first, middle, or last – with 'middle' always referring to a vowel cluster surrounded by two consonant clusters). Ideally, we would have liked to use auditory presentation of the words. However, lack of time and handy apparatus forced us to design a pencil-and-paper form of the test, which, in retrospect, seems to have certain advantages. In this *segment comparison* test, sets of words were chosen so that the spellings of the words were completely useless in making the judgment required. For example, in lists in which the subject had to decide whether the first segments of two words were identical, one list contained the word pair CHASE–CHOIR, and another list contained CHOSE–CHAIR. In this case, the degree of visual difference between the members of each pair is constant for the two pairs, since one pair is made from the other simply by switching letters; all pairs were constructed in this way. Also, if the subject used the identity of the initial letters to make his judgment, this would help him with CHOSE–CHAIR but hurt him with CHASE–CHOIR. (In other sets of words, the subject would be helped when the answer was *different* but hurt when the answer was *same*.) This kind of design goes a long way toward solving another problem in studies of segmental judgments. Specifically, when people have learned to spell words, or when they have learned spelling-sound rules, they can often make segmental judgments by imagining the spellings of the words and comparing the spellings rather than the sounds. It is hard to believe that subjects could be using such a process in this test. To do so, they would have to imagine phonetic spellings of the words, e.g. CHASE–QUIRE, and compare the relevant parts of these spellings even while they were looking right at the (misleading) correct spellings. It would seem much easier to do what they are instructed to do, i.e. compare the segments, even if this were difficult.

The *word comparison* test required subjects to make exactly the same kinds of comparisons as the segment comparison test. However, the subjects knew in advance that the two members of each pair would be phonetically identical except for the critical segment. All the *same* pairs consisted of homophones, and all the different pairs consisted of words differing only in a single segment, in a previously specified position. The same kind of design was used as in the segment comparison test, so that degree of visual similarity was completely useless as a guide to the correct response, and for each pair in one list for which the spellings suggested a correct answer, there was a pair in another list for which the spellings suggested an incorrect answer.

The word comparison test was included out of curiosity, since our hypotheses make no prediction about the extent to which it would differentiate the two groups. Whether it would differentiate the groups would depend on how the task is done. It is done in the same way as the segment comparison task, we would expect it to differentiate the groups to the same extent. If, on the other hand, if it is done by comparing sounds of whole words, our segmental analysis hypothesis would not predict any difference between the groups. (However, it is conceivable that Chinese have trouble comparing *any* speech sounds, and that this difficulty is most clearly manifest in comparing segments only because these are the most difficult for anyone to compare. By this account, Chinese ought to have difficulty even with similarity classifications in the triads test, but their impairment should be less with these classifications than with dimensional classifications.)

The segment comparison and word comparison tests might be more difficult if the subject were unfamiliar with the words used. Since the design required the use of a number of infrequent words, subjects were given practice reading all the words used in these two tests before the tests were given. This *word reading* test, the word comparison test and the segment comparison tests were all given in a single session. The word reading test served as a measure of the speed of reading the words in the last two tests. To take advantage of another chance to collect data, the words were divided into groups according to degree of regularity. Most of the words were entirely regular, but there was one list consisting of real exception words and another list consisting of words using ambiguous spelling patterns. These two lists were combined for purposes of analysis. These lists were thus far from optimal for getting a good measure of the speed of reading exception words versus regular words.

The word reading test required the subject to read 17 columns of words aloud, with about 30 words per column, as quickly as possible as in the other tests involving the reading of isolated words. After all the columns were read once, they were read again. The columns were typed, double spaced.

The word comparison and segment comparison tests are given in full in the Appendix, along with the instructions given to the subjects and the items used for practice. When the practice items were presented, any misunderstandings about the task were corrected. Each list of items contained 20 pairs of words, in a column. The subject was to place a check next to those pairs in which the critical phoneme was the same in the two words and an X next to those pairs where it was different. (Pilot studies in which subjects were asked to say 'yes' or 'no' aloud suggested that this was considerably harder, presumably because the mode of making the response conflicted with the processes used to represent the sounds of the two words.) There were two columns on each page. The column on the right contained the words matched to those on the left. For example, if the column on the left contained CHOSE–CHAIR in the 10th place, the column on the right contained CHASE–CHOIR in the 10th place. No subject reported noticing this relationship. There was one page for each test and for each segment position. The order of presenting the pages was: first segment, word comparison; first segment, segment comparison; second, word; second, segment; third, word; third, segment. The subject went through the six pages twice in the same order. Note that the subject practiced reading all the words used in the word comparison and segment comparison tests.

6 Test of the hypothesis that Phoenicians are more prone to learn rules in general

6.1 *Rule learning*

One of our hypotheses is that Phoenicians are generally better at learning rules. The rule learning test is relevant to this hypothesis. This test was a paired-associate learning experiment in which the stimuli were consonant trigrams and the responses were other consonant trigrams. Most of the letters in each response could be derived from letters in the stimulus by simple letter-letter correspondence rules. One stimulus letter, however, was paired with different letters in each response. After subjects had learned a list of criterion, they were presented with the same four pairs, plus four new pairs, and they were asked to guess at the responses to all the items. Their responses to the new pairs served as one measure of whether they had learned rules, since these responses could in large part be derived by the rules. Subjects were also asked at the end of the experiment whether they had discovered any rules during the learning phase.

The subject was told that the task was to learn four paired associates. He was shown each of the four stimuli, typed on an index card in upper case letters, and told what its correct response was. Then he was shown the four cards, in a different random order on each trial, and asked to give the response, guessing if necessary. If the subject was wrong, the experimenter gave the correct response. After the subject was correct on all four items given in a trial for two trials, the next phase of the experiment began. Here, the subject was shown eight cards (in a different random order for each subject). He was asked to produce the responses to all cards. If he did not know the response, he was told to guess, and that it might be possible to give correct responses to items he had not seen before. Finally, the subject was asked if he had noticed any correspondence between letters in the stimuli and letters in the responses. Note that all letters in the stimuli but one had a corresponding letter in the response.

All subjects were paid $2.50 per hour for the tests. The experiment was explained to each subject after all tests were completed.

7 Results and discussion

The reliability of the selection test was assessed by dividing the test into two halves, using alternate items for each half; thus, the first half consisted of the items SEAL, GOOD, ROOF and SOAK, in both the production and recognition parts of the test, and the second half consisted of HAM, SCHOOL, STAFF and JANE. The correlation across the 94 subjects between halves was 0.51, with means of 76% and 78% correct on the two halves, respectively, and standard deviations of 14% and 12%, respectively. For the production part of the test, the correlation between halves was 0.48, and for the recognition part, 0.28; the standard deviations for the reading part were about half of those in the spelling part, although the means were not much higher (78% vs 75%).

For those wanting to measure ability to use spelling-sound rules, some recommendations are in order. First, a great deal of variability in the test seems to be due to the adoption of different criteria for a 'good' response. For example, many subjects gave GOULD as a good re-spelling of the word GOOD. We scored this as incorrect, since GOULD is actually a well-known proper name not pronounced the same as GOOD. Many subjects, when asked about this, said that they had not thought of the name or had not tried of other readings of what they wrote. In a pilot study, when subjects were asked to go back and check their responses for other possible pronunciations after completing the production part of the selection test, their scores (percentage correct) improved considerably. Further, the criterion problem affected different items differently. There was only one re-spelling GOOD that we counted as correct, namely GOODE, while ROOF had a large number of possible re-spellings (resulting from various combinations of initial R, WR and RH with EUF, UEF, OOPH, EUPH, UFE, UPHE, OOF, OOFE etc.). Thus, a subject who tried hard to think of all possible answers and didn't worry much about checking them would have his score raised by ROOF and lowered by GOOD. The same problem with the criterion existed in the recognition test. In retrospect, it seems that the best test for selecting subjects would require subjects to give the single best re-spelling of a larger number of words, where 'best' is defined as the least ambiguous as to its pronunciation. For the recognition test, it might be possible to design a test in which subjects were to indicate which two of three nonsense words or words were pronounced alike. (These suggestions are offered with the need for group administration in mind; simpler tests could be designed for individual administration.) A second recommendation concerns the scoring of tests. We – as experimenters – are not necessarily Phoenicians, and books on spelling-sound rules don't contain *all* the rules. At several points in the course of the experiment, it was necessary to go back and rescore all the data when we realised that we had made errors in deciding which answers were correct. We recommend the method described above, even if it is difficult. (We will be glad to help others on similar problems.)

The main results consist of the point biserial correlations between each of the tests and the (dichotomous) Phoenician-Chinese dimension. These correlations are shown in Table 1, along with their significance levels, the group means and the number of subjects involved in each correlation. For all tests involving times, logarithms were used to calculate the correlations: the times used were also the minimum times for each *list* used in a condition. (When there were two or more lists in the same condition, the times were summed before taking the logs. The point of using logs was to adjust effects for overall speed differences among subjects, on the assumption that the effect of some variable on a subject's time would generally be proportional to the subject's time, other things equal. In general, this use of logs is conservative with respect to the hypotheses of interest.) Error rates were not transformed.

We will first discuss the results of the tests that acted more to check the selection of subjects than to find out why the groups differed. One encouraging result is the difference between the groups in the number of errors in spelling illegal words (where an error is scored when the subject's spelling is inconsistent with his own pronunciation – note, however, that the difference between groups is still significant when errors are scored when the subject's spelling is inconsistent with the experimenter's pronunciation). This indicates that the Chinese have difficulty not only with complex spelling-sound rules of the sort tapped in the second part of the selection test, but also with the most elementary letter-sound associations. Undoubtedly, the unusual context makes the task harder, leading to more errors than would otherwise occur. But many of the errors on the selection test were also of this sort: for example, Chinese gave such responses as GHAM and AM for HAM and GUD for GOOD.

The word spelling test also confirms the selection of the subjects, and shows further that the Phoenician-Chinese dimension has something to do with more everyday sorts of spelling tasks. While the groups did not differ significantly in total errors, separation of errors into those that followed the rules (phonetic errors) and those that did not (nonphonetic, see Appendix) revealed the pattern of group differences we hoped to find. Specifically, the proportion of errors (that could be clearly classified

TABLE 1 Group differences on tests

Test and measure	Point biserial correlation with group	Phoenician mean (&N)	Chinese mean (&N)
Tests primarily for selection and validation			
Word spelling (42 items)			
total errors	0.28	8.30 (13)	11.8 (10)
phonetic/(phonetic & nonphonetic)	0.38[1]	0.74 (13)	0.62 (10)
Illegal spelling (18 items)			
correct repetitions	0.33	16.3 (12)	15.5 (11)
correct spellings	0.38[1]	15.5 (12)	13.9 (11)
spelling and repetition agree	0.63[4]	17.6 (12)	15.0 (11)
Tests relevant to practice hypothesis			
Speech interference			
(interference time)/control	−0.23	1.04 (8)	1.08 (8)
(interference errors)/control	0.06	0.13 (8)	0·00 (8)
sec per list	−0.12	31.9 (8)	30.3 (8)
Homophone sentences			
(homophone time)/control	−0.27	1.00 (11)	1.04 (12)
(homophone errors)-control	−0.18	1.70 (11)	2.80 (12)
sec per list	−0.01	10.8 (11)	10.7 (12)
Categorised words			
(uncategorised time)/categorised	0.37[1]	1.05 (16)	1.09 (12)
Ambiguous spelling patterns			
(ambiguous time)/control	0.23	1.07 (17)	1.04 (13)
Tests relevant to segment-analysis hypothesis			
Free classification of syllables			
dim./(dim.+sim.), Type One	0.52[3]	0.93 (13)	0.82 (11)
dim./(dim. + sim.), same position	0.37[1]	0.97 (13)	0.93 (11)
dim./(dim. + sim.), different position	0.54[3]	0.86 (13)	0.61 (11)
dim. + sim. total	0.25	0.99 (13)	0.97 (11)
sim., Type Two	0.22	0.94 (11)	0.90 (11)
Word reading			
total sec (minimum)	0.21	106 (17)	115 (13)
ln (exception/regular)	0.07	0.10 (17)	0.09 (13)
Word comparison			
sec per item	0.42[2]	1.27 (16)	1.55 (13)
percent errors	0.38[2]	3.90 (16)	6.00 (13)
Segment comparison			
sec per item	0.54[4]	1.62 (16)	2.17 (13)
percent errors	0.43[2]	11.6 (16)	17.7 (13)
Test relevant to general rule-learning hypothesis			
Rule learning			
transfer letters (out of 18)	0.30	14.6 (14)	11.1 (10)
rules reported (out of 4)[5]	0.36[1]	3.10 (15)	2.00 (10)

[1] p < 0.05   [2] p < 0.025   [3] p < 0.005   [4] p < 0.001: all one-tailed.

[5] Subjects were scored correct on the stimulus letter associated with different response letters if they recalled two of four responses.

as phonetic or not) that were phonetic was higher for the Phoenicians. Subsequent analysis showed that this group difference was apparently due entirely to the Phoenicians' tendency to spell exception words as if they were regular; the groups did not differ in error-type tendencies on regular words. In general, the fact that Phoenicians and Chinese make different kinds of errors suggests that rules are normally used by at least some people for spelling real words.

The groups did not seem to be drastically different in intelligence or educational background. The number of responses given in the first half of the selection test averaged 19 responses for the Phoenicians and 18 for the Chinese ($r = 0.08$ for number and group membership). The number of errors made during rule learning likewise did not distinguish the two groups ($r = 0.07$). These are the best measures of intelligence we have in the data.

The main results are described simply: of the tests bearing on the major hypotheses, the ones that distinguished the groups best were Type One triads of the free classification test and the segment comparison test. Both of these results support the segmental analysis hypothesis.

More detailed analysis confirms this general account. The free classification test distinguished the groups when analysed separately for those Type One triads with the identical segment in the same position in the syllable and for those Type One triads with the position changed. Thus, this result cannot be due to a peculiarity of either type of item. Further, the groups did not differ on Type Two triads, in which the response had to be based on overall similarity.

The segment comparison test and the word comparison test bear closer examination. One might argue that the Chinese deficit in segment comparison was due to a deficit in reading isolated words. Of course, the word reading effect was smaller than the segment comparison effect, and the word reading effect was not even significant. But still, a small problem in reading isolated words could be magnified when the additional problem of segmental comparison is added to the task. To test this, we compared the correlation between group membership and segment comparison time with the correlation between group membership and word reading time (taking into account the correlation of 0.47 between word reading and sound comparison). The former correlation was significantly higher than the latter ($p < 0.05$). However, by the same method of analysis, the correlation between group membership and word comparison time was not higher than the correlation between membership and word reading time. Nor was the correlation between membership and segment comparison time higher than the correlation between membership and word comparison time. The import of these last two comparisons is that the status of the word comparison test is unclear. Because of this unclarity, two possible interpretations of the major result cannot be distinguished. One, which we prefer because of its simplicity, is that Phoenicians and Chinese differ only in their ability to compare segments, an ability used in the word comparison task as well as the segment comparison task. A second interpretation is that the groups differ both in comparing segments and in comparing whole syllables, but, since comparing syllables is easier for everyone than comparing segments, the group differences in segment comparison are greater than the differences in syllable comparison. The results most difficult to reconcile with this latter interpretation are those from the free-classification test, where all subjects preferred dimensional over similarity (whole word) classifications, but Phoenicians showed a stronger preference. (However, this result alone might be due to use of spellings of the syllables rather than sounds for classifications. Spellings would be useless in the segment-comparison test. Further, the correlation between group membership and dim./(dim. + sim.) was not significantly higher than that between membership and Type Two similarity classifications.)

One other test bearing on a major hypothesis distinguishes the groups, the categorised word test. [Note also that the effect of categorisation itself was significant across subjects; $t(28) = 6.1$.] As mentioned earlier, however, this result has two interpretations. One interpretation is that since Chinese use meanings more often in reading aloud (or in extracting phonemic codes), they have had less opportunity to learn spelling-sound rules. The second interpretation reverses the direction of cause and effect: the Chinese rely more heavily on meanings *because* they are less skilled at using rules. This second interpretation predicts that Chinese ought to be slower at reading words, since they are less skilled at one process used in reading words. The Chinese were in fact slightly slower at reading words aloud, although the difference was not significant. It seems likely that the fact that all subjects were college students acted to restrict the range of word reading speed; those who were poor at using rules were thus somewhat better than others at using other processes required for reading (a proposal consistent with the fact that Chinese were slightly *faster* in silent-reading tasks).

Another test that may have distinguished the groups is rule learning, although the results are marginal. Conceivably, the single test used was a poor measure of general rule-learning tendency. This hypothesis seems worthy of further research.

In sum, while certain small differences between groups on other tests are suggestive, the results suggest that Phoenicians are better at segmental analysis, and that there may well be no other differences between the groups that bear on the question of how the differences arose.

A comment is in order about the hypothesis attributing the group difference in use of rules to differential use of phonemic mediation in reading for meaning. The failure to find the hypothesised difference here is unlikely to be due to phonemic mediation not being manifest in the tests, since the effect of homophone sentences was significant across all subjects [$t(22) = 1.54$ for times, 3.55 for errors], and the effect of specific phonemic interference was also significant [$t(15) = 3.31$ for times, 0.22 for errors]. However, firm conclusions cannot be drawn, since the two measures of phonemic mediation were not correlated with each other across subjects. It seems likely that while these tests were sensitive to the existence of phonemic mediation, they were not good measures of individual differences in phonemic mediation. Of the two, the homophone sentence test is probably the more accurate, since it is similar to the test of Baron and McKillop (1975) on which reliable individual differences were found.

The disappointments in the data were the failure to find differences in the relative speeds at reading exception and regular words in the word reading test and the failure to find a difference in the ambiguous patterns test. The exception-regular comparison was based on only two lists of exception words (one of which consisted of words with ambiguous spelling patterns, which might not function the same as true exception words), so this need not disturb us greatly. The ambiguous pattern test also yielded differences in the predicted direction [and also showed an overall effect of list type, $t(25) = 5.4$]. Because the words used were chosen so as to be familiar to fourth grade children (Baron, 1979), it is possible that the words were so familiar to the adults that they were all read by using word-specific associations to a large extent. Thus, this failure to replicate Baron (1979) need not be very disturbing either. Possibly a test using less familiar words (e.g. VENUS–MENUS) would yield the expected effect. (It is also encouraging that the *difference* between the effect of categorisation in the categorised word test and the effect of ambiguous patterns in the ambiguous pattern test *did* distinguish the groups significantly; this at least tells us that the two groups were differentially affected by these two manipulations of difficulty.)

On the whole, the simplest interpretation of the entire set of results is that people differ in their ability to perceive segments as identical attributes of different words. Differences in the perception of speech might arise through differential experience with speech, differential development of the brain, or perhaps through more general tendencies to compare stimuli in terms of identical attributes as opposed to overall similarity (Baron, 1978; Smith and Kemler, 1977). There is little evidence on any of these points. Saffran, *et al.* (1976) have found evidence that the right hemisphere tends to perceive speech in terms of overall similarity; specifically, an aphasic patient with a left-hemisphere lesion could perceive many words but could not distinguish minimal pairs of words on the basis of phonetic distinctions. Possibly, Chinese have less developed speech areas of the left hemisphere.

We must also acknowledge, however, that the dimensional perception of phonemes might still be a result of learning spelling-sound correspondences rather than a cause. The results from the segment-comparison test made it unlikely that subjects were actually comparing spellings. However, it is possible that learning to spell by rules had essentially provided practice in detecting segments and had improved the phonemic perception of those who did learn to spell by rules. By this account, differences in knowledge of spelling-sound rules would arise from other sources, such as general differences in rule learning, or reliance on other ways of learning to read and spell. The only way to settle the issue is to do experimental studies, showing that manipulation of phonemic perception can affect learning of spelling-sound rules relying on that perception. A beginning in this direction has been made by Rosner (1971), who found that children trained in phonemic manipulations such as counting phonemes were able to learn to read about twice as fast as children who were not so trained. However, Rosner did not show that this effect was specific to the learning of spelling-sound correspondences. We hope that our present results have increased the plausibility of the causal link from phonemic perception to spelling-sound rule learning so that other studies of this question are done.

Another direction for further research concerns the individual differences we found in segmental analysis itself. These differences may have consequences for ability to learn second languages (see Carroll, 1958). They also suggest that there are two mechanisms for perceiving speech, just as there are two mechanisms for reading printed words (Baron, 1977b). One mechanism requires analysis of speech into phonemes, just as printed words may be analysed into letters. The other mechanisms might be characterised as a 'whole word' mechanism for speech perception, a process analogous to recognition of whole printed words.

8 Summary

Two groups of adult subjects were selected: 'Phoenicians' were those who were good at spelling-sound rules to produce and recognise correct spelling of words; 'Chinese' were those who made many mistakes in these tasks. Phoenicians' errors in spelling tended to be consistent with rules. Chinese tended to make errors in spelling phonologically illegal nonsense words.

Three hypotheses were advanced to explain the group difference: differential reliance on rules in reading, differential ability to discover rules in general, and differential ability to recognise common sound segments in different words. There was no evidence for the first two hypotheses, as the groups did not differ consistently in measures of speech mediation in reading or in the tendency to use rules in an artificial rule learning task. However, they did differ in two measures of the ability to recognise common segments – a test of free classification of syllables and a speeded test of judging whether two words contained an identical segment.

Acknowledgements

This work was supported by grant number MH 29453 from the National Institute of Mental Health; Jonathan Baron is the Principal Investigator.

9 Appendix: tests used

Spelling test (part of selection test)
Try to re-spell each of the words below as many different ways as you can. For example, if the word were *rye*, you could re-spell it *ri, rhi, wri, wrigh*, and so on. Make sure that each re-spelling is correct, so that if someone else wrote it you would pronounce it correctly (i.e. like the given word) on the first try. (*Note:* The words used are the same as in the pronunciation test.)

Pronunciation Test (part of selection test)

Underline each nonsense word on the right that you would pronounce the same as the word on the left (on your first try at pronouncing each nonsense word). (*Note:* italicised words are correct.)
seal – cel, sel, *seel*
ham – *hamb, hamn, hamm*, haim
good – gud, gudd, ghud, gude
school – skul, sceul, scheul, *skool*, scule, skewl, scoul, ckool
roof – ruf, *rufe, wroof, rhoof, rooph*, roogh
staff – *staph, staffe*, staphe, *staf*
soak – soce, souk, sauk, *soke*, coak, sok, sowk, *soac*, soche, *soack, soque, psoak*, soc, soch
Jane – Gane, *Jaign, Jeign*, Jan, Jaghn, Ghane, *Jain*

Word spelling test (* = nonphonetic error)

Target	Error
absence	abscence
acquitted	aquitted, acquited*
beggar	
colonel	colornel*, coronel* colnel*, coloniel*, colonel*, cornal*, colonial*
occasion	occassion*, ocassion*, occaison
pageant	pagent, pagant*
counterfeit	. . . fiet*, . . . fit
picnicking	picnicing*, picknicing*
occurrence	occurrance, occurance, occurence
endeavor	endevour, endever, endevor
unnecessary	unnecsessary*, unecessary*, unneccisary
rhythm	rhythmn, rhythem, rhythum, rythm, rythym
tomorrow	tommorrow
parliament	parliment, parliement*
until	
liar	lier
solder	sauter*, sodder, soddar
committee	

Target	Error
fiery	firey, firery*, fierey, firy
misled	mislead
ninetieth	nineith*, nineth*, ninetyth*, nintieth*, nineteeth*, ninetyeth
margarine	margerine, margerin
apparent	
angel	
psychic	psychik
inoculate	innoculate, annoculate*
stationery	stationary
principle	principal
recipe	receipe*, reciepe*
conscious	conscience*, concious
pneumonia	pnewmona*, pnemonia*, pnemonia, nemmonia
indict	endyte, indite, enditied*
penicillin	penacillen, pennicillen, penicillan, penecillin, penecilin*, pennicillan, pennicillin, penicillen, penicillian
balloon	ballon*
courageous	couragous*, corageous

Target	Error
prove	
beginning	
seize	siege*,
	ceased*,
	sieze,
	cease*,
	ceize
lose	loose*
parallel	parellel,
	paralell
dilemma	dilemna,
	dileama*,
	dilema*,
	delemia*
conscience	conscienous*,
	conscence*,
	concience,
	consciense

Illegal spelling test

nree	vree	zdlee
vwee	dlee	zvree
zdree	smree	zwee
smlee	zvwee	znwee
zbwee	dwee	mlee
thlee	hmee	sthlee

Speech interference test, examples of sentences with p, t *and* k

He talked to Ted, tripped him and told him to pay Paul or he'd kill   barn /
him   .

Take your car to town and pay your parking   lot / ticket   .

To avoid making trouble took up my every   minute / potion   .

A tear rolled down onto her   lap / dream   .

A crooked banker can totally control your   pocketbook / avenue   .

Put your bet on our track team to win every   meaning / event   .

It turned out to be a bitter pill to   take / beat   .

Ball in hand, he took a turn toward a nearby hoop and went up to make
a   dunk / top   .

Lately I have been pouring time into planning our   trip / ruling   .

To paint your boat completely will take a day or   two / bucket   .

Homophone Sentences, negative items only

Homophone	Control
A SUN is male	A sin is male
SOUL is a kind of fish	soil
An ORE is used for rowing	orb
A REIN can be a downpour	ruin
HARE is on the head	harm
An AIR can inherit money	ear
Letters and postcards are MALE	malt
A BEECH has sand	bench
A BEAT is a vegetable	belt
Boats may have SALES	salts
A BOW is an admirer	bog
Bread is made from DOE	dot
A person's way of walking is his GATE	gain
A PAIN is part of a window	pawn
A PLANE is where cattle graze	plant
A BEET is a measure of rhythm	bead
A CENT is a smell	scene
A blind man has lost his SITE	sigh
A PAIR is a kind of fruit	pier
FUR is a kind of tree	fire
The LOOT is a musical instrument	lift
STARES are in a house	starts
Three tones form a CORD	chore
A BEACH is a kind of tree	belch
A TALE is part of an animal	talk
A PANE is a hurt	pair
A 747 is a PLAIN	plate
Two things are a PEAR	pail

Free classification test

pI	te	po		be	vɛ	ke		ɪθ	es	oθ		še	čɛ	eš
be	vɛ	bo		fɪ	se	mI		ɪp	et	ɪl		še	ɛč	eš
fI	se	fo		še	čɛ	te		ab	ɛv	em		fɪ	se	of
še	čɛ	šo		θɪ	se	bɪ		ɪθ	es	ɪb		še	če	oš
θɪ	se	θo		ɪp	et	op		fɪ	se	ɪf		fɪ	se	ɪm
pɪ	te	mɪ		ab	ɛv	ob		fɪ	es	ɪf		še	čɛ	et

Key: a, b*a*t; e, b*ai*t; ɛ, b*e*t; I, b*ee*t; ɪ, b*i*t; o, b*oa*t; θ, *th*in; š, *sh*in; č, *ch*in

Ambiguous patterns test

son	maid	sun	made
on	said	on	said
none	dough	nun	doe
bone	cough	bone	cough
knows	great	nose	grate
cows	meat	cows	meat
been	some	bin	sum
seen	home	seen	home
four	no	for	know
hour	to	hour	to
to	steak	too	stake
go	leak	go	leak
rows	tow	rose	toe
cows	cow	cows	cow
sew	pear	so	pair
few	fear	few	fear
one	know	won	no
bone	how	bone	how

Word comparison and segment comparison test

Practice:
Say whether the words have the same sound in the indicated position:

First position	Middle (vowel) position	Last position
jim gym	through threw	peak pique
you ewe	week weak	dice dies
cue queue	pair par	flu flue
ode odd	die dye	damn dan
by buy	ways was	side sighed
phil pill	foul fool	sing sink
whole high	said wet	cow tow
west when	face bathe	fire store
wing who	head male	quartz has
shoe sue	food roof	lamb tim
cap kin	look mood	knife half
fork spoon	time pin	ring fun

First position: Word comparison

knot not	keel eel	
wheel heel	wring ring	
cell sell	cold sold	
whole hole	when hen	
ill kill	new knew	
where here	wrap rap	
wrote rote	what hat	
cake sake	cent sent	
knight night	kink ink	
chap cap	chord cord	
scat cat	scent cent	
cite site	sat cat	
gnat nat	gin in	
eye aye	end and	
wink ink	wrung rung	
one won	are war	
keel eel	knit nit	
wow owe	wry rye	
whine wine	thin tin	
use ease	urn earn	

Segment comparison

cite sap	site cap
chord cap	cord chap
sake cent	cake sent
ends and	eyes aye
are wart	one wont
cell sold	sell cold
uses ease	urns earn
wine whore	whine wore
cent scat	scent cat
grit rip	gnat nap
gum get	gut gem
whose hose	when hen
thin then	tin ten
chow chute	cow cute
hour out	hear eat
gone jean	joan gene
shoe sure	sue shore
chose chair	chase choir
thank than	tank tan
heir hare	here hair

Middle position: Word comparison

comb calm	bomb balm	
been bean	cheep cheap	
course coarse	sour soar	
deed dead	deer dear	
some sum	rome rum	
feat feet	head heed	
thrown throne	gown gone	
meat mate	grate grate	
ron run	sun son	
heart hart	fear far	
hare hear	ware wear	
meat meet	great greet	
four fore	sour sore	
none nun	gone gun	
fair fear	pair pear	
break brake	bleak blake	
howl hole	bowl bole	
tees ties	peer pier	
shown shone	town tone	
bought bout	taught taut	

Segment comparison

ware hear	wear hare
cheep bean	been cheap
sour fore	four sore
bomb calm	comb balm
leak greet	leek great
coarse sour	course soar
nun home	hum none
heal deed	heel dead
pear fair	pair fear
some rub	sum robe
brake lean	break lane
feat heed	feet head
howl bone	bowl hone
thrown town	thrown tone
peer lear	pier liar
grate meal	male great
taut bought	taught bout
sun rot	son rut
shone town	shown tone
heart far	hart fear

Last position: Word comparison		Segment comparison	
arc ark	lace lake	arc lake	ark lace
blue blew	sue sew	mate mat	sage sag
tow to	low lo	blue sew	blew sue
sin sink	tack tac	roll tie	role til
shoo shoe	too toe	lo tow	low to
pin pink	doc dock	inn bar	in barn
sew so	new no	tac sink	tack sin
hose hoes	dose does	tow hoe	how toe
ear earn	dam damn	shoo toe	shoe too
rage rag	bee be	tick tan	tic tank
show shoe	throw throe	dock pin	doc pink
we wee	stag stage	bloc sink	block sin
hoe how	toe tow	so new	sew no
roll role	til tie	tough doe	toe dough
barn bar	inn in	hose does	hoes dose
tic tick	ban bank	bam damn	bar darn
block bloc	sink sin	throe show	throw shoe
sage sag	bee be	lab to	lamb tom
plum plumb	so sob	stage fig	state fit
tough toe	dough doe	sag rage	sat rate

Note that in word comparisons, for same response, both words sound the same. For different response, they differ only on the critical phoneme. For segment comparisons, for same response, only the critical phonemes are the same. For different response, all phonemes are different. *Ed.*

9

Visual and Phonological Strategies in Reading and Spelling

RODERICK W. BARRON   *Department of Psychology, University of Guelph, Canada*

1 Visual-orthographic and phonological strategies in good and poor readers

There are at least two strategies which can be used with a printed word in order to obtain access to information stored in the internal lexicon. One is a visual-orthographic strategy; it is direct and involves using only a visual-orthographic code. The other is a phonological strategy; it is indirect and involves using a phonological code which is generated by applying spelling-to-sound correspondence rules. Although some investigators (e.g. Gough, 1972; Rubenstein *et al.*, 1971) have argued that a phonological code is necessary for lexical access, recent evidence (see Barron, 1978a for a review) has indicated that this is not the case, even for beginning readers (e.g. Barron and Baron, 1977). Instead, it appears that both visual-orthographic and phonological codes can be used, most likely in parallel (e.g. Baron, 1973; Coltheart *et al.*, 1977; Meyer and Ruddy, 1973).

The fact that direct visual access to the lexicon can take place suggests the possibility that learning to read produces an important change in the organisation of the internal lexicon because thereafter children will have visual-orthographic as well as phonological entries (Ehri, 1978a). This change in the lexicon has implications for spelling as well as for reading. Consider, for example, how lexical entries might be involved in strategies for reading and spelling words which are regular and irregular in their conformity to spelling rules. Regular words (e.g. GLOBE, CHURCH, SWEET) conform to spelling rules and can be read and spelled by using either a phonological or a visual-orthographic strategy. During reading, a phonological strategy could be used by applying spelling-to-sound rules to generate a phonological code which would correspond to a phonological entry in the lexicon. A visual-orthographic strategy could be used to generate a visual-orthographic code which would correspond to a visual-orthographic entry in the lexicon. During spelling, a phonological strategy could be used to generate the spelling of an item through the application of sound-to-spelling correspondence rules. A visual-orthographic strategy might be used to produce the spelling of an item by retrieving information stored in the visual-orthographic entry in the lexicon. Irregular words (e.g. SAID, BROAD, SWORD), on the other hand, are exceptions to spelling rules and cannot be read or spelled successfully by using a phonological strategy. In reading, the application of spelling-to-sound rules to irregular words could result in the generation of a phonological code which would not correspond to a phonological entry in the lexicon (e.g. Baron and Strawson, 1976; J. Mason, 1976, 1977). In spelling, application of sound-to-spelling rules to irregular words could result in the generation of a spelling for an item which would not correspond to a visual-orthographic entry in the lexicon; for example, DEBT might be spelled as DET, YACHT as YOT and SWORD as SORD.

These arguments suggest that in order to read and spell *irregular* words, it may be necessary to acquire and use lexical entries containing specific information about visual-orthographic structure. Similarly, *homophones* (e.g. SALE, SAIL; BARRON, BARON) would be difficult to comprehend and spell correctly, at least out of context, without reference to visual-orthographic entries in the lexicon as spelling rules would produce identical pronunciations and spellings for these items. Visual-orthographic entries in the lexicon may be involved in the spelling, as well as pronunciation, of *regular* English words as the application of spelling rules may depend on prior parsing of words at the morphemic level (e.g. Venezky, 1970). The *ph* consonant cluster in GRAPHIC, for example, is pronounced differently than it is in SHEPHERD where *ph* spans a morphemic boundary. Finally, it is possible that visual-orthographic entries are even involved in pronouncing (i.e. reading aloud) and spelling *non-words*. Baron (1977a, b) and Marsh *et al.* (1975) have shown that analogies to irregular words are used in pronouncing non-words (e.g. DROAD pronounced like BROAD, VAID pronounced like SAID) and Marsh *et al.* (Chapter 15) and Frith (Chapter 22) have obtained similar findings in spelling non-words.

Two experiments were carried out in order to investigate how children use visual-orthographic and phonological strategies. The first was on reading and subjects were required to decide whether or not a string of letters was a word (lexical decision task). The second was on spelling and subjects were required to write down a word after dictation. Both experiments involved comparisons of regular and irregular words and both used 4–6th grade schoolchildren (9–12 years of age) who differed in reading skill, but not in non-verbal IQ. If differences can be found which are related to reading skill, then it may be possible to be more confident that the use of visual-orthographic and phonological strategies reflect important aspects of the processes involved in reading and spelling.

2 Experiment 1: Lexical access in reading

There is indeed some evidence for individual differences in the use of visual-orthographic and phonological strategies in reading among children who have been classified as developmental dyslexics (e.g. Boder, 1971, 1973) as well as among adults with acquired dyslexia (e.g.

Marshall and Newcombe, 1973; Patterson and Marcel, 1977; Shallice and Warrington, 1975). Poor readers, who are not as seriously impaired as those classified as developmental dyslexics, nevertheless appear to differ from good readers in their reading strategies. In particular ,the poor readers appear to be deficient in their ability to use a phonological code in reading related tasks. Firth (1972), Frederiksen (1978) and Perfetti and Hogaboam (1975), for example, have shown that good readers are faster and more accurate than poor readers in applying spelling-to-sound correspondence rules when this is measured by their ability to pronounce (i.e. read aloud) nonsense and low frequency words. Using memory tasks, Liberman *et al.* (1977) and Mark *et al.* (1977) found that phonological similarity of letters and words had a greater influence upon the recognition and recall performance of their good than their poor readers. Finally, in an experiment using a lexical decision task (Barron, 1978b), good readers were slower on pseudo-homophone non-words like BAUL, which sound but are not spelled like words, than on control items like NAUL, which neither sound nor are spelled like words. The poor readers, however, did not differ on these two types of items. In addition, the use of a phonological strategy in lexical access in this experiment appeared to be related to how rapidly a phonological code could be generated by applying spelling-to-sound rules as the children with large pseudohomophone effects also tended to pronounce quickly lists of non-words.

Although the results of these studies suggest that there may be a relationship between reading skill and strategies of lexical access, particularly in the use of a phonological strategy, the visual-orthographic and phonological information in printed words has not been manipulated independently within the same task. Experiment 1 was carried out by Judith Langer for her Master's thesis at the University of Guelph with this goal in mind. Langer (1977) attempted to separate the visual-spatial characteristics of orthographic structure from its relationships with sound by varying the positional and sequential constraints on letters and letter clusters in words independently of their spelling regularity. She used a lexical decision task, and although this task does not require complete semantic processing of a word, its logic requires that the internal lexicon be consulted and Meyer and Schvaneveldt (1971) and Neely (1977) have obtained semantic priming effects with it.

Based on the evidence presented above, it might be expected that good readers could generate efficiently a phonological code by applying spelling-to-sound rules rapidly and accurately. Therefore, the phono-logical code should have the predominant influence on their lexical access. This would be indicated by subjects being faster and more accurate on regular than irregular words since the phonological code would be more likely to correspond to a phonological entry in the lexicon for regular (e.g. PINE) than irregular (e.g. BROAD) words. The extra time required to process the irregular words might be taken up by a 'spelling check' of the visual-orthographic code when the phonological code failed to match a phonological entry in the lexicon (e.g. Coltheart *et al.*, 1977; Davelaar *et al.*, 1978; Rubenstein *et al.*, 1971). Errors on the irregular words might arise from a failure of this spelling check process.

On the other hand, it might be expected that the poor readers would be relatively inefficient at generating a phonological code. Therefore, the visual-orthographic code should have the predominant influence on their lexical access. This would be indicated by subjects being faster and more accurate on words with high (e.g. THEME, COVER) than low (e.g. EMPTY, EIGHTH) summed single letter and bigram positional frequency values as well as by the absence of a spelling regularity effect. Single letter positional frequency refers to the frequency with which an individual letter appears in a particular letter position in a word of a specific length. In exactly the same way, bigram positional frequency refers to pairs of letters. Both frequency counts (Mayzner and Tresselt, 1965) are closely related and investigators (e.g. Gibson *et al.*, 1970; McClelland and Johnston, 1977; M. Mason, 1975; Massaro *et al.*, 1979) have argued that they are gross measures of visual-orthographic structure as they capture some of the positional and sequential constraints on letters and letter clusters in printed words and they can influence the visual processing of words.

2.1 *Method*

2.1.1 *Subjects.* In order to select the good and poor readers, 156 grade six children (11–12-year-olds) were given the comprehension sub-test of the Gates-MacGinitie Reading Test and the non-verbal section of the Canadian Lorge-Thorndike Intelligence Test. Using a linear regression procedure similar to that employed by Willows (1974), good readers were defined as children who obtained reading scores which were at least one-half of a standard deviation (SD = 10) above what would be predicted on the basis on their non-verbal IQ scores. Poor readers, on the other hand, were defined as children whose reading scores were at least one-half of a standard deviation below what would be predicted on the basis of their non-verbal IQs. Using this procedure and attempting to match on IQ, a total of 24 good and 24 poor readers were selected who differed significantly in their reading scores (60 and 44, respectively; t(46) = 12.93, p < 0.001), but not in their non-verbal IQ scores (102 and 103, respectively). Fourteen of the good and 12 of the poor readers were female and none of the children had been identified by their schools as having severe reading or learning disabilities. These groups of readers were similar in age, reading skill and IQ to those used by Barron (1978b).

2.1.2 *Materials.* In order to provide an empirical basis for deciding whether a word was regular or irregular in its conformity to spelling-to-sound correspondence rules, 340 words were presented to 30 undergraduates and graduate students at the University of Guelph. They were asked to imagine that they were learning English as a second language (all 30 were native speakers) and to decide whether or not they would have any difficulty in arriving at the correct pronunciation of a word the first time they read it aloud. They were further instructed to assume that they had learned the rules of pronunciation, but had not learned the actual pronunciation of any particular word. A word was classified as regular if at least 22 out of 30 subjects agreed that they would have no difficulty in pronouncing it while a word as classified as irregular if at least 22 out of 30 subjects indicated that they would have difficulty in pronouncing it.

TABLE 1   Words used in Experiment 1

Regular-high Positional freq.		Irregular-high positional freq.		Regular-low positional freq.		Irregular-low positional freq.	
fact	spend	none	words	deal	track	echo	knife
pine	state	lose	cover	drum	stuff	half	weight
list	sheet	love	marine	held	depth	pier	caught
case	slave	whom	circle	less	cloth	busy	honour
size	shade	talk	beauty	maid	broke	folk	breath
bent	tribe	walk	police	club	least	sign	knight
wide	trust	wool	league	inch	spear	bury	autumn
felt	lumber	gone	friend	crop	apart	rough	steady
main	winner	foot	couple	orbit	branch	climb	island
theme	throne	route	listen	offer	banana	flood	eighth
scale	rubber	whose	spread	silly	speech	earth	rhythm
press	market	tough	leather	fresh	escape	giant	meadow
share	member	scene	service	empty	invent	sugar	circuit
stole	strong	field	foreign	grain	expect	blood	freight
shelf	context	chalk	machine	clock	picnic	broad	unknown

The sum of the single letter and bigram positional frequency values (Mayzner and Tresselt, 1965) was calculated for each word. Then each of the two groups of regular and irregular words chosen by the above procedure was sub-divided into groups which were high and low in these frequency values. Additional constraints imposed by equating the items in word frequency (Carroll *et al.*, 1971, grade six norms) and word length (three to seven letters) resulted in four groups of 30 words shown in Table 1. These groups were regular-high summed single letter and bigram positional frequency (e.g. WIDE, TRUST), irregular-high (e.g. WHOSE, POLICE), regular-low (DEPTH, APART) and irregular-low (BUSY, EIGHTH). Finally, a non-word was generated for each word by changing one letter (vowel or consonant) in the word so that word length and summed single letter and bigram positional frequency values were preserved between the words and non-words (e.g. FACT to FICT). The non-words were all pronounceable and the location of the changed letter in the word was varied across letter position. Average frequency and word length information about the words and non-words is presented in Table 2.

TABLE 2   Word length and frequency characteristics of the words and non-words in Experiment 1

Word type	Mean summed letter positional frequency (words)		Mean word frequency	Mean number of letters per word	Mean summed letter positional frequency (non-words)	
	Single letter	Bigram			Single letter	Bigram
Regular-high positional frequency	1958	234	65	5.2	1954	228
Irregular-high positional frequency	1907	226	65	5.2	1885	190
Regular-low positional frequency	1136	131	58	5.0	1146	101
Irregular-low positional frequency	1083	94	63	5.1	1075	98

2.1.3 *Procedure.* The words were presented to the children individually on slides in lower case type. Each child was instructed to press a button when they were ready to see a word. Pressing the button resulted in the projector shutter opening, a timer starting and the word being displayed (maximum horizontal visual angle = 2.67 degrees). If the item was a word, the children were instructed to move a small lever horizontally towards the word *yes* printed on the table in front of them. If it was not a word, they moved the lever towards the word *no* printed on the table. Subjects were told whether they were correct or incorrect, but not how fast they were. Approximately 20 practice trials were given in order to acquaint the children with the procedure and apparatus. The words and non-words were presented in random order with the constraint that no more than four instances of one kind of response could appear in succession.

2.2 *Results*

The means of the median correct response times are presented in Tables 3 and 4. The results in Table 3 suggest that the good readers were using predominantly a phonological strategy in lexical access, while the

TABLE 3 Means of median response times (in msec) and mean percentage errors (in parentheses) for the good and poor readers on the regular and irregular words in Experiment 1

| | Spelling regularity | | |
	Regular	Irregular	Difference
Good reader	1108 (4.5)	1137 (8.0)	−29 (−3.5)
Poor reader	1196 (8.9)	1177 (14.9)	+19 (−6.0)

TABLE 4 Means of median response times (in msec) and mean percentage errors (in parentheses) for the good and poor readers on the high and low single letter positional frequency words in Experiment 1

| | Single letter positional frequency | | |
	High	Low	Difference
Good reader	1131 (6.0)	1115 (6.4)	+16 (−0.4)
Poor reader	1161 (12.2)	1213 (11.5)	−52 (+0.7)

poor readers were not. The good readers were significantly faster on regular than irregular words, $t(23) = 2.12$, $p < 0.05$, whereas the poor readers were slower, though not significantly. The results presented on Table 4, on the other hand, suggest that the poor readers were using predominantly a visual-orthographic strategy in lexical access, while the good readers were not. The poor readers were significantly faster on the high than the low single letter and bigram positional frequency words, $t(23) = 3.60$, $p < 0.005$, whereas the good readers were slower, though not significantly. Significant reader by spelling regularity, $F(1,46) = 4.46$, $p < 0.05$, (see Table 3) and reader by positional frequency, $F(1,46) = 10.32$, $p < 0.005$, (see Table 4) interactions were consistent with the above results. The other interactions were not significant. Finally, consistent with the results on the words, the poor readers were faster on high than low positional frequency non-words. $t(23) = 2.00$, $p < 0.05$, (one-tailed), but the good readers did not differ significantly on these items.

The percent error data are also presented in Tables 3 and 4 and show that the good readers made fewer errors than the poor readers and that both groups made more errors on the irregular than the regular words. These observations are supported by the fact that the main effects of reader, $F(1,46) = 15.34$, $p < 0.001$, and spelling regularity, $F(1,46) = 30.70$, $p < 0.001$, were the only significant effects in the analysis of variance on the error data. The spelling regularity effect for the errors suggests that the poor readers may have been able to generate occasionally a phonological code which influenced lexical access.

Although the poor readers appear to have been able to decrease their response times on the irregular words at the expense of increasing their errors, the correlation between errors and response times was not significant in this or in any other conditions in the experiment. Furthermore, when the errors were used as covariate, the difference in response time between the regular and irregular words remained nonsignificant for the poor readers.

2.3 *Discussion*

Consistent with earlier findings and confirming the hypotheses, these results suggest that the good readers used a strategy in lexical access which was predominantly phonological as their response times were influenced by spelling regularity, but not by positional frequency. Poor readers, on the other hand, appeared to be using a strategy which was predominantly visual-orthographic as their response times were influenced by positional frequency, but not spelling regularity. A phonological code is likely to be generated more slowly than a visual-orthographic code as the extra step of applying spelling-to-sound rules is required (Coltheart *et al.*, 1977). The spelling regularity effect obtained for the good readers might indicate that they can generate a phonological code more rapidly than the poor readers, thus increasing the likelihood that this code might influence lexical access. In order to investigate this possibility, 20 out of 24 of the children in each of the good and poor reader groups were required to read aloud (i.e. pronounce) the non-words used in the present experiment. This tests ability to apply spelling-to-sound correspondence rules. The procedure and apparatus were the same as in Langer (1977), except that the subjects pronounced the words and the timer was stopped by a voice activated relay. The poor readers were slower than the good readers on the pronunciation task (1414 vs 901 msec, t(38) = 3.56, p < 0.001) and made more errors 10.6 vs 5.8 percent, although this latter difference was not significant. Furthermore, the pronunciation response times were negatively and significantly correlated with the magnitude of the spelling regularity effect, r = −0.28, p < 0.05 (one-tailed). These results indicate that the use of a phonological strategy in lexical access is related to fast application of spelling-to-sound correspondence rules and are consistent with the results of Barron (1978b). The pronunciation response times were also correlated with the magnitude of the positional frequency effect. A significant positive correlation was obtained, r = +0.34, p < 0.05, suggesting that the use of a visual-orthographic strategy in lexical access is related to slow application of spelling-to-sound correspondence rules.

It is possible that the relative slowness of the poor readers in generating a phonological code may have contributed to their using primarily a visual-orthographic strategy in the present task. This does not, however, imply that the poor readers would always use this strategy as task characteristics might be changed so that it would be easier for them to use a phonological strategy than in the present experiment. Although the good readers used primarily a phonological strategy in the present task, the fact that they did not show an effect of positional frequency does not imply that they are deficient in using a visual-orthographic strategy as appears to be the case with some types of developmental and acquired dyslexia (e.g. Boder, 1971, 1973; Marshall and Newcombe, 1973). In fact, as discussed earlier, good readers must use some visual-orthographic information. Therefore, the good readers' failure to show a positional frequency effect in the present experiment may merely reflect their success with a phonological strategy in lexical access, rather than any deficiency in their use of a visual-orthographic strategy. In any case, the hypothesis is warranted that the good readers may be better able than the poor readers to use efficiently both visual-orthographic and phonological strategies in obtaining access to the internal lexicon.

3 Experiment 2: Spelling regular and irregular words

As discussed previously, it is likely that spelling is also influenced by the use of phonological and visual-orthographic strategies. Consider how these two strategies might be used in a spelling dictation task in which subjects are required to write down the spelling of a word presented auditorily. Subjects might use a phonological strategy and produce the spelling of a word by applying sound-to-spelling rules without consulting the word's corresponding visual-orthographic entry in the lexicon. On the other hand, subjects might use a visual-orthographic strategy and retrieve visual-orthographic information stored in the lexicon in order to produce a spelling. As in reading, the success of these two strategies depends on whether the words are regular or irregular. Either strategy can be used if the words are regular, but only the visual-orthographic strategy would appear to be successful in spelling irregular words. Accordingly, regular and irregular words can be used to assess the strategies subjects use in spelling. If a phonological strategy is predominant, then they should be more accurate on regular than irregular words, whereas they should be equally accurate on the two types of words if a visual-orthographic strategy is predominant.

The type of errors subjects make may also be important in analysing whether they are using visual-orthographic or phonological strategies in spelling (e.g. Nelson and Warrington, 1974). Phonologically accurate errors (e.g. spelling DEBT as DET) might be particularly informative in revealing the use of a phonological strategy as they can indicate the extent to which subjects are relying solely on sound-to-spelling correspondence rules and are not consulting visual-orthographic entries in their lexicon.

Subjects who differ in reading skill might also differ in their use of visual-orthographic and phonological strategies in spelling. Poor readers, who are deficient in the use of spelling-to-sound rules, might also be deficient in sound-to-spelling rules; consequently, they might tend to use mainly a visual-orthographic strategy in spelling. On the other hand, most spelling errors appear to be phonologically based (e.g. Frith, 1978a). Furthermore, Bryant and Bradley (Chapter 16) and Frith 1978b, 1979) have shown that poor and beginning readers, as well as good and older readers, make a large number of phonologically plausible errors in spelling. Therefore, it might be expected that both groups of readers would tend to use mainly a phonological strategy in spelling. Alternatively, the poor readers might be less likely than the good readers to use also a visual orthographic strategy just as they seem less likely to use both visual-orthographic and phonological strategies in reading. If this was the case, then both groups of readers should make more phonologically accurate errors on the irregular than the regular words, but the size of the difference should be greater for the poor readers.

Experiment 2 was carried out in order to examine these possible ways in which the good and poor readers might differ in their use of visual-orthographic and phonological strategies in spelling. Since the strategies used in reading might be related to those used in spelling, the good and poor readers were selected so that they differed in the speed and accuracy with which they could pronounce non-words. Experiment 1 and Barron (1978b) suggest that the use of a visual-orthographic strategy alone or in combination with a phonological strategy in reading depends on how quickly subjects can generate a phonological code by applying spelling-to-sound rules. Regular and irregular words were presented to the good and poor readers in a spelling dictation task. Following a procedure used by Farnham-Diggory and Simon (1975), a distraction task was interpolated between the presentation of the word and writing it down in order to make the spelling task more demanding.

3.1 *Method*

3.1.1 *Subjects*. Twenty-four good readers and 24 poor readers were used. They were made up of children in grades four, five and six (ages 9–12) and chosen from a larger group of children (N = 70). The two groups of readers had identical mean grade levels (5.2) and ages (10.8 years) and did not differ significantly in their non-verbal IQs as measured by the non-verbal section of the Canadian Lorge-Thorndike Intelligence Test (IQ = 113 for the good and 111 for the poor readers). The good readers were, however, significantly faster (7.1 vs 10.8 sec per list, $t(46) = 3.49$, $p < 0.001$) and more accurate (0.7 vs 4.2 errors out of 24 possible errors, $t(46) = 5.44$, $p < 0.001$) than the poor readers in their ability to pronounce four lists of six nonsense words (administered at the beginning of the experiment). None of the children were identified by their school as having severe reading or learning disabilities and 15 of the good readers and 13 of the poor readers were males.

3.1.2 *Materials*. Twenty regular and twenty irregular words were used. The irregular words were selected from the words reported by Venezky (1970), Langer (1977) and Baron and Strawson (1976) on the grounds that they represented a relatively small class of exceptions to the spelling-to-sound rules (e.g. PROVE) described by Venezky (1970) and/or they contained 'silent letters' which did not have any obvious morphemic basis (e.g. SWORD). The regular words, on the other hand, were chosen so as to conform to spelling-to-sound correspondence rules (e.g. GLOBE), yet still be similar to the irregular words in word frequency and length. The two groups of 20 words were each divided into two alternative lists of ten words which were approximately equal in word frequency (they ranged from 22 to 24 on the grade six norms of Carroll *et al.*, 1971) and word length (all four lists averaged 5.4 letters). The two lists of 10 irregular words were COUGH, LAUGH, ADJUST, BUSINESS, FLOOD, SWEAT, SWORD, KNEE, POLICE, YACHT and PLAID, THUMB, CANOE, CIRCUIT, PROVE, DOUBT, ISLAND, AUTUMN, TONGUE, DEBT, respectively. The two lists of regular words were STABLE, TWELVE, PROOF, BONUS, BRAVE, GLOBE, STRIKE, HERO, PRIZE, TENDER and CHURCH, GRACE, BLEED, TOOTH, THRONE, SMOOTH, SWEET, ADVICE, SMOKE, THEME, respectively.

3.1.3 *Procedure.* The subjects were tested individually. They heard each word they were required to spell on a tape recorder. Presentation of the word was followed immediately by a 15 second interpolated task which involved copying matrices of spatially transformed upper case letters (Kolers, 1969) into their correct spatial orientation. This task was fairly demanding and possibly involved both visual and verbal processing. Immediately following the end of the interpolated task, the subjects were instructed to spell the word they had heard by writing it down. After the subjects had spelled a list of words, they were shown the words visually and instructed to read them by pronouncing each item aloud. Each subject spelled one list of 10 regular and one list of 10 irregular words. The two alternative lists for each type of word, the order of the words within a list and the order of word list types (i.e. regular, irregular) were all counterbalanced across subjects.

3.2 *Results*

The subjects spelling errors were classified into four mutually exclusive categories: listening, omission, 'other' and phonologically accurate errors. Only those words which the subjects could read aloud correctly (97.5%) were used in computing the percent errors in each category. Therefore, differences in reading accuracy cannot be used to explain differences in spelling accuracy.

Spelling errors that appeared to be based upon misperceptions of words were classified as listening errors. They were relatively easy to classify as subjects almost always produced spellings that were words rather than non-words and they were often phonologically similar to the word that was presented (e.g. PIES for the word PRIZE). The percentage of listening errors ranged between 8.7 and 10.6% of the correctly pronounced words across conditions and there were no significant differences between the regular and irregular words or groups. Therefore, any subsequent differences in spelling accuracy between the type of words or the readers cannot be attributed to differences in listening accuracy.

The omission errors involved instances in which the subject failed to write down any response at all. This category of error ranged between 1.8 and 3.3% of the correctly pronounced words across conditions and appeared to originate from the subjects simply forgetting the word they were required to spell during the interpolated activity interval between presentation of the word and writing it down. Again, there were no significant differences. The category of 'other' errors included several semantic errors, but they were not analysed as they involved less than one percent of the correctly pronounced words.

The phonologically accurate errors are presented in Table 5. These errors ranged between 5.8 and 27.5% of the correctly pronounced

TABLE 5   Mean percentage of phonologically accurate spelling errors for the good and poor readers on the regular and irregular words in Experiment 2

| | Type of word | | |
	Regular	Irregular	Difference
Good reader	5.8	11.9	−6.1
Poor reader	9.3	27.5	−18.2

words across conditions and are, of course, the error category of major interest in this experiment. Table 5 shows that the poor readers made 18.2% more errors on the irregular than the regular words, while the difference between the two types of words was only 6.1% for the good readers resulting in a significant reader by spelling regularity interaction, $F(1,46) = 7.36$, $p < 0.01$. The difference between the regular and irregular words was significant for both the good, $t(23) = 2.45$, $p < 0.025$, and the poor, $t(23) = 4.85$, $p < 0.001$, readers. This interaction is consistent with the prediction that although both groups of readers use predominantly a phonological strategy in spelling, the poor readers are less likely than the good readers to use also a visual-orthographic strategy. Additional evidence consistent with this prediction comes from the fact that the poor readers made a significantly higher percentage of errors than the good readers on the irregular words, $t(46) = 3.84$, $p < 0.001$, which cannot be spelled accurately by a phonological strategy. However, the difference between the two groups of readers on the regular words, where either a phonological or a visual-orthographic strategy can be used, was not significant. Finally, the difference between the two alternative lists of regular and irregular words was not significant for either group of readers.

An analysis of those phonologically accurate errors which only involve 'silent letter' omissions (e.g. omitting the *b* in DEBT) might provide a more direct way of evaluating the poor readers' tendency not to use a visual-orthographic strategy and to rely upon a phonological strategy in spelling irregular words. It would be expected that the poor readers would make higher percentage of silent letter omission errors on the irregular words than the good readers. Accordingly, 11 out of 20 irregular words were selected for this analysis on the basis of having silent letters with no obvious phonological or morphological function. These words were ADJUST, SWORD, BUSINESS, KNEE, YACHT, THUMB, DEBT, DOUBT, ISLAND, AUTUMN and TONGUE. A mis-spelling was counted as a silent letter omission error only if the critical silent letter or letter cluster was deleted without any other letters being deleted or changed. Again, the percentage error scores were based on the number of words pronounced correctly by each subject. Consistent with the prediction, poor readers made a significantly higher percentage of silent letter omission errors (19.1%) than the good readers (7.1%), $t(46) = 2.68$, $p < 0.025$. In order to determine whether or not this difference was specific to the silent letter omission errors, the two groups of readers were also compared on the percentage of phonologically inaccurate spelling errors they made on the same silent letter irregular words. It was expected that the readers would not differ as phonologically inaccurate errors could arise from a failure of either or both visual-orthographic and phonological strategies, whereas silent letter omission errors appear to arise specifically from using a phonological, but not a visual-orthographic strategy. As predicted, the difference (3.5%) between the good (18.3%) and poor (21.8%) readers was not significant.

3.3 *Discussion*

The results of experiment two indicate that good and poor readers also differ in the strategies they use in spelling. Poor readers appear more likely than good readers to rely solely on a phonological strategy in spelling as they make more phonologically accurate errors on the irregular than the regular words compared to the good readers. They also make more silent letter omission errors on the irregular words than the good readers. The good readers, on the other hand, are more likely to use a visual-orthographic as well as a phonological strategy in spelling.

It might be argued that the subjects made more phonologically accurate errors on the irregular than the regular words because the irregular words were less familiar than the regular words, particularly for the poor readers. The regular and irregular words, however, were equated in frequency and there were not any differences between them in listening or omission errors. Furthermore, both the good and poor readers could read aloud (i.e. pronounce) all of the words which they mis-spelled. Since the irregular words appear to require a visual-orthographic entry in the lexicon in order to be pronounced, it is unlikely that the failure to spell the irregular words can be attributed to a lack of familiarity. It might be concluded, therefore, that the poor readers made more phonologically accurate errors than the good readers in spelling irregular words because they failed to use the visual-orthographic information in their lexicons which they must have used in reading those same words.

There are at least two possible reasons why the poor readers might be less likely than the good readers to use a visual-orthographic strategy during spelling. One is that the poor readers may have inadequate visual-orthographic entries in their lexicons. This does not seem very likely, at least for the irregular words in the present experiment, because adequate visual-orthographic entries are implied by the fact that both groups of readers could pronounce all of the words they mis-spelled. A second reason may be related to the characteristics of the visual-orthographic entries themselves. Given the fallibility of rule-generated spellings, it is difficult to understand why subjects would ever use a phonological strategy in spelling. It would appear to be much more efficient for them to use always a visual-orthographic strategy and produce a spelling based upon information retrieved from the visual-orthographic entry in the lexicon. It is possible, however, that the visual-orthographic entries do not actually have procedures for producing spellings as they may only influence spelling indirectly through a checking process. This checking process might operate by first compairing rule generated spellings against visual-orthographic entries in the lexicon and then correcting those spellings which fail the comparison test. Phonologically accurate errors and silent letter omission errors might arise when the checking mechanism failed to operate and this failure might be more likely to occur for the poor than the good readers. It is difficult, however, to distinguish this model from one in which visual-orthographic production processes are simply less efficient than those involved in generating spellings by applying sound-to-spelling correspondence rules. Both models would appear to be able to account for the results of the present experiment. Perhaps all that can be concluded at this point is that the reader groups appear more likely to differ in how they use the visual-orthographic information in the lexicon during spelling rather than in the adequacy of the lexical information itself.

4 Overview

Taken together, the results of these two experiments suggest that children who differ in reading skill also differ in the relative predominance with which they use visual-orthographic and phonological strategies in reading and spelling. Poor readers appear more likely to rely on a visual-orthographic strategy in reading and on a phonological strategy in spelling. Good readers, on the other hand, appear more likely to use both strategies in reading and in spelling.

The fact that the visual-orthographic strategy is used by both groups of readers in reading and the phonological strategy is used by both groups of readers in spelling suggests the possibility of an asymmetry between the strategies used in reading and those used in spelling. This asymmetry appears to be particularly marked in the performance of the poor readers as they seem to rely mainly upon a visual-orthographic strategy in reading and upon a phonological strategy in spelling. This is consistent with the conclusion of Frith (1978b, 1979) and Bryant and Bradley (Chapter 16) as they also found that children who tend to use a visual-orthographic strategy in reading also tend to use a phonological strategy in spelling.

Since good readers appear more likely to use both visual-orthographic and phonological strategies in reading and in spelling, it might be worthwhile to consider what roles a phonological strategy might play in reading and a visual-orthographic strategy might play in spelling. In reading, a phonological strategy might have several functions. One of the most obvious is that it allows children to learn new words as they can use spelling-to-sound correspondence rules to generate phonological codes which correspond to phonological entries in their lexicons. A phonological strategy might also function as a device for remembering the wording of a sentence during the process of comprehension (e.g. Kleiman, 1975; Levy, 1978), particularly when the material is difficult. It may even have a role in lexical access with irregular words as a phonological strategy might be used to focus memory access processes on only the letter or letters in a word which are responsible for the mismatch between the phonological and the visual-orthographic codes (e.g.

the *oa* in BROAD). Finally, in learning to read, a phonological strategy might even influence the acquisition of a visual-orthographic strategy. The process of learning spelling-to-sound correspondence rules might increase the likelihood that children would attend to the sequential and positional regularities of English orthography, rather than to just the information about word shape and the initial and final letters of a word. In spelling, it appears that the primary function of the visual-ortho-graphic strategy is to provide a means of spelling words which are exceptions to rule generated English spellings.

In general, a phonological strategy in reading (see also Underwood, 1978) and a visual-orthographic strategy in spelling might be viewed as serving the function of providing back-up strategies when the visual-orthographic strategy fails in reading or the phonological strategy fails in spelling, respectively. It is obvious that the phonological strategy may be particularly vulnerable to failure in spelling with, for example, irregular words and homophones since these items are unlikely to be spelled accurately by applying sound-to-spelling correspondence rules. In reading, however, the conditions whereby a visual-orthographic strategy might fail are less obvious. It is possible, however, that it may be vulnerable to failure when readers are deprived of contextual information, particularly if the words are relatively unfamiliar.

The arguments and evidence suggesting that visual-orthographic and phonological strategies may serve different functions in reading and spelling can be viewed as providing a rationale for why children might not benefit from reading and spelling programs in which too much emphasis is placed upon phonics instructions over look–say (i.e. sight–word) instruction, or vice versa. Phonics instruction might be inter-preted as providing them with the ability to use a phonological strategy and look–say instruction as providing them with the ability to use a visual-orthographic strategy. Consequently, too much emphasis on one or the other strategy might encourage children to over-specialise in one strategy and deter them from acquiring the other, and the various functions which go with it. Faulty instruction, however, may not be the only reason why children who are having trouble with reading and spelling are less likely to use both visual-orthographic and phonological strategies in reading and in spelling. A phonological strategy, for example, may be particularly hard to acquire for children who have difficulty segmenting the sounds making up words in spoken language, let alone in written language (e.g. Bradley and Bryant, 1978; Liberman *et al.*, 1977; Savin, 1972).

Finally, some qualifications should be acknowledged in interpreting the results of the present experiments. Although they can be interpreted in terms of strategies which rely only upon visual-orthographic and phonological information in words, there are certainly other levels of linguistic information represented in printed English. Graphemic, syntactic, morphemic, semantic and etymological information, for example, are also represented (e.g. Smith, Chapter 2; Smith and Baker, 1976) and subjects may be able to use strategies which employ one or more of these levels of information in reading and spelling. The visual-orthographic and phonological strategies identified in the present experiments may also involve the use of other levels of linguistic information, and with varying degrees of success. Consequently, a comprehensive theory of reading and spelling will have to include a characterisation of all of the levels of information in words as well as strategies for their use.

Acknowledgements

This research was supported by grants from the National Sciences and Engineering Research Council (A9782) and from the Social Sciences and Humanities Research Council of Canada (General Research Grant, Research Advisory Board, University of Guelph). Portions of this paper were written while I was on sabbatical leave at the Department of Experimental Psychology, University of Oxford. I thank the Department for use of their facilities and the SSHRCC Leave Fellowship program for financial support. I gratefully acknowledge the assistance of Gordon Briscoe, Christine Brown, Peter Henderson and Collen MacFadden in carrying out this research and the co-operation of the children as well as their principals, teachers and parents. I also thank Peter Bryant, Leslie Henderson, Charles Hulme and Sue Robertson for their comments on earlier drafts of this paper.

10

Visual Factors in Spelling

YVETTE J. TENNEY   *Department of Psychology and Social Relations, Harvard University, U.S.A.*

215

1 When does a word look right?

In spite of years of spelling tests in school, most English-speaking adults, from time to time, are plagued by indecision about how to spell a word. In an examination of five thousand college English compositions, Alper (1942) found that over one thousand different words were mis-spelled, usually in one particular 'hard spot' in the word. The majority of errors made sense phonetically and were not avoidable on the basis of conventional sound-to-spelling rules. They involved confusion over ambiguous vowel sounds as well as completely phonetic substitutions. These results, which are also typical of children (Masters, 1927; Simon and Simon, 1973), pose a problem. How does a good speller know that the correct spelling is HARASS and not HARRASS, ECSTASY rather than ECSTACY, NICKEL as opposed to NICKLE, SYPHILIS and not SYPHILLIS, TRANSCENDENCE rather than TRANSCENDANCE?

One possibility is that good spellers make use of subtle regularities in English orthography based on deeper level linguistic factors rather than sound-letter relationships. Chomsky (1970) has shown that uncertainty about the spelling of a word can be resolved by referring to related words e.g. SIGN–SIGNAL. This strategy, which has been known for some time (Alper, 1942), clarifies the spelling of TRANSCENDENCE (TRANSCENDENCE–TRANSCENDENTAL), but not of HARASS. A recent attempt to devise a complete set of rule-like algorithms precise enough to enable a computer to generate the spelling of any word from its sound thus far has not yielded any practical consequences (Simon and Simon, 1973).

The failure to discover sufficient regularities in spelling suggests that good spellers rely upon something else in addition to sound-to-spelling rules and linguistic strategies. The idea that spelling depends in part upon a process of visual recognition, which is developed in the course of reading, is frequently mentioned in discussions of orthography (Hendrickson, 1967; Mackworth and Mackworth, 1974) and figures prominently in a recent information processing model of spelling (Simon, 1976; Simon and Simon, 1973). As a practical consequence, one is advised to write down possible spellings for a word when in doubt in order to decide which one 'looks right'. Teachers, according to this position, should not expect children to learn to spell words that are not part of their reading vocabulary (Simon, 1976).

Although this view derives from common experience, it has not as yet been subjected to rigorous experimental scrutiny. The bulk of the evidence comes from studies of reading rather than of spelling and concerns the effects of visual configuration on word identification. If it can be demonstrated that readers are sensitive to the overall shape or *Gestalt* of a word, then indirect support would be provided for the notion that a correctly spelled word actually 'looks right'.

Several experiments involving tachistoscopic word recognition (Coltheart and Freeman, 1974; Mewhort, 1966) or same–different matching judgments (Pollatsek *et al.*, 1975; Schindler *et al.*, 1974; Well *et al.*, 1975) have shown that disrupting the familiar pattern of letters in a word, for example by alternating the case of the letters so that every other letter is capitalised, printing the words vertically instead of horizontally, rotating the word 180 degrees so that it appears inverted, or introducing gaps between the letters increases response latencies. In order to support the hypothesis that the disruption stems from inter-ference with the familiar visual pattern of the words and not just with the identification of individual letters, it is necessary to show that the manipulation does not have as large an effect on the identification of random strings of letters as it does on the processing of real words. This criterion was met in the case of alternating upper and lower case letters (Pollatsek *et al.*, 1975) and vertical writing (Well *et al.*, 1975), but may not apply to increased spacing (Schindler *et al.*, 1974) or 180 degree rotation (Well *et al.*, 1975). A more convincing case for the role of visual familiarity could be made if these manipulations were found to disrupt the processing of real words more than the processing of orthographically permissible pseudowords. This outcome was not obtained, however, in a study of case alternation (McClelland, 1976).

A different approach to the issue of whether the global appearance of a word helps to specify its meaning has been taken by Szumski (1974) and McClelland (1977). The rationale for these studies was as follows. If the visual configuration of a word contains useful information about its meaning, then subjects who are taught to associate arbitrary meanings with nonsense syllables should arrive at the meanings more quickly on a subsequent test if the words are presented in the same manner as they were during training than if their form is altered. The results of several experiments confirmed this prediction. Subjects who had learned the meaning of a word by hearing it pronounced took longer to verify the accuracy of a written statement containing the word than subjects who had been exposed to the written word during training. This difference was evident on the first couple of trials, but disappeared as subjects became familiar with the visual appearance of the word (Szumski, 1974). A similar detrimental effect on early trials was found when subjects were trained with words written with one kind of lettering (e.g. script) and were then tested with the words written with a different lettering (e.g. upper case print) (McClelland, 1977). In a related study, using real words which are normally capitalised or not, subjects took longer to read aloud an uncapitalised proper name than a capitalised name, while the reverse was true for matched words which were not proper nouns (Baron, 1977b). Altering the case of the first letter evidently disrupted the visual configuration of the word, making it more difficult to identify.

The evidence from the word perception literature, therefore, provides some support for the notion that the familiar configuration of a word plays a role in reading. One point of view, therefore, is that readers can respond to familiar English words either holistically or on the basis of orthographic or phonological analysis, depending upon the orthographic regularity of the word and on individual characteristics of the reader (Baron and Strawson, 1976). This position, however, remains open to controversy (Brooks, 1977; Pollatsek and Carr, 1979). The role of visual factors in spelling, by contrast, has been a relatively neglected topic of research. Investigations of spelling, in general, have tended to focus on correlates of individual differences in spelling and on the validity of different kinds of spelling tests. A few of these studies are relevant to the hypothesis under consideration.

Attempts to relate spelling ability to general cognitive characteristics provided no clear evidence that good spellers had a better visual memory than poor spellers (Hartmann, 1931), although good visualisers were found to be more successful than poor visualisers at avoiding at least one type of spelling error (Walker, 1974). Radakar (1963) was able to raise the spelling achievement of a group of children relative to a control group by training them to visualise words in interesting ways, such as imagining the letters to be nailed in place or flooded with illumination. Unfortunately it is difficult to separate the effects of visual imagery from the heightened motivation to learn to spell which the special training may have given the children. Ure (1969) invented a new pencil for left-handers, designed to circumvent the problem of the writing hand moving in the line of sight and obscuring the page from view. It was predicted that the spelling of these children would improve with use of the pencil because they would have a chance to become familiar with the visual *Gestalt* of the words as they wrote. Although some immediate improvement was seen, no long-range assessments were made. The immediate improvement may have occurred simply because the children were less likely to lose track of their place in the word.

A more direct way of approaching the problem might be to examine the relative difficulty of different kinds of spelling tests. The consistent finding that multiple choice tests are easier than regular dictation type tests (Moore, 1937; Nisbet, 1939; Northby, 1936) has sometimes been cited as evidence that subjects are able to judge whether a word 'looks right' or not. This comparison, however, confounds the effect of being given alternatives to choose from with the effects of being able to see how the spellings look. The superiority of written over oral spelling is also open to alternative explanation, since subjects may make errors when spelling aloud only because they have lost track of their place in the world.

In order to test the commonsense belief that the visual appearance of the alternatives helps to resolve spelling difficulties, I conducted two experiments in which the type of test, in this case multiple choice, was held constant while the physical appearance of the test words was varied. Because these experiments avoid some of the problems of interpretation of earlier studies and help to clarify the role of visual factors in spelling, they will be described in detail.

In the two experiments to be reported, subjects had to choose between the correct spelling and a common mis-spelling for a list of words. In the first experiment, the alternatives were either written in a normal way, so that subjects could compare how they looked, or they were written in a zigzag manner which distorted their appearance. In a second experiment, the alternatives were presented orally and subjects were either requested to write down both spellings before making their decision or were required to think about them. On the basis of the hypothesis that the familiar appearance aids in identifying the correct spelling of a word, it was expected that accuracy and confidence would be greater in the first condition than in the second condition for both experiments.

2 Experiment 1: Spelling alternatives seen in zigzag and normal writing

The purpose of the experiment was to compare the effects of the normal and distorted writing on the decision making process in spelling. The zigzag writing, like other kinds of distorted writing (e.g. Coltheart and Freeman, 1974), was of course expected to be more difficult to read (i.e. decode) than the normal writing. However, this difference was of no interest here. I was interested in how well subjects would be able to make the spelling decisions once they had decoded the alternatives. For this reason, it was important to ascertain that subjects could read each of the words and find the difference between the two alternatives in each case. In addition, estimates of decision time, beyond decoding time, were obtained for the two types of words by timing one group of subjects (the experimental group) on the entire task, which consisted of reading each word out loud, underlining the difference between the

TABLE 1   Two lists of words used in the construction of the normal and zigzag spelling tests

List 1		List 2	
nick*el*	(le)	insist*e*nce	(a)
chronic*le*	(al)	exerci*s*e	(z)
ses*a*me	(e)	prim*i*tive	(a)
consist*e*nt	(a)	remem*b*rance	(ber)
incompat*i*ble	(a)	rar*e*fied	(i)
stodg*y*	(ey)	att*o*rney	(ou)
f*o*rty	(ou)	ha*r*ass	(rr)
super*s*ede	(c)	correspond*e*nce	(a)
ber*s*erk	(z)	hemo*rr*hage	(rr)
*i*mitation	(mm)	privile*g*e	(dg)
independ*e*nt	(a)	absenc*e*	(s)
suppl*e*ment	(i)	ecsta*s*y	(c)
plag*i*arize	(e)	d*u*ly	(ue)
desp*e*rate	(a)	sep*a*rate	(e)
abstin*e*nce	(a)	marv*e*llous	(a)
*nine*ty	(nin)	cord*u*roy	(e)
dia*rr*hea	(rr)	zan*y*	(ey)
indel*i*ble	(a)	geni*us*	(ou)
proc*eed*	(ede)	naus*e*ous	(i)
flu*o*rescent	(ou)	cemet*e*ry	(a)
descr*i*be	(i)	reco*mm*end	(m)
si*l*houette	(ll)	vis*i*ble	(a)
bound*ary*	(ry)	hi*e*roglyphic	(y)
*c*rystal	(ch)	obsole*s*cent	(s)
questio*nn*aire	(n)	unf*or*eseeable	(or)
bro*cc*oli	(c)	av*o*cado	(a)
iso*sc*eles	(c)	syphi*l*is	(ll)
ne*c*essary	(cc)	categ*o*ry	(o)
		del*e*gate	(i)
con*s*ensus	(c)		
a*n*oint	(nn)	dorm*i*tory	(a)
commi*t*ment	(tt)	i*n*oculate	(nn)
frolic*k*ing	(c)	roo*mm*ate	(m)
to*nn*age	(n)	exist*e*nce	(a)
wit*h*held	(h)	zu*cc*hini	(cc)
transcend*e*nce	(a)	mi*s*spell	(s)
rep*e*tition	(i)	o*m*itted	(mm)

Letters in italics were replaced by the letters in parentheses to form the incorrect alternative for each word.

alternatives, and putting a check mark beside the correct spelling, and subtracting the time taken by a second group of subjects (the control group) to perform only the reading and underlining tasks. In this way, it was possible to examine the effects of the zigzag writing on the accuracy of the choices as well as on the time needed to make the decisions.

2.1 *Method*

2.1.1 *Subjects.* Subjects were thirty-two undergraduates, half males and half females. Half the subjects of each sex were randomly assigned to the experimental group and the remaining half were assigned to the control group. Each subject was seen individually and was given both conditions of the test in counterbalanced order, with the two lists also counterbalanced.

2.1.2 *Materials.* Two spelling lists of equal difficulty were compiled, each consisting of thirty-six words and thirty-six incorrect alternatives (see Table 1), which differed from the correct spelling in only one place in the word. Each of the alternatives was given as the correct spelling of the word by at least 10% of all pilot subjects on a written spelling test. Sources for the words included published lists of frequently mis-spelled words (Furness and Boyd, 1959; Kottmeyer, 1973; Masters, 1927) and spelling errors from recent student papers. Mis-spellings which reflected ignorance of conventional sound-to-spelling rules or confusion over legitimate homophones were not used. An attempt was also made to restrict the number of cases in which the correct spelling could be decided readily by linguistic analysis, e.g. the strategy of referring to a related word (as in SIGN–SIGNATURE). The last eight words of List 1 and the last seven of List 2 probably are of this type. However, whether or not such strategies are used depends on the degree of linguistic sophistication of the subjects and is therefore difficult to control.

The two spellings for each word were written one above the other, with the correct spelling randomly occurring on top for half the words in the list and on the bottom for the other half. In the zigzag condition, the letters which differed between the two alternatives were typed slightly darker than the rest, so that the choice would be clear. Examples are shown in Table 2 overleaf.

2.1.3 *Procedure.* Two practice tests, one untimed and one timed, preceded each of the tests. Subjects in the *experimental group* were instructed to do three things with each word: 1. Read the word out

loud. 2. Compare the two alternatives, letter by letter, and underline the
first pair of letters in corresponding positions which was different. 3. Put
a check mark next to the correct spelling. Subjects were told to work as
quickly as they could and were instructed to say 'ready' when they
reached the end of the list. The experimenter recorded the time using a
stop-watch. After each test, subjects were asked to estimate the number
of errors they had made. If a subject had mis-read any of the words or
underlined any of the alternatives incorrectly, the experimenter explained the mistake and allowed the subject to reconsider the spelling
decision.

TABLE 2   Sample test items as they appeared on the normal
and zigzag spelling tests

Normal test	Zigzag test
(1)	(1)
harrass	h **r** a s
	a **r** s
harass	h **r** s
	a a s
(2)	(2)
ecstacy	e s a y
	c t **c**
ecstasy	e s a y
	c t **s**
(3)	(3)
nickel	n c **e**
	i k **l**
nickle	n c **l**
	i k **e**

The procedure for the *control group* was exactly the same as for the
experimental group, except that control subjects were instructed to do
only two things with each word: read each word out loud and underline
the first letters which differed. They were told to work as quickly as
possible without taking time to decide which alternative was correct.
After each list, the experimenter pointed out any reading or underlining
errors which had occurred. After subjects had been timed on both the
zigzag and normal lists, they were given the two lists again and were
told to put a check mark beside the correct spelling for each word. They
were not timed on this task. After half the control subjects had been
tested, the procedure for the last task was changed so that the remaining

subjects read each word out loud again as they checked off the spellings. This change was introduced to check for possible mis-readings of the zigzag words seen for the second time. No errors occurred, however, confirming that subjects were able to decode all the words the second time through the list.

2.2 Results

Nineteen out of thirty-two subjects in the experiment had some difficulty deciphering the zigzag writing, as evidenced by the mis-pronunciations and word substitutions (e.g. INSTANCE for INSISTENCE) which occurred in both the experimental and control groups as the words were read aloud. These nineteen subjects made an average of one reading error apiece, excluding the words STODGY and TONNAGE which were also mispronounced on the normal lists. Subjects also had slightly more difficulty in finding the difference between the alternatives for the zigzag words as compared to the normal words. Ten subjects made an average of 1.4 underlining errors apiece with the zigzag words, while only four subjects made approximately one error apiece with the normal writing.

In order to prevent subjects from having to make spelling decisions about words which they could not decode, which would invalidate the comparison between the zigzag and normal words, subjects in the experimental group were allowed to change their spelling choices at the end of the test for the words which they had not decoded properly, after the correct pronunciation and underlinings were pointed out. Changes in spelling decisions were made following the correction of mis-readings one third of the time. Decoding errors for subjects in the control group were corrected prior to the spelling tests.

The average number of errors for the thirty-six words on the normal list, as compared to the zigzag list, was 9.56 vs 11.88 for the experimental group and 9.06 vs 12.06 for the control group. An analysis of variance with repeated measures on one factor revealed a significant main effect of list type [$F(1,30) = 15.34$, $p < 0.001$)], with no main effect of experimental vs control group ($F < 1$, $p > 0.05$), and no interaction between group and list type ($F < 1$, $p > 0.05$). The results of the analysis confirmed that subjects made significantly more errors with the zigzag writing than with the normal writing. Because the experimental and control groups did not differ from each other, and this factor did not interact with list type, data from both groups were combined in subsequent analyses.

The average number of errors which subjects estimated they had made was 5.59 for the normal list and 6.56 for the zigzag list. This difference proved to be significant [t(31) = 2.20, p <0.05]. It is interesting that the estimates, in both cases, were considerably lower than the actual number of errors made. In order to assess the effects of list type on subjects' ability to monitor their own performance, the absolute value of the discrepancy between observed and estimated errors was calculated for the two tests taken by each subject. The average size of the discrepancy proved to be significantly larger with the zigzag than with the normal writing [t(31) = 2.09, p <0.05]. Apparently subjects not only felt less confident about their decisions, but they also were less accurate in assessing the level of their performance in the zigzag condition compared to the normal condition.

The rationale for using the experimental and control groups in this experiment was to obtain separate measures of decoding and decision times for the two kinds of words. The average time taken by the experimental group to complete the decoding and spellings tasks combined was 5.63 seconds per word for the normal list and 9.27 seconds per word for the zigzag list. The time taken by the control group to perform only the decoding tasks was 3.48 and 6.58 seconds per word for the two lists respectively. Subtracting the time taken by the control group from the time taken by the experimental group yields a decision time of 2.15 seconds for each normal word and 2.69 seconds for each zigzag word. While it appears that subjects thought slightly longer about the spelling of the zigzag words than the normal words, this difference was only marginally significant [F(1,30) = 3.45, p <0.10, for the interaction between group and list type] and surprisingly small.

2.3 Discussion

The results indicated that subjects were able to make a decision on the basis of the appearance of the words in the normal condition, as predicted, and were hindered in their ability to decide on the correct spelling by the distorted appearance of the zigzag words. The opportunity to consider which spelling 'looked right' allowed subjects to give the correct answer for an average of two to three spelling questions which they otherwise would have missed. The zigzag words also lowered subjects' confidence and interfered with their ability to monitor the accuracy of their performance. Informal comments from subjects indicated that they tried to 'write the word out mentally', 'call up an impression of the word', and 'make the word look straight' in the zigzag condition. There was little evidence, however, that subjects spent more time thinking about the zigzag words, once they were decoded, than the normal words. This finding is surprising, as one would expect some loss of speed with the kinds of visualising processes that some subjects related.

One result which had not been anticipated was the difficulty which some of the subjects had simply in decoding the zigzag writing. In order to obtain additional evidence for the hypothesis that the opportunity to examine the visual appearance of a word facilitates spelling, and to avoid the decoding difficulties of the first experiment, a second study was conducted in which no attempt was made to interfere with the appearance of the word. Instead, subjects were given the opportunity either to think about the two alternatives for each word mentally or to write them down on paper before making the spelling decision. By asking subjects to report only one critical spot in the word, rather than spell the whole word aloud, the difficulty inherent in oral spelling tests, of having to keep track of one's place in the word (Brooks, 1968), was avoided.

3 Experiment 2: Is it useful to write down spelling alternatives?

3.1 Method

3.1.1 *Subjects.* Subjects were twenty-eight undergraduates, sixteen females and twelve males. Each served in both the writing and no writing conditions. The order in which the conditions were tested and the spelling tapes which were employed for the two conditions were counterbalanced across subjects.

3.1.2 *Materials.* Oral versions of the two multiple choice spelling lists used in Experiment 1 were recorded on tape. A female voice pronounced each word as it is usually spoken, rather than as it is spelled, and described the spelling alternatives in the following manner: NICKEL. Nickel begins *nick,* followed by *el* or *le*. NICKEL, is it *el* or *le*? The order in which the alternatives were named corresponded to the order in which they appeared on the written lists in Experiment 1.

3.1.3 *Procedure.* Subjects were instructed to listen to the spelling choices for the words and to say which alternative was correct. The experimenter stopped the tape after each word and waited for the subject's response. For the *writing condition,* subjects were instructed to write the word both ways on a sheet of paper before making a decision. They were told to be sure to write both alternatives for each word even when they were certain of the answer. Pencil and paper were removed for the *no writing condition,* and subjects were told simply to think as long as they liked before responding. In both conditions, subjects were required to give a confidence rating, on a scale of 1–5, along with each answer. Several practice examples preceded each of the tests. Subjects were instructed to ask for a replay of the tape whenever an item was not clear. At the end of each test, they were asked to estimate the number of errors they had made.

3.2 *Results*

The average number of errors for the thirty-six words on each test was 9.21 in the writing condition and 10.61 in the no writing condition. This difference, although small, was statistically significant [t(27) = 2.12, p <0.05]. Examination of the 1008 words written down by the subjects in the writing condition showed that an occasional subject failed to write the entire word for one or two items, stopping instead after the critical syllable. Otherwise, compliance with the instructions was excellent. In thirteen cases, or just 1% of the time, the writing revealed that subjects had not understood the choice they were asked to make (e.g. instead of HEMORRHAGE VS HEMORRAGE, a subject wrote HEMORRAGE–HEMORAGE and gave the incorrect answer *rr*). In 99% of the cases, however, the writing indicated a perfect understanding of the spelling question. It would therefore be reasonable to assume that the understanding of the task was equally high in the no writing condition.

Fifteen subjects asked for items to be replayed on the tape in the writing condition and fifteen asked for replays in the no writing condition. The average number of items which had to be repeated for these subjects was 1.9 and 1.7 respectively. Attentiveness, therefore, appeared to be similar in the two conditions.

The average number of errors which subjects estimated they had made was exactly 8.61 in both conditions. The more sensitive confidence rating for each item, introduced in this experiment, also failed to show a difference between conditions. The average confidence rating on a scale of 1–5, where 1 reflects greatest confidence, was 1.92 in the writing condition and 1.95 in the no writing condition. Confidence ratings were tabulated separately for items on which spelling errors were made. The average confidence rating for these items was 2.33 for the writing condition and 2.25 for the no writing condition, which was lower than the overall average, but similar for the two conditions. An analysis of the absolute size of the discrepancy between actual and estimated errors revealed that subjects were slightly better at assessing their performance when they wrote the alternatives than when they thought about them. This difference, however, proved to be only marginally significant (p <0.10).

3.3 *Discussion*

The results of the experiment provided further support for the hypothesis that the opportunity to inspect the visual appearance of potential spellings of a word facilitates spelling decisions. Subjects made one or two errors less, on the average, when they wrote down the alternatives than when they thought about them in their head. This difference was significant, though smaller than that found in Experiment 1. A comparison of the number of errors made in the two experiments revealed no difference between the normal condition in the first experiment and the writing condition in the present experiment (with average errors of 9.31 and 9.21, respectively) but slightly more errors in the zigzag condition of the first experiment than in the no writing condition in the second (11.97 vs 10.61), suggesting that the zigzag writing may have hindered visualisation. Neither of the differences between experiments proved to be significant, however, when analysed by tests for independent samples.

As in the first experiment, subjects tended to underestimate the number of errors they had made. The opportunity to inspect the spellings visually again reduced the discrepancy between the actual and estimated number of errors, but this time the difference between conditions was only marginally significant.

Subjects' spontaneous remarks and certain behaviors, such as asking for a pencil, closing their eyes, and writing in the air, suggested that they tried to visualise the appearance of the words in the no writing condition. While it is clear from the results of the experiment that visualising is not as effective as seeing–spelling alternatives, it is by no means certain to what extent, if any, visualisation can serve as an aid to spelling. Sartre (1966), in his philosophical work on imagination, took a negative position on this issue: 'It is for this reason that the spelling of a word cannot be decided without writing it. It is impossible for me to feel before the unreal object the change of physiognomy that the addition of one or several letters will bring'. An investigation of this question would depend upon a satisfactory means of inhibiting visualisation. While it was suspected that the zigzag condition of the first experiment might accomplish this end, there is no real evidence that it did.

4 General discussion

The results of the experiments reported in this chapter provide evidence for the heretofore unproven, but widely held belief that spelling difficulties can be resolved by seeing which of two alternative spellings 'looks right'. In particular, the results showed that imagining what two alternative spellings look like was less helpful than actually seeing them and that seeing them in unfamiliar form was less helpful than seeing them in familiar form. There could be many reasons why seeing undistorted words is helpful in spelling decisions. A particular strategy of using phonological and morphological rules was reported by a number of subjects. One pilot subject, a language major, was particularly adept at giving justifications for her decisions. For example, she knew that the correct spelling for COMMITMENT could not be COMMITTMENT because the word is obviously composed of the root *commit* and the suffix *ment*. She selected FROLICKING over FROLICING by noting that without the *k*, the *c* would have a soft sound, and picked CONSENSUS over CONCENSUS because of the related word CONSENT. This behavior suggests that inspecting a spelling alternative visually facilitates the decision making process because the speller can more easily experiment with the word, subdividing it into components and focusing attention on different parts, until the kinds of rules and regularities illustrated above can be discovered. Just imaging the word in one's head would not allow this freedom. Similarly, having to decode a word from zigzag writing would hinder experimenting with rules. In both cases, the effect would simply be one of increased cognitive load.

In order to explore this possibility, a separate analysis was made of those decisions which could be resolved by relatively well-known rules and those which could not. This classification of the words was based upon subjects' comments and on discussions of spelling regularities (Alper, 1942; Chomsky, 1970). For each word, a count was made of the number of times it had been mis-spelled when it was presented visually (i.e. in the normal or writing conditions) as compared to non-visually (i.e. in the zigzag or no writing conditions). Each of the fifteen words which seemed to be governed by relatively well-known linguistic or phonological rules (shown as the last eight words in List 1 and the last seven words in List 2) was compared with one or more of the remaining non-rule words, matched for frequency of errors in the visual conditions. The following prediction could then be tested. If subjects have difficulty in applying rules without actually seeing the undistorted words, then they should make more errors in the non-visual conditions on the rule-governed words than on non-rule words of comparable difficulty. This prediction received some support from the data. In the non-visual conditions, the rule-governed words were missed by one more subject, on the average, than the matched non-rule words. This difference did not prove to be significant. A reliable effect was found, however, when those rule-governed words which were missed by one third or more of the subjects in the visual conditions were eliminated from consideration. It made sense to eliminate these very difficult words since subjects did not seem to be able to apply the correct rules to them even under the most favorable circumstances. The seven remaining rule-governed words (REPETITION, DORMITORY, FROLICKING, OMITTED, ROOMMATE, EXISTENCE, COMMITMENT) were missed in the non-visual conditions by four more subjects, on the average, than the corresponding non-rule words ($\chi^2 = 5.97$, df $= 1$, p < 0.025). The results of this *post hoc* analysis suggest that the advantage of seeing a potential spelling can be attributed to the opportunity to make decisions based upon phonological or linguistic judgments rather than to purely visual factors. With some of the new techniques for studying individual differences in the knowledge of rules it should be possible to examine further this aspect of decision making in spelling. The work of Baron *et al.* (1978, Chapter 8) has shown that adults differ widely in their knowledge of the rules. Their findings suggest that some spellers make extensive use of this kind of analysis while others do not. Whether one tends to be more like a 'Phoenician' or like a 'Chinese' in one's approach to spelling, however, the advice is the same: Do go and get a pencil, the next time you find yourself writing with a finger in the air.

Acknowledgements

I would like to thank Gordon Riggs, Deborah Fried, Dianne Gass, and especially George Woodring for assisting with various phases of the research. The Department of Psychology at the University of Massachusetts, Amherst generously provided facilities for the second experiment.

I I

Visual Imagery and Individual Differences in Spelling

JOHN A. SLOBODA   *Department of Psychology, University of Keele, England*

1 Rules are not sufficient for perfect spelling

As with many well-learned skills, spelling seems easy to the good speller. He just *knows* that a word is spelled one way rather than another. It certainly does not *seem* to him as though rules are being applied or decisions being made. One good speller remarked: 'When you speak a word I can see it in my head as a typed image . . . the letters are black and lower case on a white background . . . no effort is required, it just happens'. Another said 'It's like being asked to remember a well-known tune . . . it's just *there* . . . there's no question of uncertainty'. And another – 'I imagine myself writing it down and I know it's right'. Comments like this suggest that some good spellers may have direct access to some sort of visual memory for words, possibly experienced as visual imagery, which might supplement or replace rule-based spelling procedures. Less good spellers would then be those who did not have access to a comprehensive visual memory. This should not be seen as contradiction of the view that proficient spelling involves knowledge of spelling rules (e.g. Simon, 1976). Rather it is an admission that spelling rules cannot do the whole job. What distinguishes the competent speller from the poor speller may well be a knowledge of spelling rules; but to become an excellent speller one needs some more specific knowledge for the cases in which the rules do not provide unique solutions. When one looks at the spelling errors of literate adults one is perhaps seeing the gap between what the rules supply and what, in the case of perfect spellers, is provided by a rapid and accurate form of spelling memory.

A major category of spelling error is the phonologically plausible error, which, if pronounced, sounds identical to or very similar to the pronounced form of the correct spelling. In a 50-word spelling test that I administered to a sample of 18 university students and staff I obtained 55 errors in the whole sample. Of these, 50 fell straightforwardly into this category (see Table 1). A very common error involved confusion between single and double consonants (e.g. PUMMICE, BALAST). Also common was a confusion between unstressed vowels, giving rise to such errors as INSISTANT, TENENT, and AVERICE. In these, and the other errors, there seemed always to be a plausible analogy for the spelling offered. For instance, subjects offering DIRTH could call on BIRTH as their analogy rather than the more appropriate SEARCH. BESEACH could be based on analogy to REACH instead of LEECH, and so on.

The only errors whose existence seems to imply other than purely phonological mechanisms were AVERIES (for AVARICE), POMMICE (for PUMICE), and LIETENANT or LEUITENANT (for LIEUTENANT).

Whilst children also make phonologically plausible mistakes of this kind, they display other types not shown by my adult sample. For instance, there are more omissions, transpositions and substitutions which significantly alter the phonological representation which would be assigned to the mis-spelling (e.g. Peters, 1967, although in this study children of high intelligence made only phonologically plausible errors).

TABLE 1   Numbers in brackets indicate the number of subjects producing each error when it occurred more than once

---

Consonant doubling errors
apraise (2)
ferets
ferretts
balast (3)
pummice (4)
chapperones

Unstressed vowel errors
chaparones
servent
averice
consistant
jackel (4)
tenent
vender
insistant (2)

Unstressed syllable errors
reble
lible (2)
hostle
decible (3)

Homophonic consonant errors
resency
pumise

Homophonic vowel errors
delaid
mislayed
mislaied
vendour
dirth (6)
beseach
mallot
tomatos

Others
averies
pommice
lietenant
lietenent
leuitenant

The elimination of such errors in literate adults suggests that adults have a well-developed knowledge of a set of correspondence rules between phonemes and graphemes. Of course, it is clear that these rules cannot be *all* they know about spelling. They must know something about orthographic constraints: for instance, they know that no English word begins with a double consonant. They are probably also sensitive to grammatical context: for instance, they do not mis-spell BLAST as BLASSED even though this is phonologically plausible. In other words, it seems a necessary characteristic of most adult spelling errors that they are phonologically plausible, but it is by no means a sufficient one. Furthermore, it seems likely that each person will differ to some extent in the sub-set of errors that he is most prone to within the class of 'permissible' errors. Whether such differences can be accounted for in a systematic manner is a question whose answer awaits serious study of individual subjects. Studies which collapse data across large numbers of subjects are unsuited by their nature to shed light on *details* of cognitive processes involved in spelling.

A quite clear example of what may be missed by looking only at group data comes from my own small sample. A type of error which occurred on seven occasions was the substitution of *-le* for a terminal *-el* (e.g. REBLE for REBEL). These errors were by four out of eighteen subjects, with one subject alone contributing three of them. The test contained four words on which such an error was possible (LIBEL, REBEL, HOSTEL and DECIBEL). The chance of spelling all four words correctly if guessing at random between *-el* and *-le* is 0.0625, therefore it is unlikely that more than one of the 14 subjects correctly spelling all four words did so by chance. Nonetheless, several of these 14 made *other* phonologically plausible errors (e.g. unstressed vowel substitutions). In contrast, the subject who made three *-le* errors made no consonant doubling errors at all, even though for the group as a whole this was the most common error. This suggests one of two things. *Either* there are subtle but systematic differences between particular confusable spellings (based on their phonological, lexical or orthographic context) which only some spellers are sensitive to, *or* such differences do not exist (or are not noticed) and different subjects have simply *learned* how to avoid particular confusions by 'rote' or by access to visual memory. If the first alternative were true one should be able to provide a set of rules for spelling troublesome word sets (e.g. FUNNEL, PUDDLE, HOSTEL, WHISTLE, LABEL, TABLE, LADLE, YODEL, TROUBLE, CAMEL, SIMPLE, APPLE) and show that subjects who spell such sets correctly do so in virtue of such rules. This would be no simple matter as one would have to take each word set as a separate case, determine whether the set could be constructed according to some rule system, and then test subjects' knowledge of such a system by, for instance, asking them to spell spoken non-words whose spelling would be predicted by the rule system in question (a technique used, for instance, by Secrist, 1976).

If, however, subjects were not using rule-based procedures but relying on memory for individual words, at least for 'difficult' cases, there would be no necessary relationship between the availability of rules to account for the spelling of a particular word set and subjects' ability to spell the set. Subjects with good visual memory would presumably have a considerable advantage here. Those with poor visual memory would need to learn to eliminate errors systematically. Individual differences could then be accounted for on the basis of past spelling history, on the assumption that certain errors will have been drawn to a subject's attention and 'worked upon'. This latter account is only plausible if there is reason to suppose that there are individual differences in visual memory for words. Evidence for such a supposition is scant, and the main aim of the experiments reported here is to obtain some evidence that the role of visual memory in receptive and productive spelling tasks is subject to individual variation.

The idea that there may be two reading 'routes', one visually based, and one using phonological mediation has polarised the psychological and pedagogical literature on reading for many years (Bradshaw, 1975; Bower, 1970; Gough, 1972; Smith, 1971; Rubenstein et al., 1971; Baron, 1973; Green and Shallice, 1976). Claims that reading uses predominantly one or other of these routes seem to have, on the whole, left unexplored the possibility that different individuals use different routes according to the constitution of their lexical memory. We may suppose that a word is recognised as a particular word when evidence for the presence of a defining set of attributes stored in memory exceeds some threshold value. It is possible that this defining set of attributes includes visual attributes, such as length, word contour, and letter contour; and that this set serves to uniquely specify one particular word. In such a case, reading could proceed by a purely visual route without phonological involvement. It is also possible that the defining set of attributes includes no visual attributes, or too few to uniquely identify one word, but includes phonological attributes, such as the nature and order of the phonemes in the word. In this case, reading would need to proceed via phonological coding, whereby letters, or letter-groups, were identified and then subject to grapheme-phoneme translation rules. In the extreme case where the *only* lexical specifications were phonological then a subject would have no way of telling which of two phonologically identical spellings was correct, whether dealing with visual input or trying to decide upon written or spoken output.

2 Experiment 1: Distinguishing between phonologically and visually similar spelling alternatives

In order to see what kind of individual variation might exist in the ability to perform a simple lexical decision task, I asked sixty literate native English-speaking adults to take part in an experiment where they were required to examine two alternative spellings of a word and then decide which of the two was correct. There were two conditions, one in which the alternatives were phonologically similar, another in which the alternatives were phonologically dissimilar. Each condition was presented on a sheet of paper containing sixty printed pairs in ten rows of six pairs each. The two members of a pair were placed one above another with leftmost letters vertically aligned, e.g.

deppress
depress

Table 2 shows a representative example of each type of alteration used. There were six alterations of each of ten types. In each type there were examplars of *both* correct spellings. For instance, the words used for the *-ancy*, *-ency* alteration were VACANCY, INFANCY, RECENCY, CURRENCY, DECENCY, and CLEMENCY. The sixty pairs were arranged on the page in random order with the correctly spelled word occurring with equal probability as the upper or the lower member of the pair. The condition containing phonologically dissimilar pairs was a control condition. Word-frequency and number of letters were matched as closely as possible with the phonologically similar condition. In addition, the visual impact of each alteration was matched as closely as possible with an alteration on the other sheet. Thus, for instance, ARRIVAL–ARRIVEL had as a control ARRIVAD–ARRIVED. In both cases there is an *e–a* alteration in the penultimate position, but only in the first case are the alternatives phonologically identical. Thus, the phonologically dissimilar condition was like the phonologically similar condition in the majority of *visual* respects.

Subjects were required to work through each sheet, marking the correct word in each pair as quickly as possible. Half the subjects attempted the control condition first, the other half in reverse order. The time taken to complete each sheet was noted, and the sheets were scored for errors after the experiment.

The whole experiment gave rise to 215 erroneous responses. Of these, 190 occurred in the phonologically alike condition. Table 2 shows the number of errors made on each alteration type. It is very clear that not all phonologically plausible alternatives are equally often chosen by subjects. The most frequent confusion (*-ent*, *-ant*) occurred 15 times more often than the least frequent confusion (*-w*, *-wh*). It is also clear that most mistakes cannot be attributed to visual similarity of alternatives. For instance, only once was a mistake made on the *-ert*, *-art* distinction as compared to 45 errors on the visually similar *-ent*, *-ant* distinction. These results show that phonological similarity is a necessary condition for receptive as well as productive spelling errors. The frequency ordering of error types is also like that obtained in a production situation. Consonant doubling and *e* for *a* confusions are most freqent. Other confusions, like *-le*, *-el*, are less common.

In order to examine differences between subjects, I obtained two measures for each subject, 't' and 'e'; t was the time required to complete the phonologically dissimilar condition *minus* the time required to complete the phonologically unalike condition; e was the number of errors in the phonologically similar condition *minus* the number of errors in the phonologically dissimilar condition.

TABLE 2

Spelling pattern variant	Alternatives				
	Phonologically similar			Phonologically dissimilar	
	Example	No. of errors		Example	No. of errors
1. -ent -ant	clement clemant	46		convert convart	1
2. -ce -se	promice promise	9		polich polish	1
3. w- wh-	weight wheight	3		sapely shapely	1
4. -er -or	paster pastor	7		parret parrot	6
5. -le -el	hostle hostel	11		assits assist	1
6. -ayed -aid	sprayed spraid	18		slayer slair	0
7. -ea- -ee-	deamed deemed	24		dearth deerth	3
8. -CC- -C-	deppress depress	33		preessed pressed	0
9. -ancy -ency	currancy currency	27		corractly correctly	0
10. -al -el	rival rivel	13		livas lives	2
	Total	191		*Total*	15

Several features of this data are of note. Firstly, no subject obtained negative values of both 't' and 'e'. Secondly the ranges of both t (-20 sec to $+83$ sec) and e (-3 to $+14$) were large. Thirdly, t and e were positively correlated ($r = 0.32$, $p < 0.01$). Subjects who were slower on the experimental sheet also tended to make more errors on it.

What these data suggest is that for many subjects, a phonologically based word identification procedure is, at the very least, preferred to a visual route. When such a procedure becomes inefficient for the task, as it must in the phonologically similar condition, then the decision task is likely to take longer, and may well fail altogether. There is no evidence from these data that there are discrete subject groups. It appears rather that there is a continuum of strategies from these who are hardly influenced by phonology to those who are highly influenced by it. Baron and Strawson (1976) in one of the few recent studies to take seriously individual differences in reading, have named subjects who fall at these two extremes 'Chinese' and 'Phoenician', respectively. Accordingly one may ask whether the Chinese-Phoenician distinction coincides with a distinction in spelling ability. Such coincidence would be expected if excellent spellers are, indeed, those who have easily accessible visual specifications for words.

To answer this question, I selected two sub-groups of subjects from the original sample of sixty, chosen so as not to overlap at all in scores on the decision task. 18 subjects agreed to return for further testing, 9 who showed little difference between the two conditions, 9 who showed a considerable difference. Table 3 summarises some data from these subjects; t1 is the time taken to finish the phonologically dissimilar condition (sec); t2 is the time taken in the phonologically similar condition; e1 and e2 are the corresponding error rates. Group A showed no significant difference between conditions whereas Group B showed a highly significant difference in both time and errors. Thus, Group B contained those who found it especially difficult to distinguish between phonologically similar alternatives, whereas it made no difference to those in Group A whether or not the alternatives were phonologically similar. Each subject was asked to rate his own spelling ability. The column in Table 3 headed 'Spelling performance rating' gives subjects' answers to this question. Eight subjects considered themselves good spellers. Seven of these were from Group A. As corroboration for this self-rating each subject was administered a spelling test of 50 words chosen from the population used in the decision experiment. The number of errors made is given in the columns headed 'Spelling test'. Group A made seven errors in all. Group B made 47 errors. It is clear, therefore, that the people in this sample finding the lexical decision between phonologically similar alternatives difficult also made spelling mistakes, and were conscious of a degree of spelling difficulty. This was despite the fact that they all enjoyed regular reading and spent much of their working lives producing written prose.

If we suppose that Group B individuals do indeed possess word recognition systems in which lexical specifications are largely phonological, then it is parsimonious to hypothesise that these same lexical specifications are used as a starting point for generating spelling codes.

TABLE 3

Group A: Small difference on error detection task

S	Time (sec) t1	t2	errors e1	e2	Spelling performance rating	Spelling test	Visual imagery rating
1.	98	92	0	1	fair	2	yes
2.	94	92	0	0	good	0	
3.	47	46	0	0	good	0	
4.	115	115	0	0	fair	3	yes
5.	90	70	0	2	good	2	
6.	65	63	0	0	good	0	
7.	70	60	0	0	good	0	yes
8.	55	66	0	0	good	0	yes
9.	38	44	0	0	good	0	yes
Means	75	72	0	0.3			

Group B: Large difference on error detection task

S	Time (sec) t1	t2	errors e1	e2	Spelling performance rating	Spelling test	Visual imagery rating
10.	80	149	0	2	fair	5	
11.	72	155	0	3	good	4	yes
12.	90	92	3	7	poor	3	
13.	103	144	0	5	poor	8	yes
14.	86	111	0	3	fair	3	yes
15.	180	195	2	6	poor	10	
16.	80	120	0	8	fair	9	yes
17.	100	137	0	4	poor	3	
18.	79	110	0	0	fair	3	
Means	97	135	0.6	4.2			

On the other hand Group A individuals could well be using visual specifications for words at both input and output, and this might account for the apparent immediacy of a spelling 'image' in good spellers.

3 Experiment 2: Effects of imagery and spelling ability on estimating the number of letters in a word

Thus, I became concerned to discover whether it could be experimentally demonstrated that imagery helped spelling performance.

Radakar (1963) carried out a study in which children were given practice at arousing clear visual images of words that they were learning to spell. They improved in spelling performance when compared against a control group who did not practise visual imagery, and Radakar concluded that visual imagery enhanced spelling performance. However, his control group indulged in 'sessions of free play and social conversation' while the experimental group were practising imagery, so it is conceivable that the improvement in spelling was contingent on concentrated attention to words rather than on the imagery as such. In addition, to say that practising imagery improves subsequent spelling performance is not to say that subjects actually *use* imagery in their spelling behaviour once the practise sessions are over. In devising my own experimental procedure I wanted to find a task involving spelling which would be helped by imagery but in which no specific instructions to image were given. In this way, I hoped to isolate spellers to whom imagery 'came naturally'. The task decided upon was one in which a subject heard a spoken word and was required to decide how many letters it contained, pressing one of 16 numbered keys to indicate his choice. The experimental arrangement was such that the reaction time between the end of the spoken word and the key-press could be measured to within an accuracy of 0.01 sec.

Clearly, if a subject is to perform this task accurately he must be able to spell the words in question (except that several of the more common spelling errors retain the correct number of letters). It also seems reasonable to suppose that visual imagery will assist performance. There is evidence that visual imagery assists other number estimation tasks such as determining the number of corners in a well-known shape (Brooks, 1968). There is also evidence that most people are able to 'subitise' small numbers of visually presented items (Jensen *et al.*, 1950). In subitising, one is able to know the quantity without consciously counting, and the span of subitising seems to be about 5 items. Subjects with clear visual images of words may be able to subitise words or portions of them, thus decreasing reaction time. Finally, there is a sense in which a visual image is a more appropriate substrate for counting than a graphemic representation which is derived from a phonological representation. Arguably, a visual image does not present its phonological credentials. Each letter is of equal status to the next, and may enter directly as a token into the counting routine. On the other hand, a letter derived from a phonological representation may not carry equal weight to its neighbour. Consider the word YELLOW. Its phonological representation might be written as Y–E–L–O, signifying four phonemic elements. In order to obtain the correct spelling, a set of transformation rules must be applied in which each phonemic element may be replaced in the 'surface' graphemic string by one or more letters.

$$Y \; - \; E \; - \; L \; - O$$
$$Y \; - \; E \; - \; LL - OW$$

In such a translation process the Y and E stand for one whole phonemic unit each, whereas each L and the O and W stand, as it were, for only half a phoneme each. In contrast, some words, like STANDS have a much simpler correspondence between phonemes and graphemes, each phonemic element being represented by exactly one letter in the grapheme string. I shall call these latter type of words 'phonemically transparent' and the former, of which YELLOW is an exemplar 'phonemically opaque'. For spellers who use phonologically based representations for deriving spellings of words I predicted that it would be more difficult for them to count phonemically opaque words than phonemically transparent ones, because at an important level of representation the number of items (i.e. phonemes) would be discrepant with the number of items (i.e. letters) being counted, thus causing, at the least, interference or slowing, and, at the most actual, underestimation of the number of letters in a word. Accordingly, my sample of words for this experiment included both transparent and opaque words. I hypothesised that visualisers should behave no differently to the two types of words, whereas the non-visualisers should perform less well on the opaque words.

The application of reaction time measurements to perceptual tasks has proved an extremely powerful tool in isolating cognitive stages in perceptual processes. One possible reason for the lack of reaction-time studies in spelling is the difficulty of finding a suitable time-interval to measure. Typically perceptual RT studies have involved the production of a unitary response (key-press or utterance) to some perceptual event. The response in a spelling task is, in contrast, a complex multi-response motor sequence extending over a significant time. If one is concerned to measure the duration of cognitive processes in spelling, one has to resolve the problem posed by the possibility of temporal overlap between cognitive and response processes. A plausible hypothesis is that a subject starts to write a word as soon as he has recognised it and generated the first letter. He then uses spare processing time while the first letter is being output to generate the second, and so on. If this model were true, then measuring RT to production onset would tell us only about recognition processes, whilst measuring to production offset would tell us only about writing processes. Spelling processes would escape the net. In fact Leslie Henderson and his colleagues (Henderson et al., 1978) have begun to systematically study writing onset and offset latencies in a transcription task, and have shown that both these measures exhibit lawful dependencies on psychologically important properties of displays. But transcription does not necessarily entail cognitive processes central to spelling, and so we await a resolution to the cluster of problems which surround the temporally extended nature of the usual spelling response.

The choice of a counting task was made, therefore, partly to avoid the problems associated with a written response, allowing instead, a unitary response of a kind familiar to students of perception. My subjects for this experiment were the two groups of subjects, A and B, isolated from the previous experiment. A hundred stimulus words were recorded on a tape of intervals at 15 seconds each preceded by a brief warning tone. The subjects were given some preliminary practise both at counting letters in words and at locating the correct one of 16 numbered keys efficiently and speedily. The tape was then set running, and the subjects worked through the complete tape without break. The

TABLE 4   Words used in Experiment 2

Phonemically transparent		Phonemically opaque	
kid	rib	eat	ebb
past	pram	word	soot
front	frost	close	snack
strong	script	growth	breast
strings	strands	strikes	crammed
unit	acid	easy	ally
visit	timid	happy	easel
moving	rusted	middle	mammal
control	convict	believe	thinker
students	distrust	pressure	stunning
italy	alibi	India	idiot
atomic	amoral	artery	airily
limited	mineral	officer	terrify
probably	skeleton	position	cavities
including	enclosing	committee	oversight
Others			
job	art	owl	eel
run	age	kit	orb
miss	alps	able	ajar
problems	bicycles	together	renowned
economics	religious	releasing	inanimate
community	certainly	porcelain	medically
experience	themselves	worshipful	tapestries
information	exterminate	development	despondency
professional	bibliography	institutions	strawberries

words were recorded in a random order, but comprised one- two- and three-syllable words of length 2–12 letters. Embedded within this population of words were thirty phonemically opaque and thirty phonemically transparent words matched for frequency, length and number of syllables. The extra forty words were used to equate the number of occurrences of each word length in the range 3–9 letters and to increase uncertainty by introducing items over a wider range of lengths. The words used in the experiment are given in Table 4.

Analysis of variance on the error distribution showed that the two groups of subjects did not differ significantly nor did performance on opaque words differ from that on transparent. There was a 4.2% error rate overall. Most subjects attributed the majority of their errors to response rather than computational error.

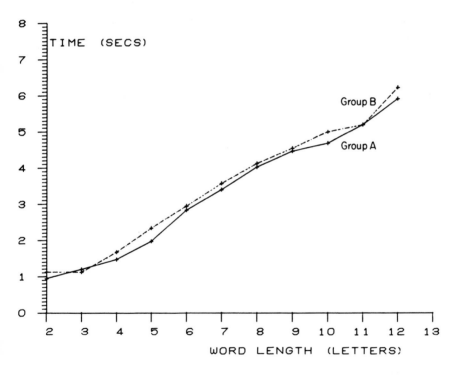

FIG. 1   Mean counting time as a function of word length. (Solid line, Group A; dashed line, Group B)

Analysis of reaction times showed only one clearly significant effect. Longer words took longer to count. Figure 1 shows the mean RT for each group of subjects as a function of word length. The function is linear with zero intercept and a slope of 0.5 seconds per letter. There is no significant difference between subject groups, word types, or any interaction of these factors.

There are many possible reasons for this lack of significant difference, and the least interesting, but most compelling is that the counting task simply does not respond to differences in spelling imagery and is therefore inappropriate as a technique for investigating the questions we are interested in. Accordingly, I sought evidence to demonstrate that the counting task could discriminate between subjects on at least one criterion, and the most obvious one seemed to be introspective report. The final column of Table 3 indicates which of the subjects in the two groups reported using visual imagery during spelling in their interview. Five of group A and 4 of group B gave definite and clear descriptions of visual imagery during spelling.

Accordingly I redivided the subjects into two groups, 'visualisers' and 'non-visualisers' on the basis of introspective report, and re-analysed the data with the new grouping. As before, the error distribution showed little of interest, but the reaction time analysis gave a significant result. The interaction between subject group (visualiser or non-visualiser) and phonemic opacity was significant [$F(1,8) = 6.87$, $p < 0.05$]. Table 5 shows this interaction. Non-visualisers take longer to count opaque words. Visulaisers take the same time for both classes of word.

TABLE 5   Mean time taken (sec) to estimate the number of letters in spoken words

Subjects	Phonemically transparent	Phonemically opaque
Visualisers	2.49	2.52
Non-visualisers	2.92	3.19

Figure 2 shows the mean time for all 100 words according to number of letters in the word for the subjects divided according to visualisation. The functions are, again, linear for the most part with equal slope, but an intercept difference of about 0.6 sec, suggests that while counting rate for the two groups is equal, visualisers are faster at establishing whatever representation it is that they count.

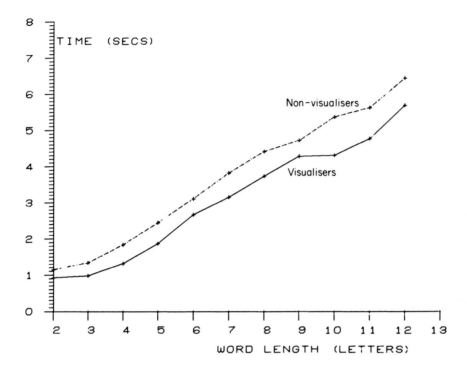

FIG. 2   Mean counting time as a function of word length. (Solid line, visualisers;
dashed line, non-visualisers)

4 Discussion

It seems that there are, indeed, individual differences in the use of
visual imagery in spelling. These differences allow 'visualisers' to exceed
'non-visualisers' at counting letters in imagined words that are
'phonemically opaque'. Nonetheless, these differences do not map on to
the differences between good and less good spellers. Therefore, it seems
unlikely that visual imagery is directly responsible for the ability of good
spellers to avoid phonologically plausible mistakes. The picture which
these results suggest is that imagery is something which operates on the
end product of a spelling process, rather than being implicated *in* that
process. Thus, some good spellers are able to image what they have
spelled: so are some poor spellers. Presumably, poor spellers will image
incorrectly spelled words. On the other hand, there are good spellers
who do not use visual imagery and are slow at counting phonemically
opaque words.

This leaves us with two problems. What *is* responsible for the large difference in spelling ability between Group A and Group B? Secondly, why are good spellers susceptible to phonemic opacity when they do not use visual imagery?

One way of resolving the first problem would be to characterise the difference between Groups A and B as a difference in *graphemic* (rather than visual) memory. On this account, good spellers store information about which letters a word contains whilst less good spellers store mainly information about which phonemes a word contains. This would still account for the pattern of results obtained in Experiment 1 since good spellers could decide between phonologically similar alternatives on the basis of graphemic specifications just as easily as on the basis of visual specifications. Indeed, one may argue that this suggestion is a more coherent one, since it is hard to know exactly what would count as a *visual* specification for a word that would, for instance, accept both AgE and aGe as instances of the same word. In certain circumstances people seem to be entirely unaware of the case in which words or letters have been presented to them (e.g. Coltheart and Freeman, 1974). A satisfying explanation for this unawareness is that words are specified at the graphemic level, and recognised if information about graphemes present in the visual input (established by visually specified letter recognition processes) matches the stored graphemic specification for a particular word. If less good spellers do not have such specifications then visual input must be further recoded into a phonemic form before it can be matched with a lexical specification.

The second problem is less easy to resolve, and what follows is merely a speculative, but hopefully testable, hypothesis. Let us assume that the output from the spelling mechanism is a grapheme string. In normal circumstances this string will act either as input to writing, typing or speaking mechanism, or as input to some visual comparison process, as in proofreading. In all these cases the time for which the grapheme string is held in memory as such is short – probably no more than one or two seconds. In the counting task of Experiment 2 subjects were spending as long as 7 or 8 seconds counting some words. This could have the consequence that the usual degree of persistence of a graphemic memory is exceeded. In this case subjects may have needed to recode, or rehearse, the word in some non-graphemic manner in order to keep it in memory. Visualisers will, no doubt, recode the word as a visual image. Non-visualisers have two plausible options. They could convert each letter into a phonologiccal code for its name, or they could hold the complete word as a phonological string (in effect 'saying the word over' to themselves). The first option seems the less attractive of the two, since it is likely to take just as long to say each letter in a long word as it is to count them. If non-visualisers need to hold words in a phonological form whilst counting them then the effect of phonemic opacity is easy to understand. A prediction from this hypothesis would be that requiring non-visualisers to perform a concurrent phonologically based task whilst doing the counting task would eliminate the difference between opaque and transparent words, since they would be forced to find some other non-phonological form in which to store the words they were counting.

If the general interpretation offered here is correct, then it follows that the role of imagery in spelling is highly task-dependent. This is because imagery does not enter into spelling as such, but it may assist a subject in a situation where one has *independent* reasons for predicting a cognitive advantage (e.g. a visual image may suffer less from interference during the concurrent performance of other mental activity).

5 Conclusion

In one sense my conclusion about the difference between good and poor spellers may seem trivial. To have a graphemic representation of a word in a lexical memory is to know what letters it contains. Being able to spell *means* knowing what letters a word contains. Thus 'having a graphemic representation' could be seen as simply an obtuse way of saying that good spellers are good spellers. Nonetheless, I believe my formulation is significant in what is *excludes*. Specifically it excludes the hypothesis that proficient spelling is a rule-governed procedure. Much writing on spelling emphasises that there exists rules which explain why particular words are spelled one way and not another (e.g. Chomsky and Halle, 1968). It is easy to slide from this admittedly significant linguistic fact to the altogether different proposition that people know how to spell *by virtue of* using these rules, whether explicitly or implicitly. Such an assumption seems very reasonable in the light of people's ability to make a passable attempt at spelling a word they have not seen before. The typical adult spelling error also suggests it. Yet it is not necessarily true of the way in which experienced and proficient spellers actually produce words they have used many times before. I believe that there is a 'null hypothesis' which is still worth maintaining in the face of more interesting and 'intelligent' models of spelling (e.g. Simon, 1976). That is that good spellers achieve their results, not by virtue of particular skills like imagery or application of linguistic rules, but by virtue of their memory for the way individual words are spelled. One might say that whilst average spellers spell by rule, good spellers spell by rote.

The problem of how these individual differences arise is one which this chapter has not addressed, although it is a very important question. Perhaps it would be premature to address this question before knowing rather more about the nature of these differences.

PART V
Spelling Errors

with an independant mind

I typed it on eage page

probbably an error

See you on Teusday

this takes ~~space~~ place in time

necessary to get more practise

12

Spelling Errors in Handwriting: A Corpus and a Distributional Analysis

ALAN M. WING and ALAN D. BADDELEY   *MRC Applied Psychology Unit, Cambridge, England*

251

1 Introduction

1.1 *Spelling errors and buffered output in handwriting*

A complaint often heard from examiners is that the exam scripts they have to mark contain frequent spelling errors. Later in this chapter we present a corpus of spelling errors (both slips and errors of convention) found in handwritten exam scripts. Our purpose, however, is not to provide an indication of the extent to which examiners are made to suffer. With interests in the psychological processes that underlie the production of handwriting, our motivation for looking at error patterns is for the possible clues they may provide to the operation of those processes. The contribution of this chapter is not intended to be a comprehensive theory of handwritten spelling errors. Instead we try to describe the errors in fairly general terms including an analysis of where errors tend to occur. Although we do make some interpretative comments of a theoretical nature we feel that a really adequate theory will have to take account of the qualitative nature of errors in addition to their quantitative distribution.

A natural taxonomy of a handwritten text might recognise sentences, words, letters and strokes. We will take this taxonomy as the bare outlines of our theoretical starting point and suppose there are corresponding levels in the information processing carried out by a person translating an idea into handwriting. On clinical grounds it has been argued (e.g. Luria, 1970) that writing depends heavily on the word-to-phoneme conversion process and even on the articulatory encoding process involved in speech. On the other hand Luria *et al.* (1970) acknowledge that words, like one's own name, that are written very frequently may be coded specifically for written output independently of the speech route. In this chapter our interest will be confined to a level of processing where individual letters are already coded and we will be concerned with questions about the involvement of short-term memory in handwriting. (A discussion of issues in the control of handwriting movements responsible for individual strokes in writing may be found in Wing, 1978.)

Why do we propose an involvement of short-term memory processes in handwriting? Most people would agree that one's thoughts or internal speech are usually ahead of the word currently being written. In reading, the eye-voice span (the amount of material which has already been fixated but has not yet been spoken) led Morton (1964) to postulate a response buffer for the temporary storage of information prior to speech output. It is thus natural to suppose that the lag between ideas and writing that allows a relatively smooth flow of writing despite revisions of opinion about word choice, is mediated by a short-term memory buffer.

As a working hypothesis we will assume single successive words are registered in the buffer. Further we will suppose that normally individual letters, rather than letter groups, are represented in the buffer in a linear fashion that corresponds to the spatial order of the letters in the written word. Output then involves retrieval of the letters encoded so that each letter is produced in turn by an appropriate sequence of hand movements. Shaffer (1976) has developed in some detail the notion of the response buffer and associated indexing control processes in the context of errors in typing and speech. The ideas he presents are in principle applicable to the sequencing of handwritten letters but they are more advanced than we would be justified in considering in our commentary on the distribution of handwritten spelling errors.

If we assume that registration of the letters in the buffer is virtually simultaneous, but the mechanical constraints of writing make serial retrieval slow, letters towards the end of a word will have been in the buffer longer than those at the beginning of the word. If there is decay of the memory trace for each letter with time there will then be difficulty in retrieval of items occurring later in each word. Errors will be more likely to occur toward the end of the word than near the beginning. With this prediction in mind, we now turn to the two studies that provide any data on the distribution of spelling errors in handwriting.

In an analysis of the spelling errors in Lee Harvey Oswald's diary, Lecours (1966) showed that where a letter is omitted from a word in which that letter occurs twice the omission is much more likely in the second as opposed to the first position. Because this finding is based on the data of just one person it is reasonable to have reservations about its generality, particularly if Lecours' diagnosis of Oswald's 'developmental dysgraphia' is accepted. However Chedru and Geschwind (1972) have reported results for words of five or more letters that also support a word position effect. A group of 21 hospitalised patients in acute confusional states and a group of 10 hospitalised controls performed various writing tasks. For words of five letters or more both groups produced more errors in the last two letters than in the first two letters.

On this promising initial note it is natural to ask whether other parallels may be drawn between the distribution of spelling errors arising from a letter storage buffer and the bow-shaped serial position curves typically obtained in studies of short-term memory, (for example see Baddeley, 1976). We might ask whether, superimposed on the increase in errors from beginning to end of the word, there is an even greater likelihood of errors in the middle of the word. Our interpretation of a concave-down, bow-shaped serial position curve could be that each item 'interferes' with neighbouring items. Since items in extreme positions have fewer neighbours they should suffer less interference of the memory trace. Later in this chapter we provide data on the probability of errors in the middle of words compared to the beginning and end.

Chedru and Geschwind classified the spelling errors they observed as omission (e.g. CLAR for CLEAR), addition (e.g. CAREFULL for CAREFUL), substitution (e.g. LAN for VAN) and inversion (reversal of two adjacent letters, e.g. LIBRETY for LIBERTY). This classification bears a strong resemblance to the types of errors found in serial list recall (for example see Conrad, 1959). An important exception is that in serial list reacll transposition errors often include non-adjacent items, an error not commonly seen in spelling errors.

Another difference between serial list recall errors and spelling errors is that the relative frequency of occurrence of transposition errors in serial list recall is typically much higher than the small proportion of inversion errors that Chedru and Geschwind found in writing. However, it should be noted that written spelling errors are often detected and corrected before the next letter is written so that many potential inversion errors may have been classified as omissions. (A corresponding ambiguity also exists between addition and substitution errors.)

On the topic of relative proportions of spelling errors by type, a potentially important result was obtained by Chedru and Geschwind on retesting their 21 acute confusional state patients after recovery. They found that whereas the frequency of omission and substitution errors decreased significantly from test to retest, there were no reliable changes in the frequency of addition or of inversion errors. This implies that the process giving rise to omission and substitution errors is separate from the process responsible for addition and inversion errors. Underlying the errors there are *at least* two processes, although there may of course be more.

1.2 *The distinction between slips and convention errors*

From an educationalist's viewpoint, remedial work on spelling usually centres on departures from conventional spelling. Typically certain words will be consistently mis-spelled and the instructor might attempt to get the writer to recognise these errors and be on guard against them. Such errors of convention are often contrasted with spelling errors that the writer would know how to correct provided the error was noticed.

Correctable errors, often attributed to carelessness or inattention on the part of the writer, are generally referred to as lapses or slips.

In the previous section we did not explicitly recognise the distinction between convention errors and slips nor did the two studies we cited. Yet our interest is in characterising processing operations in the production of writing and not in what MacKay (1970), making a related point about the validity of speech errors, referred to as prior educational deficiencies. In what follows our primary interest is therefore in slips or lapses. In practice, one cannot always be confident in classifying an error as a slip as opposed to a convention error. For example, if a word containing an error occurs only once in a text and the error is uncorrected, to show it is not a so-called educational deficiency or convention error, one would want to ask the writer to write it again or ask him whether he thinks he wrote the word correctly. Since we could not do this for the errors in our corpus we decided not to discard those spelling errors we classified as convention errors. There are a number of other reasons for analysing the convention error data. In the first place earlier studies have not attempted to separate out convention errors which means that without provision of convention error data, comparisons with our work would be suspect. Secondly, while we believe that the distinction between slips and convention errors is theoretically important, we recognise that in our analysis there will be some mis-classifications. If other grounds for classification present themselves at a later date re-analysis of the data will prove relatively easy. Finally to the extent that the classification is satisfactory, the convention error data may be used as a baseline against which the distribution of slips can be contrasted.

1.3 *The need for a systematic corpus of spelling errors*

One reason why there has been little research in the area of hand-written spelling errors is that error rates in normal people are very low. For example Van Nes (1971) reported that in text between 0.06% and 0.6% of letters were in error. Or if we want a value in terms of word involvement we may take Chedru and Geschwind's (1972) estimate that 1.1% of words written by their control group in a sentence composition task contained at least one spelling error. Such low error rates make the compilation of a corpus containing a sufficient number of cases to obtain statistically reliable data very laborious. Unless one has considerable faith in any particular hypothesis that one might want to test there is a strong temptation to take short cuts. In preliminary work it might be thought reasonable to use a small sample but without knowledge of the distributional characteristics of the population of errors it is unlikely that sampling will have obeyed systematic sampling procedures to ensure a representative sample. To obtain a large sample one might consider using data taken from situations where spelling error rates are elevated. Raised error rates could be caused by an experimental manipulation, such as the provision of a distracting, secondary task (cf. Schouten *et al.*, 1962) or they could be the result of a clinical problem as in the case of the patients in acute confusional states. We feel that the use of such data could prove a fruitful path of investigation, but that conclusions based only on elevated error rates may be limited in generality.

With these difficulties in the way of carrying out a satisfactory test even of preliminary ideas it is natural to turn to an existing published corpus of errors. The only published corpus for written spelling errors that we know of is that of Bawden (1900). Unfortunately Bawden's corpus is not large and, since no sampling details are provided, we cannot rule out selectivity in his recording of the errors. To remedy this lack we have therefore provided a full listing of our corpus of spelling errors in the Appendix.

2 Establishing the corpus of spelling errors

2.1 *Source of data*

The errors listed in the Appendix were all those found in the exam scripts of forty male, secondary school candidates applying for entrance to Cambridge colleges in engineering, mathematics or natural sciences. The exam was the General Paper of November 1976 and candidates were required to give essay-type answers to three self-selected questions. These were marked by the examiners in terms of the candidates' ability to formulate cogent arguments and to express themselves clearly in written English. Three hours were allowed for writing the examination.

After the scripts were no longer required by the examiners, forty were selected at random. A small proportion of scripts where there was reason to suspect the candidates did not possess British English as first language were excluded. The exam marks of a sub-group of 16 candidates who also wrote papers in physics and in mathematics for non-specialists are shown in the first three columns of Table 1. Given grades of below 40% are taken as failure the figures suggest the general academic abilities of the candidates was not as high as one would expect, at least of potential Cambridge undergraduates.

TABLE 1 Average and standard deviation of exam marks, general paper script length, spelling error frequencies and their intercorrelations for the 16 candidates taking physics, maths and general papers

	Exam marks in percent			Script length in lines	Spelling error frequency	
	Physics	Maths	General paper		Slips	Convention errors
Average	45.0	52.9	45.5	211.8	20.4	5.9
SD	10.8	14.7	12.7	46.9	11.2	5.3
Correlations						
Physics		0.62	0.46	−0.07	−0.35	−0.18
Maths			0.45	0.12	−0.07	−0.10
General paper				0.40	−0.39	−0.33
Script length					0.08	0.10
Slips						0.52

2.2 *Identification of errors*

Each script was scrutinised for errors by two people working independently. Altogether four scrutineers were employed, and they were all naïve about the nature of the material they were examining in relation to the statistics reported later in this chapter. (One scrutineer who in fact worked through the majority of the scripts was also employed later in word- and letter-counts of scripts, as well as in making certain checks on the accuracy of the corpus.)

In searching for errors the scrutineers were instructed to record any word that deviated from the spelling of the Oxford Concise English Dictionary. Apparent errors which could be attributed to poor letter formation rather than wrong letters were not included; this exclusion was particularly relevant to practises of a shorthand nature such as contraction of *ing* into a downward squiggle. A deviation was recognised even if the error had been corrected by the candidate. In such cases the erroneous version was recorded as the sequence of letters up to the point at which the correction was made.

For every error, the scrutineer noted the target intended by the candidate, the three words preceding the error and the three words following the error. Only one error per word was counted. The position of the error in erroneous words was taken as the left-most letter in error. Any errors occurring later in the word were ignored because of the influence detection of the error might have had on completion of the word. In many cases it was clear that errors were even detected and corrected before the next letter was written. Further information recorded about the context of the error included the distance in words of the word containing the error from the boundaries of the sentence, the number of the line on the page and the number of the page in the script. In addition to these relatively simple details, the scrutineers were required to classify each error as a slip or as a convention error. An error was categorised as a slip if (a) it was changed to the correct spelling or (b) if uncorrected, the correct form of the word occurred at least once elsewhere in the script. Otherwise the error was categorised as a convention error.

The two lists of errors for each script were checked against the script by the first author as he keyed them into magnetic disc storage files on a computer. A computer print-out of the corpus was subsequently given to the scrutineer who had worked through the majority of the scripts and she checked it for errors against the original scripts.

2.3 Overall error rates and individual differences

The total number of errors (i.e. erroneous words) in the corpus is 1185. With an average script length of 203.5 (SD = 46.8) lines, the total number of words written by the 40 candidates was in the region of eighty thousand if we allow 10 words per line. This corresponds to an error rate of around 1.5% of words written, a figure that accords reasonably well with the estimate of Chedru and Geschwind (1972) that we cited earlier.

Of the 1185 errors, 175 involve an exact repetition or several repetitions of the same error by individual candidates. Excluding the second and later (if any) repetitions within the lists of errors for each candidate reduces the number of different errors to 1076. With one exception the following analyses were carried out on this latter sub-set of the full corpus. Of these errors 847 (79%) were classified as slips and 229 as convention errors. Of the slips 616 (73%) were corrected.

Having outlined the overall rate of errors it is interesting to return to Table 1 and observe the intercorrelation matrix for the 16 candidates who wrote papers in physics and mathematics. While the exam marks correlate positively with each other, they are negatively correlated with the frequency of both types of spelling error suggesting the influence of a general educational achievement factor. Little or no correlation would, a priori, be expected between physics or maths exam marks and the length of the general paper and indeed this is the case. However the positive correlation between the general paper mark and script length is perhaps a little more surprising.

A moderate-sized positive correlation is found between the frequencies of slips and convention errors. If we want to attribute the two classes of error to different causes this positive correlation might be seen as an embarrassment since it could arise from incorrect assignment of the spelling errors into the two categories. We will consider this possibility again in a later section. However there are other reasons why the error rate of one process might affect the other. For example, candidates who realise they have difficulty with remembering conventional spellings of words may allocate more processing capacity to the determination of spelling at the cost of reduced efficiency in the storage and retrieval of the letters in the temporary storage buffer.

2.4 *Sentence and word lengths*

Basing their estimate on a variety of genres of printed text of American origin Kučera and Francis (1967) report that the average sentence length is 19.3 (SD = 12.7) words and the average word length is 4.7 (SD = 2.7) graphic characters. Corresponding estimates for a selected sample drawn from the 40 scripts are average sentence length, 26.3 (SD = 12.4) words, and average word length, 4.6 (SD = 2.5) letters. (This sample, comprising 319 observations, was made up by selecting a sentence and a word in that sentence on every page of every script, using random number tables.)

Sentences which contain errors are not reliably longer than those in the random sample. The average length of sentences containing slips is 26.2 (SD = 13.4) words and of sentences containing convention errors, 27.5 (SD = 15.2) words. On the other hand, the correct versions of words containing spelling errors are longer than those in the random sample. Furthermore, the average correct length of words containing slips (7.0, SD = 2.9 letters) is reliably less than the average length of words containing convention errors (8.8, SD = 2.4 letters).

3 Distributional analyses

3.1 *A measure of the relative position of an error*

In the following sections we present our answer to the question 'Where do errors occur?' in a simplified fashion. We have normalised the distribution of errors so that the distributions as a function of position in the word, sentence, or script are not obscured by the range of word, sentence and script lengths that actually occurred. Our measure of where an error occurred was taken relative to a division of the word, sentence or script into five regions, or as we will refer to them, positions. In cases where the length in terms of total number of elements (letters, words and lines respectively) was a multiple of 5, an equal number of elements map onto each position. Where the length exceeds a multiple of 5 by one, two, three or four elements a corresponding number of symmetrically arranged positions represent an additional unit, as shown in Table 2.

TABLE 2   Number of elements (letters, words or lines) assigned to each position under the partition of words, sentences or scripts into five equal regions. For example, if a seven-letter word contained an error on the third letter, reference to the second row shows this error would be counted in position 2. (The letter k represents the integer values, 0, 1, 2, 3 ——)

Total no. of elements	Position				
	1	2	3	4	5
$k \times 5 + 1$	k	k	$k + 1$	k	k
$k \times 5 + 2$	$k + 1$	k	k	k	$k + 1$
$k \times 5 + 3$	$k + 1$	k	$k + 1$	k	$k + 1$
$k \times 5 + 4$	$k + 1$	$k + 1$	k	$k + 1$	$k + 1$
$(k + 1) \times 5$	$k + 1$	$k + 1$	$k + 1$	$k + 1$	$k + 1$
etc.					

For those slips in which an extra letter is inserted in a word, the number of possible letter places in the erroneous word exceeds the number of letter places in the target word. In general, if a word contained more than one error we only scored the left-most (i.e. first-written) letter in the word. Thus for slips involving insertion the number of possible letter places could exceed that in the target by one. In practice it was observed that slips in which a letter was inserted before the first target letter were very rare (two cases in our corpus) compared to the number of slips in which the insertion occurred after the last letter. We therefore decided to refer to the placement of insertion errors by the place of the immediately preceding letter in the target word. (The two cases in which there was an insertion before the first letter of the target were assigned to the first position.)

When we take up in turn the question of where do errors occur in the word, in the sentence and in the script we will contrast the obtained distribution with the null hypothesis that errors are distributed with equal probability over all letters, words or lines respectively.[1] However inspection of Table 2 will show that this null hypothesis does not predict equal frequencies of error occurrence over the five positions except in the special case where the lengths are all a multiple of 5. In general the expected frequencies under the null hypothesis have to be determined according to the observed distribution of lengths. In the following analyses account of the effect of the distribution of word, sentence and script lengths on the distribution of errors expected under the null hypothesis was taken in the following manner. The expected frequencies across the five positions were determined for each word, sentence or script length as shown in Table 2 and then they were summed by position over all word, sentence or script lengths. The observed frequencies of errors summed by position over all lengths were then divided by the expected frequencies. An estimate of the probability of error by position conditional on there being an error was obtained by dividing the ratios by 5 to yield a value that, under the null hypothesis, should be 0.2 at each position.

3.2 Distribution of errors in the word

The distribution of slips and of convention errors are plotted in the lower half of Fig. 1 as a function of relative position in the word. The distribution of slips [χ^2 (4) = 161.7, p <0.001] and of convention errors [χ^2 (4) = 109.0, p <0.001] both showed significant departures from the null hypothesis. Errors are less likely to occur near the beginning or end of words than in the middle. This depression of error rate at the extremes is more marked in convention errors.

Figure 1 shows that convention errors and slips differ in position of the mode. The mode is earlier in the word for slips than for convention errors. The result for convention errors is consistent with, for example, Mendenhall (1930). He reported that when schoolchildren were given word lists as spelling tests the errors they made occurred most frequently just after the middle of the word. Jensen (1962) has suggested the distribution of (convention) errors is due to the same learning mechanisms which give rise to the classical serial position curve in serial learning tasks. Another possibility is that difficulties associated with

---

[1] In determining the distribution of errors over words, the position of just the first (leftmost) letter in error was used if a word contained more than one error. On the null hypothesis that errors occur with equal probability p over all letters, the probability of the left-most error occurring at a particular letter position n is given by $pq^{n-1}/(l-q^w)$ where $q = l - p$ and w is the word length. In fact, we used the approximation that left-most errors are distributed with equal probability, which is reasonable given the very low error rates per letter we observed.

rules for adding suffixes causes the curve to peak to the right of middle.

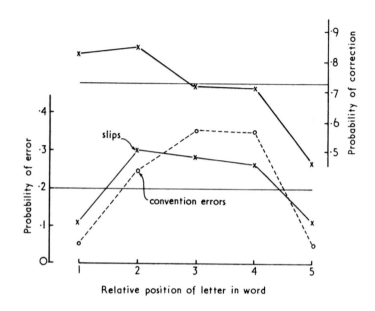

FIG. 1   Probability of error for slips (N = 847) and convention errors (N = 229) and probability of correction given a slip as a function of relative position of the left-most erroneous letter in the word

We now turn to the distribution of slips. Chedru and Geschwind (1972) found that errors are more likely in the last two letters than in the first two letters of the word. We suggested this could be due to serial retrieval from a short-term output buffer if there is temporal decay of the memory trace. However, in our corpus, we found the error probabilities in first and last positions are practically identical. We are thus inclined to favour the account of bow-shaped serial position curves given in Section 1.1 in which interference occurs only between immediately adjacent positions. What differences between the two studies might have given rise to the discrepant results on error rates at the beginning and end of the word? Methodological differences may be responsible. Certainly Chedru and Geschwind's analysis included material produced under dictation and not just spontaneously written prose. Their presentation of results doesn't allow us to assess the possible effect of production method.

It is possible that some of the difference arises in the scoring methods used. If Chedru and Geschwind scored all errors in a word (rather than the left-most) this would boost estimates of error probability in the late-serial positions. Although they state that errors could involve isolated letters as well as groups of letters their paper does not clearly indicate that multiple error locations were counted in the latter case.

Another difference in scoring procedure was Chedru and Geschwind's exclusion of words of less than five letters from their analysis. Carrying out this procedure, we found a sizeable increase in probability of slips at position 5 and little change at position 1. Moreover for word lengths 7, 8 and 9 letters, the *two* letters at each end used by Chedru and Geschwind would map onto positions 1, 2 and 4, 5 in our analysis. Pooling over both types of error we find that there are 25% more errors in the last two positions than in the first two. This is still considerably less than the seven-fold increase in error frequency evidenced in their data although the direction of the error rate changes is that predicted by the memory decay model.

In Section 1.3 we pointed out a potential disadvantage in using data obtained from situations where spelling error rates are elevated since the pattern of errors may be changed. The distribution of errors as a function of position in the word may also be linked to overall error rate. Chedru and Geschwind's data include errors from patients with high error rates and this could have contributed to the difference between our results and theirs.

In Figure 2 we compare the distributions of four types of slip as a function of position in the word. Our classification of the 847 slips was based on mutually exclusive categories of letter omission, substitution, insertion and reversal that roughly corresponded with the categories of letter omission, substitution, addition and inversion used by Chedru and Geschwind.[1] In terms of the proportion of the four types of slip we found a different ordering from Chedru and Geschwind. They observed relatively more addition errors, in fact, sufficient extra to place their estimate of addition error frequency between omissions (most frequent) and substitutions.

[1] Our four-way classification of slips by the left-most letter in error was based on the following criteria: *Omission:* a letter is omitted and is followed either by no other letter (because a break in the writing occurred to allow correction or because the omitted letter was the last letter in the target word), e.g. PRODI (PRODUCING), or by one or more of the remaining letters of the word, e.g. LIKLY (LIKELY). *Reversal:* two adjacent letters occur in reverse order, e.g. CANNTO (CANNOT). *Note:* if any 'half-completed reversals', e.g. CANNT, occur they would be classified as omissions. *Substitution:* an incorrect letter occurs followed either by no other letter, e.g. IS (IF), RAP (RADICAL) or by one or more of the remaining letters of the word, e.g. DESIREBLE (DESIRABLE). *Insertion:* an incorrect letter occurs followed by the letter that should have occurred but now occurs shifted one place to the right, e.g. REAS (RESEARCH). *Note:* if any 'incomplete insertions' without any following letter, e.g. REA, occur they are classified as substitutions.

Examination of the distributions in Fig. 2 reveals that whereas insertion errors are more likely in the final two positions 4 and 5, the other types are more likely to occur in positions 2 and 3. The substitution error distribution, if not identical to the distribution of omissions, is certainly closer to it than reversal errors. These data contrast with the recall of lists of digits for which Conrad (1959) states 'no evidence' has been found that a particular kind of error (transposition, omission, substitution, intrusion) is more likely to occur than any other kind at any particular position in the series. However if list recall errors are classified as order or item errors, according to whether the item incorrectly produced had been a member of the input sequence, order errors but not item errors show a serial position effect (Hitch, 1974). The latter corresponds well with our data on slips where the flat function for insertion errors contrasts with the bowed curves for the other 3 types of slip.

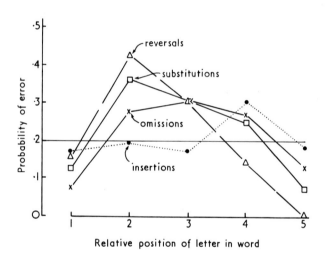

FIG. 2   Probability of error as a function of relative position in the word for slips classified into omissions (N = 412), substitutions (N = 304), insertions (N = 108) or reversals (N = 23)

What is the significance of the different distributions as a function of error type? In Section 1.1 we suggested that the interaction of error frequency with type of error found by Chedru and Geschwind implied at least two processes underlying the generation of errors. One process gives rise to omission and substitution errors, and another gives rise to errors of addition and inversion. If two error types are differently distributed through the word it suggests they are the result of different processes. (However it should be noted that the converse will not necessarily be true.) Thus our data also give support to the hypothesis that omission and substitution errors arise in a process that is distinct from the process in which insertion errors arise. Since the shapes of the distributions of insertion and reversal errors turn out to be different we now have grounds for believing there are two separate processes responsible for insertion and reversal errors.

The data on probability of correction given that any type of slip occurs are shown in the top half of Fig. 1. There is a significant effect of position in the word [χ^2 (4) $=$ 16.6, p $<$0.01]. When the slip occurs later in the word the likelihood of correcting it is much reduced. The dissociation between this function and the probability of error by position allows us to reject the idea that the process of correction is influenced simply by the likelihood of there being an error to correct. If we look at the breakdown of the correction probability data by type of error, it will be observed that the reduced correction probability at the end of the word is largely due to omission errors (see Fig. 3). Since many

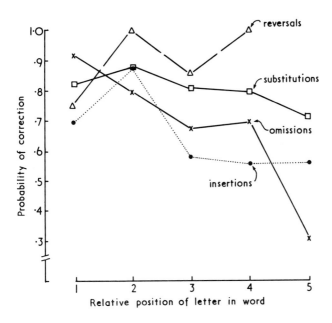

FIG. 3   Probability of correction for omissions, substitutions, insertions and reversals given a slip as a function of relative position in the word

uncorrected omission errors in position 5 left a meaningful word (e.g. letter *s* omitted from the plural) we interpret the correction data as reflecting the relative ease of finding different types of error. It is also possible that less processing capacity is available at the ends of words for monitoring errors, such capacity reduction being due to the operations needed to fetch the next word into the buffer.

3.3 *Distribution of errors in the sentence*

In presenting lists of writing errors and speech errors, Bawden (1900) suggested that many 'lapses' occurred due to 'lack of attention' which he related to fatigue. While we consider the role of fatigue in the production of spelling errors in the next section, in this section we present data that bear on another factor proposed by Bawden as contributing to errors. That factor is the 'competition' or 'divided attention' that arises when processing is required of two separate sources or, in his words, when 'two objects, either both external, one external and one internal, or both internal strive for the focal point in the field of consciousness'. As an example he mentions the apparent difficulty of attempting a conversation while composing a letter.

In one sense handwriting itself may be seen as an activity involving multiple levels of processing since, at the same time as making the movements to string out letter sequences we may be preparing the next phrase or sentence, perhaps thinking about choice of words and always holding in mind long-term directions for the prose. If we take Bawden's idea that handwritten errors arise from sharing of capacity, one might predict that error rates would be sensitive to sentence boundaries. Unless there are long pauses at the end of each sentence, as the end of one sentence is approached it is likely that the writer begins to prepare the next sentence, perhaps in terms of content or perhaps to convert it to a version encoded ready for transfer to the hypothesised temporary storage buffer. Allowing that such preparation takes some capacity away from processes responsible for the production and/or error checking of the current sentence, we might expect an increase in error rates for slips, and/or a decrease in their probability of correction at the end of each sentence.

The probability of slips and convention errors as a function of relative position in the sentence for our corpus is shown in the lower half of Fig. 4. Both the distribution of slips [χ^2 (4) $=$ 16.1, p <0.01] and of convention errors [χ^2 (4) $=$ 18.6, p <0.01] exhibit significant departures from the null hypothesis that errors are equiprobable over all words in a sentence. Error frequencies increase from the beginning to the end of the sentence. The probability of correction given a slip as a function of position in the sentence is shown in the upper part of Fig. 4. There is no significant effect of sentence position $[\chi^2\,(4) = 1.3, \text{p} < 0.2]$.

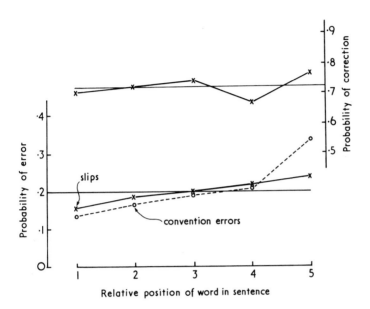

FIG. 4 Probability of error for slips and convention errors and probability of correction given a slip as a function of relative position of the word containing the error in the sentence

Although there is no evidence for the capacity sharing hypothesis in the probability of correction data, the predicted increase in the probability of slips as a function of position in the sentence is observed. But the parallel increase in convention errors is unexpected. It could indicate the existence of a factor unrelated to capacity sharing considerations that influences the distribution of errors of either type. We have checked and found that word length does not increase systematically through the sentence. If word length had changed this could conceivably have produced the parallel increase, given that slips and convention errors do involve words that are longer than average. We now consider two other possibilities.

When the frequency of occurrence of signals to be detected in vigilance tasks drops, probability of detection declines (Baddeley and Colquhoun, 1969). In the compilation of our corpus the low rates of spelling errors make it possible that some errors were missed by the scrutineers. If their ability to detect spelling errors is a function of position in the sentence such that performance improves toward the end of each sentence, the function in Fig. 4 may have nothing to do with changes in the frequency of spelling errors produced by the candidates. The only published data we know of that even begins to address this question is that of Smith and Groat (1977). In tasks requiring detection of the occurrence of every letter *e* in prose they found no changes in performance as a function of position of the word containing the letter through the sentence. However, their data were collected from people looking at printed material and the task did not involve detection of errors. We therefore carried out a brief experiment on the detectability of handwritten spelling errors.

The initial pages of the scripts of 7 candidates were checked for errors by between 7 and 9 members of the APU subject panel. The correlation over 65 errors of the relative number of subjects detecting the error with distance of the erroneous word from the beginning of the sentence was −0.15. (Each initial page contained between 6 and 11 slips and convention errors, the average place of erroneous words was in the middle of the sentence, and on average each error was detected by just over one third of the subjects.) Although the correlation is not statistically significant, the negative trend is important since it indicates that, if anything, detectability of errors declines through the sentence. We thus conclude that the sentence position effect on the production of errors is not an artefact of the scrutineers' error-checking abilities.

The motivation for attempting to distinguish between slips and convention set out in Section 1.2 was that the latter reflect educational deficiencies and not the moment-to-moment difficulties in maintaining continuous handwritten output. Unfortunately in classifying errors our scrutineers were required to use the category of convention error by default whenever an error was not demonstrably a slip. It is possible to argue that only those errors which are repeated that unambiguously demonstrate a failure to follow conventional spelling as a result of a deficit in knowledge. We therefore performed an analysis to look specifically at the distribution of occurrence of those errors where a word written incorrectly is repeated on at least one other occasion in its incorrect form by a particular individual. Repetitions were taken to include errors involving the same base even though the suffix may have differed. It will be noted that by including all the repetitions of a particular error by an individual this analysis took some examples from the corpus that were not included in preceding analyses.

The distribution of repetitions (of which there are 175 in the corpus) by position in the sentence is shown in Fig. 5. No consistent increase with position in the sentence is seen. All 1010 errors that were not repetitions are represented in the other curve which clearly shows the steady increase in error probability with sentence position. For completeness we have given the probability of correction for these latter errors as a function of sentence position in the upper part of the figure.

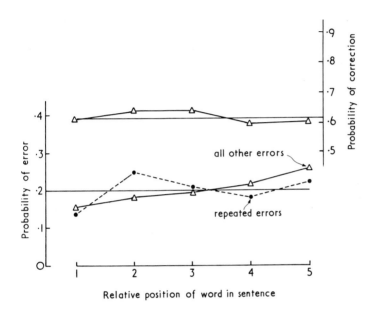

FIG. 5   Probability of error for errors occurring more than once that involve the same word in the same script (N = 175) and all other errors (N = 1010) and probability of correction given an error in the latter class as a function of relative position in the sentence

Our conclusion, then, is that with a more stringent procedure for discriminating between slips and convention errors we appear to be able to make a clearer case for the capacity sharing hypothesis. That is, the frequency of those errors that are not attributable to educational deficiency increases through the current sentence, possibly because preparation is started for the next sentence before the writing reaches the end of the current sentence.

3.4 Distribution of errors through the script

After a three-hour exam most people begin to experience general feelings of fatigue. From the noticeable decline in the neatness of the writing evident in the exam scripts, we judged our 40 candidates were probably no exception. Given Bawden's (1900) suggestion that lack of attention due to fatigue is a determinant of lapses we thought it worth looking to see whether there are more errors with progression through the script.

The probability of error as a function of relative position in the script is given in the lower part of Fig. 6. Neither convention errors $[\chi^2 \ (4) = 4.9, \ p \ > 0.2]$ nor slips $[\chi^2 \ (4) = 5.6, \ p \ > 0.2]$ showed significant departures from the null hypothesis, that errors are equiprobable across position in the script.

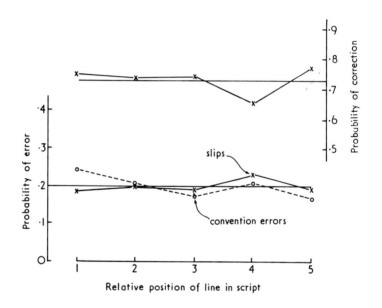

FIG. 6   Probability of error for slips and convention errors and probability of correction given a slip as a function of relative position of the line containing the error in the script

In the upper half of Fig. 6 the probability of correction given that a slip occurs, is shown as a function of position. Deviations from the marginal probability of correction, (shown by the horizontal line with ordinate 0.73), were not significant, $[\chi^2 \ (4) = 4.0, \ p \ <0.2]$.

Thus we conclude that neither the production processes nor the monitoring processes responsible for affecting error correction are sensitive to increase in levels of general fatigue, or at least to such changes as occur in the course of an exam.

4 Discussion and conclusion

It is our hope that the corpus of over one thousand spelling errors listed with their contexts in the Appendix will prove useful for the testing of theories of handwritten spelling errors. In the body of this chapter we have presented an analysis of the distribution of spelling errors and interpreted our findings in terms of the information processing that a person possibly engages in to produce handwritten prose. In particular we considered the proposal that the errors that are slips, as opposed to errors of convention, arise in a temporary storage buffer. We assumed the buffer takes as input letters, a word at a time, and the letters are retrieved serially by the process that translates them into actual movements. With the delays in retrieval that would be imposed by the mechanical constraints in writing, we suggested that the memory trace of letters later in the word might be significantly decayed. This would result in more errors with progression through the word.

This expectation was not confirmed in our data. The probability of a spelling error near the end of a word was no greater than near the beginning. The simple assumption that errors result from decay within the buffer is therefore not supported. The elevation of error probability in middle positions in the word relative to either end is however consistent with the assumption of interference between items in adjacent positions of the memory buffer. Because the function is flat we must assume the interference effect at one position is restricted to the immediately neighbouring positions. Since the unit of analysis, relative position in the word, subsumes two or even three letters in large words we are thus led to conclude interference effects are limited to only a very few adjacent letters.

When the slips in our corpus were classified by whether the error involved letter omission, substitution, insertion or reversal, in contrast to studies of short-term memory, we found rather different distributions by relative position of the letter in the word. This finding was taken as support for our earlier interpretation of Chedru and Geschwind's data on the interaction of the change in frequency of errors with error type. Errors of insertion and of reversal arise in separate processes and errors of omission and substitution arise in a process, separate from either insertions or reversals.

A detailed analysis of the letters involved in errors might prove helpful in separating out the contribution of different processes. For example, classification of letters involved in substitution errors according to whether they are phonemic, orthographic or motoric (based on similar movements, see for example Van Nes, 1971) might suggest the existence of more than one storage buffer, (or a hierarchy of representattions within a buffer). The methodological problem is, of course, that judgments of motoric similarity and to some extent orthographic similarity would involve consideration of the movements and letter structure used by individual candidates.

Because the probability of a slip increases through the sentence, operation of the temporary storage buffer that we are proposing as a source of errors should not be thought of as a passive set of processes insulated from other processes necessary for writing prose. With some reservations about the classification we achieved based on the distinction between slips and convention errors, we nonetheless feel the sentence position distribution provides support for an account of processing in which capacity is shared dynamically with other processes.

Included under 'other processes' one should probably recognise monitoring activities that check on output of the storage buffer as well as higher level activities that pass down the words for written output. The interesting questions about correction include: How and when are errors picked up? What is the nature of the concurrent reading if this is involved in the monitoring? Can such monitoring trigger errors, perhaps in the manner of a 'false alarm'? Clearly we have only just begun to scratch the surface with our distributional analysis. However, rather than apologising, perhaps we can feel the contribution of this chapter has been to do the necessary clearing of the site for the building that will follow.

Acknowledgements

We express our thanks to Susan Langmore for discussions on spelling errors and to Louise Sanders for her valuable assistance in compilation of the corpus.

5 Appendix: The error corpus

On the following pages a computer print-out of all the spelling errors found in the 40 exam scripts is reproduced. They are separated into the two classes, slips (Type 1) and convention errors (Type 2). Within this classification each candidate's errors (including targets and contexts) are grouped together in the sequence in which they occurred in the script. For each error the erroneous form of the word is given first as it was written up to the break in the written trace at which the error was corrected, if a correction was attempted. The target form of the word is then given. If shown in parentheses no correction was attempted by the candidate. When the target for a Type 1 error is shown mis-spelled this indicates a slip was made in producing a Type 2 (convention) error. The latter would thus also be listed under Type 2 errors. Some of the Type 2 targets not in parentheses appear mis-spelled. This indicates that the initial mis-spelled version was changed, but to another incorrect form of the word as shown. The context comprises the three words written immediately before the error and the three words written immediately after the error separated by (*). In the context letters or words in parentheses indicate items in the script deleted by the candidate. Punctuation marks are not indicated although sentence boundaries are identifiable by the initial capital letter. The abbreviations SQ and EQ stand for start and end of the candidate's answer to a question.

This corpus with additional quantitative information about error position etc. exists in the form of a formatted punched paper tape. It is suggested that anyone contemplating computer-assisted analysis of the corpus first contact the authors since in particular cases they may be able to make a copy of the tape available.

```
Type: 1
 1
intele intellect   pursuit of individual * it must not
censorsored (censored)   must not be * by the sponsorship
likly (likely)   which is more * to succeed than
An (Any)   is an individual * fruitless individual research
resarc research   An fruitless individual * being immediatly cur
  -tailed
immediatly (immediately)   individual research being * curtailed
  Because we
prodi producing   other way of * the results An
wull will   questions as I * state below How
no (now)   question I will * support this view
unabiguous (unambiguous)   necessarily the most * one to chose
chose (choose)   unabiguous one to * but i would
describe (described)   science may be * very sucinctly if
wa wearing   is now The * of seat belts
war wear   ensure that people * seat belts is
wa wearing   number of people * seat belts indeed
inded indeed   wearing seat belts * even the less
likly (likely)   existing cars is * to be prohibitive
posible possible   safety it is * that any inteference
inteference (interference)   possible that any * with the mechan
  -ism
malfuc malfunction   result in their * which would thus
dilema dillema   course presents the * of who is
center counter   taxation would be * productive There is
unaceptable unacceptable   think be socially * for the police
affraid afraid   or wrongly are * of the British
w vehicals   power to stop * for numerous reasons
imprisons imprison   far as to * someone for not
were whereby   introduce a system * (the) anyone who was
sould should   think that it * be a requirement
desireble desirable   would be highly * for there to
campagn campaign   present shock properganda * to (en) try to
own own   belts of their * free will EQ
 2
impo improves   before then Research * understanding but and use
reas research   use of scientific * is the indication
scient science   now obselete Applied * has more immediate
bef benefits   has more immediate * whereas pure science
itsef itself   and enlarges on * Pure research is
aswered (answered)   for immediate questions * If we had
of or   of an idea * theory is little
consup consumption   dependence continues increasing * and incre
  -asing dependence
live (life)   current way of * for as long
enevitable (inevitable)   fuels is however * and with it
ret requirement   our minimum energy * There are many
lef lesson   have learned a * from our present
envio environment   expense of our * and it seem
seem (seems)   environment and it * to be approaching
Some (So)   be nuclear power * much power from
of our   useful commodities from * environment and now
wate waste   environment harmful nuclear * which even though
a us   moral conviction in * all to be
inehaustible inexhaustible   small but comparatively * and non-d
```

```
  -etrimental potential
rap radical   hope for little * change in our
sence sense   a strictly non-political * The conservative person
culu cultures   to long past * The valuable experience
leart learnt   things to be * and gained from
consert conservative   some degree The * would argue that
pe purpose   still serve a * to maintain and
competion (competition)   women rather than * In wanting things
all also   advancement but it * serves to deter
ef ever   any change is * to occur Therefore
at as   valuable to society * the wish for
 3
elu education   time as an * At present scientists
hea here   for the encouragement * is because research
form far   specialist has had * more experience of
Cambrige (Cambridge)   SQ * Colleges Examinations General
objet object   cost when an * is to be
rasing raising   used energy in * that object Exactly
we when   can be applied * cycling up hill
usually (usual)   ontop of the * effort put in
byc bicycle   the road the * and our own
wen we   the only way * are expending energy
pedels (pedals)   in turning the * the pedals will
attacked attached   one body and * inside another body
are (area)   sensation the sensative * of the back
mircroscopic (microscopic)   nerves All these * cells would have
th to   cell must go * the right part
techiques (techniques)   by modern medical * is clearly impossib
  -le
Cambrige (Cambridge)   SQ * Colleges Examinations General
an (a)   can occur if * car hits another
inury injury   such cases the * cased could have
cased (caused)   cases the injury * could have been
concened (concerned)   leave the people * with a choice
ins incentive   insurance as an * I am very
diffuculty difficulty   point is the * in enforcing such
arr around   The only way * this problem would
wether whether   the car Indicating * or not the
diffu difficulties   were enforced then * I am sure
greater (great)   of seatbelts too * infringement of personal
 4
cannto cannot   of science one * escape the fact
symettry symmetry   these may have * about themselves that
aboit about   may have symmetry * themselves that is
prop probability   period that its * distribution of electrons
symettrical symmetrical   of electrons is * Progressing further
  still
symettrical symmetrical   that to be * an object should
fundamet fundamental   electrons and other * particles (should)
  being considered
word world   an absolutely perfect * would be extremely
ojects objects   boring or perhaps * made by man
symettrical symmetrical   man are not * because of mans
lie live   appears that we * (o) in a world
appoa approach   where many things * symmetry but nothing
aviid avoid   of science to * being swamped with
aco accomplished   individuals (have .. the discovery) have * mo
  -st of (science) the science
```

cout country people in this * are finding tha
exep except for doing nothing * signing a card
Empoymen (Employmen) to the local * office I am
6
yars (years) scientist spends five * on a project
Wen we worth is overestimated * know no other
explaratory (exploratory) science is an * and imaginative proc
-ess
Imagenation (Imagination) and imaginative process * having a h
-uch
int inventiveness choose but his * is just as
oxi oxygen the production of * was observed simultaneously
proccess process rule for the * of interpretation science
stau star formation of a * using the observations
spectoscopy (spectoscopy) the observations of * and Xray phot
-ograph
photograph (photography) spectoscopy and Xray * a scientist (h
-a) can
daubt (doubt) is to cast * upon the basic
main man of the same * after a meal
astonomy (astronomy) of modern science * being an example
be (by) etcetera (Art) An art * definition is also
tu the also a skill * basics of which
commisioner (commissioner) dictated by the * not the poet
discase discarded art can be * The conclusion must
7
any another scientific knowledge is * brushstroke added to
is it they are studying * so closely that
the that explain the part * is being studied
Scienci Scientists with one another * have become bickering
bickere bickering scientists have become * egocentric individu
-als and
political political unhappy leads to * unrest Scientific know
-ledge
og organisations made nation wide * necessary In the
convinient convenient take what is * to us We
econi economic these are for * purposes (an) or polictical
polictical (political) economic purposes (an) or * advantage
-w) both of which
furt future specifically for the * (which) plans that would
convi convenient at present extremely * to us there
a our sources or reduce * energy consumption by
it is another or what * commonly referred to
Nuclear Nuclear low impact technology * energy would offer
boma bombarding particles could be * the DNA in
shit shut power stations to * down I feel
it in could have done * the first place
convinient (convenient) A-T as a * abbreviation is simple
luv individuals enough to enable * to set up
recate relate a person to * to such a
upheavels upheavals course such great * in social structure
fantast fantasy a space age * of believing that
8
a (at) will soon need * least thrice the
urgu urgency understanding and requires * to give it
research (research) various lines of * will never meet
on of of results expected * modern science because
tw too has become far * complex for even

reas research process up scientific * is done for
manknd mankind the benefit of * and must therefore
helpfil helpful and objectives are * in research as
establishments (establishments) Most of the * which give suppor
-t
research research scientists to do * in a field
praci practicle be of direct * use The writer
possibly possibly reached (to) viable conclusions * he is (d)
also
narnc narrow the straight and * path to the
pissible possible in the shortest * time neglecting other
deadil deadliest manufacture of bigger * bombs etc reconcilable
ny hundred year twenty three * and five which
piecing (piecing) awakened by a * siren as he
5
word (world) knowledge of the * in which we
last (lasting) become a job * ten years or
tens (ten) a job last * years or more
nowa nowadays four years usual * As the expanse
than (that) my opinion is * imagination and exploration
is in a large part * (st) scientific advancement
st scientific large part in * advancements but they
ungertly (urgently) the fields most * required eg medical
reser research passes ej nuclear * and alternative technology
scie science advancements made in * (are) may well be
is in operation between specialists * more than one
indival (individual) study Thus while * work was encouraged
ad about hundred years bringing * many major advances
nuprd hundred next fifty to * years the majority
indivuals (individuals) or teams not * EU
scienic scientific which depends on * interpretation the nece
-ssary
interpart interpretation depends on scientific * the necessary
incroduction introduction interpretation the necessary * is a
simple
is its on a nill * weight must still
group ground body onto the * Any force acting
bycle bicycle force when a * is standing or
bicyl bicycle when pedaling a * along a level
upwill (uphill) Thus when pedalling * the resistance to
when (when) greater than that * pedalling on the
leval (level) pedal on the * EU
until until expansion is insignificant * the liquid begins
is it begins to boil * becomes converted into
convers converted it is being * to a gas
lighted lighter steam produced is * than air so
stem steam becoming full of * when milk boils
amot amount milk boils the * of meat needed
than that is less than * for steam Thus
tine time in a given * the vapour thus
form (formed) the vapour thus * is lighter than
than (that) vapourize it follows * when we
beyons beyond it does so * the sides of
situating situation etc in that * people should be
encourage (encouraged) people should be * to find a
fee free more money tax * then we
peice piece a ne three * sure (suddenly found them) becomes

irrationallity irrationality   the inconclusiveness and * of thi
-s past
import (important)   therefore the most * decision (in) which ef
-fects
forcasts (forecasts)   to totally different * anyway if they
indivdually individually   they were considered * On the other
consering considering   For example by * the previous fifty
milenium millenium   consider the last * as a whole
p but   towards increasing overpopulation * a far more
buts (but)   just as spectacular * takes on a
interper interpretations   whatever the different * that may be
he his   driver put on * seat belt Besides
governme government   company or the * or the participant
reat relatively   would also be * immune to the
convential conventional   injustice which less * methods tend to
it (is)   This final proposal * therefore probably the
convential (conventional)   a common and * method for achieving
9
increase increasing   Scientific facts are * all the time
obi observe   being present to * chance take its
may many   end sum of * years of careful
im information   planets and learn * regarding these Rockets
the (then)   the satellite will * communcate by radio
communcate (communicate)   satellite will the * by radio waves
determin (determine)   earths surface and * the position of
houshe household   which the average * is benefitting Originally
mu mist   was a thick * shrouding everything arround
squrting squirting   the bar by * the drink from
for four   houses of the * of them and
fw few   would find a * changes Just as
platic (plastic)   their seats a * voice from a
thoughout (throughout)   and cheers for * the hundred years
10
storey (story)   together are the * of succesful science
yeas years   dedicated individual spending * on a personal
slove solve   is known to * the problem We
Stict (Strict)   on existing knowledge * adherence to it
predicable (predictable)   a finite and * set of steps
souces (sources)   the major energy * would have three
Cites (Cities)   of large cities * by their very
partiularly particularly   deal of transportation * of food to
widesread (widespread)   this would be * so necesscay is
necesscay (necessary)   be widesread so * is mobility to
Comminites (Communities)   our present society * would become mo
-re
Plastis (Plastics)   shape and properties * can be designed
bittle brittle   soft tough or * as a replacement
insum insurmountable   no longer an * barrier to the
synbol (symbol)   is a classic * of the advance
eveywhere (everywhere)   from anywhere to * Television is certai
-nly
blnk (blink)   error in the * of an eye
tediuos tedious   be not merely * but impossible without
fundanental (fundamental)   studying the most * elements of the
precison (precision)   of the largest * instrments built by
instrments (instruments)   the largest precison * built by man
precison precision   aligned to this * so that a
wondeful (wonderful)   world Perhaps most * of all it

difficut (difficult)   and generally very * to destroy The
previouly previously   of people into * unspoilt places where
ham (harm)   even when nc * is intended they
medicin (medicine)   preposterous amounts Modern * is surely pur
-e
doubb doubtless   past Ah well * people found fault
11
rea research   wrong for all * to be like
12
ve view   of the following * c In b it is stated
somo someone   feel that if * is given a
work (works)   why a thing * can answer the
as answer   part of the * to the how
Punshment Punishment   devices Incentive schemes * Conclusion Ma
-ny people
13
build (built)   be stored and * up into an
every (ever)   up into an * increasing pyramid of
kn now   and the scientist * has to be
creatitivity (creativity)   his imagination and * but for such
Reasearch Research   to the scientist * is for the
reasearch research   backing but any * which leads nowhere
valuble (valuable)   are scarce and * not financially but
every ever   not last for * and so should
thorought thoughtlessly   not be thrown * away Financial backing
projets projects   directed at worthwhile * and not given
discovers discoveries   of men making * in their own
reas researches   team in new * to make new
whih which   its own symmetry * can be broken
emprace embrace   since it can * things which appear
abse abstract   from factual thro * In mathematics symmetry
symetrical (symmetrical)   which are perfectly * along any diame
-ter
looses (loses)   more abstract it * more and more
unsyme unsymmetrical   a completely unordered * abstract Other i
-tems
suu such   and PY In * fields symmetry is
severly (severely)   this field is * limited and definitely
limm limited   field is severly * and definitely questionable
rareley rarely   to theory and * finds requirement in
situation (situations)   arguement However practical * can be pu
-rposely
scientist (scientists)   chemically and early * believed them to
assymnetry (assymmetry)   However it is * which affects light
affets affects   is assymnetry which * light compounds which
whih which   affects light compounds * contain an assymmetric
detro dextro   to the right * the other to
syme symmetry   many things possess * flowers animals buildings
bul buildings   symmetry flowers animals * and many rely
plasing pleasing   Most symmetry is * and gives one
be (been)   electronic circuits have * minaturised transistorise
-d integrated
need (needed)   a microscope is * to view them
pinoneered pioneered   advance and has * the way to
n moon   way to the * and landing craft
is (it)   man good well * seems so Man
tens (ten)   with banks of * years ago each
tyre type   a few typwriter * keys this has

mantain maintain for people to * the computer Large
lesses losses now make such * It is however
information information produced to store * from the computer
cotries (Countrys) which aids a * economy Not only
sed send in orbit or * satellites to other
schol schools stages eg in * teaching children all
uses used computers can be * as a source
untimate ultimate mankind towards an * goal and computers
14
cons concerning explicitly the problems * the continuation of
prei periods train for extened * of time up
is (as) on the scientist * it will inhibit
wants (want) as the scientists * Necessity is the
Neccesiy Necessity the scientists wants * is the mother
suppore supported people should be * because projects have
soli solving better way of * problems than applied
insted instead a direct manner * of going indirctly
inderctly (indirectly) instead of going * in the hope
Ab Albert genius such as * Einstein and Isaac
sitt situation a very different * now Never before
being (been) of mans existence * challenged Many of
ultimatel ultimate so when the * exhaustion occurs there
exhaustion (exhaustion) when the ultimate * occurs there wil
-l

Becu Because would be inhibited * of fossil energy
been (being) of land to * a very compact
as (is) almost every point * accesible (This would) Thus our
cas caused of fossil fuel * the development of
def devices most fuel efficient * and so attitudes
ultimatel ultimate now before the * drying up of
nesse necessary that would be * would be gradual
aucomobile automobile fatality (on) in * accidents on a
increase (increased) the need for * safety measures in
safty (safety) need for increase * measures in cars
cars car mobility in the * is very limited
individual individual dictates that the * should not have
coerce coerce advances and thus * the motorist into
imple implies devices so that * that they are
infalib infallible they are not * If some part
and (an) is to provide * incentive that should
pa practical like a very * solution when one
in on this is made * the basis of
easily (easy) It is quite * to forget doing
steat seat as fastening a * belt The law
license licence of his drivers * could be inflicted
pla pleasure or individuals derive * from breaking the
inent incentive therefore be an * to break the
force forcibly to be imposed * on the motorists
15
increaseng increasing to see is * in all directions
wealh wealth all directions The * of imformation which
vaste vast produced is so * that not one
scienic (scientific) The growth of * knowledge effectively re
-sults
effectivly effectively of scientific knowledge * results in th
-e
Scientic (Scientific) been discovered previously * knowledge h

-as reach
his has previously Scientic knowledge * reach to large
reach (reached) Scientic knowledge has * to large a
to (too) knowledge has reach * large a (size) volume
science (science) secnd passage provided * is suggested to
vaste vast to be a * playing ground in
have has suggested that science * no limits and
ep experimental with facts and * data The existence
insteret (interest) of imagination and * is presumed to
secondary secondary presumed to be * to thes more
thes (this) be secondary to * more mechanical approach
widly widely is the most * accepted mechanism through
tho through widely accepted mechanism * which advances may
seccialization specialization In fact one * is met before
decisi decisions science involves The * of the post
scientic (scientific) life within the * field or other
decided (decide) he must then * what further subjects
persueded (persued) general course be * if (the) for example
special (specialize) person forced to * If (not) he is
obvious! obvious be prevented An * solution is to
thes (this) simly fcund for * problem Combined with
abo absorbed recguired to be * by even the
having (have) the trends that * been taking place
prefore before matter of time * reserves diminish This
notably (notable) be the most * ones upon society
o importance the centre of * the accumulation of
suh such would change to * a degree in
suh such mobile fossil fuels * as oils and
carboniferous carboniferous as oils and * compounds would resul
-t

vaste vast which form a * amount of consumer
recqur required the petrochemical industries * crude for the
gradual (gradually) energy that would * develop would undoubt
-edly
become (becomes) energy if it * abundant as a
hod hold tidal energies would * numerous problems such
become (become) energy would not * so available as
consumer (consumer) great value The * society that has
at advance cannot continue to * at the rate
ins injuries reduced level of * that are received
mater matter is a different * The majority of
to (that) possible to argue * a person is
by (buy) not forced to * a car which
Ultimately (Ultimately) removing his rights * taking this view
wo which such technological devices * could ultimately remove
is (his) to how he * conduct is life
bg bags he show conduct * life There are
incourage (encourage) example the inflatable * which prevent head
person (persons) would encourage those * that do not
at (as) himself at risk * I believe he
16
discipline (discipline) place in a * where men should
thougt (thought) applied science is * to give quicker
qucker quicker thougt to give * results But what
disciplines (disciplines) Years However many * would be unavail
-able

obai obtain   he managed to * amino acids This
several (several)   mean one of * things Only one
formes (forms)   present today two * of life were
asymmetrical (asymmetrical)   use for the * property of carbon
natrally (naturally)   Glucose can exist * in two forms
directio (direction)   in the same * so when glucose
atom (atoms)   these two carbon * all the glucose
diaramatically diagramatically   same direction ie * This means
that
molecul (molecul)   spiral of glucose * This means that
beeween between   glucose bond together * the first and
gluo glucose   cellulose each subsequent * molecule is invertd
invertd (inverted)   glucose molecule is * with respect to
moleculs (molecules)   formed between these * how a lattice
structu (structure)   a lattice type * can be formd
form (formed)   this way cellulose * a rigid structure
asymmetrical (asymmetrical)   other examples of * molecules in
organism
organism (organisms)   asymmetrical molecules in * which are ba
-sically
asyme asymmetry   due to the * of the carbon
prise (price)   not cause the * of the car
care car   prise of the * to rise any
idear (idea)   possibly other technological * would mean It
idear idea   that for this * if there was
diffent (different)   up However a * idear such as
idear (idea)   However a diffent * such as the
presure (pressure)   combination of no * or pressure and
idear idea   a very good * basically because I
idear idea   would want the * it wouldn't encourage
weare (wear)   every one to * a seat belt
premun (premium)   pay a lower * and then forget
douc doubt   it would no * cause extra cost
incorporatd (incorporated)   the technological device * in ones
car
20
p body   to enlarge this * of scientific knowledge
every ever   result of an * increasing body of
woking working   of imaginative individuals * in a free
fee free   working in a * situation It also
reparesents represents   The third paragraph * the opposite view
ten teams   lie with research * combining all talents
at all research teams combining * talents necessary to
aspect aspect   the only positive * of science is
thng thing   is the only * that can be
exhasted exhausted   fossil fuel are * If this should
forsee foresee   society can you * as a consequence
cond confidently   out as is * expected to happen
otter other   try to find * sources of energy
put but   is hoped for * if it should
is it for but if   should prove impractical
impractia impractical   it should prove * and solar wind
unnotic unnoticed   and possibly most * use of fossil
emp embargo   or an oil * of one kind
diswh dishwashers   our washing machines * electric irons fridge

intially (initially)   motor industries not * since many men
daminished diminished   the immediate demand * Entertainment too
would
shifts shifts   situation and perhaps * would be introduced
increases (increases)   strengths would be * thus not only
establism establishments   larger hostel type * where heating co
uld
campains campaigns   governments save it * In the long
section (sections)   out that certain * of our society
genuinly genuinely   the person who * wanted to wear
Furthermoo Furthermore   in certain quarters * it would be
may many may result in * people not wearing
17
come commercial   not distracted by * enterprise and when
as a work might represent * praiseworthy effort The
encourg encourage   considered virtuous to * research into cance
-r
im in move faster than * air and huygen's
effet (effect)   explain the photoelectric * amongst other thing
-s
awaw away   and blows them * but he knows
slih silhouettes   soil but stark * just visible against
18
detct detective   likened to a * a discovery is
den been   connection has ever * found as yet
exeption exception   space research The * to this rule
surl surely   was made then * means inquisitiveness was
mann man   be satisfied It * was not meant
restrici restriction   own conscience without * This will mean
exa exhausted   fossil fuel are * if this should
forsee foresee   society can you * as a consequence
fosscil (fossil)   or indirectly The * fuels are oil
too to   It is easy * push aside the
Nol Not   in their manufacture * all carbon compounds
aboc about   need to worry * Plastics are taking
impurite impurities   forms and the * go to industry
fl fuel   by another fossil * The ways of
maved (moved)   but has now * to better fields
th to   has also returned * the land in
simia similar   sources of energy * to this waiting
wati waiting   similar to this * to be discovered
ons on   electricity being generated * solely nuclear power
aircraft aircraft   trains boats and * we must also
19
is if   advance very rapidly * its direction is
discoverd discovery   specific line of * will be found
ideas idea   on the bright * of quarks which
particals particles   so called elementary * The aquisition of
ment (meant)   of this theory * it was possible
combination (combinations)   up of different * of a few
ther their   out more about * nature It is
feedom freedom   although lack of * can bring great
togethers (together)   individual specialists so * they will wor
-k
asymmetry (asymmetry)   or more importantly * is the fact
asymmetrical (asymmetrical)   atom can be * For example the
feed fed   an animal is * the other sort
approp appropriate   fit into the * digesting enzyme The

-s
de die mass transit would * a natural death
natrual (natural) would die a * death But what
communicate communication be the instant * around the world
wold world communication around the * Gone indeed would
remnders reminders be left with * of our profligate
electrical electrical assumes that all * and oil derived
oill oil all electrical and * derived power and
reall reality is withdrawn in * a small amount
hydroelectric hydroelectric sources such as * power wave power
undoubedly undoubtedly This power would * be very expensive
lanscape landscape return to a * dotted with windmills
wa wide Britain If a * ranging and large
occured occurred of power available * the meaning of
ide idle The present somewhat * done it all
ly living the difference between * and dying The
set seat that wearing a * belt gives better
ch clash in a car * than not wearing
unsf unsafe cars around potentially * until they are
ignton ignition on and the * is on such
efficient efficiency certainly with reduced * presenting a ha
-zard
in enforced could not be * without (either) giving it
off open population they are * to abuse The
21
knew (new) able to gain * knowledge To prevent
sient scientists so many facts * now specialise in
duy day hope that one * these researches will
revolutionised Revolutionized their scientific genius * scient
-ific thinking in
mew new they put forward * theories The information
many (main) world (today) The three * types of fossil
they the more conservative in * way they used
they the time for which * heating was left
a (at) is accustomed to * present again if
inteaded intended state was originally * for those who
na male due to the * member of the
for far welfare state are * to great at
by buy enough money to * the bare necessities
mooe more state can obtain * money (going to) than a
mooey (money) can obtain more * (going to) than a person
Thus This should be avoided * encourages laziness in
22
Utility Utility or direct thought * is the only
indidual individual day of the * is almost over
research research useruiness of scientific * because it is
usefull useful out to be * at some future
probably (probably) getting nowhere it * would be as
bicycle (bicycle) thus it the * slows down it
interisting interesting is perhaps more * is that water
at actually underlying molecules to * leave the mass
ve leave molecules to actually * the mass of
buble bubble to form a * deep below the
drik drinks on not milk * This skin traps
show should that the ignition * not work unless
all already for the reason * stated unsound if
probably probably out it would * encourage people to

lifes lives of careless peoples * All that is
Probably (probably) round the corner * still wouldnt bother
Secondly Secondly on short journeys * there are a
insure ensure how does one * that they do
23
previos previously assessing of facts * gathered for the
reas research success of scientific * solely by its
nubbers number (and) Thus the * of road accidents
pero period one ten year * compared to the
fluctuations (fluctuates) of the variables * EQ
ap opinion degree by public * or some other
24
appled applied method to be * could be found
suprly supplies of alternate fuel * are but it
to do even if goverments * not introduce energy
that than terms of energy * the production of
plactic plastic of recycling used * to make petrol
priority priorities to rearrange its * the principles would
be being the biggest change * social A good
thing (things) question and such * as sugar even
availabe available sugar even if * would be very
gra drastically energy costs go * up food prices
factr factory over automation The * with its (necessity)
in is then the worker * naturally lazy Society
25
succesful (successful) it will be * EQ
whia what scientists to investigate * they feel like
byci bicycle much when you * uphill you still
information information all the visual * of the outside
th to work The damage * their tissues is
attentin attention wont draw any * you cant have
fid fit it doesnt * the model at
women (woman) into an impulsive * who suddenly decides
walk (walks) is brilliant He * about Gerald doesnt
thing (things) totally controled by * outside of himself
character (character) I disagree the * got some real
sorted sort he has a * of timing mechanism
frips flips timing mechanism that * him about from
sli silent lone drinker a * man up at
26
paragraphs paragraph SO This * proposes that science
knowlede knowledge the boundaries of * At present he
iegures requires (A) (scientific thought *) A scientist canno
-t
resonable reasonable prevented at all * cost for the
benefites benefits science brings immediate * in comparison wi
-th
vairi various hope that the * fields will (all) converge
siaply simply this encouragement is * it says because
no (know) says because we * of no other
resar research direct route of * necessary to solve
resar research nature of scientific * and also in
an (and) it can be * quite often is
re Rises that the sun (appears) * and sets at
estabise established it has been * beyond reasonable doubt
res reasonable been established beyond * doubt for the
originaly originally phenomenon which is * observed in certain
than that quite obvious therefore * the question why

scientic scientific   used in a * context Why does
reccgnises (recognise)   the form we * a a lamp
a (as)   form we recognises * a lamp shining
lamps lamp   recognises a a * shining The question
penomenon phenomenon   of a particular * in keeping with
lamps lamp   now does the * shine by elucidating
result (results)   effect sequence that * would become apparent
ths this   intent and ultimately * implies an intelligence
onn own   removed from our * often this is
evolved (evolve)   was bound to * and adapt If
lefe life   not been there * would either never
ro wrong   cannot prove him * assuming he were
it (its)   but if answered * implications are quite
youself (yourself)   head youll find * now Time no
absolutly absolutely   matter to dust * completely unfinished EQ
complety completely   to dust Absolutely * unfinished EQ
unfinised unfinished   dust absolutely completely * EQ
27
knowledde knowledge   the amount of * that a scientist
geneus genius   allways advanced by * Science is an
shoud should   is useful he * not be given
ease easier   why it is * to cycle on
difi difficult   make it more * to cycle The
nust (must)   and the cyclist * fight this force
hardy (hardly)   The kidney has * any nerves anyway
her nerve   does have a * however This is
reconnet reconnect   brain We cannot * the eye with
plan plain   planet out of * simple stone and
pyar pyramids   list Firstly the * These are extremely
detals details   you with anymore * about something you
nonsene nonsense   This is obvious * Surely anyone who
Thirdy Thirdly   let it off * there is the
decif deciphered   still not been * The footprint is
Meditterranean (Mediterranean)   Atlantic to the * into electric
  -al energy
animals animal   pairs of (an) every * on the earth
beee been   ship must have * two miles long
const consists   the M1 itself * of a vast
hundreg hundred   long and one * yards wide and
wo who   very enigmatic people * could perform tasks
civilations (civilizations)   of the ancient * relics remain to
28
m nature   the forces of * whether it be
scientist (scientists)   used selfishly What * as a whole
mort (more)   some of the * complicated theories to
emotion (emotions)   the conveying of * that were also
lewel level   than on the * one must first
sperical spherical   Now with a * object this gravitational
earth (earths)   angles to the * surface and towards
angles (angle)   at a right * to the direction
consider (considered)   force can be * to be two
ont one   be two parts * acting horizontally the
consider (considered)   Nerves can be * to behave like
bain (brain)   impulses from the * or send an
hyge huge   congregated into one * bundle called the
prove prone   it is so * to exploitation by
wo who   by unscrupulous men * consider it to
encourge encourage   welfare state does * laziness because man
unee unemployment   who are claiming * benefits and see
all alright   all theyve done * up to now
idea (ideas)   and most noble * ever to be
29
achei achievement   be mankinds greatest * It could also
thei there   uranium hexafluoride If * had been no
find (finding)   in pipes to * tumours in a
it is   has to do * turn on his
contancts contacts   by having two * in the seat
tecl technological   advantage over the * way in that
tecln technologically   by enforcing it * as all one
30
resarc research   that of pure * Paragraph d mentions this
paintaking (painstaking)   a more meticulous * mind he works
con common   finds little in * with the impatiene
impatiene (impatience)   common with the * of the man
constitit constitutes   views about what * a scientific approach
disproo disproved   until it was * The modern view
cut culture   the field of * and religion Artists
inplications implications   with all its * The common denominato
  -r
evey every   been made in * direction so that
oftem often   in one field * receives adulation in
31
increasi increase   Science is the * in the amount
amout amount   increase in the * of organised factual
specialisises specialises   more unless he * in a limited
support (supports)   proof before he * a contension Imagination
contension (contention)   he support a * Imagination merely spee
  -ds
Imaginaiton Imagination   support a contension * merely speeds t
  -hought
thoy thought   Imagination merely speeds * but cannot instigate
by but   the short term * pure science promotes
part patronage   receive from its * of scientific endeavour
whch which   The only organ * could support such
suppart support   organ which could * such research would
spend (spent)   money could be * on more worthwhile
coure course   to such a * Even so how
proctical practical   this is not * The contention that
indivial individuals   The contention that * should be supported
it (if)   limited field Nevertheless * a individual can
individuu individual   Nevertheless if a * can cleary cope
cleary (clearly)   a individual can * cope perfectly on
lat land   While traversing flat * the only work
cyl cycle   rider and the * have to be
hg higher   the object has * energy than it
has have   only source could * been muscular exertion
worked work   equal to the * done in making
prepetual perpetual   could devise a * motion machine in
high height   back to that * which is impossible
diffucties (difficulties)   the enormous technical * to be surmo
  -unted
surmountin surmounted   diffucties to be * in transplanting an
arery arteries   join up the * and veins leaving
spontaneos spontaneously   is it contracts * even when severed
event even   it contracts spontaneously * when severed from
is its   cell to transmit * own small piece

all along piece of information * Each neuron is
reg rejoined have to be * individually an impossible
diffi different would perceive a * stimulus to the
impurs impulse of the nerve * This is necessary
wheras whereas kidneys are possible * transplants of eyes
bes belts if the seat * are not fastened
inconvi inconvenient these methods are * for the above
res reasons for the above * they are still
i ensuring surefire method of * a seat belt
one once belt is worn * these difficulties have
pilicy policy enforce such a * it would require
reguarly regularly require investigators to * observe every s
-ingle
p breaking prevent people from * their promises Clauses
Causes Clauses breaking their promises * would also have
po people stated to enable * to drive without
bea belts drive without seat * (on) in their own
increasin increase such a vast * in their duties
woud would mistaken the officer was * and there would
mistaki mistaken the officer was * be little chance
32
rel reality the messiness of * and the purity
33
offerred (offered) easier solution were * The comments offered
the that must be obvious * several brains and
crises crisis years the same * will reoccur but
is (as) energy source such * hydroelectric power or
plentl plenty since we have * of mass let
blackend blackened The pipes are * in order that
o accordingly in and act * it will be
possibly (possible) much energy as * will have to
Sciente Scientists at all costs * and engineers will
goverment (government) to which a * adhere put they
adhere (adheres) Which a goverment * but they all
chose choose who do not * to work and
facilite facilities to the same * This therefore encourages
are and with the system * would rather have
swap swamp which threatens to * the country However
countrie country to swamp the * however on the
occurance occurrence an every day * and as a
Capa Capitalism solution since obviously * was not ideal
34
basen based process of thought * on and modified
wh work wartime The scientists * is an analysis
usu usable evidence leading to * applications of a
ther their and applied have * place C is anti pure science
cycl cycle you were to * along the level
your you youre halfway there * stop pedalling You
an a back perhaps if * new eye were
keap keep new heart and * it beating Its
ch cochlea eye and the * in his ear
sout sort be used to * out light and
bean been a nerve had * Penetrated by the
alb able hear He was * to recognise objects
an (any) whether there was * way he could
mouths months after a few * Donalds behave became
behave (behaviour) few months Donalds * became changed overnig

-ht
c shown film were being * What we think
thought (thoughts) the computer Donalds * raced along at
35
beni beneficial which are most * to mankind Imagination
tie the lead we have * problem of a
the their free to direct * thoughts towards any
eaq equal in newtons is * to the product
forces (force) part of this * acts in the
dig diagrams and so in * of the kind
bonding bonded formula .. which are * together as (agglomerati
-ons) aggregates
an (and) skin is formed * the excess pressure
Cen Certainly embarassment to read * in this respect
b public ideas from the * then it is
haven have If public figures * been chosen to
severly severely required would be * changed by the
36
dratically drastically will be reduced * It is important
electricty electricity supplies unnecessarily as * is a second
-ary
cutf cutoff the period of * will probably be
shud shut period of absolute * down power could
lire like as they would * to be although
whether whether an obvious extreme * power was cut
oulawed outlawed have to be * These world surely
dratically (drastically) society would be * changed without th
-e
the (they) to live where * worked rarely leaving
reerly rarely where the worked * leaving that place
ab obvious Above are the * disadvantages of the
one once Outdoor activities would * again have to
productions production methods of energy * such as solar
desireable (desirable) is without doubt * Tests have shown
desire (desirable) seat belts are * it is necessary
sun such are other possibilities * as technological devices
divice (device) belts some technological * would be the
incouragement encouragement The method of * whereby reduced in
-surance
divice (device) with some mechanical * obviously comprehensive
policing
divice (device) the original technological * Thus a person
divice (device) to whether the * was fitted or
divice (device) could have the * removed This would
chac chance turn down the * to save some
an (and) freedom we enjoy * I think that
sle seat would flash if * belts were not
ma my only way in * opinion to encourage
enou encouragement a combination of * 1 and 2 Otherwise
37
Scc Scientists will become incomprehensible * will eventually
have
scienc scientist freedom because a * must adventure where
though (thought) can only speed * and not actually
intitate (initiate) and not actually * it its ability
idividualistic individualistic will exclude the * type of rese
-arch
rerved reserved four years is * for the scientist

-s
problem problems   of our greatest * is the feeding
depleted depleted   are rapidly being * and it is
comfortable comfortable   in safer more * air travel Even
se side   if all the * benefits of the
ree reasons   failures and the * for these of
alss also novelists let us * not forget that
knowledgeable knowledgeable   have been more * than we are
40
oly only   understanding and can * be measured by
scci science   shown financers of * should support projects
thea teams   projects not people * rather than individuals
correcte correct   told him was * His predictions although
pe predictions   was correct His * although scoffed at
recive receiving   than an experiment * up a new
     throwing   globe has been * enormous amounts of
ar organisms   organic molecules of * Under the right
oure our   state in which * meagre energy resources
b probably   world but would * be annexed by
hot (not)   would be clean * producing radioactive waste
benefit benefit   of realistic unemployment * this has done
unfortunate (unfortunate)   of the most * in our society
to too   state has developed * far too fast
beome (become)   welfare state has * the dominant feature
bi being   society instead of * the safety net
intne intended   that it was * to be it
beome (become)   it has increasingly * the supporting framework
Must (Most)   of our lives * of us go

Type: 2

1
apon (upon)   the pressure put * the scientist to
appaled (appalled)   alone in being * by this shortsighted
apon (upon)   and disagree depending * the interpretations of
dismantals (dismantles)   small child who * a watch to
presupposes (presupposes)   the question how * an answer and
propably (probably) answer will itself * assume some form
sucinctly (succinctly)   be describe very * if not fully
opperating (operating)   prevented the ignition * when the seat
sucessful (successful)   has proved remarkably * it seems people
bipass (bypass)   mechanic could probably * the system There
properganda (propaganda)   the present shock * campaign to (en)
     try

2
overwealming overwhelming   answer to the * breadth of knowledg
-e
obsolete obselete   cause are now * Applied science has
usefullness usefulness   would lose its * Science does require
persues (pursues)   with which he * his quest The
obselescence (obsolescence)   as built in * in commercial goods
satelite (satellite)   worldwide communication by * which are un
-deniably
balanced (balanced)   neophobia must be * however by neophilia

3
ballance (balance)   be allowed to * its own course
therefore therefor   have and is * better equiped to

themself themselves   turn inwards to * On a larger
stu structurisation   society is the * which occurs There
one (ones)   be the fittest * who reach there
large (larger)   live in much * groups than families
resours resources   to pool their * This would break
experents (experiments)   because many research * would either
     become
ether either   research experiments would * become useless due
in inpractical   so many are * However the statement
ou (cut) fuel   reserves run * is not entirely
wasn mans   has ruined a * private life This
bun but   the first place * in most cases
stu structure   lots the whole * of burocracy (This) Finding
fro former   different from the * ones Unless we
lif lives   to have private * we must accept
38
fas facts   know all the * which science has
remen remembered   facts be easily * by our race
stra struggle   up the mental * is honourable in
worrie worries   have no material * The thinkers needs
show should   The scientific foundations * support teams who
od order   fact finding in * to gain a
fas facts   reasons of tae * were useful research
reinfore reinforce   are needed to * our theories As
se science   order to advance * but science can
se sciences   being part of * domain eg the
prat practices   scientifically based medicinal * but noone know
-s
obtain obtained   system the results * are approximations or
afforimations (approximations)   results obtained are * or give
     only
ar our   to show that * mental model is
infite infinite   stepped onto an * merry-go-round and in
riged rigid   Even an infinitely * infinitely accurately marked
ro ruler   infinitely accurately marked * wont measure an
is it   order to describe * etc The size
me micrometers   it with calipers * etc The size
yau you   move in until * bump into the
tho through   devoted to picking * the smashed universe
descend descended   God was man * from another race
chemicall chemical   time past random * reactions had resulted
bese beside   Man stood proudly * his best machine
hes his   stood proudly beside * best machine yet
excercise exercise   a warm up * Slowly carefully man
draned drained   the blood had * from his face
settle (settled)   a paper card * back onto the
39
el exploratory   indulges in imaginative * activities Thus compl
-ete
individuals individuals   rather than sponsor * individualism is
     not
tinu tiny tiny   a stream of * particles It wait is   new theory it * however very important
particularly particular   in their own * field are far
lunar lunar   foot on the * surface said of
enough enough   with solar cells * energy can be
speial special   be stored in * batteries & (fuel) saving
successfully successfully   atmosphere can be * used in building

equiped (equipped)   is therefor better * to deal with
fatgue (fatigue)   slight feeling of * We have used
seel seal   comparatively easy to * either by natural
sensative (sensitive)   visual sensation the * are of the
sensative (sensitive)   cells each light * and having its
arguements (arguments)   are two main * against this First
exeeding (exceeding)   a car is * the speed limit
he
4

unfortunately (unfortunately)   not it is * necessary to know
practicle (practical)   always have a * use and that
occuance (occurrence)   to this ghastly * whatever you want
chauffers (chauffeurs)   all they were * road sweepers refuse
5

basicly (basically)   Science is * the building up
differant (different)   to try a * approach Although a
differance (difference)   the earth The * now is that
recieved (received)   security department he * payment for the
recieving (receiving)   reasoning that people * unemployment ben
-efit need
6

fluorishes (flourishes)   say that (a) science * better in the
unsupported (unsupported)   fall conclude that * bodies fall On
irrelevent (irrelevant)   philosophy is an * indulgence Here sur
-vival
7

seperation (separation)   the process of * of philosophy from
Spanich (Spanish)   of Velasquez the * court painter and

surplanted (supplanted)   touch cannot be * by methodical team
resionsably (responsibly)   and used more * Before we split
accessable (accessible)   is it economically * we know that
unforseen (unforeseen)   always create many * problems which can
barred (bared)   aim their fangs * their lips and
8

effects (affects)   import decision (in) which * the production
of
climatoligists (climatologists)   argued by many * that anything
cider
machinery (machinery)   a piece of * which ensured the
9

knowlegable (knowledgeable)   Financial assistance from * source
-s is usually
propell (propel)   were used to * explosive quickly and
forcasting (forecasting)   many ways from * the weather to
alow (allow)   The waves that * radio (waves) to be
forcasts (forecasts)   long range weather * are aided by
occuring (occurring)   can detect changes * in the upper
propell (propel)   been used to * man himself into
invaluable (invaluable)   that makes them * is the speed
interplanetry (interplanetary)   benefits gained by * travel may
at
arround (around)   mist shrouding everything * him visibility wa
-s
10

endeavour (endeavour)   is a human * requiring imagination and
successful (successful)   the story of * science today The
definate (definite)   main in Technology * goals are easy
versatile (versatile)   are nearly as * as people The
13

aquaint (acquaint)   for him to * himself with all
commitments (commitments)   free from all * and freedom leads
forsight (foresight)   with imagination and * leads to all
lead (led)   supervised can be * astray to other
existance (existence)   his struggle for * EQ
seperate (separate)   broken down into * branches A definition
diagonal (diagonal)   symmetry between opposite * corners thro t
he

practise (practice)   finds requirement in * is a possible
arguement (argument)   is a possible * However practical situati
-on

seperate (separate)   on as a * subject and is
proves proves   the subject but * usually useful whenever
assymetric (asymmetric)   which contain an * carbon atom a
seperate (separate)   linked to four * groups radicals possesses
prove (prove)   however these can * monotonous if overdone
monotnous (monotonous)   these can prove * if overdone so
minaturised (miniaturised)   circuits have be * transistorised i
-ntegrated and

amounts (amounts)   and wasting large * of time and
terminel (terminal)   replaced by a * linked up to
typwriter (typewriter)   of a few * type keys this
invaluble (invaluable)   and costing proving * to the majority
suceed (succeed)   which they will * for it is
proceedure (procedure)   computer language and * aiding them whe
-n

invaluable (invaluable)   but computers are * aids in the
probibilities (probabilities)   helping compute the * of over po
-Fulation
amount (amount)   do that great * of work there
loose (lose)   and even to * But are they
14

complementary (complementary)   while others are * Whatever way
one
continous (continuous)   as being the * accumulation of vast
rescvoirs (reservoirs)   accumulation of vast * of knowledge In
completly (completely)   It should be * free for the
posses (possess)   endeavours This may * a few inherent
mancue mancuver   or room to * at this present
beggining (beginning)   energy In the * this source of
accessible (accessible)   every point as * (This would) Thus our
concept

infered (inferred)   can now be * if the society
addittion (addition)   of them In * fuel consuming devices
efficient effeccient   be made more * so as to
their (there)   right direction as * is quite a
their (there)   result of this * could be a
conceive (conceive)   as we now * it EQ
Unfortunetly (Unfortunately)   fairly plausible solution * there
are a
resurect (resurrect)   so that would * the original problem
continuously (continuously)   their seat belts * This seems like
15

there (their)   are useful and * usefulness is a
there (their)   a measure of * benefit to mankind
required (required)   amount of knowledge * to be absorbed
soley (solely)   that it is * a matter of
improving (improving)   alternative forms ultimately * the situ

-ole

amounts (amounts) see the vast * of coal burnt
dissappear (disappear) fuels that would * would be the
certainly (certainly) horizons would almost * contract The wh

amount amount reality a small * of power from
available (available) power would be * This power would
available (available) a reduction of * power would be
amount (amount) decrease in the * of power available
available (available) amount of power * occurred the meaning
dissappear (disappear) Playboy society would * to be replaced
available (available) a decrease in * power is a
benifits (benefits) we had the * of plentifully available
available (available) benifits of plentifully * power EQ
amount (amount) insensitive would practically * to coercion T

-nis

certainly (certainly) so but almost * with reduced efficiency
wether (whether) the choice of * or not to
necessity (necessity) become a legal * The question is

21
definate (definite) required then a * end product is
to (too) state are far * great at present

22
suport (support) of science should * projects carried out
possesed (possessed) energy is energy * by a body
of (off) the body falls * the cliff or
sufficient (sufficient) are given a * shove by the
sufficient (sufficient) liquid are given * kicks by the
undoubtably (undoubtedly) belts is desirable * It is not
another (another) force with yet * difficult and unpleasant
license (licence) even endorse their * if on the
goverment (government) adopted by a * Goverments seem to
Goverments (Governments) by a goverment * seem to find

23
fulfilment (fulfilment) desire for intellectual * as the only
anomalus (anomalous) the possibility of * results or errors
nonprofessional (nonprofessional) better termed as * life sin
-ce public

24
definate (definite) to have a * purpose to direct
definate (definite) there is no * path for applied
definate (definite) there is a * aim in that
suprising (surprising) it is not * that the so
exaustion (exhaustion) SQ The * of fossil fuels
sucessful (successful) extent on how * the development of
goverments (goverments) result even if * do not introduce
resorces (resources) development of natural * will no longer
basicly (basically) principles would remain * unchanged The ma
-jor

strenuous (strenuous) and though doubtless * efforts would be
Luckly (Luckily) the world wars * this would require
miniature (miniature) of thing in * was observable in
suprising (surprising) it is not * that if there

25
acquire aquire (acquire) can no longer * all this knowledge
penecillin (penicillin) the discovery of * and the steam
disasterous (disastrous) That would be * A government such
tendancy (tendency) Gravity is the * for the mass
irreversable (irreversible) their tissues is * and this is

-ation for situations that would * as a result
develope (develop) that would gradual * would undoubtedly effe
develope (develop) develope would undoubtedly * the society in
-ct
effect (affect) greater Changes to * these energy systems
improve (improve) and in a * manner The values
neglegant (negligent) gears will not * unless the seat
engage (engage) owner would be * of the choice
relinguished (relinquishing) his life in * I therefore do
jeparly (jeopard) such as the * of laws in
inforcement (enforcement)

16
convienience (convenience) of time and * as well as
succesfully (successfully) be carried out * The view that
undoubtedly (undoubtedly) longer periods would * give the scie
convienience (convenience) as without the * of private transpo
-it
forseen (foreseen) but would be * and so obvious
-ly larger
forsee (foresee) smaller more efficient * or alternative
forsee (foresee) be easy to * and indeed it
successful (successful) this was not * the changes already
totalitarianism (totalitarianism) police state or * There is j
-ust
aggreement (agreement) signed such an * This alternative impli
-es
Justification (justification) measure is introduced * for puni
-shing someone
totalitarianism (totalitarianism) been said total * and any go
-verment
loose (lose) the measure would * many votes The
wheras (whereas) to wear seatbelts * they should aim

17
forseen (foreseen) is simply no (other direct) * direct pathwa
-y to
relevent (relevant) can consult any * text in a
preferance (preference) will study in * to others EQ

18
inlargement (enlargement) street as an * of human knowledge
dissappear (disappear) the three to * Of course there
polution (pollution) fool At least * would be reduced
magerine (margarine) substance similar to * EQ

19
invalueable (invaluable) a group are * and an individual
tackeling (tackling) way of * the problem Although
essentially (essentially) first approach is * analytical Vast a
-mounts
aquisition (acquisition) elementary particles The * of this t
-heory
believed (believed) experimentally reproducing conditions * to
primeval (primaeval) be present on * earth he managed

20
useage (usage) of encouraging the * of seat belts
necessarily (necessarily) as a person * stuffed full of
amount (amount) and indeed overwelming * of knowledge is
amount (amount) imagination and an * of freedom is

paraphenalia (paraphernalia) other bits of * There are also
to (too) something No thats * Lucy for Gerald
disappears (disappears) Like when he * that shows streangth
streanth (strength) disappears that shows * No not at
referance (reference) the house cross * public house He

26
to (too) available will become * great to learn
pendanty (pedantry) of analysis (and *) (A) (Scientific thou
-ght requires) a scientist
pendantic (pedantic) he is a * empiricist Imagination is
wheras (whereas) semantic problem namely * the question how
emitted (emitted) electromagnetic radiation is * by the atoms
their there had not been * life would either

27
excercise (exercise) but as an * of the mind
always (always) science is not * advanced by genius
worthwhile (worthwhile) progress is only * if it is
fourty (forty) or Cheops covers * acres of ground
allready (already) You have probably * seen yourselves Secondl
-y
definately (definitely) The footprint is * not modern If

28
eventuallity (eventuality) To combat this * the modern scienti
-st
geni genei states that individual * not teams are
truely (truly) can grasp the * wonderous concepts and
wonderous (wondrous) grasp the truely * concepts and happening
-s
truely (truly) If a man * loves something an
intellectual (intellectual) close circle of * friends but he
plebian (plebeian) let the common * in the street
truely (truly) the man who * enjoys his subjects
persueing (pursuing) only reason for * a particular branch
depprecation (deprecation) lead to a * of the work
persued (pursued) when Art is * merely for Arts
explanatory (explanatory) need pages of * notes and a
truely (truly) and all the * great composers their
allienate (alienate) soon as they * themselves from the
diss disolved charged and have * in the watery
independant (independent) the heart are * of nervous action
endochrine (endocrine) by organs called * glands These glands
controled (controlled) less control is * by these hormones
sensetive (sensitive) layer of light * cells These cells
truely (truly) or rather a * Christian state which
truely (truly) all the other * needy members of
truely (truly) those who are * parasitic in nature
critisise (criticise) that nobody can * this service If

29
unravelled (unravelled) nucleus (of) has been * The war years
orbiting orbiting levels of electrons * the nucleus and
arguments arguements Possibly the best * against technological
ways
argument (argument) were but the * is a strong

30
aff effected observes will be (limited by) * by the fact
comparitive (comparative) endeavour that in * terms bearing in
reknowned (renowned) thought Erasmus was * for the beauty
lead (led) The men who * the movement were

31
unemcompassable (unencompassable) is becoming practically * Ev
-entually in order
contempory (contemporary) from individuals since * science req
uires a
acheive (achieve) direct means to * (are visible) an objective
are
forseeable (foreseeable) sake with no * (physical) financial r
-eward The
acheived (achieved) end is being * One could cite
achi achieve skills necessary to * a specific end
replaci replacing no merit in * him by a
indispensble (indispensable) and kidneys are * organs they ar
-e

32
eazily (easily) applied science are * seen but pure
eazily (easily) the question very * becomes which would
eazy (easy) we demand an * and accurate explanation

33
imaginative (imaginative) explorer in the * and exciting adven
-ture

34
destinct (distinct) there is a * aim to work
feasi feasable before this becomes * To cut down
polishes (polishers) ovens and floor * tend to consume
reoccur (recur) same crisis will * but worse The
feasable (feasible) to create a * system in Sweden
practise (practice) the brain In * this just doesnt
seperate (separate) his thoughts and * his thinking into
seperate (separate) time split into * (person) thinking groups
learning

35
embarassment (embarrassment) always lead to * and misunderstan
-ding Moreover
embarassment embarrassment family are an * to read Certainly
exagerations (exaggerations) the truth are * The public does

36
dramatic (dramatic) also have a * effect as people
their (there) for society but * might be some
monitary (monetary) The system of * incentive might work
ensure insure comprehensive policing to * that everyone wears

37
vehicles vehicles available certainly private * and probably
public
surfdom (serfdom) of overlordship and * the situation will
burocracy (bureaucracy) whole structure of * (This) Finding a
persons

38
forseeable (foreseeable) exact in the * future of his
dissapointedly (disappointedly) far he said * There must be
existense (existence) reason for mans * EQ

39
novelists (novelists) the modern paperback * Let us also

40
Financers (Financiers) of complete freedom * of science should
Fincancers (Financiers) wars have shown * of science should
leisure leisure a lot of * time to be

13

Slips of the Pen

NORMAN HOTOPF   *London School of Economics and Political Science, London, England*

1 Introduction

Slips of the pen are of relevance to spelling on two grounds: they frequently result in spelling mistakes, and they provide clues to the processes underlying writing. In this chapter, I shall describe different types of slips of the pen and their incidence, comparing them in these respects with slips of the tongue, and then consider what they might tell us about the process of writing.

The classic study of slips of the tongue is that of Meringer who, in two books (Meringer and Mayer, 1895; Meringer, 1908), published some 1500 slips of the tongue as well as some slips of the pen and some reading errors. Although these do not constitute his complete corpus, he is alone in publishing a large sample until we come to the appendix to the collection of articles on slips of the tongue edited by Fromkin (1973). Fromkin's book testifies to the resurgence of interest in slips of the tongue, of which perhaps the first manifestation was Lashley's classic article on the problem of serial order in behaviour (1951). Lashley illustrated his thesis with examples of his own typing slips, and there have also been systematic studies of this word production situation (e.g. MacNeilage, 1964; Shaffer, 1975).

As far as slips of the pen are concerned, there has been less work. It has stemmed mainly from a different source – the psychiatric one of interest in dysgraphia and related defects (e.g. Lecours, 1966; Chedru and Geschwind, 1972). Meringer was also interested in that source of error. The co-author of his first book, Mayer, was a psychiatrist, and Mayer's collection of slips of the tongues is included in it. These appear, however, to come from normal subjects, and not from patients. Many of the slips in Freud's *Psychopathology of Everyday Life* (1914) came from the Meringer and Mayer book, whose classifications of errors served, indeed, as a stalking horse for Freud.

My interest in this field started nearly 20 years ago, and has included attempts to arrive at some kind of assessment of the frequency of the different types of slips of the pen and of the tongue by collecting systematically a number of samples.

2 Description of the samples

Author's samples. After collecting some 500 slips, analysing and classifying them, I wrote down every slip of the tongue and of the pen that I observed myself making over periods of twelve and nine months respectively. This was done in an attempt to offset the tendency only to record striking slips or ones of particular theoretical interest, and yielded 96 slips of the tongue (author's S-sample) and 111 slips of the pen (author's W-sample). The rather small number collected over such periods of time indicates one of the methodological problems involved in the collecting of slips, which is their relative rarity.

It was then necessary to compare my slips with those of others. For this I collected three more samples of speech and three of writing.

Daily life S-sample. I noted down for two years every slip of the tongue made by others in my presence that circumstances allowed me to record. This yielded 244 slips made by 111 speakers.

Meringer S-sample. In carrying out my collection, I had avoided looking at the only large collection that had been made up to that time, which was Meringer's, because I wished to see whether we arrived independently at the same classification. Having virtually completed the daily life S-sample, I turned to Meringer's two books and counted the slips he had collected. In general terms, and in spite of the difference in language, the agreement between the two collections was good. A second reason for turning to Meringer was that I had virtually confined myself as far as slips of the tongue were concerned to slips at the lexical level. In order to gain a more detailed estimate of the number of words ahead that speech was planned, it was necessary to take account of phonemic and syllable slips as well. The Meringer sample included altogether 1495 slips.

Conference S-sample. Only a few of the slips I had collected were tape-recorded so, to get a larger sample of them, I noted the slips made in tape-recordings of eight speakers giving unscripted papers at a psychology conference. This yielded a further 156 slips.

Group W-sample. This sample of slips of the pen committed by others consisted of two sub-samples. The first, the examination W-sample, was slips of the pen occurring in 14 scripts written by undergraduates in an internal psychology examination. Three problems were posed by these. The first was that of reading the handwriting, and the second that of deciding whether a mistake was deliberate or unintentional. Mistakes due to ignorance of grammar or spelling are of the former kind and should not be included, since slips of the pen are unintentional. The third problem was that of determining whether a letter, a word or part of a word that was crossed out represented a corrected slip or a change of mind on the part of the writer as to what he was trying to say. To deal with these problems, the scripts were read by two graduate students as well as myself, and classified according to a coding frame. Spelling mistakes due to ignorance were identified by seeing whether the word in question was spelled wrongly elsewhere in the same script.

If it occurred only once and was a difficult word to spell, it was accounted a spelling mistake. Judgement as to whether a word was difficult to spell or not depended upon how well the writer spelled in other places in his script. However, few cases of this kind arose. Only slips agreed by all three judges were included in the sample. If there was any doubt, the slip was excluded. These stringent criteria yielded 324 slips, which represented only about 40% of the occurrences of correction, over-writing or mis-spelling in the scripts.

As mentioned earlier, the incidence of slips of both kinds that are noticed or can be determined is rather low. Estimates based on tape-recorded data from the daily life and conference S-samples showed that slips of the tongue occurred at the rate of about 0.2%, whilst slips of the pen in the examination W-sample were at about 0.9%. In an attempt to increase the incidence of slips, a further sample of slips of the pen was collected. Ten graduate students were required to write for half an hour an answer to a controversial passage on the issue of punishment, with pressure to write fast under noisy, distracting conditions. Their answers were analysed, and the slips confirmed by discussion with the students. This, the distraction W-sample, yielded 89 slips, which represented a rate of 1.6%. Since the number of slips in this sample is rather low, it has been combined with the examination W-sample to form the group W-sample which contrasts with the samples of single individuals, such as the author's W-sample and the following one.

Monograph W-sample. The conditions under which the distraction W-sample was obtained were not conducive to noting the circumstances under which slips of the pen were produced. Unlike speech, writing – as far as its audience is concerned – takes place in privacy, and it is necessary to rely on others to collect and report on their slips of the pen. One of the judges of the examination W-sample provided a collection based on a lengthy monograph. Since every slip was noted, it qualified as a sample for determining the incidence of slips, yielding a further 175 slips.

These special samples were collected over a period of about six years, and are, as can be seen, often rather small, particularly when account is taken of the number of different categories of slip. They possess the advantage, however, that they were collected in a variety of different word-production situations. If we add to the special samples other slips collected as occasion arose, the total number of slips in my corpus is 1231 slips of the pen and 2146 slips of the tongue. In what follows I will use for quantitative analysis only the special samples described above, drawing on my other data only for qualitative analysis or illustration.

3 The classification of slips

Most slips involve either whole words and root morphemes (slips at the lexical level) or phonemes or letters (slips at the phoneme/letter level). Tables 1 and 2 show the per cent frequency of slips of the different categories for the different samples in each of these groups. Table 1 also includes a few short phrases and some bound morpheme slips. Table 2 also includes some syllable slips, as well as a few 'operation' slips of punctuation, underlining, capitalising letters and so forth.

TABLE 1   Percentages of different types of slips at the lexical level

Category	Speech				Writing		
	Author's S	Daily life S	Conference S	Meringer S	Author's W	Group W	Monograph W
Sound pattern slips	30	26	12	24	54	21	17
Stem variants	1	3	7	4	5	23	26
Anticipations	4	7	12	8	9	7	6
Repetitions	9	14	29	9	11	12	16
Transpositions	4	5	2	10	0	0	0
Immediate repetitions	0	0	0	0	2	8	2
Omissions	1	1	13	6	14	20	20
Blends	1	2	5	12	0	0	0
Semantic group	35	28	13	15	3	3	1
Other classes	16	15	8	12	2	7	12
Total no. of slips in sample (Incl. multiple classifications)	96 (103)	244 (307)	125 (154)	751 (852)	50 (55)	231 (271)	98 (105)

The number of slips in each sample is shown in the tables. However, some slips fell into more than one category, though rarely more than two, and were classified more than once. The number of such multiple classifications is indicated. The percentages given in the tables are based on totals that have been inflated in this way.

TABLE 2 Percentages of different types of slips at the phoneme/letter and syllable level

Category	Speech	Writing		
	Meringer *S*	Author's *W*	Group *W*	Monograph *W*
Anticipations	45	10	10	1
Repetitions	22	13	7	14
Transpositions	13	5	8	2
Immediate repetitions	0	1	5	2
Omissions	19	68	67	72
Other classes	0	3	3	8
Total no. of slips in sample	744	61	182	7
(Incl. multiple classifications)	(781)	(62)	(184)	(79)

My purpose in presenting these data is to compare slips of the pen with those of the tongue. There are a number of small classes which do not greatly contribute to this particular comparison, and these, with cases that have defied classification, have been lumped together under the title 'Other classes'.

Sound pattern slips. These are slips where the error word is similar in sound to the target word. Examples in writing are:

Homophones

SCENE for SEEN, NEW for KNEW, THERE for THEIR, SOLD for SOLED, WHOLE for HOLE.

Quasi-homophone

WONDER for WANDER, SOUGHT for SORT, ARE for OUR, APPOINT for A POINT

Near homophones

SURGE for SEARCH, CONSEQUENCE for COMPETENCE, THAT for THAN, A NUMBER for ANOTHER, COULD for GOOD.

Near homophones also occur in speech. Examples are: DAUGHTER for DOCTOR, RESEARCH for SEARCH, MELON for LEMON, SAUSAGES for SANDWICHES, TOP for STOP. The criterion for identifying these slips was that error and target word should have as many phonemes in common as there were syllables in the longer word, though generally the two words were of the same number of syllables. The position and order in which the common phonemes occurred had also to be the same, both between and within syllables. It might, of course, be argued that near homophones are similar in sight as well as in sound, though no one working on slips of the tongue has considered describing them in this way. In view of the homophone and quasi-homophone slips, however, the simpler theory for the present would be to attribute all these slips of the pen to similarity of sound. There are no cases of marked discrepancy favouring graphological forms such as favour phonological form with, for example, the substitution of SURGE for SEARCH.

Stem variants. These are slips where a different form of the word with the same stem is produced. Examples are REFERENTS for REFERENCE, PSYCHOANALYSIS for PSYCHOANALYST, SOCIETIES for SOCIETY'S, GROUP for GROUPED and IS for ARE. Mistakes which seemed likely to be due to ignorance of grammar or where the subject was too far from the verb for number to be easily remembered were not included. Some examples with context that were included are: 'ALTHOUGH CERTAIN RESEARCHERS SAYS . . .'; 'OBJECTS COULD BE GRASP BY PAIRS . . .'; 'CHANGE WERE MADE . . .'. With few exceptions, these examples were also cases of sound pattern similarity. However, they formed such a large class amongst slips of the pen that it was thought wise to classify them separately.

Order errors. These are transpositions, anticipations and repetitions. One example of each of these at the lexical level is given below. The first is a slip of the tongue, the rest are slips of the pen: ALL PLACES REPART for ALL PARTS REPLACED (transposition). I DO NOT SEE HOW THE FIRST (for SECOND) PARAGRAPH FOLLOWS FROM THE FIRST (anticipation), and EVEN TO GIVE TO (for THE) RESPONSE WITHOUT GAINING FOOD (repetition). Examples of these slips at the letter level are SOLUITION for SOLUTION, VAVOURS for FAVOURS and EASIAR for EASIER. In all these examples a word or a letter from another position is *substituted* for the target word or letter. Additions can also occur as in USELFUL for USEFUL and VOLOUNTARILY for VOLUNTARILY. Order errors at the phoneme/ letter level also occurred between words – generally neighbouring ones, as in ALTHOUGHT IT for ALTHOUGH IT and DEVELOP HAPITS for HABITS.

Immediate repetitions. This kind of repetition slip, known technically as a dittography, is dealt with separately because it appears to occur only in slips of the pen. At the lexical level, slips of this kind are immediate repetitions of single words, generally function words or auxiliaries. Examples at the syllable and letter level are spellings such as SENTENTENCES for SENTENCES and INTERVIEWEEE'S for INTERVIEWEE'S.

Omissions. An example of these kinds of slips in writing is: SUNDAY (for) SUNNY NOVEMBER DAY. They could be regarded as anticipation slips in the sense that words, phonemes or letters, and syllables occur earlier than they would have done had there been no omission. At the lexical level a large component is composed of single words which, as with immediate repetitions, are generally function words or auxiliaries.

Omissions at the phoneme/letter and syllable level include haplologies. For example, haplographies like REMBERING for REMEMBERING and FORBIDDENCIES for FORBIDDEN TENDENCIES, and, to coin a term, haplophonies such as BUSTARD for BUTTER, SALT AND MUSTARD.

Blends. These slips seem to arise from a speaker thinking of two words at once. Instead of saying either one or the other word, he says a blend of the two. Examples are MARMELITE, a blend of MARMALADE and MARMITE, and IN PARTICULY for IN PARTICULAR and PARTICULARLY.

Semantic group. These slips are ones where error and target word are antonymous to one another, like EARLY for LATE, or stand in a converse relationship like HUSBAND for WIFE, or are co-hyponyms. In the latter case, they may be immediately dominated by the same superordinate term, e.g. they may be meal words as in BREAKFAST for LUNCH, colour words as in RED for BLACK, greeting terms like GOOD EVENING for GOOD MORNING, or they may be dominated by a more remote term so that they are semantic cousins, as it were, rather than siblings. Examples of these are names for intervals of time like SATURDAY for JANUARY; relationship words like UNCLE for BROTHER, or geographical terms like EUROPE for BRITAIN. As can be seen, the relationship between error and target word is usually closer than is the case with many errors classified as examples of semantic paraphasia or paralexia.

4 What slips may tell us about writing

Having described the different kinds of slips, let us consider what they may tell us about word-production in writing. We can do this by considering the ways in which speech and writing are similar, as inferred from slips, and the ways in which they differ, and design a theory to account for these.

From Table 1 we can see that as far as slips at the lexical level are concerned there are clear similarities and differences between speech and writing. With rare exceptions, for all samples sound pattern slips, anticipations and repetitions are similar in frequency for the two situations. Differences are that blends, transpositions and semantic group slips are rare amongst slips of the pen. In the writing samples there was only one occurrence each of a transposition and a blend, and the few cases of semantic group slips were all cases of multiple classification. On the other hand, immediate repetitions, omissions and stem variants were rare among slips of the tongue.

At the phoneme/letter level (Table 2) slips of the tongue were more frequent amongst the order errors, particularly in anticipations and, to a lesser extent, in repetitions and transpositions, whilst omissions occurred much more frequently in slips of the pen. As with slips at the lexical level, immediate repetitions, though rare, do occur amongst slips of the pen, but are virtually non-existent in slips of the tongue. As we shall see later, the difference in frequency of the order errors is entirely due to the much greater frequency of substitution slips, where one phoneme is substituted for another. Additions of phonemes are of equal and much lower frequency both amongst slips of the tongue and of the pen.

I will now try to account for these similarities and differences, dealing first with slips at the lexical level and then with slips at the phoneme/letter level.

4.1 *Slips at the lexical level*

4.1.1 *Linguistic and motor programmes.* A number of different models, Lamb (1966), Fry (1969), Fromkin (1971), Shaffer (1976), have been presented suggesting what happens between the occurrence of the initial idea and its expression in speech. Though differing in details, they all recognise such different stages as the assembling of semantic features, lexical accessing and morphological ordering until the utterance-to-be is fully specified phonetically – that is to say, all the information required for the assembling of commands to the articulators (the linguistic programme) has been provided so that the task of realising the utterance (the motor programme) can proceed. The motor programme is itself a complex task involved with a number of stages (cf. Liberman *et al.*, 1967; Laver, in press), but not one with which we need to concern ourselves here.

Slips at the lexical level of different kinds are assumed to occur at different stages in the process of forming the programme, but there is also evidence of editing so that the utterance, though faulty, is at least phonologically respectable: to take an example of Fromkin's (1971), AN EATING MARATHON becomes A MEETING ARATHON, changing appropriately AN to A. Considerations such as these have led Fromkin and others to attribute slips at the phoneme level to errors in the linguistic and not the motor programme.

Slips are not confined to overt language behaviour. They have also been reported in silent thinking and in consciousness of what we are going to say before we say it (Meringer and Mayer, 1895; Hockett, 1968; Laver, 1969; Hill, 1972; Hotopf, in press). Sometimes, because of this, slips are corrected before we make them, a process Hockett and

Laver have described as covert editing. However, this is not the same as the editing just described which, so to speak, covers up for a slip phonetically rather than correcting it.

4.1.2 *Similarity of speech and writing.* The span ahead at which we plan speech may be gauged from anticipation slips. We measure this in syllables counting from the target word to the word ahead which was the source of the error and including both. To illustrate, in THEIR SUCCESS HAS ALSO BEEN REASONABLY SUCCESSFUL, the target word is PREDICTION, the source of the error word is SUCCESSFUL, and the span is 14 syllables. With this measure we can make a further comparison between the speech and writing samples. The spans for the daily life, conference and Meringer S-samples were 8.3, 7.7 and 6.5 syllables respectively, whilst that for the group W-sample was 6.5. The similarity in size of the spans of the speech and the writing samples is particularly striking when account is taken of the difference in speed. Speech, it has been estimated, normally proceeds at the rate of about six syllables per second (Lenneberg, 1967). A sample of ten subjects performed the same task as the distraction sub-sample of the group W-sample, writing under pressure for five minutes, and their average speed worked out as 0.75 syllables per second. A further four subjects writing as fast as they could on anything they chose averaged a speed of 0.73 syllables a second. Under these circumstances, it might have been expected that writing would not have been planned as far ahead as speech. It seems likely, however, that our utterances, whether for speech or writing, are planned in clauses rather than in the immediate constituents of clauses or in noun or verb phrases alone (Boomer and Laver, 1968).

The evidence concerning span thus suggests that the linguistic programming for writing is similar to that for speech as far as the size of the programme is concerned. The evidence for the programme being aurally encoded that comes from homophones and quasi-homophones suggests a similar common origin, and it is indeed a common experience that we occasionally mutter to ourselves or are aware of sub-vocal formulations ahead of our writing.

4.1.2 *Slips that are commoner in speech than in writing.* If the programming of writing at the lexical level is similar to that for speech, why should there be the differences that I have noted? The simplest explanation for the relative absence of blends, semantic group slips and transpositions is that the much slower rate of writing enables the programme to be more slowly constructed. Blends, which are generally of synonyms or synonymous phrases, seem to arise from hesitation between two alternative formulations. It is easier to make a choice when there is more time. Similarly, transpositions, which involve two errors in word choice, can be corrected before the second error is made and will, therefore, appear simply as anticipations. There is, as we shall see, a high rate of detection of anticipation errors. As for semantic group slips, it has been argued (Hotopf, in press) that these arise from words which are emitted before the search for the target word has reached the phonological search stage. With less pressure on time there should be fewer of them.

4.1.3 *Slips that are commoner in writing than in speech.* Turning to slips which are more frequent in writing than in speech, their greater frequency was entirely due to their being function words, auxiliaries and bound morphemes – forms which are shorter than the average word token, more frequent, usually unstressed and generally more redundant.

It has already been pointed out that the omission of single words formed a large component in the category of omissions. They constituted 87% of the omissions in the group W-sample and 70% in the only speech sample, the conference one, where the category was of more than negligible size. Of those single words that were omitted, 90% in the group W-sample and 71% in the conference S-sample were function words or auxiliaries of average lengths of 2.7 and 2.6 letters respectively. As for immediate repetitions, 79% of these in the group W-sample were of this type, average length 3.1 letters. Using t-tests, each of these three averages was significantly shorter (p <0.001) than the average word-token length of 4.7 letters according to the Kučera and Francis norms (1967).

Substitution of function words also occurred amongst sound pattern slips, and again with much greater frequency amongst slips of the pen than slips of the tongue. They formed 56% of these slips in the group W-sample, but only 5% and 1% in the daily life and Meringer S-samples respectively.

The category of stem variants also shows more errors in writing. In stem variants what differentiates error from target word is a bound morpheme (e.g. a suffix). As will be explained later, errors involving bound morphemes are treated as cases of substitutions of one word form for the other, regardless of whether the slip could be described as omission (35%), addition (20%) or substitution (43%) of the morpheme.

A possible explanation of the greater occurrence of these slips in writing is in terms of a relatively greater breakdown in syntactic structure. A feature of slips of the tongue is preservation of form class between error and target word. In the daily life, conference and

Meringer S-samples the exceptions to this formed only 10%, 15% and 7% respectively, of the total numbers of slips at the lexical level. In the group W-sample, on the other hand, exceptions formed as much as 37% of the total substitution errors, a proportion significantly larger than the largest of the S-samples, the conference S-sample [$\chi^2 = 12.29, p < 0.001$] Most of the cases of mismatch were accounted for by stem variants (31%) and anticipation, repetition or sound pattern substitutions of function words (56%). One syntactic constraint did however remain. The error word in cases of function word substitution was nearly always (93%) another function word, even though of a different form class.

As we have seen function words and bound morphemes figure prominently in these differences between writing and speech and they are, as we have noted, short, relatively unstressed and generally more redundant forms. Forms like these we might expect to be more easily overlooked than content words and their differences less easily noticed. This is suggested by studies by Healy (1976) and Drewnowski and Healy (1977) who have shown that the function words AND and THE are more likely to be omitted than the same letter strings embedded in longer words, or a content word of the same length and similar shape as AND, provided they are presented in the appropriate syntactic context. By the same token we might explain the greater involvement of function words and bound morphemes in errors as being due to their lower detectability when scanning the linguistic programme before translation into letter strings. These errors should be less likely to be detected than errors involving content words. Was there any evidence that this was so?

To answer this question it is necessary to distinguish between slips that were immediately corrected as opposed to those that were not corrected or were corrected only on subsequent reading through of the script. Therefore, corrections where an error was crossed out and the target word written above the line, or squeezed into a narrow space between words, or inserted with an arrow below to indicate its position, were not included. Only those where a word was only partially written before being crossed out or was crossed out and immediately followed by the target word on the same line were counted. Table 3 shows the incidence of immediate corrections for the different main categories of slips for three samples. Slips that were classified in more than one of the categories in the table were omitted. Consequently the numbers are reduced. The table shows that the immediate correction rate for slips of the pen was low except for anticipation and repetitions. These were significantly different from all the other categories (p < 0.01). As for function words and auxiliaries, 64% of these were not detected as compared with 44% of content words from which stem variants were excluded, a difference which is again significant [$\chi^2 = 16.41$, p $<$ 0 02].

TABLE 3   Frequency of immediate correction of slips at the lexical level

| Type of slip | Number and percentage immediately corrected | | | | | |
| | Group W-sample | | Daily life S-sample | | Conference S-sample | |
	No.	%	No.	%	No.	%
Sound pattern	44	25	36	83	10	90
Stem variants	58	17	0	0	8	50
Anticipations and repetitions	32	65	38	76	60	85
One word omissions	46	37	0	0	14	50
Semantic group	0	0	66	71	11	91

Thus, as expected in slips of the pen, omissions, stem variants and function as opposed to content words show a relatively low degree of detectability. However, unexpectedly, sound pattern slips are also often undetected. This is not due to a particularly high proportion of function words in these slips, because the detection rate of content words in this category was still lower. That slips where error and target word are similar to one another – and this applies also to stem variants – should be less likely to be detected than cases where they are different, as in anticipation and repetition slips, makes good sense, but this is incompatible with the detection rate for sound pattern slips of the tongue. Clearly here, despite the similarity between error and target word, there was no lack of detectability. Perhaps this has to do with the fact that in speech a phonological input at the lexical level is being compared with a phonological output, whereas the output with which it is compared in writing is graphological. In any case, we cannot conclude that slips that were more common in writing than in speech were those that were also less detectable due to greater similarity to the target word.

4.2 Slips at the phoneme/letter level

There are two major differences between speech and writing at the letter/phoneme level These are that, in contrast to slips of the tongue, substitutions are rare for slips of the pen. This contrast was not seen at the lexical level. On the other hand, the contrast between speech and writing in the omission of less easily detectable terms applies at both levels. At the letter/phoneme level both word-production situations produce more omissions than at the lexical level, but omissions always play a larger part in writing than in speech.

In comparing speech with writing at this level I shall mainly be using the Meringer S-sample. The main points concerning slips of the tongue made by this means have been confirmed in English and in Dutch, but the Meringer data are the only data I have available for detailed figures of incidence.

4.2.1 *Substitution slips.* Whereas substitution slips constitute 67% of slips at the phoneme/letter and syllable level in the Meringer S-sample, they only form 18% of the group W-sample (i.e. 33 slips in all) and smaller proportions of the other two W-samples. This contrasts with frequencies reported by other investigators (e.g. Lecours, 1966; Chedru and Geschwind, 1972; Wing and Baddeley, Chapter 12). To a large extent this difference is due to a different criterion used in description. Any letter slip which changed one word into another, whether by substitution, addition or omission was (with one exception) counted as a word and not a letter slip.

The first question we can ask is whether there is any evidence for phoneme slips in writing. We would expect such errors on the grounds set out in Section 4.1.1: namely, that the utterance-to-be was set up before the motor programme could be organised. Reference was made to our occasional awareness of what we were about to write before writing it. As sound plays such a marked role on the lexical level, it seems reasonable to expect this to be true for the phoneme/letter level too. However, only a few substitutions of any kind occurred at this level. Some slips indicate the influence of generalised rules of phonetic spelling such as we often get with the spelling errors of children. These are suggested by such slips of the pen as ABSALUTE, REFORENCE, EASIAR, RIDGID (a slip of my own), PREDJUDICE and NEEDENT (NEEDN'T).

There was a marked difference between substitutions in writing and in speech. One of the most regular features of slips of the tongue at the phoneme level is that the source and error phonemes are virtually always in the same position in the syllable: initial interacts with initial; medial with medial, and final with final. In contrast, over a quarter of all substitution slips of the pen fail to obey this law. This is true also for 11 out of 15 transpositions which involve adjacent letters.

4.2.2 *Omissions*. Three different kinds of omissions can be distinguished. These are between-word omissions and two different kinds of within-word omissions. Between-word omissions are ones where (generally) two words are written as one but some letters are omitted. Examples are WHETHER for WHERE THE FATHER, and (a haplography) KNEVE for KNEE LEVEL. The two different kinds of within-word omissions are those where the slip was noticed as it was being made so that the word was not completed, and those where it was not noticed at all or only noticed on re-reading so that the missing letter or letters were added above the word subsequently. Though consecutive letters might be omitted, in no case was there more than one site for omissions within a word. The first kind of omission (between-word omissions) constituted about half the slips at the letter level in the author's W-sample, the third (incomplete within-word omissions) about half in the monograph W-sample, and the second nearly half of the slips in the group W-sample. However, in the last sample nearly a third of the subjects produced no slips at all of this kind. These proportions concerning the commonest type of error at the letter level give an indication of the degree of individual differences existing in writing – at least at this level – which should warn against the rather prevalent reliance on statistics based upon single subjects in this field.

I shall deal only with the second and third types of omission – those involving single words. It should be remembered, however, that we exclude from omissions, when a complete word is written, any case where the omission results in a new word. There were a few cases of these which were attributed only to the sound pattern category, such as WORD (WORLD). The opposite WORLD (WORD) was also obtained. More important because larger are those slips that might have been classified as omissions but have instead been allocated to the category of stem variants alone. There are two reasons for this. First, all cases of addition or omission of a morpheme are also cases of substitution of words differing from one another in number, case or tense. In these, 'omissions' like PROCESS for PROCESSES were substitutions of unmarked for marked forms and 'additions' like SAYS for SAY of the reverse process. But these substitutions also occurred without additions or omissions of morphemes in irregular forms as, for example, in OURSELF for OURSELVES. Clearly, all these errors can be attributed to the same category, namely stem variants. Second, the inclusion of bound morphemes would have greatly increased the proportion of omissions occurring at the ends of words. If we do include them and compare letter omissions for words which end in one- or two-letter morphemes with those where they do not, we find that 19 out of 41 of the former (i.e. 46.3%) are omissions of the last letter or last two letters (i.e. the morphemes) as compared with 4 out of 60 of the latter (6.7%). In other words, omission of the last letter or two rarely took place unless they formed a morpheme. This is a strong argument, therefore, for classifying omissions of morphemes under stem variants at the lexical level and not as omissions at the letter/phoneme level.

4.2.3 *Letter position and detectability of omissions.* Three questions can be asked about omissions in single words. What are the features of the group as a whole; what distinguishes omissions which are immediately detected from those that are not, and what, amongst the latter, distinguishes letters that tend to be omitted from those that do not? In

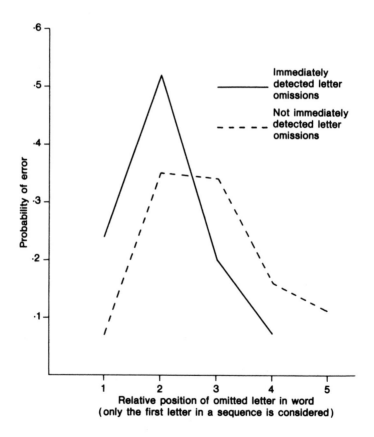

FIG. 1   Probability of error as a function of relative position for immediately detected and not immediately detected letter omission slips

answering these questions we will find similar factors operating as when we considered omissions and stem variants at the lexical level.

The words in which omissions occur are long words, averaging 8.4 letters, which is nearly double the average word token length of 4.7 letters (Kučera and Francis, 1967), a difference which is significant [$t(123) = 15.35$, $p < 0.001$]. This agrees with the data provided by Wing and Baddeley, (Chapter 12, this volume). We might consequently expect that letters would tend to be omitted, reducing a long word nearer to the average number of letters that have to be written when writing words. A serial order effect was also found – more letters being omitted in the middle than at the ends. Adopting the method used by Wing and Baddeley, Fig. 1 shows the relationship between pro-bability of omitting a letter and the position of that letter within a word. Words which were completed and those which were not are treated separately, and the same bow-shaped curve is shown for both. Of course, if bound morphemes had been included amongst omissions, there would not have been such a falling off at the end of the curve. Finally, the immediate detection rate of these errors, that is to say the proportion of words which are not completed, is at 27% a low detection rate, comparable with omissions and stem variants at the lexical level.

4.2.4 *The preservation of initial letters.* Turning to our second question, the main features which distinguish immediately detected errors from those that are not, are that the number of consecutive letters omitted is larger (1.8 rather than 1.2, $\chi^2 = 5.71$, $p < 0.05$) and that, as Fig. 1 shows, a greater proportion of the omitted letters occur early in the word. There were very few first letter omissions and none went un-detected. The first two letters on their own comprise 45% of the detected omissions in comparison with 13% of the undetected ones. These figures apply to the group W-sample, but very similar figures are shown in the monograph W-sample.

Two points of significance about this first letter effect may be brought out. First, the rarity of omissions of this letter is in agreement with studies of the tip of the tongue phenomenon. Witte (1960) found the first approximation to the target word to have the same initial phoneme as the target word in 62% of his cases, and Brown and McNeill (1966) found the first letter was the same in 57% of theirs. Looking at my data of sound pattern slips of the pen and combining the three samples, I find the initial phoneme/letter is the same in 88% of the cases. This is expressed in terms of either phoneme or letter, although in my entire corpus of sound pattern slips of the pen there were only twelve cases where – as in SEPARATED for CELEBRATED, for example – these differed. In only one of these – ONE for ON – was the match one of letters rather than of phonemes. Further light on the strength of the first phoneme/letter was unexpectedly thrown by immediate repetitions at the lexical level. If we remove cases which occurred when moving from one line or page to the next, nearly half the slips were ones where the next word started with the same letter as the repeated word. The numbers are, of course, small and we do not know the frequencies of initial phonemes or of words starting with the same phoneme following one another. Nevertheless, the odds against such a proportion occurring by chance must be considerable. It suggests that there is a word repetition effect which is much more likely to be resisted when the following word starts with a different phoneme.

Second, just as at the lexical level, words which were frequently omitted were words which were likely not to be detected, so here we have the converse relationship: letters which tend not to be omitted are ones which, when omitted, are easily detected. Similarly, studies of speech perception have shown that the initial phoneme or phonemes are more likely to be correctly perceived than later ones (Cole and Jakimik, 1978).

It may be questioned whether the primacy effect shown in the relative absence of omissions of initial letters in slips of the pen is the same as that shown in studies of forgetting. The evidence given above testifies to the important role first phonemes or letters may play in accessing words. Perhaps this also applies to production, since stuttering occurs much more frequently on the initial rather than on subsequent phonemes in words (Rieber *et al.*, 1976).

4.2.5 *Characteristics of letters likely to be omitted.* Turning to the third question – what distinguishes letters that are omitted from those that are not – three factors were considered. These were frequency in the language; ascenders (*b, d, t,* etc.) and descenders (*p, q, g,* etc.) vs the rest (*a, c, e,* etc.) on the grounds that letters that protrude above or below the line are more noticeable than those that do not; and multiple vs single occurrences of a letter in a word. This last factor was held to be important by Meringer with slips of the tongue and by Lecours (1966) with the writing errors in Lee Harvey Oswald's diary.

To carry out the analysis of the contribution of each of these three factors, only omissions in completed words were considered. This was because omissions in words which were not completed could conceivably sometimes have been cases of anticipation due, for example, to thinking of a later letter whilst about to write an earlier one and thus inserting it out of place, or cases of transposition that were stopped before the second letter was written. In the total sample of completed words there were 83 words composed of 715 letters, 100 of thich were omitted. The most frequent letters, according to the norms of Baddeley *et al.* (1960), were more liable to be omitted than less frequent ones. However, the relationship was not significant. Letters which occurred more than once in words were more liable to be omitted than those which did not. Here the relationship was significant [$\chi^2 = 5.53$, p <0.05]. Ascenders and descenders were less likely to be omitted than other letters, and this relationship was also significant [$\chi^2 = 6.36$, p <0.05]. In order to try to separate the effect of each of these variables, a regression analysis was carried out. The dependent variable was a dummy used to show whether or not the letter was omitted. Each variable was considered after the other two had been taken into account. By this method, it was found that only protruding vs non-protruding letters gave a significant relationship (p <0.05), the effect of multiple occurrence being significant only at the 10% level.

I conclude, therefore, that multiple occurrence is only a secondary factor in letter omission while perceptual prominence appears to be a primary one. It is difficult to see how the ascender/descender effect could be accounted for in terms of acoustic coding of letters waiting to be written. However, this does not imply that visual coding is necessarily involved since the letters contrast with others by the size of the movement that has to be made in their realisation. Whatever the modality in which they are encoded, we see once again evidence of the importance of detectability in making or not making a slip.

5 Conclusion

In this chapter I have set out the main differences in incidence of slips of the tongue and slips of the pen. I will now conclude with a brief consideration of the striking similarity of my results with those of Chedru and Geschwind (1972). They compared the writing and speech performance of patients suffering both from acute confusional states and attentional disorders with the performance of normal controls and of the same patients when they had recovered. They found that writing deteriorated in comparison with speech and in comparison with writing after recovery, as well as with the writing of the controls. The differences between writing and speech were the same as those I found, namely a greater frequency of omission and substitution of function words, auxiliaries and bound morphemes for writing than for speech at the lexical level, and greater frequency of omission for writing than for speech at the letter level. There was no difference at the letter level as regards additions and transpositions. The only inconsistencies of our results were in the greater frequency Chedru and Geschwind found for letter substitutions and omissions at the ends of words. It is very probable that these can be accounted for in terms of their failure to distinguish the lexical from the letter level in their analysis. Chedru and Geschwind attributed the difference to the greater complexity of writing than speech and to their patients' being less familiar with writing. Lack of familiarity is not applicable in the case of my subjects since they were university graduates and undergraduates, and were well practised in writing. As for complexity, organising the movements involved in speech is likely to be much more complex than writing, though writing demands more in the way of conscious learning. Also, there are difficulties with speech because of the speed with which words have to be accessed, which I suggested was responsible for some categories of slips being commoner in speech than in writing. This explanation also accounts for the fact that there are phoneme substitution slips which have no parallel in writing.

There are, however, two respects in which writing may be more complex than speech. These are the necessity of converting the representation of words from strings of phonemes to strings of letters, i.e. from phonologically encoded to visually or kinaesthetically encoded material. There is also the much longer delay between setting up the linguistic programme and realising it in writing, a process which would put short term memory at a premium. These difficulties could account for function words and bound morphemes being particularly prone to slips in writing. The morphemic differences might, as is the case with function words, be less easily detectable than difference of one content word from another, particularly when they are not phonologically similar. If we make the additional assumption that the response to these less easily detectable items was weaker than the response to content words, then it would be expected that they would also be more subject to short-term memory decay and interference. One criterion for the selection of Chedru and Geschwind's patients was their poor performance on a digit span test. They might therefore be expected to show reduced processing and short-term memory capacity, and hence would do less well than in their normal condition. By the same token normals, when subjected to the more sensitive test that the incidence of slips of the pen provides, similarly show a poorer performance in the particular respects considered.

The point of the study by Chedru and Geschwind was to show that there was no clinical entity called 'pure agraphia'. They hoped to show by using patients, whose confusional states were of different origins, that reported cases of this were in fact due to some global defect which they described as 'diffuse brain dysfunction'. I hope in this study to have supported them by showing that the condition can be represented as a continuum.

Acknowledgements

I wish to thank Miss Susannah Brown for help and advice on statistical treatment of the data and Miss Janet Holland, Mrs Christine Barnard and Mrs Ann Kopel for assistance in the analysis of data.

PART VI

Spelling and Development

A boy that is good
Will learn his book well
And if he can't read
Will strive for to spell.

Drawing by Wilhelm Busch (1884)
English Nursery Rhyme

The Development of Orthographic Images

LINNEA C. EHRI   *Department of Education, University of California, Davis, U.S.A.*

There is substantial disagreement among psychologists as well as teachers about the relationship between reading and spelling skills and whether they develop separately or together. The present chapter is intended to develop the idea that learning to read and learning to spell are highly related, that underlying the emergence of both capabilities is the child's growing knowledge of print as a means of representing all the words in his language. The chapter is organised into three sections. First, a theory of printed word learning is explained. Second, experimental evidence is presented to support its claim that orthographic images lie at the heart of printed word learning and enable beginners to read words easily as well as to spell words with some degree of accuracy. In the final section, evidence from various sources is discussed in order to further validate the concept of orthographic images and to clarify some of the questions and issues needing further study.

1 Word identity amalgamation theory

One of the most important capabilities in learning to read is learning to recognise printed words. Research on beginning readers performed by Shankweiler and Liberman (1972) and by Firth (1972) reveals high correlations between the ability to identify printed words and skill in reading text. However, there is substantial disagreement about which skills and experiences are most important. Some authorities stress letter-sound mapping skills (Rozin and Gleitman, 1977; Liberman and Shankweiler, 1977). Others emphasise the importance of learning to recognise printed words rapidly and automatically (LaBerge and Samuels, 1974; Perfetti and Hogaboam, 1975; Perfetti and Lesgold, 1977). Still others proclaim the centrality of learning to recognise the meanings of printed words as they participate in larger sentence and story contexts (Goodman, 1972; Smith, 1971).

Ehri (1978) has attempted to integrate some of these components into a theory of printed word learning. Rather than singling out one skill or experience, this theory makes room for the importance of several. An updated version of the theory is presented below. It is important to recognise that the theory has been fashioned as a guide for the conduct of research and hence represents an explicit but very *tentative* statement about the word learning process. At this point, its only value is heuristic, as a means of raising questions, identifying hypotheses to be tested, directing observations and experimentation, and organising information. It should not be construed as any final explanation or answer.

According to Ehri, the most important acquisition during beginning reading is learning to recognise printed words accurately, rapidly, and also completely in the sense that all the words' identities – phonological, syntactic, and semantic – are apparent when the printed word is seen. Children already possess substantial linguistic competence with speech when they start learning to read. The major task facing them is to learn how to assimilate printed language to this existing knowledge. In English, the most perceptible and dependable units of printed language are *words*, not letters or sentences, so it is at a lexical level that children work at assimilating print to their existing linguistic knowledge.

Following the suggestions of linguists (Chomsky and Halle, 1968; Langacker, 1973) the lexicon is conceptualised as consisting of abstract word units having several different facets or identities. Every word has a *phonological* identity which consists of information about acoustic, articulatory and phonemic properties of the word. (In subsequent text, these properties are sometimes referred to as word 'sounds'. It is important to note that the term 'sounds' is used in a loose sense to include articulatory gestures and abstract phonemes which are not really sounds but only correlates of sound). In addition, every word has a *syntactic* identity specifying characteristic grammatical functions of the word in sentences (i.e. noun, verb, adjective, determiner, etc.). And most words have a *semantic* identity, that is, a 'dictionary definition'. All of the foregoing identities are thought to be acquired and known implicitly as a consequence of achieving competence with spoken language.

In the course of learning to read, another identity is added to the lexicon, the word's *orthographic* form. This written unit is thought to be incorporated not as a rotely memorised geometric figure but rather as a sequence of letters bearing systematic relationships to phonological properties of the word. The term 'amalgamation' is used to denote the special way in which orthographic identities get established in lexical memory. Since beginners already know how words are pronounced, their task is to assimilate the word's printed form to its phonological structure. They do this by matching at least some of the letters to phonetic or phonemic segments detected in the word. These segments serve as 'slots' in lexical memory which are filled by images of letters seen in the word's spelling. To process and remember letter-sound correspondences effectively, readers must already be familiar with those letters as *symbols* for the relevant phonological segments they map in the word. If at least some of these letter-sound relationships are known and recognised, then there will be enough 'glue' to secure this visual symbol in lexical memory. Very likely, readers who possess more systematic knowledge about mapping relationships between letters and sounds will be better able to form a match between conventional spellings and word pronunciations and to store a complete amalgam in lexical memory.

General orthographic knowledge which is useful for setting up orthographic images includes not only information about single letter-sound relations but also information about more complex functional spelling patterns in which letters combine to map sounds within words (Venezky, 1970), about syllabic print-sound structure, and about common spelling patterns shared by sets of rhyming words (i.e. AIR, PAIR, CHAIR, HAIR, FAIR, STAIR). As the reader's repertoire of printed words grows, he becomes aware of new patterns for mapping print into speech, and these regularities are added to his knowledge of orthography as a system for mapping words. Very likely, much of this orthographic knowledge is induced as a consequence of the reader's experiences learning to read and to spell words, though some of it may result from explicit instruction about letter-sound mapping rules. However, simply being able to state a rule is not sufficient for the knowledge to become operational. The functional value of the rule must be incorporated into word learning processes. Such systematic knowledge serves the reader in several ways. It provides him with a means of decoding or spelling unfamiliar printed words. It may also speed up the process of pronouncing familiar, regularly spelled printed words (Baron and Strawson, 1976). Most importantly, it makes it easier for him to make sense of, store, and remember the spelling patterns of newly encountered words.

When printed words are stored in lexical memory, the orthographic forms are amalgamated not just with phonological identities but also with syntactic and semantic identities. Amalgamation occurs as readers practise pronouncing and interpreting unfamiliar printed words while they are reading text for meaning (Ehri and Roberts, 1979). As printed words are successfully read, orthographic images come to represent information about how the words function in phrases and sentences (i.e. what classes of words are usually positioned next to them and how they combine to form larger units) and what the words mean in various contexts. In this way, orthographic images are synthesised with syntactic and semantic as well as phonological identities and they combine to form single representational units in lexical memory.

When identity amalgamation has been achieved for particular words, the quality of the word recognition process changes. The printed form is processed as a single unit rather than as a sequence of letters to be translated into sounds (LaBerge and Samuels, 1974), and letters in words are recognised simultaneously rather than sequentially (Doggett and Richards, 1975; Terry et al., 1976). The reader can glance at a word and recognise its meaning 'silently' without needing pronunciation in order to identify it (Barron, 1978). This is because a fairly exact copy of the printed form has been stored in memory and this visual image functions as the symbol for meanings as well as sounds. When the word is seen and matched to its visual image, all of its other identities become apparent simultaneously. Once visual images are established in memory, they provide information useful for spelling as well as for reading words (Simon and Simon, 1973; Simon, 1976).

Notice how easy it is to recognise the pronunciations and meanings of the following similarly spelled words: COMB, TOMB; BEAR, DEAR; HERE, WERE, THERE; HAVE, PAVE. Readers familiar with these forms do not make errors in pronouncing them and they can recognise their linguistic identities at a glance. In fact, they may be surprised to discover that the same spelling patterns are pronounced differently depending upon which word is represented. Such spelling-sound variations do not bother word identification processes because in learning each form, readers have amalgamated letter patterns to meanings as well as to sounds. A study by Mackworth and Mackworth (1974) provides evidence that good readers are more skilled than poor readers in sorting out the appropriate lexical identities for similarly spelled word forms.

In order for these word learning processes to become operational, some preparation is essential to bring the reader to the point where the particular letters appearing in words are seen as belonging there and he can store them in memory. This preparation very likely includes some analytic capabilities: being familiar enough with the shapes and sounds of alphabet letters so that the shapes can be imagined and remembered accurately as symbols for sounds; being able to isolate relevant acoustic or articulatory segments in words and to detect systematic relationships between these sound segments and letters present in their spellings. Very likely these analytic skills must be known well enough so that the reader can co-ordinate and synthesise multiple letter-sound relations automatically without having to attend to each segment individually (LaBerge and Samuels, 1974).

Although some preparation is needed, this does not mean that printed word learning cannot begin until all the skills have been mastered. It is more likely that during acquisition, word learning ability and its relevant sub-skills interact with each other and are acquired simultaneously rather than sequentially (Goldstein, 1976; Ehri, 1978). Word reading begins but is a slow, laborious, rote process subject to forgetting initially while these skills are developing. Such practice, however, may be necessary in order to learn phonetic segmentation, letter-sound mapping relationships and how to co-ordinate them, and in order to develop visual memory for word forms. Once these prerequisite capabilities get established, words can be learned much more quickly, completely, and permanently.

1.1 *Contrast to other theories*

Before evidence for the theory is presented, it might be helpful to review how this approach contrasts with some other views of word learning. The word identity amalgamation view is distinctly different from E. J. Gibson's theory (Gibson and Levin, 1975) in that principles of memory rather than perception are invoked. The necessity of adopting memory constructs to explain how printed words are recognised is perhaps less obvious than to explain how words are spelled since the former but not the latter has the appearance of a perceptual process. However, perceptual principles such as differentiation, selective attention, detection and use of redundancy are simply *ad hoc* descriptions of the process. In contrast to memory constructs, they do not constitute a mechanism which explains or yields predictions about how readers' capabilities with words develop. Since printed words are conventional forms whose appearance deviates very little across instances and since they are seen and processed over and over again, it makes much sense to postulate the storage of specific visual information about those forms in lexical memory. Certainly, this offers a very powerful explanation. If readers know exactly how particular printed words should look, then the act of recognising them on a printed page should occur rapidly and accurately and should require little effort. This appears to characterise the capabilities of readers shown familiar printed words.

Word identity amalgamation theory resembles F. Smith's theory (1973a) in that the visual forms of words are portrayed as being stored in memory together with meanings. However, the present view differs in that words are thought to be stored as alphabetic images rather than as non-alphabetic distinctive features. Furthermore, sounds play a central role in setting up these images, according to amalgamation theory, whereas Smith argues that sound has nothing to do with the storage of print-meaning relationships.

Word identity amalgamation theory differs from a phonemic recoding view (Rubenstein *et al.*, 1971) in that another mechanism besides letter-to-sound translation is offered to explain how printed words are recognised. In contrast to the decoding view, a distinction is drawn between processing familiar and unfamiliar printed words. If readers encounter words never seen before, they apply various sound translation strategies to discover the word's identity. However, if they have successfully read the word enough times previously, then the form is familiar and does not have to be sounded out or recognised anew each time it is seen. Decoding 'strategies' are superseded by a very different process which takes much less time, one where the word is recognised in terms of its match to the form stored in memory.

A view similar to amalgamation theory is the information processing model of spelling performance proposed by D. Simon (1976). She offers some additional constructs which are compatible with and serve to elaborate the present view. Her model includes the notion of a word store containing motoric as well as auditory, visual and semantic representations of familiar words. Another component of the model is knowledge of general mapping rules relating graphemes and phonemes. The building blocks of the system are alphabet letters which, like words, are units specified multi-modally, in terms of auditory, visual and motoric representations. Correspondences among alternative alphabetic codes (i.e. upper and lower case letters) form part of the alphabetic store. Although the theories are similar, Simon does not discuss processes by which information about word spellings gets stored in memory.

2 Orthography as a representational system

We conducted one series of experiments to gather evidence that beginning readers use orthography as a representational system for storing speech sounds in memory and that this capability is important in learning to read, specifically in building up a repertoire of printed words in lexical memory. We designed a paired associate (PA) sound learning task to tap children's ability to make use of visual spellings in remembering sounds. We already knew from a previous study (Ehri, 1976) that children have difficulty remembering meaningless sounds in the absence of any mnemonics. In one or another of four PA experiments, we provided various types of mnemonic aids or sound-elaborative activities besides spellings in order to compare their facilitative effects upon sound memory (Ehri and Wilce, 1979).

In the first experiment, each of 4 different PA tasks was given to first (6 yr) and second graders (7 yr). The important features distinguishing these tasks are summarised in Table 1. In each task, the responses to be learned were 4 oral CVC nonsense syllables. The tasks differed in terms of the test cues employed and the type of mnemonic aids provided during study and feedback periods. The test cues were either meaningless but visually distinctive line drawings called squiggles, or single alphabet letters representing the first consonant in each nonsense response. The mnemonic aids shown to subjects were either correct spellings or mis-spellings of the CVC sounds. The children were given 15 trials to learn the sounds. On each trial, each of the four test cues was shown, children tried to remember the CVC sound which had been paired with it, and then the experimenter pronounced the correct sound and displayed any spelling aids. It is important to note that theoretically subjects did not have to be able to read in order to perform the task. All they had to do was remember the CVC sounds and match them up with the appropriate visual test cue. The CVC spelling aids were extra and were not present at the time of the test.

TABLE 1   Stimuli employed in the four paired associate learning tasks

Task	Test cues	Oral responses[1]	Study aid
Squiggles	⌐ᵮ	JAD	
	⊀⅄⌐	WEK	none
	⊘	SIM	
	⟋	LUT	
Initial letters	V	VAP	
	B	BEM	none
	T	TIB	
	H	HUK	
Initial letters plus correct spellings	M	MAV	Mav
	R	REL	Rel
	K	KIP	Kip
	G	GUZ	Guz
Initial letters plus mis-spellings	P	PAB	Pes
	D	DES	Dif
	N	NIF	Nug
	F	FUG	Fab

[1] The four sets of oral responses listed here were employed in all four tasks with assignments counterbalanced across subjects.

It was expected that children would be able to remember the sounds best when they were shown correct spellings and they would do worst with mis-spellings. Also, memory for the sounds was expected to be superior when letters mapping the initial sound of CVC units served as stimulus prompts than when unrelated squiggles were the prompts.

Results confirmed these predictions. In Experiment 1, children took about 6 trials to learn the sounds with spelling aids, 11 trials to learn them with initial letters but no spelling aids, and 13 trials to learn them with squiggles as test cues and with mis-spellings. These differences were statistically significant.

Experiment 2 differed only slightly from Experiment 1. The mis-spelling task was not included. Children who failed to learn the sounds in any of the tasks were replaced by children who were successful in at least one task. Only first graders were tested. Results revealed that children learned the sounds in about 6 trials with spelling aids, in 9 trials with initial letters only, and in 13 trials with squiggle test cues. These differences were statistically significant.

From these results, it was concluded that beginning readers are able to benefit from spellings in remembering sounds. The preferred interpretation for recall patterns is that sounds are remembered better because spellings provide the children with orthographic images they can use to symbolise and remember the sounds. However, some alternative explanations for the facilitative effects of spellings can be identified. Spellings may have caused subjects to repeat and rehearse the sounds one additional time. Or spellings may have clarified the separate segments in the nonsense sounds. Or some non-visual aspect of the letters may have helped.

To eliminate these possibilities, a third experiment was performed in which four variations of the PA task were employed. Rather than using squiggles or letters as stimuli, the numbers 1 through 4 prompted recall of the four CVC nonsense syllables in each task. Every child was given all of the tasks, and the order of the tasks was counterbalanced across subjects. The tasks differed in terms of the activity occurring during study and feed-back periods. After a subject had been shown the number test cue and had tried to produce the correct CVC sound, the experimenter pronounced the sound, had the subject repeat it, and then one of four events occured. Either a visual spelling was shown, or the experimenter gave the spelling orally by naming the letters, or the experimenter articulated each phonetic segment separately, or the child repeated the nonsense sound one additional time. It was reasoned that if spellings are helpful because they provide a visual image which subjects can use to remember sounds, then recall in the visual spelling condition should still be superior.

In this experiment, second graders served as subjects. They were given a maximum of seven trials to learn the sounds. Learning was terminated early if subjects reached a criterion of two perfect trials. Results confirmed predictions. Children recalled significantly more nonsense sounds when they were shown visual spellings than in the other three conditions. Performances in the latter tasks were almost identical. To illustrate, the mean number of sounds being remembered correctly by the fifth trial was: 3.1 sounds with visual spellings, 2.0 sounds with oral spellings, 1.9 sounds with phonemic segmentation, and 1.8 sounds with repetitions.

These results suggest that the visual properties of the spellings are central to their facilitative effects upon recall, presumably because they induce children to form orthographic images of the sounds and store these in memory. However, this image-forming process was merely inferred from performances in the above studies. That is, children were simply shown spellings and no mention was made of images. A fourth experiment was performed to demonstrate this effect more directly. Sound learning was compared under two conditions: when children listened to oral spellings and imagined what they looked like, and when children rehearsed the sounds several times.

In this study, second graders were given two PA tasks structured much like tasks in the previous experiment, with numbers 1 through 4 as stimulus prompts and four oral CVC nonsense sounds as responses. In the orthographic image task, the experimenter pronounced each trigram, had subjects repeat it, then the experimenter spelled it orally and had subjects close their eyes and create a visual image of the spelling. In the sound repetition task, the experimenter pronounced the word, subjects repeated it, the experimenter pronounced it again and subjects repeated it. These events took place for each of the four CVC responses on the initial study trial and then following each recall attempt. The two tasks were given in counterbalanced order to 18 children, and each completed a maximum of 7 trials to learn the sounds.

It was reasoned that if spellings facilitate recall because they provide orthographic images of sounds which can be stored in memory, then performances should be better when children are told to imagine the spellings than when they merely repeat the sounds. This prediction was confirmed. Children remembered significantly more sounds in the image condition than in the sound rehearsal condition. To illustrate, the mean number of sounds recalled correctly on the fifth trial was 2.8 sounds with images vs 2.2 sounds without. These results add to previous findings by suggesting that it is not necessary for orthographic images to be seen outside the head in order to enter memory. They can also be constructed in the learner's mind.

The first two experiments described above were conducted not only to verify the mnemonic value of orthography for beginning readers but also to determine when this capability emerges, whether it is related to the acquisition of other reading skills, most importantly, the size of the reader's lexicon of printed words, and whether it distinguishes between more and less advanced beginning readers.

Inspection of the numbers of first and second graders succeeding and failing on the spelling-aided sound learning task indicated that orthographic mnemonic capabilities emerge between the first and second year of reading instruction. Fewer first than second graders were able to benefit from spellings. Among first graders tested, 25% to 40% failed to learn the sounds in 15 trials. Among second graders, 8% were unsuccessful.

If children were going to learn the sounds in any of the 3 or 4 tasks given, it was the spelling-aided task. First graders who failed to learn the sounds with spellings never learned them in the other conditions. Even many of the successful spelling-aided learners were unable to remember the sounds without spellings. These findings are interesting in that they raise doubt about one assumption connected with the phonemic recoding view of printed word processing, namely, that beginning readers possess an effective phonemic coding system for storing and remembering sounds. Present findings indicate that, in the absence of spellings, memory for meaningless sounds is quite poor. In another study (Ehri, 1976), we found that pre-readers' memory for orally presented, single words was deficient when the words were not meaningful (i.e. OF, WERE, COULD). Combined, present and previous findings suggest that in order to be memorable, sounds must have meaning or must be symbolised by letters. Otherwise there is no coding system available for preserving the sounds in memory.

The reason why orthographic memory is thought to be important is that it enables readers to store and remember printed word forms. If this is true, then one would expect children who possess this skill to know many more printed words than those lacking it. In Experiment 1, subjects' familiarity with 27 high frequency printed nouns was assessed. In Experiment 2, 30 irregularly spelled context-dependent words (e.g. WHEN, EVERY, COULD, MIGHT, ONCE) were added to this list to insure that the size of children's printed word repertoire was being estimated rather than simply their ability to sound out unfamiliar words correctly. Clear evidence for the expected relationship emerged. The correlation between spelling-aided sound learning scores and word recognition was significant and in the case of Experiment 1 as high as -0.75.

3 Comparison of silent and pronounced letters in orthographic memory

In the sound learning experiments, the role of orthography in printed word learning was indicated only indirectly by correlational data. Some other studies were designed to collect more direct evidence that beginning readers store words as orthographic images. In the first study, a series of tasks was designed to show that children possess visual images of real words which are alphabetic and include all of the letters in a word's spelling, not just boundary letters or phonetically salient letters. Children were first shown some words to verify that they could read them. Then they were told to imagine the printed forms of each word and to decide whether it contained a particular letter. Some of the letters were constituents, some were not. Some of the constituent letters mapped single sounds in the words and some were silent. After this, subjects were surprised with a word memory task. Recall of each word was prompted with the letter given in the judgment task. It was reasoned that if beginning readers have stored familiar words as orthographic images, then they should be able to consult these images to answer questions about constituent letters, and they should have information about silent as well as pronounced constituents. Furthermore, they should be able to remember words prompted by constituent letters far better than words prompted by non-present letters.

To verify these hypotheses, 20 second graders were tested individually. A preparatory phase came first in which 15 high frequency adjectives and verbs were presented on cards for the children to identify. If subjects were unsuccessful, they were taught to read the words by representing the cards until all were correctly pronounced. Most of the words proved already familiar to the children. The mean number correct on the first presentation was 13.5 words out of 15. Eleven children required some training (i.e. a mean of 1.6 additional trials) to learn the words. After this, the subjects spent 10–15 minutes performing two filler tasks which assessed their ability to identify a set of 84 printed words and to sound out and blend some nonsense words. The letter judgment task came next. The experimenter pronounced each of the 15 words the child had recognised or been taught earlier. The child was told to form an image of the word's spelling and to indicate when he/she could see it. Then the experimenter presented a card printed with a lower case letter and told the subject to decide whether the word being imagined contained that letter. Different letters were judged for each word. Among the 15 words judged, five words contained a letter which mapped into a sound in that word (i.e. *n – kind, o – brown, r – strong, i – sick, w – sweet*), five words contained a letter which was silent in the word (i.e. *a – dead, c – black, l – talk, g – bright, e – come*), and five words did not contain the letter at all (i.e. *u – drink, z – jump, y – fast, m – hard, p – short*). All of the contained letters were in non-initial positions. The experimenter presented the words for judgment twice, each time in a different order. Then she surprised the subject with a recall task. Each letter was shown again and the child was told to remember the word he had imagined for that letter.

Results for the most part confirmed expectations. On the letter judgment task, scores were close to perfect. Mean values are given in Table 2. Though errors were few, the majority occurred with the silent letters. Scores improved slightly on the second trial. Some children commented that it was easier to judge the second time around, and response latencies appeared to be shorter. With one exception (i.e. a child who missed five), no child judged more than two letters incorrectly on the second trial.

TABLE 2 Mean correct in the letter judgment and incidental recall tasks (maximum per cell = 5)

	Letter cues			
	Sounded	Silent	Absent	Mean
Letter judgment task				
First trial	4.85	4.30	4.80	4.65
Second trial	4.95	4.35	4.80	4.70
Word recall task				
All subjects	1.70[1]	2.55[1]	0.45[1]	1.57
Subjects with perfect letter judgment scores (N = 9)	1.90	2.90	0.40	1.73

[1] MSE (32) = 0.75, Tukey pair-wise comparison value = 0.58, p < 0.05.

Informal observation of behaviours accompanying the image judgments further confirmed that it was easy for children to imagine the spellings of familiar printed words. They had no difficulty following instructions. When asked to report when they had the image, all complied, and no one claimed not to understand what he/she was supposed to do. Everyone was able to form images for most of the words, these images seemed to be formed readily, and the letter judgments were immediate. A few words required more time. For these, children would close their eyes tightly or whisper spellings to themselves. They appeared to be engaged in constructing rather than simply retrieving an image. When asked about the presence of a letter in these words, some were observed to stretch out the word as they pronounced it, either in order to find the letter or to confirm its presence in the word. Only three children reported lacking an image, and this occurred for only 1 or 2 words. As the children examined their images, some were observed to roll their eyes upward and nod their heads. If a letter was not present, they seemed to respond immediately, one child claiming 'No way!' If present, their 'yes' responses were slightly delayed as they appeared to be locating the letter in the image before answering. Eye movements and head nodding often accompanied confirming responses. These observations make it hard to doubt that the children were indeed working with images of words in their heads.

Recalling the words was somewhat more difficult than imagining spellings. Out of five words per letter category (i.e. SOUNDED, SILENT, ABSENT), the mean number of words recalled ranged between 0.5 and 2.5 words (see Table 2). Recall was very poor for words whose spellings did not include the letter prompt. Out of 20 children, 12 failed to remember any of these five words. In contrast, there were no children who failed to recall at least one word prompted by a constituent letter. These results indicate that letters comprise a relevant part of beginning readers' memory for words.

In this study, silent and pronounced letters were compared in terms of their capacity to prompt recall. This was done in order to verify that orthographic images rather than phonetic translations underlie performance. It was reasoned that if familiar printed words are stored as visual images, then all of the letters should be represented, regardless of whether they map into sound. Thus, silent letters should be as effective as sounded letters in prompting recall. An alternative possibility is that when children learn words, they translate letters into sounds and use sound to access word meanings. Those letters which correspond to sounds become the critical cues for identifying words, and they are the letters which get represented in lexical memory. If this is true, then sounded letters should serve as better retrieval cues than silent letters.

Analysis of performances in the recall task disclosed a difference, but it was the opposite of any effect expected. As displayed in Table 2, the mean number of words retrieved by silent letters was significantly greater than the mean number retrieved by pronounced letters. When the recall performance of only the best subjects was considered, that is, those who performed perfectly in judging silent and pronounced letters, the difference between silent and pronounced letter recall was even larger (see Table 2). The fact that recall was not poorer with silent letters is interpreted as support for the claim that alphabetic images of word spellings are represented in lexical memory as visual forms whose component letters do not have to map sound to be included and remembered.

Why recall should be superior with silent letters is puzzling. Several possibilities can be identified. It may be that the children spent more time or effort thinking about the silent-letter words during the letter judgment task since the presence of these letters was harder to detect. Or it may be that, unlike pronounced letters which could be verified by consulting the word's sound, silent-letter prompts forced subjects to access and examine an image of the word. Since orthographic images appear to be better mnemonics than sounds (see above discussion), word recall was superior when subjects consulted images. Another possibility is that silent-letter words were more memorable than pronounced-letter words. This could have happened since a different set of words was used in each case. A fourth possibility is that pronounced letters may have produced more intrusion errors than silent letters by causing children to think of other words containing that letter sound. Inspection of the errors, however, revealed an equal number of intrusions with each letter type, thus discounting this hypothesis. A fifth possibility is that the effect reflects a real difference. Silent letters may in fact be more salient in the images of familiar printed words. The presence of these letters is not predicted by any sound in the word and so there exists less redundancy for that letter slot in the image. As a result, these letters may have received a disproportionate amount of attention during the learning phase when the words were being stored in lexical memory.

To check on some of these explanations, another similarly designed experiment was performed. This time, a set of 10 words thought to be familiar to second graders was selected, and the same words were presented for letter judgment to two different groups of children, one group given pronounced letters to judge, the other given silent letters. Since the same words were given to both groups, we eliminated the possibility that recall differences might result from differences in our word choices. In order to make subjects in the two groups comparable in reading skill, we used their scores on a printed word reading task to form matched pairs. Members were randomly assigned to the pronounced and silent letter judgment groups. As in the previous experiment, an incidental letter judgment task was followed by a surprise letter-prompted recall task. The same sequence of tasks and task procedures were used. The new set of words plus the silent and pronounced letter prompts are listed in Table 3. Initially, the experiment was conducted with second graders. However, several of the subjects were not sufficiently familiar with the words and so their judgment and recall performances were too poor to consider. Additional pairs were recruited from the third grade (8 years) to yield a total of 19 pairs, 13 third graders and 6 second graders.

TABLE 3   List of words and letter prompts employed and number of subjects recalling each word

Words	Silent letter	Subjects (max = 19)	Pronounced letter	Subjects (max = 19)	Difference
school	h	14	c	17	−3
straw	w	10	t	5	5
wide	e	15	i	9	6
laugh	u	7	a	5	2
listen	t	14	s	4	10
friend	i	9	n	10	−1
dead	a	12	e	10	2
young	o	13	u	9	4
comb	b	18	m	12	6
bright	g	14	r	13	1
Mean		12.6		9.4	

Analysis of performances revealed that these children were already familiar with most of the 10 target words and so did not require much training. The mean number correctly read on the first word recognition trial was 8.1 words for second graders, 9.8 words for third graders. In the letter judgment task, all second graders and 5 pairs of third graders went through the task twice while eight pairs of third graders performed the judgments just once. As in the previous experiment, children judged the letters almost perfectly, with a mean of 9.8 correct for pronounced letters, and a mean of 9.4 correct for silent letters.

In the recall task, the mean number of words prompted by silent letters was again superior, 6.6 words, as contrasted to 4.9 words prompted by pronounced letters. A matched pair t-test confirmed that this difference was significant ($p < 0.05$). These findings replicate the pattern found in the previous experiment.

To further verify the superiority of silent letters as recall prompts, the number of subjects recalling each word successfully with each letter prompt was calculated. These values are reported in Table 3. Comparison of silent and pronounced letter recall for individual words revealed that the pattern favouring silent letters held for 8 out of 10 words. Thus, results appear to generalise across words as well as across subjects.

As in the previous study, it was not the case that pronounced letters elicited more word intrusions. Inspection of the number of errors in which subjects matched the wrong words to letters revealed about the same number occurring for pronounced and silent letters. Thus, greater response interference does not account for the poorer recall occurring with pronounced letters.

Another explanation for the effect was suggested by Uta Frith (personal communication). In analysing the locations of letter cues in the words in Table 3, she noticed that silent letters occurred in later positions than pronounced letters in 8 out of 10 cases. The exceptions were FRIEND and YOUNG. It may be that subjects scanned more of the orthographic image in locating silent letters than in locating pronounced letters, and that words whose images were more completely processed were better remembered. This explanation would attribute recall differences not to any special role of silent letters in images but rather to processing differences resulting from the choice of early or late letters. This possibility merits further investigation. If found to be true, it would clarify how orthographic images operate in this task, and it would suggest that silent and pronounced letters have equal status.

Results of another study using a different task to compare memory for silent and pronounced letters provided support for the equal status hypothesis. Included as part of a larger experiment (Ehri and Roberts, 1979) was a spelling task which required first graders to detect mis-spellings in 18 words thought to be in their reading vocabularies. In each mis-spelling, one non-initial letter had been deleted. For nine words, the omitted letter was silent; for nine words, a phonetic segment for the missing letter could be found in the word's sound. The child's task was to detect and correct the mis-spellings. It was reasoned that if the importance of letters in words is determined by whether they map sounds, and if word spellings are generated or remembered in terms of sound-salient letters, then missing silent letters should not be as easily identified as sounded letters. However, if orthographic images of words are stored in memory, then silent letter omissions should be as obvious as sounded letter omissions. Comparisons of the mean number of mis-spellings detected and corrected revealed equivalent means for the two sets of 9 words: $\bar{X} = 6.0$ for silent letters, 6.1 for pronounced letters, matched-pair t-test statistic $t < 1$. A tally of performances with the more easily detected mis-spellings illustrates what errors were obvious. Most children (i.e. between 25 and 36 out of 37 subjects) detected letter omissions in the following words: for pronounced letters, l – help, r – work, a – away, h – there, for silent letters, e – like, e – tree, u – your, y – play, l – tell. More than half of the children detected the following errors:

for pronounced letters, n – *find*, i – *smile*, t – *after*, s – *fish*; for silent letters, u – *house*, l – *walk*.

There are some sources of concern about these data. More of the silent than pronounced letters were located at word ends which tend to be a more salient position. Also, different words comprised the two sets, opening up the possibility that the sets were not equally familiar to subjects. Regardless of these shortcomings, the fact that beginning readers detected and corrected a majority of the silent letter omissions indicates that the visual forms of these words and not simply the pronounced letters were known. These results are consistent with the hypothesis that silent and pronounced letters are equally prominent in the visual images of words stored in memory.

4 Memory for visual forms of pseudowords

If it is true that when children learn to read words, these words are stored as orthographic images, then one would expect beginning readers to be able to read off their images and to produce correct or approximately correct spellings for familiar printed words. Acquiring the ability to spell words should develop hand-in-hand with learning to read words, even under circumstances where no opportunity is provided for spelling practice. Some preliminary studies were conducted to see just how closely related reading and spelling capabilities might be.

One experiment was designed to find out how accurately second graders would be able to spell made-up words they had been taught to read but had never written. Eight nonsense word sounds were invented. For each word, two alternative spellings were created, the spellings were printed on drawings of animals, and these were described to the children as names of the animals. Each child was shown only one of the two spellings for each picture. First, subjects practised reading the eight names until they could perform perfectly with the pictures present, then without the pictures. Also, they practised recalling the names of the pictures. Following a delay of 3–4 minutes during which they completed some math problems, they were shown the pictures and asked to write out each name. Of interest was whether original spellings would be recalled or whether children would create their own phonetic versions. It was reasoned that if, when subjects learned to read the words, they spontaneously stored orthographic forms as visual images, then their spellings should resemble the original forms. If, however, when they learned the words, they re-coded the print to speech and stored the sounds in memory, their spellings should be phonetic and not terribly faithful to the original form, particularly if it was irregular.

The words used are listed in Table 4. For each word, one of the spellings was thought to be more conventional than the other. Each of 14 children read four of the more conventional and four of the less

TABLE 4   List of nonsense names and mis-spellings

Original spellings	No. of errors	Mis-spellings[1]
1. wheople	6	wheaple (3), wheeple, whopore, whepole
weepel	4	weeple (2), weepl, wepol
2. bistion	4	bistoin, bishtin, bshistun, bitson
bischun	4	bischtun, bistchin, bischen, buchden
3. crantz	4	cantz, cranttz, crants, crand
crans	1	crane
4. ghirp	4	ghrip (2), grirp, girp
gurp	1	grup
5. juild	2	juiled, jild
jilled	0	
6. proat	2	poat (2)
prote	0	
7. lutter	1	luter
ludder	1	lutter
8. knopped	1	knoped
nopt	0	
Total	35	
(max.)	(112)	

[1] Parentheses indicate that more than one child produced this mis-spelling.

conventional spellings. The names were pronounced identically for both spellings. In cases where different pronunciations might be possible, the one used was the one suggested by the first more deviant spelling listed in Table 4.

Results revealed that children were quite accurate in their spellings: 69% of the productions were perfect. Their errors are listed in Table 4. Fewer of the deviant spellings were recalled correctly than the phonetic versions: 59% vs 80%. This suggests a greater tendency to forget more irregular forms. Inspection of the mis-spellings revealed that phonetic factors did play a role in distorting recall of original spellings though they did not account for all mis-spellings. Out of 35 errors, 60% could be considered phonetically acceptable maps while 40% failed to represent sounds in the pseudowords accurately. Further inspection of the particular letters retained in mis-spellings revealed that subjects did not completely abandon original spellings in favour of a straightforward phonetic version. This is apparent from the fact that subjects tended to preserve a salient letter pattern from the original form, and these patterns were produced only by subjects who had seen that version of the spelling. They never occurred with the other version. Whereas every mis-spelling of WHEOPLE began with *wh*, every mis-spelling of WEEPEL began with *we*. Every mis-spelling of BISTION contained *st* whereas every mis-spelling of BISCHUN had *ch*; *ch* was not produced at all in the former case. Every mis-spelling of GHIRP had an *i* and two included the *h* as well, whereas these letters never occurred with GURP. From these findings, it can be concluded that *both* visual and phonetic factors participate in the storage and production of word spellings with neither dominating to the exclusion of the other. This is consistent with amalgamation theory suggesting that the two sources of information work together in setting up orthographic images in memory.

One other study was conducted to explore subjects' visual memory for letters in pseudowords. Some better first grade readers were selected and taught to read 16 trisyllabic nonsense words such as PETRAVAMP, ROSTENLUST, NULLIBLE, TERMOLENT, MUSTURAL, pronounced with primary stress on the first syllable. The second syllable of each word was pronounced with an unstressed 'schwa' which theoretically can be spelled with any of the five vowels. In the spellings created for these 16 words, the 'schwa' sound was represented by each of the vowel letters in one or another word (i.e. each vowel occurred 4 times except the letter 'o' which appeared 5 times). Of interest was how accurately children might be able to remember these letters. It was reasoned that if sound alone determines which letters get stored, then accuracy should be poor. However, if visual properties of words are stored then these letters might be remembered better than chance.

The 16 words were taught on a memory drum using a study-test procedure. During the study trial, the child pronounced each word correctly. During the test, he or she had 3 seconds to recognise and say each word. Four training trials were given to 19 children who had demonstrated that they could read single-syllable nonsense words easily (i.e. words such as RIN, CLUS, GRAK, KEB). After each subject completed the four training trials, his memory for spellings was tested. For each word, he was shown a card with all but the 'schwa' letter printed. In place of the 'schwa', there was a hole behind which was a sliding row of vowels. Each of the vowels could be positioned in the hole to fill the slot. The child was told to pick the letter which made the word look right.

Though subjects learned to read many of the words, most did not remember the 'schwa' letters very well. The mean number of nonsense words read correctly during the fourth test trial was 10.5 (maximum = 16 words). The mean number of 'schwa' letters correctly identified on the spelling test was 6.1. By chance, one would expect about half this many, or 3.2 letters to be correct if children were selecting randomly from the set of 5 vowels. However, not all choices may have been random. A few words were correct much more often than the others (i.e. 12 or more out of 19 children were correct on PIMMICAN, SALSIFY, WEXELBAN, LIMMERPOP, whereas 9 or fewer children were correct on the other words). Thus, some of the letters may have been easy to guess based on knowledge of orthographic patterns. When the four easy words were excluded, there were only 8 subjects out of 19 who performed above a chance level, recognising between 4 and 9 out of 12 letters correctly. These results suggest that visual memory for spellings was relatively weak in this experiment, perhaps not surprisingly since the words were long and there were several to remember.

The study was designed to assess subjects' visual memory for letters which did not map into distinctive sounds. However, observation of the children's learning strategies revealed that this was in one sense a false characterisation of the task. When required to learn multi-syllabic forms, some children were observed to adopt a printed word learning strategy which *created* relevant sounds for the 'schwa' letters. During learning trials, as children were pronouncing the printed words, they sometimes separated the forms into component syllables. In doing so, they transformed unstressed into stressed syllables, and 'schwa' letters were given appropriate sound values. For example, when SALSIFY was broken into syllables and pronounced slowly, /sə/ was pronounced /si/. This strategy is noteworthy because it reveals one way that word learners might improve their memory for letters mapping into non-distinctive sounds, and it may explain how some of the children in the present study were able to remember spellings for 'schwa' sounds. By pronouncing each syllable separately with stress, they created relevant phonetic slots for the letters to fill in memory.

These observations illustrate how visual and phonetic properties of words might work together to set up and retain more accurate orthographic images in memory. As such, they are consistent with the WHEOPLE pseudoword learning study whose results pointed to an interactive view of the process. One conclusion which might be drawn from these two studies is that when both the visual and the phonological identities of words are being established in the lexicon and when the load on memory is increased beyond its capacity, the phonological representation is implanted first and the visual representation is assimilated to this form. This would account for the superior recall of phonetic spellings in Experiment 1 and also the greater success of subjects in remembering visual characteristics of words in the first than the second experiment. This possibility awaits further investigation.

5 Nature of orthographic images

Results of the studies reported here all contribute to the claim that orthographic images of words exist and that they are acquired by beginners as they learn to read. Orthographic images are thought to arise from visual experiences with words. They are not special constructions of the mind made out of something not actually seen. Evidence for a purely visual component in word memory comes from the work of McClelland (1976, 1977), Kirsner (1973), and Hintzman and Summers (1973). These studies show that visual properties of words (i.e. whether the print seen is in lower case, upper case, mixed case or script letters) are stored in memory independent of their phonetic properties.

Rayner and Posnansky (1978) and Posnansky and Rayner (1977) have conducted some tachistoscopic word processing studies with children and adults, and their evidence also supports a visual word storage view. They found that subjects who were shown drawings of common objects or animals printed with word or non-word stimuli were able to name the pictures faster when correct labels were printed on the pictures and also when non-words were printed which preserved many of the alphabetic visual features of the correct labels (i.e. horse – hcnre) though facilitation was not as great as with correctly spelled labels.

A very different type of evidence for the existence of orthographic images comes from a study by Brown and McNeill (1966). They induced a 'tip of the tongue' state in which adult subjects felt a particular word in mind but were unable to identify the word's pronunciation. Brown and McNeill found that subjects in this state were often able to identify many of the·letters in the word (i.e. initial letters were guessed correctly 57% of the time). Sometimes letter identification prompted retrieval of the word's pronunciation. The fact that letter information was available despite the absence of phonological information suggests that visual forms of words constitute a separate representation in lexical memory. The fact that letter information was connected with semantic information in the absence of pronunciations suggests that the word's phonological form is not an essential mediator of semantic information when a link between print and meaning has been established in memory.

Research reported in this chapter indicates that orthographic images provide beginning readers with fairly complete knowledge of the printed forms of words. Silent as well as pronounced letters in non-initial positions are firmly entrenched in the representations. It is interesting to note that in the picture-word facilitation study by Posnansky and Rayner (1977), the only type of printed label which facilitated picture-naming among their youngest readers (first graders) was the correctly spelled form of the word, not the forms which resembled the shape or boundary letters of the correct label (i.e. apple *vs* aggte *vs* azzme). In contrast, older readers did display some facilitation with boundary letters and shape cues. This finding for beginning readers appears to conflict with results of some previous studies suggesting that beginning readers process and remember words in terms of boundary letters (Marchbanks and Levin, 1965; Mason and Woodcock, 1973; Rayner and Hagelberg, 1975; Timko, 1970; Williams *et al.*, 1970). In these studies, a delayed recognition task was employed. Subjects were shown a single sequence of letters (e.g. CUG) and then were shown a card with several alternative letter sequences resembling the original form (e.g. CWG, OWG, OUG, CQN, JUN, JQG). They were told to select the one most like the original. Since the correct form was never included on the card, subjects were prevented from displaying accurate memory for visual forms. Thus, it is not clear from these latter studies that beginning readers' memory is limited only to boundary letters.

One rather surprising result obtained in the present studies indicated that silent letters may be more salient than pronounced letters in children's memory for words. A similar result with a proofreading task was found by Frith (1978) and hence this finding cannot be dismissed as a task specific artifact, even though it is difficult to explain. Cohen (Chapter 7) discusses a similar problem.

One reason why some silent letters may be remembered easily is that learners recognise them as an instance of a general lexical pattern characterising a number of printed words they have already acquired as orthographic images (i.e. long vowel-silent *e* pattern; short vowel-double consonant patterns; member of a family of words such as light, night, bright, fight). Though the letters themselves do not map into single sounds, in combination with other letters, their relationship to sound is recognised as regular and predictable (Venezky, 1970). Thus, they are easily remembered as an integral part of word spellings.

Another explanation for silent letter memory is that the process of storing visual word forms may be semi-autonomous in the sense that only some of the letters need to be rooted in sound in order for the entire word to enter memory. A few novel letters may be easy to learn when embedded in a familiar or predictable context. As the visual forms of words are seen repeatedly, their shape and length are stored and these characteristics create visual spaces in memory for letters to fill.

A third possibility is that children who are learning new word forms adjust their representation of the sounds in words so as to take account of as many letters as possible in word spellings. This process was suggested in the trisyllabic study where learners were observed to convert unstressed to stressed syllables so as to create appropriate vowel sounds for the letters. Also, Blumberg and Block (1975) note this strategy in the behaviour of their spelling learners who tended to segment graphemes into separate syllable units and to pronounce words as they were spelled rather than spoken even though they could read the words correctly (e.g. DISCIPLINE pronounced /dis/-/ki/-/plin/). In learning to read words like FEBRUARY and OFTEN, learners might even modify the words' pronunciation in their normal speech to legitimise the silent letters.

6 Functions of orthographic images

6.1 *Reading and spelling*

From previous as well as present research, it is apparent that ortho-graphic images are not mere epiphenomena but perform several important cognitive functions. Their main function is to ensure correct identification and production of printed words. They thus provide a close link between reading and spelling skills. In place of sound-letter principles which are utilised to generate unknown spellings, visual images can be consulted when the words are familiar printed forms. In the WHEOPLE study, children's spellings resembled the particular orthographic forms they had learned to read. The possession of alpha-betic images ensures that silent letters are included in spellings and also that the correct orthographic pattern is selected when a number of options are available (e.g. PAIR, BEAR, DARE, PRAYER, ERE, ERR). In the case of homonyms, orthographic images which have been amalgamated to word meanings enable readers and writers to distinguish which spelling goes with which meaning (Ehri and Roberts, 1979; Mack-worth and Mackworth, 1974; Mackworth, 1975).

6.2 *Verbal memory*

The contribution of orthographic images to verbal memory is indicated by the sound-learning studies of Ehri and Wilce (1979). Also, Sales *et al.* (1969) found that adults' short-term memory for six words displaying vowel variations (i.e. HICK, HECK, HACK, HOOK, HOAK, HAWK) was better when the words were seen than when they were heard. The mnemonic advantage provided by letters may be two-fold. They may offer a more memorable code than sound for preserving unfamiliar words in memory. They may serve to clarify which phonemes are being pronounced if there is any uncertainty.

The mechanism by which spellings may clarify phonemes is that they provide a means of conceptualising and symbolising words as sequences of separate sound segments. This function was apparent in the performances of beginning readers observed in a phonetic segmentation task (Ehri and Wilce, 1979). First graders listened to various words and non-words (e.g. RED, GRASS, PAG, KEST), estimated how many phonetic segments each contained, then identified the separate segments by pronouncing and marking each with a poker chip. To aid their analyses, several children spontaneously created or thought of word spellings and used these to estimate the number of segments. This strategy was verbalised when children recognised they had over-estimated the segments due to the presence of silent letters in their images. Not only BOAT with a silent *a* but also two nonsense words (/ān/and/sōt/) which subjects imagined as having silent *e*'s at the end were misjudged. The reason why children might find letters helpful is that in speech, phonemes do not exist as separate units but rather fold into each other, with properties of one often determined by the properties of adjacent sounds (Liberman and Shankweiler, 1977; Liberman *et al.*, 1977). By operating with concrete symbols for the sounds, it is easier to think of them as independent units. This conceptualisation is very likely essential in learning orthography as a speech mapping system.

6.3 *Pronunciation*

Another function of orthographic images, one not commonly recognised, is suggested by Kerek (1976) who shows that orthography can influence the pronunciation of words. Kerek proposes that when people learn how spoken words are spelled, and when spellings are not iconic with sounds (as is the case with many words in English), there is pressure to change pronunciations to enhance the iconic relationship between letter and sound (e.g. VICTUALS, previously pronounced VITTELS). Of course, the pressure works its effects slowly over time across groups of individuals due to the resistance offered by oral traditions with words. Kerek refers to this as the iconic principle of 'one graphic form – one phonetic form' (1976, p. 326). Spellings may serve to block vowel reductions so that letters mapping unstressed 'schwa' sounds become pronounced (i.e. registr*a*r, ment*o*r, th*o*rough, process*e*s, bas*e*s, juven*i*le, genu*i*ne). Words which are less common in speech than in print are particularly susceptible to change. For example, *h* is not pronounced in commonly spoken words such as HOUR and HONEST but is pronounced in words such as HUMBLE and HOMAGE. Geographical names are pronounced more like spellings by outsiders than by natives, as in Oreg*o*n pronounced with unstressed 'schwa' by local folk.

Pressure to change pronunciations may arise when new orthographic images are being formed for words whose spoken forms are less familiar and whose spellings suggest an additional or alternative phoneme. Some evidence for the iconic tendency was detected above in the spelling studies where children were observed to distort pronunciations so as to create relevant sounds for letters in words they were learning to read. Because letters are concrete units with distinct identities in contrast to sounds, they may very well dominate once they become established as symbols.

It is possible that the process of forming orthographic images is instructive for beginning readers who speak a non-standard dialect of English in which phonemes in words are deleted. As letter symbols for sounds are established in lexical memory, these speakers may learn to include the missing sounds in their word pronunciations. Such changes in speech would be expected if learning to read entails a process of amalgamating letters to phonological segments. Some evidence for this possibility is available. Desberg *et al.* (Chapter 4) examined the relationship among reading, spelling, and math achievement scores and dialect radicalism in a group of Black elementary school children. Those who had better command of standard English forms were better readers and spellers than children who did not. In contrast, achievement in math was not related to dialect. This suggests that dialect speakers may very well acquire knowledge of standard English word pronunciations primarily by learning to read and to spell words.

7 Development of orthographic images

Although the evidence is convincing that children acquire orthographic images of words as they learn to read, it is not so clear how this capability develops. According to amalgamation theory, not one but several sub-skills are involved and need to be acquired. The high correlations observed between various basic reading skills and scores on the spelling-aided sound learning task (Ehri and Wilce, 1979) indicate this. Some of the relevant sub-skills confirmed by others as being important predictors or correlates of beginning reading are: familiarity with alphabet letters and knowledge of their names (Bond and Dykstra,

1967; Richek, 1977; Speer and Lamb, 1976); knowledge of the system for deriving sounds from letter sequences (Guthrie and Siefert, 1977) Mason, 1976; Speer and Lamb, 1976; Venezky and Johnson, 1973); phonemic segmentation (Fox and Routh, 1975, 1976; Liberman, 1973; Liberman and Shankweiler, 1977; Liberman et al., 1977).

One type of experience which may contribute to the acquisition of orthographic image-forming skill is practice at inventing spellings. Such experience might promote the acquisition of children's knowledge of orthography as a speech-mapping system. This is suggested by Chomsky (1971, 1977) and Read (1971, 1973) who studied the spellings of pre-schoolers lacking much experience with the orthographic conventions of English. These children were observed to adopt a system for generating their spellings. The letters used to represent sounds were quite consistent and predictable though phonetic distinctions governing their choices were not always those used by an adult. In selecting letters, not acoustic segments but rather articulatory features were monitored. That is, the child paid attention to what his mouth was doing during word pronunciations and he abstracted from dimensions of this sort in choosing his letters. The letters chosen were ones whose names shared some feature with the sound detected in the word [e.g. *bot*, *grl*, *yl* (WHILE), *hran* (TRAIN)]. As the inventor became more familiar with standard spellings, his choices of letters to map sounds became more conventional, and morphemic patterns rather than single letter-sound mappings were adopted (i.e. past tense sound /t/ spelled first as WALKT shifted to the letter *d* and became WALKD, Read, 1971).

Such inventive spelling experiences might very well help beginning readers acquire some of the component capabilities needed to begin storing orthographic images of words, i.e. capabilities such as memory for letter shape, knowledge of letters as symbols for sounds, segmentation of words into phonemes. One possible advantage of introducing readers to the regularities of orthographic speech mapping by having them invent spellings is that they may acquire knowledge of a very flexible system which can be used to generate and justify many alternative word spelling patterns (Ehri, 1978). This may prove particularly valuable in learning to read English, a language which requires the beginner to store and remember conventional spellings which are systematic but highly variant in mapping speech (Venezky, 1970).

Spelling experiences may also enable learners to form more accurate or complete orthographic images, over and above that achieved by learning to read words accurately. Blumberg and Block (1975) found that third through sixth graders who were taught to spell words by writing them before viewing them learned the complete forms faster than children who saw and then wrote the words. Blumberg and Block speculate that the former method was more effective because it induced learners to analyse word spellings more thoroughly, particularly the parts which deviated from phonetic expectations. In another study with fifth–sixth graders, Thompson and Block (1975) found that practice in distinguishing the correct spellings of difficult words was less effective than practice in writing the words.

8 Summary

This chapter has reviewed and discussed several studies yielding evidence for the operation of orthographic images as they underlie printed word learning and create a close relationship between reading and spelling skills. Findings indicate that orthographic images can be scanned like real words seen in print, that they include all of the letters in a word's spelling, not just boundary letters or letters mapping into sounds, that silent letters may have a special status in these images. Findings suggest that the presence of orthographic images in memory increases the likelihood that the spellings produced by readers resemble single conventional forms rather than phonetic variants. In the acquisition of orthographic images, sound may provide an essential base such that learners are led to create phonological segments for unpronounced letters and unstressed vowels in order that the letters symbolising these sounds may be implanted and retained in the image. Besides their central role in reading and spelling, orthographic images were shown to have important cognitive functions facilitating verbal memory and affecting the pronunciation of words. The ability to form orthographic images as symbols for sounds was found to emerge during the first two years of reading instruction and was among the capabilities distinguishing beginning readers who had acquired large repertoires of printed words from those who had not. Though promising and provocative, the claims and findings arising from word identity amalgamation theory as well as their implications for reading and spelling instruction are preliminary and in need of further investigation. It is our hope that this chapter might provoke others to join in this investigation.

Acknowledgements

Research reported in this chapter was supported by funds from the National Institute of Education, Grant No. NIE-G-77-0009. Appreciation is extended to Lee S. Wilce who conducted the experiments.

15

The Development of Strategies in Spelling

GEORGE MARSH, MORTON FRIEDMAN, VERONICA
WELCH and PETER DESBERG   *California State University,*
Dominguez Hills and University of California, Los Angeles, U.S.A.

The purpose of this chapter is to present a developmental theory of strategies used during the acquisition of spelling along with some preliminary evidence for the theory. The theory and research presented here is an outgrowth of previous work on a developmental theory of the strategies used in reading (Marsh *et al.*, in press). The basic assumption of this approach is that there is a qualitative difference between the strategies used by young children who are just beginning to learn to read and spell and older children and adults who are proficient readers and spellers This assumption can be contrasted with the view that beginners use the same strategies as older children and adults (cf. Smith, 1971).

The differing theoretical assumptions have pedadogical implications. Since there is evidence that adults can go directly from a word's visual appearance to its meaning, some educators assume children should learn to associate a word's visual appearance directly with its meaning in reading and spelling (cf. Horn, 1969). On the other hand, a developmental approach assumes that children's strategies will change as a function of their knowledge and experience. According to this view, acquiring proficiency involves more than a quantitive improvement in accuracy, speed or 'automaticity'. It is assumed that there are major qualitative strategy shifts. In our previous work on reading we found evidence that one such strategy shift occurs early in learning to read. There is a second shift in strategies by the fifth grade. The strategies are assumed to develop as a function of the task demands which are basically determined by the structure of printed language but also partly by how that structure is presented by teachers and other adults. The sequence of strategies of reading and spelling is therefore not necessarily seen as universal and invariant, although there may be an invariant sequence of basic cognitive processing strategies as proposed by Piaget and others.

The notion of strategy has been used in different ways by different authors. What we mean by it here is active change in processing modes to accommodate task demands. This is in contrast to the emphasis on fixed structural properties in traditional information processing theories. There is considerable evidence that processing strategies based on task demands determine the outcome of information processing experiments in reading. Marsh (1978) has developed this notion in more detail.

In order to operationalise the definition of a strategy as a processing mode dependent on task structure it is necessary to do a task analysis. A task analysis of reading and spelling must involve, as a preliminary step, the description of the structure of English orthography. Fortunately,

Venezky (1970) has provided an excellent description of English spelling-to-sound system, and Hanna *et al.* (1966) have provided a description of the sound-to-spelling system. In addition, Chomsky and Halle (1968) have suggested an alternative description of the English phonotactic system which they claim is relevant to the English ortho-graphic system. However, these are *formal* linguistic descriptions, and it is important to show to what extent children and adults actually know and use these rules in reading and spelling.

Both naturalistic observational studies and experimental approaches have been used to analyse the strategies used in reading and spelling.

Biemiller (1970), Cohen (1974–75), Weber (1970) and others have used naturally occurring reading errors to infer the underlying stra-tegies in reading. Similarly, Spache (1940a) has used naturally-occurring spelling errors to infer spelling strategies. An important limitation on naturalistic observation, aside from time and energy constraints, is that it does not tell us what strategies children are using when they read or spell correctly. A particularly useful example of naturalistic observation in spelling is the work of Read (1971) on the 'invented spelling' of pre-school children who did not know how to read. This provides some interesting evidence on the natural development of spelling strategies and will be discussed later.

One widely used experimental technique, following Berko's (1958) classic study on children's knowledge of morphophonemic rules, is to use pseudoword patterns which are constructed to tap linguistic knowledge. These pseudowords have been widely used in research on both adult and child knowledge of orthographic structure in reading (Baron, 1977; Marsh *et al.*, in press; Smith and Baker, 1976; Venezky, 1974). In order to assess different strategies, it is desirable to design the pseudowords so that alternative responses are indicative of the use of a particular strategy. That is the approach employed in the present study.

The research reported here is congruent with our previous research on strategies in reading. In order to explore the relationship between strategies in reading and spelling, we will review it briefly.

1 Substitution strategies in reading and their relation to spelling

The initial strategy used when the child learning to read encounters an unknown word in context is to substitute a known word which fits the semantic and syntactic context of the sentence in which it is embedded (Weber, 1970). The substituted word may have no orthographic relationship to the printed word. This 'linguistic guessing' strategy will be of little use to the child who is required to spell a word which is in his oral vocabulary but not in his printed vocabulary. Semantic and syntactic context will however serve to disambiguate the spelling of homophones. In both reading and spelling homophones, such as SAIL–SALE, a word's visual appearance must be connected to its meaning. However, in both cases the orthographic representation is also related to the word's sound. If the speller connected the visual appearance of the word only with its meaning and not with its sound confusions such as THERE for THEIR would be rare or absent, but in fact, confusions are a common source of spelling errors (Gates, 1937).

The second substitution strategy which develops in learning to read is the use of semantic and syntactic context along with partial graphemic cues as the basis of substitution of a known word for an unknown word (Biemiller, 1970). The child often appears to rely on such cues as first letter or first and last letter to determine the substitution. Such a strategy will often lead to a correct response in reading if there is minimal orthographic overlap between the words in the print vocabulary. However, this strategy will lead to errors in spelling since the word's complete orthographic structure must be represented, when it is spelled but not when it is read. One source of evidence for this strategy is the serial position effect in spelling errors (Kooi *et al.* 1965; Wing and Baddeley, Chapter 12): letters in middle positions are less likely to be correct.

Therefore, the substitution strategies which are initially used in learning to read may be counterproductive in learning to spell. The child's reliance on semantic and syntactic context will often be successful in reading but may interfere with processing the word's orthographic representation.

2 Decoding strategies in reading and their relation to spelling

By the end of the first year of reading instruction many children have switched from substitution strategies to decoding strategies involving use of the relationship between the orthography and sound system. This switch apparently occurs naturally but is accelerated by instructional approaches which emphasise the spelling to sound relationships (Cohen, 1974–5; Barr, 1974–5). Initially, children use a sequential decoding strategy in reading in which the spelling-to-sound correspondences are treated as invariant and are processed from left to right in serial order. This strategy is successful with simple consonant-vowel-consonant (CVC) patterns and most children are able to decode novel patterns of this type by the second grade (Venezky, 1974; Marsh *et al.*, in press).

A sequential decoding strategy provides the child with useful information for spelling. In using this strategy the child must process the entire word, and could in this way build up a visual representation of the word in memory. More importantly, in using this strategy the child can use the relationship between spelling and sound to read and spell unknown words. It is expected that there might be considerable transfer between reading and spelling because of the possibility of what Baron *et al.* (Chapter 8) term associative symmetry. To the extent that spelling-to-sound correspondences are reversible the decoding strategy will be useful in spelling as well as reading. However it must be noted that spelling-to-sound correspondences are sometimes not reversible (Gould, 1976). Sound-to-spelling correspondences are also generally less predictable than the spelling-to-sound correspondences in reading. For example the rules for pronouncing the letter *k* are quite predictable (i.e. $k \rightarrow /\mathrm{K}/$ except before *n* where it is silent). On the other hand, the spelling of the phoneme $/\mathrm{K}/$ is variable and depends on the following vowel. In addition there is no simple way to predict whether or not a word begins with a silent letter *k*. The correct spelling of words with an initial silent *k* before *n* must depend primarily on visual memory.

The second decoding strategy to evolve in reading is the use of a hierarchical decoding strategy which is based on conditional rules. This strategy is necessary in order to successfully decode CVCe word patterns involving silent terminal *e* as marker for long vowel (e.g. MAT–MATE) or conditional pronunciation of letter *c* (i.e. $c \rightarrow /\mathrm{S}/$ before *i*, *e* and *y* and $c \rightarrow /\mathrm{K}/$ before *a*, *o* and *u* – CITE *vs* CUTE). This strategy develops more slowly and apparently depends on the number of exemplars in the print vocabulary. Performance on the CVCe pattern is quite high by the fifth grade but the conditional *c*-rule is not mastered completely even in a college population (Venezky, 1974; Marsh *et al.*, in press). Similar hierarchical strategies are required in spelling. For example, in spelling words with a long (free)vowel the child must use an orthographic maker to distinguish the vowel from its short (checked) alternative. There are parallel conditional rules in spelling to those described above in reading. For example, the spelling of the sound $/\mathrm{K}/$ depends on the following vowel (i.e. $/\mathrm{K}/ \rightarrow c$ before *a*, *o* and *u* and $/\mathrm{K}/ \rightarrow k$ before *i*, *e* and *y* as in CUT *vs* KIT).

3 Analogy strategies in reading

In previous studies we have found that by the fifth grade, that is, age 10, children begin to use an *analogy* strategy in reading unfamiliar words. Instead of decoding words they search for an analogue word and pronounce the unfamiliar word by analogy to the known word. This strategy can be assessed by presenting words which would be pronounced one way by a decoding strategy and another way by analogy to an irregularly spelled real word.

In an initial study by Marsh *et al.* (1977) it was found that fifth grade children used the analogy strategy as often as adults in a judgment task but not as often as adults in a production task. This suggests that even when the analogy strategy is available, it is not necessarily used. Production deficiencies are typical in the acquisition of many cognitive processing strategies. Bryant and Bradley (Chapter 16) also found this to be the case in relation to decoding strategies.

In the second study by Marsh *et al.* (in press), second grade children (age 7) were below both fifth grade children (age 10) and adults in their use of the analogy strategy. Since second grade children are capable of analogical reasoning (Sternberg, 1977) the failure of young children to use an analogy strategy may be due to the fact that they do not as yet have a sufficient store of visual word forms in memory to use the strategy productively.

Given the nature of the English orthographic system it is inevitable that phonemic decoding strategies in reading will become less than optimal as the printed vocabulary increases. Decoding strategies will not work efficiently with most polysyllabic words since the spelling of many such words is lexically based rather than phonemically based (Chomsky, 1970). There is considerable evidence that adults use analogy strategies in reading (cf. Baron, 1977a, b; Marsh *et al.*, in press).

4 Evidence for the use of phonemic strategies in spelling

The strongest evidence for the natural use of phonemic strategies in young children's spelling is the naturalistic observation of the spontaneous spelling of children who do not know how to read. A comprehensive study by Read (1971), involving twenty pre-school children, reveals a fascinating developmental sequence. The pre-school speller generally represents phonetic detail which is abstracted in conventional spelling because it is predictable. For example in English the stop phoneme /t/ is affricated before the phoneme /r/. The pre-school speller thus might spell TRUCK as CHRUK which is closer to the actual initial sound than the stop phoneme /t/ in TUCK. Similarly, since pre-consonantal nasals only have the phonetic effect of nasalising the preceding vowels they are typically omitted (e.g. DON'T is spelled DOT) and phonetic contrasts that are collapsed in speech such as intervocalic /d/ in LADDER and /t/ in LATTER are also collapsed in spelling.

In addition, the pre-school spellers invented systematic ways of representing short vowels. They use the letter name of the vowel closest to the needed vowel in place of articulation (e.g. FISH is spelled FES; FALL is spelled FELL). This system sometimes leads to overgeneralisation errors in spelling. For example a child might initially spell CAME correctly but later overgeneralise the corresponding short vowel form to produce CEME. These and the many other examples described by Read indicate that the pre-school child is very sophisticated in analysing a word's phonetic structure and in inventing clever and plausible ways of representing that structure orthographically. In fact they appear to be better at this than adults who have not been trained in phonetics. The pre-school orthographer's spellings change systematically as they gain in orthographic knowledge. The sophisticated performance of the children in these studies is somewhat paradoxical when we consider the often documented difficulty that children have in segmenting linguistic units when learning to read (e.g. Gleitman and Rozin, 1977). However, Read used a highly selected sample of pre-readers and their performance is therefore not typical of the general population of pre-school children. Phonemic spellings continue to be a major source of spelling errors even after children enter school (Gates, 1937; Masters, 1927).

Smith (1973a) has suggested that the alphabetic principle may be of much greater use to the speller than to the reader and also suggests that children may be initially using opposed strategies in spelling and reading. Evidence supporting this hypothesis comes from the difficulty which the pre-school spellers in Read's study usually had in reading their own writing.

The beginning reader uses substitution strategies which rely heavily on meaning. Reliance on these strategies may be reponsible for the initial discrepancy between reading and spelling. However by the second grade many children are using a phonemic decoding strategy in reading and so the discrepancy between strategies in reading and spelling may disappear. Frith (Chapter 22) however has reported on a sub-group of older children who use a phonemic strategy in spelling but show a great reliance on visual factors in reading. These children also have difficulty reading their own writing.

Marsh et al. (1979) have investigated the relative importance of phonemic regularity and visual familiarity in the reading and spelling performance of normal readers in the second and fourth grades, and fourth grade children who are reading at the second grade level. One major outcome of the study is that regularity of spelling-sound correspondences was more important than visual familiarity in both the reading and spelling of normal readers at both grade levels. The normal children could read and spell regularly spelled non-words which conformed to English orthographic structure as well as real regularly spelled words. Both groups were able to read and spell regular non-words better than irregularly spelled real words. Fourth grade children, reading at second grade level, read and spell irregular real words better than regularly spelled non-words. This suggests that orthographic regularity is a more important factor than visual familiarity for normal readers but the opposite may be the case for reading disabled children. Barron (Chapter 9) has obtained similar results using a lexical decision task.

5 The evidence for analogy strategies in spelling

Read (1971) reported one exception to the use of phonemic spellings in pre-school children's invented spellings. Pre-school children use a lexical rather than phonemic spelling for the plural morpheme (e.g. DOGS and CATS rather than DOGZ and CATS). However these children initially use phonemic spellings rather than lexical spellings for other morphemes such as past tense (e.g. WALKT and HOPT rather than WALKD and HOPD). The reasons for this discrepancy is not clear but it may represent early awareness of the morphophonemic basis of English spelling. It is inevitable, given the nature of the English orthographic system, that a phonemic strategy is less than optimal. Phonemic strategies will produce errors in spelling polysyllabic words which have reduced syllables (e.g. MARKET) which are lexically based (e.g. CRITICISE) or have unpredictable silent letters (e.g. KNOWLEDGE) and geminate consonants (e.g. RECESS). Simon and Simon (1973) found that by the fourth grade, children could out-perform a computer which was programmed to spell phonemically using the sequential and hierarchical rules of Hanna *et al.* (1966).

Carol Chomsky (1970) has pointed out the advantages of knowing a related word in disambiguating lexically based spellings (e.g. CRITICAL–CRITICISE; MUSCULAR–MUSCLE, etc.). Other evidence supports the hypothesis that adults rely heavily on visual or rote memory in spelling. Brown (1970) for example found that visual familiarity was more important than phonemic regularity in adult spelling. Many contributors to this volume emphasise the importance of visual factors in the spelling performance of adults. All this evidence suggests that in spelling as in reading the more experienced subject may switch from a phonemic encoding strategy in spelling unfamiliar words to a strategy based on analogy with known words in visual memory.

6 The study

6.1 *Method*

As in the previous study on reading pseudowords were used to assess the strategies used in spelling. Table 1 lists the pseudowords used in this study.

TABLE 1   Pseudowords used to assess spelling strategies

Sequential Decoding
    1. Short vowels (CVC)   FIS, JAT, CAZ
Hierarchical Decoding
    2. Long vowel (CVCe)   FISE, JATE, CAZE
                                            (alternative spellings: FYSE, JAIT, CAYZ)
    3. C-rule /K/ → *c* before *a, o* and *u* CAZICAL, CAZICISE
                                            CUSCLE, CUSCULAR
Analogy
    4. Word-pairs   CAZICAL–CAZICISE (CRITICAL–CRITICISE)
                                          CUSCLE–CUSCULAR (MUSCLE–MUSCULAR)
    5. Individual words   JATION (NATION)
                                          ZOLDIER (SOLDIER)
                                          WENGTH (LENGTH)

The spelling of simple consonant-vowel-consonant (CVC) pattern with a short vowel can be accomplished by a sequential phonemic encoding strategy. These patterns are the first to be successsfully decoded in reading and show no significant developmental change in reading from second grade through college.

The second pattern studied was the spelling of CVCe patterns with a long vowel. These patterns require the use of a hierarchical encoding strategy involving an orthographic marker to designate the vowel as free. A common orthographic marker is the final silent *e* but other spellings are legitimate (see exemplars in Table 2). Performances on the long vowel pattern in reading shows a significant developmental trend from second grade through college.

The third pattern studied was the conditional C-rule (i.e. the sound /K/ is spelled *c* before vowels *a, o* and *u*). This rule was studied in two environments – /K/ before *a* and /K/ before *u*. In both environments there are some exceptions. In the case of /K/ before /a/, Webster's college dictionary lists approximately 50 exceptions, most being low frequency words of foreign origin, (e.g. KAYAK, KANGAROO, KARATE). In addition some proper names used the variant spelling (e.g. KATE,

KAY, KATHY etc.). In the case of /K/ before *u* there are only about ten exceptions and these are words of very low frequency (e.g. KUMQUAT, KUDOS, etc.).

The development of the conditional *c* rule in reading shows a strong bias to pronounce the letter *c* as /K/ because this is the most frequent spelling. There is no significant developmental trend in this bias. There is a significant developmental increase in the pronunciation of the letter *c* as /S/ before letters *i*, *e* and *y* since exemplars on this pattern are much less frequent (Venezky, 1974; Marsh *et al.*, in press).

The fourth type of patterns were analogues to real word pairs which exemplify some of the lexical spellings discussed by Chomsky (1970), (see exemplars in Table 1). Knowledge of the relationship between lexically related words in reading shows a significant developmental trend between second grade and college. The last word types were analogies to irregularly spelled words which have no lexically related words to disambiguate the spellings (see exemplars in Table 1).

The subjects were twenty second grade children (7 yr) and thirty fifth grade children (10 yr) from the UCLA University Elementary School (UES). All subjects were reading and spelling at grade level or above. The adult subjects were thirty college students from UCLA who participated in the study to fulfil a course requirement.

The subjects were run individually and were asked to spell the pseudowords to dictation. They were given the words in random order and were asked to repeat the words as a check for misperception of the designated pronunciation. If the subject mispronounced the word it was repeated until it was pronounced correctly. The subjects were told they could use more than one spelling but to write down the best spelling first. They were asked to use print for legibility.

6.2 *Results*

TABLE 2   Mean percentage of response types

Grade	Sequential (%) Short vowel (CVC)	Hierarchical (%) Long vowel	C-rule (CVCe)	Analogy (%) Pairs	Individual
Second	68	60	66	03	0
Fifth	96	92	81	10	33
College	96	92	71	24	50

The major results are shown in Table 2 which lists the percentage of responses which correspond to the various strategies at different age-grade levels. There was a significant age–grade effect which indicates an overall developmental increase in the use of the various strategies ($F = 27.65$, df $= 2/77$, p <0.001). There was also a significant effect of word type which indicates an overall difference in the use of various strategies at a given age–grade level ($F = 149.35$, df $= 4/308$, p <0.001). The overall interaction between groups and word types was also significant ($F = 3.95$, df $= 8/308$, p <0.001). *Post hoc* comparisons were done by Newman-Keuls tests.

6.2.1 *Comparsion between grade levels.* There was a significant increase from second to fifth grade students in the number of correct spellings of simple CVC patterns which require only a sequential encoding strategy (p <0.01), but no further increase to college students.

The same pattern of results was found developmentally in the case of long vowel CVCe word patterns which require *hierarchical encoding*. In the case of the C-rule the 10-year-olds were significantly superior to both the 7-year-olds and the college students (p <0.01), who did not differ significantly from each other.

The use of the same spelling for the derivationally releated phonemes requiring an *analogy strategy* showed a monotonic developmental increase from the second grade, where it was practically non-existent, to the fifth grade where such spellings occur only 10% of the time, to college, where approximately one-fourth of the spellings are of this type. Each grade level differs significantly from the other in the use of this spelling strategy (p <0.01).

A similar monotonic trend was shown in the use of analogy strategy to spell pseudowords which have analogies to real irregularly spelled words. No second grade child gave such a response while one-third of the fifth grade responses and one-half of the college students' responses were indicative of the use of the analogy strategy.

6.2.2 *Comparisons within grade levels.* The second grade subjects' performance both on the simple CVC patterns and on the C-rule was significantly superior to their performance on the long vowel CVCe pattern (p <0.01). Either type of analogy response at this grade level was essentially nonexistent.

The fifth grade subjects and college students did not differ significantly on performance on the simple CVC spelling patterns and the more complex CVCe patterns. Their performance on the C-rule was significantly inferior to their performance on the CVC and CVCe patterns. Their performance on the analogy words was inferior to their performance on the sequential and hierarchical encoding patterns. They gave more analogy responses to the irregularly spelled words than to the systematic alterations.

The overall pattern of responding of the college students was very similar to that of the fifth graders.

6.3 *Discussion*

6.3.1 *Substitution strategy*. Even though the substitution strategy is initially dominant in reading, it was almost non-existent in the present study. Only a few responses of the second grade children were substitutions of the spelling of a known real word for one of the pseudowords. Even the youngest subjects seem to realise that a substitution strategy was not appropriate in a spelling task with no context.

6.3.2 *Sequential encoding strategy*. On the simple CVC patterns requiring a sequential encoding strategy, performance was relatively high at all grade levels. However the performance of 7-year-old subjects was significantly inferior to 10-year-olds who had reached a ceiling. This developmental shift is not found in reading where the second grade subjects do not differ significantly from fifth grade and college students in their decoding of sequential CVC word patterns.

6.3.3 *Hierarchical encoding strategy*. The long vowel requires a specific representation in a word's spelling to differentiate it from the short vowel. The most frequent spelling of the long vowel is a CVC pattern in English is the silent terminal *e*. This was by far the most frequently used orthographic marker by subjects in this study. Interestingly, in the fifth grade, spelling of these patterns has reached a ceiling whereas performance on reading the patterns has not.

In the case of the C-rule the fifth graders were superior to both second-grade and college students. The increase in performance from the second to the fifth grade is probably due to increase in the knowledge of the conditional C-rule. The decline in performance between fifth grade and college students could have been due to the increased knowledge of low frequency exceptions to this rule by the college students (e.g. KAYAK, KUDOS etc.). This explanation is *post hoc* and assumes a probabilistic use of the rule based on number of exemplars in the vocabulary. A similar *post hoc* explanation was proposed by Venezky (1974) to explain why there is no developmental increase in performance in the C-rule in reading in one instance but there is an increase in another instance. Exemplars of the reading rule that C is pronounced /K/ before *a, o* and *u* are much more frequent than exemplars of the rule $C \rightarrow /S/$

before *i*, *e* and *y* and there is no developmental increase in the first case and a sharp increase in the second case.

6.3.4 *Analogy strategy*. The use of the analogy strategy to preserve the lexical spellings of phonemes in related word pairs shows a marked developmental increase in this study as in the previous study on reading strategies. The relatively low frequency of these word pairs such as CRITICAL–CRITICISE probably accounts in part for the subjects' relatively low use of the analogy strategy with these related pairs. There are few if any high frequency word pairs which exemplify systematic spelling relationships. This reservation does not apply to the isolated irregularly spelled words since these were of relativity high frequency and were known to most of the second graders (i.e. SOLDIER, NATION, LENGTH), and yet none of them used the analogy spelling.

There appears to be a marked developmental shift in the use of analogy strategies in both reading (Marsh *et al.*, 1977) and spelling between the second and fifth grade. The analogy strategy is available by the fifth grade at least, although its use depends on a number of performance factors including availability of analogue word and type of task (e.g. *production* vs *judgement*). This indicates that by age 10 the analogy strategy is a particularly powerful and useful strategy not only in *reading* unknown words but also in *spelling*.

In summary, the results of the present study indicate that children start out with a simple sequential phonemic encoding strategy in spelling; they later develop a hierarchical encoding strategy involving the use of rules conditional on the intra-word environment (e.g. the long vowel and possibly the C-rule); they finally develop a strategy of spelling unknown words by analogy to the spellings of already known words. Except for the substitution strategies, there is considerable congruence in the development of strategies in reading and in spelling. We must conclude therefore that there are qualitative differences between the strategies used by beginners and skilled readers and spellers.

7 Pedagogical implications

The child beginning to read can take advantage of his syntactic and semantic knowledge in reading words in context. The resulting 'top down' processing however may interfere with children's learning of the orthographic structure of words or the relationship between spelling and sound. With simple invariant and reversible spelling to sound correspondences the child has an algorithm for both decoding and encoding printed words. The evidence from our previous study on reading

(Marsh *et al.*, in press) and the present study on spelling, indicates that by the second grade most children are able to deal with regular orthographic patterns successfully. The use and understanding of the alphabetic principle will probably be of greater use to the beginning reader than the beginning speller because spelling-to-sound correspondences are in general more predictable than sound-to-spelling correspondences. Performance on reading tasks is generally better than performance on parallel spelling tasks (Marsh *et al.*, 1979).

A major question is to what extent the child is able to transfer knowledge gained through reading to spelling and vice versa. One instructional viewpoint is that spelling should be 'caught not taught'. However, a review of the literature suggests that beginning strategies in reading and spelling differ. In the study by Marsh *et al.* (1979) there was no transfer between reading and spelling even though the same words and non-words were presented in the same experimental sessions. Chomsky (1971) in her article entitled 'Write First, Read Later' asserts that prior experience in spelling will facilitate learning to read but there has been no controlled demonstration that this is in fact the case.

In both reading and spelling the child must learn conditional rules based on the intra-word environment. Again, the majority of the responses given by second grade children showed successful use of a hierarchical decoding strategy and performance on this strategy is high by the fifth grade. It may be that exposure to relevant exemplars is critical in learning of higher order conditional rules such as the C-rule in reading and spelling. It is known from research on reading that children's strategies are influenced strongly by instructional strategies (Cohen, 1974–5; Barr, 1974–5). Similar studies have not been done in spelling but it is probable that an instructional emphasis on spelling-to-sound correspondences in spelling will influence children's use of phonemic encoding strategies.

The computer simulation study by Hanna *et al.* (1966) indicated that use of a large number of sequential and hierarchical phonemic encoding rules led to approximately fifty percent correct spellings. If one is an advocate of use of phonemic information in spelling this is a half-full glass; if one is an opponent, it is half empty. The Hanna *et al.* (1966) corpus consisted of over 17 000 words which means approximately 8500 word types could be spelled using approximately 300 rules. This would seem some economy over learning that many words as visual patterns.

However rule algorithms will have to be supplemented by additonal information in order to spell many words correctly. The Hanna *et al.* (1966) study used rules relating to surface phonology while Chomsky and Halle (1968) have argued that the English orthographic system is based on deep systematic phonetic structure which is lexically based. Thus a person using surface phonology might mis-spell criticise as critisize, but a knowledge of deep structure might allow him to relate criticise to the analogue word critical and thus spell it correctly. Simon and Simon (1973) argue that there are too few word pairs of this type to be useful and that such analogies will often lead to mis-spellings (e.g. REMEMBER–REMEMBERANCE; PROCEED–PROCEEDURE). It must also be noted that such word pairs are usually of very low frequency. In this study few of the children's responses preserved the spelling of the related phonemes in the non-words although 25% of the adults' spellings did. Thus teaching lexically based spellings in related word pairs may well have only limited usefulness.

However there does appear to be a major developmental shift in strategies between the second and fifth grades in both reading (Marsh et al., 1977) and spelling. This shift is towards a strategy of spelling an unknown word by analogy to a known word. In order to use this strategy productively the child must have a sufficient number of visual word forms in storage to use as analogues. It apparently takes a number of years of experience with reading and spelling to build up a sufficient visual store. Thus there is a further increase between fifth grade and college level. Spelling may be as important as reading in this regard since reading words in context can be accomplished with only partially processed orthographic information while spelling requires a complete orthographic representation.

Simon and Simon (1973) proposed a model for spelling as a serial process in which various alternative phonemic spellings are generated and the correct one selected by comparison with partial information in visual memory. The information in visual memory is derived from reading. However, our data suggest that spellers are able to go directly to visual information store because they will spell non-words by analogy to irregularly spelled real words for which there is no reasonable phonemic spelling (unless one wants to write a rule for each exception). Very proficient spellers appear to make heavy use of visual information. They also may be able to go directly from meaning to the motor output involved in writing as suggested by Smith (1973b) and Simon (1976). This latter strategy has received very little investigation.

Acknowledgements

The authors would like to thank Linnea Ehri and Richard Venezky for their helpful comments on this chapter.

16

Why Children sometimes Write Words which they do not Read

PETER E. BRYANT and LYNETTE BRADLEY   *Department of Experimental Psychology, University of Oxford, England*

One naturally thinks that a child learns to read and to write in much the same way. He learns these two skills at the same time, and from the start they are quite explicitly connected. He reads things which he has written and writes things for others to read.

But if he learns these skills in the same way one might expect him to be able to read and spell exactly the same words, and indeed to be unable to read and write exactly the same words. Yet this plainly is not true. It is not even true of adults, let alone of children. It is certainly widely acknowledged that children will often be quite unable to spell properly words which they read without hesitation (Boder, 1973) and this is obviously so with adults too. So reading and spelling cannot be completely the same thing.

However this evidence of some disconnection between learning to read and to spell can be dismissed as quite normal and rather trivial. One is producing a written word when one spells, whereas someone reading a word is merely taking it in. Production on the whole is harder than reception, especially when language is involved. There are many words and complex grammatical constructions which children have great difficulty in producing, but which they understand perfectly well, just as there are plenty of things which an adult learning a foreign language never actually speaks but always understands whenever he hears them. Yet few would suggest that learning to speak a language and learning to understand it are not intimately connected. The general suggestion is that production lags behind comprehension because production is the more difficult of the two. Another reason for spelling being the more difficult is that one can often think of two or more apparently equally valid ways of spelling a word and not know which to choose. This should hamper spelling but not reading. A child who hovers between writing FIGHT and FITE will know what the word FIGHT means when he reads it. So the fact that children sometimes cannot spell words which they do read does not on its own contradict the notion that children learn to read and to write in the same way.

But what if this sort of discrepancy between reading and spelling went both ways? Suppose that it was found that young children sometimes read words which they could not spell and also sometimes manage to spell words properly which they did not read. This surely would be strong evidence that children learn to read and to spell in different ways. No longer could one say that one skill generally precedes the other, or that one is easier than the other.

We shall be presenting some experimental evidence for this kind of discrepancy between reading and writing, and we shall argue on the basis of this evidence that when children first learn to read and to spell they do these two things remarkably independently of each other. However before presenting our evidence that children often use different cues for reading and spelling we need first to consider what sorts of cues are involved in learning these skills.

1 The cues involved in learning to read and to write

People concerned with the cues which a child must use when he learns to read and write have, broadly speaking, come up with two types of suggestion. One is that the child must be able to adopt a phonological approach: in other words, he must recognise that words and syllables can be broken down into phonetic units which correspond in various ways to individual alphabetic letters. The other suggestion is that he must be able to recognise the visual chunks or whole visual patterns which are made by written words or familiar sequences of letters.

One remarkable thing about these two very popular suggestions is that there seems to be a serious conflict between them. The first strategy involves breaking words into segments so that the written word is divided into letters and the spoken word into its phonetic structure. In contrast the second strategy eschews segments, and requires response to sequences of letters or to words as units. We obviously need to consider the two strategies in more detail.

2 The phonological strategy

Reading and spelling both involve working with the alphabetic script and the alphabetic script works by breaking words down into constituent sounds. So it seems to be almost a truism to suggest that a child must grasp the principle of how this is done if he is going to learn to read and write. It seems almost inconceivable that he will manage either skill if he does not understand, for example, that the word CAT can be broken down into the sounds *c-a-t* or that the sounds *c-a-t* add up to the word CAT.

There is, as one might expect, a great deal of evidence which does suggest that this sort of phonological awareness is essential for any one learning to read. Most of this comes from studies of backward readers, who are often very poor at dividing spoken words into their constituent sounds. One plausible way of explaining this is to suggest that they are behind in reading because they cannot appreciate smaller units than the syllable. They may fail to read because they lack an effective phonological code.

Both Savin (1972) and Liberman *et al.* (1977) have made this point.

Savin claimed that backward readers are typically bad at word games and peculiarly insensitive to rhyme: but his evidence is only anecdotal. Liberman and her colleagues offered more substantial data. Their study involved a direct attempt to get at children's ability to segment words phonetically in the form of a task in which children had to learn to tap out the numbers of phonemes in a series of words. Three taps would have been the right answer to the word CAT and two to the word IN. Although this is quite a difficult task for young children, it does seem to test the child's ability to segment sounds. Liberman and her colleagues found among a class of children that those of them who read well also learned this task with consistent ease. On the other hand it was a source of some difficulty to the children whose reading skills were relatively weak. A result like this suggests that some children are held back in reading and writing because they cannot segment words into their constituent phonemes and therefore simply cannot handle an alphabetic script which depends on this sort of segmentation.

There is however a problem about drawing conclusions from the kind of comparison which Savin (1972) and Liberman *et al.* (1977) made and it is worth noting that this is a problem which arises in very many other studies of backwardness in reading. The good and poor readers were the same age, were presumably of the same intellectual level and indeed probably seemed equal in all other respects than in their success in reading, at which of course the poor readers were much worse. The poor readers also, it seems, differed in their success in segmenting sounds.

Put like this it is easy to see that there is a problem here of distinguishing cause from effect. It may be that the difficulty with phonemes prevents the child from mastering the rationale of the alphabet and thus stops him from reading properly. But another possibility is that it is the child's experience with the alphabetic script which determines how well he manages to tap out the phonemes. So the reason for the backward readers' failure with the phoneme task may lie in the fact that they had much less successful experience with alphabetic script. In other words it may be the amount of successful experience with the alphabet which determined how well the children did on Liberman's phoneme task rather than the other way round. One can mount equally plausible arguments either way.

We (Bradley and Bryant, 1978) tried to get round this problem in an experiment in which we attempted to see how backward readers organise sounds. Our method was rather different. We simply gave children four monosyllabic words at a time (e.g. WEED, PEEL, NEED, DEED and SUN, SOCK, SEE, RAG) and asked them (after including appropriate memory controls) to tell us which contained the odd sound.

To solve this task the child must at some level understand that three of the four words have a segment in common which the fourth lacks. It is therefore another way of testing segmentation of sounds. In addition, we also gave the children ten words, one at a time, and asked them to produce a rhyming word to each one.

This was our task, but there was still the problem of ensuring that any difference between backward and normal readers was not merely the result of the difference in reading levels. We tried to solve this problem by comparing two groups with the same reading level. Both had a reading age of around $7\frac{1}{2}$ years, but one (the normal readers) was aged around 7 while the other (the backward reading group) was considerably older than this: they were around $10\frac{1}{2}$ years old. Both groups were normal in intelligence for their age and this meant that the backward readers who were older were also considerably more advanced intellectually. Thus any difference between the two groups could not be the result of a difference in reading levels, because there was no difference (Table 1c).

TABLE 1   Categorising sounds by normal and backward readers

a. Mean errors (out of 6) in the sound categorisation task

	Backward readers N 60		Normal readers N 30	
Odd word	Mean	SD	Mean	SD
Last letter different	1.15	1.43	0.17	1.11
Middle letter different	1.49	1.58	0.37	0.99
First letter different	2.62	2.26	0.67	1.188

b. Number of children producing failures to rhyme

	Total N	No. of failures										
		0	1	2	3	4	5	6	7	8	9	10
Backward readers	60	37	4	4	4	2	2	2	2	0	0	3
Normal readers	30	28	1	0	0	0	1	0	0	0	0	0

c. Reading and spelling ages and IQs of the children in these experiments

	N	Mean age	IQ (WISC) Mean	Reading age Mean	Spelling age Mean
Backward readers	60	10 yr 4 mth	108.7	7 yr 7 mth	6 yr 10 mth
Normal readers	30	6 yr 10 mth	107.9	7 yr 6 mth	7 yr 2 mth

The experiment produced a clear difference between the two groups. The backward readers, despite their overall intellectual superiority, were actually far worse at categorising sounds than were the younger normal children, as Table 1a shows. They could distinguish the different words and they could remember them, but they could not easily tell which words had some element in common and which did not. They also were far less likely to produce a rhyming word when we asked them to (Table 1b).

Our results show very clearly that many backward readers have a difficulty categorising words on the basis of their having common sounds. It could be that this difficulty would apply however small or large the unit of sound which had to be categorised. But another possibility is that the peculiar difficulty of our task for the backward readers arose from the fact that the words had to be categorised on the basis of segments which were smaller than the syllables. The backward readers might have been unable to break up those syllables into smaller units. If this were so there would be a natural explanation for their difficulty with the alphabetic script. They might be unable to arrive at the right segments.

This, in turn, suggests that the business of dividing sounds is an essential element in the way children normally learn to read and write, because it allows them to use the alphabet effectively.

3 The visual strategy

Yet it is quite difficult to reconcile this apparently plausible hypothesis with other work which appears to show that young children are often heavily dependent on recognising visual patterns while reading. The nub of these studies is that children seem to respond to visual wholes or chunks without dividing them into segments.

It makes good sense to read visual chunks rather than letter by letter. Whatever one says about the rules governing the English orthography, it is, at the level of the individual letter, highly variable since particular letters often signify different sounds in different words. But, as Eleanor Gibson has often pointed out, this variability is likely to get smaller the larger the chunk of letters which the child takes in. The letter *i* for example produces a bewildering variety of sounds in different words. Not so the sequence of letters *ight* or *ing*: these are relatively stable. So it might help a child to recognise such sequences as wholes, and even whole words as wholes, rather than having to build them up letter by letter or phoneme by phoneme.

Eleanor Gibson (1965) herself has provided some evidence that children begin to chunk in this way very soon after they begin to learn to read, but there are problems in her work of distinguishing success in reading from success in remembering, and this makes her argument somewhat tentative. But there is much stronger evidence that children who are at the very beginning stages of learning to read adopt a visual strategy which takes them straight on to the meaning of the word without any phonological intervention. This comes from the work of Barron and Baron (1977).

They worked with children whose ages ranged from $6\frac{1}{2}$ years (grade one in a Canadian school) to $13\frac{1}{2}$ years, and they gave them two tasks. In one (the sound task) the children were given a list of written words and each word was paired with a picture. Some but not all of the pictures were of objects whose names rhymed with the word with which they were paired (e.g. a pair consisting of the word HORN and a picture of corn), and the child had to mark the rhyming pairs. Obviously this is a task which involves attending to the sound patterns of the words being read.

In the other task (the meaning task) they were again given word-picture pairs, but this time they had to mark the pairs in which the word and picture meant the same thing. In fact, in order to 'mean the same', the word and the picture had to be in the same category (SHIRT–trousers) rather than to mean identical things (SHIRT–shirt). This definition of 'meaning' is an inexplicably odd part of an otherwise informative experiment.

The children were also given various kinds of interference during these tasks and the most important, for our purposes, was one which must effectively have blocked out all other phonological and articulatory activity. The children were required to say the word 'double, double, double' out aloud very quickly, and the experiment was arranged so that they did each task sometimes with this interference and sometimes without. The reason for this is simple. If the task involves some kind of a phonological strategy then the child's performance in it will be hindered by having to say 'double double'. But if the task is done purely visually this interference should have little or no effect.

As one might expect the interference did spoil the children's performance in the sound task. It did not, however, disrupt the meaning task. Even the youngest children could indicate whether the picture-word pairs had the same 'meaning' during the 'double, double' interference and when there was no interference.

This implies rather strongly that children right from the start can read some words without having to build them up from their constituent phonological elements and without, it seems, translating them into sounds at all. If Barron and Baron's result held up with a more precise meaning task, and there is no pressing reason why it should not, we could assume that children often read words on the basis of their visual patterns without heeding their phonological segments.

This is then our puzzle. On the one hand segmenting sounds, with all its obvious advantages for learning to use the alphabet and to construct words with letters on the basis of the words' constituent sounds, seems to play an important part in learning to read and write. On the other hand children often seem to read words as visual wholes. Each strategy seems to be the very antithesis of the other and yet there are good reasons for believing that both exist. Do we have to say that they simply co-exist or is there a more precise solution to this puzzle?

4 Reading and spelling

We think that there is a solution. It rests on a distinction between reading and spelling. Our idea is very simple. It is that children start learning to read and spell in rather different ways. We are suggesting that initially their reading depends very heavily on visual chunks but that they spell primarily by using phonological segments. If we are right the alphabetic principle does indeed play a part in the beginning stages of reading and spelling, but mainly in spelling.

Our hypothesis was initially prompted by a series of observations. When we looked at children spelling words, we noticed that they would often use a phonological strategy quite explicitly. If we asked them to write down the word BUN they would often say *b-u-n* out aloud while they wrote. Our confidence in the relevance of these observations was bolstered by the already considerable evidence that children take easily to a phonological strategy when they begin to spell (Read, 1971; Chomsky, 1970).

Reading, on the other hand, did not always seem like this. We encountered a great deal of informal evidence that Barron and Baron's thesis might be right. One boy for example to whom we showed the word PASTEURISED hesitated and then said WELL, YOU BOIL IT. Another informal observation centred around the observation that six-year-old children often read the word SOMETHING despite the fact that it is a long and rather complex word. We showed several children who could read it the words SOME and THING separately, and found that many could not read one of these two words and some could not read either. Here was a blatant example of a word being read as an unsegmented whole.

The simplest way to test our hypothesis that children initially learn to read and to spell in rather different ways is to give them the same list of words to read on one occasion and to spell on another. If our hypothesis is wrong there should be little discrepancy between the words they read and the words they write. But, if our hypothesis is right we should expect the children to read words which they cannot spell and, perhaps, to spell words which they do not manage to read. A two-way discrepancy of this sort would be powerful evidence for a disconnection between reading and spelling.

5 The experiments

It is quite surprising that there have been very few direct comparisons between children's reading and spelling. Standardised graded word reading and spelling tests typically employ quite different words, which makes it impossible to use these tests to compare the two skills.

It is quite interesting to see what words do occur in the two kinds of test. CUT, MAT, RUN, IN are typical words which five-year-olds spell in the Schonell spelling test and it is easy to see that these are highly regular in that they can all be constructed quite easily on a letter by letter basis. In this sense, the first words on the Schonell reading test are not often regular: LITTLE and SCHOOL are examples. One way of explaining this difference is to assume that it merely shows that reading is easier than spelling, and so that the reading test must contain harder words than the spelling test. But our hypothesis could also account for the difference since it would not matter that the very familiar words in the reading test are irregular if they are recognised as chunks. The spelling words, on the other hand, would have to be regular if children initially spell on a letter by letter basis.

The best way to sort out these two alternatives is to give children the same words to read and to spell in order to see whether they merely read more words than they spell or whether they actually read and spell different words. Boder (1973) is the only person to have made this sort of direct comparison systematically, but her main reason for doing this was to diagnose different types of 'dyslexia'.

For our first attempt to compare reading and spelling (an experiment conceived by L.B.) we simply gave two groups of children 18 words to read on one occasion and to write on another. The words were: PIN, LEG, BAD, RUB, COT, FIT, HUNT, GRAB, FLAP, DENT, CROP, SLID, UPSET, SUNLIT, CONTENT, OLDEST, UPON, PRETEND. All of these, it should be noted, are regular, in the sense that they can be constructed quite easily on the basis of the sounds associated with the individual letters.

The two groups of children were virtually the same contingent which took part in the rhyming study described earlier. Again there was a backward reading group, aged around $10\frac{1}{2}$ years, and a normal reading group of about 7 years, both with the same reading age of around $7\frac{1}{2}$ years.

One way of looking at our results is to make a crude comparison between success in reading and in spelling. As Table 2 shows both groups seem to do better in reading. This means that many children managed to read words which they could not spell. This is not surprising, given previous evidence that children read better than they spell and given our own impression that we as adults also can read words we often cannot spell. However Table 2 also shows a more surprising result which is that not all the children were better at reading than at spelling. Many children in both groups actually spelled more words correctly than they read correctly.

TABLE 2   Success in reading and spelling (Experiment 1)

	N	Mean no. of words read correctly	Mean no. of words spelled correctly
Backward readers	62	10.8	10.0
Normal readers	30	12.7	12.0

	% children reading more words than they spelled	% children spelling more words than they read
Backward readers	50	29
Normal readers	50	23

This must mean that these children at least actually do spell some words which they do not manage to read. In fact, as Table 3 shows, the vast majority of children in both groups managed to spell at least one word without succeeding in reading it. Moreover, when we looked at overall success with the individual words, we found that six of them (BAD, FIT, SLID, UPSET, COT, SUNLIT) were, *in toto*, spelled properly more often than they were read. It is interesting to note that these particular words are probably easier from a phonological point of view, because most do not contain any consonants blended within a syllable; the two adjacent consonants in UPSET and SUNLIT belong to different syllables. SLID seems to be the exception. Conversely, all the words that most often failed to be spelled were those with consonant clusters (PRETEND, etc.).

Another way of looking at the results is to note how many words each individual both read and spelled properly (RS), how many he failed both to read and spell ($\bar{R}\bar{S}$), how many he read without being able to spell ($R\bar{S}$), and finally how many he spelled but did not manage to read ($\bar{R}S$). The first two categories tell us very little about the relationship between reading and spelling. Children may or may not be using the same cues to read and spell, when they read and spell the same word properly and when they fail either to read or spell it. One cannot tell. It is the third and fourth categories, the discrepant categories, which are more definite since they would be a sign of a disconnection between the two activities.

Table 3 divides the data in this way. Notice that on average discrepant words feature more strongly in the backward reading group, but that they do occur in both groups. We also looked at the discrepant categories developmentally, and found a difference. The reading without spelling category ($R\bar{S}$) occurred at every level. However, the number of words spelled correctly but not read ($\bar{R}S$) did vary with age. The higher the age and reading level in the normal group, and the higher the reading level in the backward reading group, the less likely the children were to spell words and not to read them. We concluded that the disconnection which we had discovered between reading and spelling might be a temporary phenomenon confined in most children to the early stages of their reading and writing.

TABLE 3 Mean number of words (out of 18) in the four possible categories (Experiment 1)

	N	RS Words read and spelled	$\bar{R}\bar{S}$ Words *neither* read *nor* spelled	$R\bar{S}$ Words read but *not* spelled	$\bar{R}S$ Words *not* read but spelled
Backward readers	62	7.7	4.9	3.1	2.3
Normal readers	30	10.6	3.9	2.1	1.4

We decided also to look at the children's spelling and reading mistakes. The best way seemed to look to see how close the children came to the right word's sounds when he spelled and when he read. We looked at each mis-spelled word to see whether its first letter, its last letter and any other intervening letter were correct. In the same way we looked at the connection between the sounds of the mis-read words. Were the opening sounds, the final sounds, or any of the intervening sounds the same as in the correct word? Our hypothesis was that the children are more ready to use a phonological code when they are spelling than when they read: so we predicted that even when they erred there would be signs of more effective phonological activities in spelling than in reading.

Table 4 shows that this was the case. The number of times that the mis-read words had no phonological connection with the correct word was relatively speaking quite large. Also a far greater proportion of the spelling errors had a phonological connection with the beginning, the end, and some of the intervening sounds of the correct word. This suggests that young children tend to use what they know about sounds to construct all the word. When they read their reliance on sounds is more limited.

TABLE 4   The connection between the correct answers and the mis-spelled and the mis-read words

	No connection	Same first sound	Same last sound	Same first and last sound	Same first and intervening sound	Same first, and intervening and last sound	Same intervening and last sound
Normal readers							
Mis-spelled words (%)	4.6	4.6	0	6.6	31.6	44.8	7.9
Mis-read words (%)	10.0	13.9	0.8	12.3	26.9	23.1	13.1
Backward readers							
Mis-spelled words (%)	3.4	2.9	0.7	12.7	23.6	46.6	10.1
Mis-read words (%)	13.6	11.5	0.6	10.6	29.7	25.7	8.2

As we have already stated, this study involved only words which could be constructed on a letter by letter basis. Since our argument was that such words would lend themselves quite well to the young child's normal spelling strategies we decided on a second, rather similar experiment (conceived by P.E.B.) which included a wider variety of words. There were 30 of these: TREE, MILK, EGG, BOOK, SEE, CUT, MAT, IN, SCHOOL, SIT, FROG, BUN, RAN, OUT, BAG, TEN, PAT, CLOCK, TRAIN, LIGHT, LEG, DOT, PEN, YET, THINK, DREAM, CROWD, WEEK, KEEP, FROM.

The children were given the words to read on one occasion and to spell on another. But this time in order to check that the discrepant words (words read but not spelled or spelled but not read) did not simply happen as a result of chance variations in the child's attention we gave all the children their discrepant words once again. In practice this made hardly any difference.

We saw 50 schoolchildren who were divided into two age groups (and whose reading levels were normal for their age): 30 were 6½–7 year-olds, and 20 7–7¾ year-olds.

TABLE 5   Mean number of words (out of 30) in the four possible categories (Experiment 2)

	N	RS Words read and spelled	$\overline{R}\overline{S}$ Words *neither* read *nor* spelled	R$\overline{S}$ Words read but *not* spelled	$\overline{R}$S Words *not* read but spelled
Younger group	30	12.7	7.1	6.3	3.9
Older group	20	18.5	5.5	5.5	0.5

Table 5 gives the main results which repeat those of the first study. Again both discrepant categories occurred in the younger group, and again instances of words being spelled without being read ($\overline{R}$S) declined with age and with increasing reading skill. Thus here again we have definite evidence that at the beginning stages of reading children often read and spell in different ways.

The nature of the discrepant words also supported our ideas about phonological segments being used in spelling and chunks and wholes being used in reading. The four words which were most commonly read but not spelled (R$\overline{S}$) were SCHOOL, LIGHT, TRAIN, and EGG. The words which were most commonly spelled but not read were ($\overline{R}$S) BUN, MAT, LEG and PAT. The former words cannot easily be constructed on a letter by letter basis while the latter can. Indeed all the words which individual children spelled but did not read were, in this sense, regular. Thus now we have information about the different cues which children use in reading and spelling.

We decided on another experiment to test our idea that children spell some words without reading them, because they use the words' phonological segments when they spell but not when they read. The children, we argued, should also be able to read these same words if they could be encouraged into reading phonologically.

This is not hard to do. Nonsense words like WEF and BIP are not familiar and cannot be recognised. The only way to read them is phonetically, and, in effect, letter by letter. So we took all the 24 children in the younger group who had spelled some words without reading them. Then, in one condition, we gave the children a list of what was ostensibly a set of nonsense words, explaining at first what they were. But, embedded in this list, were all the words which these children had not read in the previous experiment and these, of course, were the words which they had neither read nor spelled ($\bar{R}\bar{S}$) and also those which they did spell but did not manage to read ($\bar{R}S$). The mean number of words which these 24 children had not read or spelled was 5.4 and of the words which they had not read but had spelled 4.9. We predicted that now the children would adopt a phonological strategy and so would begin to read the words which before they had spelled but had not read.

We also added another condition in which the same words were embedded in a list of easy meaningful words. This, we suggested, should make no difference to the child's normal dependence on recognition in reading, and, therefore should change nothing.

Our predictions were largely confirmed. In the nonsense word condition the children did now read an average of 3.5 (out of 4.9) of the words which they had previously spelled but not read ($\bar{R}S$). However the meaningful condition made no difference. Neither condition had much effect on the words which at first were neither spelled nor read correctly ($\bar{R}\bar{S}$), which suggests that if a child cannot construct a word phonetically he cannot read it phonetically either.

So we have found consistent support for our idea that children often try to read and to spell the same words in different ways, that they often depend on visual chunks when they read and phonological segments when they spell, and that they can be pushed into reading words which they previously spelled but did not read ($\bar{R}S$) by being persuaded to adopt a phonological strategy.

6 Theory of learning to read and to write

Our argument has centred around discrepancies between spelling and writing and particularly around the surprising category of words which are spelled but not read ($\bar{R}S$). But there are distinct signs from our own results that this striking disconnection between reading and spelling is a feature only of the beginning stages of learning to read and to spell. How the relations between these two skills change as the child progresses is also an intriguing question.

Our work suggests that at first children use at least two strategies, phonological and visual, and that they tend to specialise and use one strategy primarily in spelling and the other primarily in reading. We have not till now considered another strategy, the effect of context, but there is ample evidence that children use context to help them guess words when they read.

We suggest that a major change is in the extent to which a child specialises in the way he uses cues. At first there is a surprising degree of specialisation: for reading he appears to use mainly visual and probably contextual cues and for spelling mainly phonological cues. As time goes on however this specialisation declines, and our hypothesis is that it declines in both ways. They begin to read phonetically as well as visually and they also use their memory of visual chunks to help them write words. To put it another way we are arguing that the principle of associative symmetry mentioned by Baron *et al.* (Chapter 8) plays a greater part in the reading and spelling of experienced than of inexperienced readers and spellers.

The change – the use of phonological cues in reading as well as in spelling – is suggested by the fact that the older children did read virtually every word which they could spell, as well as being able to read several words which they could not spell. This could be because they continue to use visual recognition, which allows them to read words which they cannot spell, and to turn to phonological cues whenever their visual recognition fails.

But this increasing flexibility, it should be noted, may not occur in every case. In fact, the possibility of using one cue for reading and another for spelling was first demonstrated very convincingly by Frith (1976) and her work was with older children who were bad at spelling. She found that there are 12-year-old children who read well but spell remarkably badly for their age, and that these children seem to specialise in much the same way as our typical $6\frac{1}{2}$-year-old child specialises. They, too, seem to read visually and to spell phonologically. Thus these poor spellers may have failed to shed habits which are normally only associated with the beginnings of reading and spelling.

We have also encountered children of 11 and 12 who read well but spell appallingly, and we believe that there is one other interesting thing to be said about them. In our informal experience these children often begin to experience serious reading difficulties too at around the age of 13 years or so. We suggest that this is due to their being introduced to new subjects such as science subjects and therefore new words and contexts. Our hypothesis is that they can no longer rely on their twin strategies of word recognition and context, because they are faced with words which they cannot recognise in contexts which do not help. They, unlike other children, do not use the phonological strategy when visual recognition fails, and as a result are quite at a loss. These suggestions are based on experience and observation in the teaching situation, but have not been tested experimentally.

Having considered how a child manages to read words which he spells, we still have to deal with the other discrepancy, which involves words which are read but not spelled. To some extent this discrepancy will probably never disappear, since most people seem to be able to read words which they do not spell. Nevertheless there will be changes since the child will soon spell words like LIGHT or SCHOOL which cannot be constructed on a letter by letter basis.

Nothing seems to be known about how a child eventually writes words like these. One possibility is that he develops spelling 'chunks' in much the same way as he has developed reading 'chunks' earlier on. In other words he writes, so to speak, in sequence of letters. But if this is so, how does he acquire these chunks?

One idea, which certainly fits in with the suggestions of many educationalists such as Montessori, Fernald and Gillingham, is that these sequences are originally learned in the form of a pattern of movement. The stress here must be on the word 'originally' since it is clear that adults can spell all sorts of words properly without the help of a particular set of movements. Inexperienced typists can still type a word like SCHOOL correctly even if they have never done it before. But this may not be true of children who are just learning to spell sequences of letters of this kind. Again this is a suggestion which could be tested quite easily.

Our final point is a general one. The traditional view of the development of thought and intellectual skill during childhood has been that children must gradually acquire certain basic abilities which they simply do not have to begin with. However, a great deal of recent work seems to suggest that this traditional view is often wrong, and that young children frequently fail in cognitive tasks not because they lack the necessary aptitude, but because they do not know exactly when it needs to be applied (Bryant and Kopytynska, 1976; McGarrigle and Donaldson, 1974).

Our surprising discovery that $6\frac{1}{2}$-year-old children often spell words which they do not read seems to be another example. They do not read these words, but they can. They need to be shown what they can do.

PART VII
Spelling and Language Disorders

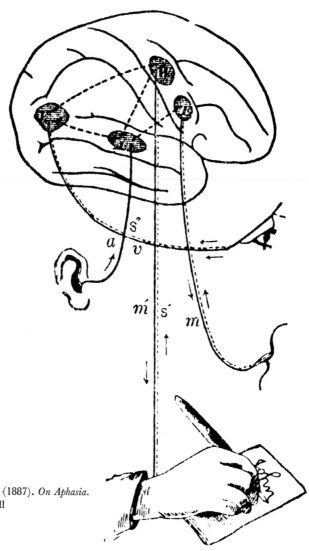

From: James Ross (1887). *On Aphasia.*
London: Churchill

17

Phonological Awareness and Phonological Representation: Investigation of a Specific Spelling Problem

TONY MARCEL   *MRC Applied Psychology Unit, Cambridge, England*

Summary A specific spelling problem was discovered in some adults attending literacy courses, some schoolchildren and three neurological patients. In initial consonant clusters containing a liquid, the liquid was omitted or misplaced inconsistently and the voicing of the stop was sometimes changed. In terminal clusters, nasal and lateral consonants were omitted. These errors are strikingly similar to deviations in the speech of young children. However the people concerned showed no obvious relation between their errors and their speech perception or production, except that they were impaired on phonetic segmentation. Two theoretical approaches are discussed. The first argues the role of processes of reflexive consciousness in literacy and proposes that these people are impaired in becoming aware of particular phonemes in certain contexts. The second proposes that, like young children, these people are indeed using a different set of features from normal adults to analyse and produce speech, but that the present tests were insensitive to this. An experiment on syllable segmentation supports the latter view. The relation between linguistic awareness, linguistic development and literacy is discussed, as well as practical implications.

1 Introduction – the problem

The work reported here was undertaken more by chance than design. Its primary concern is not spelling in general but a highly specific problem encountered by a small proportion of people. To my knowledge it has not been reported before. However, while the problem is specific, it has implications not only for the assessment and teaching of spelling and possibly reading, but for speech perception and production as well.

The study started with an initial observation by a former research student, Anita Jackson, who was acting as a voluntary tutor at an adult literacy class. In the group of people with which she was working, spelling appeared to be at least as big a problem as reading. One student, with whom she regularly practised written spelling to dictation, made some interesting errors, which upon investigation appeared to be made by some other students as well. All of these students, while their spelling had improved, seemed to have prolonged difficulties. Some of these attempts to transcribe words appear in Table 1a.

Certain words appeared to prove a continuing difficulty for these people. We can characterise these particular attempts as follows. Irrespective of the graphemic rendering of other phonemes, certain phonemes fail to be represented by any letter at all or the letter representing them is misplaced. This does not seem to be a random process. The regularity appears to be phonemic rather than ortho-

TABLE 1

a Some examples of the spelling of the adults attending literacy classes

Subject A

throat	THOAT	problem	POBLAM	blot	BOT
three	THEE	cloth	COTH	branch	BRACH

Subject B

prune	POUN	scrap	SCAP	print	PINT
thread	THEAD	glass	GASS		

Subject C

springs	SPINGS	struck	TRUCK, TUCK	help	HLEP, HEPL
fault	FAUTE	finds	FINES	ment	MET

Subject D

glass	GASSE	fruit	FIURT, FUIT	strength	STETH
quilt	QUITE	different	DIFFERWET	throne	THONE

Subject E

glove	GULVE	replied	REPIED	difficult	DIFFECOT
find	FIDE	publicity	PUPICITY	told	TOLE
against	AGAIT, AGAITAIN	sculpture	SCUPURE		

Subject F

science	SIESE, SCIENECS	cramp	CAP, CAMP	flung	FUNG
fruit	FIURT	proud	POUD	wind	WIN, WING
trunk	TUNK	blunt	BUNT	ground	GROUD
grand	GAND	drink	DINK	shrank	SHUCK, SHANK

b Some examples of the patients' spelling

J.F.		R.A.		A.E.	
bread	BAED	spot	SCOP	clot	COT
blood	BOOLD	strike	TIKE	cry	CY
plan	POLE	scrape	SCAP	strike	STIK
glove	COCK, GROVE	plan	BAN	glove	GUVE
cry	RCY	clot	GOT	find	FINE
tray	TEAY	trip	DIP	went	WET
help	HAP	bend	BAN	played	PALD, PAYD
harp	HAPE				
bent	BET, BETN				
mend	MINE				
strike	STIKE				
spring	SPING				

graphic. It concerns liquids (l and r) when preceded in initial consonant clusters by a stop, and liquids and nasals (m and n) when followed by a stop or fricative in terminal consonant clusters. On various attempts, in some cases the letter concerned is consistently omitted, in some cases it is either omitted or inserted or misplaced, and in other cases it is put in different places on different attempts. This does not seem to be well described merely as an 'order error', since it is the ordinal position of these particular letters in certain contexts which is uncertain, not that of other letters. When asked about the words in which the letter was inconsistently placed, the students said that they 'felt sure that that letter is in the word but weren't sure where to put it'. In cases where they omitted the letter consistently, these students did not appear to understand why the letter should be represented at all. This was quite striking. These students were not simply mis-spelling, they appeared not to know what certain words sounded like! Although one of the students had a noticeable dialect, none of them appeared to pronounce the words in question in an abnormal way such that one was unable to identify them. But this was with the listener's knowledge of what the target was. In spite of the apparently adequate speech of these people, their mis-spellings are most reminiscent of the speech of young children who have not yet attained adult phonology (Ingram, 1971; Smith, 1973; Dodd, 1975) and of the spellings produced by the pre-school children studied by Read (1975). Are these people abnormal in some way and in whom else is the phenomenon to be found? To answer these questions we had to know what the problem was and had to find appropriate subjects. In what follows, other problems in spelling which were exhibited by the people studied but which did not appear related to the current problem will not be discussed.

2 Mapping the phenomenon

2.1 *The tests*

In order to provide a criterion for detecting people who made errors of the type in question, a list of words and non-words was constructed. This list contained examples of words and comparable non-words (i) with both initial and terminal consonant clusters and (ii) where the consonants making up those clusters appeared singly in initial and terminal positions. As far as was possible there were two instances for both words and non-words of each type of consonant and consonant cluster. The complete list appears in Table 2.

TABLE 2 Words and non-words containing single and clustered consonants

bed	bread	amber	beb	breb	pumb
bit	brick	hungry	bol	brol	gomber
pill	blood	angler	lan	blan	tomp
pot	blade	pink	lin	blin	bimp
red	plan	sunk	rad	plid	rank
rot	played	pens	rom	plaf	runk
led	pray	suns	pog	prog	angrow
lot	prick	pence	pid	prid	onglit
dead	tray	rinse	gock	prut	strabe
dot	trip	sums	gam	grock	strup
tip	dream	mimes	kip	grem	scrot
tie	drip	scrape	kom	glame	scrit
cow	grass	scrap	dov	glud	spram
cot	great	spring	dit	clum	sprib
gun	glass	sprain	tid	clop	splot
got	glare	strike	tep	crade	splag
soap	cry	stroke	teb	crot	
hip	crate	splendid	dob	drope	
rub	clot	split	dop	drick	
hell	class		bock	trid	
bell	elbow		huck	tron	
sob	bulb		rog	elbat	
her	bold		lig	kelb	
fur	held		mot	pold	
gum	help		rad	deld	
hem	pulp		nar	rolt	
bet	herb		der	milt	
cat	harp		pell	delp	
wed	bolt		kall	colp	
hen	colt		kim	felk	
pin	milk		rom	tolk	
less	silk		vin	narb	
fuss	pork		fon	forb	
buzz	park		pozz	norp	
fuzz	heart		ruzz	darp	
scarf	hard		russ	vord	
scoot	bent		poss	vort	
stone	want		scod	sark	
pick	mend		scob	dork	
rock	bend		stap	remmed	
stick	aimed		stid	camd	
spot	hummed		spon	fent	
spin	lump		spoll	sint	
pig	camp			lond	
rug	ember			gand	

This list was used for two purposes: for initial selection of subjects and for more specific testing. For initial selection, the list was dictated. The words were presented first and subjects were informed that they were words. The non-words were presented second and subjects were told that these were not real words but were like words.

When critical and control subjects had been selected (see Section 2.2 for criterion), each subject was individually required to carry out four tasks: (*i*) *Repetition*: the entire list was read out one item at a time and the subject was required to repeat what was said. This was tape-recorded; (*ii*) *Spelling*: each item was read out and the subject was required to write out how he or she thought it was spelled. More than one attempt was allowed and the item was repeated if the subject requested it; (*iii*) *Copying*: each item was shown to the subject on a separate card typed in lower case and the subject was required to copy it; (*iv*) *Reading*: each item was shown to the subject on cards as before and the subject was required to read it. This was also tape-recorded. These four tests were always carried out in this order and with roughly a week between each.

2.2 *The people studied*

2.2.1 *Adult illiterates.* The initial observation was made at an adult literacy course. Therefore the first attempt to identify subjects was from this population. There were two main voluntary courses in Cambridge and 34 people altogether from both courses were given the first dictation test. Seven people were selected on the basis of the test. All of these to varying degrees exhibited the phenomenon. That is, they failed to represent a consonant phoneme when it was in a cluster or misplaced it in their written letter string, but did not fail to represent it when it was not in a cluster. Seven other people from the courses were selected who were willing to act as control subjects. None of the latter made any of the same type of error, but were regarded as poor spellers. Both experimental and control subjects also showed other types of spelling error where a phoneme was mis-represented. However none of these errors constituted omission of a phoneme and so they are not of immediate relevance. The ages of the experimental subjects ranged from 18 to 54, the ages of the controls ranged fron 21 to 51.

2.2.2 *'Normal' schoolchildren.* When the error was first confirmed as a definite type among the adults attending the literacy classes, Dr Margaret Peters of the Cambridge Institute of Education was consulted. One of the main reasons for doing so was that no reference to the problem had been found and it was of interest whether it had been encountered during normal schooling. Dr Peters had data available on the spelling of 920 schoolchildren from tests conducted once a year for three years (ages 8–10). This was the raw data of her 1970 study *Success in Spelling* (Peters, 1970).

While the tests employed had not been designed to examine the present problem, examination of the data from 100 children in the survey revealed what looked like twelve cases. These children appeared to show exactly the same problems as the adults on some of the critical words and this difficulty was consistent for them over the 3 years of the study. Since this study had been conducted twelve years earlier it was impossible to trace the individuals. However four schools in Cambridge agreed to allow testing of their current eight- and nine-year-old children with parents' consent.

Out of 265 children tested, fourteen were identified on the basis of the initial dictation test, eight 8-year-olds and six 9-year-olds. All of these children were at least a year behind their age norms on both reading and spelling when tested with the Schonell Graded Word Reading and Spelling tests. Fourteen children were chosen as controls. These latter children were of roughly the same reading quotient as the experimental group but were only marginally behind on spelling and none of them made equivalent errors on the consonant clusters.

2.2.3 *Patients undergoing speech therapy*. While discussing the present spelling problem, the head of the Speech Therapy department of Addenbrooke's Hospital, Cambridge, Mrs F. M. Hatfield, mentioned that she had encountered cases where consonant clusters had shown a similar problem in spelling. Over six months, using the initial dictation list, the therapists managed to identify three cases who seemed to exhibit the deletion problem. Some examples of their spelling appear in Table 1b.

Mr A. E. was 68. In August 1976 he suffered a right hemiparesis from acute cardiovascular disease, which left him with almost total expressive aphasia and limited comprehension. The speech report in January 1977 showed him to have a reduced memory span, but with no comprehension problem in everyday life, effective production of speech in sentences, able to write, especially common regularly spelled words, and while he could not read a newspaper he could understand simple written sentences.

Mr J. F. was 75. In 1975 a cerebrovascular accident left him with a mild right-sided weakness in the arm, leg and face, such that he writes with his non-dominant, left hand. He had a mild receptive dysphasia but his speech was grossly disturbed. The conclusion of the speech report was that he had a severe articulatory dyspraxia. He could imitate most phonemes in isolation, but his voluntary control of phonation was greatly impaired. His reading comprehension was good and he could spontaneously write short regular words. By September 1976 his speech had improved so that it was apparent that he was agrammatic. At the time of the current tests his dyspraxia was such that clusters could not be produced and many back plosives were fronted. However articulation was less impaired on repetition than with spontaneous speech.

Mr R. A. was 29. He suffered a left parietal depressed fracture with brain laceration. One month later on testing he had fluent speech but very little comprehension; he had no dysarthria; he had no comprehension of written material and his writing consisted of nonsensical perseverative strings of letters. At the time the current testing started, in 1977, his single word comprehension was good but his comprehension of sentences and his memory span were low. Repetition was good. His reading had improved such that he could comprehend short paragraphs. Although he was unable to write sentences to dictation, he could write single words and short phrases. His spelling was poor.

Three control subjects were chosen who were also outpatients at Addenbrooke's Hospital but who had no known dysphasic or dysgraphic symptoms. These people were 24, 68 and 73 years of age.

2.3 *Results of tests on words and non-words*

Copying. None of the subjects in any of the three groups made any errors in copying.

Repeating. None of the adult illiterates or children had any difficulty in repetition. R.A.'s repetition was nearly perfect. His only problem was in repeating non-words with initial clusters of three consonants. A. E. was also good at repetition except that he tended to repeat non-words as words. J.F.'s repetition was laboured, but, except for /g/- words, had no difficulty with cluster words.

Interestingly, two adults and three children in the control groups stumbled over repetition of items with three-consonant clusters.

Reading. The adults and children had little difficulty reading words. Some subjects in both groups had difficulty with 3-consonant clusters, and some subjects had difficulty with low frequency words (e.g. SPLENDID, EMBER). They did mis-read a few non-words as words but were able with some difficulty to sound them out correctly.

A.E. was unable to read 28 (25%) words. But he indicated that he understood 15 of these. There was no relationship between the words he could not read and their spelling or sound. He was also unable to read 24 (26%) of the non-words successfully.

R.A. was very good at reading both words and non-words. He had difficulty with ANGLER and SPRAIN, and with ANGROW, KELB, SCRIT and SPRIB.

J.F. had the same difficulty in his reading as in his repetition, that is on words and non-words with clusters, especially those with three-consonant clusters. However he indicated that he understood all of the words.

There was a small tendency amongst all three groups of control subjects to read non-words as words.

Spelling. None of the control subjects made any of the errors in question. The only exceptions to this were one adult and two children who all made order errors. But these errors involved other letters as well as the critical ones and also occurred on non-cluster words. None of the pre-selected experimental subjects failed to represent phonemes in the correct place *in non-cluster items,* even if occasionally using the wrong letter to do so. However they all made errors on clusters to varying extents and in various ways. These errors and their frequency are summarised in Table 3.

Some comments need to be made about the spelling errors.

1   The tendency to omit liquids and nasals was consistently greater when combined with an unvoiced consonant than with a voiced consonant.

2   A frequent tendency in initial clusters, but totally absent in terminal clusters, was to change the voicing of the stop consonant $(t \rightarrow d, g \rightarrow c)$. When this occurred, the liquid was never retained in the correct place and most often was deleted.

3   When letters were misplaced they were hardly ever put at the beginning of the word. One such exception appears in Table 3, where CRY becomes RCY.

4   Errors on terminal clusters with liquids in them pose a difficult problem. In most English dialects the *r* in *r* + stop merely serves to alter the vowel quality, while in a few accents it is pronounced. Thus for most British speakers MORD is a homophone of MAUDE, while for a New Yorker it is not since the *r* is pronounced. This is not the case, except in a very few cases, for the cluster *l* + stop. While in many cases a nasal + stop is actually realised in articulation as a nasalisation of the preceding vowel, most adults treat the nasal as a separate phoneme. For convenience terminal clusters of *r* + stop will not be considered further since long vowels are graphemically ambiguous (cf. PASS, FATHER, PART, PALM, AUNT).

TABLE 3 Error types and their frequency probability (in percent)

Group:	Adults		Children		Patients		Examples	
In Word/Non-word	*Wd*	*Nwd*	*Wd*	*Nwd*	*Wd*	*Nwd*	*Wd*	*Nwd*
ERROR TYPE								
On initial unvoiced stop+ liquid								
Liquid omitted	32	40	26	37	31	41	tray→tay	plid→pid
Liquid misplaced	22	18	23	10	20	05	cry→rcy	prog→porg
Stop voiced, liquid omitted	27	30	18	26	36	41	cry→gay	crade→gade
On initial voiced stop+ liquid								
Liquid omitted	26	34	20	26.	20	31	glass→gasse	blan→ban
Liquid misplaced	25	25	16	21	15	05	blood→boold	breb→berb
Stop unvoiced, liquid omitted	19	30	15	25	20	36	grass→cass	grock→cock
On initial s + unvoiced stop + liquid								
Liquid omitted	25	38	29	41	26	36	spring→sping	scrot→scote
Liquid misplaced	20	10	28	20	15	05	strike→styker	spram→sporm
Stop voiced, s and liquid omitted	15	29	12	15	41	46	scrape→gap	strabe→dabe
On terminal nasal + voiced stop or fricative								
Nasal omitted	05	17	10	20	15	31	mend→med	lond→lod
Stop/fricative omitted	11	34	19	39	26	36	hummed→hum	lond→lone
Nasal misplaced	0	0	0	0	0	0	—	—
On terminal nasal + unvoiced stop								
Nasal omitted	28	50	25	42	36	46	bent→bet	fent→fet
Stop/fricative omitted	0	0	0	0	0	0	—	—
Nasal misplaced	35	10	31	35	36	10	bent→betn	fent→fetn
On terminal liquid + voiced stop								
Liquid omitted	20	16	32	38	31	36	herb→heab	pold→pod
Stop omitted	31	32	21	34	36	41	held→hell	pold→pol
Liquid misplaced	0	0	0	0	0	0	—	—
On terminal liquid + unvoiced stop								
Liquid omitted	34	40	37	43	36	46	help→hap	delp→dep
Stop omitted	0	0	0	0	0	0	—	—
Liquid misplaced	0	0	0	0	0	0	—	—

5   Differences between words and non-words: (a) Errors of omission and voicing change were more frequent in non-words than words. However, (b) misplacings of liquids and nasals were more frequent in words than non-words.

These two tendencies could be due to either or both of two possible reasons. (*i*) The sound of lexicalised speech segments (known words) comes to be internally represented differently from that of unknown items. While for unknown speech the subject may not realise that the phoneme in question is present, in words he realises its presence but cannot access its ordinal position. (*ii*) In neither words nor non-words does the subject have any intuition that the phoneme in question is present, but in some words he or she has learned through tuition or experience that the letter happens to be in the spelling. Such people would have no basis other than rote verbal or visual memory for allotting that letter to a position. Theoretical bases for these two types of accounts will be explicated later in this chapter.

6   Differences among the spellers: Among the adult illiterates and the children there appeared to be certain individual differences.

In initial stop + liquid: Four adults and nine children tended to change the voicing of the stop. The other three adults and five children tended not to, merely deleting the liquid. Among the former group about half changed voiced to voiceless stops more often than voiceless to voiced. The other half showed the reverse tendency.

In terminal nasal + stop: Almost all subjects deleted the nasal when followed by an unvoiced stop. But only some of these, 3 adults and 8 children, deleted the nasal before a voiced stop. None of the latter deleted the voiced stop.

These two groups of subjects did not correspond to the groups treating initial clusters differentially.

As regards the patients, all three showed at least some of each type of error with terminal nasal clusters. J.F. deleted nasals before unvoiced consonants much more frequently than the other two, and R.A. misplaced nasals before unvoiced stops much more than the other two. All three made at least one error of each type on each of the initial clusters. While they appeared to have different tendencies in these cases, the data is too unclear to make any further remarks with any confidence.

7   Relationship of the errors to speech: With the exception of one patient, J.F., it appears that the problem is specifically related to spelling, in the gross sense that the tests permit. That is, one would expect that any gross deficit of speech perception or production would have shown up in the repetition test, if not the reading test. Several aspects of the data strongly suggest that the spelling problem is related in some way to

speech. Firstly, the regularity which distinguishes the individuals concerned from control subjects is omission or misplacing of a phoneme as opposed to instability of graphemic representation. Secondly, it is only certain types of phonemes, rather than types of letter, which suffer and those in specific phonetic environments. Thirdly, the transformations which take place would seem to be far more satisfactorily described by phonetic relationships than by visual relationships or purely orthographic conventions (e.g. $cr- \rightarrow g-$). Fourthly, the tendency and pattern differs between words and non-words. So far as one can tell, the only difference between the words and non-words is in the words being known and so having a lexical entry.

Another piece of evidence comes from the patient J.F. who was dyspraxic in speech in a particular way. His spontaneous speech exhibited many of the phonological impairments of his spelling. In the main, clusters were reduced and changes in voicing occurred. However this was much less evident with repetition. Why this is so is not clear. However, the connection between his speech and his spelling suggests that the spelling of the other subjects is also related to a speech problem which remains hidden. For this reason it was decided to carry out some more specific tests of speech perception and production.

3 Attempts to relate the problem to speech

One possible reason why the non-clinical groups did not appear to have problems in perception or production is that the tests and analyses were not of fine enough grain. Another possibility is that other factors masked the problems. For instance when words were presented orally there may have been good enough lip-reading cues to enable satisfactory oral mimicry (see Dodd, Chapter 19). In addition there is little reason to suppose that any aural perceptual problem would necessarily show up in reading.

Four possible types of difficulty present themselves.

(*i*) *There is an exteroperceptive difficulty.* This hypothesis holds that the perception of speech sounds is in some way abnormal.

(*ii*) *There is a productive impairment.* This hypothesis presupposes that at least for those cases where errors occur the speller is producing some form of speech (covert or overt) and relying on this code to derive his or her spelling. Further, in spontaneous production the code produced either lacks certain segments, lacks distinction between alternative segments, or distorts the segments. This could be due either to inadequate instructions for articulation or to constraints in articulation itself.

(*iii*) *There is a problem in proprioception.* This hypothesis can take two slightly different forms. In the first it may be supposed that there is an imperfect monitoring of one's own generated speech code. In the second version, the speaker has a problem in perceiving what he or she has generated. The versions differ in that, according to the first, the speaker cannot prevent himself from 'uttering' something which does not accord with his intention, while according to the second, whatever the speaker utters, he or she cannot distinguish certain features in it, whereas they can in the speech of others.

This is not the point at which to discuss the feasibility of these three hypotheses. Suffice it to say that they have all been proposed at various times and in various forms to account for both paraphasias in dysphasic patients and for phonological distortions in the developing speech of normal children (see Carrell, 1968; Fodor *et al.*, 1974, Chapter 8; Smith, 1973).

(*iv*) *There is a problem in phonetic segmentation.* This hypothesis holds that while a person may have no difficulty in the normal handling of speech, they may find it difficult to make phonetic segmentation consciously explicit. For further discussion of this see Section 4 below and Liberman *et al.* (1977).

In order to throw some light on whether any of these approaches might bear on the problem, the following tests were carried out.

3.1 *Exteroperception*

Test 1. A tape was recorded by a speech therapist who was considered a good speaker of standard English. Each word and non-word on the lists was recorded in randomised order. The subject was asked to say or indicate what each item meant. This was intended to reveal whether analysis was sufficient to access the appropriate lexical entry. Non-words were included to see if they were treated as words and, if so, what were the particular biases.

Test 2. A tape was recorded by the same speaker which consisted of minimal pairs for all critical combinations (e.g. /gra:s/vs/ga:s/; /gla:s/vs/ga:s/; /gra:s/vs/ gla:s/). An equal number of identical pairs was also recorded. The order of these pairs was randomised. Each pair was presented and the subject had to say whether they were the same or different.

3.1.1 *Results.* The performance of the adult illiterates and children was perfect. On Test 1 the patients were unable to indicate the meaning of several items. But in most of these cases they were able to respond adequately to the items which differed minimally from them. Therefore a sensory problem is unlikely. On Test 2, while not all distinctions were made, they all performed at over 90% and were able to distinguish correctly words and non-words which they failed to distinguish reliably when spelling them.

3.2 *Production*

Test 3. For each type of cluster as far as was possible a set of minimally different words was constructed, e.g. BED, RED, LED, BREAD, BLED. The subject was required to utter spontaneously each of these target words. For example the experimenter would say 'What do you sleep on?' If the subject gave a word other than the target the process was repeated until the target word was uttered. This was tape-recorded. (This produced some difficulties with the patients and in those cases, where possible, the experimenter said the word and asked first what it meant, then asked the subject to say it.) After the tapes were completed, each was played to a separate listener, not otherwise involved in the study, who wrote down what each item was. Non-target items were deleted from the tape.

3.2.1 *Results.* The speech of the adult illiterates and children enabled perfect identification of the targets. There were several items which the patients could not produce. However all the words which A.E. and R.A. produced were easily identifiable. J.F., by contrast with his performance on repetition, produced forms which showed distortions which, according to their transcription, were congruent with his spelling.

3.3 *Proprioperception*

Test 4. Each tape with a subject's own utterances on it was played back to him or her at least one week after it had been recorded. The subject was asked to indicate the meaning of each item. The object of this was to see how subjects' perception of their own speech compared with their perception of another's speech.

3.3.1 *Results.* Once again the adult illiterates' and children's understanding of their own speech was perfect. A.E. and R.A. were unable to identify several items which they had produced. But these were predominantly words they had had difficulty in producing spontaneously. With these few exceptions they were able to identify correctly the meaning of all their own productions. J.F.'s performance was striking. He was able to identify *all* the words he spontaneously produced, even the distorted ones. That is, given the target CLOCK for production in Test 3 with the cue 'it shows the time', the transcription of his production was /kʰɒk/. Yet his identification of it was 'to tell the time.'

3.4 *Phonetic segmentation*

Test 5. The same tape was presented as for the same–different judgments in Test 2, and the subject had to say which item had more sounds (i.e. phonemes) in it, or whether they both had the same number of sounds. This task was explained to subjects by the experimenter using two examples each of initial CCV vs CV and terminal VCC vs VC.

Test 6. A tape was presented, again recorded by the same speaker, which had one example of each consonant in isolation and of each critical cluster permutation. The subject was required to tap once for each phoneme in the item. This is the task used by Liberman *et al.* (1977). The experimenter demonstrated what was required by tapping to examples such as /b/, /bʌ/, /bʌt/.

Test 5 was directed at seeing whether the addition of the critical phonemes in clusters was perceived as adding any sound. Test 5 might be adequately performed but extra phonemes in clusters might be consciously interpreted as adding extra duration rather than extra segments. Therefore, Test 6 was directed at seeing whether phonemes in clusters could be perceived as an extra segment as opposed to merely adding temporal length.

3.4.1 *Results.* On each of these tests, both control and experimental subjects tended to underestimate the number of phonemes in clusters as compared to single consonant items. However, according to analysis of variance, this tendency was much greater in all the experimental groups. On Test 5, the interaction between number of erroneous 'same' judgments and control versus experimental groups was significant ($p < 0.001$ for each group). On Test 6, the interaction was also significant between insufficient taps to cluster items, non-cluster items and control vs experimental groups ($p < 0.001$ for each group).

3.5 *Comments*

With the exception of the patient J.F., there appeared to be no relation between spelling and either the perception or production of speech. The only test which showed some relation was that which required judgment of number of sounds and that which required explicit phonetic segmentation.

However the similarity of the mis-spellings to two other phenomena is striking. The first of these is the incidence in child speech of every one of the deviations that appear in the present spelling (see Tables 1 and 3). Of course misplacing of letters is discounted. Examples of these from a single corpus appear in Table 4.

TABLE 4   Examples of child forms from Smith (1973)

On unvoiced stop + liquid		
Liquid omitted	tree	→ /tiː/
Stop voiced, liquid omitted	tree	→ /diː/
On voiced stop + liquid		
Liquid omitted	grape	→ /geip/
Stop unvoiced, liquid omitted	green	→ /kʰiːn/
On s + unvoiced stop + liquid		
Liquid omitted	strawberry	→ /tˢɔːbəriː/
Stop voiced, *s* and liquid omitted	spring	→ /biŋ/
On nasal + voiced consonant		
Nasal omitted	and	→ /æd/
Consonant omitted	mend	→ /mɛn/
On nasal + unvoiced consonant		
Nasal omitted	went	→ /wɛt/
On liquid + voiced stop		
Liquid omitted	hold	→ /uːd/
Stop omitted	cold	→ /goːl/
On liquid + unvoiced stop		
Liquid omitted	help	→ /hɛp/

The second phenomenon is the 'spontaneous' spelling of the pre-schoolchildren studied by Charles Read (Read, 1975). The two pieces of orthography most relevant were the children's reduction of *tr*-clusters and nasal clusters. Nasal consonants were omitted before terminal stops and initial *tr*- was rendered as a single affricate equivalent to /č/. In the latter case some of the children felt that 'the first sound' of /tr-/ words was more similar to that in words starting with /č/ than to that in words starting with a non-cluster /t/. Read argues that these spellings indicate the children's intuitions as to which phonological distinctions are most important, especially when there are not enough letters to represent all distinctions.

If the present mis-spellings are related to these phenomena of children's speech perception and production, is it in the state of linguistic awareness possessed by the present group and the mechanisms underlying it, or in the state of their speech itself which is not apparent to adult hearers? Firstly, while these people are able to judge gross aspects of the sounds of words (whether they are the same or different), what they have trouble with is in making conscious judgments about specific aspects of the sounds of the words which lead to mis-spellings (their absolute and relative number of phonemes). But secondly, while their speech perception and production is adequate for distinguishing and understanding words whose critical components they spell alike, this does not mean that the distinctions are made *in the same way* as adult speakers and listeners. J.F. was able to identify his own 'mis-pronunciations'. Maybe the other subjects were behaving like him but in a non-obvious way.

4 Two theories

4.1 *Consciousness and spelling*

This approach to the problem is an attempt to deal with all those subjects *other than J.F.*, and is based on the following consideration. While the mis-spellings bear a striking relationship to the forms produced in speech by young children in the course of acquiring adult phonology, there was little evidence that the speech perception and production of the spellers with whom we are concerned deviates in a relevant way from adult forms. (In the next section, the sensitivity of the relevant indices will, however, be questioned.)

The motivating theme of what follows is the distinction between those activities which involve only 'primary linguistic activity' and those which involve 'secondary linguistic activity'. Basically this corresponds to our *use* of language and our *reflexive awareness* of language. The first in no way implies the second. Several authors (Klima, 1972; Mattingley, 1972; Savin, 1972; Donaldson, 1978) have drawn attention to this distinction and discussed its relevance to literacy. Donaldson especially has shown how much developmental-research has suffered from confusing the two. To take an example which is closely related to our present concerns, the fact that all people who adequately perceive and produce speech are at some level of description segmenting and combining phonemes stands side-by-side with the fact that not only are most people unaware of this but that many people have great difficulty in understanding what they are doing. This is not merely a difficulty in intellectually grasping the concept. Such people have unusual difficulty in learning secret languages such as Pig Latin (Savin, 1972) which require paying attention to phonetic segments, and intentionally splitting them and recombining them.

Indeed the abovementioned authors amongst others have drawn an intimate connection between literacy and locutionary awareness.

Let us carry this argument further and onto slightly more specific grounds. By the age when formal tuition of reading usually begins, the perception and production of speech are automatic and unconscious activities, such that users' awareness and intentions focus most of the time on semantics and pragmatics. However for the learning of reading and spelling, what is required is a conscious representation of speech which can be intentionally manipulated. That is, in order to understand the concepts of phoneticisation and alphabeticisation when conveyed by a teacher (see Rozin and Gleitman, 1977) one needs to be able to attend to and consider the sound, as opposed to the meaning, of one's own speech. Certainly if one has to read or spell new words, then one needs a representation of a segment of speech which can be maintained consciously, which can be considered and upon which intentional operations can be performed, as opposed to it merely being processed further, i.e. lexically and syntactically.

Elsewhere (Marcel, 1979) I have proposed that perceptual processing needs to be distinguished from conscious percepts. Processing of sensory input is automatically and non-selectively carried out to the highest level of analysis (e.g. semantic) available to the perceiver. However a conscious representation of sensory information involves an act of 'recovery'. Processes of perceptual analysis (and production) automatically pass their products to other processes whereby information is recoded. They also leave a record of their analysis or recoding and it is this information which is recovered. Recovery is selective in that phenomenal experience of one aspect of environmental input or self-generated output requires information at the desired level of code to be transferred or copied to a representation where it can be matched to hypotheses and 'considered'. Figure 1 will serve to illustrate this for speech.

Now, for speech information to be mapped onto graphemes, or at least for those mappings to be learned and understood, it is essential that that information is in a code which can be segmented into units which can correspond to graphemes, i.e. phonemes. The first problem which might occur, even with a system for perception and production which is functioning perfectly, is that information represented in B or C may not be easily recoverable in units suitable for A. For example, take the string of units in B: $-B_1$, B_2, B_3, B_4. The units in this code may be perfectly segmentable and 'perceptible' by, say, lexical devices for word recognition, but may not be so for recovery by A. This may not usually be of any great importance, but suppose that the process of recovery is not

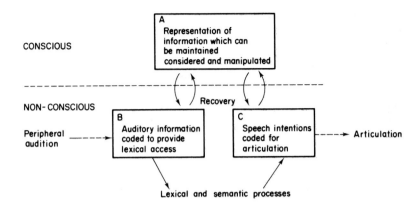

FIG. I   Conscious representation distinguished from automatic processing of speech

optimally sensitive or is unusually distractable by a B unit which is in a dominant relationship to another adjacent B unit. Suppose B_1 is more salient than B_2 and masks it when adjacent. In this case what may be recovered and transferred to the representation in A is B_1 B_3 B_4. This idea entails that some phonemes can dominate others when in a certain relationship – not so that they will prevent correct lexical identification of the string, but such that when recovery is suboptimal the masked phonemes cannot be consciously retrieved. Is this notion at all plausible? It is analogous to one view of central or backward pattern masking in vision. It has been found that where one pattern follows another, and shares certain features with it, at certain temporal separations it is impossible to decide what was in the first stimulus – for example, what letters were in a letter string. Yet it has been shown (Marcel, 1979) that the masked word has been sufficiently analysed to access its lexical and semantic entry without the subject's awareness. There is also evidence to suggest that one pattern may interfere with the recovery of another simultaneously present pattern depending on their spatial relationship. Thus one letter of a string is more recoverable than another next to it. Furthermore, and most relevant for present concerns, there are marked differences between individuals in the critical separations, temporal and spatial, of masking and masked patterns.

By analogy, it may be that for some individuals certain phonemes will effectively mask certain other phonemes when they are in a particular relationship. Thus stops may mask immediately following liquids, and stops and fricatives may mask immediately preceding liquids and nasals. While such masking will not prevent the lexical utilisation of the masked phoneme, it will prevent awareness, and certain individuals will be more susceptible than others to this.

The problem of recovery would of course be much more serious if the code of the unconscious representation differed from that of the requisite conscious representation. Several authors have suggested that the way that non-conscious or tacit knowledge is coded differs qualitatively from that in which conscious or explicit knowledge is coded (Polanyi, 1966; Turvey, 1974; Marcel, 1979). In the present case this is entirely possible. What is required for the mappings involved in reading and spelling is a phonemic code, since the units involved are beneath the level of syllables, indifferent to phonetic or allophonic variation, and certainly above the level of acoustics. Indeed it may be that we can only be conscious of the form of speech sounds in terms of phonetics or phonology but not in terms of acoustics. However it is by no means clear that the descriptive code which gives access to the lexicon is phonemic. Indeed there is little reason to assume it is other than acoustic. A special problem thus arises, since acoustic segments are not co-extensive with phonetic segments, and due to co-articulation the number of acoustic segments is usually less than the number of phonetic segments.

What does this kind of account buy us? To return to the original observations, those people who deleted letters representing the phonemes in question did not seem to be aware that those phonemes were there. In the case of words, they may have known, through tuition or through informal encounters with the word when reading, that the letter is in the spelling of the word. But if they did not know the spelling by heart (i.e. have it lexically stored)[1], then they appeared to have no basis for allotting it a particular ordinal location in their spelling. It should be remembered that in non-words misplacings of deletable letters hardly ever occurred. In non-words there would be no basis for deciding what letters to use other than the consciously perceived sound of the utterances. Thus the phonemes would be omitted as opposed to misplaced, as indeed they were.

According to this account the very reason why the experimental subjects do so badly on tasks requiring judgments of length and phonemic segmentation is that these tasks reflect recovery of un-

[1] It is assumed, as in other chapters, that the spelling of a word may be stored along with other information at the entry for that word in an internal lexicon. It is lexical information which underlies normal writing. No assumption is made that lexical output information is equivalent to that which permits lexical access. There are various options as to the way such information may be held: (*i*) in some speech code, e.g. as a string of letters, phonemes, syllables or morphemes, (*ii*) 'visually', as an ordered set of letters or graphemes or as a whole orthographic chunk. The differences between these options lie in their consequences for retrieval.

conscious information as opposed to the normal processing of that information, and it is in this recovery, or the availability of the relevant information for recovery, that these people are 'impaired'.

This approach can be applied to several other phenomena discussed by Marcel (1979). One that can be briefly mentioned is the extreme difficulty people have in learning the skill of phonetic transcription. Transcribers find it difficult to attend to the phonetic form of utterances and to avoid being biased by the lexical values. If lexical and semantic analyses do proceed automatically and one normally attends to the higher, more functionally useful levels, then it would be difficult to recover phonetic aspects uninfluenced by higher level knowledge.

The hypothesis which has been advanced above, that of locutionary awareness, was designed to account for the spelling of those people whose speech *appeared* to be normal, or at least not correlated in detail with the phonology of their spelling. Its motivation lies in the general consideration of the importance of linguistic awareness. However it does not really deal with the patient J.F. whose speech was impaired in ways related to his spelling. More seriously, it does not account comfortably for phonemic changes in the spelling other than deletions and misplacings, i.e. changes in articulatory voicing ($/k/\rightarrow/g/$) and even placing values ($/tr/\rightarrow/g/$) of letters.

Indeed one major feature seems at variance with the masking hypothesis. In initial clusters deletions were less frequent in the presence of a voiced than an unvoiced stop, and in terminal nasal clusters not only was deletion of the nasal much less frequent before a voiced than unvoiced stop, but voiced stops themselves were frequently deleted instead of the nasal, whereas this never happened with unvoiced stops. Intuitively it seems that voiced stops are more perceptually salient than unvoiced stops and that, if so, they should be more, not less, effective in masking liquids clustered with them. There is no formal evidence for this but two informal experiments do support this intuition. In the first experiment people were simply asked to listen to minimal pairs of non-words ($/kæm/$ and $/gæm/$, $/ket/$ and $/ked/$) and to judge which initial or terminal sound was most perceptually salient. For initial clusters the results clearly favoured voiced stops, for terminal clusters the results were not clearcut. In the second experiment lists of the same non-words were tape-recorded by a single speaker and subjects were required to detect a target phoneme by pressing a button as quickly as possible. Reaction times measured from temporally and acoustically equivalent points (segment onset) favoured voiced rather than unvoiced versions of stops in all cases. According to Foss and Swinney's (1973) account of phoneme monitoring, this would suggest that voiced stops are indeed phenomenally more dominant or more accessible to conscious recovery. The specific version of the masking hypotheses presented above is thus discredited.

An alternative approach is presented in the next section which tries to account for all subjects and all errors by reconsidering certain theoretical and testing assumptions.

4.2 *Acoustics, syllable structure and acquisition of phonology*

As we noted above, the spelling patterns exhibit a striking similarity to deviations from adult phonology which appear at certain stages of children's speech. However, the speech perception and production of these spellers, with the exception of J.F. did not appear to correspond to their spelling. Indeed it appeared to be normal to the extent that they could perceptually distinguish and correctly identify as well as normal adults, and produce speech which was correctly identified both by themselves and normal adults.

However it will be argued that the conclusions that their speech was normal may be based on a mistaken view of child phonology and that the tests carried out were inadequate. The predominant approaches to child phonology are based on the observation that while the child distinguishes and identifies adult speech adequately, its productions do not match the adult forms. The most widespread view of child language is that the child perceives speech in terms of adult phonological distinctions, but has output problems in producing a phonetic copy of adult speech. This could be due to either of two things: (*i*) All aspects of perception are adequate, but realisation is distorted either through insufficient development of motor intentions or because of insufficient development of the articulature which realises these intentions. (*ii*) The monitoring of production is impaired either through inadequate feedback from productive stages prior to ultimate articulation or through inadequate perception of that feedback.

Kornfeld (1971a, b, 1977; Kornfeld and Goehl, 1974) has argued that these accounts are both wrong, at least for certain stages of the child's language. While at certain points the child can distinguish between his own production and adults' forms (see Morton and Smith, 1972), at others the situation is rather more complicated.

Consider the following exchange (from Kornfeld, 1974):

Adult: (pointing to a picture) What's that?
Child: That's a [wæbɪt].
Adult: No, say [ræbɪt], not [wæbɪt].
Child: But I didn't say [wæbɪt]; I said [wæbɪt]!

Linguistic theories are often based on the adult treatment of the two [wæbɪt]'s produced by the child as the same; that is, /r/ becomes [w]. But if the child treated his own /w/'s as cases of /r/, he should treat other people's /w/'s in the same way and not reject the adult's 'errors'.

There are two clues to the solution of this particular problem. Firstly, several investigators (Klein, 1969; Kornfeld, 1971a; Hawkins, 1973) have shown by acoustic and spectrographic methods that the [w]-like sounds produced in *r*-words are consistently different from the [w]-sounds produced by the same child in *w*-words. Secondly Goehl and Golden (1974) have shown that such children reliably identify their own productions. When children were presented with pictures of minimal word-pairs like WING and RING, and an adult said the words, they made no errors in identifying the pictures. The children were then asked to name each picture. When recordings of these utterances were then played back with the picture pairs, the *w/r* children were significantly better than adults and other non-*w/r* children at identifying words from their own recordings.

Kornfeld proposes that children acquiring phonology are using the same features both to perceive and produce speech, but that set of features is different from the adult's. Can this idea be applied to the present phenomenon? Its application would take the following form. The abnormal spellers are using a different set of features from normal adults to perceptually distinguish the clusters in question. They are also using that set of features to produce speech. That set of features does not yield separate segments corresponding to those letters omitted in spelling. However normal adult listeners interpret the speech of these people as containing those phonemes.[1]

In order to specify those features it is necessary to provide plausible reasons both for cluster reduction and the particular influences of voicing and alterations of voicing. While some languages have syllables both with and without consonant clusters and some languages only have syllables without clusters, no languages have *only* syllables with clusters. In addition, Fujimura (1975) has argued on computational grounds that the syllable is best viewed as a core with affixes. In terms of the principle of 'vowel affinity' Fujimura has argued that the consonant further from the vowel in 2-consonant clusters is the basic one and the

---

[1] In contrast to the above, Dodd (Chapter 19) has provided a case where spelling is based on a phonological code (sound or speech) and yet differs from the speller's speech. Further, in that case while the perception of speech distinctions was accurate their production was not. However that population was profoundly deaf and perception was via lip reading. Plainly the children in her study could not have been using *acoustic* information as the present subjects are argued to be doing.

one nearer the vowel is the affix. If it is true that CV- and -VC syllables are more 'basic' than CCV- and -VCC, then this might be the child's initial internal model and we would have good reasons for expecting reduction. Coupled with this tendency to reduce, Kornfeld (1977) has argued that the young child's 'phonological' identification of consonant segments will be determined largely by predominant acoustic cues present in adult utterances. Before the child has learned which cues signal, say, voicing in particular combinations, he will rely on those which are 'primary' (Klatt, 1973). Older children and adults can rely on their knowledge of morpheme structure constraints and syntactic and lexical knowledge. Evidence that children who reduce clusters are indeed using different features has been provided by Menyuk (1971). What might the acoustic cues be?

Considering clusters as a whole, Haggard (1973) has shown that the durations of liquids and nasals are reduced in initial and terminal clusters and more so in general when the other consonant is unvoiced. Also, to take initial segments, for single consonants the most reliable cues for voicing are in voice onset time (VOT) and the transition of first formant (F_1). But cue values are changed by consonant additions in clusters. Thus in the cluster /gr-/, the VOT value indicates a single, voiceless aspirated stop ([k^h-]). With voiceless stops + /r/, the lengthened VOT and lowered F_1 frequency produced by the /r/ both indicate a single, voiced consonant. If turbulence and loudness are used, /tr-/ might be analysed as a single unvoiced stop with aspiration or as an affricate (see Kornfeld, 1977).

In the case of terminal nasal clusters, spectrographic records show that with a voiced stop (TEND) there is a distinct segmental realisation of the nasal, but with an unvoiced stop (TENT) there is not (see Fujimura, 1975). The explanation for this is that the articulatory demands of voiceless stops and fricatives are in conflict with those of a nasal. In order to accumulate the air pressure which will identify a voiceless consonant on release, the velum must close. But for a nasal it must open. For voiceless stops and fricatives preceded by a nasal, and to some extent a lateral (/-lt/), the velum remains open for a shorter time than otherwise. Further, nasalisation of pre-consonantal vowels is a secondary cue to a nasal consonant, and since vowels are longer before voiced than unvoiced stops, vowel nasalisation is more obvious in the former case. These factors plus other differences between final voiced and unvoiced consonants predict dropping of the nasal more with unvoiced stops, and perhaps even dropping of the stop when it is voiced.

It is interesting that each of the above predictions appears in the spelling. Particularly with regard to voicing changes and voicing environments, the above type of considerations gives a more exact account than that in terms of masking. This is particularly the case with terminal clusters. It will be remembered that deletions of nasals and laterals were more frequent when followed by voiceless plosives and fricatives. In contrast the only occasion when the nasal was retained and the following consonant was deleted was when the latter was voiced.

Is it plausible that the people in this study were in fact analysing and producing speech in the manner of children at particular stages of the acquisition of phonology? In Read's study, mentioned above, the same type of spellings were obtained and were based on his children's perception of phonological distinctions. If attaining adult forms is a matter of learning it might be that the schoolchildren and adult illiterates in this study have learned to *approximate* adult distinctions, but, instead of abandoning one feature set in favour of another, have merely modulated the original set of features. As far as the patients are concerned, J.F. was dyspraxic of speech and the therapist's report notes similar difficulties with sounds to those of children. Hatfield and Walton (1975) point out that individual differences in dyspraxic speech may be due to reflection of different stages of child speech and that patients may simultaneously retain many features of a fully acquired speech system. Luria (1947, 1950) has described patients similar to A.E. and J.F. who are quite capable of normal speech perception but unable to break a word down into its succession of sounds and who may omit phonemes or confuse their order in speaking and writing. Another consideration which is consistent with a return to an early form of speech coding is that, as noted above, lexical, semantic, morphemic and syntactic knowledge may contribute to achieving adult phonological distinctions. The present patients had all at one point lost such knowledge to some extent.

If the 'developmental' notions above are valid, then in what way are the people we are concerned with different from normal speakers and why was it not apparent in their speech? The answers to both questions would appear to be the same. These speakers, while they approximate the adult phonological distinctions in their productions (as far as the adult ear is concerned), have not attained, or, in the case of the patients, have possibly *lost* the abstract features of the normal English speaker. The features which they choose as primary to categorise and generate speech are determined by acoustic cues. While the set of distinctive features in their speech sounds does not correspond to the adult set of phones or phonemes, they are not as radically different as young children's. Normal speakers, hearing them in terms of their own phonemic distinctions, classify them into their own lexical and syllabic categories. Smith (1973) presents arguments that distinctive features (see Chomsky and Halle, 1968) provide a better account of children's phonology than phonemes. But he also notes that phonemes *as well as* distinctive features are necessary as units of representation. What is suggested here is that normal adults, for whatever reason, classify in terms of phonemes while the deviant spellers classify in terms of distinctive features, reducing syllables to CV- and -VC where possible. To test the validity of this account it would be necessary to analyse the speech of these people in a more exact acoustic manner than by the normal adult ear (e.g. spectrographically), and to test their perception by manipulating the relevant distinctions in artificially produced speech.

4.3 *The influence of subjective syllables*

As a final comment in this section let us return to one of the potential motivations for cluster reduction. This was the idea that syllable structure is conceived of as basically initial CV- or terminal -VC with concatenated additions. One reason for emphasising the syllable is that it appears to be a more 'natural' unit for speech perception and production than the phoneme (Savin and Bever, 1970) and is certainly an easier unit to use in teaching reading (see Gleitman and Rozin, 1977; Rozin and Gleitman, 1977; Liberman *et al.*, 1977). While it is debatable whether the morpheme or the syllable is the more appropriate unit (see Smith, 1973; Chomsky and Halle, 1968), the argument is not crucial for the present point. If it is the case that phoneme omission is partially due to tacit intuitions about syllable or morpheme structure, then it might be the case that there should be a smaller tendency to omit in cases where the consonants of a cluster are treated as belonging to two separate syllables and especially to two morphemes.[1] Indeed Haggard (1973) has shown that duration of consonants in clusters is less reduced when they are separated by a morpheme boundary. One way to test this is to examine clusters in the middle of words as opposed to at the beginning and end of words. As a first informal test I returned to the large sample of spellings in the raw data of Margaret Peters' (1970) survey. For those children who consistently showed the relevant deletions in initial and terminal clusters, it was immediately obvious that they showed this tendency to a much smaller degree (as far as the corpus permitted such a comparison) in internal clusters such as ALPINE, MOUNTAIN, ANSWER, APPROVAL. The problem arises however as to how to know what is the subjective syllable boundary. Indeed this is one of the main problems

---

[1] This idea and its test were suggested to me by Gillian Cohen.

with defining the syllable as a unit. One possible solution to this problem is to examine the temporal and rhythmic segmentation of letters when people spell words orally. If the representation of words from which they are spelled is speech-based or influenced by a phonological code (see Henderson, Hotopf, Chapters 5 and 13), then speech-based subjective segmentations should show themselves in the output of this information when 'read off' from the representation. A list of words was constructed with internal clusters comparable to most of the clusters in the previous lists. As far as possible these clusters did not correspond to morpheme boundaries. These words appear in Table 5.

TABLE 5   Words used to test syllabification hypothesis

petrol	elder	mattress	boulder
wardrobe	balcony	squadron	falcon
zebra	vulgar	cobra	amalgamate
public	writer	cobbler	enter
April	under	oppress	abandon
reply	member	topless	number
negro	temper	tigress	hamper
sacred	donkey	decree	tinker
reckless	anger	seclude	finger
piglet	crimson	igloo	damsel
melba	plimsole	Albert	samson
helping	panzer	palpitate	lenses
falter	pencil	Walter	fancy

Normal adult spellers were then asked to orally spell each one, starting their output as fast as possible after the word was uttered. If they had been allowed time before starting, they might have transferred all items held in a syllabically segmented form to an unsegmented list of letter names in a 'pre-output buffer' (Shaffer, 1976) and so mask any underlying structure. These responses were tape-recorded. The recordings were then played to another set of observers, with white noise added to impede the identification of the spoken letters. This second set of observers were asked to indicate where temporal or rhythmic breaks occurred (i.e. longer pauses). There was a large degree of agreement as to these boundaries. For the most part they were placed between the two consonants constituting the internal cluster in question. At this point it was only possible to test four of the original subjects, two of the adult illiterates and two of the children. They were asked to spell the words in this list. Out of 26 items, no subject made more than three

errors of deletion of the type made by that subject in equivalent initial
and terminal clusters, though they did reverse the order of the cluster
letters on several items. While this experiment is informal and the
validity of the techniques of construction are dubious, it does suggest
strongly that the views advanced in this section have relevance to the
spelling problem and to speech perception and production.

5 Conclusions and implications

5.1 Phonological features, phonological awareness and literacy

The two approaches presented above are essentially (*i*) that the
abnormal spellers code speech in the same way as normal adults, but
differ in their linguistic awareness, specifically in the recovery of
phonemes in particular contexts, and (*ii*) that the abnormal spellers
code speech differently from normal adults in that they are using a
different set of features which, due to the adult classification system are
not apparent in their speech but are manifested in their spelling. While
the latter hypothesis is favoured in that it accounts for specific aspects of
the data, it is not inconsistent with and does not exclude the general
aspects of the 'consciousness' hypothesis. Indeed the effect of 'subjective
syllables' indicates a synthesis of the two approaches. Since cluster
effects were decreased when clusters spanned two syllables, syllables
must be functionally segmented by these people. However in many of the
two-syllable words used to test the idea, the two phonemes would not
have been made more acoustically distinct than when in a single
syllable. Therefore it is most plausible that the effect is due to the syllable
serving as a basis for conscious segmentation. Thus while tacit assumptions about syllable structure allow acoustic and articulatory factors to
determine perception within syllables, they tend to prevent these factors
operating across subjective syllable boundaries.

Marshall and Morton (1978) have recently argued that linguistic
awareness is intimately involved in the development itself of the child's
speech feature system, although which is chicken and which is egg is not
clear. But more importantly, not enough attention, in fact hardly any,
is paid to the importance of linguistic awareness and phenomenal
consciousness in the acquisition of reading and spelling. I have discussed
this elsewhere (Marcel, 1978). But it is of note that most of the other
contributions to this book treat spelling and reading simply as aspects of
an information-processing system. That is, they ignore (*i*) the importance
of reflexive awareness in learning the 'nature of the game' in the first
place, and (*ii*) the fact that much spelling is an intentional activity as

opposed to merely being the output of a passive system. This is not to deny that there are automatic aspects of spelling. When I am writing this now my awareness is not at the level of the orthography, until an error is detected, and those chapters which deal with such automatic non-conscious processes in the skilled writer (e.g. Hotopf, Wing and Baddeley) cannot be faulted on this score. However, while the nature of the skilled system is very useful knowledge, and can serve usefully as a diagnostic tool and as theoretical language, it is hard to see how it can help us to teach, i.e. how to help a learner achieve that skilled state (see Marcel, 1978, for fuller discussion). What the theoretical discussions of the present problem have served to do is to emphasise the potential relevance to spelling research and analysis of two kinds of factors not normally discussed – (*i*) that the speller may have problems in conscious recovery of what is to be spelled, in what evercode it is represented (cf. the problem of *recovering* a visual code encountered by the patient in Morton's chapter), and (*ii*) that the speech code used by the speller may not be the same code as that used by the teacher.

The accounts presented in Sections 4.1 and 4.2 lead to an interesting speculation about reading and spelling in general. It is now commonly assumed that phonemic perception is a prerequisite for learning to read and spell with alphabetic writing systems. However the psychological validity of the phoneme as the actual 'unit' of perception and production is dubious (see Savin and Bever, 1970; Liberman *et al.*, 1967, for some associated problems). That rhyming, alliteration and language games, which appear to be based on the phoneme, exist in non-literate groups does not imply that the phoneme is their basis. It may just be that it is more convenient to think and explain in terms of phonemes than in terms of the featural variants from which phonemes are an abstraction. Indeed the phonetic distinctions of the acoustic signal that are made (i.e. are lexically significant) in any one linguistic environment are in a sense arbitrary. The allophones of /d/ which are significant in some African languages are not significant for us, and distinctions we make are irrelevant for others, such as /l/ and /r/ for Japanese. In this sense the acquisition of each language's adult phonology is a problem-solving process for the child. It can be argued that the ability to perceive in phonemic terms is necessary for the invention and understanding of an alphabet. However, although the alphabet is the most efficient way of reading and writing, Gelb (1963) has suggested that it has been invented only once in all history. This would imply that the representation of speech on which it relies (the phoneme) is rather unnatural. In whatever way the alphabet was first invented, it is possible that for each learner today, *the concept of the phoneme* (tacit if not explicit) *comes from rather than leads to the particular alphabetic system with which he or she is confronted.* This is an extremely important point whose implications for literacy and linguistic awareness need no emphasis.

5.2 *Practicalities*

For the people studied, what look like 'order errors' are not due to an impairment to their representation or memory of order, but to their having no consciously accessible basis (phonemic) at all for allotting one of the letters to its proper location in the first place. The problem is that in many of the current analyses and assessments of spelling the status of categories such as 'order errors' is doubtful. The categories used appear to aspire to be atheoretical. But this is the problem – descriptive categories cannot avoid implying theories. What I am pleading for is that categories should be explicitly seen as diagnostic rather than 'descriptive'. Most current spelling tests seem to be compiled on a normative basis (e.g. of an item's difficulty or predictive value) and the analyses of the errors are *post hoc*. Since this limits their classificatory or heuristic utility, one is led to wonder what their pedagogic value is.

Lastly, it is important to draw attention to techniques of teaching spelling. When we first searched for the abnormal spellers in the two adult literacy courses, we could only find them in the original class. But at that time we only looked at spelling of real words. When we included spelling of dictated non-words, we immediately identified three people in the second class. One of the main differences between the courses is teaching methods. In the first, the ethos was to encourage if not insist that pupils 'listen to the sound of what they said'. For the people examined here, since they appear to have an inadequate phonological representation, phonological techniques can hardly be expected to help. The critical words provided a continuing problem. In the second class, one of the main methods of teaching people with continuing difficulty was to adopt visual techniques based on the suggestions of Fernald (1943), Hillerich (1977) and Peters (1975). One of these, for example, is short-term visual memorisation, which encourages rote learning of a visual memory of the spelling of certain words. Of course it is hardly useful to apply this technique to items other than real words. But this is what they appeared to have been helped with. It is only when these people have to rely on sound, which they are forced to do with non-words, that we might expect errors of phonology. I am not advocating that visual techniques should replace phonological techniques. Far from it. As far as is possible with a given language, phoneme-grapheme rules are a powerful tool to donate. The point is that, until we know how to alter the cognitive state of learners (e.g. remediate problems such as the present one), what is taught and how it is taught must be matched to the learner as he or she is. To obtain the diagnostic tools to describe the individual learner appropriately is a prime task for psychology.

Acknowledgements

I would like to acknowledge the help given to me by the following people: Margaret Hatfield, Tricia McLoughlin and Corinne Garvie of the Speech Therapy Department at Addenbrooke's Hospital; The Cambridge Education Authority; Anita Jackson, Margaret Peters, Judy Kornfeld and Uta Frith.

18

Spontaneous Spelling by Language-Disordered Children

RICHARD F. CROMER   *MRC Developmental Psychology Unit, London, England*

405

Most of the investigations that have been made into the processes used in spelling have been carried out by examining the spelling errors of normal children or children with reading difficulties. From the error patterns observed, various processes are inferred which the children are thought to use in generating their responses. However, the evidence for these processes is indirect. By extending these studies to groups with known deficits it may be possible to find more direct evidence of underlying processes used in spelling. This is because particular defects may prevent particular spelling strategies from being used. At the same time, however, these very defects may result in the adoption of certain other spelling strategies, and these might serve as clues to the nature of more basic deficits.

The main purpose of this study, then, is to examine and compare the spelling of various groups of linguistically handicapped children. Since the spelling of some of these groups of children has not been studied before, and especially since one of these conditions is rare, the complete list of spelling errors is given in the appendix to this chapter. This will enable any interested reader to re-classify, re-interpret, and otherwise make use of the data.

1 The study

1.1 *The five groups of children*

Five groups of children were tested. The main group of interest is a receptive aphasic group (R), composed of six totally aphasic children. Their ages at the time of the study ranged from 7:6 to 16:1, with a median age of 12:0. These children can neither comprehend nor produce oral language. Two of the children are what are termed 'developmentally aphasic' in that they never possessed language. The remaining four had developed some language before deterioration, for unknown reasons, occurred. The ages of onset of language deterioration of these four children were 3:6, 4:0, 4:6 and 5:0.[1] It cannot be too strongly

[1] The data were originally collected in order to study the linguistic structures used by various language-disordered groups. It should be noted that the receptively aphasic children reported here are a sub-set of those reported in Cromer (1978a, b). Two of the children reported in the earlier studies had some small hearing loss. These children are not included here. Furthermore, in those earlier studies of linguistic structure, it was necessary to eliminate children who had only produced lists of words or who produced writings so disorganised linguistically that the language structure could not be analysed. While they were eliminated from those analyses, they were nevertheless included here since the present interest is in their spelling, not their sentence structure. For these reasons the median ages and ages of onset reported here differ slightly from those in the earlier reports since some of the actual children included differ.

emphasised that these children are of a special type, not to be confused with so-called 'aphasic' children found in most studies in the literature. Many children with varying types and degrees of language disorder have been labelled 'aphasic'. By contrast, the children in this group are totally aphasic. Either from birth or from an early age they have neither comprehended nor produced language, although most of them can produce and comprehend single words which are semantically correct in the sense of being appropriate to the situation. They are bright and interested and give the appearance of being frustrated by their lack of communicative ability. In addition, they meet the four criteria used by Griffiths (1972) to provide a working definition of developmentally aphasic children: the failure of the normal growth of language function when deafness, mental deficiency, motor disability and severe personality disorder can be excluded.

Although these children are not necessarily alike in their abilities, they nevertheless share the crucial feature that they are essentially languageless, at least in terms of oral comprehension and production. The children in this special group have, however, been taught to read and write, but they are still handicapped in these abilities. The linguistic analyses that have been made on their written language (Cromer, 1978a, b) suggest an underlying cognitive deficit which may be partly responsible for or at least associated with their language disorder. In other words, their disability manifests itself not only in oral language, but in their written language. It may even affect performance on other, non-verbal tasks (Cromer, 1978c). This is in contrast to theories that have proposed that their deficit is specifically auditory in nature (Eisenson, 1968; Mark and Hardy, 1958; Rosenthal, 1972; Tallal and Piercy, 1975).

A second group can be called the expressive (or executive) aphasic group (E), and is composed of five children who have an expressive language disorder but whose comprehension is relatively unaffected. The age range of these children is 8:5 to 12:0, with a median age of 12:8. A third group, the speech-disordered group (S), is composed of six children with a variety of expressive speech disorders including dyspraxia for speech and neurological dysarthria. The ages of these children range from 10:8 to 14:3 with a median age between 12:11 and 13:0. All three groups, R, E and S, are from the same residential school for children with language disorders. They are thus from a common daily environment, and are exposed to the same teaching methods.

A group of six congenitally profoundly deaf children (D) were obtained from a class of 10-year-olds in a school for the profoundly deaf. Their ages ranged from 9:11 to 10:8, with a median age of between

10:5 and 10:6. Hearing loss varied from 90 to 120 dbs. Finally, six children were randomly chosen from a class of 9½ to 10½-year-olds in a normal school to form the group of normals (N). All of the children in the five groups were of normal intelligence – as ascertained from non-verbal tests of intelligence in the case of the various language-disordered groups and the deaf.

1.2 *Methodological considerations*

Much of the research on spelling is based on standardised spelling tests or on the use of specific words that children are asked to spell. Usually the child attempts to write words that have been spoken by an examiner, and an analysis is made of the amount and types of spelling errors that he makes. Such testing, in spite of yielding data relatively more amenable to analysis than spontaneously written samples, nevertheless has an important drawback. The child, it can be argued, by having first heard a spoken form, may be more likely to attempt to encode that form by sound-to-graph correspondence strategies than by other possible means. These sound-based strategies, which in the remainder of this article will be termed 'phono-graphical' patterns, may not necessarily be the only manner by which the child spells in his spontaneous writing. Differences among groups of children with various types of language disorders may thus be masked in analyses based on the collection of spelling samples by such means. It is of some interest, then, to study the spelling of language-disordered children without the bias introduced by having the child first hear the word. This is especially important in this study where the interest is not so much in the spelling errors themselves but in the light such errors may throw on the processes which these children use in coping with a language-related task – and these processes may differ from one type of language-disordered group to another.

One of the main problems in analysing spontaneous spelling data is that of equating in some manner the words used by the subjects. In the present study, this problem was addressed by using a standardised experimental procedure. Small groups of children watched silent, non-verbal puppet shows.[1] The puppet shows were carefully designed to elicit various morphological and sentential structures. Each show lasted for approximately two minutes and contained from four to five animals engaged in a number of actions with various material props. At the conclusion of each puppet show, the children were instructed to write a

---

[1] Further details of the administration and content of the puppet shows can be found in Cromer (1978a, b). I would like to thank Maria Black, a linguistics student, who helped with the administration of these shows.

description of the story they had just seen enacted. They were given as much time to write their descriptions as they wanted. This usually ranged from 30 to 45 minutes. At the beginning of the first puppet show, the four hand puppets were introduced and the name of each was written on the blackboard. Thus the child had in front of him, written as a list on the blackboard, the words 'a wolf, a monkey, a duck, a duck'. This constituted the only verbal or written aid to the child.[1] The second show consisted of a number of small toy animals moved through the actions of the plot. The names of the animals were not given, and nothing was shown in written form on the blackboard. Again, the children were allowed as much time as they wanted to write their description of the story.

1.3 *Predictions*

Both the receptive aphasics and the deaf are primarily learning language 'by eye'. In its written form, they are thus more likely to be influenced by the visual shapes of the words. It was therefore predicted that both of these groups would have relatively more spelling errors that could be classified as visual errors, than the other three groups, E, S and N.

Although the deaf and the receptive aphasic children are alike in certain respects in that the language input they receive is primarily visual, they may differ in crucial ways in the use they can make of that input. Any language problems the deaf have are secondary to their auditory disorder. It has been argued that the deaf can make use of a phonological code even when their input is visual (Dodd, Chapter 19). If this is true, then the deaf children in this study should make a sizeable proportion of phono-graphic spelling errors. This should be true as well of the receptive aphasic children if their problem is also purely auditory as some theorists have suggested. However, I have argued that the receptive aphasic children, in contrast to the deaf, have a language problem due to processes more basic than a purely auditory defect (Cromer, 1978a, b). If this is true, the formation of a true phonological code would be affected, and this would result in fewer phono-graphical spelling errors than the deaf and other groups.

[1] Originally, the project was not concerned with spelling abilities. During one testing session with the group of receptively aphasic children, two children indicated that they would like a word finger-spelled for them. This was allowed. It did not, however, affect the spelling results. One of these children was eliminated from the analysis since it was found that he had some hearing loss. The other child, in spite of having the word FRIGHTENED finger-spelled for him, nevertheless spelled it incorrectly when he wrote it. It is important to note in this regard the large number of incorrect spellings by children in all groups of the words WOLF, MONKEY and DUCK, even though these were clearly written on the blackboard in front of them.

Finally, since both the expressive aphasic and speech-disordered groups are characterised by problems with production, it was predicted that the quality of their phono-graphic errors would differ from the other groups. Phono-graphic errors by children in other groups should be found generally to represent the sounds of the intended word. By contrast, it is predicted that the phono-graphic errors by the E and S groups will be less accurate in representing their target words.

2 Spelling error differences

Each of the stories written by the child was scored separately. A count was made of the total *different* words used in the story. The number of *different* spelling errors was then noted. Thus, if the same word was identically mis-spelled again and again by the child, it was only scored once. The different words and different errors were summed across stories, and the errors were scored as a percentage of the total number of different words attempted. Table 1 shows the numbers and mean percentages of mis-spelled words by the five groups. It can be seen that the means of the R and D groups are lower than the E and S groups and differ significantly from them (Mann-Whitney U $= 21.5$, p < 0.005, 1-tail). But neither of these combined groups differs significantly from the N group. The normal group contains both good and poor spellers and thus overlaps with both extremes.

TABLE 1   Total numbers of different words attempted, total number of different mis-spelled words, and mean precent of different words mis-spelled by the five groups of children

Group	n	Total no. of different words	Total no. of different mis-spellings	Mean % of mis-spelled words
Receptive	6	376	23	6.18
Deaf	6	456	30	6.39
Normal	6	733	101	14.20
Expressive	5	179	45	23.29
Speech-disordered	6	865	188	25.52

These differences can be seen more clearly by classifying each individual child as regards his spelling ability. This was defined in terms of the five categories shown in Table 2. If the groups are combined as before, then 75% of R and D children are good or fair spellers, as are

66.7% of N children. But only 18.2% of E and S children are good or fair spellers. This low percentage differed significantly from the others (p < 0.01, compared to R and D, and p < 0.05 when compared to N). None of the children in the R and D groups are poor or very poor spellers, but 33.3% of the N children are (p < 0.05). And 54.5% of the E and S children are poor or very poor spellers (p < 0.01 when compared to the R and D group).

TABLE 2   Classification of spelling ability in the five groups

Classification (% errors)	Number of children in each group				
	R	D	N	E	S
Good (0–5)	3	2	1	1	1
Fair (5–10)	1	3	3	0	0
Middling (10–15)	2	1	0	2	1
Poor (15–20)	0	0	1	0	1
Very poor (20+)	0	0	1	2	3

In summary, the receptive aphasic and deaf children, like many normal children, were good or fair spellers, whereas very few expressive aphasic or speech-disordered children were. More interestingly, none of the receptive aphasic and deaf children were poor or very poor spellers. In this, they differed significantly from both the normals and the expressive aphasic and speech-disordered children. In other words, receptively aphasic and deaf children tended to be good spellers; expressively aphasic and speech-disordered children tended to be poor and even very poor spellers. And the group of normal children contained both good and poor spellers as might be expected of the 'normal' population at large. This, incidentally, can be taken as an indication that the present sample was representative in this regard. It might seem strange that the very group that is most impaired in language (R), as well as the deaf, were good at spelling. Some hints as to why this may be so can be found in an analysis of the spelling errors that were made.

3 Analysis of spelling errors

Rather than differences in level of spelling, the question of main interest was whether the groups differed in the quality of their spelling errors.

Therefore, each mis-spelled word was categorised into one of seven major categories:[1]

1 *Phono-graphical errors:* The mis-spelled word resembles in some respect the sound of the target word when pronounced. An example of an error judged to be similar in sound is CAIM for CAME. This category of spelling error is in fact composed of several sub-types as shown in the Appendix.

2 *Visual errors:* These errors preserve the general shape or look of the word, where pronunciation would not lead to a similar sound (e.g. ENOUGTH for ENOUGH, and THSES for THERE). This category is also composed of several sub-categories as shown in the Appendix.

3 *Morphological errors:* These errors have to do with problems in the morphological form of the word. An example would be LAUGHTED for the target word LAUGHED.

4 *Spelling rule errors:* Errors categorised here include suffix-adding rules (e.g. CHASEING for CHASING), doubling rules for final letters (e.g. BITTING for BITING), the end-*e* rule (e.g. BITE for BIT), and other arbitrary spelling conventions.

5 *Segmentation errors:* The main problem with these words is an incorrect segmentation, usually one word written as two, as in A WAY for AWAY.

6 *Form errors:* Here, the main error is in the form of an individual letter or letters, as in *b*/*d* letter reversals.

7 *Unclassifiable:* This waste basket category mainly was composed of either illegible words or of words for which no logical target word seemed discoverable.

Within the context of known stories, it was fairly easy to identify the intended target for most mis-spelled words. All spelling errors were listed followed by their assumed target word. Two judges then classified these words in terms of what they felt to be its single major error.[2] On initial scoring, the overall agreement between the judges on the 507 mis-spelled words was 84.2%. The words on which the two judges differed were then discussed until they agreed as to the major error. A complete list of all the errors as classified into each category can be found in the Appendix to this chapter.

The error types for each child were scored in terms of the percentage of his total errors, since some children made few and some made many

[1] Most of these major categories were in fact made up of several sub-categories. However, too few errors in each sub-category made such a fine-grained analysis not worthwhile, and only the overall categories will be considered here with the exception of a later breakdown of the phono-graphical errors.

[2] I would like to thank Margaret Snowling for her help in scoring the error types.

overall errors (range = 0–54). Since these scores were then analysed to see whether the error patterns differed from one another by group, children with two or fewer errors were then eliminated from this analysis. This was necessary because, for example, a child with only one spelling error would put a weight of 100% into the entry for error types for which he made his one error. This constraint resulted in the elimination of two receptive aphasic children, two deaf children, and one expressive aphasic child.

Table 3 shows the mean percent of errors of each major error type made by children in the five groups. It can be seen that the R group have fewer phono-graphical errors than the other groups. The mean percent phono-graphical errors by the R group, 38.50, differs significantly from the overall mean of the children in the other four groups,

TABLE 3 Mean percent of spelling errors of each major error type by children in five groups

	Error types						
	Phono-graphical	Visual	Morphological	Spelling rule	Segmentation	Form	Unclassifiable
R (n = 4)	38.50	15.50	0	31.25	0	5.50	9.00
D (n = 4)	62.25	15.75	8.25	13.75	0	0	0
N (n = 6)	56.67	2.08	1.50	27.92	11.50	0	0.67
E (n = 4)	59.50	4.00	0	13.50	3.12	2.00	17.50
S (n = 6)	61.50	11.00	1.33	4.33	9.00	0.33	12.00

59.80 (Mann-Whitney U = 12, p < 0.025, 1-tail). None of the means of these other four groups (ranging from 56.67 to 62.25) differ significantly from one another.

It can also be seen that both the R and the D groups appear to make higher percentages of visual errors than the other groups, but this is based on too few errors to analyse for statistical significance. There is further evidence, however, that the R and D groups are using a visual code for their spelling more often than the other groups. If in writing one is making use of the visual characteristics of the word, there should be few errors in segmentation. Again, Table 4 shows that no child in the R and D groups ever made this type of error, while some children in all other groups did make such errors.

Other error types shown in the table were made up of too few errors to make a meaningful comparison, with the exception of arbitrary spelling rule errors. Only normal children consistently made a fair number of spelling errors of this type, with all normal children contributing to the overall percentage. In all other groups, some children never made

such errors, while some children made a few, generally less than normal
children. The high percentage in the R group is due to one child, all of
whose spelling errors were of this type.

It was predicted that children with productive speech and language
difficulties (the S and E groups) would be less accurate in representing
their target words than would be children in the other groups. In order
to assess this, the errors in the phono-graphical category were sub-
divided into three major sub-types. Errors were rated as phono-
graphically similar if in general they preserved the sound of the target
word. By contrast, errors were classified as phono-graphically distant if
they varied more widely from the sounds of the target word. The third
category within the phono-graphical error type was composed of syllable
omissions and syllable transpositions. It was found that no rigorous
definition of similarity in terms of number of phonological differences
seemed subjectively adequate to capture the notion of phono-graphical
similarity and distance. Therefore, the 107 errors in these two categories
were systematically randomised and given to three judges with no training or experience in spelling analysis. Their task was merely to give
what they supposed to be the target word of the child for each error.
The errors were typed in columns and were thus out of context except
that each judge was given a verbal synopsis of the two puppet shows so
that he would be familiar with the types of materials the children were
describing. The rationale was that errors which had earlier been classified as phono-graphically similar should be close enough in sound to
the target word to yield a significantly greater likelihood of judges
identifying the target than errors that were phono-graphically distant.
This was upheld. The three judges correctly identified 65.8%, 65.8%
and 71.2% of the phono-graphically similar targets, but only 2.9%,
5.9% and 5.9% of the phono-graphically distant targets. This appears
to validate the subjectively defined notion of phono-graphical similarity
and distance.

Children in the R and D groups *never* made phono-graphically distant
errors. In this respect they differed significantly from the N, E and S
groups respectively (Mann-Whitney $U = 8$, $p < 0.025$, 1-tailed; $U = 4$,
$p < 0.025$, 1-tailed, and $U = 4$, $p < 0.005$, 1-tailed). The mean percents
of phono-graphical errors that were phono-graphically distant for the
E and S groups were 16.67 and 16.50, and while these were higher than
the mean for the normal children, 10.67, these three groups did not
differ significantly from one another. Thus, the prediction that children
with productive speech and language difficulties might experience more
difficulty in their phonological code as reflected in a greater percentage
of phono-graphically distant spelling errors was only partially upheld

in that they had significantly more errors than receptively aphasic and deaf children. But they did not significantly differ in this respect from the children in the normal group.

4 Discussion

The study of spelling errors in various groups of language-disordered children may be useful in highlighting processes they use in more general language tasks. In this study, it was found that receptively aphasic children and profoundly deaf children, in spite of being at a lower level of language competence than normals and than other groups of language-disordered children, nevertheless evidenced significantly fewer spelling errors than these other groups in their spontaneous writings in standardised situations. This at first appears paradoxical, but it may reveal something of the nature of the way these two groups deal with language input. The error analysis revealed that both the receptive aphasic and the deaf children seemed to rely slightly more on vision for their spelling patterns than children in the other groups. This was evidenced both in their greater number of visually similar errors and in the fact that they never made segmentation errors. However, these two groups themselves differed. The receptively aphasic children can hear (all children with any hearing loss had been carefully excluded from the group) and the profoundly deaf children cannot. Yet the profoundly deaf appear to make as much use of a phonological code, as reflected in phono-graphical spelling errors, as the normal children and children in the speech-disordered and expressive aphasic groups. This lends support to Dodd's claim (Chapter 19) that profoundly deaf children can indeed construct and make use of a phonological code. By contrast, only the receptively aphasic children make significantly fewer errors of a phono-graphical type. One possible interpretation is that they are less adept at using any kind of phonological code. It is important to notice that 'phonological' is a *linguistic* term, and not based on acoustic properties alone. That is, the possession of a phonological code implies the ability to make linguistically relevant categorical judgments based on sound-related differences in whatever manner or modality these are perceived. That the profoundly deaf appear to construct such a code means that their problem is not a linguistic deficit in the deeper sense of that term. The receptively aphasic children in this study, however, evidence some deficit in this regard. If this is true, then some doubt is cast on theories of receptive developmental aphasia which claim that the deficit is specifically auditory in nature.

It must again be emphasised that the receptive aphasic group of children in this study is a very special group. What most other studies in the literature refer to as aphasic children would in fact be included mainly in the expressive aphasic or speech-disordered groups studied here. There is great difficulty in finding children who fit the full definition of receptively developmentally aphasic children as defined in this study. Indeed, there were only a handful in the south of England who were so completely aphasic without known traumatic injury and yet had normal intelligence, no hearing loss, and no motor disability or personality disorder that could be construed as possibly causal of their condition. This was originally the group of interest in this study, and the control groups were limited to similar numbers. Thus, the comparisons and conclusions are based on very small numbers – a total of 29 children in the five groups. It is therefore necessary to view the results with caution and to treat these findings as tentative.

5 Appendix: corpus of spelling errors

Below are listed all of the spelling errors by major and subordinate categories. The assumed target, from context, is shown in parentheses. '?' indicates either problems of legibility or uncertainty concerning the assumed target. The letters and numbers following the parentheses indicate the group and child. Errors of the type RAN for the target RUN which appear occasionally, were only included when in context they were deemed to be true spelling errors and not due to faulty morphology on the part of the child.

1 Phono-graphical errors

1.1 *Phono-graphically similar*

Generally similar in sound
  (in British English pronunciation)

ERROR	TARGET		ERROR	TARGET
agae	(again) S5		caim	(came) S1
agang	(again) S6		caridg	(carriage) N3
agine	(again) E4		chaged	(chased) S2
alone	(along) S4		changed	(chased) S2
are	('oh' or 'ah') N1		choob	(tube) N3
baak	(back) S6		con	(come) S1, S6
basked	(basket) D1		conplane	(complain) S2
baskes	(basket) R3		continner	(container) E4
basking	(basket) D1		cud	(could) S5
begain	(began) S2		did'en	(didn't) D3
boles	(balls) N3		doun	(down) N3

ERROR	TARGET
dunk	(duck) S5
dust	(just) N3
emptey	(empty) E4
evreone	(everyone) S3
fate	(fight) S1
fome	(from) S1
foue	(four) S1
frighting	(fighting) S4
fritened	(frightened) R6
fritte	(fright) N1
gett	(get) S2
gom	(come) S1
has	(as) S2
his	(as) S2
hourse	(horse) D3
house	(horse) D5
imamgine	(imagine) N4
jumbed	(jumped) N6
kart	(cart) S2
lack	(like) S1
litll	(little) S5
lotss	(lots) N3
miky	(mickey) S2
momky	(monkey) S6
moncy	(monkey) N3
monekey	(monkey) R7
mongky	(monkey) N3
on	(and) S5
oun	(one ?) S5
owway	(always) S5
pik pom	(ping pong) S3
pord	(poured) N3
pult	(put) N3
roan	(round) E4
sow	(so) N3
sowe	(show) E1
ther	(they) E4, S1
there	(they) S5
thort	(thought) N3
thut	(thought) S5
tray	(try) E4
wald	(would) N3
wan	(when) S1
wend	(went) S6
wicid	(wicked) N3

ERROR	TARGET
woof	(wolf) D6
woof	(wolf's) D6
woted	(wanted) S5

Near homophones

ERROR	TARGET
off	(of) N4, S2
to	(too) N2, S4, S5
to	(two) R6, N1, N3, S3
two	(to) N5

Vowel substitutions

ERROR	TARGET
an	(in) S6
anuther	(another) N3
ap	(up) S1, S5
bay	(boy) E1
bean	(been) N3
beg	(big) S6
busket	(basket) D1
camal	(camel) N1
caw	(cow) S1
cheaky	(cheeky) S2
cilender	(cylinder) N2
creaped	(creeped) N3
fall	(fell) S2
fallow	(follow) D3
fallowed	(followed) D3
full	(fell) S6
gat	(get) S1
gat	(got) S1
got	(get) E5
it	(at) S2
iven	(even) N3
meny	(many) N3
nats	(nets) S6
nit	(net) S6
not	(net) S6
pack	(pick) E5
puck	(pick) E5
ran	(run) S2
se	(so) S6
sew	(saw) S1, S6

ERROR	TARGET	ERROR	TARGET
somo	(some) S1	son	(soon) S5
tabe	(tube) E2	soner	(sooner) S5
tamper	(temper) S2	sudenly	(suddenly) N3
tap	(top) S1	the	(then) N1, N2, N5
than	(then) S3	the	(there) S5
thes	(this) S1	the	(they) S5
thet	(that) S3	thee	(three) S1
tirid	(tired) R6	ther	(their) E2
uther	(other) N3	ther	(there) N1, E4, S1
wake	(woke) S2	to	(top) N2, S2
walf	(wolf) N3	wak	(weak) S1
wis	(was) E1	waking	(walking) N3
		wat	(what) N3
		were	(where) N1
		wich	(which) N6
		wof	(wolf) R7

Letter omissions

ERROR	TARGET
a	(and) S4
a	(at) E5
agan	(again) D5, N3
alon	(along) N3
alwas	(always) N 3
an	(and) S2
belive	(believe) N5
came	(camel) R2
carrige	(carriage) N6
cat	(cart) R7
com	(come) D3
empted	(emptied) S4
for	(four) N3
frend	(friend) N3
gon	(gone) N3, S5
hevier	(heavier) N3
hevy	(heavy) N3
insted	(instead) N1
is	(his) S2, S6
me	(met) N2
meet	(met) S3
mischif	(mischief) N3
mokey	(monkey) D5, S5, S6
monky	(monkey) R2, N2, N3
nice	(nicer) S2
now	(know) S5
plese	(please) S3
quck	(quack) R6
som	(some) S6

1.2 *Phono-graphically distant*

ERROR	TARGET
a	(up) N2
aagmints	(argument) S3
a gold	(again) S1
anoy	(another) S5
argy	(angry) S2
backt	(basket) E2
dolis	(balls) E1
eept	(empty) E4
ented	(emptied) N1
exeted	(except) N1
feelableness	(feebleness) S2
gate	(cart) S1
gute	(cart) S1
happe	(help) S1
harde	(helped) S1
havre	(heavy) S5
hope	(help) S6
many	(monkey) S6
miscefers	(mischievous) N3
nall	(? now) S1
palls	(pulling) S6
pallse	(pull) S6
palt	(put) N3
sate	(chased) S1
some	(saw) S5

ERROR	TARGET		ERROR	TARGET
sow	(soon) S5		it	(in) S6
the	(that) S5		monkeg	(monkey) R7
to groud	(around) D2		nok	(know) S5
tot	(top) N6		now	(down) S5
use	(was) S6		peel	(? fell) S2
warth	(with) S1		runis	(runs) R6
we	(was) S5		soms	(some) S1
we	(when) S2		standed	(started) S3
you	(who) S1		thses	(there) E1
			wife	(wire) S1

1.3 *Sound-related syllable errors*

Syllable omissions

ERROR	TARGET
cinder	(cylinder) S2
gine	(again) E4
imaging	(imagining) S5
long	(along) E4
mines	(minutes) E4
rembered	(remembered) S2
suddley	(suddenly) D6
ther	(other) E4

Syllable transpositions

ERROR	TARGET
amanals	(animals) D3
amanls	(animals) D3
molar	(moral) S3

2 Visual errors

2.1 *General visual errors*

ERROR	TARGET
chacse	(chase) E4
eeg	(egg) S5
eegs	(eggs) S5
egg	(eye) S5
enougth	(enough) N4
finth	(fight) S3
fired	(friend) S5
firind	(friend) S6

2.2 *Letter transpositions*

ERROR	TARGET
atfer	(after) S5
crat	(cart) S6
korss	(cross) S6
loin	(lion) D5
naer	(near) S5
sotp	(stop) R6
tried	(tired) D4, S2
wofl	(wolf) S6

2.3 *Other order errors*

ERROR	TARGET
arothe	(other) E4
beaucse	(because) D3
saw	(was) S6
sorty	(story) R7
surpisered	(surprised) D1
tairn	(train) S3
thougth	(thought) S3

3 Morphological errors

ERROR	TARGET
angar	(angry) S3
founded	(found) S2
frighted	(frightened) D6
laughted	(laughed) D6
slowlyer	(slower) N2

4 Spelling rule errors

4.1 *Suffix-adding rules*

ERROR	TARGET
biger	(bigger) S5
bitting	(biting) R2, R4, N2
bravly	(bravely) S2
chaseing	(chasing) R4, E2, E4
emptyied	(emptied) N5
fliing	(flying) N1
gating	(getting) S5
geting	(getting) R4, S5
heavyer	(heavier) N6
hidding	(hiding) S2
neting	(netting) N3
ploded	(plodded) S2
poped	(popped) N1
puting	(putting) R4, E4, S5
stoped	(stopped) N5
storys	(stories) N4

4.2 *End-e rule*

ERROR	TARGET
bake	(back) E4
bite	(bit) D1, D2, D3, D4, D6, E4
chas	(chase) N3
don	(done) N3
duke	(duck) E4
dukes	(ducks) E4
hom	(home) S1
tak	(take) S1

4.3 *Spelling conventions*

ERROR	TARGET
acros	(across) N3
animall	(animal) N4
beter	(better) N3
cammel	(camel) N6
puling	(pulling) N3
roled	(rolled) N3
tigger	(tiger) N2
wel	(well) N3

4.4 *Apostrophe rules*

ERROR	TARGET
arnt	(aren't) E4
ball's	(balls) N1
ball's'	(balls) N1
dont	(don't) S3
duck's	(ducks) N3
foxes	(fox's) N1
foxs	(fox's) N4
have'nt	(haven't) D3

5 Segmentation errors

ERROR	TARGET
a con	(again) S1
a cross	(across) S2
a gine	(again) E4
a long	(along) S2
alright	(all right) S4
a nuther	(another) N3
anymore	(any more) N2
any more	(anymore) E4
a wane	(away) S1
a way	(away) E4, S4
every thing	(everything) N4
in to	(into) N3, N4, N5, S1, S2, S3
some thing	(something) S5
with out	(without) N5

6 Letter form errors

ERROR	TARGET
buck	(duck) R6
dnck	(duck) E1
duck	(back) S1
hospilal	(hospital) R6

7 Unclassifiable

ERROR	TARGET
an	(?) S6
arer	(?) S1
bag	(? bad) E1

ERROR	TARGET	ERROR	TARGET
bol	(?) N3	?ow	(now?) S6
bole	(?) N3	p	(?) E1
cash	(chase? catch?) E5	paes	(?) S1
cdmd	(?) R6	ripid	(?) S2
charch	(chase? catch?) S5	sane	(?) S3
dan	(man?) E1	seond	(second? again?) S3
diga	(big?) E1	slid	(should) S5
drte	(?) E1	thing	(thought? think?) S5
duc?k	(duck?) S6	thro	(three? other?) S1
endadeing	(?) S1	waiht	(which?) S6
fon	(far?) S5	wain	(putting?) S1
frond	(floor? ground?) S3	wakkup	(?) S1
gat	(?) S6	wet	(?) S1
lav. 1	(?) E1	what	(went? walked?) S3
lu	(?) R2	whith	(?) S6
nafe	(another?) S1	whlf	(? Note: not 'wolf') S6
nearlly	(? Note: not 'nearly') S2	wnet	(?) S6

19

The Spelling Abilities of Profoundly Pre-lingually Deaf Children

BARBARA DODD   *MRC Developmental Psychology Unit, London, England*

Since the linguistic and academic competence of the deaf often shows severe retardation (Ivimey, 1977) one would also expect poor spelling performance. It is very surprising therefore that such empirical studies as have been done, suggest that the spelling abilities of the deaf are not retarded. In fact Gates and Chase (1926), Templin (1948), Hoemann *et al*. (1976) and Markides (1976) have found that they can spell remarkably well, and in some cases better than age-matched normally hearing children.

One simple explanation for this surprising finding put forward by Gates and Chase (1926) is that hearing may detract from spelling accuracy in languages lacking exact phonemic-graphemic correspondence. It is possible to argue that there are so few invariant phoneme-grapheme correspondences in English orthography that a phonological code for generalising spelling patterns is of little use. However, against this is the fact that there certainly are rules of phoneme-grapheme translation which are essential for the spelling of unfamiliar or nonsense words not seen or written before.

In an alphabetic system spelling rules provide a means for the graphic representation of sound. English orthography has developed a mixed method of grahpically symbolising speech. One level of representation is based on current pronunciation, and involves the ability to segment speech into abstract discrete sounds which can be translated into graphic symbols by use of 'regular' spelling rules. This ability may be primarily dependent upon a phonological code. The other level of representation is based on rules derived from past pronunciation, historical accident, syntax, etymology, etc. These rules are often thought to be dependent upon stored graphemic rather than phonemic information.

Research into the roles of graphemic and phonological information in the spelling abilities of hearing children seems to indicate that both sources are necessary for normal development. Boder (1973) identified a group of children from those referred for spelling and/or reading difficulties, who seemed unable to use phonological information (dysphonetic dyslexia). They were unable to analyse words phonetically. They were poor at reading nonsense and novel words, and when spelling they omitted syllables and added extraneous letters. Another group was identified who seemed unable to use graphemic information (dyseidetic dyslexia). These children could tackle nonsense words but had a very poor sight vocabulary. Nelson and Warrington (1974) also found that those dyslexic children with a linguistic deficit made phonologically poor errors, while others, without an apparent linguistic deficit, made phonologically good errors.

If both graphemic and phonemic information are necessary for normal reading and spelling development, one could hypothesise that deaf children, if they lack phonological information and exclusively rely on graphemic information, should perform like dysphonetic dyslexic children. However, there is little evidence for such a similarity. It is true that deaf children are often reported to have retarded reading abilities (e.g. Conrad, 1972a). However, there is evidence that some deaf children develop average reading skills (Markides, 1976) and Furth (1966) has argued that reading disability in the deaf is a symptom of their general linguistic incompetence rather than a specific consequence of deafness. Also, as already mentioned, many deaf subjects have been shown to develop at least average spelling abilities.

Day and Wedell (1972) investigated the types of spelling errors made by a group of normally hearing children with no special spelling difficulties. They divided the group into three sub-groups: those whose auditory memory was better than their visual memory, those whose auditory and visual memories were equal, and those whose visual memory was better than their auditory memory. There was no significant difference between the number of errors made by the three groups – only in the type of error made. Children whose auditory memory was superior, made more letter insertions, omissions or inversions of adjacent letters, children whose auditory and visual memories were equal applied the rules of phoneme-grapheme associations, and children whose visual memory was superior made more syllabic confusion errors. If the deaf rely heavily on graphemic memory they might perform like this last group. This hypothesis is supported by the following experiment. Conrad (1964) used a memory task to try to determine the type of memory code used by deaf children when remembering words. When he compared the type of confusions made by deaf and hearing children, he found that the deaf confused words that looked similar, whereas the hearing children confused words that sounded similar. Conrad concluded that the deaf were using a visual-alphabetic (i.e. graphemic) code for words.

The hypothesis is also supported by Hoeman et al. (1976) who examined the frequency of error types for deaf children, and compared these data with Mendenhall's (1930) for hearing children. For the deaf, omission errors were the commonest, followed by substitutions, transpositions and additions. The normal data showed substitution as the commonest error type, followed by omissions, additions and transpositions. However, the actual percentage scores for error types did not differ greatly between the two subject groups and Hoemann et al. concluded the pattern to be similar. They also reported that the deaf

produced only 19% phonetic errors (mis-spellings that could be pronounced the same as the correct spelling), a figure which contrasts
sharply with Mendenhall's data for normal subjects where about 75%
of the errors were phonetic mis-spellings. This would seem to indicate
that when reproducing spelling patterns for real words the deaf subjects
did not rely on phonological information, and/or phoneme-grapheme
rules. However, the fact that 19% of their errors were phonetic indicates
that some such information may have been used, and that an explanation solely in terms of a graphemic code is not wholly appropriate.

Gibson *et al.* (1970) found that when they presented nonsense words
which were either pronounceable (GLURCK) or non-pronounceable
(CKURGL), deaf subjects, like the normal controls, were able to remember
the pronounceable ones better. Since they assumed that sound mapping
(a phonological code) was not available to the deaf, they concluded that
they were using orthographic rules, which could not cope with illegal
spellings like CKURGL. This is not the same as using a graphemic code,
since this should not have resulted in a difference between the two
classes of stimuli. However, there is now evidence that profoundly pre-
lingually deaf children can use a phonological code. Recent experiments
have shown that errors which deaf and partially hearing children produce in spontaneous speech are consistently rule governed and follow
much the same pattern as that of young hearing children (Dodd, 1976;
Oller and Kelly, 1974; West and Weber, 1973). What type of information do profoundly pre-lingually deaf children use to develop a phonological system? A series of experiments (Dodd and Hermelin, 1977) was
carried out to try to determine whether deaf subjects who had acquired
a degree of skill in phonological processing which enabled them to
match homophones and identify rhymes were doing so on the basis of
written representations, kinaesthetic feedback from the vocal apparatus,
lexical information or lip read cues. The results indicated that the deaf
subjects were primarily dependent upon a visual input from lip reading.
Thus a phonological code can be abstracted from information in either
the auditory modality (hearing) or the visual modality (lip reading).

1 The relationship between spelling and speaking

It seems probable that if the deaf can use a phonological code which
allows them to develop a phonological system like that of young hearing
children, and hence to appreciate rhymes and match homophones, then
that phonological coding capacity might also be used for spelling tasks.
Speaking and writing, being the two most commonly used output pro-

cesses of language, should be closely related, since they express, in most languages, the same phonological, syntactic and semantic information. However, Avakian-Whitaker and Whitaker (1973) suggest that spelling, being a derived ability, is less automatic and makes greater demands on language mechanisms. It is less time-bound, allowing for the detection and correction of errors, and it is more conventionalised, permitting less free variation than speaking. For these reasons, they concluded that spelling behaviour provided a more direct representation of underlying phonological processes. Thus a spelling task which forces the use of a phonological code may provide a measure of phonological competence for the deaf. Further, a comparison of the two phonological output tasks, speaking and spelling, may provide information which will clarify the organisation of phonological processes in deaf children.

The nature of the relationship between spelling and speaking has not been extensively investigated, and what work exists is contradictory. Schonell (1934) found that if a child consistently pronounced inaccurately he not infrequently spelled inaccurately, and the nature of his written errors had a remarkable similarity to the nature of his spoken errors. Orton (1937) and Pass (1950) have reported the same finding. However, Carrell and Pendergast (1954) and Ham (1958) examined the relationships in terms of specific articulatory disorders, and found no direct link. Carrell and Pendergast (1954) found no specific relationship between errors of speech and errors of spelling for the articulatory disordered children, and when these children were compared with a control group of normally articulating children, it was found that they made the same number and type of spelling errors. Ham (1958) found that words which were mis-articulated were more likely to be mis-spelled than words pronounced correctly, but there was no relationship between the sound mis-articulated and the spelling error. The child who said WABBIT for RABBIT was more likely to spell it incorrectly than a child who pronounced it correctly, but the spelling error would not involve the *w*/*r* substitution.

Thus, the nature of the relationship between speaking and spelling is unclear and in need of further investigation. Similarly, the evidence regarding the type of codes deaf children are able to use for spelling tasks is limited, and far from unequivocal. The research, then, presented in this chapter examines three aspects of the spelling behaviour of some profoundly pre-lingually deaf children who have been educated by the oral method. It is concerned primarily with the coding mechanisms the subjects were able to use. The three questions asked were:

1 To what extent do deaf children normally use phonemic and graphemic information to generate spelling patterns for real words?

2   Can deaf children recode nonsense words presented in written form in a phonological code for memory storage?

3   Can deaf children spell nonsense words encoded phonologically by lip reading and, if so, does their written output match their spoken output of the same words?

2 Experiment 1

This experiment was designed to answer the question: to what extent do deaf children normally use phonological and graphemic information to generate spelling patterns for real words? Normally hearing children make fewer errors on words which have a direct phoneme-grapheme correspondence (e.g. PROBLEM) than they do on words which do not (e.g. STOMACH). This has been taken as an indication of the use of a phonological code for generating spelling patterns (Schonell, 1932). If the deaf do not use this phonological information, but rely heavily on a graphemic memory store, then they should make as many errors on words which are phonetically spelled as they do on words which are non-phonetically spelled.

2.1 *Subjects*

There were two groups of ten subjects. The normal subjects, who had a mean age of 14 years 7 months, attended a comprehensive secondary school in London; there were six girls and four boys. The profoundly deaf subjects, had a mean age of 14 years 6 months; there were five girls and five boys. Their mean hearing loss for the better ear was 99.3 dbs, range 87 to 114 dbs, over the speech range. The school the deaf children attended was a grammar school, and therefore the children were likely to be more academically competent than the average deaf adolescent, although all children were pre-lingually deaf.

2.2 *Procedure*

All subjects were tested on 18 words taken from the Schonell Spelling Test. Three words were randomly selected from each of the last three levels of Test 1A (Irregular words), i.e. non-phonetically spelled, and 1B (Regular words), i.e. phonetically spelled (see Table 1). The subjects were instructed to write down the words said (i.e. the deaf had to lip read the stimuli), when presented in a meaningful sentence frame. The total number of errors from this task was used to match the subject groups.

TABLE 1   Real word spelling test

Regular	Irregular
latest	purple
punish	poetry
remember	juice
unbroken	awful
problem	special
visited	stomach
unexpected	scissors
promotion	separate
instructed	receipt

2.3 Results

2.3.1 *Quantitative analysis*. An analysis of variance was carried out for the two subject groups and for the correct scores of the two types of words from the Schonell test. Since the groups had been matched on the total number of errors, the groups term was by definition non-significant. However, there was a significant difference between the number of errors made for phonetically and non-phonetically spelled words ($F = 9.1$; df = 1, 18; $p < 0.01$). There was also a Groups × Word Type interaction ($F = 6.4$; df = 1, 18; $p < 0.025$). Subsequent Newman-Keuls tests showed that normal children made fewer errors (12.2%) when spelling phonetically spelled words than when spelling non-phonetically spelled words (37.7%), at the 0.025 level of significance, whereas the deaf performed equally well when spelling the two different types of words (28.8% vs 27.2%).

2.3.2 *Qualitative analysis*. Any classification of spelling errors is arbitrary and arguable. However, it is possible to compare data from different subject groups in order to assess the similarity of error types made. The following categories were devised for the analysis:

Pure phonetic – errors which could arise from strict phoneme-grapheme association either for a whole word, e.g. PERPAL for PURPLE, or for part of a word, e.g. SPECAL for SPECIAL.

Context phonetic – errors which could arise from the implementation of higher order phoneme-grapheme rules, e.g. PROMOSION for PROMOTION where the rule /s/ before *ion* is sounded as / ʃ / as in PENSION.

Transpositions – errors where the correct letters were written but in the wrong order, e.g. RECIEPT for RECEIPT.

Additions and deletions of 1 or 2 letters – errors where letters were added or deleted which would *not* give rise to a phonetically plausible pronunciation, e.g. VISISTED for VISITED.

Refusals

Others

The data presented in Table 2 indicate that the major source of errors for the normal group were phonetic mis-spellings, whereas the major source of errors for the deaf were simple refusals.

TABLE 2   Types of errors made in the spelling of real words: mean % scores

Error types	Deaf	Normal
Pure phonetic	7.4	46.7
Context phonetic	3.7	8.9
Transpositions	5.5	6.7
Additions + deletions of 1 or 2 letters	7.4	17.8
Refusals	64.8	2.2
Others	11.1	17.8

The results, both quantitative and qualitative, confirm previous studies with hearing children. They relied heavily on direct phoneme-grapheme correspondence for generating spelling patterns for real words. They made more errors in words where this correspondence was not direct, and most errors were such as to establish a direct correspondence. In contrast, it was found that the deaf relied on a different strategy which resulted in an equal number of errors for words spelled phonetically and non-phonetically. Thus it would seem unlikely that the deaf were using phonologically coded information for this type of spelling task. Since the most common error type for the deaf subjects was a refusal to attempt words, despite encouragement to guess, there is no relevant data on which to base speculations about the type of alternative strategy used. However, it seems reasonable to assume, and consistent with previous studies (Conrad, 1972a; Hoemann *et al.*, 1976), that a graphemic code was used. The lack of difference between regular and irregular words could be explained by the use of such a code.

3 Experiment 2

This experiment asked the question: can deaf children be forced to recode nonsense words presented in written form, in a phonological code for memory storage? Obviously they can convert graphemes to phonemes because they can read words aloud, but this task may not require the capacity to store phonological information gained from reading.

The experimental method was devised to force the use of a phonological code in one condition, and the use of a graphemic code in another condition and also to elicit responses which would give an indication of what type of code the subjects were using. Thus, nonsense words had to be used since familiar words would already be stored in the preferred code. The nonsense words were either short or long, since visual memory is subject to a memory load effect (Paivio, 1971), and if a graphemic code is being used then short words should be remembered better than long words. The nonsense words were also either phonetically regular or irregular since, if a phonological code was being used, then words with unambiguous phonetic spelling should be remembered better than those with unusual phoneme-grapheme correspondence. With a graphemic code there should be no differences.

In order to manipulate the use of a particular code two interference tasks were used. In one condition the subjects were asked to perform an interference task involving phonological processes, which would hopefully force them to remember the experimental words in a graphemic store. In the other condition, the subjects were asked to perform an interference task involving graphemic processes, which would hopefully force them to remember the experimental words in a phonological store.

3.1 Subjects

The same children as in Experiment 1 acted as subjects for Experiment 2.

3.2 The stimuli

Two sets of 16 nonsense words were devised. In each set eight words could be generated unambiguously by phonetic spelling, e.g. PLAF, and eight words could not be generated unambiguously by phonetic spelling e.g. CHRISAL. These two sets correspond to regular and irregular words. Four of each type were short, consisting of four or five letters, and four of each type were long, consisting of six or seven letters (see Table 3). Each word was stencilled using a 10 mm stencil, in black ink on a 9 × 13 cm white card. These words were used for the experimental task. Another set of 50 nonsense words which had the same characteristics was prepared for the interference tasks.

TABLE 3   Nonsense words used in Experiment 2

'Regular'		'Irregular'	
Short	Long	Short	Long
plaf	bravel	fype	beraph
klug	herkon	phim	syntic
vust	methon	yigh	folumn
narg	glinst	kohn	yeight
frimp	prevend	moubt	whilper
steeg	cronide	wrike	koreign
shorm	fralomp	pyraf	chrisal
hinks	yoldern	knalk	schogar

3.3 *Procedure*

3.3.1 *Task 1: Remembering nonsense words after phonological interference.*
The subjects were told and shown in written form: 'I am going to show
you some nonsense words. They aren't real words, they are made up
ones. I want you to remember them, because you are going to have to
write them down – here. But before you write them down you have to
repeat other made up words that I will say'. Thus, the subject was
shown one of the experimental nonsense words and given time to read
it, i.e. about two seconds. He then repeated three other nonsense words
said by the experimenter from the 'Interference Pack'. The interference
task was timed as taking from 10 to 15 seconds. Subjects then had to
write down the words they had seen.

3.3.2 *Task 2: Remembering nonsense words after graphemic interference.*
The subjects were told: 'I am going to show you some nonsense words.
They aren't real words, they are made up ones. I want you to remember
them, because you are going to have to write them down – here. But
before you write them down you have to copy three other words that I
will show you'. Thus, the subject was shown one of the experimental
words, given time to read it, i.e. about two seconds. He was then shown
three words one at a time from the 'Interference Pack', and wrote them
down. This interference task was timed at between 15 and 20 seconds.

Subjects were given practice in both conditions before experimental
testing to familiarise them with the tasks. The order of presentation of
the two experimental packs of words, and the two conditions (phonological interference and graphemic interference) were randomised.
There were 16 trials per condition. Each child received both conditions
in balanced order.

3.4 *Results*

Since the levels of difficulty of the two types of interference were not controlled, and cannot therefore be considered equal, it is not meaningful to directly compare the amount recalled. Thus, each interference task will be considered separately.

3.4.1 *Remembering nonsense words after phonological interference.* An analysis of variance compared the ability of deaf and normal subject groups to remember regularly and irregularly spelled nonsense words after phonological interference. The results showed that the groups performed equally well (deaf 63%; normal 56%), and that there was no advantage for one of the word types, and no interaction between the subject groups and the types of words. However, another analysis of variance which compared the ability of the subject groups to remember short and long nonsense words revealed that both groups could remember the short words better than the long words (68% vs 51%; $F = 7.6$; $df = 1, 18$; $p < 0.025$). There was no interaction between the subject groups and word length.

3.4.2 *Remembering nonsense words after graphemic interference.* An analysis of variance compared the ability of the subject groups to remember regularly and irregularly spelled words after graphemic interference. The results showed no difference between the groups (deaf 39%; normal 38%), but both groups were able to remember how to spell the 'regular' words better than the 'irregular' words (46% vs 30%; $F = 15.0$; $df = 1, 18$; $p < 0.01$). There was no interaction between the subject groups and word type. A similar analysis compared the ability of the subject groups to remember how to spell short and long words. It revealed no significant differences; the groups performed equally well and there was no advantage for short words.

The results indicate that it was possible to manipulate the code in which nonsense words were stored for both groups of subjects by the use of interference tasks. When subjects could not use a phonological code to store the target words because of the interference task of imitating nonsense words vocally, they had to rely on some form of memory store where short words were remembered better than long words. Since the stimuli were nonsense words it is unlikely to include linguistic information, and was probably visual. Paivio (1971) found that sequential shortterm memory is less efficient than verbal memory, and thus, the subjects' ability to remember short words better than long words lends support to the hypothesis that the words were stored visually.

When children's visual memory was subjected to interference by asking them to copy nonsense words, they were forced to remember the target words in terms of a phonological code, and thus, those words which could be generated by direct sound-letter correspondence rules, e.g. PLAF, were better remembered than those which could not, e.g. CHRISAL. This result throws doubt on the conclusion of Gibson *et al.* (1970) that the deaf use an orthographic rather than a phonological code. An orthographic code would work equally well for all words in the present task, since both the 'regular' and 'irregular' nonsense words in the present experiment were orthographically legal (e.g. CHRISAL is legal, but CKURGL is not). Yet the deaf subjects were clearly better able to remember the words with direct grapheme-phoneme correspondence. This finding agrees with that of Chen (1973) who found that pronounceability was a predictor of learning trigrams for deaf subjects. She concluded that her deaf subjects were compensating for their lack of hearing by using information gained from lip reading experience. Therefore, there seems to be evidence that deaf subjects are able to use phonological information to remember spelling patterns, and that they naturally do so where a graphemic code is unavailable.

So far, the spelling tasks which can elicit the use of a phonological code in deaf subjects have all been memory tasks where the stimuli were presented in written form. A more convincing demonstration of the deaf children's ability to use a phonological code would be to ask them to write down nonsense words from a lip read stimulus, since in such a stimulus no graphemic information is available.

4 Experiment 3

This experiment asked the question: can deaf children graphemically represent nonsense words which they had to encode via lip reading, and if so, does their written output match their spoken output of the same words? Only those nonsense words were used that had an unambiguous phoneme-grapheme relationship.

4.1 *Subjects*

Twelve profoundly pre-lingually deaf children, with a mean age of 14 years 5 months, acted as subjects. They attended a secondary school for the deaf in London; there were eight boys and four girls. Their mean pure tone hearing loss for the better ear was 92 dbs, range 81 to 117 dbs over the speech range. The school encouraged the children to lip read and use spoken language.

4.2 *Procedure*

The subjects were told and shown in written form: 'I am going to say some words. They are not real words. They are nonsense words. Non-sense words are made up words, like PREEL. I want you to say the word that I say, and then write it down'. Practice trials were then given to familiarise subjects with the task, and to ascertain that they understood what was required. Subjects sat opposite the examiner across a three-feet wide table in a quiet room in the school building. The spoken responses were recorded, stereophonically, on a Uher Royal tape recorder.

4.3 *The stimuli*

The stimuli consisted of 24 legal nonsense words, 12 of which were of CCVC form, and 12 CVCC form.

4.4 *Scoring*

4.4.1 *Written response.* Since there were three consonants per word, each word was given a score out of 3, which indicated the number of consonants correctly represented, e.g. LISK for YISK would be scored as 2. Vowels were not scored since they are difficult to transcribe accurately. Either member of the voice/voiceless pairs (p/b, t/d, f/v, s/z) were scored as correct, since lip read inputs give no information about voicing, e.g. FUMP for VOMP would score 3. Where subjects interpolated an extra sound, e.g. SKELP for SKEL, a point was subtracted. Thus SKELP scored 3 for the inclusion of the letters $s\ k\ l$, but a point was subtracted for the p, leaving 2. Similarly, a point was subtracted for an extra 'consonant' syllable, e.g. LESHAIN for KLUSH scored 1.

4.4.2 *Spoken response.* A speech pathologist transcribed tapes of the subjects' spoken responses twice. Where disagreements occurred in the two transcriptions the tapes were listened to again and a decision made. Where it was impossible to be sure of a reliable transcription, the word was scored as 0. To gain a measure of reliability of the transcription, another judge transcribed two subjects, i.e. 48 of the words, chosen at random from the tapes. When the transcriptions were compared it revealed an agreement of 88.2%. The transcriptions of the children's utterances were analysed in the same way as were the written responses.

4.5 *Results*

4.5.3 *Quantitative analysis.* The mean number and range of consonants correctly represented when subjects were asked to spell and say nonsense words from a lip read input are shown in Table 4. There was no significant difference between the number of consonants correctly represented in the written and spoken conditions.

TABLE 4   Number of consonants correct

Possible score	Written response 72	Spoken response 72
Mean no. of consonants correct	29.4	33.4
Range	23–34	24–48

4.5.4 *Qualitative analysis.* A qualitative comparison of those consonants included in the written and spoken responses was made, and a difference score obtained for each word, for each subject. For example, one subject wrote TEEK but said /ti/ for the stimulus word STEEG, therefore the difference score was 1, since *k* occurred in the written response but was deleted in the spoken response. The mean difference score was 22.2 (total possible 72). Thus 30% of the actually presented consonants were correctly represented when the word was spoken – but not when written, or when written – but not spoken, i.e. there was a large mis-match between the two output conditions from a single lip read input.

In order to account for this mis-match the written and spoken responses were compared to determine whether or not the subjects were consistently representing sounds and clusters in one way when spelling but in another when speaking. A data summary appears in Table 5.

A series of related tests was performed on the raw data for each of the ten most frequently occurring phonological features listed in Table 5. They compared the most commonly used representations for these features given by a subject when writing and when speaking. When there was a significant difference in the quality of the responses in the written and spoken conditions, it is indicated by [1] in Table 5. The six features that showed such a difference are described below.

m. When the subjects were writing they were likely to represent *m* correctly, e.g. MULTH for MULTH, but when speaking the M was often substituted by *b*, e.g. /bʌlθ/ for MULTH (t = 3.7; df = 11; p < 0.01).

kl clusters. When subjects were writing they reduced the *kl* consonant cluster to *l* frequently, e.g. LUG for KLUG, but when speaking they often reduced the cluster to *k*, e.g. /kʌg/ for KLUG (t = 2.5; df = 11; p < 0.05).

s + C initial clusters. The most common cluster reduction strategy for both written and spoken responses was to represent *s* + C consonant clusters by the C, e.g. TEEG for STEEG. However, when writing subjects chose to represent the cluster by *s*, e.g. SATH for SLATH significantly more often than when speaking (t = 3.02; df = 11; p < 0.025). With *s* + C final clusters the pattern of errors was similar for written and spoken responses.

TABLE 5   Percentage scores: qualitative analysis of written and spoken responses

Feature	Written response			Spoken response		
	Correct	Preferred substitute	Other substitutes	Correct	Preferred substitute	Other substitutes
/m/						
*m*ulth, sna*m*, *m*ilt	64¹	*b* = 28	8	28	*b* = 67	5
/k/ clusters		*k* = 11				1= 25
*kl*ong, *kl*ug, *kl*ush	17	1 = 50¹	other = 22	22	*k* = 42	other = 11
/s + C/ clusters, initial		*s* = 38¹			*s* = 23	
*s*teeg, *sk*el, *sn*am,						
*sl*ath	10	C = 42	10	10	C = 44	23
/s + C/ clusters, final			*s* = 6			*s* = 8
shu*sp*, yi*sk*, da*sp*, yi*st*	10	C = 56	other = 28	17	C = 56	other = 19
Final velars /k, g/						
stee*g* klu*g*, tro*g*	61	ø = 25¹	14	44	ø = 50	6
nasal + C clusters		C = 31	total cl		C = 28	total cl
vo*mp*, ga*nk*, cha*nk*	8	nasal = 42¹	ø = 19	22	nasal = 8	ø = 42
/C + r/ clusters		C = 28			C = 8	
th*r*ib, *pr*uv, t*r*og	36¹	*r* = 22	14	67	*r* = 14	11
/f, b + l/ clusters		C = 17			C = 38	
*fl*un, *bl*oot	79		4	54		8
/l + C/ clusters		*l* = 6			*l* = 23	
the*ld*, go*lsh*, mi*lt*,						
mu*lth*	6	C = 35	53	15	C = 31	31
/p, b/						
*p*ruv, *b*loot	96	*m* = 4		92	*m* = 4	4

¹ Significant difference between written and spoken responses. C, consonant; ø, deletion; cl, cluster.

Final velar *k, g*. While there was no significant difference between the number of correct representations of *k, g* finally for the two conditions, if subjects made an error, than it was more likely to be a deletion, e.g. /tro/ for TROG, when speaking, than when writing (t = 3.00; df = 11; p < 0.025).

Nasal and C clusters. When writing subjects most frequently represented nasal and consonant clusters by the nasal, e.g. vom for vomp, but when speaking they were likely to delete the entire cluster, e.g. /gæ/ for gank (t = 3.63; df = 11; p < 0.01).

C + r clusters. When speaking subjects were more likely to represent C + r clusters correctly, than when writing.

4.6 Discussion

The results show that profoundly pre-lingually deaf children can use a phonological code to generate spelling patterns for nonsense words. This must be so since they could encode visual (lip read) information and represent it in articulatory and graphemic forms. They reached an impressive level of performance with only lip read nonsense stimuli. When they made errors these were, for most phonological features, highly consistent and sometimes appeared to reflect output strategies rather than perceptual difficulties. For example, it is often assumed that the cause of the deaf's frequent substitution of /b/ for /m/ in spontaneous speech (Dodd, 1976) is the inability to perceptually distinguish between the bilabial sounds /p, b, m/. However, the comparison of written and spoken outputs from a single lip read input shows that subjects frequently represented /m/ and /b/ correctly when spelling, but when speaking both were articulated as /b/.

Thus, there is a mis-match between perception and production in the phonological systems of the deaf. This mis-match between perceptual and productive abilities is still a controversial topic in the theoretical discussions of young normal children's phonological development, although it seems generally accepted that perceptual distinctions precede productive distinctions (Ingram, 1976). Since there is evidence that the phonological strategies used by deaf children are similar to those used by normal children (Oller and Kelly, 1974; Dodd, 1976) it is not necessarily surprising to find that deaf children's speech does not always reflect perceptual limitations, but rather the application of phonological rules on output. Features which demonstrated the use of production rules which gave rise to errors that could not be accounted for in terms of perceptual difficulties, were m, kl clusters, and nasal + C clusters.

Similarly, it was not necessarily true that the deafs' writing reflected only their perception of the stimuli. For example, when writing C + r clusters subjects frequently reduced the cluster to either the consonant or the r, yet when speaking they often pronounced the cluster correctly. The phonological features which demonstrated this phenomenon were C + r clusters and kl clusters.

Therefore it must be evident that there was also a mis-match between the two output systems. Information which was included in the spoken output was not included in the written output, and vice versa. It follows that, at least for the deaf, the two output systems are organised separately, and that the strategies governing the generation of the two outputs differ.

5 Summary and conclusion

The research presented in this chapter has been concerned with the type of information deaf children use to generate spelling patterns in three different tasks. They were first asked to spell familiar words from a lip read input, and the pattern of errors showed that they did not distinguish between words which had a direct phoneme-grapheme correspondence and those which did not. This result suggests that deaf children normally remember how to spell all familiar words in much the same way that hearing children remember only those words which have no direct phoneme-grapheme correspondence (e.g. by rote, use of linguistic information, orthographic rules, etc.). Hearing children seem to make use of phoneme-grapheme correspondence rules for most words. This results in correct spelling of regular words and characteristic misspellings for irregular words. It also enables them to spell any nonsense word.

When the same deaf subjects were asked to remember nonsense words, which were presented in written form, and to write them down after an interference task which involved the copying of other nonsense words, they were apparently able to use phoneme-grapheme correspondence rules. As they performed as well as a hearing control group, they must be credited with the ability to extract and store phonological information derived from graphemic input. While this potential ability is not usually tapped in the standard spelling test using real words, it can be elicited in spelling tests of real unfamiliar or of nonsense words, and similarly in reading tests.

The third task demonstrated that another group of deaf children could extract novel phonological information from a single visual (lip read) input, and then use it in different output systems, i.e. spelling and speaking, each expressing the same information, but in specific and not necessarily identical ways. This experiment provided additional evidence that the deaf can use a phonological code, derived from a lip read input to perform a complex cognitive operation.

It is therefore not necessarily surprising that the deaf often have average spelling abilities, since they have been shown to be able to use both phonological and graphemic codes, although the second is probably the preferred code for most tasks. The results also indicate that the development of a phonological code is not specific to the auditory modality, but can also be derived from visual (lip read) information. Thus, a phonological code may be an abstract code, able to be realised in two different ways – speaking and writing.

PART VIII

Spelling and Dyslexia

THE MOSYIRIS
chaniages
One very GOStley
night I when t into
the attic. Har
a gess want I saw?
I saw an ant
more than five
feet long it was
a red ant it
started shoting
asid at me.

20

Lexical and Non-lexical Processing
of Spelling in Dyslexia

PHILIP H. K. SEYMOUR and CONSTANTINOS D.
PORPODAS   *Department of Psychology, University of Dundee, Scotland*

1 Introduction

A competent reader and writer of English appears to possess two conceptually distinct types of knowledge of English spelling. On the one hand he knows about the *regularities* of spelling, that is the reliable relations between graphemic patterns and pronunciation (called the grapheme-phoneme correspondences) which characterise a substantial proportion of English words (Gibson *et al.*, 1962). On the other he possesses a large amount of knowledge about the spellings of specific words which may be regarded as *lexical* or morphemic in nature. The first type of knowledge is exemplified when he reads regularly spelled non-words, such as SPRILK or BLORDS, with conventional pronunciation, or writes them to dictation. The second is indicated by his ability to read and write 'irregular' words, such as EYE, EWE, BLOOD, ISLAND, SWORD, LAUGH, BEAUTY, to choose between the alternative spellings of homophones, such as SALE and SAIL, or to make numerous decisions as to which of a number of possible spellings is the correct one for a particular word. (See N. Chomsky, 1970; C. Chomsky, 1970; Klima, 1972; Gleitman and Rozin, 1977 and the chapters by Barron, Henderson and Chard and others in this volume for discussions of aspects of spelling which are not explicable in terms of grapheme-phoneme correspondence rules.)

These two aspects of spelling are rather clearly distinguished in modern Japanese script. There are two types of phonetic script, called *Kana*, which represent syllabic components of Japanese words, and an ideographic script, called *Kanji*, which represents meanings or concepts (Sakamoto and Makita, 1973). Children begin by learning to read the Kana script, which is characterised by very regular grapheme-syllable correspondences, but replace the Kana versions of many content words by Kanji ideographs as they progress through school. This system is considered to be highly successful, and it is claimed that cases of severe reading disability are very rare in Japan (Makita, 1968).

In written English the phonetic and lexical-semantic aspects of spelling are merged in a single script. A child learning to read English must therefore realise that spelling serves in part to signal pronunciation, though not in an entirely regular fashion, and in part to signal lexical identity or syntactic function (Gleitman and Rozin, 1977). This view about the dual nature of English spelling has been taken to imply that skilled reading might depend on the development of two functionally distinct processing systems, a *grapheme-phoneme translation channel* which can transform regular spellings into syllabic speech codes, and a *lexical-semantic channel* which is capable of recognising individual words or morphemes and of translating the visual input into a semantic or phonological representation. Studies of patients who appear to have lost one of these functions while partially preserving the other provide neuropsychological support for this two-channel theory (Marshall and Newcombe, 1973; Shallice and Warrington, 1975; Marshall, 1976; Marcel and Patterson, 1978).

Analogous arguments can be developed with regard to the production of written spelling. It seems that people possess a capability for non-lexical spelling which is exemplified when they write nonsense words or spell real words with attention to their sounds rather than their meanings (e.g. LARF, NITE). However, as has been emphasised by Simon and Simon (1973), the existence of a substantial arbitrary and morphemic element in English spelling makes it clear that a non-lexical *phoneme-grapheme translation channel* of this kind could never provide an adequate basis for spelling competence. For this we have to assume the existence of a lexically-indexed store which can be accessed for retrieval of information about the correct spellings of individual words.

In developmental dyslexia we find cases of children who, despite adequate intelligence, motivation and social advantage, nonetheless encounter extreme problems in mastering the fundamentals of reading and spelling (see Critchley, 1970; Hermann, 1959 and the following chapter by Nelson). We considered that it would be worthwhile to examine instances of this disorder within the framework of the two-channel model of reading and spelling functions. Thus, we may ask whether a dyslexic child possesses operational lexical and non-lexical systems for reading and written spelling, and whether his impairment affects the development of one type of system more than the other. We may note that some schemes for classifying sub-types of dyslexia have been formulated in just these terms. For example, Boder (1973) defined the *dysphonetic* dyslexic as a child who had difficulty with non-lexical spelling and the *dyseidetic* dyslexic as one who lacked a sight vocabulary or word-specific spelling memory.

Implicit in Boder's classification is the suggestion that we might look for determinants of dyslexia by considering on the one hand disorders affecting visuo-spatial operations on written language (Orton, 1937; Hermann, 1959) and on the other disorders affecting the processing of spoken language. This latter view, which has received considerable emphasis in recent years (see Vellutino, 1977; Rozin and Gleitman, 1977 and Bryant and Bradley, Chapter 16) states that reading difficulties may stem from defects in 'phonological awareness', especially the capacity to segment spoken language into units which are appropriate for coding in written spelling. Indeed, Sakamoto and Makita (1973) have pointed out that one important difference between Western alphabetic scripts and Japanese is that the former code phonemes whereas the Kanas represent larger syllabic units which are more easily perceived by young chidren.

2 Method

The remainder of this chapter will report an experimental investigation of reading and spelling processes in normal and dyslexic subjects which was designed to explore some implications of the two-channel model and also to contribute to the debate concerning the spatial or linguistic basis of dyslexia. The study took the form of an extended series of experiments. These involved the individual testing over a period of some months of members of a small group of dyslexic subjects. Table 1 gives

TABLE 1   Details of ages, intelligence levels and reading and spelling ages of the dyslexic and control subjects tested in the experiments

| Subject | Age | Intelligence level | | | | Reading age | | Spelling age |
		Ravens matrices %ile	Verbal IQ	Wechsler Perform- ance IQ	Overall IQ	Schonell	Neale	Schonell
Dyslexic children								
LA	8:7	>95	117	131	125	7:4	7:6	6:6
AR	9:10	>95	110	122	117	8:0	8:7	7:9
GD	9:7	>95	112	111	112	7:7	8:2	7:6
JM	9:10	>95	112	91	101	8:1	8:2	8:0
X̄	9:5					7:8		7:5
Dyslexic adults								
RN	20:0	—			130			
BS	17:0	—			119			
Younger controls								
(N = 8)	7:2	>95				7:9		7:6
Older controls								
(N = 8)	9:4	>95				12:1		11:2

the initials of each subject, together with details of their ages, intelligence and reading and spelling attainment. There were four dyslexic boys, LA, AR, GD and JM, who were attending primary schools in Dundee and who were also receiving remedial instruction on account of their reading and spelling difficulties. It can be seen that they were of above average intelligence (as assessed by the WISC and Ravens Matrices) but that they were retarded by 1–2 years on the Schonell reading and spelling tests. We also tested two adult subjects, RN and BS, who had well-established histories of reading and spelling problems.

The dyslexic children were contrasted with two groups of capable readers aged 7 years and 9 years (N = 8 in each case). The 9-year-old group (which will be referred to as the Older Control Group or the Chronological Age, CA Control) consisted of boys whose age and intelligence were similar to those of the dyslexics although their reading and spelling attainment was at the 11–12-year-old level. The 7-year-old boys were intelligent children in the second and third years of primary schooling whose reading attainment was considered by their teachers to be at the level expected for their age and which was shown by the Schonell tests to correspond approximately to the level achieved by the dyslexic subjects. This group will be referred to as the Younger Control Group, or the Reading Age (RA) Control.

The advantages of using both Reading Age and Chronological Age Controls are discussed in Chapters 16 and 21 in this volume. If the dyslexic subjects are found not to differ from their CA Controls on a particular task we will conclude that they are unimpaired in the psychological functions required for the successful performance of that task. If they are shown to differ from the CA Controls but not from the RA Controls we will say that an impairment has been demonstrated but that it is no greater than would be predicted on the hypothesis that the child has been deprived of much of the experience of written language which would normally be acquired by a reader of his age. Only if the dyslexic performance can be shown to differ either quantitatively or qualitatively from that of both the RA and the CA Controls will we conclude that the experiment is tapping an area of dysfunction which possibly makes a causal contribution to the disorder.

3 Graphemic-pictorial dissociation

Some preliminary experiments were conducted with the aim of determining whether the reading deficiency of the dyslexic children was apparent in visual information processing tasks in which the stimuli were either linguistic (graphemes) or non-linguistic (object pictures).

In a study of physical identity judgements rows of 2–7 letters or pictures were displayed and the subjects were instructed to respond 'Yes' if the items were identical (e.g. AAAAAAA) and 'No' if there was a different item. The dyslexic children responded as rapidly as their Chronological Age (CA) Controls when classifying pictures but at about the level of their Reading Age (RA) Controls when classifying graphemes.

This result suggests (*i*) that the visual processing channel for graphemes is functionally distinct from the channel for processing objects, and (*ii*) that the visual deficit of the dyslexic children is specific to the graphemic system. An experiment on naming of pictures of objects and reading of their written names tended to confirm this conclusion. Our dyslexic subjects were equivalent to their CA Controls in object naming, but were slower, more error prone, and more affected by variations in word length than their RA Controls when asked to vocalise the printed names of the same objects. On the other hand we did find that judgements as to whether or not a letter or picture of an object was normally oriented were delayed, being at the level of the Reading Age Controls for objects and somewhat slower than this for graphemes. It seems arguable, therefore, that our subjects were unimpaired in gestalt processing of objects, but that they suffered a general deficiency in the processing of orientation which may have contributed to a selective defect in the channel for analysis of visual features of graphemes.

Nonetheless, the delays observed when the dyslexics vocalised the written object names were too great to allow us to dismiss them as a simple consequence of a delay in graphemic encoding. Further, we cannot explain this effect in terms of word retrieval processes (cf. Denckla and Rudel, 1976) since the words were all successfully and rapidly produced in the object naming task. The implication is that the defect is located in the intervening stages, i.e. in the grapheme-phoneme or lexical-semantic channels, and the remainder of this chapter will report experiments designed to focus on the functioning of these systems.

4 The non-lexical channel

According to the two-channel hypothesis a competent individual's knowledge of English spelling is in part represented in a non-lexical grapheme-phoneme translation channel. We assume that this channel handles the naming of symbols and, more significantly, the transformation of regularly spelled letter arrays into syllabic speech codes. Regularity is in one respect a property of *orthography*, being concerned with the repeated occurrence of certain letter groups or 'spelling patterns' in particular positions in words of a given length. It is also a matter of *pronounceability*, that is the ease with which the array can be mapped onto a phonotactically acceptable speech representation. (See Mason, 1975; Gibson *et al.*, 1962; Spoehr and Smith, 1975; Rubenstein *et al.*, 1975 and Henderson and Chard, Chapter 5.)

We made the assumption that an operational grapheme-phoneme translation channel must possess capabilities for: (*i*) visual recognition of spelling patterns, and (*ii*) retrieval of corresponding phonemic representations. The system must also achieve a spatial-temporal transformation, so that spatial position in the graphemic input is properly related to temporal position in the speech output. The logical structure of a system of this kind is shown diagrammatically in Fig. 1. It is proposed

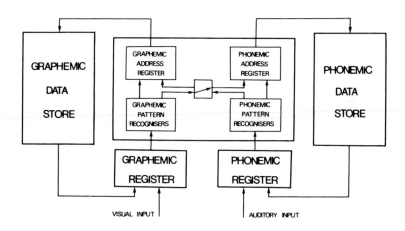

FIG. 1   Schematic representation of the grapheme-phoneme translation channel

that the array of letters to be translated is initially represented as a spatially structured code in a *graphemic register* which is viewed as a post-iconic visual short-term memory specialised for the maintenance and manipulation of graphemic information. During translation the graphemic code is sampled in a spatially disciplined manner by a system of graphemic *pattern recognisers* which respond to visual characteristics of letters and spelling patterns. The pattern recognisers may be linked to a register of addresses of locations in a phonemic data store. If the evidence accumulated in a recogniser passes a threshold, and if the link is traversed, a code will be retrieved and entered into a *phonemic register* (an acoustic short-term memory system). The process can operate in reverse, in which case elements in the phonemic register provide input to the phonemic pattern recognisers. If these are linked to the addresses of locations in a graphemic data store a visual representation of letters or spelling patterns will be retrieved.

Figure 1 illustrates a number of ways in which the grapheme-phoneme translation system of a dyslexic child could be defective. On the graphemic side there might be a deficiency of spatial coding in the register, or inadequacies in the pattern recognisers, or an impoverishment of the graphemic data store or its addressing mechanism. The phonemic side of the system, as the repository of 'phonological awareness', might be defective in terms of the speech categories identified by the phonemic recognisers or established in the data store, and could suffer from a temporal coding deficiency affecting the phonemic register.

A series of experiments was conducted with the aim of investigating some of these loci. The materials for these studies were non-words of regular or irregular orthography. Our assumption was that non-words are not normally processed in the lexical system, and that they may therefore provide reasonably uncontaminated information about the non-lexical channel. All of the experiments were undertaken by the two dyslexic adults in addition to the four dyslexic boys and two groups of control subjects.

4.1 *Graphemic comparisons*

The first experiment was designed to investigate visual processes occurring at the level of the graphemic register in Fig. 1. The questions considered concerned (*i*) the *directional* control of processing in this system, and (*ii*) its sensitivity to variations in *orthographic regularity*. A graphemic comparison task was used. The subjects were presented in a tachistoscope with pairs of 5-letter arrays printed one above the other and were instructed to respond 'Yes' to physically identical arrays (i.e. those containing the same letters in the same positions) and 'No' to arrays containing one or more different letters. There was a total of 120 trials, equally divided between 'same' arrays and 'different' arrays, and between orthographically regular items, such as SLART SLART, and irregular items, such as LRTSA LRTSA. The materials were selected from the list given by Chambers and Forster (1975).

On 'different' trials the arrays either differed at all positions or at only one position. The function relating the 'different' RT to the position of this single difference was examined in order to test for directed left-to-right graphemic processing (cf. Henderson and Henderson, 1975). The function was somewhat bow-shaped in the data of the Older Controls but exhibited a clear left-to-right trend having a slope of about 330 msec per letter pair in the results of the Younger Controls. This finding was closely matched by the dyslexic children who also showed a clear left-to-right trend with a slope of about 360 msec per letter pair. In order to assess the sensitivity of the directional process to letter orientation we repeated the experiment using mirror-image arrays. This manipulation effectively reversed the direction of processing in the control subjects (see also Well *et al.*, 1975). However, this reversal did not occur in any of the dyslexic subjects other than LA, and the most frequent pattern (also shown by the adult subject, BS) was for the mirror-image arrays to be processed left-to-right.

The experiment provides further evidence, therefore, for qualitative distinctions between the dyslexics and their controls in the processing of disoriented symbols. However, the general conclusion that the dyslexics perform very much like their RA controls in graphemic tasks is confirmed.

4.2 *Orthographic regularity effects*

According to the model in Fig. 1 a code established in the graphemic register may access a stored image of itself via the graphemic pattern recognition and addressing systems. It has been suggested by Seymour and Jack (1978) that a process of *graphemic enhancement* of this kind may be at least partially responsible for the familiarity effects which are found in graphemic comparison tasks (see Henderson, Chapter 5). It is well-established that adult subjects match orthographically regular non-words more rapidly than irregular non-words (Barron and Pittenger, 1974; Chambers and Forster, 1975). If this regularity effect is interpreted in terms of the graphemic enhancement hypothesis its occurrence becomes evidence for graphemic storage of spelling pattern information whereas its non-occurrence is evidence for impoverishment of such storage.

Table 2 summarises the mean 'same' RTs for responses to physically

TABLE 2 Mean 'same' reaction times (in msec) for matching orthographically regular and irregular non-word displays

Subjects	Regular	Irregular
CA Control	1269	1687
RA Control	2308	2621
Dyslexic children	2543	2596
Dyslexic adults		
RN	2444	2628
BS	2124	2260

identical regular and irregular arrays. It can be seen that the regularity effect was replicated in the data of both of our control groups. However, it was quite absent in the results of the dyslexic children, and was not found to be significant in individual tests on the RTs of the two adults.

This result suggests that the dyslexic subjects differ qualitatively from their RA Controls with regard to storage or accessibility of visual representations of spelling patterns. We cannot at this stage say why this should be so, since the impoverishment could reflect deficiencies in graphemic representation or storage *per se*, or in the linguistic categories in terms of which the contents of the store are defined and indexed.

4.3 *Grapheme-phoneme translation*

In a second experiment the rate and accuracy of functioning of the grapheme-phoneme translation channel was studied. The task of vocalising printed non-words of regular spelling was used for this purpose (cf. Frederiksen and Kroll, 1976). The items were 150 single syllable non-words, 4, 5 or 6 letters in length which were derived by rearrangement of the vowel and consonant spelling patterns found in a sample of regularly spelled English words of varying frequency. The words were all based on a C–V–C structure and the sizes of the initial and terminal consonant clusters were systematically varied. Examples are STAM, REAST, SPOOCH, STROAT and PRAIST. The full set of 150 items was used to test the dyslexic subjects and the Older Controls. This was considered to be too extended a test for the Younger Controls who were given a shortened list of 90 words. Reaction times for each response were measured, and the sessions were tape recorded to allow subsequent identification of errors.

A summary of the results of this experiment has been given in Fig. 2. A trend over all subject groups, also reported by Frederiksen and Kroll (1976), was for RT and error rate to increase as a function of non-word length. It can be seen that the dyslexic boys were similar to their RA Controls with regard to error rate, but that their reactions were substantially slower, both in general level and in the steepness of the function relating RT to word length. This slowing of response was also evident in the data of the two adult subjects. RN's average RT was similar to that of the Younger Controls but the slope of the word length function was steeper (433 msec per letter). In BS this delay of reaction was extreme. Although his responses were accurate for more than 90% of the non-words his mean RTs were of the order of 10–11 sec, and the length effect was about 2000 msec per letter.

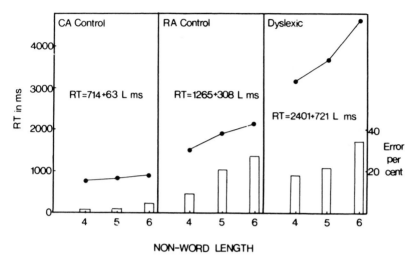

FIG. 2 Vocal reaction times (in msec) and error percentages for naming of regular non-words plotted to show the effect of word length

From this we can conclude that our dyslexic subjects possessed operational grapheme-phoneme translation channels but that the systems were in each case impaired with regard to their speed of functioning. The retardation seems too great to be explained solely in terms of delays in the graphemic system since the processing time per letter in the naming experiment was about double the time per letter pair in the graphemic comparison experiment. Further, since the effect occurred for the adult subjects as well as for the dyslexic boys, and since the dyslexics were clearly differentiated from their RA Controls, it seems that the delay of translation cannot be accounted for in terms of limitations of reading skill or experience with written language.

4.4 Phoneme-grapheme translation

An assessment of the efficiency of non-lexical phoneme-grapheme translation was made by presenting our subjects with a sequence of spoken non-words (the same as those used in the reading experiment) and asking them to spell them in writing. As has been noted by Nelson in this volume the scoring of errors in written spelling is subject to a number of difficulties. We considered that it would be sufficient for our purposes if each response was assessed in terms of its phonological acceptability, and if the frequencies of errors in the initial or terminal consonant cluster or in the medial vowel cluster were then determined.

The overall frequencies of error were 19% for the Older Controls, 51% for the Younger Controls, 25% and 24% for RN and BS, and 68% for the four dyslexic boys. These scores were in each case substantially greater than the frequencies observed in the naming task (see Fig. 2), indicating that subjects failed to write many of the non-words which they read correctly. A summary of the data classified by location of error has been given in Fig. 3. It can be seen that the great majority of errors occurred on the vowel spelling patterns. The frequency of these errors increased with word length, and was higher in the dyslexic and Younger Control group than in the Older Control group. Comparisons between the dyslexic children and the Younger Controls showed no significant difference for the 5- and 6-letter words, although the effect

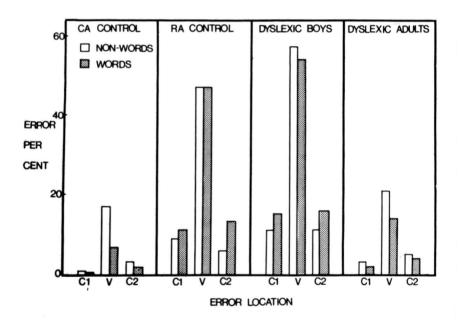

FIG. 3   Percent error rates for initial consonant, vowel and terminal consonant positions in written spelling of regular words and non-words

for 4-letter words was significant, as was the difference in overall error frequency.

The predominance of vowel errors is in agreement with the findings reported by Shankweiler and Liberman (1972) for performance on a reading test. These authors noted that mis-perception of vowels was less frequent than mis-perception of consonants in listening tasks but more frequent in reading tasks. They argued that the effect might depend on the diversity of orthographic patterns used to represent individual vowels, and that this might in turn relate to aspects of the perception of vowel sounds, particularly their continuous, non-categorical nature.

4.5 *Conclusions*

These experiments serve to demonstrate that our dyslexic subjects were deficient in the area of non-lexical spelling knowledge. They differed radically from their CA Controls on each of the functions we examined, and from their RA Controls in terms of sensitivity to orthographic regularity, slowness of grapheme-phoneme translation, and liability to error in phoneme-grapheme translation.

5 The lexical-semantic channel

According to the two-channel theory competent reading involves concurrent processing in the non-lexical grapheme-phoneme channel and in a second system which is *lexical* in that the units it deals with are words or morphemes and *semantic* in that it provides a direct route by which visual words may access information about meaning and logical structure. This channel may be represented as a *logogen system*, as defined by Morton (1968, 1969), which contains pattern recognisers for visual and auditory words and which mediates retrieval of semantic and phonological codes.

A diagram of the possible structure of the system is shown in Fig. 4. This includes sets of graphemic, phonemic and semantic pattern recognisers which may optionally be linked to phonological, semantic and graphemic address registers. The solution differs in certain respects from Morton's earlier formulations and also from his more recent proposals in favour of a functional separation of the word recognition and speech production systems (Morton, 1977). In Fig. 4 access and exit functions are contained within a single logogen system, although access is mediated by the graphemic pattern recognisers and exit depends on the addressing of locations in the phonological data store. The graphemic and phonemic registers may also be linked by the non-lexical translation channel diagrammed in Fig. 1 (although this is not represented in the figure).

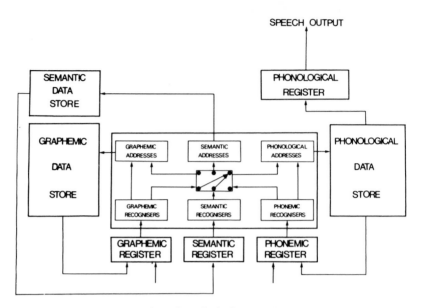

FIG. 4   Schematic representation of the lexical-semantic system

When established in competent readers the lexical-semantic system gives rise to a number of effects which are well-documented in the experimental literature. These include (*i*) word superiority effects, (*ii*) word frequency effects, and (*iii*) spelling regularity effects. The *word superiority effect* is an advantage, in either accuracy or latency, enjoyed by real words over non-words (see Henderson and Chard, Chapter 5). The *frequency effect* is an advantage enjoyed by words which occur with high frequency in written English over those which occur with lower frequency. The *regularity effect* is a disadvantage noted when words of irregular spelling are contrasted with words of regular spelling (Baron and Strawson, 1976; Barron, Chapter 9).

5.1 *Lexical effect on graphemic comparison*

Chambers and Forster (1975) provided evidence for the occurrence of lexical effects in the graphemic comparison task. Their adult subjects matched words faster than non-words, and matched words of high frequency faster than words of low frequency. These effects can be interpreted in terms of the graphemic enhancement hypothesis of Seymour and Jack (1978). According to this view graphemic representation of a word may result in access to the graphemic store and retrieval of word pattern information which benefits the comparison process. Seymour and Jack presented evidence to show that the facilitation was dependent on visually mediated lexical access, and also that it could be complicated by semantic influences on the judgemental process.

A graphemic comparison experiment was conducted with our control and dyslexic subjects to test for these effects. The displays were pairs of regular and irregular non-words under one condition, and pairs of words of high or low frequency under the other, e.g. CHAIR CHAIR and TORCH TORCH. There were 20 'same' pairs in each frequency class, and 20 'different' pairs, making a total of 80 displays. The items were selected from the list given by Chambers and Forster (1975), and the non-word set (also consisting of 80 displays) contained orthographically regular items derived from the words and irregular items derived by rearrangement of letters.

The question of principal interest is whether 'same' judgements show either a word superiority effect or a word frequency effect. Table 3 gives a summary of the RT data. Both groups of control subjects were significantly affected by orthographic regularity, and this effect was

TABLE 3   Mean 'same' reaction times (in msec) for matching words of high and low frequency and non-words of regular and irregular spelling

Subjects	Words		Non-words ·	
	High frequency	Low frequency	Regular spelling	Irregular spelling
CA Control	883	922	1006	1087
RA Control	1110	1153	1119	1239
Dyslexic children				
LA	2453	2652	2519	2480
AR	1555	1690	2626	2930
GD	2994	3205	1510	1309
JM	1206	1345	1483	1357
$\bar{X}$	2052	2223	2034	2019
Dyslexic adults				
RN	999	1036	1094	1188
BS	2402	2181	1323	1362

again found to be absent from the data of the dyslexics. The lexical effects were not significant for the Younger Controls, but there was evidence of facilitation in the matching of high frequency words by the Older Controls. Some lexical effects were also evident in the results of the dyslexics. In the adult subject, BS, we can see a consistent *reversal* of the normal effects, words being matched less rapidly than non-words, and words of high frequency less rapidly than words of low frequency. The reversal of the word superiority effect was also significant in the data of GD. All of the subjects other than BS showed evidence of a word frequency effect and this was significant in individual tests on the results of LA and GD.

5.2 *Lexical effect in word naming*

These results contrasted with our findings for orthographic regularity and offered a preliminary indication that our dyslexic subjects possessed operational visual word recognition systems. A subsequent study provided clear confirmation of this conclusion for the two adult subjects, RN and BS. They were asked to name 150 regularly spelled words which varied in frequency of usage and length (4, 5 or 6 letters). The items were the base-words used in the derivation of the non-word set described earlier, and therefore matched the non-words orthographically. Mean naming RTs were 621 msec for RN and 778 msec for BS, and effects of both frequency and length were relatively slight. The RTs appear close to the normal range for this task and were similar to those of Older Controls. A striking feature was the extreme contrast between these results and those obtained with the non-words, especially for BS. Confronted with a non-word, such as FOAST, he struggled for many seconds before determining its pronunciation, whereas his response to a real word of equivalent structure, such as ROAST, was direct and rapid.

This contrast between words and non-words was not shown by the dyslexic boys. Their error rate (about 22%) and the processing rate per letter (averaging 774 msec) were similar to those observed in the non-word study. On the other hand, some facilitation was evident in their reactions to high frequency words. This suggests the involvement of the lexical channel although we cannot say whether the frequency effect was contributed by the visual word recognition system or by the phonemic recognisers and phonological addressing system (see Fig. 4).

We also used the regular words and non-words in a lexical decision experiment in which subjects reported 'Yes' if the letter string displayed was a word and 'No' if it was a non-word. Despite their efficiency in word naming both RN and BS were subject to a delay of reaction in this task. This was also true of the dyslexic boys, but the main feature of their performance was a strong tendency toward false classification of words as non-words. This trend was related to the word frequency variable, and the error frequencies were consistently higher than those of the Younger Controls.

5.3 *Naming words of irregular spelling*

These results suggested that the two adult dyslexic subjects possessed well-established and extensive systems for lexical recognition and naming of English words (equated with the graphemic pattern recognisers in Fig. 4, and the link to the phonological address register), but that this system was restricted in scope in the younger subjects, who were consequently forced to rely on the grapheme-phoneme channel in reading. On this view, we would expect the children to have particular difficulty in reading words of *irregular* spelling, such as LAUGH, BEAUTY, ISLAND, which are unlikely to be translated correctly by the non-lexical channel, although such difficulties should not be encountered by the adult subjects.

We accordingly assembled a new list of 182 words which contained equal numbers of regular and irregular items which varied in length (3, 4, 5 or 6 letters) and in frequency (high or low). Examples of high frequency irregular words are: EYE, KNOW, SWORD, BEAUTY and examples of low frequency items are: EWE, ACHE, AISLE and RESIGN. Each cell of the 2 × 2 × 4 design was represented by 12 words, apart from the two low frequency 3-letter lists which contained 7 items only (on account of a difficulty in finding examples of low frequency irregular 3-letter words). The Older Controls and the dyslexic subjects were tested for speed and accuracy of naming the words on the complete list, and the Younger Controls were tested with an abbreviated list of 80 words.

Figure 5 presents the naming RTs of the Older and Younger Control subjects plotted to show the effects of word length, word frequency, and spelling regularity. The Older Controls named irregular words about 50 msec less rapidly than the regular words, thus confirming the findings of Baron and Strawson (1976). This regularity effect interacted with effects for word frequency and word length, chiefly on account of the inversion of the length effect for low frequency irregular words. As anticipated, the dyslexic adults performed very much like the Older Controls. They made virtually no errors, and the mean RTs were 617 msec for RN and 907 msec for BS. Given our earlier demonstration of an impairment of non-lexical grapheme-phoneme translation in these subjects we can feel reasonably confident that their responses were mediated entirely by the lexical-semantic system. Hence, we would not expect to find a facilitating effect of spelling regularity (on the assumption that the regularity effect shown by normal readers depends on concurrent activity in the lexical and non-lexical systems). Tests for a regularity effect were made on the individual data, but were not found to be significant in either case.

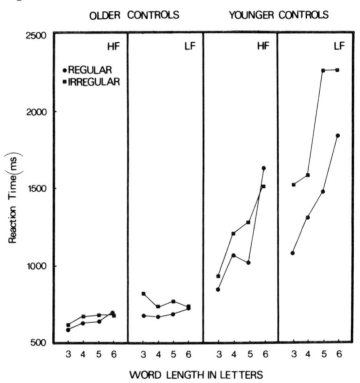

FIG. 5 Vocal reaction times (in msec) for naming regular and irregular words of varying length and frequency by the Older and Younger Control subjects

As can be seen in Fig. 5, the Younger Control subjects showed word length effects (averaging about 200 msec per letter) for both regular and irregular words. There was a strong effect of spelling regularity on RT and error rate, and this interacted with word frequency. For high frequency words spelling irregularity produced an increase in RT of 93 msec and an increase in error rate from 1–9%. With low frequency words the RT effect was 467 msec, and error rate increased from 11–35%. Examination of the results of the dyslexic boys indicated that their RTs, averaging well over 3 sec, were significantly greater than those of their RA Controls, and that they were more liable to error (often failures to respond or production of neologisms) on high frequency words, rates being 7% for regular words as against 27% for irregular words.

5.4 *Conclusions*

Two main conclusions are suggested by these findings: (*i*) The dyslexic adults, RN and BS, possessed a fully operational link between an extensive visual pattern recognition system for words and the phonological addressing system. They used this route in the naming of English words of regular or irregular spelling, thus by-passing a deficient grapheme-phoneme translation channel. There was a hint, in the lexical decision experiment, that the semantic retrieval function might nonetheless be impaired, and it would be worthwhile to investigate this possibility in the future. (*ii*) The dyslexic children were found to be sensitive to the factors of lexicality and word frequency in the graphemic comparison and word naming tasks. This suggests that the lexical channel was operational, although it seems to have been impaired both with regard to the time required for translation and the range of vocabulary covered by the visual word recognition system. The dyslexic boys were inferior to their RA Controls in these respects. This suggests that their lexical deficiency was not wholly explicable in terms of a delay in graphemic processing or the limitations of reading skill or experience associated with their disorder.

6 Coding and production of spelling

It was argued at the beginning of this chapter that the two-channel model was in principle applicable to an analysis of the production of written spelling. We have already shown that our subjects possess a capability for non-lexical phoneme-grapheme translation. This non-lexical channel could play an important part in spelling production, although errors would occur frequently if it was not supported by a lexical system giving access to spelling facts about individual words (Simon and Simon, 1973).

The points at issue here can be illustrated by means of a diagram of the possible structure of a lexical channel for spelling production. This is shown as Fig. 6, and takes the form of a logogen system through which currently active phonological, semantic or graphemic codes may access word-specific spelling information. A key question concerns the nature of the codes held in the word-specific store. Does it contain complete or partial representations of spelling, and is it associated with a particular sensory modality? A complete representation would be one which

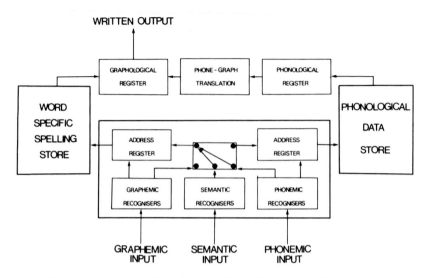

FIG. 6   Schematic representation of system for spelling production, showing a non-lexical phone-to-graph channel and a lexical system for accessing spelling information in a word-specific store

detailed all of the letters making up a word in their correct order of output. A partial representation might detail only those facts which could not be derived by application of the phoneme-grapheme rules in the non-lexical phone-graph translation channel. The information could be visual in character (implying that the word-specific spelling store may be equated with the graphemic data store in Fig. 4), but could also consist of phonemically represented lists of letter names, or more abstract structures.

6.1 *Graphemic coding of spelling*

A small experiment previously reported by Seymour and Porpodas (1978) provides some pointers regarding the graphemic-phonemic distinction. This study tested for a bias in favour of graphemic coding when analytic operations were performed on representations of the spellings of regular and irregular words. The task required the subject to make decisions about either the shape or the sound of letters whose positions in target words were specified by digit probes. The shape decisions depended on whether or not the letter possessed an ascender/descender, and the sound decisions on whether or not its name rhymed with *ee*. The judgements were in each case indicated by the closure of

one or other of two switches. Ten 5-letter target words were used, 5
regular and 5 irregular. On each trial the subject heard an instruction
('shape' or 'sound') followed by the target word. A probe digit, 1–5,
was then presented, visually under one condition of the experiment and
auditorily under the other, and the RT was recorded from onset of the
probe to closure of the switch. The subjects were 7 competent readers,
aged 11 years, from the same school as our Older and Younger Control
groups. The auditory and visual conditions each involved 100 trials
(2 instructions × 10 words × 5 positions).

Average RT in this experiment was about 1700 msec with an error
rate of about 5%. Responses to auditory probes were 400 msec faster
than responses to visual probes. This modality effect was independent
of the effects of decision type, regularity and probe position which are
presented graphically in Fig. 7. It can be seen that the RT increased

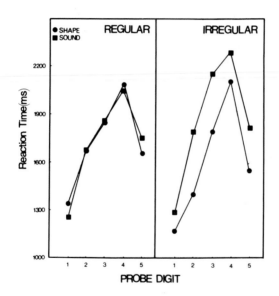

FIG. 7   Reaction times (in msec) for shape and sound judgements in the digit probe
task

over the first four positions and declined at the fifth. The slope of the
increasing function averaged 288 msec per position. Decision type interacted significantly with regularity, and it can be seen from the figure
that this was because shape decisions were faster than sound decisions
for irregular words but not for regular words. The experiment was also

completed by a group of dyslexic boys, aged 12–17 years. Their results were qualitatively similar to those of the competent readers, but they made more errors and the RT increased at a rate of about 700 msec over the first four positions. They did not show a decision × regularity interaction. However, their RTs were in general faster for shape decisions than for sound decisions.

We interpret this experiment as suggesting that letter-specific information about words of irregular spelling may be maintained in permanent storage by competent readers in a predominantly graphemic format. The study with the dyslexic boys appears not to substantiate the hypothesis that children with spelling difficulties have a special deficiency in this kind of storage, although further research on this point is needed.

6.2 Directional coding

Seymour and Porpodas (1978) also explored the possibility that permanent memory representations of spelling may be organised within the framework of a *structural* code which specifies relations of adjacency and precedence existing between individual letters. This code has both spatial and temporal aspects, indicating the locations of letters in a horizontal array and the serial order of their generation in written or oral spelling. Thus, although there may be a graphemic element in spelling representations, this should not be taken to imply gestalt or image qualities. At the structural level the representation possesses a dynamic property of *directional polarisation* which strongly favours serial production in a left-to-right first-to-last order (cf. Bryden's, 1967, discussion of directional biases in reports of tachistoscopically presented letter arrays).

A second probe experiment was conducted with the aim of examining this directional aspect of the spelling code. On each trial the subject was given the instruction 'Forward' or 'Backward' followed by a target word. We again used a set of 10 words, all 5 letters in length, half of regular spelling and half of irregular spelling. The probe was a visually presented letter from the target word, and the subject responded by naming the letter before or after it. The response 'nothing' was required for a backward probe of the first letter or a forward probe of the last letter. The subjects were the 7 boys tested in the previous experiment, and the session involved 100 trials (2 instructions × 10 words × 5 positions).

The mean RT in this task was 1390 msec with errors on fewer than 4% of trials. There was a regularity effect which was independent of the position and direction effects and their interaction. Forward instructions produced faster responses than Backward instructions, but this directional effect was limited to the third, fourth and fifth letter positions. The position effect itself reflected the rapid responses to the first letter position. This experiment was also undertaken by the group of secondary school dyslexic boys. They were slower and more error prone than the competent readers and the directional effect was quite absent from their data.

The experiment indicates, therefore, that there is an important dynamic or directional element in the coding of spelling which may well be defective in dyslexic subjects.

6.3 *Spelling regular words*

Our proposal so far is that competence in written spelling may depend on the combined activity of a non-lexical phoneme-grapheme channel and a lexical system which mediates access to a word-specific data store. We have further suggested that representations held in the permanent store contain spatial-temporal structure and possibly a graphemic form of coding for individual letters. A first question to be asked concerns the extent of the contribution of the lexical system to the spelling of regular words. Although these words conform to phoneme-grapheme correspondence rules their spelling remains to a degree undetermined on account of the range of acceptable alternative vowel and consonant realisations which are available in English (cf. Henderson and Chard, Chapter 5). We would anticipate, therefore, that word-specific information would normally be established for regular words, and that the growth of this form of storage would be related to word frequency.

In order to test this expectation our original groups of dyslexic and control subjects were asked to write to dictation the items on the list of 150 regular words which were used in the naming experiment described earlier. It will be recalled that these words varied in length (4, 5 or 6 letters) and in frequency (high, medium or low), and that they were based on the same C–V–C spelling structures as the non-word set. We can therefore determine whether there is a lexical effect on production of regular spelling by considering (*i*) whether or not subjects make fewer errors in spelling words than non-words, and (*ii*) whether accuracy in spelling words is affected by word frequency.

The data relevant to the word/non-word comparison have been summarised in Fig. 3. The Older Control subjects showed a significant word superiority effect, error rate being 7% with words as against 19% with non-words. This advantage was absent from the results of the Younger

Controls (52% vs 51%) and the dyslexic boys (66% vs 68%). The word frequency effect was significant for the Older Controls, but not for the Younger Controls. All four dyslexic boys made fewer errors with high frequency words than with words of medium or low frequency. Thus, we can conclude that the Older Control subjects probably made use of the lexical channel when spelling regular words, but that the Younger Control subjects did not. The performance of the dyslexic subjects was at the same level as the least competent of the Younger Controls. The results were also analysed with regard to word length and location of errors. The pattern was very similar to that found with the non-words, showing that error frequency increased with word length and that errors on the vowel cluster predominated. About 20% of the errors made by each subject were classifiable as phonetically appropriate spellings (e.g. BEEM, TRANE, GREEF), but the proportions of these errors (relative to each subject's total error rate) were similar in the control and dyslexic groups.

6.4 *Spelling irregular words*

The dyslexic and control subjects were also given the list of regular and irregular words to spell. The writing of the irregular words offers a strong test of the availability of word-specific spelling information. In the absence of such information the word will be spelled by applying phone-graph translation rules, and errors (which will often approximate phonetically correct spellings) will occur. If the subject possesses a lexically indexed word-specific store his error rate on irregular words will fall below 100%, and his errors may reflect a partial knowledge of the correct spelling of the word.

Table 4 presents a summary of the error frequencies obtained for the regular and irregular words of high and low frequency. We can see that the Older Control subjects and the dyslexic adults, RN and BS, were able to write substantial numbers of irregular words correctly. There was, nonetheless, a consistent tendency for accuracy to be greater for regular than for irregular words, and for words of high frequency than for words of low frequency. The errors were classified as phonetically correct spellings or as phonetically incorrect spellings which included an appropriate idiosyncratic element. For example, BS wrote AKE, EACO, BEUTEY, ANKOR, RESINE, WEPON (phonetically correct errors) and SOWRD, BIULD, TOUNGE, HAISTEN, MUCLE (errors giving evidence of partial word-specific information). Both he and RN showed a tendency for the phonetic errors to predominate with low frequency irregular words, and for the idiosyncratic errors to predominate with the high frequency words. The errors made by the Older Controls in spelling low frequency irregular words were also predominantly phonetic.

TABLE 4 Percent error rate in spelling words of high and low frequency and regular and irregular spelling

Subjects	High frequency		Low freuqency	
	Regular	Irregular	Regular	Irregular
CA Control	1	7	7	16
RA Control	22	59	32	79
Dyslexic children				
LA	58	81	67	81
AR	44	79	56	91
GD	35	77	56	79
JM	27	46	49	74
$\overline{X}$	41	71	57	81
Dyslexic adults				
RN	0	12	2	14
BS	10	27	16	28

Table 4 also reports the data of the Younger Controls and the dyslexic children. These show strong effects of both word frequency and spelling regularity. The control and dyslexic subjects had an error rate of about 80% on low frequency irregular words, and these errors were more often phonetic than idiosyncratic. With high frequency irregular words, the error rates of LA, AR and GD exceeded those of any of the Younger Control subjects. Thus, the dyslexics were impaired relative to their RA Controls in spelling common irregular words, indicating a retardation in the establishment of word-specific storage which is not explicable in terms of limitations of language experience.

6.5 *Conclusions*

These experiments suggest that the normal course of spelling development involves the establishment of permanent storage for word-specific representations of both regular and irregular words extending over a progressively widening range of vocabulary. We have presented evidence which indicates that the spelling code contains a dynamic element and possibly graphemic information about letters. It may well be that the code is most closely related to the actions required for written production of spelling, although further research will be needed to validate this suggestion. As far as the dyslexic subjects are concerned, the picture is similar to the one obtained from the studies of lexical processing in reading. There is an operational lexical system for spelling, but its resources, in terms of stored word-specific information, are limited to a restricted vocabulary range.

7 Discussion

7.1 *Two-channel model of reading*

In this chapter we have discussed the reading and spelling performance of developmentally dyslexic subjects within the framework of the two-channel model advocated by Marshall and Newcombe (1973) and Shallice and Warrington (1975). This theoretical approach differs from the position adopted in many previous analyses of dyslexia in that it emphasises a distinction between *lexical* and *non-lexical* processing rather than between visual and auditory or spatial and linguistic cognitive functions.

Our analysis of the performance of the four dyslexic boys suggested that they possessed operational lexical and non-lexical channels but that both systems were to a greater or lesser degree impaired. This conclusion is in agreement with the 'double-deficit' hypothesis outlined by Nelson (Chapter 21). In the two adult subjects, RN and BS, the picture was somewhat different, since their data demonstrated a persisting impairment of the non-lexical grapheme-phoneme channel combined with generally efficient functioning in the lexical channel (at least in word naming tasks).

The dyslexic boys differed from their Reading Age Controls with regard to speed of lexical and non-lexical translation and also in liability to error in lexical translation. This implies that their deficiency cannot be dismissed as a simple reflection of their limited skill in reading or reduced experience with written language. Similarly, the adult subjects, RN and BS, compared well with the Older Controls on the word reading tests, but were distinctively different in the non-word naming task. Again, this means that the non-lexical channel operated less efficiently than we would expect from a consideration of the level of reading skill exhibited by these subjects.

7.2 *Language deficit hypothesis*

We may ask whether a persisting impairment of the non-lexical translation system could be explained on the basis of the language deficit hypothesis of Vellutino (1977), Bryant and Bradley (Chapter 16) and Liberman and her associates (Shankweiler and Liberman, 1972; Liherman *et al.*, 1977). A deficiency in segmentation of speech into phoneme-sized units would certainly be most damaging to the development of the grapheme-phoneme channel, since it would mean (*i*) that the codes held in the phonemic data store of Fig. 1 were inappropriate (e.g. they might be syllabic rather than phonemic), and (*ii*) that the graphemic categories to be recognised and stored were poorly defined. A case can be made out, therefore, for interpretation of both the delay in grapheme-phoneme translation and the absence of orthographic regularity effects in graphemic comparison in terms of a defect in phonemic segmentation.

The relevance of this hypothesis to the delay in the development of the lexical system is less obvious. We assume that dyslexic children are well able to segment language at the level of words. Further, our experiments on object naming suggested that our subjects were not deficient in word finding or speed or speech production. Thus, we can argue that the phonological storage and addressing system in Fig. 4 probably functioned normally, and that the lexical categories represented in the visual word recognition system and its associated graphemic data store were well-formulated. Against this, it could be maintained that the visual recognisers are responsive to units of written language which are *smaller* than words, e.g. root morphemes and grammatical particles (cf. Gibson and Guinet, 1971; Murrell and Morton, 1974; Taft and Forster, 1977). In this case, a deficiency in *morphemic segmentation* could disrupt the development of the lexical channel.

A further possibility is that the development of the lexical pattern recognition system depends critically on the functioning of the nonlexical channel. The learning of Kanji ideographs can be assisted by printing a Kana transcription above each new character (known as Furigana) (see Sakamoto and Makita, 1974). The formation of visual word recognisers might be similarly facilitated if an efficient grapheme-phoneme channel was available to assist the identification of words and to act as a short-term memory capable of maintaining a durable and precise graphemic representation. According to this theory, the dyslexic subjects are not deficient in their capacity to form pattern recognisers for visual configurations, and might be expected to possess a fully developed system for visual object recognition, and to establish a comparable system for words in due course. Our findings of efficient object naming by the dyslexic children and of rapid vocalisation of words by the dyslexic adults are consistent with this view, as are the results of studies suggesting that disabled readers may be quite successful in learning Chinese ideographs (Rozin *et al.*, 1971) or other unfamiliar symbols (Vellutino *et al.*, 1975).

7.3 *Visual deficit hypothesis*

According to Figs 1 and 4 translation to a speech code via either the lexical channel or the non-lexical grapheme-phoneme channel depends on prior formation of a visual code in the graphemic register. Deficiencies in the visual encoding or representational functions could be responsible for slow reactions in reading tasks and also for defective development of the graphemic pattern recognition and storage systems. Our results argued against a *general* visual processing deficit, but in favour of a *selective* impairment of the graphemic channel (since the dyslexics appeared normal when making identity judgements about objects but impaired when making similar judgements about letters).

A selective impairment of the graphemic channel might be regarded as secondary to the linguistic deficiencies discussed in the previous section. An alternative possibility is that the impairment derives from a defect in the coding of *orientation*. Gibson (1965) has emphasised that this property is more significant for recognition of alphabetic symbols than for recognition of objects. Our experiments indicated that the dyslexic children had difficulty in discriminating normally oriented symbols from their inverted or reflected forms, and that this defect extended to discrimination between normal and inverted pictures of objects. We also found that the children made frequent reversal errors in writing. LA made several errors of this kind, reversing letters such as Z, J, g, p, when writing single letters to dictation. Taking the spelling experiments as whole, each dyslexic child made about 12 such errors (mainly *b–d* confusions) as against a total of 3 errors by the two groups of control subjects.

It is important to consider whether deficiencies which can be localised in the graphemic processing system provide an adequate explanation for the delays of reaction observed in the word and non-word naming tasks. Our position on this issue was that the graphemic deficit, as indexed by the identity judgement and graphemic comparison tasks, probably contributed to these delays but that it could not wholly account for them. The level of RT shown by the dyslexics in the graphemic tasks was very similar to that of the Reading Age Controls, but their reactions in the word naming tasks were substantially slower.

Our assumption that graphemic registration necessarily precedes access to the pattern recognition systems in both the lexical and the non-lexical channels is called into question by the results of the adult

PROCESSING OF SPELLING IN DYSLEXIA

subject, BS. This subject showed delays of reaction in the graphemic tasks and in the grapheme-phoneme translation tasks, but reacted rapidly when processing real words through the lexical channel. The implication is that BS was impaired in carrying out *analytic* operations on graphemes, but that this impairment was not disruptive of the process of lexical word recognition.

7.4 *Spelling production*

Our theoretical analysis suggested that spelling production might be viewed as being functionally distinct from reading. For reading, the critical requirement is the development of *pattern recognisers* which are responsive to visual characteristics of English words and spelling patterns. Spelling depends on *permanent storage* of information about letter identity and sequence. Our observation that spelling competence lagged behind reading competence for all subject groups confirmed that the existence of a pattern recogniser for a word (or spelling pattern) need not imply the availability of the spelling structure in permanent storage. Indeed, BS successfully read virtually all of the words we presented to him but nonetheless made many errors in spelling these same words. Given our assumption that his reading was entirely dependent on the lexical channel, we can infer that storage of spelling information in the word-specific data store of Fig. 6 is at least partially independent of the development of the pattern recognisers.

Description of the nature of the spelling codes held in the word-specific store remains a topic for future research. Our preliminary studies suggested that there might be a graphemic element in the code, but that there was also a dynamic property which we called *directional polarisation*. The dyslexic subjects were deficient in the storage of such codes, as shown, for example, by their tendency to make more errors than their Reading Age Controls when writing high frequency words of irregular spelling.

7.5 *Structural coding hypothesis*

In discussing the coding of spelling we argued that information about individual letters was organised within the framework of a *structural code* which specified spatial/temporal properties of location, adjacency, precedence and succession. The experiments described by Seymour and Porpodas (1978) suggested that dyslexic subjects might well be subject to a general deficiency in this form of coding, shown by delays in accessing locations in spelling structures (and other sequences), and by the absence of a directional effect (difference between forward and reverse shifts). Our study with the mirror-image letters indicated that directional processing of letter arrays was connected with their orientation. When confronted with a mirror-image array normal readers switched to a right-to-left processing strategy, but the dyslexic subjects did not. A possibility exists, therefore, that a link can be found between the coding of the orientation of individual letters and the directional polarisation of a letter array, and that this type of coding is likely to be deficient in dyslexia.

A deficiency of this kind could affect spatially directed processes, such as graphemic comparison and grapheme-phoneme translation, and also the storage of directionally polarised spelling codes. It would also be expected to affect other coding systems of analogous logical structure, such as the number system, time labelling systems, and perhaps temporal ordering of speech segments. The hypothesis has the potential, therefore, to explain defects in grapheme-phoneme translation, spelling, arithmetic, and in acquisition of concepts of left–right orientation and clock and calendar time, and merits careful experimental investigation in the future.

8 Summary

In this chapter we have discussed 1. the applicability of the two-channel model to the analysis of reading and spelling functions in developmentally dyslexic subjects, and 2. the extent to which the disorders exhibited by our subjects might be interpreted in terms of either (i) the speech segmentation hypothesis, or (ii) the structural coding hypothesis. The general conclusion was that a speech-based defect could account for certain aspects of the reading and spelling difficulties, but that it would not be sufficient to explain the full range of results we have reported. We are therefore inclined to pursue the notion of a structural coding deficit, and to explore some of its wider cognitive implications.

Acknowledgements

The research described in this chapter was conducted by Mr C. Porpodas with the assistance of a post-graduate award from the University of Dundee and a research grant from the Scottish Council for Research in Education. We are most grateful for the help and co-operation given by our subjects and by their parents and teachers during the conduct of the research. The assistance given by the Tayside Dyslexia Association, by the Headmistress, staff and pupils of the Park Place Primary School, Dundee, and by Miss Catriona Collins of George Watson's College, Edinburgh, is most gratefully acknowledged.

2 1

Analysis of Spelling Errors in Normal and Dyslexic Children

HAZEL E. NELSON   *Department of Psychology, The National Hospital for Nervous Diseases, London, England*

In order to avoid making premature implicatins for the aetiology or associated symptomatology of developmental dyslexia, for the purposes of this chapter the term dyslexia will be used to refer to:

A failure to develop literacy skills to a level commensurate with the child's age and level of general intellectual functioning which occurs despite adequate socio-cultural opportunity and teaching, and which cannot be attributed to brain damage or to some emotional or personality disorder.

The main object of this chapter is to present the results of a new spelling test that yields a qualitative analysis of errors with direct theoretical implications for theories of dyslexia.

1 Critique of spelling error classification schemes

Obviously the utility and validity of the inferences which can be drawn from an analysis of spelling errors is limited by the way in which the errors have been analysed and by the reliability of the analysis. At one time considerable interest was shown in the types of spelling errors produced by children and many different ways of classifying these were devised. Spache (1940a) made an extensive and critical survey of a number of these classification schemes and subsequently devised his own Spelling Errors Test (Spache, 1955). In a very thorough review of spelling tests Shores and Yee (1973) note that this is the only test available that enables the child's responses to be analysed qualitatively by measuring his tendency to make different types of error, and it is certainly an improvement on the unstandardised and often hopelessly subjective error analysis schemes previously available. If one considers some of the more serious criticisms that have been levelled against error analysis schemes then one begins to appreciate just how difficult it is to construct a system that would enable all errors to be classified in a reliable and useful way.

First the error frequency measures are often subject to unreliability because the error types are not uniquely defined and mutually exclusive. For example under some schemes it may be impossible to decide in any objective way whether errors should be scored as separate errors of addition and omission or as errors of substitution, and whether they occur as separate letter errors or as syllable errors. When the fundamental structure of a word is distorted by multiple errors objective classification becomes even less reliable as it is left to the examiner to decide where one error stops and another begins. Although the inclusion of an 'unrecognisable' or 'incomplete' category is a common one in classification schemes, it is not a sufficient safety net into which all badly mis-spelled words can be thrown because it is left to the examiner to decide whether or not the word is 'unrecognisable'. In practice, then, it is generally impossible to identify the individual elements within a multiple error word with any degree of objectivity or reliability. How-ever, this serious limitation can be avoided if the error word is treated as a single whole unit rather than as a number of separate errors. If the whole word is treated in an all-or-none fashion, being classified accord-ing to whether or not it meets certain specified criteria, then it becomes as easy to deal with a badly distorted error word as it does to deal with an error word that has only a minor inaccuracy.

Another common disadvantage of error classification schemes is that they are not suitable for quantified analysis since only few errors are made in each category stipulated. Most schemes specify somewhere between 10 and 20 categories or sub-categories of errors (see Spache, 1940, for several examples) which often serve to describe in detail the exact nature of the error made. For example, one system scores separately the substitution of k for hard c and the substitution of s for soft c. Given that the number of errors per child available for statistical analysis is limited, then the number of error categories must also be strictly limited.

A third general criticms of many spelling error schemes lies in the way which the results of the individual child are interpreted relative to his peers. If good and poor spellers attempt exactly the same words then the quality of the good spellers' errors will be judged from relatively few errors, and from errors which have occurred on words almost within their capabilities. In contrast, the quality of the poor spellers' errors will be judged from many errors, and these errors will include some on words which are way beyond their capabilities and for which they can do little better than offer a random guess. There is no good theoretical reason to assume that words which are almost within the child's spelling vocabulary and words which are far in advance of his spelling skills will be mis-spelled in the same sort of way. Indeed, experience suggests that if a word is much too difficult for a child he is more likely to produce a grossly mis-spelled error, or produce only part of the word. Also, some words are especially prone to a particular type of error, e.g. SON is often mis-spelled as SUN but other mis-spellings of SON are extremely rare. Thus if error types obtained from different words are compared, such error tendencies of specific words may seriously bias the results.

Fourthly, there is a danger that inappropriate norms are used. If the individual child's errors are compared with the errors made by children of the same age, one makes the assumption that the relevant factor in determining the 'normal' pattern of errors is chronological age rather than level of spelling achievement. However, the generally accepted theories of cognitive development argue for a fixed and necessary order in the development of cognitive skills, and this would imply that it is level of spelling achievement that is the relevant factor in determining the types of error made rather than chronological age. Hence, it would be more appropriate to compare the poor speller with younger children of the same spelling ability than with those of the same age with superior spelling ability. Only then can one be sure whether there is an abnormal pattern of errors such as might indicate some particular weakness of the poor speller. Therefore the ways in which spelling error patterns may change with age and achievement level must be established before the significance of the individual child's results can be evaluated.

Bearing these criticisms in mind the 'Word Equated Spelling Test' (W.E.S.T.) was devised in order to enable the errors made by children to be analysed with objectivity and reliability and to explain as well as to describe the nature of the errors. The choice of error categories was determined by the specific intention of using this test to investigate the spelling deficits in dyslexic children. It was guided by analyses of the mis-spellings made by adult patients with acquired spelling deficits.

An important study in this respect was carried out by Kinsbourne and Warrington (1964) who compared groups of adult patients with cerebral lesions on oral spelling tasks. They found that the quality of the mis-spellings produced by dysphasic patients reflected their underlying language dysfunctions whilst the quality of mis-spellings produced by patients with finger agnosia reflected their underlying sequencing difficulties.

If different underlying cognitive dysfunctions can produce different patterns of spelling errors in the acquired dyslexias then it seems reasonable to propose that the dysfunction(s) underlying the developmental dyslexias could also be reflected in the quality of the spelling errors produced. According to this rationale and in order to test some popular theories of developmental dyslexia the following three error categories were chosen: (i) order errors, which may be considered to reflect sequencing problems, (ii) phonetically inaccurate errors, which may be considered to reflect auditory-linguistic problems, and (iii) orthographically illegal errors, which may be considered to reflect visual-linguistic problems. Each of these three areas of deficit has been specifically postulated as a primary cause of developmental dyslexia.

TABLE 1   Word Equated Spelling Test (W.E.S.T.)

My	044	Put	040	Air	021	Able	010
It	044	Sky	031	Said	110	Eight	021
No	022	Ago	040	Mark	011	Honey	010
As	040	Free	020	Shot	030	Fruit	020
Be	000	Cake	020	Skin	021	Crown	021
Box	040	Girl	120	Act	030	Uncle	000
Do	020	Add	011	Mile	021	Children	130
Yes	010	Oil	010	Die	030	Knew	010
Love	140	Fast	021	Head	220	Every	120
Run	040	Nice	021	Why	002	Grasp	021
Was	010	Age	021	Care	010	Suit	020
Its	040	Kill	010	Dress	021	Knife	010
Old	030	Town	030	Few	011	Would	020
Hot	040	Been	010	Pain	010	Angel	310
Now	011	Who	310	Use	011	Speak	000
With	130	Much	041	Knee	010	Fail	010
Blue	020	Ask	020	Held	020	Sign	000
Her	030	Year	130	Done	000	Castle	010
Ice	030	About	030	Mean	000	Wrong	010
Say	010	Shoe	020	People	120	Circle	020
Friend	320	Sword	010	Prayer	010	Probably	000
Taste	000	Health	010	Example	010	Autumn	010
Area	000	Ought	011	Journey	020	Neither	200
Sigh	011	Measure	000	Really	000	Tongue	400
Laugh	020	Label	310	Tomorrow	010	Pleasant	000
Ocean	010	Bridge	100	Lying	000	Attitude	000
Double	010	Kitchen	120	Ancient	000	Success	000
Early	010	Thought	021	Science	010	Seize	210
Public	010	Colour	100	Guard	310	Built	000
Movement	010	Quiet	310	Beauty	110	Debt	010
Breath	031	Fifty	012	Policy	000	Height	200
Judge	110	Answer	200	Accept	000	Foreign	400
Loss	010	Address	000	Honour	000	Precious	100
Already	000	Figure	200	Patient	100	Professor	000
View	210	Travel	004	Special	000	Business	200
Coffee	000	Clothe	000	University	000	Campaign	011
Nevertheless	010	Several	010	Except	000	Aerial	000
Calm	000	Allow	000	Territory	000	Possess	000
Gain	010	Complete	010	Society	001	Committee	000
Banana	020	District	030	Theatre	210	Possession	000

2 The W.E.S.T., a new spelling test[1]

The W.E.S.T. comprises 160 words which provide a comprehensive selection of phoneme-grapheme equivalents encountered by children at different achievement levels. There was no intentional bias in the selection of the words except that words thought to be particularly susceptible to order errors (e.g. WHO, LABEL) were specifically included. There are some 20 words for each year of spelling achievement from a basal age of 5.3 years. An overall level of spelling achievement is calculated from the number of words correctly spelled and the first 20 misspelled words are taken for error analysis. The special feature of the W.E.S.T. is that each word has been classified according to its propensity to result in particular error types. This is indicated by 3 digit numbers, as shown in Table 1, and explained in detail in Section 2.4. The words are dictated.

2.1 Standardisation

The W.E.S.T. was administered to all the children in five year groups (age range $5\frac{1}{2}$–12 years) at three suburban council schools. Out of these 176 children 137 could write at least 25/26 letters of the alphabet dictated in random order, in both nominal and phonetic forms. This latter group formed the standardisation sample (mean age 9.2 years, SD 1.6). The first three columns of the Schonell Graded Word Spelling Test (Form A) was also administered and the scores pro-rated to give spelling age equivalents (mean Schonell S.A. 8.8 years, SD 1.3). The two spelling tests, which used two entirely different sets of words, were highly correlated (r = 0.95), which indicates good concurrent validity for the new test. This is supported by the similarity in correlation between age and spelling score on both tests (both r = 0.7).

2.2 Error categories

The first 20 incorrectly spelled words are taken for error analysis. A mis-spelled word is considered as a whole and classified according to presence or absence of each of the following independent error categories.

Category OR: Order errors. An order error is present if all and only the letters of the stimulus word are given, but are given in the wrong order. For example: SEY for YES, WHIT for WITH, YSA for SAY.

Category PI: Phonetically inaccurate errors. A phonetically inaccurate error is present if the error word shows the omission, addition or substitution of some phonemic element. For example: AG for AGO,

---

[1] A test manual is available from the author

OILED for OIL, OOTS for ITS. A mis-spelling was not considered to be phonetically inaccurate as long as it could possibly represent the component phonemic elements, even if the choice of grapheme was a most unlikely one. For example: NEYES for NICE and NOWA for NOW.

Category OI: Orthographically illegal errors. An orthographically illegal error is present if the written word contains some grouping of letters which cannot possibly be found within the English orthographical system, and which the child can never have seen in this order or position in his reading experience. For example: NEDH for HEAD, CKAK for CAKE, SHOHW for SHOE.

The error categories are mutually independent but not exclusive. Thus it is possible to obtain errors that score positively on more than one error type (e.g. WSA for SAW would score positively on all 3 error categories); also it is possible to obtain errors that score negatively on all three error types (e.g. BATE for BAIT).

TABLE 2   Normative data for W.E.S.T.

Age range (yrs)		Age	No. of words correct	Spelling age[1] equiv.	Analysis of first 20 errors		
					OR[2]	PI[2]	OI[2]
6.5– 8.4	Mean	7.5	42	7.5	1.8	8.1	3.2
n = 47	SD	0.5	24	1.2	1.5	4.1	2.2
8.5–10.4	Mean	9.0	74	9.1	2.2	6.9	2.4
n = 42	SD	0.3	27	1.4	1.4	4.1	1.7
10.5–12.0	Mean	11.2	113	11.1	2.7	3.5	1.3
n = 48	SD	0.3	33	1.7	1.9	3.6	1.6

Correlation data

CHRONOLOGICAL AGE (CA) VS
PI errors, r = −0.53 (p < 0.001)
PI errors, with SA held const.,
Partial r = −0.08 (N.S.)
OI errors, r = −0.38 (p < 0.001)
OI errors, with SA held const.,
Partial r = −0.01 (N.S.)

SPELLING AGE (SA)[1] VS
PI errors, r = −0.66 (p < 0.001)
PI errors, with CA held const.,
Partial r = −0.47 (p < 0.001)
OI errors, r = −0.51 (p < 0.001)
OI errors, with CA held const.,
Partial r = −0.37 (p < 0.001)

[1] Spelling age = No. correct/19.6 + 5.3 yrs.
[2] OR, order error; PI, phonetically inaccurate; OI, orthographically illegal.

2.3 *Normative data*

Table 2 shows means and standard deviations for the quantitative and qualitative measures that can be obtained from the W.E.S.T. It also shows the correlations of two of the error types with Chronological Age and with Spelling Age (number of words spelled correctly). These correlations are important as they give clear support for the notion that spelling level is the relevant factor when considering error types and not chronological age. Normally, these two factors vary together: an older child normally has a higher spelling attainment. However, the technique of partial correlation allows one to estimate the effect of these two factors separately. Thus, when spelling level is partialled out, (or held constant), then no effect remains that might be due solely to age. On the other hand, when age is partialled out (or held constant), then a substantial effect remains that must be due just to spelling level.

Order errors could not be interpreted in this way because the test had a bias towards the inclusion of order error producing words, and therefore their true relationship to either CA or SA could not be assessed. Given the bias of the present word list the number of order errors obtained were very few. The most striking type of order error, where change of grapheme order represents a change of phoneme order (e.g. WAS–SAW) occurred predominantly in younger children. Order errors for older children tended to be restricted to words where an alternative and more common spelling pattern would still preserve the correct sound (e.g. LABLE–LABEL, NIETHER–NEITHER).

2.4 Individual word analysis

For each individual word in the W.E.S.T. all the mis-spellings which had been made by the standardization sample were collected together. The percentage of those words which contained an order error was calculated, and similarly the percentage of words containing a phonetically inaccurate error and the percentage containing an orthographically illegal error. These percentages were converted to a 5 point scale, so that $0-19\% = 0$, $20-39\% = 1$ etc. In this way each word was classified by a three digit number which described the frequency with which the three different types of error occurred in the normal population when errors were made on that particular word. These numbers are shown in Table 1, the first digit always refers to order errors, the second to phonetically inaccurate errors and the third digit to orthographically illegal errors. Thus a word classified as 400 would be one which, if spelled incorrectly, was very likely to result in an order error rather than any other. A word classified as 000 would be one that, if spelled incorrectly, would result in some other error than that assessed by the 3 error categories used here.

Given this analysis it is possible to compare the spelling performance of children who had been given different words. For each error made it is possible to take into account the error tendency of the particular word.

The following scoring method does this very simply. We take a mis-spelled word (say FREIND for FRIEND). We classify it in terms of the 3 error categories: order inaccurate – yes, phonetically inaccurate – yes, orthographically illegal – no. We give a score of 4 for presence and a score of 0 for absence of an error type. This produces a 3 digit number, in our case 440, which can be subtracted from the 3 digit number given for FRIEND in Table 1, namely 320. The resulting difference score, −1 −2 0, shows us that this error is quite typical for that word. Difference scores of −4 or +4 in any error category show us at a glance that the error is atypical. The difference scores can be summed up over the 20 error words of each child, and this gives an average tendency for typical or atypical errors.

3 Spelling error analysis in normal and dyslexic children

In this comparison study the more sophisticated difference scores gave identical results to the simple percentage scores which do not take error propensities of individual words into account. Therefore only the simple analysis will be reported here which gives a straightforward description of the occurrence of the 3 error types in the first 20 mis-spelled words.

The W.E.S.T. was administered to a consecutive series of 30 children who had been referred to the Psychology Department of the National Hospital, Queen Square, and had been diagnosed as having develop-mental dyslexia according to the definition given at the start of this chapter. Full details of the criteria for group selection are given else-where (Nelson, 1978), but it should be noted that all the dyslexic chil-dren were able to read and write to dictation all the individual letters of the alphabet and all had W.I.S.C. Full Scale IQs of at least 85 (the mean Full Scale IQ was 105).Since the normative data clearly indicated that error tendencies in normal children are determined by level of spelling achievement rather than by chronological age, 30 control sub-jects were chosen to match the 30 dyslexic subjects on spelling achieve-ment level. Each dyslexic child was matched with a control child whose spelling age equivalent was within a half a year of the dyslexic child's spelling age and was within one year of the control child's own chronological age. This latter requirement ensured that all the control subjects were 'average' spellers. The control group was necessarily younger than the dyslexic group.

The first twenty spelling errors made by each child on the W.E.S.T. were scored qualitatively, as described previously, and the results are given in Table 3.

TABLE 3   Comparison of dyslexic and control subjects

	Dyslexics (n=30)		Controls (n=30)		t	p<
	Mean	SD	Mean	SD		
Chronological age (years)	11.10	2.40	7.72	1.00	5.39	0.001
No. of words correct	46.60	29.20	47.00	25.40		NS
Spelling age	7.68	1.49	7.70	1.29		NS
Spelling retardation	3.42	0.93	0.02	0.36	11.20	0.001
Analysis of first 20 errors						
Order error	1.57	1.31	1.87	1.43	0.59	NS
Phonologically inaccurate	7.05	4.45	7.17	3.86	0.08	NS
Orthographically illegal	3.60	1.50	2.67	1.95	1.44	NS

First, the frequency of *order errors* was low in both groups, occurring on average in less than ten percent of the errors analysed. There was no significant difference between the groups in the frequency of occurrence of order errors. Indeed, the slight trend in the means and standard deviations would be consistent with fewer and less extreme tendencies to produce order errors amongst the dyslexic subjects than amongst their normally spelling, matched controls.

Secondly, in both groups more *phonetically inaccurate mis-spellings* were made than either of the other two error types. Nevertheless since these errors occurred in only just over thirty-five percent of the total errors made, the majority of the mis-spellings was phonetically accurate. This error category also failed to show a significant difference between the groups.

Thirdly, in both groups the incidence of *orthographically illegal* mis-spellings was low, occurring on average in less than eighteen percent of the total errors. Although the dyslexics tended to make more of these errors than the control group, these differences were not sufficient to reach even the ten percent level of significance.

Re-ordering the words according to their relative difficulty for the dyslexic subjects produced an essentially similar order to that established in the standardisation study, with no individual word proving substantially harder or easier for the dyslexic subjects as a group.

In the present study the dyslexic children did not produce more extreme patterns of error tendencies than the controls, as shown by the similarities in the standard deviations obtained. Thus it could not be argued that the failure to find an excess of one or other type of spelling error in the dyslexic group as a whole was due to the counter-balancing effects of different sub-groups of dyslexia within this total group.

The finding that the quality of the dyslexic children's spelling is essentially normal has some important implications for theories about the aetiology of developmental dyslexia. Clearly none of the three theories that postulate primary sequencing, auditory-linguistic or visual-linguistic problems is compatible with this result. Each of them would have predicted an increased incidence of a specific type of spelling error for dyslexic children.

4 Implications for theories of dyslexia

4.1 *Sequencing problems*

A notion that has been greatly popularised by the public media is that developmental dyslexia is due to an underlying ordering or sequencing deficit. But when the spelling errors of dyslexic children were specifically analysed with respect to the occurrence of letter order errors it was found that not only did the group of dyslexic children as a whole fail to produce more order errors than the matched controls, but also there were no individual children in the group with abnormal tendencies to make this type of error. This is similar to Nelson and Warrington's (1974) results obtained using the words of the Schonell Graded Word Test where this type of error was also found infrequently in the dyslexic children's scripts. This result clearly renders untenable any suggestion that the primary cause of developmental dyslexia is a difficulty with letter ordering or sequencing.

It is perhaps surprising that the notion of impaired sequencing ability became so popular when the few objective studies of the quality of literacy skills that were available in the literature (e.g. Tordrup, 1966) had suggested that letter order errors did not play a significant part in the difficulties experienced by poor readers and spellers. It is perhaps curious that the weight of the evidence cited in support of the impaired sequencing notion appears to have been derived from aspects of the dyslexic child's functioning other than his literacy skills. For example a characteristic feature of a dyslexic child's performance on the W.I.S.C. is a particularly poor Digit Span score, often accompanied by a poor Coding score (e.g. Rugel, 1974). Although several authors follow Bannatyne (1966) in considering these two sub-tests to be principally testing sequencing ability this could be an unwarranted assumption; indeed it may well be that they are better considered as principally testing short-term memory and/or attentional processes, as suggested by Cohen (1959), and Bortner and Birch (1969). A detailed investigation of memory functions in dyslexic children (Nelson, 1978) confirmed that there were deficiencies in their short-term or primary memory systems. Thus without positive evidence to the contrary it seems unnecessary to invoke a sequencing deficit to account for the poor digit span scores when there is the simpler explanation of a less efficient primary memory system to account for the poorer performance.

Studies of normal adults have shown that if the primary memory system is over-loaded this can result in the subject sacrificing information about the order of the material in an attempt to retain more information about the content (e.g. Buschke and Hinricks, 1968). If dyslexic children are compared with control children of the same chronological age on a recall task involving sequential material then they are being compared with children who have a greater primary memory capacity: and if the primary memory systems of the dyslexic children are under greater stress, then one might expect them to produce more sequencing errors. Hence the occurrence of sequencing errors by dyslexic children in a memory task need not necessarily imply a sequencing deficit. It could be due to a poor memory capacity and the normal trade-off of order information for content information.

Letter order errors are commonly associated with letter orientation errors (b–d–p–q), and despite the evidence that these two types of error are independent of one another both in writing (Lyle, 1969) and in reading (Liberman *et al.*, 1971) they are frequently treated as though they were but different manifestations of a single process disorder. Letter orientation errors are commonly attributed to an inability of one cerebral hemisphere to dominate the other, but this notion is based on a naïve and invalid conception of how the cerebral cortex functions. It is supposed that when a child looks at a letter the images formed in each cerebral hemisphere are mirror images of one another, and therefore if one hemisphere cannot 'dominate' the other the child will have to cope with two conflicting images and may sometimes choose the 'reversed' image. But although the anatomical arrangement of the cells in the visual primary cortex are 'mirrored' in the left and right hemispheres, the visual projections to the primary cortex can only be considered to be 'mirror-images' as far as the external observer is concerned (in much the same way the visual projections would appear to be inverted to the external observer). When the information is transferred from the projection areas for processing and interpretation in other parts of the brain, the information from the two hemispheres is combined and there is no longer any simplistic spatial equivalence between the object perceived and the site of cortical excitation. So this commonly held notion of why letter reversal errors could occur in dyslexic children is clearly untenable on theoretical grounds. At the more pragmatic level it has been convincingly argued (e.g. Vernon, 1957), that the errors actually made by dyslexic children could not be adequately explained in terms of a confusion of mirror images.

In view of these considerations one must wonder how letter orientation and order errors came to be associated with developmental dyslexia, and why it became popularly accepted that the prolific production of these errors was almost a cardinal feature of the disorder. One plausible explanation is that the dyslexic children have been compared inadvertently with an inappropriate norm. This could produce a particularly striking effect with the letter reversal errors. We know that letter reversals are not uncommon before the alphabet has been learned, and that these mistakes gradually disappear from the normal child's writings as his over-learning of the alphabet increases until they are virtually never found after about 8–9 years of age. In such a situation the occurrence of a letter reversal in a child of 9+ years might well strike the tester as being of potential significance, unless he also takes into account that the level of alphabet mastery and spelling is only at the 6+ year equivalent level. Similarly, the occurrence in an older child of a letter order error which involves a phoneme order error might well strike the tester as being of potential significance unless he also takes into account the much younger spelling age of that child.

4.2 *Visual-linguistic problems*

The visual aspect of reading is a very immediate and obvious one and thus it is not surprising that a number of theories of developmental dyslexia have been based on notions of impairment in the visual perception and/or analysis of written words. Inherent in the visuo-perceptual deficit hypotheses is the assumption that the spelling disability of dyslexic children is a result of inaccurate revisualisation of the forms of the words. On these grounds one might expect to find a relatively increased incidence of orthographically illegal errors. However, the results only showed a non-significant trend for the dyslexic children to produce more orthographically illegal errors than their controls. This result is in keeping with the increasing body of evidence that visual perception and recall are not major factors in determining reading disability (Vellutino *et al.*, 1975).

In any case one must seriously question the assumption that know-ledge of a word's spelling is retained as a visual image in some long-term visual memory store in view of evidence to the contrary that has come from neuro-psychological research. Studies of patients with unilateral brain lesions have clearly demonstrated that memory for purely visual material is mediated by the non-dominant hemisphere whilst memory for verbal material is mediated by the dominant hemisphere (e.g. Milner, 1971). Since studies of both neurological patients and normal adults using tachistoscopic presentation of material to one or other hemisphere have shown that reading and spelling skills are functions of the dominant hemisphere, it seems most unlikely that they depend on visual images stored in the visual memory system of the non-dominant hemisphere.

4.3 *Auditory-linguistic problems*

Since the auditory aspects of learning to read and spell are so important it has also been supposed that developmental dyslexia might be due to deficiencies in the auditory processes. However, Hammill and Larsen (1974) concluded from their comprehensive survey of the literature that the evidence failed to confirm the assumptions that particular auditory skills were essential to the reading process, or that substantial numbers of children actually fail to read because of auditory perceptual deficits. If the dyslexic child's difficulties were due to poor auditory perception then one might expect to find some evidence of phonemic errors in their reading and spelling. This was not borne out in the present study where the dyslexic children made no more phonetically inaccurate errors than would be expected in view of their overall level of spelling achieve-ment.

In their study of adult patients who had acquired a spelling deficit as the result of a cerebral lesion Kinsbourne and Warrington (1964) found significant abnormalities in the quality of the spelling errors produced by the two groups of patients. But since the quality of the dyslexic children's errors was essentially normal, one must conclude that there is no evidence of any specific deficits underlying their difficulties of the sort found in adult patients with acquired spelling impairments. In this respect the results are consistent with the generally accepted view that developmental dyslexia cannot be attributed to a discrete focal lesion affecting only a specific and restricted aspect of the reading and spelling processes.

The dysphasic patients in Kinsbourne and Warrington's study made significantly more phonetically inaccurate errors in their spelling than the non-dysphasic patients, and it was argued that the abnormal production of this type of error reflected the underlying language impairments. So the normal quality of the dyslexic children's spelling errors implies that their literacy retardation cannot be attributed to a developmental dysphasia *per se*. In an earlier study of spelling errors made on the Schonell G.W.S.T. Nelson and Warrington (1974) suggested that the reading and spelling difficulties of the dyslexic children should be considered in the context of their other language weaknesses, which include lower Verbal than Performance IQ on the W.I.S.C. and histories of delayed speech development (Warrington, 1967). As data were not available from normal children at that time it was not possible to stipulate how the literacy and language weaknesses might be related, but as the result of the present study it would appear that the literacy retardation should not be attributed directly to the language retardation. Rather the results would be in keeping with the operation of some other factor or factors which affected both language and literacy development. The possibility that these factors may be in specific memory processes of dyslexic children has been considered and evidence for this notion has been obtained (Nelson, 1978).

5 The dual route of reading hypothesis

In adult subjects two ways of reading have been identified, the graphemic-phonemic route in which the written stimulus is converted into the phonological equivalent before the meaning is accessed, and the direct graphemic-semantic route in which the word's meaning is elicited directly by the written stimulus. The skilled reader normally relies heavily on the direct route (Coltheart *et al.*, 1977), though even at this level the effects of the two routes may be additive in obtaining the meanings of less common words. In childhood, when reading and spelling skills are still developing, it could be argued that the phonemic route will play a much more important role. If a word is not established in the child's so-called 'sight vocabulary' (i.e. can be read as a whole unit, by the direct route) then it must be read by the phonemic route, that is by decoding the written stimulus into the appropriate phonemic equivalents and reblending these to make the whole word. For further discussion of these processes in relation to adults and children respectively the chapters by Cohen and Bryant and Bradley can be referred to (Chapters 7 and 16).

There is good reason to suppose that the phonemic route of reading involves short-term memory. As a written word is decoded into its phonemic elements these must be held in some temporary store before being re-blended into the whole word. In view of the duration and accuracy of storage required, and more particularly in view of the phonological nature of the material to be stored, the primary memory system is clearly the most suitable for this temporary storage. However the direct route of reading relies more heavily on the semantic memory system since it involves accessing material that has been acquired by and is stored within the semantic memory system.

6 The dual route of spelling hypothesis

The acquisition and practice of spelling skills in children and adults have received considerably less attention in the literature than reading skills. The theory that will be considered here is that, just as in reading, there are two routes of spelling, namely a phonemic-graphemic route which operates by translating the phonemic elements of the word as spoken into their graphemic equivalents and a direct semantic-graphemic route.

During the development of spelling ability the many ways in which the different phonemes can be represented by written letters have to be learned together with certain rules about the English orthography (e.g. when to drop a final *e* before adding *ing*). Apart from such general rules, specific information pertaining to the spelling of an individual word also has to be learned. In this latter case the information would be associated with a particular lexical entry. The information stored in this way could be just one part of the word (e.g. that the /I/ in STREET is represented by *ee*) or it could be the whole written word.

Bearing in mind the limitations set by the amount of general and specific information about spelling that is stored in semantic memory, the phonemic route for spelling would proceed via the spoken word by analysing this into its constituent phonemic elements and then converting these into their appropriate graphemic equivalents. In the English orthography this latter stage is far from simple, particularly where vowel sounds are concerned, because there are often several ways of graphemically representing a particular phoneme. In this case, reference must be made back to the lexical entry which provides word specific spelling information. In this way it is possible to check which of the graphemic alternatives is the appropriate one for that particular word. If the spelling of the whole word had been stored, then the direct route for spelling could operate, i.e. directly from the lexical entry not via a phoneme conversion stage. As with reading, efficient spelling probably relies on the additive effects of both spelling routes.

7 Differences between reading and spelling

Although there are very obvious parallels between the dual route theories of reading and spelling one would be quite wrong to regard the spelling process merely as the reverse of the reading process. In adult subjects a reading impairment following a cerebral lesion can occur independent of a spelling impairment, and vice versa. Thus reading and spelling processes can be distinguished at an anatomical level. At a functional level also there are a number of important differences. First, the number of phoneme alternatives for any one grapheme is generally fewer than the number of grapheme alernatives for any one phoneme. Hence reading via the phonemic route is simpler than spelling via the phonemic route. For example, the written word STREET could only be pronounced in one way, whereas the spoken word /strɪt/ could reasonably be written as STREAT, STRETE or STREET. Secondly, in normal reading the end product must be real words which are stored in their phonological form. With legal non-words there are often many ambiguities of pronunciation and stress, but this 'real word' constraint greatly reduces the number of possible sound equivalents that are tenable for particular letter strings. Indeed, if it were not for this constraint relatively few words could be read by the phonemic route alone. In spelling, on the other hand, there does not appear to be an equally strong constraint to assist selection of appropriate grapheme equivalents. There are illegal and legal sequences of letters in English orthography (e.g. the /k/ sound at the beginning of a word cannot be represented by *ck*) but it is not clear how well this knowledge is mastered by a child or the average adult. The spoken form of a 'real word' is usually more practised and hence more familiar than the written form. Therefore, whereas the phonemic route of reading enables most written words to be read correctly because the subject can readily eliminate the phonemic possibilities that would not form a real word, the phonemic route of spelling does not to the same extent allow elimination of different graphemic possibilities. There is a third difference between reading and spelling that also indicates that reading is the easier task. Whereas the reader may recognise a word on the basis of a few letters only, the speller must accurately reproduce all the letters of the word.

8 Causes of spelling retardation

Children with developmental dyslexia, according to the definition given at the beginning of this chapter, are retarded in both reading and spelling development. One of the complicating factors in any investigation of the possible causes of the spelling difficulties in dyslexic children is knowing to what extent the spelling deficits could be secondary to the reading deficits. When reading and spelling are mature skills, reading ability can become impaired (e.g. as the result of a cerebral lesion) without necessarily affecting spelling ability. However, whilst these skills are developing poor reading ability will inevitably have some effect on the development of spelling ability both by limiting the opportunity for learning and by affecting the ability of the child to accurately monitor his own written work. But it is unlikely that what can often be a very severe spelling retardation could be accounted for merely in terms of a secondary effect of the reading retardation.

An hypothesis to account for the dyslexic children's spelling problems which can be tentatively put forward on the basis of the essentially normal quality of their spelling errors is that their main difficulty lies in the *acquisition* of spelling knowledge by the semantic memory system. Furthermore it is suggested that once this knowledge has been acquired it can be accessed normally by both spelling routes. This would explain why there are no more phonetically or orthographically inaccurate errors than one would expect given a certain level of knowledge. Thus there is a case for a learning rather than a retrieval problem. This would be consistent with the results of a study (Nelson, 1978) which showed that dyslexic children had difficulty with the acquisition of new semantic information but had no apparent difficulty with accessing well-established semantic information.

Although most children referred for literacy problems are retarded in both reading and spelling, a number of children have never had any difficulty with reading and are retarded only in spelling (e.g. Naidoo, 1972). In these latter cases the spelling difficulties are certainly not secondary to reading retardation, and in this respect these children form a particularly interesting group. Unfortunately, too few of these children have been assessed on the present spelling test to furnish reliable results but an earlier study (Nelson and Warrington, 1974) which looked at the spelling errors made on the Schonell Spelling Test, found that these children made significantly fewer phonetically inaccurate errors than another group of children, retarded in spelling as well as in reading. Thus in the spelling-only retarded children the phonemic analysis aspect of spelling appears to have developed more in keeping with chronological age than with overall level of spelling ability, but the ability to refer back to specific word information stored in semantic memory to decide on correct graphemic representations appears to be impaired. Thus the hypothesis could be put forward tentatively that these children have a specific retrieval rather than a learning problem, in contrast to the reading-and-spelling retarded children who appear to have a learning rather than a retrieval problem.

In the Nelson and Warrington (1974) paper it was pointed out that, unlike the reading-and-spelling retarded children, the spelling-only retarded children did not show any evidence of any other verbal weaknesses and in particular their vocabulary levels were not impaired. These results, together with their normal acquisition of reading knowledge, would support the hypothesis that the spelling-only retarded children do not have a general weakness in acquiring semantic information.

In summary, the hypothesis suggested to account for *classic dyslexia*, which involves both reading and spelling problems, differs from that suggested for specific spelling retardation. The qualitative analysis of spelling errors made on the W.E.S.T. has complemented other evidence from memory studies to indicate that the most likely deficiency in classic dyslexia lies in the acquisition of spelling knowledge. It has also indicated that access via both phonemic and direct routes are in keeping with the performance level and hence that neither route is specifically impaired. Retrospective interpretation of the error analysis on words from the Schonell test has enabled the suggestion to be made that a possible cause of *specific spelling retardation* lies in the access to specific semantic-graphemic information whilst the phonemic analysis of words and the knowledge of general phoneme-grapheme equivalences are intact. This hypothesis is speculative and awaits further testing but further support is provided by Frith (Chapter 22).

Probably the most immediately useful consequence arising from the qualitative analysis of spelling errors which was the main object of this chapter is the doubt it has cast on several traditional theories of dyslexia. In particular there was a singular lack of evidence for any sequencing difficulties, or specific visual or auditory-linguistic difficulties in the spelling errors made by dyslexic children.

Acknowledgements

This study formed part of a Ph.D. thesis (London University), and I am indebted to Dr E. K. Warrington for her supervision of this work. I should like also to thank the headteachers and staff of the schools in which the W.E.S.T. was standardised.

22

Unexpected Spelling Problems

UTA FRITH   *MRC Developmental Psychology Unit, London, England*

1 Good readers who are atrocious spellers

Are reading a word correctly and writing a word correctly two sides of the same coin? Or are they separate processes which have little in common? Both make up visible language: reading means recognising words that have been written; writing means producing words that will be read. One is meaningless without the other. Learning to read should imply learning to spell, and learning to spell should imply learning to read. In the past, teachers only taught spelling, and assumed that their pupils would automatically acquire the ability to read. Today, the reverse of this idea can be seen: teachers often only teach reading, and believe that spelling will naturally follow. However, if there really was such a close relationship between reading and writing a word correctly, people who can read excellently but spell atrociously should not exist.

Yet there are such people who have not a trace of reading difficulties, but are seriously handicapped by their inability to spell. For this inability, neither lack of intelligence, nor lack of education can be blamed. There was the research student who confidently spelled SOTHERN in the belief that this word at least she knew as she saw it daily when travelling on Southern Region trains. There was the university professor who on a trip abroad wanted to write BRITAIN, a word which he had seen a thousand times before, but could not then remember whether to spell it BRITON, BRITTEN or BRITAIN. Neither of these people at any stage of their life had had a reading problem. On the contrary, they were exceptionally precocious in learning to read and were avid readers.

There are also cases of people with persistent spelling disability who have had previous reading problems which they managed to overcome. These seem to be about as frequent as persistent reading problems (Naidoo, 1972; Nelson and Warrington, 1974). Although the incidence of specific spelling problems is unknown, a conservative estimate might be about 2% of the population. This estimate is based on the relative ease of finding subjects.

It is well established that there is a positive correlation between reading and spelling performance. A review of several large scale studies is provided by Malmquist (1958), with correlations ranging from 0.50 to 0.80. The size of even the highest estimate suggests that a third of the variance is unaccounted for and, therefore, a prediction of spelling on the basis of reading performance in individual cases would not be very accurate. Discrepancies are bound to occur quite often, and they can occur at all levels of ability. Thus, a child whose reading performance is well above average and whose spelling is only average for its age, can be said to have unexpected spelling problems. What is unexpected in unexpected spelling problems is that on the one hand the person can recognise and read a word very well, but on the other hand cannot recall the correct sequence of letters when trying to write the same word.

2 The three groups of subjects defined

In order to get some understanding of this dissociation, I started by asking two questions: Do those poor spellers who are good readers make different kinds of errors from those poor spellers who are at the same time poor readers? Do poor spellers who are good readers recognise words differently from other good readers? To answer these questions I selected 29 out of about 120 twelve-year-olds from three South London secondary schools. This age group seemed suitable, as by that stage children can quite reliably be assessed as good or poor at reading and spelling. The children selected were of comparable and at least average verbal intelligence. This presumably guaranteed that there were no gross differences in intellectual skills that might (uninterestingly) account for differences in educational attainments. They were selected on the basis of their reading and spelling performance, in order that they could be divided into three groups, A, B and C, as shown in Table 1. Performance is expressed in terms of quotients with a mean of 100 taking chronological age into account, in order to show the attainments of the present samples relative to the general population.

TABLE 1   The three subject groups defined. Age 12:2 (range 11–13)

	A Good readers Good spellers		B Good readers Poor spellers		C Poor readers Poor spellers	
	10		10		9	
	Mean	SD	Mean	SD	Mean	SD
Reading quotient	106	(6)	101	(9)	81	(10)
Spelling quotient	109	(6)	90	(10)	83	(9)

Group A had children who were good at both reading and spelling, that is at least average for their ages.

Group B had children who were good at reading, with a reading level statistically identical to that of Group A, but relatively poor at spelling, with a level statistically identical to Group C. They, therefore, show a dissociation between reading and spelling skills, and so constitute the unexpectedly poor spellers on which this chapter focuses its attention.

Group C had children who were relatively poor at both reading and spelling, that is below average for their age. Since their intelligence level would lead one to expect a higher level of academic attainment, they are, in fact, unexpectedly poor readers. By this operational definition they may be termed dyslexic without implying a disease entity.

To test reading and spelling attainment, I used the Schonell graded word lists (Schonell, 1942). Thus, reading here means being able to recognise single words and pronounce them correctly. Spelling here means being able to write down the correct letter sequence of single words. Oral spelling was not required, so that difficulties in naming letters or keeping track of letters can be ruled out in accounting for poor performance. Silent reading of prose was also assessed (Frith, 1978b). Speed and comprehension were similar for Groups A and B, and both were superior to Group C. This confirmed the assessment in terms of single word reading.

3 Phonetic and nonphonetic spelling errors

One outstanding characteristic of many of the spelling errors obtained with the Schonell graded spelling test was that they preserved the sound of the target word. They were phonetic (in the layman's sense of the term). Some typical errors on arbitrarily selected words may illustrate the distinction between phonetic and nonphonetic errors:

Target word	Phonetic	Nonphonetic
cough	coff, cof	couge, coft
search	serch, surch	sherch, suach
freeze	freez, freas	frezze, fizze
instance	instants, instence	instinst, insants
attendance	attandance, attendence	attance, attence
interfere	interfear, interfeer	inteffer, interfy
allotment	alotmont, alotmeant	aloment, attolment
capacity	capasaty, capasertee	capisdy, cassaty
resource	resorse, resorce	recourse, recorse
courteous	curtious, curtius	couterious, curtess

Inevitably, such a categorisation is to some extent subjective. To mitigate this problem, the errors were classified twice by two judges. Mis-spellings on which no agreement was reached amounted to about

5% of the errors. As far as possible the task was done blind as to the group membership of the child. For each child the error types were expressed as a percentage of total errors. This qualitative comparison, which is quite independent of spelling level, is shown in Table 2.

TABLE 2   Percentage of phonetic and nonphonetic errors when spelling real words

Type of error	A Good readers Good spellers	B Good readers Poor spellers	C Poor readers Poor spellers
Phonetic	73	67	45
Non-phonetic	23	29	49
No agreement	4	4	6

Since good spellers tend to make errors on other, more difficult words than poor spellers, the qualitative comparison between poor and good spellers can be misleading. Nelson (Chapter 21) has pointed out that one word, if mis-spelled, may typically result in a phonetic error, while another may result more often in a nonphonetic error. Since Groups B and C on the whole attempted and mis-spelled the same words, this problem is avoided in the critical comparison.

Although Groups B and C made the same number of spelling errors [an average of 21.2 (range 15–24) for Group B, and an average of 21.3 (range 17–24) for Group C], they showed a different pattern in terms of error types: Group B made more phonetic errors ($t = 4.24$, $p < 0.01$) and fewer nonphonetic errors ($t = 3.40$, $p < 0.01$).

Group A was not strictly comparable to Groups B and C as their errors were produced on more difficult words that were not attempted by the other two groups. However, although they were significantly superior to Group B in terms of spelling attainment, the two groups were similar in their patterns of error types – both having an overwhelming majority of phonetic mis-spellings. This contrasted significantly with Group C, who showed an almost equal proportion of phonetic and non-phonetic errors.

There was another result which distinguished the two types of poor spellers: Group B were more consistent in their mis-spellings, that is 41% of their mis-spellings were identical when they were tested with the same list a few weeks later, compared to only 23% of Group Cs. Such qualitative differences, in spite of quantitative similarities, are evidence that unexpected spelling problems are different from spelling problems combined with reading problems, and should be approached by different remedial methods.

What can we infer about the spelling strategy of unexpectedly poor spellers? It seems that they are concerned to retain the correct sound of a word even if they do not retain the correct spelling. They can use sound-to-letter correspondence rules, but they do not seem to know the precise letter-by-letter structure of a word. Unfortunately, relying on sound-letter correspondence rules in English is not a very satisfactory strategy, as discussed in many chapters of this book (e.g. Desberg, Elliott and Marsh; Baron, Treiman, Wilf and Kellman). Group C who had more nonphonetic mis-spellings, and hence must be worse at using sound-letter correspondence rules, managed nevertheless to do as well as Group B on the spelling test. One might deduce from this that in languages with strictly phonetic orthographies Group B would not exist. However such languages are rare.

4 Phonetic spelling of nonsense words

A possible test of the hypothesis that Group B has no problem in using phoneme-to-grapheme correspondence rules while Group C does have such problems is spelling of non-words. For nonphonetic renderings it is clear that such rules could not have been used. For phonetic renderings, on the other hand, regardless of the specific choice of grapheme, one might conclude that such rules have been used. As before, phonetic spelling here is to be understood in its naïve sense, namely to indicate that the letter string can be pronounced plausibly to give the original correct sound. The term phonetic is not used here in its technical meaning, namely regarding the physical – that is, either acoustic or articulatory – features of speech sounds.

A list of 20 nonsense words was dictated. Each word was pronounced very clearly three times. These nonsense words were all possible English words, as they were derived from real words with a change of a few letters only: e.g. ZATEST (LATEST), USTERAND (UNDERSTAND), RITUATED (SITUATED), DETARDED (RETARDED), REKIND (REMIND).

As with real words, Group B was equal to Group A in terms of phonetically acceptable spellings, and significantly better than Group C. Group A produced 93% phonetically acceptable spellings and Group B 85%, while Group C produced only 67%. Thus the hypothesis is confirmed that Group B has no problems using phoneme-to-grapheme rules, in contrast to Group C which does have such problems.

5 Preferred phonetic spellings of nonsense words

The main problem of Group B when spelling real words, was that they spelled them by phoneme-to-grapheme rules, producing a phonetic version, but could not recall the exact letters of specific words. Thus, they might spell the word SEARCH like BIRCH, like PERCH or like LURCH, all of which sound correct but look wrong. With a nonsense word like HERCH any phonetic version would be correct. Hence, they were good at spelling nonsense words and poor at spelling real words. However, one aspect of the results pointed towards the fact that nonsense words, too, have favoured spellings. With good spellers at least, some phonetic versions seem more conventional than others. I noticed that the phonetic, that is correct, responses given by good spellers were mostly identical with my own spellings of the nonsense words, which they, of course, had never seen. They had only heard the nonsense words when they were dictated. There was considerable agreement in this group with each other and with me as to what letters to choose to spell the nonsense words. This was not the case for the poor spellers of Groups B and C. They had a reasonable amount of disagreement with each other and with me, so that different children used different letters, thus spelling nonsense words phonetically but unconventionally. The results are shown in Table 3. The differences between Groups A and B (t = 2.46, p < 0.01) and A and C (t = 3.23, p < 0.01) were significant.

TABLE 3   Percentage of phonetic and nonphonetic responses when spelling nonsense words

	% responses			
Type of response	A Good readers Good spellers	B Good readers Poor spellers	C Poor readers Poor spellers	Examples
Phonetic – conventional	90	75	60	USTERAND
Phonetic – unconventional	3	10	7	ASTERAND
Nonphonetic	7	15	33	AUSTERAN

How did the good spellers come to the remarkably high agreement on how to spell a nonsense word such as ZATEST? The most straightforward explanation is that they did this by analogy to the base word LATEST. If so, this would imply that good spellers aged twelve do not use a pure phoneme-to-grapheme strategy even when spelling regular nonsense words. Apparently they also take into account the letter sequence of the presumed base word. Of course, it is possible that poor spellers do the same. However, even if they recognise the analogous base word, they do not necessarily know how to spell it and are, therefore, not helped as good spellers are. This could be tested readily by asking children to say the analogous base word for a variety of nonsense words.

One implication of the results is that the technique of using nonsense words is far from being a stringent test of knowledge and application of phoneme-grapheme rules. There appears to be a strong possibility of by-passing such rules. As Marsh, Friedman, Welch and Desberg (Chapter 15) have found, this strategy is increasingly used from age ten to college level.

6 Three stages in the spelling process

The spelling errors found with real and with nonsense words allow us to derive some important details about the process of spelling. The majority of errors were phonetic mis-spellings. This implies three stages. First, there must have been a correct analysis of the speech sounds, that is, the approximate phonemes have been derived. Second, the phonemes must have been converted into graphemes by appropriate conversion rules or, possibly, by analogies rather than rules. The third stage implied by phonetic mis-spellings is that the conventionally correct graphemes out of all the phonetically plausible graphemes have to be selected. The failure indicated by phonetic mis-spellings can thus be located at the very end of the spelling process, at a stage beyond phoneme-to-grapheme rules.

This failure seems characteristic of most of the few spelling errors made by good spellers (Group A), and most of the many spelling errors made by unexpectedly poor spellers (Group B). It also applies to a large proportion of the spelling errors of the other poor spellers (Group C). However, another large proportion of their errors can be attributed to failure at the phoneme-to-grapheme stage. This includes errors due to not knowing certain spelling rules, for instance the final e rule (e.g. BIT is written instead of BITE). They pre-suppose that the child has analysed the correct phonemes, but in this case did not know that without the final e the preceding vowel is short and hence pronounced quite differently. Most of the nonphonetic errors were probably failures at this stage of the spelling process, and this is what one would expect during the acquisition period of spelling. Baron et al. (Chapter 8), however, have found even with adults that there are marked individual differences in spelling.

While there are formulations of spellings rules (a list of about 14 major rules appears, for example, in *Webster's New Collegiate Dictionary* there is no definitive systematic description. From considerations of statistical frequency, a different picture emerges of what the rules are than comes from purely historical or linguistic considerations. For these reasons a proper analysis of spelling errors of this type is difficult.

A small proportion of the nonphonetic errors may have been due to failure at stage one: the incorrect phoneme was derived from the speech sound. This could be the case for such errors as AMOT for AMOUNT, or GROUD for GROUND. As N. Smith (1973) and Dodd (1974) have shown, the omission of the nasal consonant before a stop consonant is characteristic of an early stage of phonological development in children and, therefore, if it occurs in older children it is indicative of phonological problems. Marcel (Chapter 17) discusses the relevance of cluster reduction errors to spelling and their possible causes. Looking specifically for cluster reduction errors in another study, I found this significantly discriminated good spellers from poor spellers at age seven. At the twelve-year-old level such errors were rare, but nevertheless occurred in all but one of the Group C children. The characteristic nonphonetic spelling errors of language-disordered children are described in Chapter 18, by Cromer and these can clearly be accounted for by phonological deficits.

The error analysis suggests that members of Group C suffer from problems at an earlier stage of the spelling process than Group B, possibly at the phoneme stage. Since Group C can be considered a mildly dyslexic group, this fits in with recent suggestions that there are phonemic problems in developmental dyslexia (Snowling, in press). In this volume, different theories of developmental dyslexia are discussed in the chapters by Nelson, and Seymour and Porpodas.

The distinction between Groups B and C is similar to the distinction made by Nelson and Warrington (1974) (see also Nelson, Chapter 21) and Sweeney and Rourke (1978). In each case, two groups of poor spellers were compared, and were found to differ in the level of the phonetic accuracy of their mis-spellings. On the basis of evidence from other tests, these authors agree in their conclusions that the deficit of the groups corresponding to Group C here is primarily a language deficit – in contrast to the other (B) groups, whose problem is decidedly not a linguistic one. The precise nature of their problem, however, still appears to be an open question.

7 Stage three: beyond sound-letter correspondence rules

From the spelling error analysis it appears that unexpected spelling problems are mainly due to a failure at stage three. This stage is the most puzzling in the whole spelling process, since it is arguable whether it is governed by rules at all. Sloboda (Chapter 11) points out that there is little evidence to reject the hypothesis of rote learning for perfecting spelling at this level. Nevertheless, it cannot be ruled out that there are rules based on deep levels of linguistic analysis that determine the choice of grapheme at this stage of spelling. That this may be true for some words and some individuals at least is suggested by Tenney's findings (Chapter 10).

Against rote learning is the observation that children do use graphemic rules (i.e. rules not based on sound) and analogies when spelling novel words. An example might be the use of -*ed* to indicate past tense, even though phonetically -*t* would be more appropriate. Against linguistic rules is that they are complex and of a large and unknown number, or that they are known by hindsight only. For example, one should theoretically know how to spell NATION (rather than NASHEN) because of the morphological relationship to NATIVE; on the other hand, one probably only knows about the relationship because one can spell NATION. Also there are pitfalls where relationships give misleading cues. For example, PRONUNCIATION, which might be spelled PRONOUNCIATION as it relates to PRONOUNCE; SPATIAL, which might be spelled SPACIAL as it relates to SPACE; DECEIT, which might be spelled DECEIPT as it relates to DECEPTION.

However many rules one may state, there always remain words that are purely arbitrary in their spelling. This may be especially true for English, with its many underlying languages and long history of spelling and spelling reforms (Venezky, Chapter 1). However, exceptions to rules can be found in the orthography of most languages. Rather than speak of rules, one might speak of different orthographic systems that underlie English through the different underlying languages and spelling traditions. Knowing these systems would enable one to handle stage three of spelling. This purely orthographic knowledge is not the same as lexical or semantic or morphological knowledge, and not the same as word-specific memory. It would undoubtedly depend on rote memory, but once acquired could be generalised and used in rule-governed ways. Unexpected spelling problems could then be attributed to ignorance of the basic orthographic systems in English, and not be attributed to rote learning failure, nor to some linguistic failure. To understand the notion of orthographic systems, the chapters by Smith and Baker are highly relevant.

In the English dictionary one can find words derived from almost all European and many non-European languages. However, historically the most important sources are Latin, Greek, German and French. Each of these has characteristic spelling rules, so that if one knows the origin of a word one has a set of constraints on possible graphemes (e.g. *k* and *w* never occur in words derived from Latin). Much of this knowledge is not explicit, and not open to conscious introspection. Yet such techniques as stress assignment and spelling reform tasks, as used by Smith and Baker, indicate that the knowledge is there. They have shown that there is remarkable sensitivity to the language origin of words. This sensitivity is remarkable because it appears to be achieved without much explicit instruction. The obvious way in which this could be learned is through reading: by looking at written or printed words carefully – that is their letter-by-letter sequences – we gain incidental knowledge of the orthographic peculiarities of the different underlying systems. From this we should predict that good spellers and unexpectedly poor spellers show different reading strategies. We could then be more precise about the possible cause of unexpected spelling failure. Such failure may be the result of a particular reading strategy – a strategy that succeeds without detailed attention to the letter-by-letter structure of words. This is reminiscent of hypotheses put forward by Henderson (Chapter 5) and by Marsh *et al.* (Chapter 15). Reading strategy differences would clearly provide a viable hypothesis for stage three spelling failure. For this reason, the remainder of this chapter is concerned with word reading differences between Groups A and B.

8 Reading strategies in good and poor spellers

8.1 *From print to meaning and from print to sound*

On the Schonell Graded Word Reading Test, Groups A and B achieved similar scores (see Table 1). However, a similar level can be achieved by qualitatively different strategies. As many authors have argued in other chapters, there are two (at least) distinct ways of recognising script or print: one 'by eye', which goes directly from print to meaning; the other 'by ear', which goes first from print to sound and then from sound to meaning. For a full discussion see Cohen, Barron, and Morton, Chapters 7, 8 and 9. From the overall score we cannot say which strategy was used.

By presenting nonsense words to be read, to some extent one can test for the ability to use grapheme-to-phoneme correspondence rules and thus for reading 'by ear'. A rational approach to reading nonsense words would be to use such rules; however, reading by analogies to real words is also possible. The nonsense words to be read were English-like and derived from real words. Each word exemplified a particular grapheme-to-phoneme rule, e.g. *c* before *e* becomes /s/ (LAUCER for SAUCER). If the critical graphemes were pronounced incorrectly, an error was scored regardless of the rest of the word. Conversely, if the critical grapheme was pronounced correctly, no error was scored even if the rest of the word was incorrect.

Group A made 11% reading errors, and Group B 24%, which was significantly more. The difference is surprising since the groups had achieved the same attainment level on word recognition. Most of the words on which the nonsense words were based had been read correctly by these children. Yet, Group B made letter to sound translation errors in about a quarter of the nonsense words. This suggests that they had not read the corresponding real words by such translation rules, but by look-and-say strategy, thus by-passing grapheme-to-phoneme translation.

When reading can proceed 'by eye', as with the recognition of words in sight vocabulary or with silent reading of text for meaning, Groups A and B cannot be differentiated. However, when reading has to proceed 'by ear', as for instance in the reading of critical grapheme-to-phoneme correspondences in nonsense words, the groups can be differentiated. A series of experiments that provides the evidence (Frith, 1978b) included reading text aloud and silently; reading mis-spelled words that preserved sound and those that did not; judging word pairs that did or did not rhyme, and judging sentences that did or did not sound correct. Group B did slightly worse, yet consistently so, whenever they had to go from print to sound, but were equal to Group A when they had to go from print to meaning.

8.2 *Reading with partial cues*

Since good spellers are well versed in converting print to sound, if this is required, one might hypothesise that they are fast and accurate with a strategy that can be described as reading by full cues. By this I mean taking account of all cues available in a word, including its letter-by-letter structure. Reading by full cues would entail attention to sound. It would also provide a good basis for acquiring spelling skills.

Reading by partial cues can be contrasted with this, and might be characteristic of Group B. It capitalises on the redundancy present in written language, in that many elements in a word are not essential to its recognition. Such a strategy is plausible, simply on the grounds that one can recognise fragmented or distorted words, and also that one often misses typing, printing or writing errors. Strong support for such a partial cue strategy is provided by letter cancellation tasks, which clearly show that attention in the reader varies systematically with the position of the letter in the word (Smith and Groat, 1979). Thus, whether a letter will be missed or detected can be predicted. Using partial cues for reading can only be possible when reading 'by eye', since reading 'by ear' demands attention to all letters in the word in the right order. On the other hand, the cues that are sampled by a visual-spatial approach need not be in any particular order. Words can often be recognised on the basis of minimal cues, e.g. first letter and overall length. If this does not lead to recognition, there might be repeated sampling of different parts of the stimulus until the word is recognised. There is no doubt that reading by partial cues is economical and successful in most normal reading situations. However, it would provide less opportunity for acquiring knowledge of the underlying spelling systems. It would also provide a poor basis for the letter-by-letter programme necessary for spelling production. Thus, a strong preference for reading by partial cues and/or a dislike for reading by full cues (i.e. using a redundant strategy) might result in someone being a good reader, yet an atrocious speller.

8.2.1 *Reading mis-spelled and partially obliterated text.* Consistent with the hypothesis of preference for partial cue reading is the observation that Group B is handicapped when reading mis-spelled words, which was true even when reading their own spelling mistakes (Frith, 1978b). This should be so since the partial cues they select from seriously mis-spelled words could often be misleading. Group A, who usually attend to more detail, should have a better chance of finding an error and of ignoring a misleading cue.

One can also predict that incomplete words, containing fewer redundant elements but no misleading ones, would not be more difficult to read for Group B than for Group A. This can be contrasted with reading mis-spelled words, containing redundant and potentially misleading cues, a condition which apparently is more handicapping for Group B than Group A. To test this prediction I used the same words and omitted the same letters, but in the 'partial cue' condition I replaced those letters by inverted triangles, and in the 'mis-spelled' condition I replaced them by other phonetically plausible letters. The choice of letters omitted was dictated by the availability of a reasonable phonetic substitute, for example:

myles – m▽les; ennergee – e▽erg▽; cood – co▽▽d; steddy – st▽▽dy

It is obvious that the letters that were retained can in no way be claimed to be the same partial cues that the children would have selected themselves during reading. For this reason alone, one would expect this condition to be much harder than normal text.

As the examples show, the same partial cues were available in both conditions, but only one condition had potentially misleading cues, the substituted letters, and these were not misleading to children who adopted a phonetic strategy. The words were presented in connected prose based on the GAP reading test (McLeod, 1970). Three paragraphs, each 60 words long, were used: 34 words were selected for the two distortions; 21 words, almost all short words that were difficult to mis-spell phonetically, were correctly spelled. There were also five gaps in all versions of the text where the omitted word had to be guessed. This was meant to induce reading for meaning. The child was asked to read as if the text were normal, and was given some practice sentences first. Any word that the child did not guess within four seconds or guessed wrongly was supplied by the experimenter. The groups did not differ in reading errors on any condition, and both groups made only few errors. Therefore, the time taken to read was used for the analysis. Each child read the two distorted text conditions and a normal version, each time using a different text for each condition. The order of conditions and stories was, of course, balanced. Example sentences of the two conditions are:

> Boo▽s he▽p us . . . . . le▽ ▽n and incre▽se our kno▽l▽dge.
> Boocks hellp us . . . . . lerne and increse our knolidge.

The results confirmed the predictions. Group B was slower (43.8 seconds) than Group A (30.9) on the phonetically mis-spelled condition ($t = 2.3$, $p < 0.05$), fully consistent with previous results (Frith, 1978b). In contrast, the two groups took identical times (57.9 and 58.5 seconds) to read aloud the partially obliterated text, although this was quite hard for both. Thus, as predicted, Group A lost their advantage over Group B.

Again fully consistent with previous results (Frith, 1978b), Group B took significantly longer (36.0 seconds) than Group A (26.6) to read the normal text aloud ($t = 2.2$, $p < 0.05$). This should be so since a full cue strategy is needed when reading aloud, and this would favour Group A. Reading aloud does not allow skipping of redundant elements (e.g. word endings, function words) in the text, while this skipping may occur in silent reading.

8.2.2 *Detecting a mis-spelled word.* The partial cue hypothesis also predicts that Group B should perform less well than Group A when attention to all the letters and their sound equivalents is essential, as for example in proofreading. A related, if highly artificial, task is to search for a particular mis-spelling among other mis-spellings of the same word. In the present experiment, the word DEVELOPING was used since it lends itself to many different, yet still plausible, mis-spellings. The experiment was a visual search task, where a subject has to search for a particular target embedded in a long list of words that are confusable with the target. There were four lists of 25 words, all variants of DEVELOPING. These were identical in all respects except for the identity of the target and how often it occurred. The target DEVELLOPING was embedded in arbitrary positions in one list, and the target DEVOLEPING in exactly the same positions in another list. Each target occurred twice in one list, and eight times in another.

Both targets should be highly confusable with the correct version and with the other spelling variants used, since they were all minor deviations that might easily pass unnoticed. However, DEVELLOPING sounds similar to the correct version and to most of the spelling variants, while DEVOLEPING sounds different. This fact should make the target DEVOLEP-ING more discriminable and hence easier to detect. Group A, using full cues including sound in reading, should, therefore, find it easier to detect the different sounding than the similar sounding one. On the other hand, Group B, using partial cues, should find both equally hard to detect.

The lists had an unusual graphic appearance as shown in this shortened sample:

> dEveLoPpinG
>   DeveLOuPiNg
> DEvELopInG
>   deVellOupINg
>   dEvELLoPIng
>   DaVeLOpIng
> davElOUpiNG
>   DEvEloPinG

The random case and margin changes were meant to discourage such strategies as simply looking for specific letters in specific places. The target was typed in lower case at the top of the page. The children were simply asked to 'find this' while scanning through the list, and were told to place a tick ($\sqrt{}$) next to the target whenever it occurred. Since the task was quite difficult, four practice lists were given, using different words.

The results confirmed the predictions. There were errors of omission and commission, which were combined for the two trials with each target. In the case of the target word sounding similar to the distractor words, Groups A and B were alike, with 2.8 and 2.9 errors on average.

However, in the case of the target word sounding different, A did much better than B (1.1. vs 2.8 errors). This interaction was significant ($\chi^2 = 7.9$, p <0.01). Nine out of ten good spellers had fewer errors for DEVOLLOPING than for DEVELLOPING as targets, while half of Group B had fewer errors with one target and half with the other. Because of the relatively high incidence of errors, which sometimes entailed that less than the whole list was scanned, time scores were not considered trustworthy.

Obviously the good spellers took advantage of the heightened discriminability that resulted when the target differed phonetically from the other words. The poor spellers may not have sufficiently analysed the targets to notice and take into account the phonetic dissimilarity. We can conclude that in this task unexpectedly poor spellers did not opt for a strategy that involved careful letter-by-letter analysis and thus, necessarily, grapheme-to-phoneme conversion, even though this would have been an advantage. There is no reason to believe that this result is specific to the test word DEVELOPING, but obviously a variety of words would need to be tested before generalisations could be safely made.

8.2.3 *The reversed context effect: A technique for studying the internal representation of spellings.* The visual search task was used in another experiment to compare the effect of a mis-spelled as opposed to a correctly spelled target. Correct spellings may have a privileged status, and this would help when scanning for them. As Henderson (Chapter 5) has pointed out, once a word – that is its orthographic structure – has become familiar and is memorised, it can never again be seen with naïve eyes. One way to study the familiarity of word spellings is by analogy to single letters in a visual search paradigm that leads to the reversed context effect (Frith, 1974). This is illustrated below:

ı   NNNNИNNNN

ıı   ИИИИNИИИИ

It takes longer to search for a normally orientated letter embedded in a context of mirror image letters (line ii) than it takes to search for a reversed letter in a context of normal letters (line i). It is easier to spot the 'odd-one-out' if it is also an odd-one-out in terms of one's previous experience. Likewise, deviant forms can become acceptable if they are frequent, and normal forms become hard to distinguish from them. We can look at correctly and incorrectly spelled words in the same way:

i   PERCEIVE   PERCEIVE   PERCIEVE   PERCEIVE   PERCEIVE
ii   PERCIEVE   PERCIEVE   PERCEIVE   PERCIEVE   PERCIEVE

The same effect should be obtained with words, if the correct spelling has a privileged status.

The experiment reported here uses the word SEPARATE and its common mis-spelling SEPERATE. These two spellings look and sound similar, and unless one delves into the Latin origin (SE-PARARE) of the word there is no obvious rule to decide on *a* as opposed to *e*. It is relevant that the difference between the two stimuli concerns an unstressed indeterminate sound in the middle of the word. All these factors are associated with low detectability (Smith, Chapter 2; Wing and Baddeley, Chapter 12). One would, therefore, expect that only a person using full cues would take notice of this vowel. A person using partial cues would be vague about the identity of a letter that in any case is likely to receive very little attention in the word. With the same amount of reading experience, Group A might have gained familiarity with the critical *a* in SEPARATE, since they can readily use full cues when reading, but Group B might not, since they strongly prefer partial cues when reading. Thus SEPARATE might have privileged status for Group A, leading to the reversed context effect, but not for Group B.

The SEPARATE task was similar to the DEVELOPING task as the same procedure and instructions were used. Again there were random margins and case alterations. There were four lists, 30 words long, with two, four, eight and ten targets. All the distractor words had identical spellings, and this made the task much easier than the previous one. Only three and four children in each group made any errors at all. The children were not told what the correct spelling of SEPARATE was and, indeed, only few could write the word correctly: five of Group A and three of Group B. A reversed context effect, if any, must therefore be due to reading rather than writing experience.

All ten of the good spellers were faster with an incorrect target, and thus showed a clear reversed context effect and hence evidence of a special status of the correct target. With the poor spellers in Group B, no such systematic effect could be seen. About half the children were slower with the correct targets, and half were slower with the incorrect targets. This significant interaction ($\chi^2 = 6.62$, p < 0.05) suggests that good spellers (at least for the word SEPARATE) possess the kind of orthographic representation that is akin to the representation that one has for familiar letters. There was no systematic effect of whether or not the children could spell the word.

One possible implication of this result is that good spellers can easily be made uncertain about the correct spelling of a word that they know well. Simply, frequent exposure to an incorrect version can make a good speller waver. Apparent instability of spelling knowledge has anecdotal support: examiners sometimes report that their spelling ability has been rendered considerably poorer by reading through examination scripts.

A stage three deficit in spelling could be related to a lack of letter-by-letter representations as opposed to representations that consist of partial cues just sufficient for the identification of the word. Poor spellers often report that they learn spellings by deliberate enunciation of all the letters in a word – often at variance with its normal pronunciation. This strategy is, of course, one that entails attention to the letter-by-letter sequence of words, so that the correct letters are remembered in the correct order. It also often includes the use of stress on a normally unstressed syllable (e.g. sep*a*rate), and thus ensures that even twilight places of the word are attended to. Ehri (Chapter 14) discusses this strategy and its implications.

8.2.4 *Reading by eye and writing by ear.* The reading results have suggested that the unexpectedly poor spellers read 'by eye', while the spelling results have suggested that they write 'by ear'. Very similar conclusions were reached by Bryant and Bradley (Chapter 16) for beginning readers. Is this discrepancy in strategies an explanation of the discrepancy in reading and writing performance? It is certainly not a satisfactory explanation, since the same evidence also indicates that Group A prefers to read 'by eye' and to spell 'by ear'. There is reason to believe that there is similar specialisation for input and output processes in general, as both make demands on the system that are often incompatible with each other (Frith and Frith, in press).

It can be argued that reading 'by eye' is the method of preference at all stages of reading acquisition, and at all levels of reading ability (e.g. Frith, 1978). This strategy enables one to read a phrase such as MINUTE STEAK (m*i*nute or min*u*te?); it is fast and efficient for both regular and irregular words. Its limitation is evident with nonsense words, but even here, as we have seen, an analogy strategy may go a long way.

On the other hand, on the present evidence of spelling errors (see also results by Sloboda, and Barron, Chapters 11 and 9) and of slips of the pen (Hotopf, Chapter 13), and on the evidence of nonsense word spellings by the deaf (Dodd, Chapter 19), we must conclude that a sound-based strategy is dominant in spelling. The puzzling question is why spelling should not also be done by a potentially efficient visual strategy? One could argue that spelling by ear is so often misleading that spelling by eye should be recommended as a generally better strategy. There must be reasons why such a potentially advantageous strategy is not obviously preferred.

A theory relating hearing and time on the one hand and seeing and space on the other, put forward by O'Connor and Hermelin (1978), suggests what these reasons might be. Sound has specific affinity to temporal processes, and it follows that the auditory modality is ideally suited to letter-by-letter representation. Knowing the correct sequence of letters is what is meant by spelling. Vision has specific affinity to spatial processes, and it follows that the visual modality is ideally suited for spatial representation of familiar words. Reading a word means identifying it on whatever cues or aspects of the stimulus are sufficient to get it right. The more minimal the cues need to be for correct identification, the more economical the process. Thus, reading by partial cues is as good or better a strategy as reading by full cues if the aim is recognising familiar words.

The case of Gail, presented by Morton (Chapter 6), allows a direct glimpse of how a purely visual-orthographic strategy for spelling might work. The striking characteristics are that letters are written down in a peculiar order, and there are almost always gaps in words. The first observation is entirely consistent with O'Connor and Hermelin's theory, i.e. lack of sequential information. The second observation is consistent with the hypothesis that only partial but not full information of the written word is available. It is tempting to speculate from this that reading by eye is essentially the same as reading by partial cues, and reading by ear is essentially the same as reading by full cues. Speculations on the neuropsychology of these processes might suggest that the left hemisphere governs phonological or full cue strategies, while the right hemisphere governs visual or partial cue strategies in reading and spelling.

It may seem far-fetched to talk about a neurological basis for such a highly artificial skill as spelling. Yet, neuropsychological studies (e.g. Sasanuma and Fujimura, 1972; Sasanuma, 1975; Pizzamiglio and Black, 1968) clearly indicate that brain damage in specific areas has specific effects on spelling. Langmore (1979) studied the spellings produced by Broca's aphasic patients, with brain lesions of the anterior part of the dominant (usually left) hesmisphere. She found that they were unable to spell nonsense words and that almost all of their misspellings of real words were nonphonetic, yet visually similar to the target word. She concluded therefore that the patients were not able to use phoneme-to-grapheme conversions but spelled via exclusive use of a visual memory strategy. Similarly, Wapner and Gardner (1979) found that Broca's aphasic patients produced phonetically unacceptable spellings and only patients with posterior lesions (Wernicke's and anomic aphasics) were able to produce phonetically acceptable ones. Langmore speculates that spelling in Broca's aphasics reflects processes available to the intact right hemisphere. Investigations of right hemisphere capabilities (Gazzaniga and Sperry, 1967; Levy, 1974; Levy *et al.*, 1971; Zaidel, 1978) indicate that this hemisphere does not use phonological information or phoneme to grapheme rules. Hence the strategy for spelling is limited to visual memory. Thus, another way of viewing the pervasive dichotomy of phonological and visual strategies in spelling would be to see them as left vs right hemisphere language processes. Whether or not this would provide a basis for the contrast of full vs partial cue strategies in reading and writing remains to be seen. These strategies may well be linked to more general cognitive strategies, for instance analytical (needing full cues) and holistic (possibly only using partial cues) strategies.

9 Summary

At the outset of this study I asked the question: do poor spellers who are good readers spell differently from other poor spellers? The answers provided by the experiments are clear-cut. Unexpectedly poor spellers do make different kinds of spelling errors. Their mis-spellings are consistently phonetic. We must, therefore, conclude that their problem is located at a late stage of the spelling process. To be precise, it is the stage beyond the bounds of sound-to-letter rules. Faced with equally plausible phonetic alternatives, they cannot reliably decide which grapheme is the correct one for a particular word.

The other poor spellers were a group that could be considered mildly dyslexic since both their reading and spelling attainment was retarded and not in keeping with their general intelligence. These children, in contrast to the unexpectedly poor spellers, have problems at an earlier stage of the spelling process. A sizeable proportion of their mis-spelling is inconsistent and also not phonetic. Thus, they could presumably benefit from learning phoneme-to-grapheme rules, and also phoneme analysis. Clearly, this approach would be inappropriate with the unexpectedly poor spellers. They, on the other hand, would benefit from learning the letter-by-letter structure of words. This may be a matter of rote learning, and of knowing the constraints imposed by the orthographic systems that underlie English. It is likely that this knowledge is normally incidentally learned through reading. Obviously, careful reading, based on full cues, would result in better learning than careless reading based only on partial cues.

The second question asked was whether poor spellers who are good readers read differently from other good readers. Again, the answer from a series of experiments was that they do indeed differ in their reading strategies. The difference was not detectable in the tests used for word recognition or for silent reading of prose. Thus the groups equal each other in translating print to meaning. It is possible that with more sensitive tests of silent reading of longer texts an advantage in speed would be shown by the unexpectedly poor spellers. This is at least supported anecdotally. However, in certain conditions of reading, the strategy used by the unexpectedly poor spellers is revealed as deficient in some sense. They were handicapped whenever it was necessary to translate print into sound, for instance when reading aloud, or reading nonsense words. I argued that the efficiency of good spellers under such conditions of reading is a by-product of their habitual attention to full cues, which could also be associated with slow reading. Conversely, the inefficiency of poor spellers under such conditions is a by-product of their habitual use of partial cues in reading, which on the other hand could result in especially fast reading.

Whatever one may hypothesise about the acquisition of letter-by-letter knowledge of words, whether rote learning or rule learning, partial cues are an insufficient basis to form output programmes that generate the correct letter-by-letter sequence of words. If minimal cues are used for word recognition, the reading process is highly efficient: however, only limited information becomes available through it to the spelling process. Thus, there is a cost in the elegant economy and speed of reading by partial cues: poor spelling. There is, on the other hand, an immense pay-off to the good speller in the wealth of linguistic knowledge provided by the written word – that is, its orthography, independently of the spoken word. In this sense, reading a word correctly and writing a word correctly ideally should be two sides of the same coin, and learning to read should imply learning to spell. However, such a close relationship can only be obtained if the reading process itself mimics the spelling process.

Acknowledgements

I would like to thank Jocelyn Robson for carrying out the experiments, Chris Frith for thinking them out with me, Daphne Hutchins for putting them into writing with me and Leslie Henderson for criticising them. I am grateful to Beate Hermelin and Neil O'Connor (my ideal Type A and Type B spellers) for essential stimulation and discussion.

Bibliography

This collection of references contains the references cited in the various chapters. In addition it contains references that, although not used in this volume, should not be overlooked as contributions to the study of cognitive processes in spelling. This area of research is still young enough to encourage the degree of presumption conveyed by the word 'bibliography'. However, the student of spelling may wish also to consult bibliographies on reading.

ALBROW, K. H. (1972). *The English Writing System: Notes Towards a Description*. London: Longman

ALLINGTON, R. (1978). Sensitivity to orthographic structure as a function of grade and reading ability. *Journal of Reading Behavior* (in press)

ALLPORT, D. A. (1979). Word recognition in reading: a tutorial review. In BOUMA, H., KOLERS, P. A. and WROLSTAD, M. (Eds), *Processing of Visible Language*, I. N.Y.: Plenum Press

ALPER, T. G. (1942). A diagnostic spelling scale for the college level: its construction and use. *The Journal of Educational Psychology*, **33**, 273–290

ASCH, S. E. and EBENHOLTZ, S. M. (1962). The principle of associative symmetry. *Proceedings of the American Philosophical Society*, **106**, 135–163

AVAKIAN-WHITAKER, H. and WHITAKER, H. A. (1973). The spelling errors of children with communication disorders: a preliminary classification. *Linguistics*, **115**, 105–118

BAKER, R. G. and SMITH, P. T. (1976). A psycholinguistic study of English stress assignment rules. *Language and Speech*, **19**, 9–27

BAKER, R. G. and SMITH, P. T. (1977). The psychological reality of English stress assignment rules. In DRACHMAN, G. (Ed), *Salzburger Beiträge zur Linguistik*, 4. Salzburg: Wolfgang Neugebauer

BAKER, R. G. and SMITH, P. T. (1978). Sound patterns and spelling patterns in English. In CAMPBELL, R. N. and SMITH, P. T. (Eds), *Recent Advances in the Psychology of Language, Part B. Formal and Experimental Approaches*. N.Y.: Plenum Press

BANNATYNE, A. D. (1966). Diagnostic and remedial techniques for use with dyslexic children. *Word Blind Bulletin*, **1**, nos 6 and 7

BANNATYNE, A. D. and WICHIARAJOTE, P. (1969). Relationship between written spelling, motor functioning and sequencing skills. *Journal of Learning Disabilities*, **2**, 4–16

BADDELEY, A. D. (1966). Short term memory for word sequences as a function of acoustic, semantic and formal similarity. *Quarterly Journal of Experimental Psychology*, **18**, 362–365

BADDELEY, A. D. (1976). *The Psychology of Memory*. N.Y.: Harper and Row

BADDELEY, A. D. and COLQUOHOUN, W. P. (1969). Signal probability and vigilance: a reappraisal of the 'signal rate' effect. *British Journal of Psychology*, **60**, 169–178

BADDELEY, A. D., CONRAD, R. and THOMSON, W. E. (1960). Letter structure of the English language. *Nature*, **186**, 414–416

BADDELEY, A. D. and HITCH, G. J. (1974). Working memory. In BOWER, G. H. (Ed), *The Psychology of Learning and Motivation: Advances in Research and Theory*, **8**. N.Y.: Academic Press

BARATZ, J. C. (1969a). Bi-dialectal task for determining language proficiency in economically disadvantaged children. *Child Development*, **40**, 889–901

BARATZ, J. C. (1969b). Teaching reading in an urban negro school system. In BARATZ, J. C. and SHUY, R. W. (Eds), *Teaching Black Children to Read*. Washington D.C.: Center for Applied Linguistics

BARGANZ, R. A. (1974). Phonological and orthographic relationships to reading performance. *Visible Language*, **8**, 101–122

BARON, J. (1973). Phonemic stage not necessary for reading. *Quarterly Journal of Experimental Psychology*, **25**, 241–246

BARON, J. (1974). Facilitation of perception by spelling constraints. *Canadian Journal of Psychology*, **28**, 37–50

BARON, J. (1975). Successive stages in word recognition. In RABBITT, P. M. A. and DORNIC, S. (Eds), *Attention and Performance*, V. London: Academic Press

BARON, J. (1977a). What we might know about orthographic rules. In DORNIC, S. and RABBITT, P. M. A. (Eds), *Attention and Performance*, VI. Hillsdale, N.J.: Erlbaum

BARON, J. (1977b). Mechanisms for pronouncing printed words: Use and acquisition. In LABERGE, D. and SAMUELS, S. J. (Eds), *Basic Processes in Reading: Perception and Comprehension*. Hillsdale, N.J.: Lawrence Erlbaum

BARON, J. (1978). Intelligence and general strategies. In UNDERWOOD, G. (Ed), *Strategies in Information Processing*. London: Academic Press

BARON, J. (1979). Orthographic and word-specific mechanisms in children's reading of words. *Child Development*, **50**, 60–72

BARON, J. and MCKILLOP, B. J. (1975). Individual differences in speed of phonemic analysis, visual analysis, and reading. *Acta Psychologica*, **39**, 91–96

BARON, J. and THURSTON, I. (1973). An analysis of the word-superiority effect. *Cognitive Psychology*, **4**, 207–228

BARON, J. and STRAWSON, C. (1976). Use of orthographic and word-specific knowledge in reading words aloud. *Journal of Experimental Psychology: Human Perception and Performance*, **2**, 386–393

BARR, R. (1974–5). The effect of instruction on pupil reading strategies. *Reading Research Quarterly*, **10**, 555–582

BARRON, R. W. (1978a). Access to the meanings of printed words: some implications for reading and learning to read. In MURRAY, F. B. (Ed), *The Recognition of Words: IRA Series on the Development of the Reading Process*. Newark, Del.: International Reading Association

BARRON, R. W. (1978b). Reading skill and phonological coding in lexical access. In GRUNEBERG, M. M., SYKES, R. N. and MORRIS, P. E. (Eds), *Practical Aspects of Memory*. London: Academic Press

BARRON, R. W. and BARON, J. (1977). How children get meaning from printed words. *Child Development*, **48**, 587–594

BARRON, R. W. and HENDERSON, L. (1977). The effects of lexical and semantic information on same–different visual comparisons of words. *Memory and Cognition*, **5**, 566–579

BARRON, R. W. and PITTENGER, J. B. (1974). The effect of orthographic structure and lexical meaning on 'same'–'different' judgments. *Quarterly Journal of Experimental Psychology*, **26**, 566–581

BAWDEN, H. H. (1900). A study of lapses. *Psychological Review Monograph Supplements*, **3**, 1–121

BEARD, R. (1977). Teachers' and Pupils' Construing of Reading. Paper presented at the 2nd International Congress on Personal Construct Theory. Oxford

BEAUVOIS, M.-F. and DEROUESNE, J. (1978). Phonological alexia. A study of a case of alexia without aphasia or agraphia. Paper presented at the *Meeting of the European Brain and Behaviour Society*. London

BESNER, D. and JACKSON, A. (1975). Same–different judgements with words and non-words: a word superiority/inferiority effect. *Bulletin of the Psychonomic Society*, **6**, 578–580.

BEREITER, C. and ENGLEMANN, S. (1966). *Teaching Disadvantaged Children in the Pre-school*. Englewood Cliffs N.J.

BERDIANSKY, B., CRONNELL, B. and KOEHLER, J. JR. (1969). Spelling-sound relations and primary form-class descriptions for speech-comprehension vocabularies of 6–9 year olds. *Technical Report No. 15*, Los Alamitos, California: Southwest Regional Laboratory

BERKO, J. (1958). The child's learning of English morphology. *Word*, **14**, 150–177

BIEMILLER, A. J. (1970). The development of the use of graphic and contextual information as children learn to read. *Reading Research Quarterly*, **6**, 75–96.

BLOCK, K. K. (1978). *Some Instructional Tests of a Cognitive Spelling Model*. Pittsburgh: University of Pittsburgh, Learning Research and Development Center, Publication No. 1978/18

BLOOMER, R. H. (1956). Word length and complexity variables in spelling difficulty. *Journal of Educational Research*, **49**, 531–535

BLUMBERG, P. (1976). The effects of written attempts prior to correct visual presentation on spelling acquisition and retention. *Contemporary Educational Psychology*, **1**, 221–228

BLUMBERG, P. and BLOCK, K. K. (1975). The effects of attempting spelling before feedback on spelling acquisition and retention. Paper presented at the meeting of the American Educational Research Association, Washington, D.C.

BODER, E. (1971). Developmental dyslexia. Prevailing diagnostic concepts and a new diagnostic approach. In MYKLEBUST, H. R. (Ed), *Progress in Learning Disabilities*, **2**. N.Y.: Grune and Stratton

BODER, E. (1973). Developmental dyslexia: a diagnostic approach based on 3 atypical reading-spelling patterns. *Developmental Medicine and Child Neurology*, **15**, 663–687

BOND, G. L. and DYKSTRA, R. (1967). The cooperative research program in first-grade reading. *Reading Research Quarterly*, **2**, 5–142

BOOMER, D. S. and LAVER, J. D. (1968). Slips of the tongue. *British Journal of Disorders of Communication*, **3**, 1–12

BORTNER, M. and BIRCH, H. G. (1969). Patterns of intellectual ability in emotionally disturbed and brain damaged children. *Journal of Special Education*, **3**, 351–369

BOTEL, M., HOLSCLAW, C., CAMMOROTA, G. and BROTHERS, A. (1971). *Spelling and Writing Patterns* (Rev. edn). Chicago: Follett Educational Corporation

BOWER, T. G. R. (1970). Reading by eye. In LEVIN, H. and WILLIAMS, J. P. (Eds), *Basic Studies on Reading*. N.Y.: Basic Books

BRADSHAW, J. L. (1975). Three interrelated problems in reading: a review. *Memory and Cognition*, **3**, 123–134

BRADSHAW, J. L. and NETTLETON, N. C. (1974). Articulatory interference and the mown-down heterophone effect. *Journal of Experimental Psychology*, **102**, 88–94

BRADLEY, L. and BRYANT, P. E. (1978). Difficulties in auditory organization as a possible cause of reading backwardness. *Nature*, **271**, 746–747

BRICKER, A., SCHUELL, H. and JENKINS, J. (1964). Effect of word frequency and word length on aphasic spelling errors. *Journal of Speech and Hearing Research*, **7**, 183–192

BRIGGS, D. G. (1969). Deviations from standard English in papers of selected Alabama Negro high school students. Unpublished doctoral dissertation. University of Alabama. Available from University Microfilms Ann Arbor Michigan No. 69–6528

BROOKS, L. (1967). The suppression of visualization by reading. *The Quarterly Journal of Experimental Psychology*, **19**, 289–299

BROOKS, L. (1968). Spatial and verbal components of the act of recall. *Canadian Journal of Psychology*, **22**, 349–368

BROOKS, L. (1977). Visual patterns in fluent word identification. In REBER, A. S. and SCARBOROUGH, D. L. (Eds), *Toward a Psychology of Reading*. Hillsdale, N.J.: Erlbaum

BROOKS, L. (1979). The form of knowledge of spelling-sound correspondences. In VENEZKY, R. L. and KAVANAGH, J. (Eds), *Cross-language Conference on Orthography, Reading and Dyslexia*. Baltimore: University Park Press

BROWN, H. D. (1970). Categories of spelling difficulty in speakers of English as a first and second language. *Journal of Verbal Learning and Verbal Behaviour*, **9**, 232–236

BROWN, J. (Ed.) (1976). *Recall and Recognition*. N.Y.: Wiley

BROWN, R. and FRASER, C. (1963). The acquisition of syntax. In COFER, N. and MUSGRAVE, B. S. (Eds), *Verbal Behavior and Learning Problems and Processes*. N.Y.: McGraw Hill

BROWN, R. and McNEILL, D. (1966). The 'tip of the tongue' phenomenon. *Journal of Verbal Learning and Verbal Behavior*, **5**, 325–337

BRYANT, P. E. and KOPYTYNSKA, H. (1976). Spontaneous measurement by young children. *Nature*, **260**, 773

BRYDEN, M. P. (1967). A model for the sequential organization of behavior. *Canadian Journal of Psychology*, **21**, 37–56

BUSCHKE, H. and HINRICKS, J. V. (1968). Controlled rehearsal and recall order in serial list retention. *Journal of Experimental Psychology*, **78**, 502–509

CABAN, J. P., HAMBLETON, R. K., COFFING, D. G., CONWAY, M. T. and SWAMINATHAN, H. (1978). Mental imagery as an approach to spelling instruction. *Journal of Experimental Education*, **46**, 15–21

CAHEN, L. S., CRAUN, M. J. and JOHNSON, S. K. (1971). Spelling difficulty – a survey of the research. *Review of Educational Research*, **41**, 281–301

CALFEE, R. C., LINDAMOOD, P. and LINDAMOOD, C. (1973). Acoustic-phonetic skills and reading – kindergarten through twelfth grade. *Journal of Educational Psychology*, **64**, 293–298

CALFEE, R. C., VENEZKY, R. and CHAPMAN, R. (1969). Pronunciation of synthetic words with predictable and unpredictable letter-sound correspondences. *Wisconsin Research and Development Center for Cognitive Learning, Technical Report No. 71*

CAMP, B. W. and DOLCOURT, J. L. (1977). Reading and spelling in good and poor readers. *Journal of Learning Disabilities*, **10**, 300–307

CARBONELL DE GROMPONE, M. A. (1974). Children who spell better than they read. *Academic Therapy*, **9**, 281–288

Carnegie Endowment for International Peace (1919). *A Manual of the Public Benefactions of Andrew Carnegie.* Washington, D.C.: Carnegie Endowment for International Peace

CARRELL, J. A. (1968). *Disorders of Articulation.* N.J.: Prentice-Hall

CARRELL, J. A. and PENDERGAST, K. (1954). An experimental study of the possible relation between errors of speech and spelling. *Journal of Speech and Hearing Disorders,* **19**, 327–334

CARROLL, J. B. (1958). A factor analysis of two foreign language aptitude batteries. *Journal of General Psychology,* **59**, 3–19

CARROLL, J. B., DAVIS, P. and RICHMAN, B. (1971). *The Word Frequency Book.* N.Y.: Houghton, Mifflin Co., American Heritage Printing Co.

CHAMBERS, S. M. and FORSTER, K. I. (1975). Evidence for lexical access in a simultaneous matching task. *Memory & Cognition,* **3**, 549–559

CHEDRU, F. and GESCHWIND, N. (1972). Writing disturbances in acute confusional states. *Neuropsychologia,* **10**, 343–353

CHEN, K. (1973). Pronouncability in verbal learning of the deaf. *The Journal of Psychology,* **84**, 89–95

CHOMSKY, C. (1970). Reading, writing and phonology. *Harvard Educational Review,* **40**, 287–309

CHOMSKY, C. (1971). Write first; read later. *Childhood Education,* **47**, 296–299

CHOMSKY, C. (1977). Approaching reading through invented spelling. In RESNICK, L. B. and WEAVER, P. A. (Eds), *Theory and Practice of Early Reading.* Hillsdale, N.J.: Erlbaum

CHOMSKY, N. (1970). Phonology and reading. In LEVIN, H. and WILLIAMS, J. P. (Eds), *Basic Studies on Reading.* N.Y.: Basic Books

CHOMSKY, N. and HALLE, M. (1968). *The Sound Pattern of English.* N.Y.: Harper and Row

CLARK, H. H. (1973). The language-as-fixed-effect fallacy: a critique of language statistics in psychological research. *Journal of Verbal Learning and Verbal Behavior,* **12**, 335–359

CLARK, H. H. and CLARK, E. V. (1977). *Psychology and Language. An Introduction to Psycholinguistics.* N.Y.: Harcourt Brace Jovanovich, Inc.

CLARK, R. G. B. and MORTON, J. The Effects of Priming in Visual Word Recognition. (In prep.)

COBB, L. (1831). *A Critical Review of the Orthography of Dr. Webster's Series of Books for Systematick Instruction in the English Language.* N.Y.: Collins and Hannay

COHEN, A. S. (1974–75). Oral reading errors of first grade readers taught by a code emphasis approach. *Reading Research Quarterly,* **10**, 616–650

COHEN, H. (1959). The factorial structure of the W.I.S.C. at ages 7–6, 10–6 and 13–6. *Journal of Consulting Psychology,* **23**, 285–299

COLE, R. A. and JAKIMIK, J. (1978). Understanding speech: how words are heard. In UNDERWOOD, G. (Ed.), *Strategies of Information Processing.* London: Academic Press

COLTHEART, M. (1979) Review of Gibson, E. J. and LEVIN, H. *The Psychology of Reading. Quarterly Journal of Experimental Psychology,* **29**, 157–167

COLTHEART, M. (1978). Lexical access in simple reading tasks. In UNDERWOOD, G. (Ed.), *Strategies of Information Processing.* London: Academic Press

COLTHEART, M., DAVELAAR, E., JONASSON, J. T. and BESNER, D. (1977). Access to the internal lexicon. In DORNIC, S. (Ed), *Attention and Performance,* VI, N.Y.: Academic Press.

COLTHEART, M. and FREEMAN, R. (1974). Case alternation impairs word identification. *Bulletin of the Psychonomic Society*, **3**, 102–104

COLTHEART, M., HULL, E. and SLATER, D. (1975). Sex differences in imagery and reading. *Nature*, **253**, 438–440

COLTHEART, M., PATTERSON, K. and MARSHALL, J. (Eds) (in press). *Deep Dyslexia.* London: Routledge, Kegan and Paul

CONRAD, R. (1959). Errors of immediate memory. *Birtish Journal of Psychology*, **50**, 349–359

CONRAD, R. (1964). Acoustic confusion in immediate memory. *British Journal of Psychology*, **55**, 74–84

CONRAD, R. (1972a). Short-term memory in the deaf: a test for speech coding. *British Journal of Psychology*, **63**, 173–180

CONRAD, R. (1972b). Speech and reading. In KAVANAGH, J. F. and MATTINGLY, I. G. (Eds), *Language by Ear and by Eye.* Cambridge Mass.: MIT Press

CORCORAN, D. W. J. (1966). An acoustic factor in letter cancellation. *Nature*, **210**, 658

CORCORAN, D. W. J. and WEENING, D. L. (1968). Acoustic factors in visual search. *Quarterly Journal of Experimental Psychology*, **20**, 83–85

CRITCHLEY, M. (1970). *The Dyslexic Child.* London: Heinemann

CRITCHLEY, M. and CRITCHLEY, E. A. (1978). *Dyslexia Defined.* London: Heinemann

CROMER, R. F. (1978a). The basis of childhood dysphasia: a linguistic approach. In WYKE, M. (Ed.), *Developmental Dysphasia.* N.Y. and London: Academic Press

CROMER, R. F. (1978b). Hierarchical disability in the syntax of aphasic children. *International Journal of Behavioral Development*, **1**, 391–402

CROMER, R. F. (1978c). Hierarchical ordering disability and aphasic children. Paper presented at the First International Congress for the Study of Child Language, Tokyo

CRONNELL, B. A. (1970). Spelling-to-sound correspondences for reading *vs* sound-to-spelling correspondences. *Technical Note TN 2-70-15.* Los Alamitos, California: Southwest Regional Laboratory

CRONNELL, B. A. (1973). Black English and the spelling of final consonant clusters. Unpublished doctoral dissertation. University of California, Los Angeles

CROWDER, R. G. (1978). Memory for phonologically uniform lists. *Journal of Verbal Learning and Verbal Behavior*, **17**, 73–89

DAVELAAR, E., COLTHEART, M., BESNER, D. and JONASSON, J. T. (1978). Phonological recoding and lexical access. *Memory and Cognition*, **6**, 391–402

DAY, J. B. and WEDELL, K. (1972). Visual and auditory memory in spelling: an exploratory study. *British Journal of Education*, **42**, 33–39

DENCKLA, M. B. and RUDEL, R. G. (1976). Rapid 'automatized' naming (R.A.N.): dyslexia differentiated from other learning disabilities. *Neuropsychologia*, **14**, 471–479

DERWING, B. L. (1977). On recognising morphemes in derived words: an experimental study. In DRACHMAN, G. (Ed.), *Salzburger Beiträge zur Linguistik*, Vol. 4. Salzburg: Wolfgang Neugebauer

DESBERG, P., MARSH, G., SCHNEIDER, L. and DUNCAN-ROSE, C. The effect of social dialect on auditory sound blending and word identification. *Contemporary Educational Psychology.* (In press)

DESBERG, P., MARSH, G. and STANLEY, A. (1977a). Sentence repetition as a measure of social dialect. Paper presented at Western Psychological Association Meeting, Seattle, Washington

DESBERG, P., MARSH, G. and WOLFF, D. (1977b). Relationship between non-standard dialect and academic achievement. Paper presented at Third International Conference on Educational Testing, Leyden, The Netherlands

DEWEY, G. (1970). *Relative Frequency of English Spellings*. N.Y.: Teachers College Press, Teachers College, Columbia University

DEWEY, G. (1971). *English Spelling. Roadblock to Reading*. N.Y.: Teachers College Press, Columbia University

DODD, B. (1974). The acquisition of phonological skills in normal, severely subnormal and deaf children. Unpublished PhD thesis, University of London

DODD, B. (1976). The phonological systems of deaf children. *Journal of Speech and Hearing Disorders*, **41**, 185–198

DODD, B. and HERMELIN, B. (1977). Phonological coding by the prelinguistically deaf. *Perception and Psychophysics*, **21**, 413–417

DOGGETT, D. and RICHARDS, L. G. (1975). A re-examination of the effect of word length on recognition thresholds. *American Journal of Psychology*, **88**, 583–594

DOLBY, J. L. and RESNIKOFF, H. L. (1964). On the structure of written words. *Language*, **40**, 167–196

DONALDSON, M. (1978). *Children's Minds*. Glasgow: Fontana

DREWNOWSKI, A. and HEALY, A. F. (1977). Detection errors on *the* and *and*: Evidence for reading units larger than the word. *Memory and Cognition*, **5**, 636–647

DUBOIS, J., HÉCAEN, H. and MARCIE, P. (1969). L'agraphie "pure". *Neuropsychologia*, **7**, 271–286

DUNN-RANKIN, P. (1968). The similarity of lower-case letters of the English alphabet. *Journal of Verbal Learning and Verbal Behavior*, **7**, 990–995

DYKSTRA, R. (1966). Auditory discrimination abilities and beginning reading achievement. *Reading Research Quarterly*, **1**, 5–34

EHRI, L. C. (1976). Word learning in beginning readers and prereaders: Effects of form class and defining contexts. *Journal of Educational Psychology*, **68**, 832–842

EHRI, L. C. (1978). Beginning reading from a psycholinguistic perspective: Amalgamation of word identities. In MURRAY, F. B. (Ed.), *The Development of the Reading Process*. International Reading Association Monograph (No. 3). Newark, Del.: International Reading Association

EHRI, L. C. (1979). Linguistic insight: Threshold of reading acquisition. In WALLER, T. G. and MACKINNON, G. E. (Eds), *Reading Research: Advances in Theory and Practice*. N.Y.: Academic Press

EHRI, L. C. and ROBERTS, K. T. (1979). Do Beginners Learn Printed Words Better in Contexts or in Isolation? *Child Development* (in press)

EHRI, L. C. and WILCE, L. S. (1979). The mnemonic value of orthography among beginning readers. *Journal of Educational Psychology*, **71**, 26–40

EISENSON, J. (1968). Developmental aphasia: A speculative view with therapeutic implications. *Journal of Speech and Hearing Disorders*, **33**, 3–13

FARNHAM-DIGGORY, S. (1978). How to study reading: Some information processing ways. In MURRAY, F. B. and PIKULSKI, J. J., *The Acquisition of Reading: Cognitive Linguistic and Perceptual Prerequisites*. Baltimore: University Park Press

FARNHAM-DIGGORY, S. and SIMON, H. A. (1975). Retention of visually presented information in children's spelling. *Memory and Cognition*, **3**, 599–608

FASOLD, R. W. (1969). Orthography in reading materials for Black English speaking children. In BARATZ, J. C. and SHUY, R. W. (Eds), *Teaching Black Children to Read*. Washington, D.C.: Center for Applied Linguistics

FERNALD, G. M. (1943). *Remedial Techniuqes in Basic School Subjects*. N.Y.: McGraw-Hill

FICHTNER, E. G. (1976). The pronunciation of the English < NG > : A case study in phoneme-grapheme relationships. *TESOL Quarterly*, **10**, 193–202

FINK, R. (1974). Orthography and the perception of stops after S. *Language and Speech*, **17**, 152–159

FILOLOGY COMMITTEE OF THE SIMPLIFIED SPELLING BOARD. (1920). *Handbook of Simplified Spelling*. N.Y.: Simplified Spelling Board

FIRTH, I. (1972). Components of reading disability. Unpublished doctoral dissertation. University of New South Wales, Kensington, N.S.W., Australia

FIRTH, J. R. (1935). The technique of semantics. *Transactions of the Philological Society*, 36–72

FISHMAN, E. J., KELLER, L. and ATKINSON, R. C. (1968). Massed versus distributed practice in computerized spelling drills. *Journal of Educational Psychology*, **59**, 290–296

FODOR, J., BEVER, T. and GARRETT, M. (1974). *The Psychology of Language*. N.Y.: McGraw-Hill

FOLLICK, M. (1965). *The Case for Spelling Reform*. London: Pitman Press

FORSTER, K. I. (1976). Accessing the mental lexicon. In WALKER, E. C. T. and WALES, R. J. (Eds), *New Approaches to Language Mechanisms*. Amsterdam: North Holland

FOSS, D. J. and SWINNEY, D. A. (1973). On the psychological reality of the phoneme: perception, identification and consciousness. *Journal of Verbal Learning and Verbal Behavior*, **12**, 246–257

FOX, B. and ROUTH, D. K. (1975). Analyzing spoken language into words, syllables and phonemes: A developmental study. *Journal of Psycholinguistic Research*, **4**, 331–342

FOX, B. and ROUTH, D. K. (1976). Phonemic analysis and synthesis as word-attack skills. *Journal of Educational Psychology*, **68**, 70–74

FRANCIS, H. (1973). Children's experience of reading and notions of units in language. *British Journal of Educational Psychology*, **43**, 17–23

FRANKLIN, B. A scheme for a new alphabet and a reformed mode of spelling. In BIGELOW, J. (Ed.), *Franklin's Works*, Volume IV, 1887–1888. N.Y. (First published 1768)

FREDERIKSEN, J. R. (1976). Decoding skills and lexical retrieval. Paper presented at the annual meeting of the Psychonomic Society, St. Louis

FREDERIKSEN, J. R. (1978). Assessment of perceptual decoding and lexical skills and their relation to reading proficiency. In LESGOLD, A. M., PELLEGRINO, J. W., FOKKEMA, S. D. and GLASER, R. (Eds), *Cognitive Psychology and Instruction*. N.Y.: Plenum Press.

FREDERIKSEN, J. R. and KROLL, J. F. (1976). Spelling and sound: approaches to the internal lexicon. *Journal of Experimental Psychology: Human Perception and Performance*, **2**, 361–379

FREUD, S. (1914). *The Psychopathology of Everyday Life*. London: Fisher Unwin

FREYBERG, P. S. (1970). The current validity of two types of spelling test. *British Journal of Educational Psychology*, **40**, 68–71

FRITH, U. (1974). A curious effect with reversed letters explained by a theory of schema. *Perception and Psychophysics*, **16**, 113–116

FRITH, U. (1976). How to read without knowing how to spell. Paper presented to the British Association for the Advancement of Science, Lancaster

FRITH, U. (1978a). Spelling difficulties. *Journal of Child Psychology and Psychiatry*, **19**, 279–285

FRITH, U. (1978b). From print to meaning and from print to sound or how to read without knowing how to spell. *Visible Language*, **12**, 43–54

FRITH, U. (1979). Reading by eye and writing by ear. In KOLERS, P. A., WROLSTAD, M. and BOUMA, H. (Eds), *Processing of Visible Language*, I. N.Y.: Plenum Press

FRITH, U. and FRITH, C. D. (in press). Relationships between reading and spelling. In VENEZKY, R. L. and KAVANAGH, J. F. (Eds), *Orthography, Reading and Dyslexia*. Baltimore: University Park Press

FROMKIN, V. A. (1971). The non-anomalous nature of anomalous utterances. *Language*, **47**, 27–52

FROMKIN, V. A. (Ed.) (1973). *Speech Errors as Linguistic Evidence*. The Hague: Mouton

FRY, D. B. (1969). The linguistic evidence of speech error. *BRNO Studies in English*, **8**, 69–74

FUJIMURA, O. (1975). Syllable as the unit of speech recognition. *I.E.E.E. Transactions on Acoustics, Speech, and Signal Processing*, **23**, 82–87

FUJIMURA, O. (1976). Syllables as concatenated demisyllables and affixes. Paper presented at 91st meeting of the Acoustical Society of America, Washington

FURNESS, E. L. and BOYD, G. A. (1959). Real spelling demons for college students. *College English*, **20**, 292–295

FURTH, H. G. (1966). A comparison of reading test norms of deaf and hearing children. *American Annals of the Deaf*, **111**, 461–462

FUSARO, J. A. (1978). Grapheme-phoneme and phoneme-grapheme correspondences. *Perceptual and Motor Skills*, **47**, 171–174

GATES, A. I. (1937). *A List of Spelling Difficulties in 3876 Words*. N.Y.: Teachers College Press, Columbia University

GARDNER, J. L. (1973). *Reporting Glory*. N.Y.: Charles Scribner's Sons

GATES, A. I. and CHASE, E. H. (1926). Methods and theories of learning to spell tested by studies of deaf children. *Journal of Educational Psychology*, **17**, 289–300

GAZZANIGA, M. D. and SPERRY, R. W. (1967). Language after section of the cerebral commissures. *Brain*, **90**, 131–148

GELB, I. J. (1963). *A Study of Writing*. Chicago: University of Chicago Press

GENTRY, J. R. and HENDERSON, E. H. (1978). Three steps to teaching beginning readers to spell. *The Reading Teacher*, **31**, 632–637

GIBSON, E. J. (1965). Learning to read. *Science*, **148**, 1066–1072

GIBSON, E. J. and GUINET, L. (1971). Perception of inflections in brief visual presentations of words. *Journal of Verbal Learning and Verbal Behavior*, **10**, 182–189

GIBSON, E. J. and LEVIN, H. (1975). *The Psychology of Reading*. Cambridge, Mass.: M.I.T. Press

GIBSON, E. J., PICK, A. OSSER, H. and HAMMOND, M. (1962). The role of grapheme-phoneme correspondence in the perception of words. *American Journal of Psychology*, **75**, 554–570

GIBSON, E. J., SHURCLIFF, A. and YONAS, A. (1970). Utilization of spelling patterns by deaf and hearing subjects. In LEVIN, H. and WILLIAMS, J. (Eds), *Basic Studies on Reading*, 57–73. N.Y.: Basic Books

GILOOLY, W. B. (1972). The influence of writing-system characteristics on learning to read. *Reading Research Quarterly*, **8**, 167–199

GLEITMAN, H. and GLEITMAN, L. (1970). *Phrase and Paraphrase: Some Innovative Uses of Language*. N.Y.: Norton

GLEITMAN, L. R. and ROZIN, P. (1977). The structure and acquisition of reading, I: Relations between orthographies and the structure of language. In REBER,

A. S. and SCARBOROUGH, D. L. (Eds), *Toward a Psychology of Reading*. Hillsdale, N.J.: Erlbaum

GOEHL, H. and GOLDEN, S. (1974). A psycholinguistic account of why children do not detect their own errors. Ms, Department of Speech, Temple University

GOLDMAN, E. (1956). *Rendezvous With Destiny*, revised edition. N.Y.: Vintage Books

GOLDSTEIN, D. M. (1976). Cognitive-linguistic functioning and learning to read in pre-schoolers. *Journal of Educational Psychology*, **68**, 680–688

GOODGLASS, H. and HUNTER, M. (1970). A linguistic comparison of speech and writing in two types of aphasia. *Journal of Communication Disorders*, **3**, 28–35

GOODMAN, K. S. (1970). Reading, a psycholinguistic guessing game. In SINGER, H. and RUDDELL, B. (Eds), *Theoretical Models and Processes of Reading*. Newark, Del.: International Reading Association

GOODMAN, K. S. (1972). Orthography in a theory of reading instruction. *Elementary English*, **49**, 1254–1261

GOUGH, P. (1972). One second of reading. In KAVANAGH, J. F. and MATTINGLY, I. G. (Eds), *Language By Ear and By Eye*. Cambridge, Mass.: M.I.T. Press

GOULD, S. M. (1976). Spelling isn't reading backwards. *Journal of Reading*, **20**, 220–225

GOYEN, J. D. and MARTIN, M. (1977). The relation of spelling errors to cognitive variables and word type. *British Journal of Educational Psychology*, **47**, 268–273

GRAHAM, L. W. and HOUSE, A. S. (1970). Phonological oppositions in children: a perceptual study. *Journal of the Acoustical Society of America*, **49**, 1971

GREEN, D. W. and SHALLICE, T. (1976). Direct visual access in reading for meaning. *Memory & Cognition*, **4**, 753–758

GRIFFITHS, P. (1972). *Developmental Aphasia: An Introduction*. London: Invalid Children's Aid Association

GRIMES, J. (1979). Design of new orthographies. In VENEZKY, R. L. and KAVANAGH, J. (Eds), *Orthography, Reading and Dyslexia*. Baltimore: University Park Press

GROAT, A. (1979) The use of English stress assignment rules by children taught either with traditional orthography or with the initial teaching alphabet. *Journal of Experimental Child Psychology* **27**, 395–409

GUTHRIE, J. T. and SIEFERT, M. (1977). Letter-sound complexity in learning to identify words. *Journal of Educational Psychology*, **69**, 686–696

HAAS, W. (1969). *Alphabets for English*. Manchester: University Press, U.K.

HAAS, W. (1970). *Phonographic Translation*. Manchester University Press, U.K.

HAAS, W. (Ed.) (1976). *Writing Without Letters*. Mount Follick Series, Vol. 4. Manchester University Press, U.K.

HAGGARD, M. (1973). Abbreviation of consonants in English pre- and post-vocalic clusters. *Journal of Phonetics*, **1**, 9–24

HALL, R. A. (1961). *Sound and Spelling in English*. N.Y.: Chilton

HALLE, M. (1969). Some thoughts on spelling. In GOODMAN, K. S. and FLEMING, J. T. (Eds), *Psycholinguistics and the Teaching of Reading*. Newark, Delaware: International Reading Association

HAM, R. E. (1958). Relationship between misspelling and misarticulation. *Journal of Speech and Hearing Disorders*, **23**, 294–297

HAMMILL, D. D. and LARSEN, S. C. (1974). The relationship of selected auditory perceptual skills and reading ability. *Journal of Learning Disabilities*, **7**, 429–434

HANNA, P. R., HANNA, J. S., HODGES, R. E. and RUDORF, E. H. (1966). *Phoneme-Grapheme Correspondences as Cues to Spelling Improvement*. Washington D.C.: U.S. Government Printing Office.

HANNA, P. R., HODGES, R. E. and HANNA, J. S. (1971). *Spelling Structure and Strategies.* Boston: Houghton Mifflin

HARDY, M., SMYTHE, P. C., STENNETT, R. G. and WILSON, H. R. (1972). Developmental patterns in elemental reading skills: phoneme-grapheme and grapheme-phoneme correspondences. *Journal of Educational Psychology,* **63**, 433–436

HARDYCK, C. D. and PETRINOVICH, L. F. (1970). Subvocal speech and comprehension as function of difficulty level of reading material. *Journal of Verbal Learning and Verbal Behavior,* **9**, 647–652

HARTMANN, G. W. (1931). The relative influence of visual and auditory factors in spelling ability. *Journal of Educational Psychology,* **22**, 691–699

HATFIELD, F. M. and WALTON, K. (1975). Phonological patterns in a case of aphasia. *Language and Speech,* **18**, 341–357

HAUGEN, E. (1966). *Language Conflict and Language Planning: The Case of Modern Norwegian.* Harvard: Harvard University Press

HAWKINS, H. L., REICHER, G., ROGERS, M. and PETERSON, L. (1976). Flexible coding in word recognition. *Journal of Experimental Psychology: Human Perception and Performance,* **2**, 380–385

HAWKINS, S. (1973). Temporal coordination of consonants in the speech of children: preliminary data. *Journal of Phonetics,* **1**, 181–217

HEALY, A. F. (1976). Detection errors on the word *the*: Evidence for reading units larger than letters. *Journal of Experimental Psychology: Human Perception and Performance,* **2**, 235–242

HÉCAEN, H. and ALBERT, M. L. (1978). *Human Neuropsychology.* N.Y.: Wiley

HENDERSON, L. (1975). Do words conceal their components letters? A critique of Johnson (1975) on the visual perception of words. *Journal of Verbal Learning and Verbal Behavior,* **14**, 17–29

HENDERSON, L. (1977). Word recognition. In SUTHERLAND, N. S. (Ed.), *Tutorial Essays in Psychology,* Vol. I. Hillsdale, N.J.: Erlbaum

HENDERSON, L. (1978). Pandemonium and visual search. *Perception,* **7**, 97–104

HENDERSON, L. and CHARD, M. J. (1976). When are words easier targets to detect than single letters? Unpublished manuscript

HENDERSON, L. and CHARD, M. J. (1978). *Word Recognition.* Final report to the Social Science Research Council on grant no. HR 3301

HENDERSON, L., CHARD, J. and CLARK, A. (1978). Spelling as a transcription process. *Abstract Bulletin of the British Psychological Society,* **31**, 67–68

HENDERSON, L. and HENDERSON, S. E. (1975). Visual comparison of words and random letter strings: effects of number and position of letters different. *Memory & Cognition,* **3**, 97–101

HENDRICK, B. J. (1932). *The Life of Andrew Carnegie,* 2 volumes. Garden City, N.Y.: Doubleday, Doran & Co.

HENDRICKSON, O. D. (1967). Spelling: a visual skill. *Academic Therapy Quarterly,* **3**, 39–42

HERMANN, K. (1959). *Reading Disability.* Copenhagen: Munksgaard.

HERRMANN, D. J. and McLAUGHLIN, J. P. (1973). Language habits and detection in very short-term memory. *Perception and Psychophysics,* **14**, 483–486

HILL, A. A. (1961). Grammaticality. *Word,* **17**, 1–10

HILL, A. A. (1972). A theory of speech errors. In FIRCHOW, E. S. *et al.* (Eds), *Studies Offered to Einar Haugen.* The Hague: Mouton.

HILLERICH, R. L. (1977). Let's teach spelling – not phonetic misspelling. *Language Arts,* **54**, 301–307

HINTZMAN, D. L. and SUMMERS, J. J. (1973). Long-term visual traces of visually presented words. *Bulletin of the Psychonomic Society*, **1**, 325–327

HITCH, G. J. (1974). Short-term memory for spatial and temporal information. *Quarterly Journal of Experimental Psychology*, **26**, 503–513

HOCKETT, C. F. (1968). *The State of the Art*. The Hague: Mouton

HODGES, R. E. (1972). Theoretical frameworks of English orthography. *Elementary English*, **49**, 1089–1079

HODGES, R. E. (1977). In Adam's fall: a brief history of spelling instruction in the United States. In ROBINSON, H. A. (Ed.), *Reading and Writing Instruction in the United States: Historical Trends*. Newark, Del.: International Reading Association

HOEMANN, H. W., ANDREWS, C. E., FLORIAN, V. A., HOEMANN, S. A. and JENSEMA, C. J. (1976). The spelling proficiency of deaf children. *American Annals of the Deaf*, **121**, 489–493

HOLMES, D. L. and PEPER, R. J. (1977). An evaluation of the use of spelling error analysis in the diagnosis of reading disabilities. *Child Development*, **48**, 1708–1711

HOLT, J. (1964). *How Children Fail*. London: Pitman

HOOLE, C. (1660). *A New Discovery of the Old Art of Teaching School*. London: Andrew Crook. (Facsimile reproduction by the Scolar Press Ltd., Menston, England, 1973)

HORN, T. D. (1969). Spelling. In EBELS, R. L. (Ed.), *Encyclopedia of Educational Research* (4th edition). N.Y.: Macmillan

HOTOPF, W. H. N. (1971). What light do slips of the tongue and of the pen throw on word production? Unpublished paper: London School of Economics

HOTOPF, W. H. N. (in press). Semantic similarity as a factor in whole word slips of the tongue. In FROMKIN, V. A. (Ed.) *Errors in linguistic performance: slips of the tongue, pen and hand*. N.Y.: Academic Press

INGRAM, D. (1971). Phonological rules in young children. *Papers and Reports on Child Language Development*, **3**, Committee on Linguistics, Stanford University

INGRAM, D. (1976). *Phonological Disability in Children. Studies in Language Disability and Remediation*, **2**. London: Edward Arnold Ltd.

IVIMEY, G. P. (1977). The perception of speech – an information processing approach (Part 3 – Lipreading and the Deaf). *The Teacher of the Deaf*, **1**, 90–100

JACKSON, A. and MORTON, J. The effects of priming on auditory word recognition. (In prep.)

JAMES, C. T. (1974). Vowels and consonants as targets in the search of single words. *Bulletin of the Psychonomic Society*, **2**, 402–404

JAMES, C. T. and SMITH, D. E. (1970). Sequential dependencies in letter search. *Journal of Experimental Psychology*, **85**, 56–60

JARVELLA, R. J. and SNODGRASS, J. G. (1974). Seeing ring in rang and retain in retention: on recognising stem morphemes in printed words. *Journal of Verbal Learning and Verbal Behavior*, **13**, 590–598

JENSEN, A. R. (1962). Spelling errors and the serial position effect. *Journal of Educational Psychology*, **53**, 105–109

JENSEN, E. M., REESE, E. P. and REESE, T. W. (1950). The subitising and counting of visually presented fields of dots. *Journal of Psychology*, **30**, 363–392

JOHNSON, N. F. (1975). On the function of letters in word identification: some data and a preliminary model. *Journal of Verbal Learning and Verbal Behavior*, **14**, 17–29

JOHNSTON, J. C. (1978). A test of the sophisticated guessing theory of word perception. *Cognitive Psychology*, **10**, 123–153

JOHNSTON, J. C. and McCLELLAND, J. L. (1973). Visual factors in word perception. *Perception and Psychophysics*, **14**, 365–370

JOHNSTON J. C. and McCLELLAND J. L. (1974). Perception of letters in words: seek not and ye shall find. *Science*, **184**, 1192–1194

JORDAN, J. (1964). *The Awful Spellers Dictionary*. (Brit. Ed.) London: Wolfe

JORM, A. F. (1977). Children's spelling processes revealed by transitional error probabilities. *Australian Journal of Psychology*, **29**, 125–130

JUOLA, J. F., LEAVITT, D. D. and CHLOE, C. S. (1974). Letter identification in word, nonword and single letter displays. *Bulletin of the Psychonomic Society*, **4**, 278–280

KATZ, L. (1977). Reading ability and single-letter orthographic redundancy. *Journal of Educational Psychology*, **69**, 653–659

KAUFFMAN, J. M., HALLAHAN, D. P., HAAS, K., BRAME, T. and BOREN, R. (1978). Imitating children's errors to improve their spelling performance. *Journal of Learning Disabilities*, **11**, 33–38

KELLY, G. A. (1955). *The Psychology of Personal Constructs*. N.Y.: Norton

KEREK, A. (1976). The phonological relevance of spelling pronunciation. *Visible Language*, **10**, 323–338

KINSBOURNE, M. and ROSENFELD, D. B. (1974). Agraphia selective for written spelling. *Brain and Language*, **1**, 215–225

KINSBOURNE, M. and WARRINGTON, E. K. (1964). Disorders of spelling. *Journal of Neurology, Neurosurgery and Psychiatry*, **27**, 224–228

KIRSNER, K. (1973). An analysis of the visual component in recognition memory for verbal stimuli. *Memory and Cognition*, **1**, 449–453

KLATT, D. (1973). Voice onset time, frication, and aspiration in word-initial consonant clusters. *R.L.E. Quarterly Progress Report No. 109*, M.I.T., 124–135

KLEIMAN, G. M. (1975). Speech recoding in reading. *Journal of Verbal Learning and Verbal Behavior*, **14**, 323–339

KLEIN, R. (1969). Acoustic analysis of the acquisition of acceptable [r] in American English. Paper presented at the 1969 S.R.C.D. Convention, Santa Monica, California

KLIMA, E. S. (1972). How alphabets might reflect language. In KAVANAGH, J. F. and MATTINGLY, I. G. (Eds), *Language by Ear and by Eye*. Cambridge, Mass.: M.I.T. Press

KNOELL, D. M. and HARRIS, C. W. (1952). A factor analysis of spelling ability. *Journal of Educational Research*, **46**, 95–111

KOLERS, P. A. (1969). Reading is only incidentally visual. In GOODMAN, K. S. and FLEMING, J. T. (Eds), *Psycholinguistics and the Teaching of Reading*. Newark, Del.: International Reading Association

KOOI, B. Y., SCHUTZ, R. D. and BAKER, R. L. (1965). Spelling errors and the serial position effect. *Journal of Educational Psychology*, **56**, 334–336

KORNFELD, J. R. (1971a). What initial clusters tell us about a child's speech code. *R.L.E. Quarterly Progress Report No. 101*, M.I.T., 218–221

KORNFELD, J. R. (1971b). Theoretical issues in child phonology. *Proceedings of the 7th Annual Meeting of the Chicago Linguistics Society*, University of Chicago

KORNFELD, J. R. (1977). Implications of studying reduced consonant clusters in normal and abnormal child speech. In CAMPBELL, R. N. and SMITH, P. J. (Eds), *Recent Advances in the Study of Language: Language Development and Mother-Child Interaction*. NATO Conference Series, III 4A. N.Y.: Plenum Press

KORNFELD, J. R. and GOEHL, H. (1974). A new twist to an old observation: kids know more than they say. *Proceedings of the 10th Annual Meeting of the Chicago Linguistics Society*, University of Chicago, 210–219

KOTTMEYER, W. Spelling list for literate adults. Reproduced in MAEROFF, G. I. The latest word on poor spellers. *The New York Times*, August 4, 1973, p. 25

KOTTMEYER, W. and CLAUS, A. (1968). *Basic Goals in Spelling* (4th edn). N.Y.: McGraw-Hill

KRUEGER, L. E. (1970). Search time in a redundant visual display. *Journal of Experimental Psychology*, **83**, 391–399

KRUEGER, L. E. (1975). Familiarity effects in visual information processing. *Psychological Bulletin*, **82**, 949–974

KRUEGER, L. E., KEEN, R. H. and RUBLEVICH, B. (1974). Letter search through words and nonwords by adults and fourth-grade children. *Journal of Experimental Psychology*, **102**, 845–849

KUČERA, H. and FRANCIS, W. N. (1967). *Computational Analysis of Present-day American English*. Providence, R.I.: Brown University Press

KYÖSTIÖ, O. K. (in press). Is learning to read and write easy in a language in which the grapheme-phoneme relationship is regular? In VENEZKY, R. L. and KAVANAGH, J. F. (Eds), *Orthography, Reading and Dyslexia*. Baltimore: University Park Press

LABERGE, D. and SAMUELS, S. J. (1974). Toward a theory of automatic information processing in reading. *Cognitive Psychology*, **6**, 293–323

LAMB, S. M. (1966). Linguistic structure and the production and decoding of discourse. In HALL, V. E. (Ed.), *Brain Function. III – Speech, Language and Communication*. Cambridge: Cambridge University Press

LANGACKER, R. W. (1973). *Language and its Structure*. N.Y.: Harcourt Brace Jovanovich

LANGMORE, S. (1979). The written spelling deficit in Broca's aphasics. Unpublished preliminary report of a doctoral dissertation, Northwestern University, Evanston, Ill.

LANGER, J. L. (1977). The effects of spatial frequency and pronunciation regularity on good and poor readers' performance on a lexical decision task. Unpublished masters thesis. University of Guelph

LASHLEY, K. S. (1951). The problem of serial order in behavior. In JEFFRESS, L. A. (Ed.), *Cerebral Mechanisms in Behavior*. N.Y.: Wiley

LAVER, J. D. M. (1969). The detection and correction of slips of the tongue. Work in Progress, 3, Department of Phonetics and Linguistics, University of Edinburgh

LAVER, J. D. M. (in press). Monitoring systems in the neurolinguistic control of speech production. In FROMKIN, V. A. (Ed.) *Errors in linguistic performance: slips of the tongue, ear, pen and hand*. N.Y.: Academic Press.

LECOURS, A. R. (1966). Serial order in writing – a study of mis-spelled words in "developmental dysgraphia". *Neuropsychologia*, **4**, 221–241

LEE, W. R. (1960). *Spelling Irregularity and Reading Difficulty in English*. Windsor, Berks.: N.F.E.R. Publishing Co. Ltd.

LEFTON, L. A. and SPRAGINS, A. B. (1974). Orthographic structure and reading experience affect the transfer from iconic to short-term memory. *Journal of Experimental Psychology*, **103**, 775–781

LENNEBERG, E. H. (1967). *Biological Foundations of Language*. N.Y.: Wiley

LESLIE, R. and CALFEE, R. C. (1971). Visual search through word lists as a function of grade level, reading ability and target repetition. *Perception and Psychophysics*, **10**, 169–171

LESTER, R. (1941). *Forty Years of Carnegie Giving*. N.Y.: Charles Scribner's Sons

LEVITT, J. (1978). The influence of orthography on phonology: a comparative study (English, French, Spanish, Italian, German). *Linguistics*, **208**, 43–67

LEVY, B. A. (1975). Vocalization and suppression effects in sentence memory. *Journal of Verbal Learning and Verbal Behavior*, **14**, 304–316

LEVY, B. A. (1978). Speech processing during reading. In LESGOLD, A. M., PELLEGRINO, J. W., FOKKEMA, S. D. and GLASER, R. (Eds), *Cognitive Psychology and Instruction*. N.Y.: Plenum Press

LEVY, J., NEBES, R. D. and SPERRY, R. W. (1971). Expressive language in the surgically separated minor hemisphere. *Cortex*, **7**, 49–58

LEVY, J. (1974). Cerebral asymmetries as manifested in split-brain man. In KINSBOURNE, M. and SMITH, W. L. (Eds), *Hemispheric Disconnection and Cerebral Function*, Springfield, Ill.: Charles C. Thomas

LIBERMAN, A. M. (in press). Orthography and phonemics in present-day Russian. In VENEZKY, R. L. and KAVANAGH, J. F. (Eds), *Cross-Language Conference on Orthography, Reading and Dyslexia*. Baltimore: University Park Press

LIBERMAN, A. M., COOPER, F. S., SHANKWEILER, D. P. and STUDDERT-KENNEDY, M. (1967). Perception of the speech code. *Psychological Review*, **74**, 431–461

LIBERMAN, I. Y. (1973). Segmentation of the spoken word and reading acquisition. *Bulletin of the Orton Society*, **23**, 65–77

LIBERMAN, I. Y. and SHANKWEILER, D. (1977). Speech, the alphabet and teaching to read. In RESNICK, L. B. and WEAVER, P. A. (Eds), *Theory and Practice of Early Reading*. Hillsdale, N.J.: Erlbaum.

LIBERMAN, I. Y., SHANKWEILER, D., LIBERMAN, A. M., FOWLER, C. and FISCHER, F. W. (1977). Phonetic segmentation and recoding in the beginning reader. In REBER, A. S. and SCARBOROUGH, D. L. (Eds), *Toward a Psychology of Reading*. Hillsdale, N.J.: Erlbaum

LIBERMAN, I. Y., SHANKWEILER, D., ORLANDO, C., HARRIS, K. S. and BERTI, F.B. (1971). Letter confusions and reversals of sequence in the beginning reader. *Cortex*, **7**, 127–142

LURIA, A. R. (1947). *Traumatic Aphasia*. Moscow: Academy of Medical Science of the U.S.S.R.

LURIA, A. R. (1950). *Psycho-physiological Features of Writing*. Moscow: Academy of Psychological Science of the Russian Soviet Federative Socialist Republic

LURIA, A. R. (1966). *Higher Cortical Functions in Man*. N.Y.: Basic Books

LURIA, A. R. (1970). The functional organisation of the brain. *Scientific American*, **222**, 66–78

LURIA, A. R., SIMERNITSKAYA, E. G. and TUBYLEVICH, B. (1970). The structure of psychological processes in relation to cerebral organisation. *Neuropsychologia*, **8**, 13–19

LYLE, J. G. (1969). Reading retardation and reversal tendency: a factorial study. *Child Development*, **40**, 843–933

MACKAY, D. G. (1968). Phonetic factors in the perception and recall of spelling errors. *Neuropsychologia*, **6**, 321–325

MACKAY, D. G. (1969). The repeated letter effect in the misspellings of dysgraphics and normals. *Perception and Psychophysics*, **5**, 102–106

MACKAY, D. G. (1970). Spoonerisms: the structure of errors in the serial order of speech. *Neuropsychologia*, **8**, 323–350

MACKAY, D. G. (1972). Input testing in the detection of misspellings. *The American Journal of Psychology*, **85**, 121–127

MACKWORTH, J. F. (1975). A new reading test for grade 1. *Bulletin of the Psychonomic Society*, **6**, 143–145

MACKWORTH, J. F. and MACKWORTH, N. H. (1974). Spelling recognition and coding by poor readers. *Bulletin of the Psychonomic Society*, **3**, 59–60

MACNEILAGE, P. F. (1964). Typing errors as clues to serial ordering mechanisms in language behavior. *Language and Speech*, **7**, 144–159

MAKITA, K. (1968). The rarity of reading disability in Japanese children. *American Journal of Orthopsychiatry*, **38**, 599–614

MALMQUIST, E. (1958). *Factors Related to Reading Disabilities in the First Grade of the Elementary School*. Stockholm: Malmquist and Wiksell

MALONE, K. (1925). A linguistic patriot. *American Speech*, **1**, 26–31

MANELIS, L. (1974). The effect of meaningfulness in tachistoscopic word perception. *Perception and Psychophysics*, **16**, 182–192

MANN, H. (1839). Spelling. *The Common School Journal*, **1**, 354–357

MARCEL, A. J. (1978). Prerequisites for a more applicable psychology of reading. In GRUNEBERG, M. M., MORRIS, P. E. and SYKES, R. N. (Eds), *Practical Aspects of Memory*. London: Academic Press

MARCEL, A. J. (1979). Conscious and unconscious perception: the effects of visual masking on word processing. *Cognitive Psychology* (in press)

MARCEL, A. J. and PATTERSON, K. E. (1978). Word recognition and production: reciprocity of clinical and normal studies. In REQUIN, J. (Ed.), *Attention and Performance*, VII. Hillsdale, N.J.: Erlbaum

MARCHBANKS, G. and LEVIN, H. (1965). Cues by which children recognize words. *Journal of Educational Psychology*, **56**, 57–61

MARK, H. J. and HARDY, W. G. (1958). Orienting reflex disturbances in central auditory or language handicapped children. *Journal of Speech and Hearing Disorders*, **23**, 237–242

MARK, L. S., SHANKWEILER, D. and LIBERMAN, I. Y. (1977). Phonetic recoding and reading difficulty in beginning readers. *Memory and Cognition*, **5**, 529–539

MARKIDES, A. (1976). Comparative linguistic proficiencies of deaf children taught by two different methods of instruction – manual versus oral. *The Teacher of the Deaf*, **74**, 307–347

MARMUREK, H. C. (1977). Processing letters in words at different levels. *Memory and Cognition*, **5**, 67–72

MARSH, G. (1969). *Conceptual Skills in Beginning Reading*. Technical report No. 18, Southwest Regional Laboratory, Los Alamitos, California

MARSH, G. (1978). The HIP approach to reading. In MURRAY, F. (Ed.), *Efficient Processing in Reading*. Newark, Del.: International Reading Association

MARSH, G., DESBERG, P. and COOPER, J. (1975). Developmental changes in strategies for pronouncing nonwords. Paper presented at the Psychonomic Society Meeting, Denver

MARSH, G., DESBERG, P. and COOPER, J. (1977). Developmental changes in reading strategies. *Journal of Reading Behavior*, **9**, 391–394

MARSH, G., FRIEDMAN, M. P., DESBERG, P. and SATERDAHL, K. A. (1979). Comparison of reading and spelling strategies in normal and reading disabled children. Paper presented at the NATO conference on Intelligence and Learning, July, York

MARSH, G., FRIEDMAN, M. P., WELCH, V. and DESBERG, P. A cognitive-developmental approach to reading acquisition. In WALLER, T. and MACKINNON, G. E. (Eds), *Reading Research: Advances in Theory and Practice*, Vol. 2. N.Y.: Academic Press (in press)

MARSHALL, J. (1976). Neuropsychological aspects of orthographic representation. In

WALES, R. J. and WALKER, E. (Eds), *New Approaches to Language Mechanisms*. A collection of psycholinguistic studies. Amsterdam: North-Holland

MARSHALL, J. C. and MORTON, J. (1978). On the mechanisms of Emma. In SINCLAIR, A., JARVELLA, R. J. and LEVELT, W. J. M. (Eds), *The Child's Conception of Language*. Berlin: Springer-Verlag

MARSHALL, J. C. and NEWCOMBE, F. (1966). Syntactic and semantic errors in paralexia. *Neuropsychologia*, **4**, 169–176

MARSHALL, J. C. and NEWCOMBE, F. (1973). Patterns of paralexia: a psycholinguistic approach. *Journal of Psycholinguistic Research*, **2**, 175–199

MARX, M. H. and MARX, K. (1976). Learning to spell as a function of trial-and-error performance or observation. *Bulletin of the Psychonomic Society*, **8**, 153–155

MASON, G. (1957). Word discrimination and spelling. *Journal of Educational Research*, **50**, 617–621

MASON, G. E. and WOODCOCK, C. (1973). First graders' performance on a visual memory for words task. *Elementary English*, **50**, 865–870

MASON, J. (1976). Overgeneralization in learning to read. *Journal of Reading Behavior*, **8**, 173–182

MASON, J. (1976). The roles of orthographic, phonological and word frequency variables on word–nonword decisions. *American Educational Research Journal*, **13**, 199–206

MASON, J. (1977). Questioning the notion of independent processing stages in reading. *Journal of Educational Psychology*, **69**, 288–297

MASON, M. (1975). Reading ability and letter search time: effects of orthographic structure defined by single-letter positional frequency. *Journal of Experimental Psychology: General*, **104**, 146–166

MASSARO, D. W. and KLITZKE, D. (1977). Letters are functional in word identification. *Memory and Cognition*, **5**, 292–298

MASSARO, D. W., VENEZKY, R. L. and TAYLOR, G. A. (1979s). Orthographic regularity, positional frequency, and visual processing of letter strings. *Journal of Experimental Psychology: General*, **108**, 107–124

MASTERS, H. V. (1927). *A Study of Spelling Errors*. Iowa City, University of Iowa Studies in Education, **4**, 138, Whole

MATHEWS, M. M. (Ed.) (1931). *The Beginnings of American English*. Chicago: University of Chicago Press

MATHEWS, M. M. (1966). *Teaching to Read, Historically Considered*. Chicago: University of Chicago Press

MATTINGLY, I. G. (1972). Reading, the linguistic process and linguistic awareness. In KAVANAGH, J. F. and MATTINGLY, I. G. (Eds), *Language by Ear and by Eye*. Cambridge, Mass.: M.I.T. Press

MAYZNER, M. S. and TRESSELT, M. E. (1965). Tables of single-letter and digram frequency counts for various word length and letter position combinations. *Psychonomic Science Monograph Supplements*, **1**, 13–32

McCLELLAND, J. L. (1976). Preliminary letter identification in the perception of words and nonwords. *Journal of Experimental Psychology: Human Perception and Performance*, **2**, 80–91

McCLELLAND, J. L. (1977). Letter and configuration information in word identification. *Journal of Verbal Learning and Verbal Behavior*, **16**, 137–150

McCLELLAND, J. L. and JOHNSTON, J. C. (1977). The role of familiar units in perception of words and nonwords. *Perception and Psychophysics*, **22**, 249–261

McEWEN, G. D. (1953). *How To Be a Better Speller*. N.Y.: Crowell

McGarrigle, J. and Donaldson, M. (1974). Conservation accidents. *Cognition*, **3**, 341–350

McLeod, J. (1970). *Gap Reading Comprehension Test*. London: Heinemann

Melmed, P. J. (1970). Black English phonology: the question of reading interference. Unpublished PhD thesis, University of California, Berkeley

Mendenhall, J. S. (1930). *An Analysis of Spelling Errors: A Study of Factors Associated with Word Difficulty*. N.Y.: Teacher's College, Columbia University

Menyuk, P. (1971). Clusters as single underlying consonants: evidence from children's productions. Paper presented at the International Congress of Phonetic Sciences, Montreal

Meringer, R. (1908). *Aus dem Leben der Sprache: Versprechen, Kindersprache, Nachahmungstrieb*. Berlin: Behrs Verlag

Meringer, R. and Mayer, K. (1895). *Versprechen und Verlesen: Eine Psychologische-Linguistische Studie*. Stuttgart: Goschensche Verlagsbuchhandlung

Mewhort, D. J. K. (1966). Sequential redundancy and letter spacing as determinants of tachistoscopic recognition. *Canadian Journal of Psychology*, **20**, 435–444

Meyer, D. E. and Gutschera, K. (1975). Orthographic versus phonemic processing of printed words. Paper presented at Psychonomic Society Meeting, Denver

Meyer, D. E. and Ruddy, M. G. (1973). Lexical-memory retrieval based on graphemic and phonemic representations of printed words. Paper presented at the meeting of the Psychonomic Society, St. Louis

Meyer, D. E. and Schvaneveldt, R. W. (1971). Facilitation in recognizing pairs of words: evidence of dependence between retrieval operations. *Journal of Experimental Psychology*, **90**, 227–234

Meyer, D. E., Schvaneveldt, R. W. and Ruddy, M. G. (1975). Loci of contextual effects on visual word-recognition. In Dornic, S. and Rabbitt, P. M. A. (Eds), *Attention and Performance*, V. London: Academic Press

Milner, B. (1971). Interhemispheric differences in the localization of psychological processes in man. *British Medical Bulletin*, **27**, 272–277

Mohr, J. P. (1976). An unusual case of dyslexia with agraphia. *Brain and Language*, **3**, 324–334

Molen van der, H. and Morton, J. (1979). Remembering plurals: units of coding and form of coding during serial recall. *Cognition*, **7**, 35–47

Moore, J. E. (1937). A comparison of four types of spelling tests for diagnostic purposes. *Journal of Experimental Education*, **6**, 24–28

Morison, E. E. (1951). *The Letters of Theodore Roosevelt*, 8 volumes. Cambridge, Mass.: Harvard University Press

Morton, J. (1964). The effects of context upon speed of reading, eye movements and eye–voice span. *Quarterly Journal of Experimental Psychology*, **16**, 340–354

Morton, J. (1968). Considerations of grammar and computation in language behaviour. In Catford, J. C. (Ed.), *Studies in Language and Language Behavior*. Progress Report No. VI, University of Michigan

Morton, J. (1969). The interaction of information in word recognition. *Psychological Review*, **76**, 165–178

Morton, J. (1970). A functional model for memory. In Norman, D. A. (Ed.), *Models for Human Memory*. N.Y.: Academic Press

Morton, J. (1977). Perception and memory. In *Cognitive Psychology Memory (part I) Course D303 Block 3 Units 13–15*. Milton Keynes: Open University Press

Morton, J. (1979a). Word recognition. In Morton, J. and Marshall, J. C. (Eds), *Psycholinguistics Series II*. London: Elek

MORTON, J. (1979b). Facilitation in word recognition: experiments causing change in the logogen model. In KOLERS, P. A., WROLSTAD, M. E. and BOUMA, H. (Eds), *Processing of Visible Language*. N.Y.: Plenum Press

MORTON, J. and PATTERSON, K. E. (in press). A new attempt at an interpretation or an attempt at a new interpretation. In COLTHEART, M., PATTERSON, K. E. and MARSHALL, J. C. (Eds), *Deep Dyslexia*. London: Routledge and Kegan Paul

MORTON, J. and SMITH, N. V. (1972). Some ideas concerning the acquisition of phonology. In *Proceedings of the Colloque International du C.N.R.S. 206, Current Problems in Psycholinguistics*. Paris: Editions du CNRS

MOSKOWITZ, B. A. (1973). On the status of vowel shift in English. In MOORE, T. E., *Cognition and the Acquisition of Language*. N.Y.: Academic Press

MURRAY, E. (1919). The spelling ability of college students. *Journal of Educational Psychology*, **10**, 357–376

MURRELL, G. A. and MORTON, J. (1974). Word recognition and morphemic structure. *Journal of Experimental Psychology*, **102**, 963–968

MYKLEBUST, H. R. (1973). *Development and Disorders of Written Language, II, Studies of Normal and Exceptional Children*. N.Y.: Grune and Stratton

NAIDOO, S. (1972). *Specific Dyslexia*. London: Pitman

NELSON, H. E. (1974). The aetiology of specific spelling disabilities. In WADE, B. and WEDELL, K. (Eds), *Spelling: Task and Learner*. University of Birmingham, Educational Rewiew. Occasional Publications. No. 5

NELSON, H. E. (1978). Spelling development and memory functions in childhood dyslexia. PhD Thesis, University of London

NELSON, H. E. and WARRINGTON, E. K. (1974). Developmental spelling retardation and its relation to other cognitive abilities. *British Journal of Psychology*, **65**, 265–274

NEELY, J. H. (1977). Semantic priming and retrieval from lexical memory: roles of inhibitionless spreading activation and limited capacity attention. *Journal of Experimental Psychology: General*, **106**, 226–254

NEISSER, U. (1954). An experimental distinction between perceptual process and verbal response. *Journal of Experimental Psychology*, **47**, 399–402

NISBET, S. D. (1939). Non-dictated spelling tests. *British Journal of Educational Psychology*, **9**, 29–44

NOBLE, G. L. (1971). Joseph Mayer Rice: critic of the public schools and pioneer in modern educational measurement. (Doctoral dissertation, State University of New York at Buffalo, 1970), *Dissertation Abstracts*, **31/109-A**, p. 4503. (University Microfilms No. 71-06100)

NORTHBY, A. S. (1936). A comparison of five types of spelling tests for diagnostic purposes. *Journal of Educational Research*, **29**, 339–346

O'CONNOR, N. and HERMELIN, B. (1978). *Seeing and Hearing and Space and Time*. London: Academic Press

OLIVER, P. R., NELSON, J. M. and DOWNING, J. (1972). Differentiation of grapheme-phoneme units as a function of orthography. *Journal of Educational Psychology*, **63**, 487–492

OLLER, D. K. and KELLY, C. A. (1974). Phonological substitution processes of a hard of hearing child. *Journal of Speech and Hearing Disorders*, **39**, 65–74

O'NEAL, V. and TRABASSO, T. (1976). Is there a correspondence between sound and spelling? Some implications for Black English speakers. In HARRISON, D. S. and TRABASSO, T., *Black English: A Seminar*. Hillsdale, N.J.: Erlbaum

ORTON, S. T. (1937). *Reading, Writing and Speech Problems in Children*. N.Y.: W. W. Norton

PAIVIO, A. (1971). *Imagery and Verbal Processes*. N.Y.: Holt, Rinehart and Winston

PARTRIDGE, E. (1966). *Origins*. London: Routledge and Kegan Paul

PASS, M. F. (1950). An inquiry into the relationship between spelling and articulatory defects in high school freshmen. Masters Thesis, University of Alabama

PATTERSON, K. E. and MARCEL, A. J. (1977). Aphasia, dyslexia and the phonological coding of written words. *Quarterly Journal of Experimental Psychology*, **29**, 307–318

PEAKE, N. L. (1940). Relation between spelling ability and reading ability. *Journal of Experimental Education*, **9**, 192–193

PERFETTI, C. A. and HOGABOAM, T. (1975). The relationship between single word decoding and reading comprehension skill. *Journal of Educational Psychology*, **67**, 461–469

PERFETTI, C. A. and LESGOLD, A. M. (1977). Coding and comprehension in skilled reading and implications for reading instruction. In RESNICK, L. B. and WEAVER, P. A. (Eds), *Theory and Practice of Early Reading*. Hillsdale, N.J.: Erlbaum

PERSONKE, C. and KNIGHT, L. (1971). Proofreading and spelling: a report and a program. In PERSONKE, C. and YEE, A. H. (Eds), *Comprehensive Spelling Instruction*. Scranton, Pa: Intext

PERSONKE, C. and YEE, A. H. (1966). A model for the analysis of spelling behaviour. *Elementary English*, **43**, 278–284

PETERS, M. L. (1967a). The influence of reading methods on spelling. *British Journal of Educational Psychology*, **37**, 47–53

PETERS, M. L. (1967b). *Spelling: Caught or Taught*. London: Routledge and Kegan Paul

PETERS, M. L. (1970). *Success in Spelling*. Cambridge Institute of Education

PETERS, M. L. (1975). *Diagnostic and Remedial Spelling Manual*. London: Macmillan

PETTY, W. T. (1957). Phonetic elements as factors in spelling difficulty. *Journal of Educational Research*, **51**, 209–214

PIERRO, P. S. (1967). An investigation of visual form perception and eidetic imagery in students who read well and spell poorly. *Dissertation Abstracts* (Northern Illinois University), **27** (9-A), 2894–2895

PITMAN, SIR J. and ST. JOHN, J. (1969). *Alphabets and Reading: The Initial Teaching Alphabet*. London: Pitman

PIZZAMIGLIO, L. and BLACK, J. (1968). Phonic trends in the writing of aphasic patients. *Journal of Speech and Hearing Research*, **11**, 77–84

PLESSAS, G. P., and DISON, P. A. (1964). Spelling performances of good readers. *California Journal of Educational Research*, **16**, 14–22

POLANYI, M. (1966). *The Tacit Dimension*. Garden City: Doubleday

POLLATSEK, A. and CARR, T. H. (1979). Rule-governed and wholistic encoding processes in word perception. In KOLERS, P. A., WROLSTAD, M. and BOUMA, H. (Eds), *Processing of Visible Language*, I. N.Y.: Plenum Press

POLLATSEK, A., WELL, A. D. and SCHINDLER, R. M. (1975). Familiarity affects visual processing of words. *Journal of Experimental Psychology: Human Perception and Performance*, **1**, 328–338

POSNANSKY, C. J. and RAYNER, K. (1977). Visual-feature and response components in a picture-word interference task with beginning and skilled readers. *Journal of Experimental Child Psychology*, **24**, 440–460

PRINGLE, H. F. (1931). *Theodore Rooosevelt, A Biography*. N.Y.: Harcourt, Brace and Co.

PYLYSHYN, Z. (1973). What the mind's eye tells the mind's brain: a critique of mental imagery. *Psychological Bulletin*, **80**, 1–24

RADAKAR, L. D. (1963). The effect of visual imagery upon spelling performance. *Journal of Educational Research*, **56**, 370–372

RAYNER, K. and HAGELBERG, E. M. (1975). Word recognition cues for beginning and skilled readers. *Journal of Experimental Child Psychology*, **20**, 444–455

RAYNER, K. and POSNANSKY, C. J. (1978). Stages of processing in word identification. *Journal of Experimental Psychology: General*, **107**, 64–80

READ, C. (1971). Preschool children's knowledge of English phonology. *Harvard Educational Review*, **41**, 1–34

READ, C. (1973). Children's judgements of phonetic similarities in relation to English spelling. *Language Learning*, **23**, 17–38

READ, C. (1975). *Children's Categorization of Speech Sounds in English*. NCTE Research Report No. 17. Urbana Ill.: National Council of Teachers of English

READ, C. (1978). Writing is not the inverse of reading for young children. In FREDERIKSON, C. H., WHITEMAN, M. F. and DOMINIC, J. F. (Eds), *Writing: The Nature, Development and Teaching of Written Communication*. Vol. 1, *Writing: Process, Development and Communication*. Hilldsale, N.J.: Erlbaum

REED, D. W. (1970). A theory of language, speech and writing. In SINGER, H. and RUDDELL, R. B. (Eds), *Theoretical Models and Processes of Reading*. Newark, Del.: IRA

REID, J. F. (1958). An investigation of 13 beginners in reading. *Acta Psychologica*, **14**, 295–313

RICE, J. M. (1893). *The Public School System of the United States*. N.Y.: Century Co.

RICE, J. M. (1897). The futility of the spelling grind. *The Forum*, **23**, 163–172, 409–419

RICE, J. M. (1898). *The Rational Spelling Book*. N.Y.: American Book Co.

RICE, J. M. (1913). *Scientific Management in Education*. N.Y.: Hinds, Noble and Eldridge

RICHEK, M. A. (1977–78). Readiness skills that predict initial word learning using two different methods of instruction. *Reading Research Quarterly*, **13**, 200–222

RIEBER, R. W., SMITH, N. and HARRIS, B. (1976). Neuropsychological aspects of stuttering and cluttering. In RIEBER, R. W. (Ed.) *The Neuropsychology of Language*. N.Y.: Plenum Press

RIEMER, G. (1970). *How they Murdered the Second "R"*. London: Pitman

ROSENTHAL, W. S. (1972). Auditory and linguistic interaction in developmental aphasia: evidence from two studies of auditory processing. In INGRAM, D. (Ed.), *Papers and Reports on Child Language Development: Special Issue: Language Disorders in Children. No. 4*, 19–34

ROSNER, J. (1971). Phonic analysis training and beginning reading skills. Learning Research and Development Center, University of Pittsburgh. Publication 1971/19

ROSS, S. B. (1971). On the syntax of written Black English. *TESOL Quarterly*, **5**, 115–122

ROURKE, B. P. (1978). Reading, spelling, and arithmetic disabilities: a neuro-psychological perspective. In MYKLEBUST, H. R. (Ed.), *Progress in Learning Disabilities*, Vol. IV. N.Y.: Grune and Stratton

ROURKE, B. P. and ORR, R. R. (1977). Prediction of the reading and spelling performances of normal and retarded readers: a 4-year follow-up. *Journal of Abnormal Child Psychology*, **5**, 9–20

ROZIN, P. and GLEITMAN, L. R. (1977). The structure and acquisition of reading, II: The reading process and the acquisition of the alphabetic principle of reading.

In REBER, A. S. and SCARBOROUGH, D. L. (Eds), *Toward a Psychology of Reading*. Hillsdale, N.J.: Erlbaum

ROZIN, P., PORITSKY, S. and SOTSKY, R. (1971). American children with reading problems can easily learn to read English represented by Chinese characters. *Science*, **171**, 1264–1267

ROZIN, P., BRESSMAN, B. and TAFT, M. (1974). Do children understand the basic relationship between speech and writing? The mow-motorcycle test. *Journal of Reading Behavior*, **6**, 327–334

RUBENSTEIN, H., LEWIS, S. S. and RUBENSTEIN, M. A. (1971). Evidence for phonemic recoding in visual word recognition. *Journal of Verbal Learning and Verbal Behavior*, **10**, 645–657

RUBENSTEIN, H., RICHTER, M. L. and KAY, E. J. (1975). Pronounceability and the visual recognition of nonsense words. *Journal of Verbal Learning and Verbal Behavior*, **14**, 651–657

RUGEL, R. P. (1974). W.I.S.C. subtest scores of disabled readers. *Journal of Learning Disabilities*, **7**, 57–64

RUSSELL, D. H. (1955). A second study of characteristics of good and poor spellers. *Journal of Educational Psychology*, **46**, 129–144

SAFFRAN, E. M. and MARIN, O. S. M. (1977). Reading without phonology: evidence from aphasia. *Quarterly Journal of Experimental Psychology*, **29**, 515–525

SAFFRAN, E. M. ,MARIN, O. S. M. and YENI-KOMSHIAN, G. H. (1976). An analysis of speech perception in word deafness. *Brain and Language*, **3**, 209–228

SAKAMOTO, T. and MAKITA, K. (1973). Japan. In DOWNING, J. (Ed.), *Comparative Reading*. N.Y.: Macmillan

SALES, B. D., HABER, R. N. and COLE, R. A. (1969). Mechanisms of aural encoding, IV: Hear, see, say–write, interactions for vowels. *Perception and Psychophysics*, **6**, 385–390

SANTA, J. L., SANTA, C. A. and SMITH, E. E. (1977). Units of word recognition: evidence for the use of multiple units. *Perception and Psychophysics*, **22**, 585–591

SARTRE, J. P. (1966). *The Psychology of Imagination*. N.Y.: Washington Square Press. Translated by B. Frechtman

SASANUMA, S. (1975). Kana and Kanji processing in Japanese aphasics. *Brain and Language*, **2**, 369–383

SASANUMA, S. and FUJIMURA, O. (1971). Selective impairment of phonetic and non-phonetic transcription of words in Japanese aphasic patients: Kana *vs* Kanji in visual recognition and writing. *Cortex*, **7**, 1–18

SASANUMA, S, and FUJIMURA, O. (1972). An analysis of writing errors in Japanese aphasic patients: Kanji *vs* Kana words. *Cortex*, **8**, 265–282

SAVIN, H. B. (1972). What the child knows about speech when he starts to learn to read. In KAVANAGH, J. F. and MATTINGLY, I. G. (Eds), *Language by Ear and by Eye*. Cambridge, Mass.: M.I.T. Press

SAVIN, H. B. and BEVER, T. G. (1970). The nonperceptual reality of the phoneme. *Journal of Verbal Learning and Verbal Behavior*, **9**, 295–302

SCHINDLER, R. M., WELL, A. D. and POLLATSEK, A. (1974). Effects of segmentation and expectancy on matching time for words and nonwords. *Journal of Experimental Psychology*, **103**, 107–111

SCHONELL, F. S. (1932). *Essentials in Teaching and Testing Spelling*. London: Macmillan

SCHONELL, F. S. (1934). The relation between defective speech and disability in spelling. *British Journal of Educational Psychology*, **4**, 123–129

SCHONELL, F. (1942). *Backwardness in the Basic Subjects*. London: Oliver and Boyd

SCHOUTEN, J. F., KALSBEEK, J. W. H. and LEOPOLD, F. F. (1962). On the evaluation of perceptual and mental load. *Ergonomics*, **5**, 251–260

SCHWARTZ, M. F., SAFFRAN, E. M. and MARIN, O. S. M. (1979). Fractioning the reading process in dementia: evidence for word specific print to sound associations. In COLTHEART, M., PATTERSON, K. E. and MARSHALL, J. C. (Eds), *Deep Dyslexia*. London: Routledge and Kegan Paul

SCHWARTZ, S. and DOEHRING, D. G. (1977). A developmental study of children's ability to acquire knowledge of spelling patterns. *Developmental Psychology*, **13**, 419–420

SCOTTISH COUNCIL FOR RESEARCH IN EDUCATION (1961). *Studies in Spelling*. London: University of London Press

SCRAGG, D. G. (1974). *A History of English Spelling*. Manchester: University Press

SCRIBNER, S. and COLE, M. (1978). Literacy without schooling: testing for intellectual effects. *Vai Literacy Project, Working Paper No. 2*, Laboratory of Comparative Human Cognition, The Rockefeller University

SCUDDER, H. E. (1881). *Noah Webster*. Boston: Houghton, Mifflin, and Co.

SEARS, D. A. (1969). Engineers spell acoustically. *College Composition and Communication*, **20**, 349–351

SECRIST, R. H. (1976). Internalization of English orthographic patterns. *Visible Language*, **10**, 309–322

SEYMOUR, P. H. K. (1973). A model for reading, naming and comparison. *British Journal of Psychology*, **64**, 35–49

SEYMOUR, P. H. K. and JACK, M. V. (1978). Effects of visual familiarity on 'same' and 'different' decision processes. *Quarterly Journal of Experimental Psychology*, **30**, 455–469

SEYMOUR, P. H. K. and PORPODAS, C. D. (1978). Coding of spelling by normal and dyslexic readers. In GRUNEBERG, M. M., SYKES, R. N. and MORRIS, P. E. (Eds), *Practical Aspects of Memory*. London: Academic Press

SHAFFER, L. H. (1975). Control processes in typing. *Quarterly Journal of Experimental Psychology*, **27**, 419–432

SHAFFER, L. H. (1976). Intention and performance. *Psychological Review*, **83**, 375–393

SHALLICE, T. and WARRINGTON, E. K. (1975). Word recognition in a phonemic dyslexic patient. *Quarterly Journal of Experimental Psychology*, **27**, 187–199

SHALLICE, T. and WARRINGTON, E. K. (in press). Single and multiple component central dyslexic syndromes. In COLTHEART, M., PATTERSON, K. E. and MARSHALL, J. C. (Eds), *Deep Dyslexia*. London: Routledge and Kegan Paul

SHANKWEILER, D. and LIBERMAN, I. Y. (1972). Misreading: a search for causes. In KAVANAGH, J. F. and MATTINGLY, I. G. (Eds), *Language by Ear and by Eye*. Cambridge, Mass.: M.I.T. Press

SHIMRAT, N. (1973). The impact of laterality and cultural background on the development of writing skills. *Neuropsychologia*, **11**, 239–242

SHOEMAKER, E. C. (1936). *Noah Webster, Pioneer of Learning*. N.Y.: Columbia University Press

SHORES, J. H. and YEE, A. H. (1973). Spelling achievement tests: what is available and what is needed? *Journal of Special Education*, **7**, 301–309

SIMON, D. P. (1976). Spelling – a task analysis. *Instructional Science*, **5**, 277–302

SIMON, D. P. and SIMON, H. A. (1973). Alternative uses of phonemic information in spelling. *Review of Educational Research*, **43**, 115–137

SIMONS, H. D. (1975). Transformational phonology and reading acquisition. *Journal of Reading Behaviour*, **7**, 49–59

SIMPLIFIED SPELLING BOARD (1906). *Simplified Spelling*, first edition. Washington, D.C.: U.S. Government Printing Office

SKEEL, E. E. and CARPENTER, E. H., JR. (Compiler and editor) (1958). *A Bibliography of the Writings of Noah Webster*. N.Y.: Arno Press

SMITH, E. E. and HAVILAND, S. E. (1972). Why words are perceived more accurately than nonwords: inference versus unitization. *Journal of Experimental Psychology*, **92**, 59–64

SMITH, E. E. and SPOEHR, K. T. (1974). The perception of printed English: a theoretical perception. In KANTOWITZ, B. (Ed.), *Human Information Processing: Tutorials in Performance and Cognition*. Hillsdale, N.J.: Erlbaum

SMITH, F. (1971). *Understanding Reading: A Psycholinguistic Analysis of Reading and Learning to Read*. N.Y.: Holt, Rinehart and Winston

SMITH, F. (1973a). Alphabetic writing – a language compromise? In SMITH, F. (Ed.), *Psycholinguistics and Reading*. N.Y.: Holt, Rinehart and Winston

SMITH, F. (Ed.) (1973b). *Psycholinguistics and Reading*. N.Y.: Holt, Rinehart and Winston

SMITH, H. A. (1975). Teaching spelling. *British Journal of Educational Psychology*, **45**, 68–72

SMITH, L. B. and KEMLER, D. G. (1977). Developmental trends in free classification: evidence for a new conceptualization of perceptual development. *Journal of Experimental Child Psychology*, **24**, 279–298

SMITH, N. B. (1965). *American Reading Instruction*, revised edn. Newark, Del.: International Reading Association

SMITH, N. V. (1973). *The Acquisition of Phonology: A Case Study*. London: Cambridge University Press.

SMITH, P. T. and BAKER, R. G. (1976). The influence of English spelling patterns on pronunciation. *Journal of Verbal Learning and Verbal Behavior*, **15**, 267–285

SMITH, P. T. and GROAT, A. (1979). Spelling patterns, letter cancellation and the processing of text. In KOLERS, P. A., WROLSTAD, M. and BOUMA, H. (Eds), *Processing of Visible Language*, I. N.Y.: Plenum Press

SNOWLING, M. (in press). The development of grapheme-phoneme correspondences in normal and dyslexic readers. *Journal of Experimental Child Psychology*

SPACHE, G. (1940a). A critical analysis of various methods of classifying spelling errors. I and II. *Journal of Educational Psychology*, **31**, 111–134, and 204–214

SPACHE, G (1940b) The role of visual defects in spelling and reading disabilities. *American Journal of Orthopsychiatry*, **10**, 229–237.

SPACHE, G. (1940c). Characteristic errors of good and poor spellers. *Journal of Educational Research*, **34**, 182–189

SPACHE, G. (1955). *Spelling Errors Test*. Gainsville, Fla.

SPEER, O. B. and LAMB, G. S. (1976). First grade reading ability and fluency in naming verbal symbols. *The Reading Teacher*, 572–576

SPOEHR, K. T. and SMITH, E. E. (1973). The role of syllables in perceptional processing. *Cognitive Psychology*, **5**, 71–89

SPOEHR, K. T. and SMITH, E. E. (1975). The role of orthographic and phonotactic rules in perceiving letter patterns. *Journal of Experimental Psychology: Human Perception and Performance*, **1**, 21–34

SPYROPOULOS, T. and CERASO, J. (1977). Categorized and uncategorized attributes as recall cues: the phenomenon of limited access. *Cognitive Psychology*, **9**, 384–402

STALLER, J., BUCHANAN, D., SINGER, M., LAPPIN, J. and WEBB, W. (1978). Alexia without agraphia: an experimental case study. *Brain and Language*, **5**, 378–387

STANNERS, R. F. and FORBACH, G. B. (1973). Analysis of letter strings in word recognition. *Journal of Experimental Psychology*, **98**, 31–35

STANOVICH, K. E. and BAUER, D. W. (1978). Experiments on the spelling-to-sound regularity effect in word recognition. *Memory and Cognition*, **6**, 410–415

STEINBERG, D. D. (1973). Phonology, reading, and Chomsky and Halle's optimal orthography. *Journal of Psycholinguistic Research*, **2**, 239–258

STERNBERG, R. J. (1977). Componential investigations of human intelligence. Paper presented at the NATO Conference on Cognition and Instruction, Amsterdam, The Netherlands

STEWART, W. A. (1969). The use of negro dialect in the teaching of reading. In BARATZ, J. C. and SHUY, R. W., *Teaching Black Children to Read*. Center for Applied Linguistics. Washington D.C.

SWEENEY, J. E. and ROURKE, B. P. (1978). Neuropsychological significance of phonetically accurate and phonetically inaccurate spelling errors in younger and older retarded spellers. *Brain and Language*, **6**, 212–225

SZUMSKI, J. M. (1974). The effects of specific visual experience on rapid visual word identification. Master's thesis, McMaster University, Hamilton

TAFT, M. and FORSTER, K. I. (1977). Lexical storage and retrieval of polymorphemic and polysyllabic words. *Journal of Verbal Learning and Verbal Behavior*, **15**, 607–620

TALLAL, P. and PIERCY, M. (1975). Developmental aphasia: the perception of brief vowels and extended stop consonants. *Neuropsychologia*, **13**, 69–74

TAYLOR, J. A., MILLER, T. J. and JUOLA, J. F. (1977). Isolating visual units in the perception of words and nonwords. *Perception and Psychophysics*, **21**, 377–386

TEMPLIN, M. (1948). A comparison of the spelling achievement of normal and defective hearing subjects. *Journal of Educational Psychology*, **39**, 337–346

TEMPLIN, M. (1954). Phonetic knowledge and its relation to the spelling and reading achievement of fourth grade pupils. *Journal of Educational Research*, **47**, 441–454

TERRY, P., SAMUELS, S. J. and LaBERGE, D. (1976). The effects of letter degradation and letter spacing on word recognition. *Journal of Verbal Learning and Verbal Behavior*, **15**, 577–585

THOMPSON, M. D. and BLOCK, K. K. (1975). The effects of three types of practice formats and two degrees of learning on the spelling performance of elementary school students. Paper presented at the American Educational Research Association, Washington, D.C.

THORNDIKE, E. L. (1903). *Educational Psychology*. N.Y.: Science Press

THORNDIKE, E. L. (1914). *Educational Psychology*, Vol. III. (*Mental work and fatigue and individual differences and their causes*). N.Y.: Teachers College, Columbia University

THORNDIKE, E. and LORGE, I. (1944). *The Teacher's Word Book of 30,000 Words*. N.Y.: Teacher's College, Columbia University

TIMKO, H. G. (1970). Configuration as a cue in the word recognition of beginning readers. *Journal of Experimental Education*, **39**, 68–69

TORDRUP, S. A. (1966). Reversals in reading and spelling. *Slow Learning Child*, **12**, 173–183

TOWNSEND, A. (1947). An investigation of certain relationships of spelling with reading and academic aptitude. *Journal of Educational Research*, **40**, 465–471

TRAGER, G. L. (1974). Writing and writing systems. In SEBEOK, T. A. (Ed.), *Current Trends in Linguistics*, Vol. 12. The Hague: Mouton

TREIMAN, R. and BARON, J. Segmental analysis ability: development and relation to reading. In WALLER, T. G. and MacKINNON, G. E. (Eds), *Reading Research: Advances in Theory and Practice*, Vol. 2. N.Y.: Academic Press. (In press)

TURVEY, M. T. (1974). Constructive theory, perceptual systems and tacit knowledge. In WEIMER, W. B. and PALERMO, D. S. (Eds), *Cognition and the Symbolic Processes*. Hillsdale, N.J.: Erlbaum

TZENG, O. (in press). Reading in the nonalphabetic writing system: some experimental studies. In VENEZKY, R. L. and KAVANAGH, J. F. (Eds), *Orthography, Reading and Dyslexia*. Baltimore: University Park Press

UNDERWOOD, B. J. and SCHULTZ, P. W. (1960). *Meaningfulness and Verbal Learning*. Philadelphia: Lippincot

UNDERWOOD, G. (1978). Memory systems and the reading process. In GRUNEBERG, M. M., SYKES, R. N. and MORRIS, P. E. (Eds), *Practical Aspects of Memory*. London: Academic Press

URE, D. (1969). Spelling performance of left-handed schoolchildren as affected by the use of a pencil modified to increase visual feedback. *Journal of Experimental Child Psychology*, **7**, 220–230

VACHEK, J. (1973). Written language. *Janua Linguarum*, Series Critica 14. The Hague: Mouton

VALLINS, G. H., revised by SCRAGG, D. G. (1954). *Spelling*. London: Deutsch

vanHEUVEN, V. J. (in press). Some aspects of Dutch orthography and reading. In VENEZKY, R. L. and KAVANAGH, J. F. (Eds), *Orthography, Reading and Dyslexia*. Baltimore: University Park Press

VAN NES, F. L. (1971). Errors in the motor program for handwriting. *I.P.O. Annual Progress Report*, **6**, 61–63

VELLUTINO, F. R. (1977). Alternative conceptualisations of dyslexia: evidence in support of a verbal-deficit hypothesis. *Harvard Educational Review*, **47**, 334–354

VELLUTINO, F. R., SMITH, H., STEGER, J. A. and KAMAN, M. (1975). Reading disability: age differences and the perceptual-deficit hypothesis. *Child Development*, **46**, 487–493

VENEZKY, R. L. (1967). English orthography: its graphical structure and its relation to sound. *Reading Research Quarterly*, **2**, 75–105

VENEZKY, R. L. (1970). *The Structure of English Orthography*. The Hague: Mouton

VENEZKY, R. L. (1974). Language and cognition in reading. In SPOLSKY, B. (Ed.), *Current Trends in Educational Linguistics*. The Hague: Mouton

VENEZKY, R. L. (1976). Notes on the history of English spelling. *Visible Language*, **10**, 351–365

VENEZKY, R. L. and JOHNSON, D. (1973). Development of two letter-sound patterns in grades one through three. *Journal of Educational Psychology*, **64**, 109–115

VERNON, M. D. (1957). *Backwardness in Reading*. Cambridge: Cambridge University Press

WADE, B. and WEDELL, K. (Eds) (1974). Spelling: task and learner. *Educational Review*. University of Birmingham, Occasional Publications. Whole No. 5

WALKER, B. S. (1974). Vividness of imagery and spelling errors. *Perceptual and Motor Skills*, **39**, 823–825

WALL, J. F. (1970). *Andrew Carnegie*. N.Y.: Oxford University Press

WALLACH, M. A. (1963). Perceptual recognition of approximations to English in relation to spelling achievements. *Journal of Educational Psychology*, **54**, 57–62

WANG, W. S. Y. (in press). Language structure and optimal orthography. In VENEZKY, R. L. and KAVANAGH, J. F. (Eds), *Orthography, Reading and Dyslexia*. Baltimore: University Park Press

WARFEL, H. R. (1936). *Noah Webster, Schoolmaster to America*. N.Y.: Macmillan

WAPNER, W. and GARDNER, H. (1979). Study of spelling in aphasia. *Brain and Language*, **7**, 363–374

WARREN, C. E. J. and MORTON, J. *The Effects of Priming on Picture Recognition*. (In prep.)

WARREN, R. M. (1971). Identification times for phonemic components of graded complexity and for spelling of speech. *Perception and Psychophysics*, **9**, 345–349

WARRINGTON, E. K. (1967). The incidence of verbal disability associated with reading retardation. *Neuropsychologia*, **5**, 175–179

WAUGH, N. C. (1970). Associative symmetry and recall latencies: a distinction between learning and performance. In SANDERS, A. F. (Ed.), *Attention and Performance, III. Acta Psychologica*, **33**, 326–337

WEBER, R. M. (1970). First grader's use of grammatical context in reading. In LEVIN, H. and WILLIAMS, J. P. (Eds), *Basic Studies on Reading*. N.Y.: Basic Books

WEBSTER, N. (1783). *A Grammatical Institute of the English Language, Part I*. Hartford, Hudson and Goodwin. (Facsimile reprint No. 89, Scolar Press, Menston, England, 1968)

WEBSTER, N. (1789). The reforming of spelling. In *Old South Leaflets*, Vol. VIII, No. 196. Boston: Directors of the Old South Work (1908)

WEBSTER, N. (1806). *A Compendious Dictionary of the English Language*. New Haven: Sidney Babcock

WEBSTER, N. (1828). *An American Dictionary of the English Language*. N.Y.: S. Converse

WEBSTER, N. (1831). *The American Spelling Book*. Middletown, Conn. (Facsimile reprint with an introductory essay by Henry Steel Commager, Bureau of Publications, Teachers College, Columbia University, 1958)

WEIGL, E. (1974) Neuropsychological experiments on transcoding between spoken and written language structures. *Brain and Language*, **1**, 227–240

WEIGL, E. (1975). On written language: its acquisition and its alexic-agraphic disturbances. In LENNEBERG, E. H. and LENNEBERG, E. (Eds), *Foundations of Language Development*, Vol. 2. N.Y.: Academic Press

WEIGL, E. and FRADIS, A. (1977). The transcoding process in patients with agraphia to dictation. *Brain and Language*, **4**, 11–22

WELL, A. D., POLLATSEK, A. and SCHINDLER, R. M. (1975). Facilitation of both 'same' and 'different' judgments of letter strings by familiarity of letter sequence. *Perception and Psychophysics*, **17**, 511–520

WEST, J. and WEBER, J. A. (1973). A phonological analysis of the spontaneous language of a 4-year-old hard of hearing child. *Journal of Speech and Hearing Disorders*, **38**, 25–35

WHEELER, D. D. (1970). Processes in word recognition. *Cognitive Psychology*, **1**, 59–85

WILLIAMS, J. P., BLUMBERG, E. L. and WILLIAMS, D. V. (1970). Cues used in visual word recognition. *Journal of Educational Psychology*, **61**, 310–315

WILLOWS, D. M. (1974). Reading between the lines: selective attention in good and poor readers. *Child Development*, **45**, 408–415

WING, A. M. (1978). Response timing in handwriting. In STELMACH, G. E. (Ed.), *Information Processing in Motor Control and Learning*. N.Y.: Academic Press

WINNICK, W. A. and DANIEL, S. A. (1970). Two kinds of response priming in tachistoscopic recognition. *Journal of Experimental Psychology*, **84**, 74–81

WITTE, W. (1960). Mnemische Determination und Dynamik des reproduktiven Tatonnements. *Psychologische Beiträge*, **4**, 179–205

WOLF, C. G. and ROBINSON, D. O. (1976). Use of spelling-to-sound rules in reading. *Perceptual and Motor Skills*, **43**, 1135–1146

WOLFRAM, W. and FASOLD, R. W. (1974). *Social Dialects in American English*. Englewood Cliffs, N.J.: Prentice-Hall Inc.

WOLFRAM, W. and WHITEMAN, M. F. (1971). The role of dialect interference in composition. *The Florida FL Reports* 9 (Fall), **59**, 34–38

ZAIDEL, E. (1978). Concepts of cerebral dominance in the split brain. In BUSER, P. and ROUGEUL-BUSER, A. (Eds), *Cerebral Correlates of Conscious Experience*. Elsevier: North-Holland Biomedical Press

ZECHMEISTER, E. B. (1972). Orthographic distinctiveness as a variable in word recognition. *American Journal of Psychology*, **85**, 425–430

Author Index

Subject Index

Please note: f indicates one further page after the page number and ff indicates two or more pages after the page number